Canadian
Performance
Documents
and Debates

Canadian Performance Documents and Debates

A Sourcebook

Edited by

ANTHONY J. VICKERY,
GLEN F. NICHOLS, and
ALLANA C. LINDGREN

Foreword by
JERRY WASSERMAN

UNIVERSITY *of* ALBERTA PRESS

Published by

University of Alberta Press
1–16 Rutherford Library South
11204 89 Avenue NW
Edmonton, Alberta, Canada T6G 2J4
amiskwaciwâskahikan | Treaty 6 | Métis Territory
uap.ualberta.ca | uapress@ualberta.ca

LIBRARY AND ARCHIVES CANADA
CATALOGUING IN PUBLICATION

Title: Canadian performance documents and debates : a
    sourcebook / edited by Anthony J. Vickery, Glen F. Nichols,
    and Allana C. Lindgren; foreword by Jerry Wasserman.
Names: Vickery, Anthony J., editor. | Nichols, Glen Freeman,
    1961– editor. | Lindgren, Allana, editor. | Wasserman, Jerry,
    1945– writer of foreword.
Description: Includes bibliographical references and index.
Identifiers: Canadiana (print) 20220166668 |
    Canadiana (ebook) 20220166714 |
    ISBN 9781772126044 (softcover) |
    ISBN 9781772126204 (EPUB) |
    ISBN 9781772126211 (PDF)
Subjects: LCSH: Performing arts—Canada—History—Sources. |
    LCSH: Theater—Canada—History—Sources. | LCSH:
    Canadian drama—History and criticism—Sources.
Classification: LCC PN2301 .C36 2022 | DDC 791.0971—dc23

First edition, first printing, 2022.
First printed and bound in Canada by Friesens, Altona, Manitoba.
Copyediting and proofreading by Joanne Muzak.
Indexing by Stephen Ullstrom.

University of Alberta Press is committed to protecting our
natural environment. As part of our efforts, this book is printed
on Enviro Paper: it contains 100% post-consumer recycled fibres
and is acid- and chlorine-free.

This book has been published with the help of a grant from the
Canadian Federation for the Humanities and Social Sciences,
through the Awards to Scholarly Publications Program, using
funds provided by the Social Sciences and Humanities Research
Council of Canada.

University of Alberta Press gratefully acknowledges the support
received for its publishing program from the Government of
Canada, the Canada Council for the Arts, and the Government of
Alberta through the Alberta Media Fund.

Canadä  

Contents

Thematic Table of Contents

Reactionary and Colonialist Art

Foreword

THEATRE HISTORY TEXTS have traditionally come in two kinds: anthologies of plays and narrative histories containing some play excerpts. This volume represents both a synthesis of those two genres and something new, a mix-and-match documentary approach that substitutes "performance" for "theatre" and lays out a progressive agenda for the study of Canadian performance in historical contexts.

The editors and contributors have taken an eclectic, holistic approach. This book is not Brockett's *History of the Theatre* for Canada. Though it moves chronologically from what has often been considered "the first Canadian play" in 1606 to the generally assumed beginnings of "modern" Canadian theatre in 1967, it doesn't attempt to be comprehensive in its coverage. New topics like circus, fancy dress balls, vaudeville, amateur ballet, drag, and mummering are included. Many of the usual suspects—Charles Mair, Merrill Denison, Gwen Pharis Ringwood, Gratien Gélinas, James Reaney, John Coulter, George Ryga— are not.

By no means has every element of the currently canonical been expunged. Included are texts from and essays on material relatively familiar to the study of Canadian theatre history in its heretofore traditional form: *Acadius, or Love in a Calm*, Sarah Anne Curzon, Little Theatre, Herman Voaden, Oscar Ryan (though not the usual *Eight Men Speak*), Lister Sinclair and CBC radio drama, Robertson Davies and the *Massey Report*, Tyrone Guthrie and the Stratford Festival, and Marcel Dubé. Analyses and translations are sometimes strikingly new, though the principals are generally recognizable.

But from the margins of Canadian performance history George Cockings, Pauline Johnson, and Marjorie Pickthall have been recuperated and invited to the party; so too William Tremayne, Yvette O. Mercier-Gouin, Claude Gauvreau, and Lorris Elliott. And from the remote, outermost margins come some definite newbies: Chinese Canadian theatrical entrepreneur Sam Kee, vaudeville dancer Evelyn Geary, and Quebec circus performers Ricardo the Human Fly and Miss Victory the Human Cannonball. And John Nihei, who staged his own Japanese adaptation of Friedrich Schiller's *William Tell* for his fellow Japanese Canadian internees in British Columbia's Tashme camp during the Second World War.

Many of these playwrights, producers, and performers are being introduced to me here for the first time, and I find it a disorienting experience. Imagine someone inviting you on a tour of the place where you've lived most of your life and showing you bars and restaurants you've never seen before, neighbourhoods you've never visited, entire landscapes you never knew existed. It's disorienting, but also thrilling.

In revisiting the old and introducing the new, these scholars are hyper-conscious of their responsibility to call out the racism and colonialism that inevitably infect many of the performance tales they tell. If Cockings's *The Conquest of Canada* marks "the racist beginnings to both Canadian theatre and Canadian politics"; if blackface minstrelsy in nineteenth-century Toronto was "the performance of hate"; if a 1930s pageant to welcome British royals to Winnipeg was marked by Indigenous absence, why mark those phenomena for inclusion and analysis in a text like this? Because if we don't learn from history, we're doomed to repeat it.

One of the most exciting elements of this book for me is the way it builds its histories upon those that came before it. I had the good fortune to enter the ranks of Canadian theatre scholarship in the early 1980s when the first generation of Canadian theatre historians was doing their pioneering work, founding the Association for Canadian Theatre History (now the Canadian Association for Theatre Research), and passing the torch to my generation. Among those groundbreaking scholars cited here are Eugene Benson and Len Conolly, Mary Brown, Murray Edwards, Chad Evans, Richard Plant, and Ann Saddlemyer.

Many of the authors in this book began their research in that era, taught and mentored by those first-generation pioneers. This collection is studded with their expertise: Stephen Johnson on Canadian minstrelsy, Kym Bird on Curzon, Anton Wagner on Voaden, Alan Filewod on workers' theatre, John Jackson and Howard Fink on radio drama, and Denyse Lynde on Newfoundland. Even more exhilarating is to see the current generation of Canadian performance scholars revisiting and revising the work of those who first blazed the trail: the way, for example, Heather Davis-Fisch builds on Patrick O'Neill's original research into shipboard theatricals.

Two of the most eloquent entries begin and end the collection, reminding us how Canadian theatre and performance are implicated in what might be this country's greatest historical injustice: its treatment of Indigenous people. Expanding, reinterpreting, and correcting some of my own work on Marc Lescarbot and *The Theatre of Neptune*, Jill Carter considers the ways the Mi'kmaq may have intervened in the French performance of *Neptune* on that November day in 1606, performing her own Indigenous intervention and resistance to settler readings of this originary theatre-historical moment.

Canadian Performance Documents and Debates: A Sourcebook concludes with one of the all-time great Canadian performers and performances: Chief Dan George's profound "Lament for Confederation," delivered on the occasion of the 1967 Centennial. His is a prescient call for the kind of redress and reconciliation so frequently cited and desperately needed in Canada today—perhaps the "new ceremony of welcome" that Jill Carter suggests this book itself may, in some ways, hopefully embody.

JERRY WASSERMAN
Actor, theatre scholar, Professor Emeritus of English and Theatre (University of British Columbia), Vancouver, August 2021

Acknowledgements

WHEN WE STARTED THIS PROJECT, we were unaware that we would meet and collaborate with so many wonderful people whose collegiality and commitment fill the pages that follow.

We extend a heartfelt thank-you to our contributors. Working with such an insightful, good-natured, and dedicated group of scholars has been one of the most enjoyable aspects of this project and has affirmed our belief that we are truly lucky to be members of the Canadian performance history community.

In the fall of 2017, we held a workshop at the University of Toronto. We wanted to gather scholars from across the country to discuss Canadian performance sources. This meeting marked a pivotal moment in our thinking about the book and strongly influenced its eventual contents and structure. We are deeply grateful to everyone who enabled or participated in this event. In particular, we thank Dr. Tamara Trojanowska, the then director of the Centre for Drama, Theatre and Performance Studies, for providing space for the workshop. Dr. Stephen Johnson helped to arrange for four amazing University of Toronto graduate student assistants: thanks to Kelsey Jacobson, who oversaw the catering and kept the schedule running on time, and to David DeGrow, Grace Smith, and Sara Robbins for their superb note-taking. At the University of Victoria, Claire Carolan and Elizabeth Wellman ensured that the travel plans and accommodations for the workshop attendees were in place.

Along the way, other students have contributed to this project. Kennedy Longaphie, a student researcher at Mount Allison University, carefully researched and created transcriptions of the mummering plays and *Acadius*. Lindsay Robinson and Kyra Oser at the University of Victoria similarly provided skilled research support for several chapters. Kate Jordan, a student at Dalhousie University, conducted research at the Dalhousie Archives so we could include a photograph of the Theatre Arts Guild in Halifax.

We are indebted to colleagues across the country who offered advice and support. Notably, we owe thanks to Stephanie Ballard, Dr. Dorothy Williams, Dr. Roberta Barker, Dr. Joanne Muzak, and colleagues in the Gatherings Partnership.

Several executors granted permission to reproduce many of the sources that appear in this book. Their assistance made all the difference. We are sincerely grateful to Madame Thérèse Gouin Décarie (Yvette Mercier-Gouin estate) as well as the Mercier-Gouin family, Jean Kamimura (John Nihei estate), Line-Sylvie Perron (Maurice Perron estate), Anne-Marie Sicotte (Gratien Gélinas estate), Rosalind Shuster (Frank Shuster estate), Aura Vaucrosson (Lorris Elliott estate), Dr. Anton Wagner (Herman Voaden estate), Michael Wayne (Johnny Wayne estate), Janine Carreau (Estate of Pierre and

Claude Gauvreau), and Dr. Ray Ellenwood on behalf of the Claude Gauvreau estate.

We were lucky to encounter so many archivists and arts administrators who took an interest in our project, often alerting us to unusual material or helping us to locate copyright holders. This list of stalwart professionals includes Anna-Karyna Barlati of the École Nationale de Cirque; Adele Benoit and the Black Theatre Workshop; Amy Bowring at Dance Collection Danse; Crystal Braye at the Wooden Boat Museum of Newfoundland and Labrador; Maryann Chach, Sylvia Wang, and Mark Swartz of the Shubert Archives; Mary Haegert at the Houghton Library, Harvard University; Christine Schindler at the Stratford Festival Archives; Theressa Takasaki at the Japanese Canadian Cultural Centre; and Lisa Uyeda at the Nikkei National Museum and Cultural Centre.

More generally, the staff at the following institutions provided essential assistance in locating many of the documents that appear in this sourcebook: Archival and Special Collections, University of Guelph; Bibliothèque et Archives nationales du Québec; City of Vancouver Archives; Hamilton Public Library; Libraries and Archives Canada; McCord Museum; Memorial University of Newfoundland Folklore and Language Archives; Ottawa Little Theatre; Real Estate and Facilities Management, City of Vancouver; Royal Winnipeg Ballet Archives; Special Collections and Archives, University of Waterloo; and William Ready Division of Archives and Research Collections, McMaster University.

University of Alberta Press has been a staunch champion of this project from its inception. Peter Midgley instantly understood the potential of this sourcebook and energetically encouraged us in our pursuit to rethink the narratives and primary source documentation that have traditionally defined the field. Thanks also to Mat Buntin for his wonderful support and sage guidance through the production process. We are particularly indebted to the two anonymous readers the University of Alberta Press invited to review our manuscript. Their insightful feedback and incredible generosity have improved this collection enormously.

We also gratefully acknowledge the financial support of the Social Sciences and Humanities Research Council of Canada as well as the University of Victoria's Office of Research Services, and Mount Allison University.

Finally, as always, our families have been our biggest supporters. They have been the disembodied hands that passed cups of coffee—and the occasional glass of wine—to us during our marathon Zoom meetings. They have graciously refrained from complaining as stacks of research materials grew in our homes, sometimes tumbling to the floor, sometimes tripping the unexpecting. They have, throughout the multi-year process that preceded this publication, never asked when we would be finished. Instead, they continuously cheered us on. For these and so many other familial blessings—thank you.

Introduction

Documenting and Debating Performance in Canada

ALLANA C. LINDGREN, GLEN F. NICHOLS, & ANTHONY J. VICKERY

A SOURCEBOOK ALWAYS HAS TWO SUBJECTS: the topic it addresses and
the cultural moment in which it is published. *Canadian Performance Documents
and Debates: A Sourcebook* offers a selection of playscripts and reproduced
archival materials that provide insight into theatrical activities from the
seventeenth century to the early 1970s. This range of material encourages
readers to consider the many ways that performance has been defined and
documented over a span of more than 350 years. At the same time, this sourcebook reflects the contemporary view that communities, confederations,
colonies, and nations are mutable concepts—social experiments with ever-
changing and often-contested ideological parameters and protocols. Our
intention has not been to create a definitive, or even a comprehensive, historical overview of the country's theatrical past, but rather to facilitate
twenty-first-century debates about how performance and its material
remnants can raise important, yet vexing, questions about "Canada" in its
many permutations.

To help pursue the double focus of this volume, an impressive group of
leading and emerging scholars, artists, and arts administrators has been gathered. The result is a vibrant and varied mix of voices and perspectives that
complements the diversity of tones, styles, and convictions conveyed through
the performance documents examined in this collection. Some of the contributors were invited to provide new English translations of theatrical texts in
acknowledgement that translations are always historically situated and interpretative. Others were asked to write introductions for each chapter as a way
to rethink the artistic and sociopolitical significance of well-known plays and
theatrical events. Still others were requested to write introductions to initiate
conversations about documents and modes of performance that traditionally have not received much attention. Indeed, several of the primary sources
included in the collection are appearing in print for the first time.

The contributors highlight several issues and themes that will resonate
with contemporary readers. Several discuss a sense of apprehension about
gender and race that is present in the documents they introduce. Others foreground how economic factors have tacitly determined the feasibility and
contours of creativity. Still others grapple with how government agendas and
political allegiances have impacted human rights as well as artistic expression. The mobility of ideas is also broached by some contributors who explore
how theatrical trends that circulated transculturally were localized and then
relaunched. While many of these topics reflect the perspectives of the people

who created the documents reprinted in these pages, they also exemplify the twenty-first-century interests of the editors and writers who have contributed to this sourcebook—twenty-first-century interests that ultimately shape (some might say skew) how the past is viewed.[1]

Contexts

Previous Collections

Acknowledging the influence of choice and interpretation in the creation of a collection of historical documents also means considering the broader implications of canon formation. To assemble a sourcebook is to select, and to select is to include and exclude content based on a set of deliberate or unwitting criteria. To date, there is no other sourcebook of historical materials related to performance in Canada, but a brief perusal of a few previously published drama anthologies discloses related and sustained priorities. For instance, several anthologies use celebratory and patriotic language to affirm the existence of historical cultural activity. One example was compiled by James Huston, whose four-volume *Le répertoire national, ou Recueil de littérature canadienne* (1848–50) was originally issued by subscription and features over 1,600 pages from newspapers and magazines, which were mostly published in Lower Canada. The collection covers a range of literary genres, including drama, and in the preface, Huston is clear in his desire to pay tribute to Canada and its culture: "Après avoir fait de longues et attentives recherches et consulté plusieurs écrivains distingués, nous nous sommes convaincu que la republication d'un bon choix des meilleurs écrits canadiens ferait honneur au pays et à ses écrivains" (Huston 1893, i).[2]

The editors of early English-language anthologies emphatically position their volumes as agents in the creation of a Canadian drama tradition. Notably, Vincent Massey's two-volume *Canadian Plays from Hart House Theatre* (1926–27) explicitly expresses the editor's goal to "give birth to a drama really Canadian in spirit and, therefore, worthy of Canada" (Massey 1926–27, vii). Caught between the acknowledgement that "drama is inseparable from the stage" and the reality that no local professional theatre industry existed when his anthology was published, he calls upon the "perpetuation and the spread [of] play-producing societies…throughout the Dominion" to secure "the growth of what we can call a real national drama" (vi). Massey's introduction outlines key anxieties that similarly motivate later collections. His starting position presupposes the need for a "national" theatre, defined as something that is cohesively "Canadian in spirit" (vii). The achievement of that spirit is challenged by two pressing issues: that "Our theatres are under alien influences" and that "We accept in the main what Broadway sends us" (v). In short, Massey articulates qualms voiced by several subsequent anthology editors: a desire to contribute to the formation of a singular, unified national theatre in the face of perceived foreign cultural dominance and a lack of

1. Ric Knowles makes a similar point in his article "Just the High Points? A Canadian Theatre Chronology": "History, of course, is always seen from the vantage point of the present, structured most often by the question of how we got to be where we are now" (1998, 74). Similarly, this sentiment is echoed by Robert Lecker in his consideration of the politics underpinning literary anthologies: "As texts that unite editors and their publishers with teachers and their students, national literature anthologies mediate between critical values, material realities, and pedagogical goals. They act as matrixes that display the tensions, doubts, and ideals attached to crucial historical moments in the cultures that produce them. In this sense, they are narratives in their own right. Every anthology tells a story about how it came into being, and about how it means to be" (2013, 8).

2. "After conducting long and careful research and consulting with several distinguished writers, we are convinced that republishing a good selection of the best Canadian writing would honour the country and its writers." For an overview of the history of theatrical publishing in Quebec, see Forsyth 1989.

national (or even local) artistic infrastructure—issues compounded by disdain for populist forms of theatre.

Massey and most of the editors of English-language drama anthologies who follow him do not probe the term "Canadian." For Massey, Canadian plays are Canadian not because "they may have been given mechanically a Canadian 'atmosphere,' nor because they may deal with Canadian history or politics—but Canadian because the dramatists are good Canadians" (1926–27, vi). Herman Voaden's 1930 collection of *Six Canadian Plays* is similarly motivated by essentialism, assuming the existence of single unified "Canadian" character: "Our innate ideality should force itself on our art, changing our expression till it is in line with our fundamental character" (Voaden 1930, xxiii–xxiv). Fulfilment of that character is to be achieved by distancing our theatre from American culture of "materialism and success" in favour of British "poise and restraint" (Voaden 1930, xix).

By the 1960s, the narratives in the introductions of some English-language drama anthologies published in Canada began to assert cultural nationalist sentiments in more self-assured tones. In 1960, for example, Stanley Richards, an American playwright and anthologist who conducted the Western Ontario Playwriting Seminar in the late 1950s, published a collection of ten one-act plays entitled *Canada on Stage*. In his introduction, Richards claims that "more and more (and finer) plays are being written by Canadian authors. And, salubriously, a majority of these plays are finding their way to Canadian stages and to stages beyond the boundaries of the Dominion" (1960, ix). He asserts that Canadian playwrights are "maturing and enjoying sudden acceptance," which will further encourage them to write "more about the Canadian way of life" (xi).[3]

The national confidence, turbulence, enmity, and angst of the late 1960s and 1970s—bolstered by and expressed through nationalistic Centennial celebrations, Expo 67, the 1970 October Crisis and the growing separatist movement in Quebec, the federal policy of multiculturalism, the 1972 Canada–Soviet Hockey Summit Series, anti-Americanism, the 1976 Summer Olympics in Montreal, and the 1976 election of the Parti Québécois, just to name a few social accelerants—were felt in the pages of anthologies published during this period. The surge of patriotic pride, for instance, is evident in Connie Brissenden's introduction to *Now in Paperback: Six Canadian Plays of the 1970's*, published in 1973: "For the first time in our history," Brissenden writes, "we have a strong contingent of theatre-writers—strong in talent and in numbers—of whom we can be proud...Canadian plays are no longer the exception but the mainstays of our theatres" (1973, 7).

Perhaps not surprising given the pressing issues of the day, editors of English-language drama anthologies during this period seem to be urgently preoccupied with the task of defining what it means to be Canadian. In particular, from approximately the 1970s on, the issue of defining Canada

4. See volume 3, *Albertan Dramatists* (1984), edited by Denis Salter; volume 4, *Manitoba Dramatists* (1986), edited by Douglas Arrell; and volume 7, *West Coast Comedies* (1998), edited by Alan Filewod.

through examinations of its diversity was a guiding factor in the creation of English-language drama anthologies published in Canada. Rolf Kalman's five-volume anthology *A Collection of Canadian Plays* (1972–78) offers a range of contemporary plays, including plays for young audiences (volume 4) and English translations of plays from Quebec (volume 5). Unlike Kalman's series, the scope of Anton Wagner's four-volume anthology, titled *Canada's Lost Plays* (1978–80), has a larger temporal span by including plays written between 1606 and 1960. Wagner's series reclaims several "lost" plays by bringing them back into print. Like Kalman's publications, *Canada's Lost Plays* covers a diverse range of topics, including drama in the nineteenth century, women's theatre, drama in the early twentieth century, and theatre in Quebec.

Yet, despite this reorientation to broader inclusion—no matter how limited it might appear to twenty-first-century readers—there remain echoes of Massey's unquestioned understanding of the existence of a containable and stable definition of "Canadian" that underpinned the editors' elusive attempts to define the term. In *Encounter: Canadian Drama in Four Media* (1973), Eugene Benson ventures beyond stage drama to include other types of scripts while counselling that "plays should be Canadian plays in the sense that they must say something about Canada and the people who live in Canada" (1973, 1). According to Andrew Parkin in the introduction to *Stage One: A Canadian Scenebook* (1973), "In Canada today there is a curious mixture of attitudes about Canadian culture. There is a demand for things Canadian, the continuing search for identity, the surge of nationalism, the cult of 'this land,' and mixed in with it all, modesty about the real achievements, together with dependence on foreign opinions" (1973, ix). Correspondingly, in *Contemporary Canadian Drama* (1974), Joseph Shaver informs his readers that "differing greatly in approach and technique, nearly all of these plays deal—in varying degree— with the problem of identity and the desire to 'belong,' a theme which may, just possibly, be one of the characteristics of Canadian drama" (1974, 1).

Other anthologies of the time focus on individual regions, including Connie Brissenden's *West Coast Plays* (1975) and *Prairie Performance: A Collection of Short Plays* (1980), which was edited by Diane Bessai. Some of the volumes in the New Canadian Drama series published by Borealis Press were similarly dedicated to the plays of specific regions.[4] While the emphasis during this period was on regional voices, Pamela Hawthorn, the managing director of the New Play Centre, which published Brissenden's *West Coast Plays*, reminded readers in her introduction to that publication that the theatrical conversation generated by these anthologies was, for the most part, still national in nature: "In January 1972 I was asked to join a growing but still fledgling organization whose aim was to develop and promote B.C. plays. This organization was the New Play Centre and from my first meeting with its founders, Sheila Neville and Douglas Bankson, I became swept up in the fervour surrounding the Canadian Playwright. This fervour, born out of a new national awareness

5. Wasserman subsequently added a second volume (1993) and both volumes have been reissued in five editions up to 2013.

of the need for a strong Canadian identity, has made it an easier, but never simple task to gain long overdue attention for the homegrown play" (7).

In Quebec, a parallel sense of cultural conviction regarding French-language theatre was apparent in publications like Jan Doat's *Anthologie du théâtre québécois: Le théâtre canadien de langue française de ses origins à nos jours 1606–1970* (1973) as well as *Anthologie thématique du théâtre québécois au xixe siècle* (1978), edited by Étienne-F. Duval (with the collaboration of Jean Laflamme). This latter publication was followed shortly by Duval's *Le jeu de l'histoire et de la société dans le théâtre québécois 1900–1950* (1981).

The years 1984 and 1985 marked the apex of omnibus-type anthologies that sought to map Canadian drama with the publication of three collections: Richard Plant's *Modern Canadian Drama* (1984), Richard Perkyns's *Major Plays of the Canadian Theatre 1934–1984* (1984), and Jerry Wasserman's *Modern Canadian Plays* (1985).[5] All three convey optimism that, as Plant states, "Canadian drama has come of age" (1984, 26) and as Perkyns concurs, "the impetus and the opportunities are now available more than ever for Canada to produce dramatists whose work can without shame stand beside that of playwrights in countries where drama has more traditionally been accepted as part of a nation's culture" (1984, 17).

In 1993, and reflecting the critiques of canon formation that sparked vehement debates among scholars, Alan Filewod's *The CTR Anthology: Fifteen Plays from* Canadian Theatre Review appeared in print. Filewod oriented his introductory statement away from previous nationalistic and celebratory impulses and instead invited readers to consider how the choices over the years about which plays to publish in the *CTR* (*Canadian Theatre Review*)—the source publication for his anthology—constructed narratives not only about the plays they contextualized, but also about the nation and its shifting theatrical interests: "All canons enshrine identifiable values and in this *CTR* is no exception. At the same time every addition to or rehabilitation of the canon both expands and subverts notions of Canadian theatre. The *CTR* canon represented here offers several narratives of Canadian theatre. In particular, these plays can be read in terms of the evolution of *CTR*'s discourse of nationalism and the regionalism as the defining conditions of modern Canadian drama, and as an expression of the changing nature of theatrical practice in Canada" (1993, xii).

Since the publication of *The CTR Anthology*, English-language drama anthologies have tended to couple national coverage with a focus on the specific demographics of playwrights, often representing communities that have been traditionally marginalized. Diversity, in other words, has continued to occupy editors' interest, with an expansion of the parameters and definitions of diversity that guided previous anthologies. Among the many collections that have followed this approach are *Beyond the Pale: Dramatic Writing from First Nations Writers and Writers of Colour* (1996), edited by Yvette Nolan, Betty Quan, and George Bwanika Seremba; *Staging Coyote's Dream: An Anthology of First Nations*

6.   The literature debating canon formation is extensive. An early example is Von Hallberg 1984. For conversations within the Canadian context, see Lecker 1991 and 2013.

Drama in English (2003), edited by Monique Mojica and Ric Knowles; *Love, Loss, and Longing: South Asian Canadian Plays* (2015), edited by Dalbir Singh; *Queer Play: An Anthology of Queer Women's Performance and Play*, edited by Moynan King; and Q2Q: *Queer Canadian Performance Texts* (2018), edited by Peter Dickinson, C.E. Gatchalian, Kathleen Oliver, and Dalbir Singh, just to name a few.

Canon Formation

The recent proliferation of anthologies that explore the intersections between identity politics and drama is, in part, the result of the impassioned debates about canon formation that ricocheted through universities in the 1980s and 1990s as scholars argued over the proposition that aesthetic standards are determined in ways that enable the continuation of discriminatory social hierarchies and the normalization of exclusionary practices.[6] Rejecting the notion of a universal understanding of excellence, some scholars queried how canons function as "the instruments of entrenched interests" (Von Hallberg 1984, 2).

Given that anthologies—and sourcebooks—inevitably participate in the project of canon-making because of the processes of selection, preservation, and dissemination, one can conclude that a collection like *Canadian Performance Documents and Debates: A Sourcebook* inevitably will be contentious not only in terms of material that has been excluded, but because some of the included documents contain ideas that might be viewed as noxious from a twenty-first-century perspective. The past, however, is always contentious for the very reason that attitudes and values are mutable. Yet, by contextualizing historical performance documents, the introductions in this publication demonstrate that there is a fundamental difference between trying to understand the past and promoting beliefs that are no longer acceptable. To this end, Gerald Graff offers wise advice in *Beyond Culture Wars*: "The best solution to today's conflicts over culture is to teach the conflicts themselves, making them part of our object of study and using them as a new kind of organizing principle to give the curriculum the clarity and focus that almost all sides now agree it lacks" (1992, 12). In this way, the hope is that the documents included in this collection and the introductions that accompany them will spark productive debates about how people use performance to assert particular values and what those values tell us about the people who have lived in different time periods in the lands now known as Canada.

The Plurality of "Canada"

Before proceeding further, it is worth noting that the phrase "the lands now known as Canada" is neither straightforward nor without debate. In fact, perhaps one of the most controversial aspects of this volume for twenty-first-century readers will be the use of the word "Canada." A collection of theatrical performance documents that extends back to 1606 needs to acknowledge that over the four centuries covered in this volume, the meaning of "Canada" and

7. Denis Salter makes this point
in his article "The Idea of a
National Theatre." See Salter
1991, 71–72.

the ideas it connotes have been in continual flux. A reductively unified or even singular "Canada" is therefore conceptually, if not geographically, a misnomer. Or, as theatre historian Denis Salter has written, the canon is "endlessly deferred" in the same way that "the very idea of 'Canada'" is an ultimately unattainable and unstable entity (1991, 90).

In this light, querying the validity of assembling performance activities and the resulting documentation within a national context is reasonable. One response is that many of the documents in *Canadian Performance Documents and Debates: A Sourcebook* invite a consideration of the plurality of Canada through their direct or indirect engagement with concerns related to collective identities. Readers are, therefore, encouraged to parse the term "Canada" as it appears throughout the volume to determine how it has been used to perpetuate or challenge an unacknowledged shorthand for shifting values and priorities that benefit some demographics while discriminating against others.

Along the same lines, the view taken in this collection is that the words "nation" and "national" are not synonymous with "nationalism," though none of these terms is neutral.[7] The intent is not to glorify Canada's theatrical past, but to understand its artistic and ideological complexities—to see what the remnants of performance can tell us about the values, debates, and priorities of artists and their audiences at different moments in time. Therefore, unlike previous anthologies that have tried to define or idealize the nation, *Canadian Performance Documents and Debates: A Sourcebook* offers readers the opportunity to grapple with the conflicts, contradictions, and multiplicity of perspectives that accrue in the collection as a means to understand how ideas about "Canada" have reverberated in the past.

Without question, the period examined in this sourcebook can be—and should be—interrogated. Readers might question why this publication only stretches to the early 1970s, but this choice is deliberate. Beyond the debates about Canada that the nationalist festivities and conflicts of the late 1960s and early 1970s facilitate, this fertile artistic period and its aftermath, which fostered the rapid expansion of professional theatre as part of the growth of alternate theatre, and dance companies that resulted from the international dance boom and the rise of the independent dance artist, has arguably received more scholarly attention than the performance activities of earlier decades and centuries. In this light, *Canadian Performance Documents and Debates: A Sourcebook* is an attempt to encourage renewed critical interest in the pre-Centennial past.

Performance

Another term in need of attention is "performance." This collection differs from prior anthologies in that it not only includes drama but also offers a sampling of dance, opera, and popular entertainment forms such as circus and vaudeville. This expanded focus displaces the traditional dominance of text-based theatrical activities while simultaneously acknowledging the rich diversity of the performing arts that have been practiced during the period under consideration and dismantling the artificial distinctions between so-called high and low art. To accommodate this multidisciplinary focus, the term "performance" is used instead of "theatre," even though the documents chosen for this sourcebook are all theatrical in one or more ways.

Furthermore, use of the term "performance" intentionally nods towards performance studies, which similarly embraces artistic activity that extends beyond text-based drama and the tiered ranking of the arts according to discriminatory values that trace their origins to colonial projects. Indeed, in an effort to upend the long-standing industrialized Western hegemony, performance studies scholarship is frequently oriented towards intercultural exchanges instead of examples of creative expression indebted exclusively to Eurocentric artistic traditions. The range of races and cultural communities represented in these pages fits within and furthers performance studies' intercultural approach.

Yet, despite respecting the precepts and ethics that inform performance studies scholarship, this volume does not test the elasticity of the word "performance" to the extent that many proponents of performance studies would counsel. As Richard Schechner, one of the founders of performance studies, has suggested, the field is all-encompassing:

> Performance *as an overall category must be construed as a "broad spectrum" or "continuum" of actions ranging from ritual, play, sports, popular entertainments, the performing arts (theatre, dance music), and everyday life performances to the enactment of social, professional, gender, race, and class roles, to healing (from shamanism to surgery), and to the various representations and construction of actions in the media and the Internet. There is no historically fixable limit to what is or is not "performance." Along the continuum, new genres can be added, others can be dropped. The underlying theoretical claim is that any action can be framed, presented, highlighted, or displayed as a performance. (2002, xi–xii)*

Canadian Performance Documents and Debates: A Sourcebook does not follow Schechner's definition, and instead focuses exclusively on materials created for explicitly artistic performances intended for the edification or enjoyment of the performers themselves, or a live audience, or readers in the case of a closet drama such as *Sweet Girl Graduate* or a government brief such as "A Dialogue on the State of Theatre in Canada."

Sources related to ceremonies and rituals have not been included, even though many religious and cultural rituals involve dialogue, characterization, plot, dance, and other elements closely associated with theatrical performance. Furthermore, there are no pre-contact examples in the collection. The earliest case study is *The Theatre of Neptune*, which was penned

by Marc Lescarbot, a seventeenth-century French writer and lawyer. The
seemingly infinite expansiveness of the word "performance" is not conflated
with religious rites in order to be sensitive to the critique that using artistic
terminology to discuss cultural practices potentially distorts the sacred nature
of the latter as the words "theatre" and "performance" equate too easily with
"entertainment" and "diversion"—thereby potentially trivializing expressions
of spirituality. These distinctions between religious and cultural ceremonies,
theatrical productions and performance are not just matters of terminological
nuance, but involve the vital acts of reclaiming ownership and control by
traditionally marginalized communities whose cultural practices have long
been oppressed or co-opted.

Following the logic of this argument, one might reasonably query the
appropriateness of the representations of Indigenous Peoples in *Canadian
Performance Documents and Debates: A Sourcebook*. Almost all were created by
artists of European heritages. The culturally ersatz pan-Indian costuming
at the fancy dress balls held in Ottawa during the nineteenth century, for
instance, exemplify the kind of appropriation and control that has long
dictated what Indigenous Peoples (or their theatrical stand-ins) could say and
do while influencing how they were viewed by the rest of the population.

Informing this collection is an apprehension over the appropriateness of
including now-odious depictions of Indigenous Peoples as well as other racial
groups and women. That is, does the inclusion of these examples participate in the continued demoralization of these groups? Ultimately, *Canadian
Performance Documents and Debates: A Sourcebook* has been guided by the view
that bigoted values and actions need to remain a visible part of the archival
and documentary records. To do otherwise is to risk abetting the erasure of
evidence of Canada's long history of prejudice. That said, the choice to end the
sourcebook with Chief Dan George's powerful "Lament for a Confederation,"
which was delivered to crowds in Vancouver who had assembled to celebrate
one hundred years of Confederation on July 1, 1967, gives the last word to an
Indigenous artist.

Mediated Performance

In addition to thinking about the implications of the terminology used in this
volume, readers are encouraged to consider the sources or, more accurately,
how performance and the past are mediated through the documentation
that represents them. For instance, the photographs, theatrical programs,
handwritten notes, and so on presented in this volume are obviously repro-
ductions—not the originals. While these kinds of copies are valuable to study
when thinking about the topics examined in this book, it is important to
acknowledge that the materiality of the originals, which inevitably convey
information about the source, is missing. It is not possible to reproduce the
original paper stock of the fancy dress ball photographs, for instance. The
original size of the petitions against "blackface" clowns has been altered to

fit the dimensions of this sourcebook. The resolution of the newspaper articles related to mummering has been digitally improved. While these details
might seem minor, as theatre and performance scholar Peggy Phelan asserts,
"performance's life is only in the present. Performance cannot be saved,
recorded, documented, or otherwise participate in the circulation of representations of representations: once it does so it becomes something other
than performance" (1993, 146). Or, as theatre historians Charlotte Canning and
Thomas Postlewait similarly suggest, "the representation seeks to be an objective image of the thing itself, yet it cannot avoid being, in some capacity, a
subjective distortion of that thing" (2010, 7).

If recording performance means creating something that is inescapably
not the performance in question, and if making archival materials accessible
generally involves the dissemination of copies of documents related to but not
the performance itself, this double-distancing should not dissuade readers
from engaging with the sources reproduced in these pages. Ultimately, all
historical study is based on the material or digital vestiges of past events
or actions. How, in other words, do we understand the First World War, or
the stock market crash of 1929, or the signing of the Proclamation of the
Constitution Act of 1982 except through the photographic or moving images,
objects, written accounts, and oral histories that have been generated during
or in the wake of these events?

The "alteration" of performance through representation that Phelan,
Canning, and Postlewait all allude to is further magnified in some of the editorial choices that have been made in this sourcebook. For instance, excerpts
instead of the entire texts of two plays—*The Conquest of Canada; or the Siege of
Quebec* and *The Man Who Went*—have been chosen because both plays are quite
lengthy. Moreover, neither is a likely candidate for theatrical production in
the near future, so providing a performance-worthy script is not the purpose
of their inclusion in this collection. Instead, the excerpts are intended to help
to focus the reader's attention on certain aspects of the plays. For example, the
excerpts from *The Conquest of Canada; or the Siege of Quebec* provide an opportunity to consider how the playwright's dramaturgical style and use of language
affects characterization. The dialogue from Act IV, in particular, conveys the
effects of battle on the characters and in so doing solicits empathy from audience members, thereby potentially bypassing critical engagement. The final
scene from *The Man Who Went* exemplifies the resolution of all plot points: a
dramaturgical feature that is typical of well-made plays. The final scene also
returns to the play's underpinning thematic interest in the issue of empire.
The concluding moment, in which love is playfully depicted as a way to tighten
"the bonds of the Empire," offers twenty-first-century readers a chance to
consider the political implications of theatrical comedy and laughter. Ideally,
these excerpts will inspire readers to read the complete text for each of these
plays. Knowing, however, that excerpting is tantamount to editing and can

lead to a misrepresentation or unintentional interpretations of a play, the accompanying introductions carefully contextualize these theatrical works while offering thorough bibliographies so readers can consult other scholarly perspectives.

Similarly, including a translation that takes artistic liberty with the original was also an intentional decision. Specifically, in translating Marcel Dubé's *Zone* from French to English, Aviva Ravel, an accomplished playwright, made substantive changes to the plot. As Sylvain Lavoie notes in his astute introduction, Ravel's choices alter the play in several ways. The characters' diction and setting more directly convey their socioeconomic circumstances in the English version. Ravel also revised the plot to lessen the religious allusions. Finally, she altered the plot at a critical moment in the play. Consequently, readers and audience members who engage with the play only in English will experience a different *Zone* than those who know the play in French. Ravel's version, although a distinctly bold example, invites debate about how all translations inevitably modify their original source texts.

Contents

The ordering of the sources is another editorial choice. While the chronologically arranged table of contents can help to historicize the sources, offering a temporal signpost that situates individual events and practices within specific moments in time, readers are cautioned that this arrangement is not intended to suggest a linear trajectory of social or artistic development. To counter any impulse to interpret the arrangement of the chapters as an evolutionary account of performance, the following thematic groupings and the Thematic Table of Contents should help readers to focus on the issues that the chapters flag.

Clothing/Costuming

This collection contains documentary evidence of how clothing and costumes have enabled theatricalized performances of the self. The four fancy dress balls hosted by the governors general from 1876 to 1898 provide a fascinating glimpse into a popular form of entertainment for the upper classes. As Cynthia Cooper suggests in her introduction to the archival photographs reproduced in Chapter 7, "Dressing up in costume offered the extraordinary experience of transcending the limitations of fashionable dress and one's public self." As such, the images offer a record of fantasized histories, nationalistic agendas, gender transgressions, and racial drag while exemplifying how portrait photography and cutting-edge photographic techniques were important contributors to these escapist expressions of identity.

In his introduction to documents related to John Herbert and Tracy Roberts in Chapter 22, J. Paul Halferty similarly shows how cross-dressing/drag performances enabled gay men to express their gender identities and undermine constricting and punitive social norms. In this way, the archival images included in this collection demonstrate how clothing, body styling, and subversion of gender expectations through performance were simultaneously dangerous, liberating, and galvanizing for Toronto's gay/queer communities.

Community Building

No less politicized are the chapters outlining how performance functioned as the conduit for community building. Louis Patrick Leroux's overview of circus practices in Quebec from the late eighteenth century to the mid-twentieth century in Chapter 4 provides an insightful contribution to the history of popular performance while establishing that there has been a long history of circus performers from Quebec. These performers have not only contributed to the various evolving iterations of circus, but have been embraced as emblematic of the daring theatrical talent in Quebec. In particular, as Leroux notes, Louis Cyr is a stellar example of the mobilizing power of celebrity by becoming a symbol of strength and endurance that has rallied pride within Quebec.

In another example from Quebec, resistance to authority is a dominant theme in *Zone*, a play that helped to launch the career of Marcel Dubé, an important and prolific writer from Montreal. In his introduction to Chapter 28, Sylvain Lavoie encourages readers to consider the parallels between how the play explores the conflict that pits youth against the police in the mid-twentieth century and Quebec's own sociopolitical turbulence under Maurice Duplessis—a connection that no doubt was recognizable for many audience members who attended performances of the play in the early 1950s.

As Denyse Lynde outlines in her introduction to Chapter 25, mummering in Newfoundland has a long history of community building. Primarily a Christmastime tradition, mummering can take many forms, including groups of people who don homemade costumes and visit neighbours as well as parades and the performances of scripted plays that usually involve hero-combat narratives. Despite the multiple stylistic iterations of mummering, the localization of theatrical tradition that results from communal creation and close engagement between performers and their audiences remains constant. The demarcations of participating communities are revised and reinforced through each mummer performance.

Erin Hurley examines the attempt to create a sense of bicultural—if not entirely bilingual—harmony during Expo 67. In other words, she explores an attempt to fashion a sense of cultural unity through performance for national and international visitors to the world's fair in Montreal. Specifically, in her introduction to Chapter 30, Hurley foregrounds *Katimavik-Revue*, a fifty-minute variety satire about Expo 67 and its visitors that was created by Gratien Gélinas with Johnny Wayne and Frank Shuster. Performed in French and English, *Katimavik-Revue* "pointed to national and linguistic distinctions and reconciled them in spectacle."

William Andrew Tremayne's play *The Man Who Went* is a good example of
the well-made play genre infused with Canadian references. In his introduction to the excerpt included in Chapter 12, Anthony J. Vickery examines how
the play uses this European dramatic form to subtly counter the stereotypes of
Canadians as less urbane than their European counterparts. Placed against the
backdrop of the First World War, the play projects an image of a Canada that
is modern and daring while simultaneously supporting continuance of the
British Empire.

Economics

Several of the chapters remind readers that artistic achievement has often
been influenced by non-artistic factors, including economics. The documents
Anthony J. Vickery contextualizes in Chapter 10, which focuses on Winnipeg's
Walker Theatre, illuminate the business operations of a lively and successful
Canadian theatre on the touring circuit during the early twentieth century.
The documents also provide insight into the intersections between interna-
tional transportation, the economic exigencies of touring, and the nationalist
factors that influenced dealings with business colleagues in the United States.

Chafing against commercialization and in addition to providing a forum to
renounce gender and racial discrimination, theatrical productions have also
given voice to the class struggle. Oscar Ryan's *Unity*, which was produced by
the Workers' Experimental Theatre in 1933, is an example of the international
agitprop style. In its use of cartoonish characters and choral mass chanting,
the play is an unabashed critique of capitalist excess. In Chapter 18, Alan
Filewod details the political context of the play's premiere and outlines how
this kind of performance generated combustive conflict between artists and
the authorities.

Experimentation

Some of the chapters explore how artists have pursued experimentation with
artistic forms of expression. In *Rocks: A Play of Northern Ontario*, Toronto playwright Herman Voaden launched the artistic style he later named symphonic
expressionism—a non-realistic, multimedia approach to production that
synthesized music, lighting, spoken dialogue, choral speech, ritualized gestures,
and dance. Drawing on Voaden's own writings, Anton Wagner indicates in
Chapter 17 that the playwright was deeply influenced by the Group of Seven,
whose paintings sought to articulate an aesthetic that matched the Canadian
landscape and placed art in the service of cultural nationalism. In adapting
new artistic ideas initiated in Europe, the Little Theatre Movement in Canada
was similarly motivated by nationalist impulses. In his introduction to
Chapter 13, Paul J. Stoesser explores how scenography and theatre architecture supported the ideals of the Little Theatre Movement, which theatrically
advanced a sense of national cohesiveness.

One of the ways that the proponents of the Little Theatres in Canada distinguished their artistic activity from the productions staged by their larger, more commercial, counterparts was in their adoption of more modest performance spaces, which helped to recalibrate the actor-audience relationship in more intimate terms. This goal animated the design of the Festival Stage at the Stratford Festival in Stratford, Ontario, as well. Drawing on a range of archival documents, Liza Giffen examines the importance of the thrust stage to the history of the Stratford Festival in Chapter 27. Developed by Tyrone Guthrie, the British director, and the designer Tanya Moiseiwitsch, the Festival Stage created what Giffen calls a "communion-like effect of actor-audience interaction" in which the closer proximity of artist and spectator made nuanced performances possible while simultaneously accommodating realist and ritualistic conventions.

Within Quebec, linguistic experimentation expanded the contours of artistic expression. As Ray Ellenwood notes in his introduction in Chapter 23 for *Bien-être*, translated into English by Ellenwood as *The Good Life*, playwright Claude Gauvreau was a member of the Montreal Automatists, an interdisciplinary group of artists dedicated to artistic experimentation intended to bypass rationality in order to access the unconscious. By extending Automatist tenets to theatre in *The Good Life*, Gauvreau decoupled sound and meaning, language and action. Confused, audiences initially responded with laughter, but Gauvreau's "explorational language" remained steadfastly unapologetic in its rejection of the artistic status quo. As Ellenwood indicates, Gauvreau's plays, including *The Good Life*, are now seen within Quebec as classics; their experimental impulse, exemplary of Quebecois artistic innovation.

Gender

Another way that the chapters can be placed in conversation with each other is by exploring how several lend themselves to discussions about gender politics. In particular, a number of the chapters—including the chapters for *Historical Pageant* and the *Happy and Glorious* concert—showcase women's artistic accomplishments, and several of the accompanying introductions examine performance-related documentation against the backdrop of social debates about the rights and social agency of women, including *Sweet Girl Graduate* by Sarah Anne Curzon. In her introduction to this play, which appears in Chapter 8, Kym Bird helps the reader to understand the nuanced contours of progressive thinking regarding the rights of women in Canada near the end of the nineteenth century, showing how Kate Blogg, the play's protagonist, fights for the opportunity to study at "Toronto University" at a time when the issue of female education was fervently debated.

The question of women's rights is also central to Lister Sinclair's radio play *Hilda Morgan*. Radio dramas were a popular genre in Canada during the early twentieth century. In particular, the Radio Drama Department of the CBC, under the leadership of Andrew Allan, produced exciting and often provocative productions. *Hilda Morgan*, which told the story of a woman's unwed pregnancy, was one such program. In Chapter 24, John Jackson and Howard Fink discuss how the aural world of radio plays could powerfully engage listeners' imaginations; technology mediated, but also intensified, the listeners' involvement. Therefore, it is perhaps not surprising that *Hilda Morgan* unleashed a passionate debate about female morality and autonomy.

In addition to Curzon, *Canadian Performance Documents and Debates: A Sourcebook* includes plays by a number of other female playwrights. Yvette Mercier-Gouin was one of the most successful. Her play *Cocktail*, included in this collection in a new English translation by Glen F. Nichols and introduced in Chapter 19 by Christl Verduyn, was hugely successful when it premiered in 1935. Moreover, Mercier-Gouin raised a family while establishing her career in theatre. In contrast to her personal achievements, she uses *Cocktail* to examine female desire for more autonomy, mirroring many women's frustrations with gender strictures in the 1930s. Marjorie Pickthall was another successful female playwright. During her lifetime, she attained national and international recognition. In her introduction to Pickthall's *The Wood Carver's Wife* in Chapter 14, Moira Day deftly sets the shifting responses to the play within their theatrical and sociohistorical contexts, noting Pickthall's frustration as a female writer and her belief that "as a man you could go ahead and stir up things *fine*."

Pickthall is not the only artist highlighted in this sourcebook who experienced success tempered by stresses related to gender. At a time when there were limited professional opportunities for dancers in Canada, Evelyn Geary's career provides insight into the daily realities of female vaudeville performers. As Amy Bowring details in her introduction to Chapter 15, female vaudeville performers were applauded onstage, though criticized as having loose morals for performing professionally. They generally enjoyed good incomes and had more financial independence than most other women, but also had gruelling rehearsal and performance schedules.

Government Regulation and Intervention
Largely absent from previous Canadian performance histories, the documentation related to Cantonese opera in Vancouver similarly raises opportunities to think about how West Coast culture was affected by the transnational nature and the financial dynamics of theatrical performance during the early twentieth century. Although the border between the United States and Canada appears to have been fairly fluid for Corliss Powers Walker and the New York firm of Marc Klaw and Abraham Erlanger (with whom Walker had a booking agreement), Canadian immigration officials tasked with enacting race-based policies strictly regulated the ability of Cantonese opera performers to enter the country as Wing Chung Ng discusses in his introduction for Chapter 11.

Another significant instance of the federal government influencing performance was set in motion with the decision to establish internment camps during the Second World War. Documents related to John Nihei, whose adaptation of *William Tell* was performed within the confines of a Japanese internment camp in British Columbia, are included in this collection. As Cody Poulton and Jordan Stanger-Ross highlight in their introduction to Chapter 21, the play's theme of deliverance from tyranny inevitably resonated with Nikkei audiences while underscoring the vulnerability of minorities and encouraging discussion about the limits of democracy within wartime Canada.

One example of an artist advocating for more government financial support of the performing arts involves Robertson Davies, a well-known Canadian playwright, novelist, journalist, editor, and professor. When asked to write a submission for the Royal Commission on National Development in the Arts, Letters and Sciences—which was more commonly known as the Massey Commission after Vincent Massey, the commission's chair—Robertson Davies responded with "A Dialogue on the State of the Theatre in Canada." Structured as a conversation between two fictional theatre artists, "A Dialogue" outlines the deficiencies in mid-twentieth-century Canadian theatre while advocating for a national theatre modelled on European ideals. As James Hoffman suggests in his introduction to Chapter 26, Davies's perspective unquestioningly promotes a colonial orientation. The dramatic presentation of Davies's argument points to the effectiveness of theatrical dialogue to engage and instruct while his directive for creating a national theatre, particularly his caution against strict government involvement, was adopted by the Massey Commission in its report.

Performance as Resistance

There are numerous examples of performance used as a form of resistance in this volume. In the 1840s, for instance, members of the Black community in Toronto petitioned City Council to ban the performances of blackface clowns, whose provocative racist routines were injurious to their reputations and encouraged violence toward them. As Stephen Johnson asks in his introduction to Chapter 5, these documents raise important questions that not only demonstrate how popular entertainment has been used to construct and normalize racial stereotypes, but also query government's responsibility and ability to regulate these performances. While the petitions are evidence of aestheticized and systemic racism in Toronto, they also tell the story of Black attempts to exercise agency within a civic bureaucracy.

Created more than a century later and demonstrating how the act of making art can be an assertion of racial agency, *How Now Black Man* by playwright Lorris Elliott creatively claims theatrical space for the Black diaspora. Clarence Bayne is a charter member of the Black Workshop (later renamed the Black Theatre Workshop, the oldest continuously operating Black theatre company in Canada), which produced *How Now Black Man*. His introduction to Chapter 29 provides both a critical assessment of Elliott's play and an impassioned personal remembrance of the ambition, struggle, and early success of the Black Theatre Workshop.

Several of the other chapters also engage with race. Many of the pre-twentieth-century chapters and documents, for instance, provide insight into Canada's long history of racial intolerance. Notably, this sourcebook offers an excellent new translation of *The Theatre of Neptune* by Daniel J. Ruppel and VK Preston, along with an introduction to Chapter 1 by Jill Carter (Anishinaabe-Ashkenazi) that rethinks the play's previous status as an unquestioned originary text. Specifically, Carter analyzes how this 1606 text not only prescriptively conjures mutually accepted hierarchical encounters between Indigenous Peoples and Europeans during the seventeenth century, but also how it can help readers to parse the racial implications of the more recent Canada 150 celebrations. Likewise, in dramatizing General James Wolfe and the 1759 British campaign to capture Quebec as part of the Seven Years' War in his play *The Conquest of Canada; or the Siege of Quebec*, George Cockings praises the valour of all men serving in the British military. In his introduction to Chapter 2, Glen F. Nichols contextualizes Cockings's nationalistic adulation while drawing the reader's attention to the racist and imperialist assumptions that inform the play.

Acadius, or Love in a Calm (1774) serves as an important example of British garrison theatre, demonstrating how this kind of play served as a diversion for military personnel while blending local references with British theatrical genres. In his introduction to Chapter 3, which models how to read the social and theatrical importance of a play when only fragmentary evidence remains, Justin A. Blum explores how the racial impersonation and cross-dressing in the play facilitate a consideration of eighteenth-century social mores.

Another military production that contains pertinent information about race is *Zero, or Harlequin Light*. In Chapter 6, Heather Davis-Fisch introduces images related to this theatrical pantomime, which was performed in the Arctic in 1851 to amuse the naval squadron searching for traces of the Franklin Expedition. At one point in the action, the script indicates that a character called Fox transforms into the ship's young Inuk navigator and interpreter. There is no record of the reception of this part of the pantomime, but Davis-Fisch investigates the racial implications of this action, thereby raising questions about attitudes towards race within British society at the time.

The Theatre of Neptune, *The Conquest of Canada; or the Siege of Quebec*, and *Zero, or Harlequin Light* are not the only chapters that address representations of Indigenous Peoples. As a poet and literary recitalist, E. Pauline Johnson (Tekahionwake) was a beloved Indigenous celebrity, but as Sasha Kovacs notes in her introduction to Johnson's "A Red Girl's Reasoning" in Chapter 9, subsequent scholarship has construed Johnson's performance practices as evidence of self-imposed cultural assimilation. Through her insightful reading of Johnson's short story "A Red Girl's Reasoning," Kovacs challenges this perspective, offering a new way to interpret the documentary evidence that illuminates Johnson's Indigenous activism.

The text of Chief Dan George's "Lament for Confederation," included in this collection and introduced by Jenn Cole (mixed-ancestry Algonquin) in Chapter 31, is not only a record of its author's unwavering integrity, but also speaks to the ongoing discrimination against Indigenous Peoples in Canada. Yet, like the petitions signed by members of Toronto's Black community in Stephen Johnson's introduction for Chapter 5, "Lament for Confederation" was an assertion of defiance and determination, and Chief Dan George's performance of this speech with his children at the Empire Stadium in Vancouver on July 1, 1967, can be viewed as proclaiming a new age of Indigenous activism.

Reactionary and Colonialist Art

While the sources related to Voaden, the Little Theatres, the Stratford Festival, and Gauvreau are evidence of a desire to push back artistic boundaries, other documents serve as reminders that performance is not always forward-looking. *Historical Pageant* was an extravagant theatrical spectacle produced in Toronto to celebrate Canada's Diamond Jubilee in 1927. As Allana C. Lindgren discusses in her introduction to Chapter 16, the event was written, arranged, and choreographed by Amy Sternberg, a successful dance teacher, and was staged through the efforts of over three thousand people, including five hundred performers, many of them members of the Imperial Order Daughters of the Empire (IODE). Presenting scenes intended to represent important moments from Canada's history, this highly applauded spectacle is a revealing example of how women associated with the IODE used a theatrical performance to advocate enthusiastically for a continued strong colonial affiliation with the British Empire.

A further example of the ways in which female artists have placed their art in the service of colonial ties is the 1939 *Happy and Glorious* pageant. In her introduction to Chapter 20, Erin Joelle McCurdy describes how the Winnipeg Ballet Club, which would later become the Royal Winnipeg Ballet, the longest continually running ballet company in North America, made its first appearance as part of this concert, which had been organized in honour of King George VI and Queen Elizabeth, who were touring North America. The dancers performed *Grain* and *Kilowatt Magic*. These two choreographic works conveyed nationalist pride and promoted the prairies as resource rich and ready to affirm ties with the British as the world marched ever closer to another globalized war. In this way, *Grain* and *Kilowatt Magic* serve as reminders of how dancers' bodies have been used to signal political allegiance.

Final Thoughts

Canadian Performance Documents and Debates: A Sourcebook is neither comprehensive nor definitive. As the Thematic Table of Contents indicates, individual chapters fit within more than one category, creating opportunities to expand the analysis offered here. Moreover, the contributors' introductions provide specific readings of the documents they introduce, but their comments do not preclude other—even contradictory—readings. Instead, through the questions they ask, the modes of analysis they employ, and the historical and artistic connections they make through contextualization, they offer useful models of engagement. To this end, readers are encouraged to make their own connections between the chapters. For instance, how might reviewing the documents related to the Walker Theatre in tandem with Cantonese opera productions in Canada help us to think about how attitudes toward race and ethnicity have exerted subtle and not-so-subtle influences on the economics of touring? What might be learned about modes of advocacy by putting the agit-prop strategies in *Unity* in conversation with the use of characterization and dialogue in "A Dialogue on the State of the Theatre in Canada" by Robertson Davies? In addition, any number of other case studies can be easily chosen. Indeed, the hope is that readers will be inspired by the different examples included in this book to seek out other neglected sources to augment our collective understanding of past performance practices and their cultural meanings while continuing to query how sourcebooks contribute to historical debates that continue to resonate today.

Bibliography and Further Reading

Arrell, Douglas, ed. 1986. *Manitoba Dramatists*. New Canadian Drama 4. Ottawa: Borealis.

Benson, Eugene, ed. 1973. *Encounter: Canadian Drama in Four Media*. London: Methuen.

Bessai, Diane, ed. 1980. *Prairie Performance: A Collection of Short Plays*. Edmonton: NeWest.

Brissenden, Connie, ed. 1973. *Now in Paperback: Six Canadian Plays of the 1970's*. Toronto: Fineglow Plays.

———. 1975. *West Coast Plays*. Vancouver: New Play Centre/Fineglow.

Canning, Charlotte, and Thomas Postlewait, eds. 2010. *Representing the Past: Essays in Performance Historiography*. Iowa City: Iowa State University Press.

Dickinson, Peter, C.E. Gatchalian, Kathleen Oliver, and Dalbir Singh, eds. 2018. *Q2Q: Queer Canadian Performance Texts*. Toronto: Playwrights Canada.

Doat, Jan, ed. 1973. *Anthologie du théâtre québécois: Le théâtre canadien de langue française de ses origines à nos jours 1606–1970*. Québec, QC : Éditions La Liberté.

Duval, Étienne-F., ed. (with the collaboration of Jean Laflamme). 1978. *Anthologie thématique du théâtre québécois au XIXe siècle*. Montréal: Leméac.

———. 1981. *Le jeu de l'histoire et de la société dans le théâtre québécois 1900–1950*. Trois-Rivières, QC: Collection Théâtre d'hier et théâtre d'aujourd'hui.

Filewod, Alan, ed. 1993. *The CTR Anthology: Fifteen Plays from Canadian Theatre Review*. Toronto: University of Toronto Press.

———. 1998. *West Coast Comedies*. New Canadian Drama 7. Ottawa: Borealis Press.

Forsyth, Louise H. 1989. "Publishers: French-Language Drama." In *The Oxford Companion to Canadian Theatre*, edited by Eugene Benson and L.W. Conolly, 437–39. Toronto: Oxford University Press.

Graff, Gerald. 1992. *Beyond Culture Wars: How Teaching the Conflicts Can Revitalize American Education*. New York: W.W. Norton.

Hawthorn, Pamela. 1975. Introduction to *West Coast Plays*, edited by Connie Brissenden, 7–8. Vancouver: New Play Centre/Fineglow.

Huston, James. 1893. "Préface de la première édition." In *Le répertoire national, ou Recueil de littérature canadienne*, vol. 1, i–viii. Montréal: J.M. & Cie. Libraires-Éditeurs.

Kalman. Rolf, ed. 1972–78. *A Collection of Canadian Plays*. 5 vols. Toronto: Bastet Books.

King. Moynan, ed. 2017. *Queer Play: An Anthology of Queer Women's Performance and Play*. Toronto: Playwrights Canada.

Knowles, Ric. 1998. "Just the High Points? A Canadian Theatre Chronology." In *Theatre Memoirs: On the Occasion of the Canadian Theatre Conference*, edited by Angela Rebeiro and Pat Bradley, 74–89. Toronto: Playwrights Union of Canada.

Lecker, Robert. 2013. *Keepers of the Code: English-Canadian Literary Anthologies and the Representation of Nation*. Toronto: University of Toronto Press.

Lecker, Robert, ed. 1991. *Canadian Canons: Essays in Literary Value*. Toronto: University of Toronto Press.

Massey, Vincent, ed. 1926–27. *Canadian Plays from Hart House Theatre*. 2 vols. Toronto: Macmillan.

Mojica, Monique, and Ric Knowles, eds. 2003. *Staging Coyote's Dream: An Anthology of First Nations Drama in English*. Toronto: Playwrights Canada.

Newman, Gerald. 1960. "Gumdrops and Maple Sugar." *Canadian Literature* 5 (Summer): 70–72.

Nolan, Yvette, Betty Quan, and George Bwanika Seremba, eds. 1996. *Beyond the Pale: Dramatic Writing from First Nations Writers and Writers of Colour*. 1st ed. Toronto: Playwrights Canada.

Parkin, Andrew. 1973. "Theatre and Drama in Canada: An Emerging Tradition." In *Stage One: A Canadian Scenebook*, edited by Andrew Parkin, ix–xvi. Toronto: Van Nostrand Reinhold.

Perkyns, Richard, ed. 1984. *Major Plays of the Canadian Theatre 1934–1984*. Toronto: Irwin.

Phelan, Peggy. 1993. *Unmarked: The Politics of Performance*. London: Routledge.

Plant, Richard, ed. 1984. *Modern Canadian Drama*. Markham, ON: Penguin.

Richards, Stanley, ed. 1960. *Canada on Stage: A Collection of One-Act Plays*. Toronto: Clarke-Irwin.

Salter, Denis. 1991. "The Idea of a National Theatre." In *Canadian Canons: Essays in Literary Value*, edited by Robert Lecker, 71–90. Toronto: University of Toronto Press.

Salter, Denis, ed. 1984. *Albertan Dramatists*. New Canadian Drama 3. Ottawa: Borealis Press.

Schechner, Richard. 2002. Foreword to *Teaching Performance Studies*, edited by Nathan Stucky and Cynthia Wimmer, ix–xii. Carbondale: Southern Illinois University Press.

Shaver, Joseph. 1974. *Contemporary Canadian Drama*. Ottawa: Borealis.

Singh, Dalbir, ed. 2015. *Love, Loss, and Longing: South Asian Canadian Plays*. Toronto: Playwrights Canada.

Voaden, Herman, ed. 1930. *Six Canadian Plays*. Toronto: Copp-Clark.

Von Hallberg, Robert, ed. 1984. *Canons*. Chicago: University of Chicago Press.

Wagner, Anton, ed. 1978–1980. *Canada's Lost Plays*. 4 vols. Toronto: Canadian Theatre Review Publications.

Wasserman, Jerry, ed. 1985. *Modern Canadian Plays*. Vancouver: Talonbooks.

1 : *The Theatre of Neptune* (1606)

Addressing Neptune, *Welcoming Redress*

JILL CARTER

ON NOVEMBER 14, 1606, Marc Lescarbot celebrated the return of French explorers Seigneur de Poutrincourt and Monsieur de Monts[1] to Port Royal, a French colony newly established on the shores of the Annapolis Basin, with a pageant[2] of his own devising. Lescarbot's *Neptune* has, for some, marked the birth of Canadian theatre on territories that have been stewarded by the Mi'kmaq[3] since time immemorial, and it invoked a key origin story that still exercises a curious force on the Canadian imaginary. (Indeed, Canada remembers its theatrical origins with every reference to Halifax's celebrated Neptune Theatre.)

In 1956 *The Theatre of Neptune's* re-enactment (fallaciously) marked "the birth of the theatre in North America" (Stanton and Banham 1996, 214). And plans for its 2006 re-enactment, which were to be accompanied by a commemorative stamp and a *Heritage Minute* television spot, were cancelled in the wake of ensuing backlash, initiated by Optative Theatrical Laboratories' *Sinking Neptune* (2006)—a performative intervention, denouncing the play as a celebration of genocide (see Optative 2006).

Born and educated in France, Marc Lescarbot was a lawyer, translator, poet, and historian, best known, perhaps, for his written account of early French encounters in the "New World." An idealistic nature and adventurous spirit infuse Lescarbot's writings in which he explains how his disenchantment with the corruption he had encountered professionally within the French legal system had driven him to accept his friend[4] Seigneur de Poutrincourt's invitation to accompany him to the newly established colony at Port Royal in 1606 (Biggar 2005, 11).

The colonists at Port Royal had endured a tortuous winter in 1606, so in August of that year, de Poutrincourt set off to find a more temperate site upon which to locate the settlement, appointing Lescarbot as interim leader. As autumn descended, fears escalated. Had de Poutrincourt met with accident? Would he return? To quell mounting unrest, Lescarbot hastily penned *The Theatre of Neptune*, channelling the restless energy of the colonists into an ordered project of hope and "jollity" (Lescarbot 2005, 116).

There may be little to impress in these "rhymes made hastily" (Hicks 1926, 216).[5] Nonetheless, Lescarbot has left us a political document—archiving a historic event of pageantry that worked kinaesthetically upon witnesses and

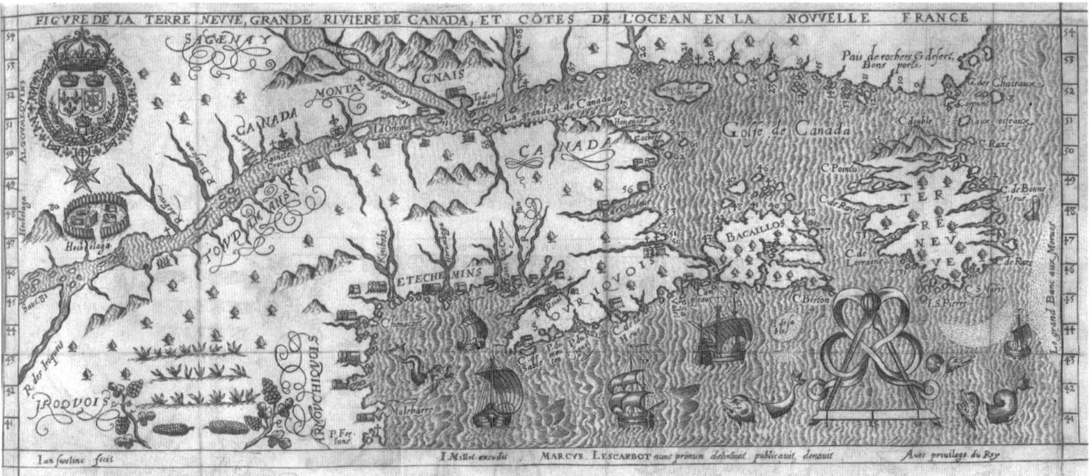

FIGURE 1.1: *Map of New France and the St. Lawrence River drawn by Marc Lescarbot, 1609. Originally published in* Histoire de la Nouvelle France: Contenant les navigations, découvertes, & habitations faites par les François és Indes Occidentales & Nouvelle-France...: Avec les tables & figures d'icelle.

Item 0296-002, E609 L624h. Courtesy of the John Carter Brown Library.

identify themselves with the nouns "Lnu" (singular) or "L'nuk" (plural).

4. De Poutrincourt was also a former client of Marc Lescarbot (Muddiman 1912, 281).

5. Lescarbot employed alexandrine verse: twelve syllable lines, stressed on the sixth and final syllable, and matched in rhyming couplets. This translation breaks from his prosody and employs blank verse.

6. See Van Oostveldt and Bussels (2017) for their excellent treatment of the spectacle from ancient Rome through seventeenth-century France.

7. Michel de Pure was a chaplain in the French court of Louis XIV. His 1668 *Ideas about Ancient and New Spectacles* concerns itself with the opulent effects ("visual and auditory") of these performative events and their effect on the senses of the witnesses (see Van Oostveldt and Bussels 2017, 215).

8. Small boats, equipped with sails and oars. Upon approaching land, the larger ship would drop anchor and its crew would row to shore in this compact vessel.

9. We cannot know for certain whether Lescarbot's spectacle was actually staged in the manner he indicates in his

participants alike, rousing a sense of awe and establishing in their enraptured senses unswerving faith in the power of their nation and devotion to its rulers.[6] The premise of *The Theatre of Neptune* is simple: as the long-awaited de Poutrincourt returns to his colony, the sea-god Neptune and his Tritons praise his courage and bless the French project of empire building. Graciously acceding to divine will, the Indigenous Peoples, through four representative "Sauvages," welcome the French captain with offerings to him from the bounty of the land and with a final plea (from one unsuccessful hunter) for bread. So received, the returning hero inserts himself into the performance with some improvised words of thanks, and *visitor becomes host* signalling his sovereignty over all the lands and their bounty, as he invites all to the feast that has been prepared in his honour.

A "De Purist"[7] would, no doubt, have been awed by Lescarbot's sublime maritime setting. There, unshaken by nature's fury, the French ship waited calmly to accept its royal due from those whimsical creatures (gods and "Sauvages"), braving the ocean's fury in their pinnaces[8] to meet their long-awaited leader and extend their tribute. Here, within Lescarbot's mise en scène, human powers against a backdrop of foaming white caps, mountainous sea swells, howling wind, and endless grey skies are as much serenaded by the natural powers as they are by Lescarbot's verse. Wind and water sing in the ears. Nostrils are tickled by the salty tang of seawater. Looking out from the shore of Port Royal, one is dwarfed by eternity, as the sea bows to the French adventurers so favoured by the gods.[9]

stage directions, or whether it
was even staged at all. Several
scholars have argued against
the likelihood that it could
have been staged on the waters
of the Annapolis Basin in
November (see Wright 2013, 8),
while Alan Filewod has argued
that Lescarbot's elaborate
stage directions might more
accurately be received as a
compilation of select remem-
brances of particularly
resonant moments and quaint
devices drawn from masques
the lawyer had attended in
Europe (cited in Wasserman
2006, 33). It is worth considering, however, that the
Annapolis Basin is a sheltered
harbour. It was (and remains)
protected from the November
gales that would have otherwise disrupted an outdoor
performance on the water. And
experienced marine travellers
(Indigenous and European)
who were accustomed to navigating in canoes, pinnaces, and
tall ships would certainly have
been able to navigate with
grace and ease through the
basin's shifting currents over
the course of a few short
hours. Finally, as I reflect on
my own limited experience
with the Great Lakes Canoe
Journey, I have every
confidence that those who
were called to declaim upon
the waters could quite securely
maintain their balance in the
exquisite birchbark canoes
crafted by their Indigenous
hosts and remain erect as they
delivered their lines. My own
experiences have demonstrated
to me that the traditionally
crafted *wiikwaas ciimaan*
(birchbark canoe) cradles its
human cargo securely,
responds with agility to its
navigator, and is not easily
capsized.

10. Under European international
law, the rites of "Discovery"
were observed through a
series of speech acts, during
which an articulation of
ownership (i.e., "I claim these

FIGURE 1.2: *Gourd likely of Mi'kmaq origin, ca. 1610, engraved with the arms of Seigneur de Poutrincourt and Charles Robin, Vicomte de Coulonge. The gourd is believed to be a gift from Sagamos Membertou to Robin, his godfather, following his baptism.*
Courtesy of the Stewart Museum (Montreal, Quebec).

This performative reception—a "visible sign of the contract between [European] ruler and subject town" (Wasserman 2006, 24)—constitutes a performance of de jure[10] sovereignty over Mi'kma'ki. The spectacle is concluded; its writer and original performers are long dead. Still, four centuries after its abandonment and decay, contemporary visitors to the reconstructed Port Royal will encounter, by way of welcome, "the arms of France, encircled with crowns of laurel" with the mottos of Henri of Navarre, M. de Monts, and M. de Poutrincourt, inscribed upon its gates (Lescarbot quoted in Hicks 1926, 216). Lescarbot's spectacle continues to inscribe an insistent force on contemporary hearts and minds: his ephemeral gesture of welcome remains archived in the restored symbols of French authority and Occidental thought inscribed upon the lands of the Mi'kmaq Confederacy. The message of these symbols is clear: the gracious host—sovereign holder of title to the lands he occupies— welcomes the visitor to *his* abode.

Were any of the "Sauvage" characters who sailed out to meet de Poutrincourt on that day members of the Mi'kmaw Confederacy? If so, are we to take their involvement as a passive relinquishment of Mi'kmaw sovereignty? It is a generally accepted trope that the Mi'kmaq would have lacked the linguistic ability to perform Lescarbot's rhyming French couplets. But they had traded, warred, ratified treaties, and shared resources with many other Indigenous nations long before contact. They would have *had* to be polyglots. Moreover, by the sixteenth century, the Mi'kmaq had become master builders and navigators of the European pinnace. Indeed, petroglyphs in Nova Scotia's Kejimkujik National Park provide textual evidence that by the seventeenth century, Mi'kmaw sailors were being engaged to crew European ships (Whitehead 2015, 7). There can be little doubt that these allies spoke French. And if they did not read Roman orthography, what matter? Perfect recall was a trait common within and necessary to the continuance of every Indigenous nation across the continent; it certainly proved itself a trait possessed in abundance by the Mi'kmaq who memorized countless prayers and catechisms under the tutelage of the Jesuits (see, for example, Schmidt and Marshall 2006). Surely, Lescarbot's rhyming couplets could pose no insurmountable challenge to these orators.

Might participation in an act of welcoming have provided some means (not apprehended by the French) to assert Mi'kmaw sovereignty over Mi'kma'ki— to subtly subvert France's performance of "authority and right to determine the proceedings that occur[red] within [Mi'kmaw] space" (Robinson 2016, 16)? Inarguably, that space and proceedings therein were being dramaturged by the French "guests." Where then lay the greatest opportunity to stage an eloquent intervention that would be received and understood by the human and nonhuman witnesses in their territories: in the act or in the refusal to act? Is it conceivable that the Mi'kmaq would stand aside and allow French man to welcome French man to the territories within which he held no right of welcome? This is a question which remains open, and for which we may never arrive at a definitive answer.

Regardless, the impact of Lescarbot's spectacle upon the Canadian imaginary remains virulently potent. Amidst the official rhetoric of "reconciliation," this root origin story pushes against Indigenous claims to sovereignty and Indigenous demands for self-determination and self-governance, as settlers continue to maintain that their relationship with these lands "pre-dates their arrival and validates their occupation" (Elder Daniel Francis quoted in Optative 2006). Consider Prime Minister Justin Trudeau's (2017) confident assurances to the populace during Canada's sesquicentennial celebrations: "Canada and the idea of Canada goes [*sic*] much further back than just 150 years. For thousands of years, in this place, people have met, traded, built, loved, lost, fought, and grieved. They built strong communities. They worked hard to make better lives for their kids and learned to lean on their neighbours."

Indeed.

So firmly rooted is this mythos in the hearts and minds of Canadians that while *The Theatre of Neptune* and the particulars of its performance may be forgotten, its spirit and intent continue to direct settler attitudes, even four centuries later. Perhaps, then, *this* sourcebook effects more than a new translation of the tired trope of conquest.

Perhaps it performs *a new ceremony of welcome*. After all, the remembrance, revival, and dissemination of this obscure origin story may indeed prepare the way for a new story of redress, repair, and re-creation. In bringing *The Theatre of Neptune* to a new generation of readers, we may at last expose the roots of a poisonous belief and thereby effectively begin to treat the disease of settler entitlement that impedes the crucial project of conciliation between settler-guests and their Indigenous hosts.

Bibliography and Further Reading

Bakker, Peter. 1989. "'The Language of the Coast Tribes Is Half Basque': A Basque-American Indian Pidgin in Use between Europeans and Native Americans in North America, ca. 1540–ca. 1640." *Anthropological Linguistics* 31 (4): 117–47.

Biggar, Henry. 2005. Introduction to *Nova Franca: A Description of Acadia 1606*, edited by Henry Biggar, ix–xiii. London: Routledge.

Black-Rogers, Mary. 1986. "Varieties of 'Starving': Semantics and Survival in the Subarctic Fur Trade, 1750–1850." *Ethnohistory* 33 (4): 353–83.

Bohaker, Heidi. 2014. "Indigenous Histories and Archival Media in the Early Modern Great Lakes." In *Colonial Mediascapes: Sensory Worlds of the Early Americas*, edited and with an introduction by Matt Cohen and Jeffrey Glover, 99–140. Lincoln: University of Nebraska Press.

Champlain, Samuel de. 1925. "Part I: The Voyages, 1613; Book II, 1608–1612." In *The Works of Samuel de Champlain: 1608–1613*, edited by Henry Biggar, 2:1–236. Toronto: Champlain Society.

Corbière, Alan. 2017. "Presentation at Manitoulin Island Summer Historical Institute." Ojibwe Cultural Foundation, August 18, 2017.

Delâge, Denys. 1993. *Bitter Feast: Amerindians and Europeans in Northeastern North America, 1600–64*. Translated by Jane Brierly. Vancouver: UBC Press.

Deloria, Philip Joseph. 1998. *Playing Indian*. New Haven, CT: Yale University Press.

Dickason, Olive Patricia. 1984. *The Myth of the Savage: And the Beginnings of French Colonialism in the Americas*. Edmonton: University of Alberta Press.

Ellingson, Ter. 2001. *The Myth of the Noble Savage*. Berkeley: University of California Press.

Fournier, Hannah. 2001. "Une Entrée Vice-Royale au Nouveau Monde: Le Théâtre de Neptune de Marc Lescarbot." In *Les arts du spectacle dans la ville (1404–1721)*, edited by Marie-France Wagner and Claire Le Brun-Gouanvic, 137–57. Paris: H. Champion.

Frisch, Andrea. 2015. *Forgetting Differences: Tragedy, Historiography, and the French Wars of Religion*. Edinburgh: Edinburgh University Press.

Ganong, William Francis. 1889. "The Economic Mollusca of Acadia." Reprinted from Bulletin No. VIII of the Natural History Society of New Brunswick. St. John, NB: Barnes & Co.

Greer, Allan. 2018. *Property and Dispossession: Natives, Empires and Land in Early Modern North America*. New York: Cambridge University Press.

Halberstam, Jack, and Tavia Nyong'o. 2018. "Introduction: Theory in the Wild." *South Atlantic Quarterly* 117 (3): 453–64.

Hicks, R. Keith, trans. 1926. "Le Theatre de Neptune," by Marc Lescarbot. *Queen's Quarterly*, no. 34, 215–23.

Holdraft, T. Rose, Elizabeth Perry, Susan Haskell, Diana Loren, and Christian J. Hodge. 2007. "A Rare Native American Sash and Its Paper Label 'Belt of the Indian King Phillip. From Col. Keyes': A Collaborative Study." *European Review of Native American Studies* 21 (2): 1–8.

Hornborg, Anne-Christine. 2008. *Mi'kmaq Landscapes: From Animism to Sacred Ecology.* Burlington, VT: Ashgate.

King, Thomas. 2003. *The Truth about Stories: A Native Narrative.* Toronto: House of Anansi Press.

Lescarbot, Marc. 1609a. *Histoire de la Nouvelle France: Contenant les navigations, découvertes, & habitations faites pare les François és Indes Occidentales & Nouvelle-France...: Avec les tables & figures d'icelle.* Paris: Chez Iean Millot.

———. 1609b. *Les muses de la Nouvelle France: À Monseigneur le Chancellier.* Paris: Chez Iean Millot.

———. 1609c. *Noua Francia: Or the Description of That Part of Neuu France, Which Is One Continent with Virginia [...].* Translated by Pierre Erondelle. London: George Bishop.

———. 1926. "Le Theatre de Neptune." Translated by R. Keith Hicks. *Queen's Quarterly,* no. 34, 215–23.

———. 1927. *Neptune's Theatre: The First Existing Play Written and Produced in North America.* Translated by Edna Lake Bourne Holman. New York: Samuel French.

———. 1927. *The Theatre of Neptune in New France, Presented upon the Waves of Port Royal the Fourteenth Day of November, Sixteen Hundred and Six, on the Return of the Sieur de Poutrincourt from the Armouchiquois Country.* Translated by Harriet Taber Richardson. Boston: Houghton Mifflin.

———. 1980. "Theatre of Neptune." Translated by Renate Benson and Eugene Benson. In *Canada's Lost Plays,* edited by Anton Wagner, 35–43. Toronto: Canadian Theatre Review Publications.

———. 2004. *Les muses de la Nouvelle-France de Marc Lescarbot: Premier recueil de poèmes Européens écrits en Amérique du Nord.* Edited by Bernard Emont. Paris: Harmattan.

———. 2005. *Nova Francia: A Description of Acadia 1606.* Edited by Henry Biggar. Translated by Pierre Erondelle. London: Routledge.

———. 2007. *Voyages en Acadie, 1604–1607: Suivis de la description des moeurs souriquoises comparées à celles d'autres peuples.* Edited by Marie-Christine Pioffet. Éd. critique. Québec: Presses de l'Université Laval.

Linklater, Tanya Lukin. 2016. "Slow Scrape (2012–2015)." *Dance Research Journal* 48 (1): 24–28.

Muddiman, Bernard. 1912. "Marc Lescarbot." *The Academy and Literature 1910–1914,* no. 2104, 218–82.

Narbonne, Andre John. 2012. "An Aesthetic of Companionship: The Champlain Myth in Early Canadian Literature." *Ariel: A Review of International English Literature* 42 (2): 75–98.

Optative Theatrical Laboratories (Radical Dramaturgy Unit). 2006. *Sinking Neptune.* Nova Scotia Script. Accessed May 3, 2018. http://www.optative.net.

Otto, Paul. 2013. "Wampum, Tawagonshi, and the Two Row Belt." *Journal of Early American History* 3 (1): 110–25.

Parsons, Christopher M. 2018. *A Not-So-New World: Empire and Environment in French Colonial North America.* Philadelphia: University of Pennsylvania Press.

Paul, Daniel N. 2006. *We Were Not the Savages: A Mi'kmaq Perspective on the Collision between European and Native American Civilizations*. New twenty-first-century edition. Halifax: Fernwood Press. First published 1993 by Nimbus Publishing.

Peers, Laura Lynn, and Carolyn Podruchny, eds. 2010. *Gathering Places: Aboriginal and Fur Trade Histories*. Vancouver: UBC Press.

Preston, VK. 2015. "Un/becoming Nomad: Marc Lescarbot, Movement, and Metamorphosis in Les Muses de La Nouvelle France." In *History, Memory, Performance*, edited by D.M. Dean, Yana Meerzon, and Kathryn Prince, 54–68. New York: Palgrave Macmillan.

———. 2020. "Convening Muses and Turning Tables: Reimagining a Danced Politics of Time in Jordan Bennett and Marc Lescarbot." In *Futures of Dance Studies*, edited by Susan Manning, Janice Ross, and Rebecca Schneider, 269–85. Madison: University of Wisconsin Press.

Reid, Jennifer. 2010. "The Doctrine of Discovery and Canadian Law." *Canadian Journal of Native Studies* 30 (2): 335–59.

Robinson, Dylan. 2016. "Welcoming Sovereignty." In *Performing Indigeneity: New Essays on Canadian Theatre*, vol. 6, edited by Yvette Nolan and Ric Knowles, 5–32. Toronto: Playwrights Canada Press.

Ryder, Huia (in collaboration). 1979. "Biencourt de Poutrincourt et de Saint-Just, Jean De." In *Dictionary of Canadian Biography*, vol. 1. Toronto: University of Toronto / Université Laval, 2003–. Accessed August 11, 2018. www.biographi.ca/en/bio/biencourt_de_poutrincourt_et_de_saint_just_jean_de_1E.html.

Schmidt, David L., and Murdena Marshall, eds. 2006. *Mi'kmaq Hieroglyphic Prayers: Readings in North America's First Indigenous Script*. Halifax: Nimbus Publishing.

Seed, Patricia. 1995. *Ceremonies of Possession in Europe's Conquest of the New World, 1492–1640*. New York: Cambridge University Press.

Stanton, Sarah, and Mark Banham. 1996. *Cambridge Paperback Guide to Theatre*. Cambridge: Cambridge University Press.

Trudeau, Justin. 2017. "Prime Minister Trudeau Celebrates Canada Day on Parliament Hill." YouTube video, July 1, 2017, 2:39–3:05. https://www.youtube.com/watch?v=liliBBHDQzsZs.

Van Oostveldt, Bram, and Stijn Bussels. 2017. "The Sublime and French Seventeenth-Century Theories of the Spectacle: Toward an Aesthetic Approach in Performance." *Theatre Survey: The Journal of the American Society for Theatre Research* 58 (2): 209–32.

Wasserman, Jerry. 2006. "Introduction: Marc Lescarbot and the Spectacle of Empire." In *Spectacle of Empire: Marc Lescarbot's Theatre of Neptune in New France (400th Anniversary Edition)*, edited by Jerry Wasserman, 11–43. Vancouver: Talon Books.

Welch, Ellen R. 2011. "Performing a New France, Making Colonial History in Marc Lescarbot's Théâtre de Neptune (1606)." *Modern Language Quarterly* 72 (4): 439–60.

Whitehead, Ruth Holmes. 2015. *Niniskamijinaquik (Ancestral Images): The Mi'kmaq in Art and Photography*. Halifax: Nimbus Publishing.

Williams, Carol, ed. 2012. *Indigenous Women and Work: From Labor to Activism*. Urbana: University of Illinois Press.

Wright, Kailin. 2013. "Politicizing Difference: Performing (Post)Colonial Historiography in *Le Théâtre de Neptune en la Nouvelle-France* and *Sinking Neptune*." *Studies in Canadian Literature / Études en littérature canadienne* 38 (1): 7–30.

The Theatre of Neptune in New France[1]

MARC LESCARBOT

Translation by V K PRESTON & DANIEL J. RUPPEL

Performed on the tides of Port Royal[2] on November fourteenth sixteen-hundred and six for the return of Lord de Poutrincourt from the lands of the Armouchiquois.[3]

Neptune begins veiled in blue cloth, wearing high boots, his hair and beard long and hoary. He holds his Trident in his hand and is seated on a chariot fitted in his colours.[4] The said chariot is drawn over the waves by six Tritons[5] until it pulls up beside the shallop[6] that the Sieur de Poutrincourt and his people were using to leave the ship and come ashore. As they secure the shallop, Neptune begins as follows.

NEPTUNE. Stop, Sagamos,[7] stop right here
    And listen to a God who cares for you.
    If you know me not, Saturn was my father,
    And Jupiter and Pluto—I'm their brother.
    Among we three was the Universe split,   (12)[8]
    Jupiter got the sky, Pluto got Hell,
    And I, the greatest chance-taker, got the sea as my share,
    And with it the government of that soggy inheritance.
    Neptune is my name, Neptune, one among the
    Most powerful gods beneath the vaulted sky.
        If a man wants a happy fortune,
    He had better implore Neptune's protection.
    Because whosoever stays cooped up at home
    Deserves only the name "cook."[9]
        I bring the Flemish on their journey
    To China as swiftly as the wind.
    I make it so a man, borne on my waters,
    Might see the unknown torches of another pole,
    Breaking the bounds of the Torrid Zone,[10]
    Where the tides of the liquid element boil.
    Without me the King of France would never have received
    That triumphal present from the Persian—a superb elephant:[11]
    And without me none of France's fighting men
    Would have planted their arms on the lands of the Levant.[12]
    The Portuguese who chance my waves
    Would stagnate without me, fame-less, in closed rivers,
    Having never stolen off with the beauties of the Dawn[13]
    That the senseless world now maddeningly adores.

1. "The Theatre of Neptune" is the third poem in Marc Lescarbot's collection of verse *Les muses de la Nouvelle France* (pages 11–21; hereafter, *Muses*). This translation uses Lescarbot's 1609 first edition of the *Muses of New France*. Existing translations are by R.K. Hicks (1926), Edna Holman (1927), Harriet Taber Richardson (1927), as well as Eugene Benson and Renate Benson (1982). The latter two also appear in Jerry Wasserman's *Spectacle of Empire* (2006). This translation published with permission from Daniel J. Ruppel and VK Preston, and with thanks to the John Carter Brown Library for the use of their special collections.

2. A reconstruction of the French "Habitation" thought to resemble the performance site now stands near Annapolis Royal in Nova Scotia. On contested histories of this land and period, see also Bohaker 2014; Delâge 1993; Greer 2018; Parsons 2018; Paul 2006; and Peers and Podruchny 2010.

3. The French colony of Port Royal was built at the turn of the seventeenth century on Mi'kmaq lands (Mi'kma'ki) on the shores of what is now called the Bay of Fundy. In the Mi'kmaq language, these Atlantic homelands were Wabanahk ("Dawnlands"). These the French called La Cadie, or Acadia. De Poutrincourt's journey to the "lands of the Armouchiquois" took him to rival nations at the edge of what is now Cape Cod, Massachusetts. Lescarbot called the Mi'kmaq people the "Souriquois," a name

likely derived from the mixed Basque-Algonquin tongue spoken by Indigenous and European traders before the French arrival. See Bakker 1989, 121–23.

4. In the Renaissance pageants Lescarbot draws upon, marchers often honoured their patron by wearing colours identified with that person, town, or guild. The sea-god's "chariot" was likely a boat arranged in such regalia.

5. In Roman mythology, Triton was the son and subject of the sea-god Neptune. He was often accompanied by "Tritons" in Renaissance pageants, costumed as merfolk and carrying tridents, with reputations for salacious, libidinous behaviour. Lescarbot may have seen images of similar pageants, such as one that honoured King Henri II and Catherine de Medici in Rouen (1550), which featured Neptune in a "chariot" on the River Seine alongside Indigenous "Brazilians" (Tupinamba).

6. "Chaloupe" can refer to a range of small boats used for navigating coastlines or, as in this case, for travelling between an anchored sailing ship and the shore.

7. Lescarbot's text includes several words he termed "Sauvage" and translated in the book's margins. The author renders "Sagamos" as "Captain," implying that the Indigenous rulers were of a similar rank to de Poutrincourt and not sovereign kings like Henri IV.

8. The translators include page numbers that align with the Bibliothèque et Archives nationales du Québec's digitized version of Lescarbot 1609b.

9. Lescarbot uses the rhymed words "cazanier" (homebody) and "cuisinier" (cook) tauntingly, the way a modern English speaker might use "chicken," underscoring social stratification of his era.

In short, without me the merchant, pilot, and mariner
Would still be home packed up as if in a basket
Barely able to leave their province.
Princes could never bring aid to one another
If I set them apart with my deep-running waters.
And without me, even you with your great deeds,
All your exploits in the French war,[14]
You'd never have had the pleasure of coming to this land.
For it was I who carried your vessels on my back   (13)
When you had the will to pay me a visit.
Lately it was I who a hundred times
Preserved you, your people, and your ship from Fate.
For I will always second your plans,
And wish that your efforts not be in vain,
For your courage has ever been constant,
As you came from afar in search of this shore,
To establish a French Kingdom here,
And uphold within it my statutes and my laws.[15]
    By my sacred Trident, by my scepter, I swear
I will take care to favour your project.
As for myself there will be no rest
Until in all these parts I see my tides
Heaving with the weight of ten thousand ships
That do all that you desire in a blink of an eye.
Go, then, happily,[16] and follow your path
Where fate leads you: for I see destiny ahead
Preparing for France a flourishing Empire
In this New World, that will sound at a great distance
The immortal renown, of De Monts, and of yourself,
Under the mighty reign of HENRY your King.[17]

Neptune having finished, a burst of trumpets begins to sound, encouraging the Tritons to speak. The Sieur de Poutrincourt held his sword in hand, not returning it to his scabbard until after the Tritons have spoken as follows.

FIRST TRITON. You (great Sagamos), you can call yourself happy
    For a God promises you favourable assistance
    In this important business you bravely undertake   (14)
    As with a vigorous heart you force Aeolos's[18] violence,
    Who, fickle and inconstant,
    Adesquides[19] one moment, and envious the next,
    Always ready to put you and yours in harm's way.
        Neptune, that great God, will make this jealousy
    Disperse like smoke into the air

10. The "Torrid Zone" desig-
nates the tropics while the
"unknown torches" (l.31)
suggest constellations of
the southern hemisphere.
These stars were unknown to
Europeans before Portuguese
explorers sailed across the
equator in the 1400s.

11. According to legend, the
Abbasid caliph Harun al-Rashid
gave Charlemagne a live
elephant as part of a diplomatic
exchange around 800 CE.

12. This line refers to the
Crusades, wars in which
European armies seized the
Holy Land. Lescarbot linked
the Crusades to the projects
of conversion and settlement
in North America, pleading
for the establishment of "the
Muses in a New France, trans-
marine, and Occidental, for
the conversion of the infidel
peoples" (Lescarbot 1609b, 6).

13. Europeans have long referred
to the "Near" or "Middle" East
as the "Levant" (literally, where
the sun rises). L'Aurore (Dawn)
here refers to the "Far" East
(Asia), where the Portuguese
had established colonies.
However, as Wabanaki
terms for the region around
Port Royal also translate as
"Dawnlands," this reference
might encourage his reader to
see La Cadie as a new "Levant."

14. The "French War" is a polite
reference to the decades-
long civil wars (the "Wars
of Religion") that ended
eight years before Lescarbot
sailed for Port Royal.
Though Neptune praises de
Poutrincourt's military deeds,
he does not mention that the
governor fought against King
Henri IV.

15. It may seem odd for Neptune
to say "*my* statutes and *my*
laws." However, in this play
Neptune seems to speak as
a surrogate for King Henri
IV (r. 1589–1610) as well as
the Christian God, reflecting
contemporary royal propa-
ganda calling the French King
"the true Image of God."

And we his envoys, in spite of Aeolos's efforts
Make your courage heard
As fame, already in flight in every land.
SECOND TRITON. If Jupiter is King in the heavens,
Governing you men down here,
Neptune is so in our realm
To the same effect, and we
Who serve him have great desire
To see the time and the day
When you receive the pleasure of your work
After you've finished your course,
So that these coasts may soon
Resound with the glory
Of mighty Neptune: and so
You may eternalize your memory.
THIRD TRITON. France, you may rightfully
Honour the devotion
Of your children, in whom courage
Shows itself far greater in this age
Than ever in centuries of old.
They take ardent care
To blaze your praise forth
Out to the most foreign of peoples,
Engraving your immortal renown
Even onto this mortal world.
    Bring aid, then, and give favour
To this praiseworthy enterprise.
As Neptune offers his support,
Which will always maintain your people
Against any human force
That might muster against you.
"We must never reject
The good a God would bring us."
FOURTH TRITON. Those who never risk themselves
Reveal their cowardly souls,
But the one with a brave heart, who scorns
The fury of the swelling waves
For a purpose filled with glory
Makes everyone believe easily
He is belted and clothed
With courage and virtue,
And he does not want silence
To hold his name in forgetting.[20]

(15)

Thus your name (great Sagamos)
Will resound over these tides
From this moment on as over the waves
You discover this new world,
And plant the name of France within it
As well as the Majesty of your Kings.

A Gascon delivers these verses in more or less his own language:[21]

FIFTH TRITON. So here's what I want to say
  About the old man Neptune
  The other day he was off braggin'   (16)
  And making himself out to be a silver fox.[22]
      Not so long ago he played the lover
  To entice a young girl
  All polite and gentle
  Who pursued him, by god!
      But don't you make so much
  Of guys with grey beards
  For in all these "enterprises"
  We should ban the "trot" along with the "gallop."
SIXTH TRITON. Long Live HENRI the great King of the French
  Who now makes live under his laws
  The nations of his New France,
  And under whom we have the hope
  Of seeing Neptune revered here soon
  As he was once honoured
  By his subjects on the Gaulish coast,
  In all the places where the brave courage
  Of their ancestors once carried them.
  Neptune for his part will also ensure
  That their descendants will work without deception
  To ornament their beautiful enterprise,
      He shall favour all their plans,
  And make them prosper on his waters.

*This done, Neptune draws back, making room for an approaching canoe in which
there were four Sauvages,*[23] *each bringing a gift for Poutrincourt.*[24]

The first Sauvage offers a quarter of an Elk or Moose, saying the following:

FIRST SAUVAGE.[25] On behalf of the Sauvage peoples   (17)
  That fill these lands
  We come to render the homages[26]

---

16. *"Heureusement"* refers not only to an emotional state, but also to the luck, good fortune, or happenstance that causes it. Thus, here, "happiness" resonates with "fate" and "destiny" in the next line, and with the larger theme of godly favour, felicity, or Providence.

17. Henri IV reigned from 1589 to 1610, but his succession was contested until 1598. Pierre Du Gua de Monts was named governor of Acadia in 1603—a title he would delegate to de Poutrincourt before the 1606 expedition joined by Lescarbot.

18. In Greco-Roman mythology, Aeolus was "Keeper of the Winds" as well as colonizer of the Aeolian Islands.

19. Lescarbot translates *"adesquides"* as "friend," identifying the term as a *("[m]ot de Sauvage")* in his margin notes.

20. French Kings declared policies of forgetting (*"oubliance"*) during moments of peace in the long Wars of Religion. These policies were intended to quell the desire for vengeance and facilitate a "forgetting" that there had ever been attempts to challenge royal rule. On the theme of "forgetting" in contemporary tragic drama, see Frisch 2015.

21. Henri IV was born in a region called Gascony. Lescarbot presents this verse in the king's local dialect, though he declares the bawdy verse only "rather close" to Gascon.

22. "Silver-fox" translates the Gascon *"bergalant."* The term references King Henri, whose reputation as a "player" was the source of this nickname *"le vert-galant."*

23. The translators leave *"Sauvage"* untranslated. This follows Daniel N. Paul (Mi'kmaq), Georges Sioui (Wendat), and Olive P. Dickason (Métis) on the complexities translating this word. See Dickason 1984; Paul 2000. In early seventeenth-century French,

the word did not convey the same pejorative connotations as its modern English cognate. Influenced by European myths of "Wildmen" (*hommes sauvages*) who lived in the woods, French accounts use "*sauvage*" as a term for the inhabitants of the Americas. By naming his speakers "*Sauvages*," not *Souriquois* (i.e., Mi'kmaq), Lescarbot implies these characters stand in for myriad Indigenous groups. For recent reconsiderations of these terms, see also Halberstam and Nyong'o 2018.

24. Gift-giving in North America was a ritual rather than an economic affair. This distinction was profoundly misunderstood by Europeans, who had different conceptions of gifts and payment. See Black-Rogers 1986. On reciprocity and gifts, see Otto 2013, 112.

25. Most scholars of *The Theatre of Neptune* assume that the "*Sauvage*" roles were played by Europeans, in costume, making them instances of what Phillip Deloria terms "playing Indian." See Delorai 1998.

26. "*Rendre les Hommages/Deuz*" refers to the ceremonial duty of vassals (i.e., lesser nobility) to honour their lords by swearing fealty. The ritual affirms the reciprocal duties and rights of the feudal relationship. Lescarbot repeatedly affirms the nobility of the inhabitants of the Americas, titling a chapter "The Sauvages are Truly Noble," though "noble" could have mixed connotations. See Lescarbot 1609a, 256; 1609c, 274; Ellingson 2001, 21–22.

27. *Fleur-de-lys*, a stylized lily flower, is the symbol of the French monarchy featured on the king's coat of arms and on flags flown by French ships. This symbol embodies the "majesty" of the king, even if he is not physically present. The line suggests that

Due to the sacred Fleur-de-liss[27]
Which in your hands represents
Your Prince's majesty,
Anticipating that this province
Will flourish in piety
In civil mores, and all things
That serve in establishing
That which is beautiful, and rest
Upon a Royal government.
   Sagamos, if of our services
You have some devotion,
We sacrifice them to you
And to your progeny.
   Our means are catch from the hunt
Which we offer with our hearts full,
Since living always in your grace
Is all that we desire.

The second Sauvage, holding his bow and arrow in hand, gives beaver skins for his present, saying:

SECOND SAUVAGE. Here is the hand, the bow, and the arrow,
   Which made the deadly breach
   In this animal, whose skin
   Would make a good coat
   (Great Sagamos) that suits your height.
     Receive then from my littleness
An offering that to your greatness
I convey with the best of my heart.

The third Sauvage offers Matachiaz,[28] that is, sashes [or belts] and bracelets made by his mistress's hand, saying

THIRD SAUVAGE. It's not only in France   (18)
   That Cupid gives orders,
   But in New France,
   As among you, he also lights
   his brazier: and with its flames
   Roasts our poor souls,
   And plants the pilgrims' staff.[29]
     My mistress having news
That you would arrive soon
Told me that out of love for her
I should come to find you

de Poutrincourt is holding a royal banner or flag. On the day of this performance, the king's arms were hung above the door of the fort along with those of de Poutrincourt and de Monts. See Lescarbot 1609a, 617, excerpted below. The symbolic act had legal consequence in French rituals of military victory and the possession of land (Seed 1995).

28. Carol Williams addresses the "profound history of women's beading literacy in continent-wide inter- and intracultural diplomacy and trade" in *Indigenous Women and Work* (2012, 7). Craft, Tanya Lukin Linklater writes, "is de-valued within art hierarchies due to its association with domesticity, culture, and utilitarianism." She continues, "trade beads conjure a past of ill-gotten land gains in the Americas, international trade routes, and Indigenous women's appropriation of trade beads in indigenous designs. We are reminded of a historical global economy" (2016, 25). On seventeenth-century Indigenous belts, sashes, and Abenaki beading, see Holdraft et al. 2007. Lescarbot writes of beads in his *Histoire* (1609a, 730–43), and William Ganong adds that women's porcupine beadwork was dyed with "black, white and red colours" and used alongside glass tubes brought from France. See Ganong 1889, 13–14.

29. The *bourdon* was a pilgrim's staff with a gourd on top.

30. As used here and below, "caress" implies favour or election. Alan Corbière observes that "carress," as a form of cleansing and care related to hearing, appears in historical Indigenous records as well as practices. See Corbière 2017.

31. These stanzas deploy a striking rhyming pattern of words ending in "esse," a feminine suffix in both French and English often

And offer you
This small work
That her hand has knowingly made.
　　Receive, then, with merriment
This gift I present to you
Filled with the noble kindness
Of the love of my lady
Who is now in distress,
And will have no release
Unless I run quickly to tell her
Of the caress[30]
Your highness has given me.[31]

The fourth Sauvage, unlucky hunting in the woods, appears with a harpoon in hand. Making his apologies, he then says he is on his way to fish.

FOURTH SAUVAGE. Sagamos, pardon me　　　　　　　　(19)
　　If I come in this way,
To present myself to you
Without presents at all.
Fortune does not always favour
A good hunter.
Which is why, having recourse
To a more tractable master,
After having so many times
Invoked Fortune
And thrust myself into the thick of woods,
I am leaving to follow Neptune.
　　Leave Diana[32] in her forests
Giving her caress to whom she will,
I now have too many regrets
Of having lost my youth
Following her through valleys,
Over mountains, and across plains,
With a thousand labors,
Always hoping in vain.
　　Now I will go to see
Whether by the coast
I cannot find
Something with which to furnish your kitchen:
And meanwhile if in your shallop
Somewhere you have got
A bit of caracona[33]
Furnish some for me and my troupe,

designating women's work and professions.

32. Roman goddess of hunting associated with wild animals, archery, and the moon.

33. Lescarbot translates "*caracona*" in his page margin as "bread" ("*pain*").

34. In Roman mythology, Proserpina is abducted by Pluto and forced to become his wife. Her cyclical motions between the world of the living and the dead are reflected in the seasons. Her pregnancy is not featured in traditional mythology, but Lescarbot seems to suggest a connection between her giving birth and the coming of winter. The cannonade itself reflects a common trope in descriptions of royal entry ceremonies, further connecting this performance with performative, legal rituals of civic homage and royal domination.

35. "*gaillarde humeur*" points to a ribald mood, associated with the playfulness, courtship, satirical jests, and fashionable, fast-paced dances (*Gaillards*). Linked with the humours ("*humeur*") the passage also has medical overtones. Lescarbot calls the "Theatre of Neptune" a "*gaillardise*" in his *Histoire*, as does explorer Samuel de Champlain, who sailed with de Poutrincourt and mentioned this event in his *Voyages* (1613).

36. "Like a land with no water." Cf. Psalm 142:6: "*Expandi manus meas ad te anima mea sicut terra sine aqua tibi*" (*Vulgate*): "I stretch forth my hands unto thee: my soul thirsteth after thee as a thirsty land. Selah" (*KJV*). The French word "*alterez*" (here, "parched") also means "changed" or "transformed." The tides of the Bay of Fundy, amongst the most massive tidal transformations in the world, dramatize both of these meanings.

37. This "K" is unclear. Bernard Emont reads this as "Karolous," a type of coin

After the Sieur de Pourtrincourt thanked Neptune for his wishes for the good of France, the Sauvages were also thanked for their good will and devotion (20) and invited to come to Fort Royal for caracona. In this instant, Neptune's troupe sings what follows in a four-part harmony:

True Neptune give us
Assurance against your waves
And make it so one day we might all
See one another again, in France.

The music complete, a trumpet sounds and each participant goes their separate ways: Cannons boom from all directions, making such a thunderous sound that it seems like Proserpina is giving birth: this is caused by the multiplicity of Echoes sent from one cliff to another, which last for a quarter of an hour.[34]

The Sieur de Poutrincourt having reached the Royal Fort, found a companion in gallant spirits[35] *steadfastly waiting for him, saying the following.*

After desiring your return to this place
For so long (Sagamos), the brooding sky has finally
Had pity on us and shown us your face
Thus making incredible grace appear.
   Up, then, roasters, butlers, cooks,
Kitchen hands, pastry chefs, stew-makers, and tavern-masters,
Pile up pots, and platters, and dishes,
That we may give these folks their full quarter, each
I see them parched, Sicut terra sine aqua[36]
Hurry boy, and bring each one their K.[37]
Cooks, are these ducks not yet on the spit?
Let's slaughter these chickens, Let's skewer that goose,
Look, here come many good companions
Hardy in their teeth and in their guts.
Come on in, Gentlemen, you are welcome here
May we each, before drinking, sneeze out
Our cold humours and so disperse them
To fill our brains with sweeter vapours.[38]

       (21)

I beg the reader's forgiveness if these rhymes are not as well fashioned as more delicate men may desire. They were done hastily. Nonetheless, I wanted to include them here, both for how they serve our history, and to show that we lived joyously. More on these acts can be found at the end of chapter 45, book 2, of my History of New France, *page 617.*[39]

Lescarbot mentions in a later poem (Lescarbot 2004, 146). He interprets this to mean that the actors were paid for performing in the show. Harriet Taber Richardson translates "K" as "portion," adding that "the portion was 3 pints per person," and stressing the account of vast quantities of food and drink (1927, 27).

38. Medical science in Lescarbot's time relied on Galenic "humoral" theory, which stated that health was the balance of four bodily humours. The "colder" humours (melancholy and phlegm) would be prevalent in Acadian November, and so if one wanted to be cheerful and optimistic (sanguine), it was best to release them, perhaps by sneezing, before consuming more chilly wet beverages.

39. Lescarbot enterprisingly links this collection of verse to his longer historical writing. His chapter on festivals, "On Songs and Dances" (*Des danses and chansons*) in *Histoire*, seems to suggest that the "Theatre of Neptune" is already a kind of re-enactment of Greek solemnities and festivals. He praises ancient Greek politicians for holding public solemnities and dance competitions in honour of the god of the sea. See Lescarbot 1609a, 847; Preston 2015.

40. "One protects two." The motto of Henri IV, signifying the two kingdoms of France and Navarre.

41. This "crown of laurels," worn by generals celebrating triumphal processions, makes the door to the fort into a sort of "triumphal arch."

From Lescarbot's *History* (1609a, 617):

After a great many perils (that I hesitate to compare to either Ulysses or Aeneas, so as not to soil our sacred voyages with impurity), the Sieur de Poitrincourt arrived at Port Royal on the fourteenth of November, where we received him joyously, and with a solemnity entirely new in those parts. At the point at which we awaited his return (with great desire, and even more besides, because he arrived so late and as we were in danger of having some confusion), I took it upon myself to perform [representer] some gaillardises, going before him as we do. And this was quickly written in French rhythms, which I have included among the Muses of New France under the title THEATRE OF NEPTUNE, *to which I refer the reader. In addition, for honoring this return and and our action, we placed above the door of our Fort the Arms of France, surrounded with crowns of laurels (of which there are a great quantity along the edges of these woods) with the King's device:* DUO PROTEGIT UNUS.[40] *And above the coat of arms of the Sieur de Monts the inscription* DABIT DEUS HIS QUOQUE FINEM: *and those of the Sieur de Poutrincourt with this inscription,* INVIA VIRTUTI NULLA EST VIA, *each of these also encircled with crowns of laurels.[41]*

2 : *The Conquest of Canada; or the Siege of Quebec* (1766)

Canadian Drama before Canada

GLEN F. NICHOLS

1. On p. 12 of his epic poem *War* (1762) he says, "Just as I reach'd the years to mark me man, / The present war to burn afresh began." The Seven Years' War, which is the subject of that piece, began in 1754 and spread globally in 1756; if Cockings was born in the early 1730s, he would have reached his maturity (age twenty-one) about 1755.

ALTHOUGH WRITTEN AND PERFORMED by a British bureaucrat stationed in the New England colonies to the south, *The Conquest of Canada; or the Siege of Quebec: An Historical Tragedy in Five Acts* was almost certainly the first play set in what would become Canada. By depicting significant current events, the play is an important window into the period's theatrical as well as geopolitical conditions, even though the depictions of these are highly problematic by today's standards.

George Cockings was born in England in the early 1730s.[1] As a young man he worked for the British government in Boston. By the 1770s he had returned to Britain, working as the registrar for the Society of Arts, Manufactures, and Commerce until his death in 1802. In his spare time, he wrote poetry inspired by the martial themes that thrilled him as a boy (Cockings 1762, 10). *The Conquest of Canada*, his second work and only play, was published in 1766 (London), and reprinted in 1772 (Philadelphia) and 1773 (Albany). One might wonder how a play written in Boston by a British citizen comes to be included in a volume of "Canadian" drama and performance documents; however, it is important to remember that this was a period when there was neither a "United States" nor a "Canada" as we know them. The "Canada" of the title was the name in use for nearly two hundred years by the time of the play to identify the region we now know as "Quebec." There is no universal understanding of what makes a "Canadian" work of art, and indeed the presence of troubling works such as this one, among numerous others in this volume, encourages readers to unpack the assumptions about geography and history, as well as race and identity that go to the heart of any study of drama and performance. The significance of *Conquest* is to add to that discussion, while also reminding us that our modern concerns around race and identity have very deep roots.

Late eighteenth-century theatre was in a state of change and effervescence. The restricted forms of neoclassicism and sentimentalism of the generation before were mixing with newer genres and ideas. Typical of plays for its time, Cockings apologizes in his foreword "To the Public" for not respecting the unities of "Time, Place, and Circumstances," acknowledging the classical forms but composing a piece that moves fluidly across time and space, compressing events for dramatic effect.

The play upholds aspects of sentimentalism in that there are no wholly bad characters. Even the "enemy" is clearly depicted with redeeming qualities. At the same time, the language and structure of the play look forward to Romanticism's affection for Shakespeare. The play is composed in relentlessly regular iambic pentameter blank verse, familiar to readers of Shakespeare's plays. Even the ordinary sailors, who learn the rumours of the impending expedition in their local "drinking house," speak in iambic pentameter. The only exception is the extended ballad Ned sings for his friends in this scene (Act I, scene 5). In form, the play moves effortless across continents and time. It even suggests the further developments of melodramatic theatre in the profound emotionalism of relationships (e.g., Peyton and Ochterlony, as well as Wolfe and Sophia), and in the very humanized heroics of Wolfe that bring to mind the Romantic plays of Schiller such as *William Tell*.

The play focusses on the character of General James Wolfe, who led the British campaign against Quebec in 1759 as part of the global conflict of the Seven Years' War. It begins with scenes of Wolfe saying goodbye to his wife and mother (curiously, and despite Cockings's insistence the play be a "representation of real and genuine facts," Wolfe actually never married). Then, reminiscent of Shakespeare's *Henry V*, the play presents alternating scenes of English and then French military preparations, depicting the British as serious and rational, while the French are shown as vain and argumentative: the play is expressly written, as was all his poetry, to "give deserved applause to these gallant countrymen of ours" (Cockings 1766, iv). Acts III, IV, and much of V depict scenes of battles that happened throughout the summer of 1759. The first of these is the attempt by the French to set fire to the British fleet soon after they arrive at Quebec in late June. The representation of the abortive offensive at Montmorency Falls in August downplays the British failure to hold the landing by depicting the melodramatic wounding of two dear friends, Captain Ochterlony and Lieutenant Peyton. Finally the battle on the Plains of Abraham, which took place on September 13 and ends with British victory despite the deaths of Wolfe and Montcalm, takes up much of Acts IV and V. The play concludes back in England when the joyful news of the victory, tempered by that of Wolfe's death, is brought to Wolfe's wife and mother.

The portions of the play included here represent about 20 per cent of the original. The decision was made not to reproduce the entire play because the play is very lengthy and presenting excerpts better focuses the reader's attention on key stylistic and thematic issues.

The first excerpt, which consists of part of the first act (scene 3), depicts General Wolfe's farewell to his wife, Sophia. Although she never existed in real life, it provides an opportunity for Cockings to portray the sentimental and humane side of the general.

The second selection comes from Act III (scene 2) and depicts the naval battle where the British thwart French attempts to burn the invading fleet by sending fireships downriver at them. In his 1989 description of *Conquest*,

FIGURE 2.1: *Benjamin West,* The Death of General Wolfe, *oil on canvas 152.6 × 214.5 cm, 1770.*

Gift of the 2nd Duke of Westminster to the Canadian War Memorials, 1918; Transfer from the Canadian War Memorials, 1921.
National Gallery of Canada, Ottawa.

Richard Plant notes several performances of the play in America and possibly Canada in the late eighteenth century (1987, 149). This scene is good evidence of the play's potential as a stage work, rather than closet drama: it contains little coherent dialogue and depends on layered action, with multiple characters coming on and off reporting off-stage events (in particular the main battle scenes), and stage directions indicating the placement of speakers "behind the scenes" and the need for scenes to "close" when changing locations.

Taking a very different perspective, the two scenes included here from Act IV depict the effects of battle on different individuals. The first (scene 1) moves into Quebec itself and offers a glimpse of the terrible British bombardment of the city from the point of view of a cloister of French nuns. The scene humanizes the "enemy" who have suffered the terrifying destruction and who fear what will happen to them if the British take over the town. The scene is designed to impress the viewer not only with the effectiveness of the British military assault, but also with their expected compassion since Lady Abbess reports that the citizens of recently captured Louisbourg were treated very well by the conquering British and she expects to be treated similarly with "so much Humanity, / And good Manners." The second scene from Act IV (parts of scenes 2 and 3) depict the relationship between two wounded officers, Peyton and Ochterlony, who at first refuse to be parted from each other to receive medical aid. Their friendship and loyalty mean more to them than death itself. The final scene here (Act V, scene 5) depicts the wounding of Montcalm and the death of Wolfe. This highly romanticized depiction can be compared to the famous painting *The Death of General Wolfe* by Benjamin West. The painting is almost exactly contemporary with this play (painted in 1770) and, as it hangs prominently in the National Gallery of Canada, also speaks to the power of these works to inform the modern imaginary and our sense of ourselves (see Figure 2.1).

Although the Seven Years' War—of which this siege was one small part—may seem distant to today's readers, it was a global conflict with significant geopolitical outcomes. The taking of Louisbourg, for example, given the consideration of the fort as "impenetrable," and its key strategic importance to French control of North America, was a landmark event. And Cockings's repeated allusions to this British victory, as well as to other recent battles and war heroes, both military and naval, speaks to the current importance of these world-changing events. To Cockings, these are worthy of the "historical tragic" form because the events are as "great in themselves, as any in our times, and amply worthy of being registered in the annals of fame, as rival actions of those patriotic deeds, of the so much admired ancient Greeks and Romans!" (Cockings 1766, iv). Its repeated reprinting suggests Cockings's approach struck a chord for his contemporary readers as well.

For the modern reader, however, the play is deeply flawed by its inherent racism. The several Aboriginal Allies of the Canadian forces, members of the "Seven Canadian Nations" (Jaenen 2007), played a significant role in these historical events. Yet they are treated only glancingly in the play and described in the most derogatory racist terms by Cockings, whose interest is vaunting the heroics of his colonial nation's forces before the hostile European enemy. One is correct to decry the play for this element. As a result, the play is an important reminder of the racist beginnings to both Canadian theatre and Canadian politics, and a call to us today to ensure our theatre and politics move beyond these foundations.

Bibliography and Further Reading

Cockings, George. 1762. *War: An heroic poem, from the taking of Minorca by the French, to the raising of the siege of Quebec, by General Murray.* Boston: Printed by S. Adams. Canadian Institute for Historical Microreproductions, microfiche #64940.

———. 1766. *The Conquest of Canada, or, the Siege Of Quebec: An Historical Tragedy of Five Acts.* [Microform]. London: n.p. Canadian Institute for Historical Microreproductions, microfiche #61747.

Jaenen, Cornelius J. 2007. "Seven Nations." In *The Canadian Encyclopedia.* Accessed August 3, 2017. https://www.thecanadianencyclopedia.ca/en/article/seven-nations.

Knight, John Joseph. 1887. "Cockings, George." In *Dictionary of National Biography*, vol. 11, edited by Leslie Stephen. London: Smith, Elder & Co.

MacLeod, D. Peter. 2008. *Northern Armageddon: The Battle of the Plains of Abraham*. Toronto: Douglas & McIntyre.

Parkman, Francis. 1883. *Montcalm and Wolfe*. Markham: Viking-Penguin, 1984. Reprint. Boston: Little, Brown.

Plant, Richard. 1987. "Drama in English." In *The Oxford Companion to English-Canadian Theatre*, edited by Eugene Benson and L.W. Conolly, 148–69. Toronto: Oxford University Press.

The Conquest of Canada; or the Siege of Quebec

An Historical Tragedy of Five Acts[1]

GEORGE COCKINGS

CHARACTERS

MEN

Wolfe,[2]

Leonatus, Three *English* Generals

Britannicus[3]

First *Caledonian* Chief,

Second *Caledonian* Chief.

Ochterlony,[4]

MacDonald,[5] Three Officers, in the Troops of *Great Britain*.

Peyton,[6]

Montcalm,[7]

Levi,[8] Three *French* Generals.

Bougainville,[9]

WOMEN.

Sophronia, Wolfe's mother

Sophia, Wolfe's wife[10]

Land and Sea Officers, Soldiers, Sailors, Nuns, etc. The first Act in *England*, and during great Part of the rest of the Play, in *America*, at *Quebec*, and Places adjacent.

[…]

ACT I, SCENE THREE

Scene draws, and discovers WOLFE, *and* SOPHIA, *sitting.* SOPHIA'S *Parlour.*

SOPHIA. Then I find, Sir, you prefer the Noise and
    Danger of the Battle, and Fatigues of
    A foreign Campaign, to the quiet Enjoyment
    Of your Friends in Safety in your native Country?
WOLFE. Madam, you already know my Sentiments:
    Our Monarch, Good, and Gracious as he is,[11]

In me reposes special Trust; in me,
Great-Britain, and her Patriots confide:
With Joy, my faithful sturdy Soldiers wait
To hail me General: No sluggish Thought
Shall ever Harbour in my Breast, to cause
Me to recede from my firm Purpose.

SOPHIA. I think not of altering your Purpose
For the War; perhaps that would be a Task
Too hard:—
And yet methinks we might expect a more
Lasting Pleasure than we yet have had, in
Your company, and Friendship, that we might
Add more Esteem, and heap new Favours on
The Man, whose Actions have rendered him so
Deserving.

WOLFE. By Honour spurr'd, and an emulating
Thirst for Fame, to stand inroll'd 'mongst *Britain's*
Worthies, I re-affirme the martial Toil.—
Whilst all *Britannia's* Sons, are rous'd to Arms,
And burn with generous Ardor to revenge,
And redress their Country's Wrongs; shall I fit
Tamely down, and dose a life of Sloth away?

WOLFE and SOPHIA rising.

SOPHIA. Such Sir, has ever been your active Course
Of Life, and such your shining Deeds, they spread
A Blaze of Glory round, that pale Envy's
Self must keep a silent Distance, and with
Mute Indignation gnaw the galling Chain.
You're scarce return'd from *Louisbourg*, and yet
Seem longing for another Undertaking.
Has nothing Charms to stay you longer here?

WOLFE (*Aside.*) Such Charms!—the Fair! the kind Enquirer has!
I scarce know how to flee their magic Pow'r!
(*To her.*)
[…]
All my ambition, Madam, centers in
Yourself: And I esteem my Honour well
Insur'd, and cannot doubt Success, since while
I range the savage Continent, Maiden
Innocence, will plead with kneeling Eloquence,
My Cause with Heav'n.—
Active as the rising Flame, my gladden'd

Soul transported! soars upon the Wings of
Exultation, sweetly reflecting on
My future Bliss!

SOPHIA. Your Happiness I measure by the soft
Transports I enjoy: now show'd I feel a
Sweet Foretaste of mutual Delight, did
Not Honour Rival me, (at present,) in
Your Esteem, and smile triumphant in the
Conquest she has made, mixing some jealous
Anxious Pangs with that overflowing Flood of Joy.

WOLFE. That rival Mistress shortly must depart,
And you remain sole Charmer of my Soul.
No greater Joy has Fate in Store! since you
Are pleas'd to give me but a distant Hope!
To bid me conquer! and make my Fame your
Theme! and promise me you'll smile Applause on
Each praise worthy Deed!—

SOPHIA. Long wou'd I fain detain you here, and with
Persuasive Kindness, strive to beguile your
Resolution for this foreign War: But
Being honour'd with the Royal Confidence,
And public Approbation, and drawn by
Glory's animating Call, I cannot
Wish you to relinquish that high Claim of
Honour which fires your Soul; may your guardian
Angel go forth with you to the Battle;
Avert each rapid Bullet as it flies;
And ward far off the mortal Steel: and oh!
May you return with Vict'ry crown'd, to bless
My longing Eyes again.—

WOLFE. Dear as you've ever been, this last kind Speech
Makes you shine more amiable; rend'ring
You dearer to my Soul, by Sympathy
Of Sentiment.—Madam, I take my Leave:—
(*Embracing her tenderly. Embracing her a second Time.*)
Dear! dear Maid! Farewell!

Exit WOLFE, SOPHIA *attends him to the Door; looking eagerly after him.*

SOPHIA (*Sola.*) He's gone! (*Weeps.*) and yet he seem'd as if about
To stay; and often backward cast such tender
Speaking Looks of sweet Distress, as if his
Soul had been upon the Wing to quit its
Body, and fix its Habitation here.

The thrilling Eloquence so charm'd my Senses,
I thought my Soul about to blend with his;
And such an unwonted pungent Pang he
Gave my Heart at parting! as if he there
Till then had grown; and thence was dragg'd by some
Superior force!   (*Exit* Sophia.)

***

ACT III, SCENE TWO

*The Stage darken'd, and two men placed behind the Scenes, with speaking Trumpets,
one at the Front, and one at the inner End of the Stage. A Ship to appear.*

FRONT MAN. Make a Signal immediately for all the Ships
    Boats, and all the Fleet to mann Ship!
INNER TRUMPET. Bear a Hand! bear a Hand my Lads!
    Mann the Boats! and pull up!
    The Fire-ships[12] are coming down the Stream upon us!
    (*Boatswain pipes forward in the Ship.*)
    All Hands, Hoy!
    Pipes a Midship, at the middle or main Hatchway.
    All hands, Hoy! tumble up, tumble up; there below!
    Pipes abast, or at the after Hatchway.
    All Hands Hoy!

*A great Noise within of Long-boat[13] men; Yaulers, away,[14] a running fore and aft,
and clattering of the Oars.*

    Out Barge, Hoy! a running, whurrow, whurrow,[15]
    Whurrow, whurrow, Pipes to Lower, Pipes to stop.
FRONT TRUMPET. Bargemen, jump into the Barge, and wait further Orders:
    Get the Fire Engine in Readiness there!
    Chearly my boys! Chearly!
    Three or four Boats clap along-side of that
    Headmost Fire Ship, and tow her ashore on the
    Larboard[16] side of the River.
    (*As he speaks, a Light appears on the left Side of the Stage. After a Pause.*)
    Have you book'd the Grapples Men?
SAILOR ANSWERS. We have her as safe as a Thief in a Halter;[17]
    But the Tide runs strong.
FRONT TRUMPET. Pull up briskly, half a Dozen Boats more there,
    And tow her plump ashore!

12. Ships or vessels loaded with combustible material would be set on fire and floated in the direction of enemy ships with the intent of setting them on fire. This was the strategy attempted by the French against the British fleet at Quebec.
13. A smaller open vessel that could be rowed by pairs of sailors.
14. A small oared boat used as tender to large ships, so here the sailors are preparing and setting off in the yawls in preparation to divert the fireships.
15. An onomatopoeic cry, which seems to be unique to Cockings's work here.
16. Starboard: the right-hand side of a sailing vessel.
17. Restraining headgear, perhaps a noose.

After a small Time, the Sailors huzza; one bawls out, She's safely stow'd away.

FRONT TRUMPET. There let her grow;
    She makes a fine Illumination:
    Clear your Grapples, and get off in the Stream
    In Readiness.

Inner Trumpet, Lieutenant Hatchway, Front Trumpet, Halloo.

INNER TRUMPET. Here's a whole Fleet of Fire Ships, and Fire Floats.[18]
    Coming round the Point:
    The French are trading with *Lucifer* I think,
    And have borrow'd th' infernal Coast of him
    For this Night's Service.
FRONT TRUMPET. If they've borrow'd his Imps[19] likewise
    To Conduct the Machinery, we have a Parcel
    Of brave hardy Tars,[20] that will play their Parts
    Manfully in the Scene, and grapple with
    Any Terrors which can float upon the Water!
INNER TRUMPET. Order more Assistance here;
    They're coming down upon us six Knots!
    And will be close on Board of us in an Instant!
    (*As he speaks, a great Light appears.*)
FRONT TRUMPET. Row up there one whole Division of Boats!
    My brave Fellows! behave like *British* Seamen;
    There's warm Duty for ye!
A SAILOR ANSWERS. Never Fear, Sir!
    We'll tow them ashore, if the Grapples hold,
    Or we'll fry like Sausages in the Flames!
    (*All Whurrow, Whurrow.*)
FRONT TRUMPET. One whole Division of Boats; take up
    That Fire Ship near the Two Decker, and tow
    Her to Starboard; and be sure mind to grapple
    The Floats which miss the headmost Division,
    And touch them ashore.
FIRST OFFICER. (*Within.*) Be ready with the Fire Engine!
    Get up Oars, Poles, and Booms there!
    And mann the Starboard Side well!
SECOND OFFICER. Brace all the Yards; sharp fore and aft!
    And mann the Shrouds and Yards with Pole Ax
    Men to clear the Fire Ships Grapples!
FIRST OFFICER. Run both Tiers of Guns out double shotted,
    And bring them all to bear upon the Fire Ship!
    Carpenters! stand by to cut the Cables!

SECOND OFFICER. Pull up your Starboard Oars briskly my Lads!
    And keep her well to Starboard of us:
    Take Care; don't fall athwart the Ship's Hawse
    Astern of us.

Sailors bawl out, Whurrow, whurrow: Never fear, Never fear.

SECOND OFFICER. She goes clear of us:
    They have her under Command.

Inner Trumpet, Lieutenant Hatchway, Front Trumpet, Halloo.

INNER TRUMPET. I can perceive no more Fire Floats and Fire Ships
    Coming; that whole Division may be employ'd
    In picking up such as pass'd the Point.
FRONT TRUMPET. They are all clapp'd on Board by this Time,
    And greatest Part of them landed on *Terra Firma:*[21]
    The most Mischief they've done us, was just
    To singe one of the Ships Sides as they pass'd.

All the Sailors within, Huzza! Huzza! Huzza! Scene closes; Lights descend.

***

ACT IV, SCENE ONE

A NUNNERY, A LADY ABBESS, and TWO NUNS.

LADY ABBESS. Oh how welcome seems the returning Day,
    After this Night of Horrors!—
1ST NUN. (*Crossing herself.*) Blessed *Mary* defend us, from all the
    Threat'ning Dangers of the succeeding Night!
2D NUN. (*Crossing herself.*) May all the holy Angels, and Host of
    Saints, be our Protection this Day; and the
    Ensuing Days, until our Army drives
    The Enemies away.
LADY ABBESS. Heav'nly Father!— (*Crossing herself.*)
    Such another Night, for all the World I
    Wou'd not choose to pass!—
    Amidst the Dispolation of our own Guns
    In the Garrison, (so near us) and the
    Continual Discharge from *Point Levi,* and
    The *British* ships, of Mortars and Cannon,
    The City seem'd to reel; nay, the very

Ground trembled under us! whilst the whole Air
Felt one unintermitted Shock; and in
The undulating Space, long hung the hoarse
Growing Sound, like distant Thunder.
1ST NUN. Good heav'ns!—
How dreadful was the Scene within our Walls—
Debarr'd the chearing Company of the
The more intrepid Sex, to sooth our Souls, and
Calm our Fears, each Sister gave herself for lost!
2D NUN. How Shocking thro' the Gloom of Night, wou'd the
Discharge of their Artill'ry, and Mortars,
Flash like Lightning, against our Walls, and gleam
Horrible thro' the long Range of all our
Cells! and then to raise us from the trembling
Stupor into which the Sight had thrown us,
Instantly, the terrific Roar roll'd over Head!
1ST NUN. Methinks I yet hear the battering of
The Balls! and see the Shells, (like Meteors)
With their flaming Tails, descending thro' the air!
LADY ABBESS. The shrieking Sisterhood, (like a Flock of
Frighten'd Doves, trembling! and scatt'ring from an
Eagle sousing down) oft as they heard the
Warning Voice; a Shell! or Flight of Shells! in
Doleful Accents pierce their Ears, saw the
Flaming Show'r aloft, fell prostrate! kneel'd! and
Pray'd! or ran almost each a different
Way, as Fear suggested; seeking Shelter,
And dubious of the Event!—and from our
Apartments, as they burst around us, broke
Forth a terrifying Scream!—
1ST NUN. To this without our Walls, in a dismal
Concert, rung the Groans, and Cries, of dying
People!—Houses tumbling into Ruins!—
Or perishing in Flames;—Fearful Mothers,
With their Children crying, and thronging in
Heaps; not knowing where to fly for present
Security, and calling loud on all
The Saints for help.
LADY ABBESS. Alas! in vain!—
For over Head would rise another Show'r
Of Shells, and send them screeching Headlong to
A distant Spot!—many too slowly fled;
For Death, with unrelenting Haste, follow'd
At their Heels, and as a Peasant cuts thro'

A grassy Meadow, so he mow'd down the
Crowd!—

2D NUN. Oh! terrible!—if they shou'd take the City
And we shou'd fall into the Hands of these
Rough *Englishmen*!

1ST. NUN. I'm shock'd at the Thought!—

2D NUN. The very Idea harrows up my Soul!—
And darts a Tremor thro' every Nerve!

LADY ABBESS. I hope it will not happen as you Fear,
We have all the Saints on our Sides, to pray
For us; the bold General *Montcalm*, (who
Has often beat them) and twelve thousand *French*
Soldiers, with a *Canadian* Militia,
And some Thousands of Indians, to fight for
Us, and they are not half our Number.

2D NUN. But still my good Lady they may beat us;
And then alas what may we expect will
Be the Consequence!

1ST NUN. (*To Lady Abbess.*) Our Confessors, Father *Dominic*, and
Father *Francis*, have told us strange Things.

LADY ABBESS. Perhaps our good Fathers were a little
Too rash in forming their Judgments, or were
Misinform'd. What their whole Nation is, I
Cannot say; but I'm told by a Lady,
Who was at *Louisbourg* when taken by them,
That the Officers behaved with the greatest
Civility and Politeness to all,
But in a more peculiar Manner, to
The religious Ladies, and Orders, of
All Sorts; kept the strictest Decorum in
The Town, among their Soldiers, and stuck most
Honourably to their Capitulation,
Injuring none, after the Deliv'ry
Of the Forts and Town.

1ST NUN. (*To Lady Abbess.*) I'm greatly Shock'd at what our Confessors
Have told us!

LADY ABBESS. My dear Children, discard these Fears:—I hope
The Governor will not give up the Town;
But if he should, let this calm all our Doubts:
These are the Men, who treated their captive
Enemies with so much Humanity,
And good Manners, at *Louisbourg*.

2D NUN. (*To Lady Abbess.*) How know you that, Madam?

LADY ABBESS. From the same Lady, who inform'd me of
　　Their former Behaviour. I trust we're safe
　　From personal Insult: for where the true
　　Spirit of Brav'ry inspires the Breast of
　　Any Commanders in Chief, a manly
　　Generosity accompanies it;
　　And they'll keep the Troops under their Command,
　　In good Order and Discipline.
2D NUN. Heav'n hear my Pray'r, and grant they may!
　　For I'm almost at my Wits End!—
LADY ABBESS. But for your further Comfort, my ghostly
　　Father tells me, we are by and by to
　　Have a general solemn Procession,
　　To the Church of Misericordia, to
　　Deprecate the Ruin which threatens us,
　　From this Invasion of our Enemies:
　　Let us retire my Children, and join with
　　Them in their Petitions for Victory.
　　This is our last, our best Resource, in all
　　Our Dangers. (*Exeunt omnes.*)

***

ACT IV, SCENE TWO

Point LEVI

Curtain falls, Thunders, and a Discharge of Artillery, and small Arms, Drums beating, and a Shout of Battle, Curtain rises, and discovers Capt. OCHTERLONY, *and Lieut.* PEYTON, *lying wounded among several dead Soldiers; Mr.* PEYTON'S *Leg shatter'd near his Knee, he being armed with a Fusee,* [22] *and a Dagger.* [23] *Drum beats a Retreat.*

Enter a SERJEANT, *and some* GRENADIERS, *as retreating.*

SOLDIER. Oh! dismal Sight of Grief! here wounded lie
　　Our Captain and Lieutenant!
SERJEANT. We'll bear them off, tho' thousands dam the Pass.
　　(*Speaking to* Ochterlony, *and reaching him his Hand.*)
　　Rise worthy Sir, and on my Back ascend;
　　Proud as a Miser bears his Load of Pelf, [24]
　　Forth rushing from a House inwrapt in Flame,
　　My willing Shoulders shall sustain your Weight;
　　Thro' crimson Floods, and numbers of the Slain:

Another will your good Lieutenant take;
The rest all Opposition shall defy,
'Till we in Safety shall depose our Charge,
Rescu'd from Death, and far from scalping Foes.

OCHTERLONY. My gen'rous Men, I ever Thought you brave,
And worthy of the Fame our Troops have gain'd;
I feel I have my mortal Wound receiv'd,
Should I retard your quick Retreat, you're lost:
I am not therefore worth the Hazard of
Your Lives, which yet may be of Service to
Your Country, and in future Days revenge
My Fall. Here let me lie, in painful Joy,
Reflecting on my Soldiers proffer'd Love;
But bear the gallant *Peyton* from the Field,
I know his Valour, and I love the Man!
Perhaps the Foe may one Day feel his Worth,
And you his Gratitude.

SOLDIERS. We'll take you likewise, Sir.

OCHTERLONY. Soldiers, no more: I will not hazard Lives
So precious to *Great Britain*, and my King;
Nor at so great a Price, will dearly buy
A few short painful useless Moments here:
But oh! fulfil my last, my best Request!
Preserve my Friend; defend his precious Life;
And bear him safely hence!

OCHTERLONY reclines on a dead Body. Soldiers move towards Mr. PEYTON.

PEYTON. Stand off Soldiers! nor think to take me hence.
Oh! can I bear the cruciating Thought!
How shall I when amongst our Troops arriv'd,
E'er cast a Look of warm Reflection back,
And in Idea see my gallant Friend,
My *Ochterlony*! whilst alive forsook!
And by his *Peyton* too! Oh, then to see him
Drown'd in Blood! by savage Foes incircled,
Screaming aloud th' infernal Yell of Joy:
Then see the Tomax sink into his Head;
His Body mangled; and his Scalp torn off,
Whilst he perhaps is vainly calling on
His absent Friend!—
No *Peyton* near, to dart like Lightning on
Them! and with remorseless amicable

Fury, tread them down among their Kindred
    Fiends below!
SERJEANT. Consider, Sir, reject not Timely Aid,
    Tho' fractur'd be your Bone, Vigor remains,
    And Youth, and Time, may give that Part new Strength;
    Besides, you yet may serve your Country.
PEYTON. Serjeant, thou spok'st a Dagger to my Heart:
    For Safety, and for Life, my Country calls.
    Then who shall *Ochterlony* save! — (*Pausing a little.*)
    It is resolv'd:—and here will I remain.
    (*Speaking now in a commanding Tone:*)
    Soldiers, with Speed retreat while yet you may!
SERJEANT. Farewel, ye brave and much lov'd Officers;
    We'd gladly bear you hence, and with our lives
    At Stake defend you both wou'd, you consent;
    But here we can no longer safely stay,
    Our Duty to our Country calls us hence;
    For from their lofty Trenches like a Flood,
    The *Frenchmen* pour o'er *Montmorenci's* Field,
    And like grim Furies from th' infernal Coast,
    The cruel savage Bands are straggling round.
    (*The Indians yell.*) Hark!
    They yell the Transport which they'll soon enjoy
    Amidst the scalping Scene! we promise this,
    Our Friends once more rejoin'd, we'll rouze them to
    Avenge your Cause. (*Exeunt Soldiers.*)

SCENE THREE

Manent OCHTERLONY and PEYTON.

OCHTERLONY. Oh, my dear Friend, e'er 'tis too late, be gone.
PEYTON. Persuade me not, for I am fixt as Fate:
    Watchful and fierce, as is the Dragon said
    To stand, and guard the bright Hesperian Tree;[25]
    So will I guard thee from the savage Foes:
    Perhaps some Foe of manly Sentiment,
    By Providence directed, may approach;
    At least, before I die, amongst the Scalpers
    I'll so spread a gloomy Scene of Slaughter, and
    Fall with thee amidst a glorious Ruin!

*An Indian Yell, OCHTERLONY attempts to rise, and PEYTON begins to load his
Fusee; the Scene closes in the mean Time.*

26. Anstruther is a fishing village
on the east coast of Scotland.

***

ACT V, SCENE FIVE

*Scene closes, Drums beat a short March on both sides then a Point of War; a
Discharge of Artillery and small Arms, a Shout of Battle, and Indians yelling: Scene
draws and discovers General* WOLFE *wounded in the Wrist; an Officer attending.*

OFFICER. You bleed, Sir.
WOLFE. The ball graz'd my Wrist.
OFFICER. Shall a Surgeon be call'd to dress the Wound, Sir?
WOLFE. Call no Surgeon to a Wound so slight as this.
    (*Taking out his Handkerchief, and wrapping it round his Wrist.*)
    We waste the precious Moments! whilst all are
    Upon the Wing to Honour! See, where the
    Anstruthers[26] and *Caledonians*, with a
    Mutual Emulation, hew thro' the thick
    Obstructing Ranks of *Frenchmen*; and as they
    Lift their burnish'd Steel, they fling a transient
    Gleam of Terror round!
    And see, where every other Corps with
    Bayonets fix'd, to close Engagement throngs!
    Let us my Friend among'em speed, and in
    Their Front rush foremost to their Goal of Glory!

Exeunt, in haste. A Shout of Battle, Indians yelling.

Scene draws. LEVI *and a French Officer in Disorder.*

LEVI. The Battle will be irretrievably
    Lost, without a sudden Turn!
    Gen'ral *Montcalm*, and others are wounded!
    The Wings give Way! the main Body is broke!
OFFICER. The Indians faintly squall their horrid Yell
    Of Onset! and in their thick Ambushment
    Riveted Agape, they gazing stand as
    Thunderstruck!
LEVI. Heav'ns! that such a Handful of Men should work
    So much confusion!
    Run!
    Rally the broken Troops, and make them stand;
    Whilst I head and spirit up the main Corps,
    'Till *Bougainville*'s Reinforcement arrives.

Exeunt severally, in Haste.
MONTCALM *brought in by two, his Thighs wrapp'd up and bloody.*

MONTCALM. Each *Englishman* this Day behaves, as if
    He wore *Medusa's*[27] head! with Gorgon Frowns
    They look some *Frenchmen* pale and stiff with Horror!
    Whilst with averted Looks, others retreat
    With a mercurial Speed!
1ST. SOLDIER. Where'er they face, our Troops retreat;
    Or else they pierce and hew a Lane of Carnage out.
2D. SOLDIER. Our Army dares as far as Men can do:
    But who can stand the Charge of these
    Impetuous *Britons*!
    The Day is theirs! *Quebec* must fall!
MONTCALM. And *Canada* is lost!—Alas my Country!—
    As the roaring Thunder, on the rapid
    Wings of keen Light'ning, bursts resistless thro'
    The sturdy oaken Grove, scorches, and rives,
    And lays its stubborn Honours low, so the
    Furious *Britons* break thro' our thickest Ranks!
    And as a cold Blight nips tender Blossoms,
    The fierce *Wolfe* blasts all the former Honours
    Of my Life! he tears with greedy Hand the
    Fading Laurels from my Head! and rises
    Into Glory, whilst in Disgrace I set!
    Bear me into *Quebec*. (*Exeunt.*)
MONTCALM. (*As they go off.*)
    Canada shakes!—my Country bleeds!—my Honour's lost!
    (*Groans, oh—*)

[...]

As they go off, four Soldiers, bearing General WOLFE; *an Officer attending.*

WOLFE. Here let me rest awhile:—
    My Wounds grow painful.—
    (*Speaking to the Officer.*)
    Pray tell me, Sir, how goes the Battle?
    For hearing is the chiefest Sense I've left:
    A chilly Damp of Gloom hangs o'er my Sight,
    And seems to wrap me in a waking Dream.
OFFICER. Firm as a Rock amidst the Billows plac'd,
    Our little Army stands the furious Charge
    Of their ten Thousand veteran Troops!

28. Admiral Richard Howe, 1st Earl
Howe, captured Cherbourg,
amongst other victories on the
continent in 1758.

And at an awful trembling Distance held,
The savage yelling Bands, (with Horror struck)
Howl out their Rage against the gallant *Howe*,[28]
And his small Corps of Infantry, yet dare
Not come within the Fascination of
Their Eyes, nor meet the piercing Terrors of their Frowns!

WOLFE. Discern you this for certain?
Mock me not I beg with vain delusive
Hopes in my last Moments.—

OFFICER. (*Clapping his Hand to his Breast.*)
Upon my Honour, Sir,—I discern it well.

WOLFE. Now Fate retard thy Speed!
Oh Death inexorable! stop! stop thy Dart!
Already levell'd at my Breast! that my
Good Soul may take its Flight, amidst the Shouts
Of my victorious Countrymen! (*Groans.*)

OFFICER. Now Front to Front they close, and Man to Man
They stand, and urge the steely Arguments
Against each others Breasts! Pikes, Bayonets,
And Halberts meet, and clash together!
Others with batt'ring Firelocks clubb'd, engage,
And pound to Death their rough Opponents! and
All around the glitt'ring Deaths, in Show'rs of
Steel descend!

WOLFE. I'll lay me back,—— and rest awhile,
Perhaps this cooling Tremor may wear off.

*Lays back against a Soldier, (sitting for that Purpose:) as he falls back groans,—and
lies as dead.*

[...]

A shout of Victory, *and* Indians *yelling.*

WOLFE. (*Raising himself in Haste.*)
Who runs?—that Sound recall'd me into Life!—
Surely my fearless *Britons* do not run!—
Now I'm well!—bear me into the Battle!—
Amidst the greatest Rout there set me down!
My Soldiers will not leave me!
The glorious Tumult of the War, has Charms
To stay my flitting Soul some short Moments!
And the bright Implements of Death shall give

New Day to my benighted Eyes, and light
    Me where to snatch at Victory with my dying Grasp!
OFFICER. Your Fears are needless, Sir:
    For in a total Rout the Foe is fled:
    Your Soldiers chace them headlong to their Walls!
    They kill! run down! and take at Pleasure! and
    Never was Victory more compleat!
WOLFE. My Glory's Race is run!—my County's serv'd!
    Quebec is conquer'd —Great *George* is Victor!—
    I wish no more; and am compleately satisfy'd. (*Dies.*)

 Acadius, or Love in a Calm (1774)

The Lost Play at the Beginning of English Drama in Canada

JUSTIN A. BLUM

PERFORMED IN HALIFAX in the first half of 1774, *Acadius, or Love in a Calm* was probably the first play both written and performed in English in what is today Canada. Its obvious importance to the history of Canadian theatre and drama has, however, been obscured by the fact that no text of the play has survived. We know the play only from a succession of news items published in Halifax in *The Nova Scotia Gazette and Weekly Chronicle* that are reproduced here: these include a list of characters, the play's prologue, and summaries of two of the play's three acts. While we have only an incomplete picture of the play's narrative arc, together these documents allow us to analyze the role of theatre and drama in colonial society, while providing a picture of a play written by someone well attuned to the conventions of British drama in the period but also open to trends in popular entertainment that were emerging in the North American context.

In the 1770s, theatre was an important part of the cultural life of Halifax, a city that had been founded less than twenty-five years earlier (1749) as a bastion of British colonialism in Nova Scotia. While a group of professional actors from the colonies that would shortly become the United States of America visited Halifax in 1768, theatre would remain a primarily amateur affair until touring companies began to include Halifax in their regular itineraries in the nineteenth century, a practice that began only once the Intercolonial Railway was established in 1876 (O'Neill 1989, 389). Before this time most theatrical performances, including *Acadius*, were put on by officers of the British garrison. Such performances were popular throughout both French and British colonies in North America, with soldiers imitating the lively theatrical culture of the imperial capitals as a way of passing the winter months and providing social occasions for members of both military and civilian colonial elites (Londré and Watermeier 1998, 104–05). Prior to the construction of permanent and dedicated theatres, these performances used improvised spaces like a large room at the Pontac Inn and coffee house, where *Acadius* was probably staged (O'Neill 1989, 388). Realistic stage sets of the kind that became increasingly common in the nineteenth century were still relatively rare and innovative in the second half of the eighteenth even in places like London (Holland and Patterson 1995, 262); however, if *Acadius* was performed as the summary suggests it was written, with at least eight changes

FIGURE 3.1: *Halifax from Fort Needham, Edward Hicks, ca. 1780.*
Accession number 1979-147, no. 614. Courtesy of Nova Scotia Archives.

of scenery between six distinct locations in the first two acts, even stages like
those at the Pontac must have been capable of at least some scenic flexibility.

Theatre during the eighteenth century was not without controversy,
both in England and the colonies. There was a long association in British
culture between professional actors and vagabonds or, in the case of female
performers, prostitutes; while important London performers like David
Garrick and Sarah Siddons were attempting to change these associations
by leading lives of middle-class propriety, a strong anti-theatrical prejudice
persisted and would become especially pronounced in the North American
colonies. By announcing that all profits from the performance would go to
"poor *Housekeepers* or the late *sufferers* by Fire," as well as invoking classical
references like the Greek actor Thespis and the nine Muses, we can see the
anonymous author of *Acadius* attempting to claim a respectable status for the
play and its performers by invoking charitable motives and classical ante-
cedents to counter "the opposition to the stage of some who were Puritan in
sentiment" (Fergusson 1950, 426).

Apart from the objections of those with a fundamental moral opposition to
the theatre, eighteenth-century drama could also cause controversy when it
engaged in satire of recognizable people. Throughout the late eighteenth and
early nineteenth centuries, journalists in the British colonies that would eventually become Canada often published dramatic pamphlets and dialogues to

1. Along with the Tories, the Whigs were one of the two major political parties in early eighteenth-century England. The nominal excuse for the 1737 Licensing Act was *The Golden Rump*, which satirized both politician Sir Robert Walpole and King George II, whose posterior is referred to in the title of the play. No script of the play survives, and many historians and critics think that Walpole invented, or possibly even commissioned, the offending script as a pretext to bring in theatrical censorship (Thomson 1993, 130).

make political arguments and attack political foes (Plant 1989, 150). Given the public nature of a play when it moved from page to stage, British authorities were always wary of the use of theatre to satirize political authority and attack the social elite; indeed, satirical attacks made from the stage against the Whig[1] political establishment had provided part of the pretext for the 1737 Licensing Act, which sought to establish strict censorship over the London theatre.

Anxiety about political or social critique from the stage in the context of colonial Halifax may well be why the February 1, 1774, news item that provides the play's cast list also contains assurances from the play's author that it would contain no directly recognizable depictions of individual Haligonians, despite rumours "that *this Comedy* contains *undue* reflections on this Country or *Personal* ones, on some of its inhabitants or Residents." The author's defence is made partially on the grounds of neoclassical theory, the dominant theatrical aesthetic of the eighteenth century, which insisted on the distinct separation of comic from tragic dramas. Within this theoretical regime comedies should be, as the author of *Acadius* puts it, "*probable, natural,* and *diverting*" but also of "a strict *Moral* tendency"; the writer's defence somewhat undermines itself in the assertion that "the CHARACTERS…are too *outré* to be *personal* on any Persons *here* or *elsewhere*, within the circle of the Author's acquaintance." The paradoxical implication is that the characters are, as neoclassical ideals would insist, based in nature, but also so exaggerated that no reasonable person could possibly think him- or herself to be depicted in them. While we cannot confidently know whether any actual Halifax merchants or British officers were alluded to in *Acadius*, the manner in which the author felt required to assure the public that they were not—and indeed to repeat the assurance in the prologue published a week after the cast list—suggests that anxieties about the social and political role of theatre were held in the North American colonies no less than in the colonial centre of London.

The surviving summary suggests a play firmly in the tradition of the English comic theatre that emerged after the Restoration of the British monarchy in 1660. The drama is both complicated in its layering of disguise and deception, and relatively simple in the overall movement of its plot such as we can reconstruct it. The play concerns the dual machinations of its title character, a British officer ardently in love with a young woman named Louisa Frankport, and of Louisa's father, a Halifax merchant who has been financially ruined by the wreck of a ship in which he had invested large sums of borrowed money. The play begins with a party in the Frankport household, where we discover that the merchant is about to depart for England to evade his creditors, while Acadius has disguised himself as a female slave of African descent to infiltrate the household and woo Louisa. Opening exchanges between Frankport and his wife, Louisa's stepmother, reveal the troubling sexual politics of slavery as she suspects him of having purchased "Sophie," who is in fact the cross-dressed Acadius, to gratify his sexual desires.

Acadius is involved in two further subplots that are also laid out in the first act. In the first of these, he promises to help reunite Fortune, an actual African slave in the Frankport household, with his wife Phebe, who has been sold and sent to England. In the second subplot, Acadius schemes to help his relative Jenny Chowder, a young woman who has become pregnant by the Master of the merchant ship *Albion* on which the Frankports intend to sail. Acadius's plan to help Jenny involves dressing her up in his uniform and claiming that she is her own brother in order to first secure passage aboard the *Albion*, and later convince the Master, who has jilted her, to follow through on a promise of marriage. The motif of cross-dressing becomes vertiginously complicated in this plot strand when the Master, who is at first suspicious of Jenny when she presents herself as her "brother," relents and promises to smuggle "him" on board disguised as a woman. The act ends when the drunken Master interrupts the Frankports' party to announce that conditions are right for the *Albion* to sail, allowing Frankport to board just steps ahead of the Sheriff's Officers, whom his creditors have engaged to arrest him for his debts.

The second act takes place aboard the *Albion*, which is just off the coast of Nova Scotia and unable to make progress toward England due to a lack of wind (the "calm" of the title). Acadius, still disguised as Sophie, reveals himself to Louisa in a comic wooing scene, while the drunken Master discusses their becalmed situation with the Frankports and other members of the crew. Jenny Chowder, having resumed her female dress, reveals that the ship has sprung a leak; Acadius then steals the Master's pistol and locks him and most of the passengers below decks before taking the ship's longboat and escaping to a nearby naval vessel with the Frankports and a few sailors. The act ends with sailors of the British Navy coming aboard the *Albion* to rescue the rest of the passengers, including Fortune, who has passed out from intoxication, and the Master of the *Albion*, who first threatens to throw Jenny Chowder out a porthole window before making a rapid reversal and promising to marry her instead.

In its comic tone, use of cross-dressing, and pursuit of young romance in the face of generational objections, the play closely mirrors the long tradition of Restoration comedy most familiar in plays like Aphra Behn's *The Rover*. However, while many plays in this tradition feature leading female characters disguised as men (in an era when full skirts were the norm, such "breeches parts" allowed the audience its best opportunity to view the legs of actresses), having the male lead cross-dressed as a female, and particularly as a female slave, is unusual. This, along with the use of a "*Negro song* newly wrote and set to Musick of four verses" to open the play, links *Acadius* to the tradition of blackface minstrelsy that would emerge as a major form of popular entertainment on both sides of the Atlantic in the early nineteenth century. The musicians and dancers in these variety shows were mostly white men who "blacked up," applying make-up mixed with burnt cork to darken their skin. The same device was certainly used for the actor playing Acadius; and indeed, it is likely that Fortune and Phebe were also played by white actors in black-face. This form of racial impersonation—uncomfortable for us today—was widely accepted in the period; its prominence in a play where Acadius also expresses abolitionist sentiments and seems to express a genuine friendship for Fortune are markers that the politics of race in the eighteenth century were no less complicated and contradictory than they are today.

At the moment of this writing, it appears the summary of the third act of *Acadius* was never published. Colonial papers appeared in relatively small numbers, often on irregular schedules, and with frequent changes of editorial direction and title that make it difficult to be certain if present-day archival collections are complete. Given the play's relatively conventional plot, it is probably safe to conclude that the play would have ended with marriages either accomplished or in prospect between Acadius and Louisa, as well as between Jenny Chowder and the Master of the *Albion*. Characters like Guttle, Guzzle, and the merchant Frankport would likely have received a comedic comeuppance for their social missteps and questionable business manoeuvres. The most intriguing question is how the storyline of Fortune and Phebe would have been resolved: the conventions of Restoration and eighteenth-century comedy would almost certainly mean their reunion as a couple, but did they end the play emancipated or still enslaved? The open questions about *Acadius* make it an instructive example of one of the realities of theatre history: prior to the emergence of "modern drama" in the late nineteenth century, the over-whelming majority of plays written and performed in Canada and around the globe were unpublished and survive only, if at all, in second-hand accounts and other fragmentary evidence like the advertisement, prologue, and chapter summaries reproduced here.

Bibliography and Further Reading

Brooks, C.J. 2008. "Chapter 9B: All You Need to Know About Life Jackets." In *Survival at Sea for Mariners, Aviators, and Search and Rescue Personnel*. NATO Science and Technology Organization. https://www.sto.nato.int/publications.

Dow, Howard M. 1879. "Three Children Sliding on the Ice." In *Two Songs Nursery Rhymes*. Boston: White, Smith and Company. https://www.loc.gov/item/sm1879.04284/.

Fergusson, C. Bruce. 1950. "The Rise of the Theatre at Halifax." *Dalhousie Review* 39 (4): 419–27.

Holland, Peter, and Michael Patterson. 1995. "Eighteenth-Century Theatre." In *The Oxford Illustrated History of the Theatre*, edited by John Russel Brown, 255–98. Oxford: Oxford University Press.

Horace. 1926. *Satires, Epistles, the Art of Poetry*. Translated by H. Rushton Fairclough. Cambridge, MA: Loeb Classical Library.

Hume, Robert D. 2014. "The Value of Money in Eighteenth-Century England: Incomes, Prices, Buying Power—and Some Problems in Cultural Economics." *Huntington Library Quarterly* 77 (4): 373–416.

"Life Preservers." 1857. In *The Encyclopaedia Britannica, or Dictionary of Arts, Sciences, and General Literature*. 8th ed. Vol. 13. Edinburgh: Adam and Charles Black.

Londré, Felicia Hardison, and Daniel J. Watermeier. 1998. *The History of North American Theater: The United States, Canada, and Mexico From Pre-Columbian Times to the Present*. New York: Continuum.

McCullogh, A.B. 1983. "Currency Conversion in British North America, 1760–1900." *Archivaria*, no. 16, 83–94.

The Nova Scotia Gazette and Weekly Chronicle. Halifax, NS: Printed by Anthony Henry, 1770–1789. Spool 5687. Reel 2. February 1 & 8, and April 12 & 19, 1774.

O'Neill, Patrick B. 1989. "Theatre in Nova Scotia." In *The Oxford Companion to Canadian Theatre*, edited by Eugene Benson and L.W. Conolly, 388–94. Oxford: Oxford University Press.

Plant, Richard. 1989. "Drama in English." In *The Oxford Companion to Canadian Theatre*, edited by Eugene Benson and L.W. Conolly, 148–69. Oxford: Oxford University Press.

Rewa, Natalie. 1989. "Garrison Theatre." In *The Oxford Companion to Canadian Theatre*, edited by Eugene Benson and L.W. Conolly, 222–24. Oxford: Oxford University Press.

Thomson, Peter. 1993. "Magna Farta: Walpole and *The Golden Rump*." In *Humour and History*, edited by Keith Cameron, 100–30. Oxford: Intellect.

Acadius, or Love in a Calm[1]

ANONYMOUS

PERSONS OF THE DRAMA &c.

Of a new Comedy of three Acts, proposed to be acted in the Theatre in this Town, intituled:

"Acadius, or Love in a Calm."[2]

MEN

FRANKPORT,	A *Merchant* in dubious Circumstances.
ACADIUS,	A Subaltern *Officer*,[3] in Love with Frankport's Daughter.
MASTER,	Of the ALBION, a Merchantman.
CAPTAIN,	Of a Man of War.[4]
FORTUNE,	Negro Servant to Frankport.
GUTTLE & GUZZLE,[5]	*Two Londoners*, Passengers in the ALBION,
SCENTWELL & SAVEALL,	Frankport's Creditors.

WOMEN

MRS FRANKPORT,	Wife to Frankport & *Step*-Mother to his Daughter.
LOUISA,	Frankport's Daughter.
JENNY CHOWDER,	A young Woman, betrothed to the Master of the Albion.
PHEBE,	Wife to Fortune.

Sheriff's Officers—Passengers—Cabin Boy and Ship's Dog.

N.B. It being given out, that *this Comedy* contains *undue* reflections on this Country or *Personal* ones, on some of its Inhabitants or Residents: THE AUTHOR thinks proper to assure the Public; that the FABLE of it is, an entire Fiction; and tho' *some* part of the PLACE of *Action* may on a general Construction, *rather* be fixed in this *Province*, than any other part of the Continent of *America*, yet it *cannot* be absolutely so. —THE MORAL has a strict *Moral* tendency. The EPISODES and INCIDENTS (he presumes[6]) are *probable*, *natural*, and *diverting*. —And the CHARACTERS, *he insists*, are too *outré* to be *personal* on any Persons *here* or *elsewhere*, within the circle of the Author's acquaintance —The CATASTROPHE[7] is strictly agreeable to the *principles* of *Comedy*.[8] —And the SOLE INTENT of his writing it, was for its being twice acted, for the BENEFIT[9] of poor *Housekeepers* or the late *sufferers* by Fire—The first time at 1s. and the other at 2/6[10] each Person.

---

1. As transcribed from *The Nova Scotia Gazette*, February 1, 1774, 3. Microform texts transcribed with the assistance of Kennedy Longaphie, research assistant, Mount Allison University. The text printed here maintains the spelling and punctuation of the original 1774 printing, including variations in spellings. Apparent typographical errors have been corrected silently, with footnotes indicating the original.
2. A nautical term for a period during which a ship is unable to sail due to a lack of wind; such a vessel is said to be "becalmed."
3. Any officer in the British military hierarchy below the rank of captain. In the eighteenth-century navy the primary distinction among subalterns was between commissioned officers, who held royal commissions and were invariably considered gentlemen, and warrant officers, who might have started their careers as enlisted seamen and come "through the ranks." Acadius is almost certainly one of the former, and so would hold the rank of either master or, most probably, lieutenant.
4. Generic name for a large sailing warship of the British Navy.
5. "Guttle" is an archaic term meaning to drink or eat loudly and/or greedily; "guzzle," still in use, is a synonym that refers to drinking only. The use of names that express characteristics—in this case the gluttony of the two characters—is a common feature of comedy after the Restoration and is also expressed in the names "Scentwell" and

"Saveall" for two upright, honest businessmen.

6. "persumes" in original.

7. Based on a Greek word meaning something like . "unravelling," "catastrophe" was used to describe the final part of a classical tragedy. It did not necessarily have the connotation of "disaster" that the term carries in contemporary English, so the author's use of this word in the context of a comedy does not indicate that the ending was unhappy.

8. Neoclassical principles were first articulated by early modern Italian humanists and were most fully (and rigidly) elaborated in seventeenth-century France. Widely observed in Europe throughout much of the eighteenth century, they held that comedy and tragedy should be entirely distinct.

9. Performances from which proceeds were given to a particular individual or cause. Professional actors frequently received one or more "benefits" as part of a contract, from which they got all the proceeds but for which they often had to pay expenses; in this case, the benefit is a charitable one.

10. The ticket prices quoted here are 1 shilling for the first performance, and 2 shillings and 6 pence for the second. In the eighteenth century there were 12 pence in a shilling, and 20 shillings in a pound, so the second price is exactly 1.5 times the first. Comparisons of monetary value over historical time are difficult to make accurately; in this case, the difficulty is compounded by the fact that Halifax had its own currency—also denominated in pounds, shillings, and pence—that was used throughout British colonies in North America between 1760 and 1820, with an average value of approximately £1.11 Halifax to £1 British throughout the period (McCullogh 1983, 84).

***

[As transcribed from *The Nova Scotia Gazette*, February 8, 1774, p. 3.][11]

PROLOGUE.[12]
To the new Comedy of ACADIUS, etc. mentioned in our last.

In *less*, than half, MAN's Post Deluv'an AGE;[13]
In this SEPTENTRION[14] Clime, there was no STAGE:
No *Sock'd* or *Buskin'd*, THESPIS,[15] in a Cart;
In DROLS or PLAYS, e'er *played*, any Part,
But *Interludes*, in *savage Nupt'al strain*;
Were *often heard*, throughout the whole DOMAIN:
As were the WARHOOP, and *knell*, DEATH SONG;
In *voices*, hoarse or shrill, *Stentor'an*[16] strong!
The MUSES, then, *knew not*, these *frozen Climes*;
So sent no Cargo, HERE, of *Prose* or *Rhymes*.
But ARTS and TRADE, at length being wafted o're [sic],
From BRITISH ISLES to this ACAD'AN Shore[17];
DICIPLES, then, of the PARNASS'AN[18] TRAIN;
Adventure'd, over, the ATLANTIC Main:
Some came from *all* the Muses, saving one,
Her Name, I think, Is THALIA,[19] she sent none:
(Tho' Patroness of *smiling* COMEDY,
Of *laughing* FARCE, and *pleasing* MELODY)
'Till lately, *one* of ANCIENT BRITISH, Birth,[20]
Came HERE; with fine Song, second handed, Mirth;
Which growing *stale*, to keep the FROLICK, up,
Resolv'd one Night, on COMIC *food* to sup:
Food *Al'ment'ry*, on which *poor* POETS *feed*,
And *live* upon, thro' LIFE, a life, of need:
A *hearty* MEAL's, *digestion* did begat;
A *Theatric, Comic,* (but ill shaped) BRAT.
    CALLED,
"Acadius, or Love in a Calm."
A Name, fictitious, and so is the PLOT,
Character' and Incident'; and what not?
No PLACE of *Action*, do we dare to *name*,
At *Personal*, REFLECTION, do not aim.
We think it meet to let YOU, understand;
He is *Amphib'ous*, rear'd at *Sea* and *Land*:
So, when in *Scenes*, or *Dress*, in ought we fail;
Let FANCY, those supply, connect the TALE.
We serve up, VIANDS,[21] *solid*, call'd, a PLAY;

Accurate figures for Canada don't exist, but Robert D. Hume estimates that average family income in Britain was roughly £46 in 1760, with more than half of families subsisting on less than £26 per year throughout the eighteenth century (2014, 375–76), so even the lower ticket price of 1 shilling would have made the performance of *Acadius* an event restricted to the relatively well-off in Halifax society.

11. This Prologue has also been partially reproduced in Fergusson 1950, 419–20.

12. Prologues and epilogues, often written from the point of view of the playwright, were a common feature of British comedies after the Restoration.

13. The time since the supposed occurrence of the biblical Noah's flood.

14. An obsolete term meaning "northerly."

15. Reputed to be the first actor and tragic playwright in ancient Greece; the tradition that he travelled around the Greek city states in a cart is documented in the *Ars Poetica* of the Roman writer Horace, which describes how Thespis "carried his pieces in wagons to be sung and acted by players with faces smeared with wine-lees" (1926, 275–77). Classical actors in both Greece and Rome were associated with special footwear including "socks" and "buskins."

16. Loud or solemn; these verses describe the non-dramatic performance traditions of the First Nations in a way that dismisses them as "savage" while showing fascination with their power.

17. Acadia refers to an area comprising part of the present-day Canadian Maritime provinces, Quebec, and Maine, that was colonized by French settlers in the seventeenth and early eighteenth centuries. The British gained control of

---

Yet YOU, the JUDGES, will be apt to, say,
'Tis a *flimsy*, Mess; of *hot–cold–wet–dry*:[22]
Kickshaw![23] or *Soup maigre*[24]! or *Pudding Pye*![25]
Or a *Salmagundy*![26] –or–*any thing*;
Toss'd, up, in, Three, Soup, Plates, call'd Acts. we bring*
In *aid* of BILLIARDS, DANCING, CARDS, & SONG,
To shorten, WINTER EVENINGS, *cold* and *long*;
Be it so—if *pleased* applaud; if not be merry;
And I'll be, your *humble Servant*, VERY.

*In allusion to to [*sic*] Mr. Pope's *redicule* in his Essay on Criticism,[27] of some Poets, using ten mono-syllables in one Line.
†*† The *Author* before he leaves this Country says, that he intends to favour us, with the EPILOGUE, and the FABLE or STORY on which the Comedy is wrote.

***

[As transcribed from *The Nova Scotia Gazette*, April 12, 1774, p. 1.]

HALIFAX, April 11

The following is a short *Abstract* of the new Comedy called ACADIUS or Love in a Calm.

The *first Act* opens, with a Scene of a Dining Room in *Frankport*'s House, the cloth just laid for dinner by *Fortune* a negro man, and *Acadius* as a negro woman, servants to *Frankport*. They sing a *Negro song*, newly wrote and set to Musick, of four verses, the following being the first, we give as a specimen of it:

"The Negroes *farewell* to America."[28]
"Now, farewell my Massa, my Missey adieu!
"More *blows* or more *stripes* will I e'er take from you;
"Or will me *come* hither, or thither me *go*;
"No help make you *rich*, by de sweat of my brow.
"*Yankey doodle*[29]*, yankey doodle, dandy, I vow,*
"*Yankey doodle yankey doodle etc...bow, wow wow!*"

Which ended—*Acadius* speaks much in praise of Liberty; by way of recapitulation of some former discourse between them, and makes several promises of his friendship towards *Fortune*, to carry on the character, *Acadius* had assumed and among others the recovery of his wife *Phebe*, who had been sold and carried away to England. *Frankport* and his *wife* appearing, *Fortune*, as it had been before concerted kisses and fondles *Acadius*—Mrs *Frankport* charges them with wasting their time in dalliance, and beats 'em off. This

this territory after the War of Spanish Succession and officially deported most French residents between 1755 and 1762. The name "Acadius" would seem to be a reference to this territory.

18. Mount Parnassus, in Greece, was the traditional home of the Muses, nine sisters responsible for inspiring artistic and intellectual creativity.

19. The precise names and domains of responsibility for each of the nine Muses vary among sources, but Thalia is indeed listed by the Greek poet Hesiod as the Muse of comedy and pastoral poetry.

20. Original: "Brith."

21. From the French "*viande*," meaning "meat," the archaic English word "viand" refers to any item of food.

22. The Ancient Greek philosopher Aristotle believed that all matter was composed of four elements—earth, wind, water, and fire—each of which was defined as possessing two of the following characteristics: hot, cold, wet, and dry. This became the basis for the "humoral" theory of medicine, which was widely popular from antiquity to the eighteenth century, and held that illness was caused by imbalances between bodily fluids that also possessed these characteristics; remedies prescribed under the humoral theory included variations of diet and removing blood or other fluids from the patient.

23. Generic word for a dish that was fancy, but not necessarily nourishing; this was especially applied to foreign foods. In this and the subsequent culinary comparisons, the author is ironically disparaging his play.

24. Literally "thin soup," this term refers to a vegetable broth with few other ingredients added to it.

25. Throughout the eighteenth and nineteenth centuries, the term "pudding pye" (or "pudding

occasions a very warm altercation between *Frankport and his wife*, in which she compares the *state* of negroes with Brute beasts. He argues the contrary speaks highly of their fidelity and utility—she now in terms of asperity and jealousy intimates his having had *criminal conversation*[30] with his female negroes and charges him with purchasing *Acadius* (who goes under the name of *Sophy*) for the amusement of his leisure hours and that *Fortune*, under a colour of an *amour* with her was to *foster* the children she should bear; He now becomes very irascible and threatens her with correction. Some of the company invited to dinner being come, he proposes a reconciliation, she rejects it and goes off in a rude and angry manner.—*Frankport* is amazed at her behaviour, and whilst he is musing thereon, his daughter *Louisa* enters; and having learned the occasion of his uneasiness, endeavours to pacify him; and having dreamed that the *Albion* in which they were to sail for England was at sea and had took fire, she endeavours to persuade him to postpone his voyage—He speaks very lightly of dreams, and argues that the contrary appearances if any, were generally the result.—That it was more probable a *Leak* might happen instead of a *Fire*, as her bottom had not been surveyed for some time.—He opens to her the cause of his going to England which was, that he had ventured almost his whole Property in one ship, which he concludes to be lost, not having heard of her for near twelve months, and that he never intended to return, but apply for employment, in some public office.—*She* assures him of her doing every thing to produce him not only the necessaries, but the comforts of life; he thanks her in very *pathetick*[31] terms of *Paternal* affection, and she comforts him with many *filial* assurances of the performance of her promises.—*Fortune* comes in and informs them—that some of the company who were invited were arriv'd; *Frankport* and his *Daughter* go out with *Fortune*. The scene now changes to another apartment in *Frankport*'s house. —*Acadius* & *Jenny* Chowder (a Relation of *Acadius* under a promise of marriage *pregnant* by the *Master* of the *Albion*, & dress'd in a suit of his) now appear; after some little raillery pass'd between them in respect to their *Masquerade appearance* and their adventures, settle the *Terms* of their behaviour towards each other on ship board, and the Plan for obtaining justice from the master in England; and perceiving the *Master* approaching she goes out to meet him—and the scene changes to the street, where the master (attended by the ship Dog) and *Jenny* have a conference.—*She* assumes the character of her *Brother* whom the *Master* had never seen; he entertains some suspicions of the deceit and attempts to be familiar with her; but is interrupted by the Dog, and some persons approaching—*She* informs him that she and her *sister* had been decoy'd from England by an uncle and had both ran away from him; that being pursued, *her sister* not being able to avoid being taken, had drown'd herself. —The *Master* is *pleas'd* at the event, agrees for her passage, and undertakes to get her onboard in a suit of his sisters cloaths, and they go off to put his design in execution, —The scene now changes to *Frankport*'s dining room, the cloth just remov'd and the usual *Toasts* and *etiquet* of a polite ceremonial table *sans*

pie") was used in different regions of Britain to refer to a variety of desserts, often with a custard-based filling.

26. Usually spelled "salmagundi," this is not a specific dish but rather a category of dishes that entered British cuisine in the early seventeenth century. A traditional salmagundi is a salad containing a combination of meats, seafood, vegetables, nuts, fruits, and herbs dressed with oil, vinegar, and other spices; it thus has the connotation of being "a hodgepodge."

27. Alexander Pope's *An Essay on Criticism*, published in 1711, was an important work of English neoclassical theory and criticism. Written in verse in imitation of Horace's *Ars Poetica*, it argues for the value of classical literature and drama as a model while insisting that poets and critics should focus on the overall aims of the poet, rather than making inflexible rules on the basis of technical features like metre and structure.

28. The inclusion of songs in plays was a long-standing characteristic of much of British theatre—there are songs included, for instance, in many of Shakespeare's plays. This particular song is an early example of the imitation of African American dialect in songs about slavery and plantation life, a genre that would become widely popular in the nineteenth century in the context of blackface minstrelsy.

29. The song "Yankee Doodle" was sung before the American Revolution by British soldiers to mock the perceived gullibility of colonial militiamen who had been born in North America; during the revolution, this song about a country bumpkin was ironically adopted as an anthem by soldiers in the rebelling armies.

cinerité is introduced. *Guttle* a Welchman and *Guzzle* an Irishman[32] ([who] are concerned in several droll scenes in the remainder of the piece) and two other passengers in the *Albion* are now first introduced to the audience; the two *former* give a *specimen*, of their characters the *first* picking a bone long after the cloth is removed and *both* drinking out of turn; a *Gentleman* being given[33] and one of the Passengers inadvertently giving a married lady, who was lightly talk'd of, a *Peal* of laughter ensues,[34] which subsides on the *Master* of the *Albion's* appearance somewhat in liquor; He joins the company, is called upon for a *song*, at the close of which, a *Sailor* enters, and informs 'em the wind and tide serve—*Frankport*, takes leave of the company, among whom are *Scentwell* and *Saveall*, two of his creditors who behave in a seeming *very pathetic* manner at parting altho' they had engaged two *Sheriff's Officers* to arrest *Frankport* for Debts he had just before secured payment; all the company having departed, the *officers* are introduced, and the *manoeuvres* of an *English* spunging house[35] are shewn in very strong colours. —*Frankport* is enraged at this behaviour, and closes, the *first act* with these lines:

Speaking of the *Sheriff's Officers*, who he says are

> *Bred* in the *bruis'd* and rotten parts of *law*,
> *Nourish'd* by the corrupted part, a *flaw*;
> *Law* was first *planted* in *hallowed* ground.
> No *viper* practicer could then be found:
> But *now* round all its branches *myr'ads* cling;
> From thence *recoil*, & more than *bite* they *sting*.

— *To be continued* —

***

[As transcribed from *The Nova Scotia Gazette*, April 19, 1774, p. 3.]

HALIFAX, April 19

EXTRACT *from the new Play*, ACADIUS.

The second *Act*, opens with the *Scene* of the *Cabbin* on-board the *Albion*, with Candles light up, it being about Midnight[,] The *Master* and several of the Passengers very merry over their Bottle. The *Master* being much in liquor, retires, with a promise of returning—*Acadius* not finding *Jenny Chowder* on board, comes in and enquires of *Fortune* concerning Her, who giving *Acadius* no information, He goes out to seek her; and the *Scene* changes to the *Steerage*,[36] where the *Master* is tippling alone—*Mr.* and *Mrs. Frankport* come in to *Him* and enter into a conversation about the Calm they were in;

and *Frankport* asks the *Master* if he did not feel the ship in some agitation, as she cross'd the Bar,[37] the *Master* tacitly acknowledges he did, but says it was occasion'd by an *Eddy*—*Frankport* proposes to go upon Deck, as it was a fine Night, and the Passengers were so vociferous and in great jollity, in the Cabin, and is attended by his *Wife*—The *Scene* now *changes* to the *State Room*, where *Acadius*, as a Negro girl attends *Louisa*, who begins to undress for bed—an opportunity now offering, *Acadius* very artfully draws from her, *Her opinion* of Him, which being a favourable one, and *She* being stimulated by Him, with an assurance of his Love (which he pretends he had discovered by being a Servant in the House where he lodg'd) declares a *Passion* for *Him* and as it was a Calm and the Ship near Land, proposes to escape on shore in the Ship's Boat, and fly to *Acadius's* arms—*He* now discovers[38] himself, *She* is surpriz'd and shrieks out—Her *Father* comes in and enquires the cause of her behaviour, which *Acadius* very a-propos and naturally ascribes to a *Rat*, which had run across the Cabin into the Steerage—*Frankport* goes out to kill it.—*Acadius* now resumes his addresses and prevails upon *Louisa* to give *Him*, her hand; and whilst he kneels and kisses it, *Mrs. Frankport* comes in, and is amaz'd at his posture and *devotion*—*He* wittily turns off the real intention, to his learning his Prayers from *Louisa*, and kissing her hand as a dutiful and submissive return of Thanks, which *Mrs Frankport* believes—now is introduc'd a *specimen* of an *American* Mistress's *capricious* and *tyrannical* behaviour to a *Slave*, in very natural and lively colours: *Acadius* behaving awkwardly, is corrected, *Louisa* interposes; a rupture between the Mother and the Daughter in *Law*,[39] being likely to break out, the *latter* departs, and is follow'd by the *former*, who threatens to make a complaint to her Husband of *Louisa's* behaviour— The *Scene changes* to the *Steerage*; where the *Master* and a *Sailor* by a very new and extraordinary method determines the *Day* of the Week and Month to be Saturday the 31st June, which the *Master* enters in the *Log Book*, as the Day of departure—*Jenny Chowder* now appears, and *announces*, that the Ship has sprung a *Leak*! Her appearance and in Her natural dress, more *amazes* the *Master* than the information of the Leak; *He* is going to heave her over board thro' a Port-hole—Her *cries* summon *Frankport* and others into the Steerage, which prevents his attempt from being carried into execution, and they now learn the dangerous situation they were in; and *Acadius*, for the first time finds *Jenny* safe on-board and in her proper Dress, instead of his Cloaths, at which he expresses his astonishment, intermixt with much secret Pleasure—The *Master* is now become *sober*, and gives the necessary directions to save the Ship; but in as mild terms as possible, lest the whole Company, some whereof were in liquor and others in Bed, shou'd be alarmed and occasion confusion; & *his* own & *sole* preservation seeming to ingross his whole attention; *Acadius* takes an opportunity of *seizing* his Fire Arms and *securing* Him and all the rest, save *Mr.* and *Mrs. Frankport*, *Louisa* and two or three Sailors, between Decks: They go off in the Long boat to a *Man of War*, who had for some time appear'd at a little distance and was becalm'd.—The *Scene* now *changes* to the Cabin,

30. "Conversation" was a euphemism used in laws and legal cases to refer to sexual intercourse. Criminal conversation statutes allowed one partner in a marriage to sue for damages against anyone with whom the other partner had an adulterous relationship. In practice this usually meant husbands suing their wives' lovers: in a famous case in 1769, Lord Grosvenor was awarded £10,000 in damages in a suit against his wife's lover, the Duke of Cumberland, who was the brother of King George III. The notion that Mrs. Frankport might seek damages against her husband's slave is obviously intended as an absurd joke.

31. In this period, "pathos" and "pathetic" did not have the negative association they carry today; here and elsewhere the term indicates only "full of emotion."

32. Stereotypical depictions of Welsh and Irish characters for comic effect were another traditional element of British drama common in the Elizabethan theatre, and they remained current through the nineteenth century.

33. That is, having a toast offered in his honour.

34. Elaborate toasts and rules of etiquette for both eating and drinking predominated in polite society in the eighteenth century. In eating after the tablecloth has been removed, drinking at the wrong time, and offering a toast to a married woman, Guttle and Guzzle show that, while they are British, they are outsiders to polite English society.

35. In the eighteenth and nineteenth centuries, people who could not pay their debts could be put into debtors' prisons until they made good. "Sponging houses" were places of temporary confinement in which debtors might be confined before appearing

where several of the Passengers remain in much jollity; the Master *breaks* into them and informs 'em of their situation; they, one and all are immediately cast down into the *lowest degree of despondency* and *fear*,—confess their sins, and pray; the *Welchman* in his native Language; and the *Irishman* in Latin and crossing himself;[40] and at length bursts out into this exclamation: "*Oh hone! Oh hone! What a fool was I, to trust all my two feet off the solid Land, on this boggy Floor, that won't be eisy!*"—*Guttle* and *Guzzle* eat and drink, as 'tho they had done neither, for a whole Month. *Fortune* who attends them having got drunk, falls asleep on the Floor—*Guttle* and *Guzzle* now go out to put on their cork and air Jackets[41] and jump out at the State Room window, and swim to shore— The *Master* and *Jenny* who attends him closely and behaves very tenderly towards him, and who had been a considerable time in a separate, whispering and very serious confabulation together, now speak out—She hints to *Him*, that his present *Distress*, was a *Judgement* upon *him*, for the wrong He had done Her; *He* thereupon very solemnly promises to marry *Her*, if *they* should escape to shore—whilst they are in this *Dilemma*, a noise is heard on Deck, and some Sailors enter, who come to carry them on board the *Man of War*, where *Frankport* and *his Family* were arrived—*Fortune* who is still asleep is with much difficulty awoke and carried off on a *Sailor*'s back, who, after taking out his chaw of Tobacco; in the Tar[42] style sings: (to the tune of "three Children sliding on the Ice upon a Summers Day"[43])

Well, now you're *up*, you'll *quiet* lay,
You're *safe*, as safe can *be*;
And if you 'tempt to *run away*,
I'll throw you in the *Sea*.
    I'll be d——d if I don't.

And thus endeth the second Act.

in court; the relationship between sponging houses and debtors' prisons was similar to that between local jails and prisons in our present legal system.

36. The lower, closed deck of the ship, in which cargo and passengers not able to afford individual cabins would sail.

37. Bars of sand form naturally at the point where many rivers flow into the ocean or another large body of water; to "cross the bar" was to leave the shelter of the harbour for the open seas.

38. In this context, "discover" means "to reveal" rather than "to find."

39. "Daughter in Law" is here synonymous with step-daughter, a usage that was common before the twentieth century.

40. Prayers in Latin and the act of crossing himself mark Guzzle as a Catholic.

41. Life preservers of this sort would have been relatively novel in 1774: a mid-nine-teenth-century edition of the *Encyclopedia Britannica* notes that "in the year 1764 the attention of the British public was particularly called to the floating powers of cork, by some experiments which were made with cork jackets on the Thames, together with some comparative experi-ments on air-jackets" ("Life Preservers" 1857, 440). Several forms of personal flotation device, usually vests made of cork, were commercially avail-able by the early nineteenth century, but British commer-cial vessels like the *Albion* were not legally required to carry one for each passenger until 1888 (Brooks 2008, 2).

42. "Tar" or "Jack Tar" was a common categorical name for a British Navy sailor, much like the use of "Tommy" for British soldiers during the First World War. Tar figures frequently appeared on stage, and in the nineteenth century an entire

style of nautical melodrama
emerged to depict the exploits
of brave British sailors.

43. Many variations of this
nursery rhyme beginning
with the lines "Three children sliding on the ice / Upon
a summer's day / As it fell out
they all fell in, / The rest they
ran away" were published
with sheet music during the
nineteenth century. A digital
facsimile of an example from
1879 by the composer Howard
M. Dow can be seen on the US
Library of Congress website.

4 : Early Quebec Circus (1797–1950s)

Performance beyond Language

LOUIS PATRICK LEROUX

TO SPEAK OF QUEBEC CIRCUS TODAY is to immediately conjure up images of the New-World commercial "reinvention" of circus, with its radicalized athletic exploits and heightened physicality. One also thinks of fantastical narrative and design: a marriage of theatre and dance to traditional circus disciplines. Today's billion-dollar industry is largely based in Montreal with its "big three": Cirque du Soleil, Cirque Eloïze, and Les 7 doigts de la main (7 Fingers). In addition, TOHU, a circus-devoted theatre in the round and producer of the Montréal Complètement Cirque international festival boasts forty smaller companies and collectives, and there are two state-funded professional schools (the National Circus School in Montreal and the École de cirque in Quebec City), multiple feeder schools, government subsidies for non-commercial companies, and an increasing variety of hybrid artistic forms.

The circus scene in Quebec has grown into a complex ecosystem involving artists, athletes, the business sector, and governments swelling with pride and advocating creativity and artistic know-how as a national and commercial virtue. And yet, nothing in the history of Quebec circus anticipated Montreal becoming a hub for circus production, training, and research by the turn of the twenty-first century. No one could have imagined that a nation obsessed with its very survival, culturally and linguistically, would have embraced a theatre of physical feats, of exploits and prowess that largely function beyond logocentrism.

Circus in Quebec before 1967, however, was closer to our nostalgic images of North American "traditional" tent-based circuses and smaller performative feats unencumbered by fanciful themes, narratives, or costumes. Ringling Brothers and Barnum & Bailey Circus regularly toured to Quebec with its big-top shows, often taking local talent with them on the road.

English-fashioned modern circus came to Quebec by way of the United States. In fact, we can reconstitute the tale of the origins of circus in Quebec with the historical trip of Ricketts's Circus up north to Quebec in 1797 (Figure 4.2). A mere thirty-seven years after Montreal capitulated to the conquering English colonial forces, Philadelphia-based Ricketts's Circus was travelling upstate New York to Albany, but decided to continue all the way across the border to the new British-controlled colony. In Montreal, they found an eager, ideal audience made up of a few distinct populations: on the one hand,

Counterclockwise from top left:

FIGURE 4.1: *Advertisement for L'Hippozoonomadon! Originally published in La Minerve, August 16, 1862, 4.* Courtesy of Bibliothèque et Archives nationales du Québec.

FIGURE 4.2: *Ricketts's Circus poster, ca. 1797.* MS Thr 1835 (Folder 385), Houghton Library, Harvard University.

FIGURE 4.3: *Louise Armaindo and Velocycle. Photograph by J. Wood, ca. 1883.* Courtesy of the author.

francophones whose theatrical infrastructures were in their infancy and, on the other hand, the new ruling classes comprised of the English administration and military, as well as the Scottish commercial class. All three populations mingled at this "modern circus," a new form following British officer and showman Philip Astley's popular mix of acrobatics-based equestrian acts and theatrical performances. The master of ceremonies was none other than actor, dancer, and acrobat John Durang, later claimed as both "America's first dancer" and "America's first native-born to make a lifelong career in the theatre" (York County 2015; see also Brooks 2011). Durang was functionally trilingual as his parents spoke French (they were from Alsace) and he had grown up in German-speaking Pennsylvania. He managed to entrance the audience and bridge the communities by addressing everyone, from the former German mercenaries who were rewarded by the British with land to the French-speaking population who could not get enough of this new form of entertainment. Ricketts's Circus played for a full eighteen months in Montreal, then performed an additional three months in Quebec City, later returning to Montreal for a repeat engagement on its return trip to the United States. It would be the first of many forays by American circus into Quebec.

In the nineteenth century, when foreign circuses and specialized acts toured regularly throughout Quebec, Quebec produced its own talented performers, including athlete Louise Armaindo, who later became a cycling champion (Figure 4.3). Armaindo was a high-level high-wheel racer, a champion *pedestrienne* (competitive speed-walker), and early circus performer. Born Marie Louise Brisebois in Sainte-Anne-de-Bellevue, she later moved to Chicago where she performed with the circus while also developing as an athlete. She first performed briefly as a trapeze artist but soon became a strongwoman. In her monograph about Louise Armaindo, Margaret Ann Hall (2018) writes that the athlete lifted 760 pounds before an audience at the Chicago Athenaeum, and that she handled Indian clubs and dumb-bells with great dexterity and strength. She reportedly also assumed the role of Zoe, the "Human Cannonball." Her later success as a professional athlete, especially as a *bicyclienne* at a time when cycling was gaining both in popularity and social acceptability, was regularly reported in American papers. In 1883 alone, "she was reported to have cleared $4,000 through her bicycling" (Hall 2018, 85).[1] Much of the time, she competed against men. Nevertheless, in spite of her achievements, Louise Brisebois/Armaindo has proven to be an elusive figure in both sports and circus histories.

One of the most important nineteenth-century circus creators from Quebec was Louis Cyr. Figure 4.4, a poster from John Robinson's Circus, features the legendary French Canadian strongman and his acolyte, "the French Hercules" Horace Barré. They were both from Quebec and quickly rose to leading acts. The poster acknowledges the pivotal place and prestige they had acquired. The undisputed "Strongest Man on Earth" could be challenged before every show. Contestants were enticed by a $25,000 challenge (this was an era when

2. As a comparison, Lillian Russell, a popular star in variety and musicals, was engaged by Sam S. Shubert in 1904 to perform in a musical comedy entitled *Lady Teazle* for $600 per week as well as 50 per cent of the net profits (Contract between Sam S. Shubert and Lillian Russell, October 24, 1904, Shubert Archives, New York City).

3. Following the civil unrest of the 1837–38 Patriot Rebellions in Lower Canada (now Quebec), Lord Durham was sent by Britain to assess the troubles. His report proposed some progressive notions such as "responsible government," but he is mostly remembered in Quebec for having presented the hypothesis of "two nations at war" and recommending a systematic assimilation and political dilution of the French Canadian population. Amongst the major implementations of the report was the Union Act of 1841, which unified the two colonies of Upper and Lower Canada. Durham's colonialist and dismissive statement that French Canadians were without culture nor history provoked a veritable social, cultural, historical, and political awakening in that population that continued well into the twentieth century.

a decent salary was about $5 a week). His "value" was advertised on the poster that read "engaged at the princely salary of $2000 a week." Cyr's salary marks his value as equal to, if not greater than, one of the most famous entertainers of the day.[2] Before Cyr, strongmen did not typically lead the circus parade through town, nor were they headliners. Cyr, however, had great stage charisma as well as incredible skill and strength. He also was a leading act in the Ringling Brothers' show before returning to Quebec, a rich, world-renowned performer. With Horace Barré, he founded the Cirque Cyr-Barré in 1899, bolstering what was then a growing confidence and advocacy for French Canadian culture, know-how, and figures of success and strength in the wake of Lord Durham's report and the Canadian government's deliberate strategy to weaken and assimilate its French-speaking population.[3] Figures such as Cyr and Barré, in addition to the numerous other strongmen and strongwomen from Quebec (including Cyr's wife and daughter), contributed to a discourse speaking to "a heritage of strength" and exceptionalism. Indeed, Louis Cyr became a mythical figure in Quebec lore.

A decade after Cyr left Ringling Brothers, Léon DuPerré, who developed a balancing unicycle act with two other acrobats and toured with this act for Norris and Row Circus starting in 1906, joined "The World's Greatest Circus" in 1908. Working with Ringling, who then bought out their rival Barnum & Bailey Circus, the Quebec-born artist quickly found his place within the growing company. He married his artistic partner under a big top and, after a few years of touring with the major American circuses, created his own troupe, "Leojoe" (Figure 4.5), with four other artists, and then "Leo Trio" with his wife Adrienne and an American partner.

Afterwards, the DuPerrés ended up being "Dupree and Dupree," touring nonstop until 1919, living a bohemian, yet luxurious life until the exhaustion of the punishing tour (one contract was for fifty-five consecutive weeks in fifty-five different cities, playing both Shea's and Keith's syndicated theatres) led to the couple's eventual divorce. Léon DuPerré developed a new act with Chicago-based cyclists Bill and Genevieve Levering, touring constantly during the 1920s until he fell in love with their daughter with whom he eloped. The couple started their own act as "Dupree and Merrill," touring throughout North America until the stock market crash of 1929 precipitated the couple's retirement from show business. They eventually settled in Montreal. DuPerré's life was a typically tumultuous, if particularly successful, example of life in the circus in that era.

The early to mid-twentieth century mostly saw the rise of multitalented individuals who, after demonstrating a prolixity of talents and ability, at one point defined and exploited their singularity. These athletes of exception were often charismatic entertainers with a devil-may-care attitude. While they usually toured with large American circuses, they also entertained a solid provincial network of venues, some traditional, others more unexpected.

FIGURE 4.4: *Louis Cyr on poster of John Robinson's Circus, ca. 1898.* Library of Congress.

FIGURE 4.5: *Troupe Leo Trio at Dominion Park, ca. 1913.*

© Léon DuPerré fonds, Bibliothèque de l'École nationale de cirque.

FIGURE 4.6: *Ricardo, acrobat and contortionist ca. 1931.* Item P322, S3, D5-23, P9, Paul-Émile Duplain fonds. Courtesy of Bibliothèque et Archives nationales du Québec.

FIGURE 4.7: *Miss Victory, the Human Cannonball at Parc Belmont, June 13, 1944.* Item P48, S1, P9933, Conrad Poirier fonds. Courtesy of Bibliothèque et Archives nationales du Québec.

One example is Alphonse Richard, also known as Ricardo L'homme-mouche, or as his English business card read, "The Famous Ricardo, Human Fly Man." The photograph reproduced here was his official headshot from which postcards were printed and distributed as promotional material (Figure 4.6). It was taken shortly after his spectacular 1930 crossing of the tumultuous Jacques-Cartier River on a high wire without a net or safety cable. The crossing included dancing and acrobatics on the wire. The event essentially launched his career and prompted him to move to Montreal. He constantly performed throughout Quebec for six years in theatres, parish halls, and public parks, most notably at the Parc La Fontaine. He died at the age of thirty after suffering a fall before an agitated crowd when he climbed the exterior brick wall of Hotel Chicoutimi in what is now Saguenay, Quebec, with his bare hands, a feat he had done countless times across the province until that fateful day in September 1936.

Miss Victory, the Human Cannonball, was a featured performer at Parc Belmont in the 1940s (Figure 4.7). This was an era in which high-diving ponies performed alongside acrobats and trapeze artists. Through the 1950s, 1960s, and early 1970s, the park boasted tantalizing "freak shows," most notably Peter Kortes's *Sideshow* as well as Sam Alexander's *Strangest Show on Earth*. The park would essentially become an amusement park over the years before being eclipsed by La Ronde on Île Sainte-Hélène, inaugurated for Expo 67 and which still operates today as an amusement park and midway.

Parc Belmont, created during Montreal's heyday as the "Paris of North America" and owned in part by the Trudeau family (whose scions, both Pierre Elliott and his son Justin, would later become prime ministers of Canada), was the last in a series of historically significant parks in which artists performing traditional circus disciplines were featured. Montreal boasted a tradition of public parks for amusement (not yet amusement parks as we understand them today). The first such park was the Jardin Guilbault, which featured Quebec's first circus acrobatics school in addition to extensive botanical gardens and a *glaciarium*, or ice rink. Jardin Guilbault was later followed by the creation of Parc Sohmer. Both parks exemplified the model of an urban "*parc champêtre*" based on music, artistic and acrobatic displays, strolling, and dining. Parc Dominion, a "trolley park" owned and managed by the local tramway company and inspired by Coney Island, introduced mechanical rides and focused on thrilling experiences rather than spectatorship and performances. Parc Dominion, which was Canada's largest amusement park, survived two fires but did not survive the Depression. Of this sequence of amusement parks, Parc Belmont bridged several eras and carried with it many traditions, including the regular performance of traditional circus acts.

The Baillargeon brothers (Jean, Paul, Adrien, Lionel, Charles, and Antonio) displayed feats of strength and classic hand-to-hand acrobatics and gymnastics (Figure 4.8). A typical program would feature Charles pulling a school bus with his teeth, as well as all six brothers performing acrobatics and creating

FIGURE 4.8: *The Baillargeon brothers, 1951.*

Item P833, S2, D150, La Presse fonds, Bibliothèque et Archives nationales du Québec.

elaborate human pyramids. In addition, guest performers specializing in balancing and acrobatics were showcased. Jean, displaying "muscular control" by lifting a ton, would then be followed by his brother, Adrien, who did a 3,000-pound lift on a platform. The finale usually involved Paul, who lifted a 1,400-pound horse with his bare hands. The Baillargeon brothers' careers spanned from the early 1940s to the mid-1970s, during which time they went from vaudeville artists to performing acrobats and strongmen to professional wrestlers. Paul had the most successful North American career and Adrien, "the Big Frenchman," moved to the United States, becoming a household name in the northeastern states, eventually settling in Louisiana where he stoked Cajun pride around his wrestling feats.

From Louis Durand to Ricardo-L'homme-mouche—without forgetting the DuPerrés, the Baillargeon Brothers, and many other artists not discussed here—the story of Quebec circus before 1967 is one of exceptional athletes with artistic flair, practicing multiple sports or working in many circus disciplines. There were very few specialists given that artists needed to display an aptitude in more than a single discipline or specialty to survive. The history of these early circus activities is also the story of artists and athletes leaving

Quebec in search of success or, when they remained, living a life on the road out of economic necessity.

Ringling Brothers and Barnum & Bailey Circus stopped their big-top shows in 1956 but returned to Montreal one last time in 1967, at the world's fair, Expo 67. Putting on a show of spectacular excess, they staged a parade of animals heading from downtown onto the Expo site and performed twenty-six shows that summer. Traditional circuses continued to tour in Quebec on a smaller scale: the Shriners had their suburban circus, and Quebec companies emerged as well, most notably Cirque Gatini in the 1970s, until an elephant trampled its trainer during a performance in 1979, in part marking the end of an era in Quebec in which traditional, animal-based circus was seen as innocent fun for the family.

From this point on circus would be "reinvented" (or at least reconsidered), recontextualized at a pivotal moment in Quebec society where artists mostly invested in the project of an independent nation were spurned by the Quebec population who voted "no" in the first referendum on the separation of Quebec from Canada in 1980 and then again in 1995. Theatre, in this new political climate, would become international, physicalized, image-based; hybrid forms of dance and a newly reconceived form of circus would emerge in a nation discovering that its creativity and artistic know-how could transcend language and reach audiences and influence circus production internationally.

Bibliography and Further Reading

Baillargeon, Marie-Ginette. 2013. "My Father the Wrestler as a Socio-cultural Icon or Papa, the Big Frenchman." *Revue de recherche en civilisation américaine*, no. 4. http://journals.openedition.org/rrca/539.

Batson, Charles. 2014. "Pink, Cirque, and the Québécisation de l'industrie." *Québec Studies* 58 (1): 25–44.

Bordez, Claude, and Giovanni Iuliani. 2002. *Dernier tour de piste*. Chicoutimi, QC: Éditions JCL.

Boudreault, Julie. 2016. "Are Quebec Circuses of Foreign Origin?" In *Cirque Global: Quebec's Expanding Circus Boundaries*, edited by Louis Patrick Leroux and Charles R. Batson, 55–68. Montreal and Kingston: McGill-Queen's University Press.

Bourassa, André-G. 2004. "Entrée des artistes." *L'Annuaire théâtral: Revue québécoise d'études théâtrales*, no. 35, 177–203.

Brooks, Lynn Matluck. 2011. *John Durang: Man of the American Stage*. Amherst, NY: Cambria Press.

Burger, Beaudoin. 1974. *L'activité théâtrale au Québec (1765–1825)*. Montréal: Parti pris.

Clairoux, Jacques. 2009. "Des hommes forts aux artistes de la piste: L'invention du cirque Québécois." *Cap-aux-Diamants: La revue d'histoire du Québec*, no. 97, 16–19.

Desbiens, Raymond. 2010. *Le retour du Roi du cirque au Québec. Ricardo "L'homme-mouche" 1906–1936*. Self-published (Presses Borgia).

DuPerré Rouseau, Léonne. 1989. *Une histoire d'amour avec le Show Business: Léon DuPerré 1886–1943*. Self-published typescript. Gatineau, QC: Éditions J. Oscar Lemieux.

Gaudet, Sylvain. 2009. "Un haut lieu de la culture populaire à Montréal au XIXe siècle: Le Jardin Guilbault." *Cap-aux-Diamants: La revue d'histoire du Québec*, no. 97, 25–29.

Hall, M. Ann. 2018. *Muscle on Wheels: Louise Armaindo and the High-Wheel Racers of Nineteenth-Century America*. Montreal and Kingston: McGill-Queen's University Press.

Jacob, Pascal. 2016. "The Québécois Circus in the Concert of Nations: Exchange and Transversality." In *Cirque Global: Quebec's Expanding Circus Boundaries*, edited by Louis Patrick Leroux and Charles R. Batson, 25–35. Montreal and Kingston: McGill-Queen's University Press.

Kantorowski, Frédérik. 2016. "Le cirque est en ville." In *En scène! 1865–1979*, Publications du Québec, 1–21.

Lamonde, Yvan, and Raymond Montpetit. 1986. *Le parc Sohmer de Montréal, 1889–1919. Un lieu populaire de culture urbaine*. Montréal: Institut québécois de recherche sur la culture.

Leroux, Louis Patrick. 2016a. "Epilogue: Circus Reinvested." In *Cirque Global: Quebec's Expanding Circus Boundaries*, edited by Louis Patrick Leroux and Charles R. Batson, 284–93. Montreal and Kingston: McGill-Queen's University Press.

———. 2016b. "Introduction: Reinventing Tradition, Building a Field: Quebec Circus and Its Scholarship." In *Cirque Global: Quebec's Expanding Circus Boundaries*, edited by Louis Patrick Leroux and Charles R. Batson, 3–20. Montreal and Kingston: McGill-Queen's University Press.

———. 2016c. "A Tale of Origins: On the 'Invention' of Cirque and Where Québécois and American Circus Cultures Meet." In *Cirque Global: Quebec's Expanding Circus Boundaries*, edited by Louis Patrick Leroux and Charles R. Batson, 36–54. Montreal and Kingston: McGill-Queen's University Press.

Lévesque, Réjean, and Kathy Paradis. 1997. *Hommage aux célèbres frères Baillargeon*. Cap-Saint-Ignace, QC: La plume d'oie.

Massicotte, Édouard-Zotique. 1909. *Athlètes canadiens-français. Recueil des exploits de force, d'endurance, d'agilité des athlètes et des sportsmen de notre race, depuis le XVIIIe siècle. Biographies-Portraits-Anecdotes-Records*. Montréal: Librairie Beauchemin.

———. 1937. "Coins historiques du Montréal d'autrefois: Le Jardin Guilbault." *Cahiers des Dix*, no. 2, 142–46.

Moy, James S. 1980. "The First Circus in Eastern Canada." *Theatre Research in Canada* 1 (1): 12–23.

Ohl, Paul. 2013. *Louis Cyr, biographie*. Montréal: Libre expression.

Proulx, Steve. 2005. *Les saisons du Parc Belmont 1923–1983*. Montréal: Libre Expression.

United States Consular Reports: Labor in America, Asia, Africa, Australasia, and Polynesia. 1885. Prepared by the Department of State. Washington, DC. https://babel.hathitrust.org/cgi/pt?id=inu.30000116794706&view=1up&seq=9.

Whittman, Matthew. 2012. *Circus and the City: New York, 1793–2010*. New York: Bard Graduate Center.

York County Historical Center. 2015. "John Durang: Forming America on Stage." http://johndurang.yorkhistorycenter.org/.

5 : Petitions against Performances of "Jim Crow" (1840–1843)

Roots of American Blackface Minstrelsy

STEPHEN JOHNSON

1. For further discussion of these petitions, see Johnson 2017, 254–79.

FROM 1840 THROUGH 1843, a group of Toronto's citizens, most of them representatives of its Black population, submitted petitions to their city council, requesting the banning of a certain kind of performer that, they argued, was damaging their reputation and inciting racial violence toward them.[1] The performer they protested was the blackface clown, the venue was the circus, and the law they appealed to for protection was a new licensing act meant to control the activities of travelling performers within the city limits. This episode in the history of performance in Canada raises questions that remain relevant: What is the relationship between a government and its citizens when it comes to controlling public performance? How do governments control the performance of hate and the incitement toward violence in theatrical presentations? And at what point do social satire and mockery become unacceptable in society? The story of these petitions and the performances they were intended to prevent is a story of the presentation of race, the persistence of tradition, and the prospects of changing the perceptions of people toward one another.

The performers being protested were clowns dressed as if they were southern plantation slaves at a time before the Civil War when slavery, though strongly protested by an abolitionist movement, had only recently been abolished in the British Empire and was still firmly entrenched in the southern United States. These performers played to the extremes of what we still imagine as "clown-like" behaviour, dressed in patchwork and stripes with make-up that made them grotesque, comic, or both, turning them into fantastical creatures. At the same time, they dressed and enacted ethnic and racial stereotypes. This combination of clowning and stereotypes resulted in a demeaning mockery of people—some of whom had only recently arrived in Toronto, and some of whom were long-time residents—who were powerless to protest.

Of these "take-offs" (as they are called in the petitions), the most powerful and the longest lasting was the blackface clown "Jim Crow," who presented himself as an authentic depiction of the "slave." With his halting walk, his accent, his out-of-control song and dance, and his uneducated "character" incapable of understanding civilized speech and manners (who attempted to put on airs but always got it wrong), this character became a mainstay

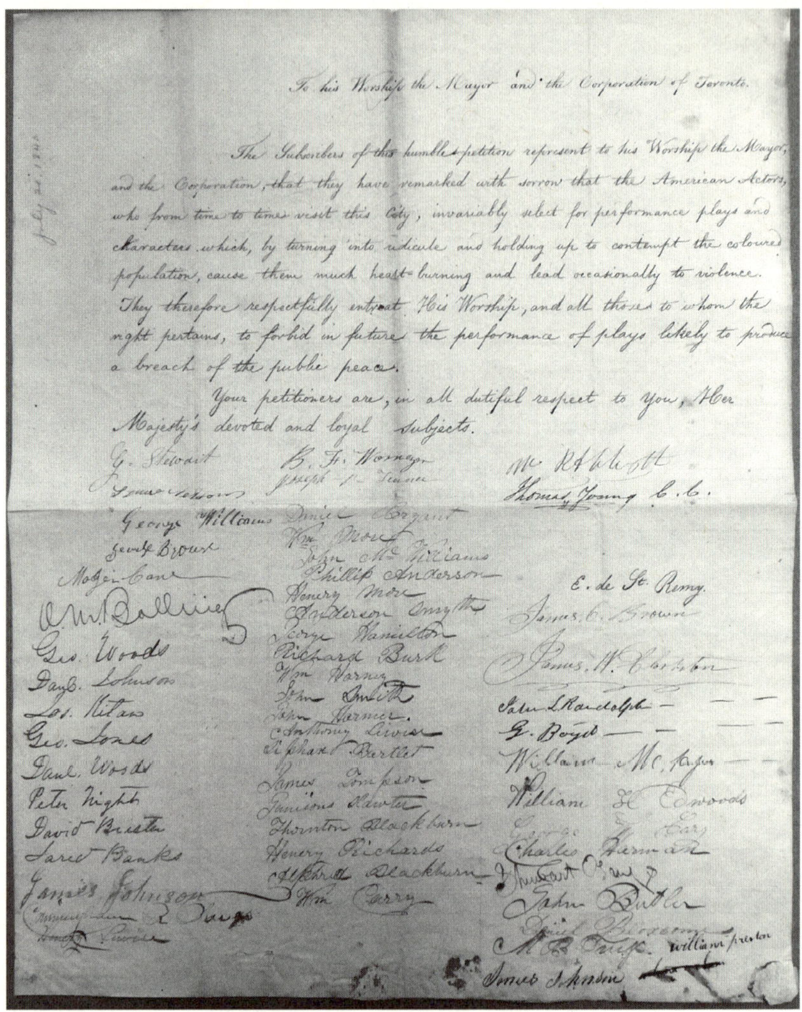

FIGURE 5.1: *Petition 1840: The first petition submitted to the Toronto City Council, dated July 20, 1840. Metropolitan Toronto Archives.*

of popular culture. Most important, and with the longest surviving legacy, was the face, which featured dark black make-up made of burnt cork mixed with grease that was highlighted with a wide red circle around the mouth to depict large, protruding lips. The costume also included a close-cropped curly wig. The image of the blackface clown was at once abstract, with clown-like features that bore no resemblance to any group or region, and yet very much a reference to a specific group in society and, in this particular case, in the audience.

The roots of this character reach far back into Western European culture, to images of the devil in medieval theatre, to the "Harlequin" figure in Italian Commedia dell'Arte, and to images of the Moor in early modern performance, all of which used black masks or make-up. But this is also a character of folk

FIGURE 5.2: *T.D. Rice as "Jim Crow": A widely circulated image of Thomas Dartmouth Rice, who was a very successful performer in the 1830s, popularizing (and claiming to have invented) the role of "Jim Crow."* From the cover of the sheet music for "The Original Jim Crow" (New York, E. Riley, n.d.).

culture, where "blacking up" was used as a way of obscuring identity while making a mockery of traditional and empowered society during carnivals and, in Canada, Halloween. It was not that this figure was entirely new to the citizens of Toronto in 1840, but much about the context was new and that made many people see this figure in a new light.[2]

At this time, an increasing number of Americans of colour were escaping from slavery in the southern United States, some into British North America. The idea of "Canada" as a welcoming place for the "fugitive slave" has been

FIGURE 5.3: *Richard Pelham as "Jim Crow": An image of Richard (Dick) Pelham as a performer in the Virginia Minstrels, one of the first minstrel shows, in 1843. From the cover of the sheet music for* The Celebrated Negro Melodies, as Sung by the Virginia Minstrels, *arranged by Th. Comer (Boston, 1843). Source: https://www.loc.gov/item/2016647558/.*

FIGURE 5.4: *The circus in the early 1840s: A "typical" circus from the mid-nineteenth century. This shows the Hippotheatron Circus, New York City, in September 1865, housed in a wooden structure, but with the same configuration as a travelling canvas tent. The circus appearing in Toronto in 1840 had a similar origin (New York) and form of entertainment. Note: Figures shown are not to scale; the venue was much smaller than it appears.* Circus Images, 1766–1939 (MS Thr 693 [82]), Harvard Theatre Collection, Harvard University.

1865
Sep. 25
INTERIOR VIEW OF THE HIPPOTHEATRON, FOURTEENTH STREET.

overstated, and an increase in the numbers of Black Americans arriving in Toronto no doubt increased the stress of relations between Toronto's white population and its long-resident Black settlers. Also at this time, improved transportation led to an increase in the number and kind of entertainments flooding across the border. American popular culture was then what it is now, a kind of juggernaut, overwhelming other cultures because of the country's large population, the entrepreneurial model of its "show business," and the technology used in disseminating its "brands." In the early 1840s, the new technology was the circus tent, the brand was blackface, and the citizens of Toronto really had no way to stop its arrival.

The circus tent as a performance venue was more disruptive than we imagine because it was a temporary building to which the normal rules did not apply. There was no cultural habit that prevented people of different classes and races from attending together, unlike other venues in the city, and so we can imagine an unusual audience that would not normally be together watching a performance. The circus was in the round, where audiences could see each other, and included a variety of performances with broad appeal. Among the characters was the clown, such as the Jim Crow figure, who provided rough verbal and physical mockery of all the other acts and who also talked directly to the audience, often making use of local events in his humour.

So consider the event in Toronto: a group of citizens who normally did not share a performance space together are assembled in a circus tent, and out into the ring runs Jim Crow, a clown whose task is to mock a particular minority. Sitting in the audience are members of this minority, visible to all, and no doubt mocked directly. Not everyone was shocked—remember that this blackface clown had been a part of the culture for some in the audience— but the direct reference to a group of fellow citizens, and audience members, was new. And despite the protests to the city council, nothing apparently could be done.

Toronto had only recently been incorporated as a city and was undergoing a complete renewal, building sewers and roads, improving sidewalks, and rewriting many of its bylaws. The city council was preoccupied, certainly, and ill-equipped to handle a complaint such as this petition. But it is clear from the city minutes that they did not simply dismiss these petitions. The greater problem was that they had just changed the law, bringing in Toronto's first real licensing act to control performances in the city. Unfortunately, the law allowed for some control over individual performers, including blackface minstrelsy, but it restricted itself to what happened on the streets of Toronto, and not inside a circus tent. It also had no provision to stop a performance before it began; if the licence was paid, the performance could be given, and nothing could be done until there was some actual physical violence. In two ways, then, this law had no teeth. It couldn't stop a performance in anticipation of an attack on its citizens and, anyway, it couldn't enter the tent. The city council couldn't help this situation even if it wanted to do so.

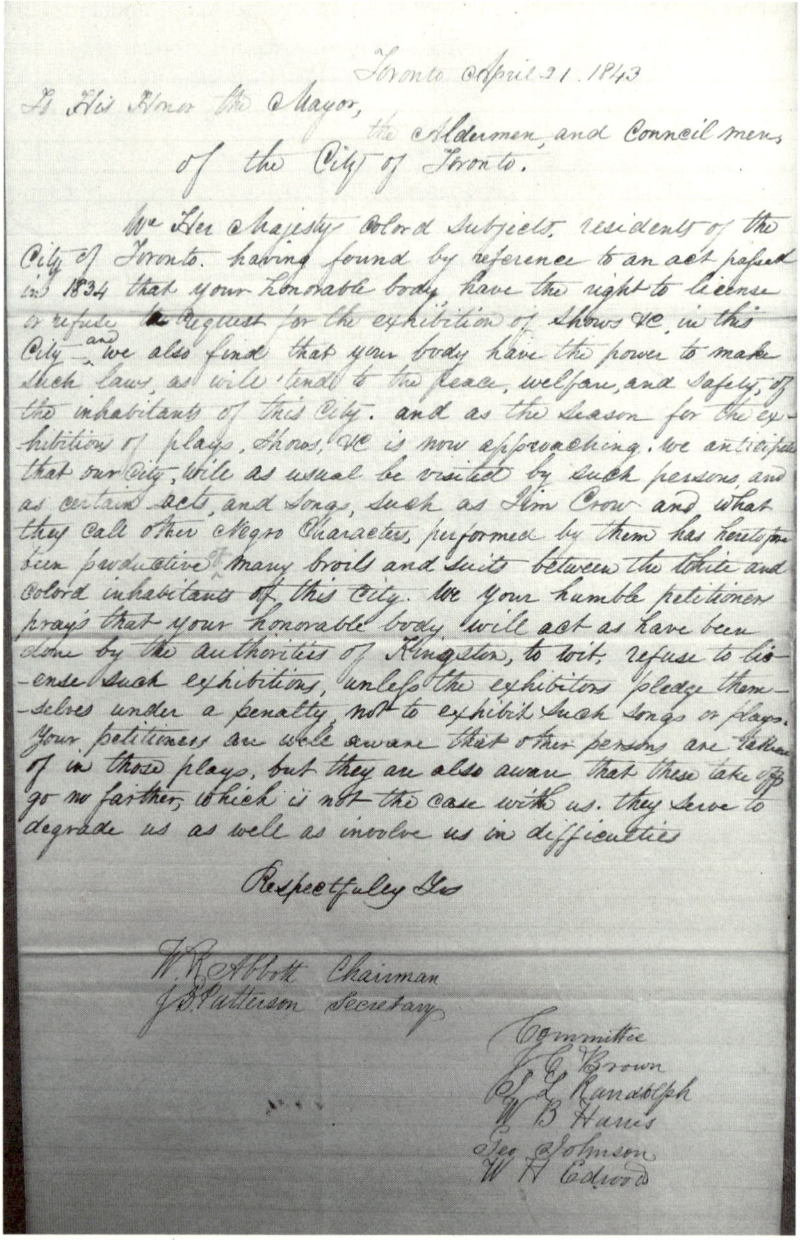

Toronto April 21. 1843

To His Honor the Mayor,
the Aldermen, and Council men,
of the City of Toronto.

We Her Majesty Colord Subjects. residents of the City of Toronto. having found by reference to an act pased in 1834 that your honorable body have the right to license or refuse the Request for the exhibition of Shows &c. in this City — and we also find that your body have the power to make such laws, as will tend to the peace, welfare, and Safety, of the inhabitants of this City. and as the Season for the exhibition of plays, Shows, &c is now approaching. we anticipate that our City, will as usual be visited by Such persons, and as certain acts, and Songs, such as Jim Crow and what they call other Negro Characters, performed by them has heretofore been productive of many broils and suits between the white and Colord inhabitants of this City. We your humble petitioners prays that your honorable body will act as have been done by the authorities of Kingston, to wit; refuse to license such exhibitions, unless the exhibitors pledge themselves under a penalty, not to exhibit Such Songs or plays. Your petitioners are well aware that other persons are taken of in those plays, but they are also aware that these take offs go no farther, which is not the case with us. they serve to degrade us as well as involve us in difficulties

Respectfuley Yrs

W. R. Abbott   Chairman
J. P. Patterson   Secretary

Committee
J. C. Brown
C. L. Randolph
W. B. Harris
Geo C Johnson
W. H. Edward

FIGURE 5.5: *Petition 1843: The fourth and last petition submitted to Toronto City council, dated April 21, 1843.* Metropolitan Toronto Archives.

FIGURE 5.6: *Legacy of the offending clown: Image of minstrel show performers in formal dress. The Ethiopian Serenaders, 1846.* Miscellaneous sheet music covers, author's collection.

The documents reproduced here were created by this combination of events and help to tell its story. The first petition (Transcript 1 and Figure 5.1) was presented to city council by both Black and white citizens. It is formal, respectful, and reads as if the signatories had an expectation of success. It advocated for the censorship of a figure that was extreme in its race hatred, and in its demeaning depiction of any local black citizenry, something that can be seen in the two images of Jim Crow. The first (Figure 5.2) shows the most famous of these performers, T.D. Rice, who popularized the character internationally. The second (Figure 5.3) shows Dick Pelham, who in fact was the performer travelling to Toronto just as the first petition was submitted. The difference in the imagery clearly shows the difference in the kind of performance: whereas Rice is shown with some humanity, Pelham's is an extreme, grotesque, and frightening image—just the kind of distortion the citizens of Toronto were trying to stop. Compounding the distortion, Pelham crossed the border performing with a circus, an intimate space that promoted the participation of audiences and disrupted their normal segregation (Figure 5.4). The petition didn't work, in large part because of the theatrical licensing law, the opening of which is reproduced here (Transcript 2). By the fourth try, the petition has become quite different (Transcript 3 and Figure 5.5). It is submitted by members of the Black population only and expresses desperation and a fear of physical violence.

The petitions did not prevent the return of the Jim Crow character. On the contrary, by the end of this decade he had become the main attraction of a new genre of performance, the "minstrel show," which sold itself as an "authentic" depiction of southern plantation slaves and therefore of a Black population

FIGURE 5.7: *Legacy of the offending clown: Image of minstrel show performers in plantation dress. The Virginia Minstrels, 1843.* Miscellaneous sheet music covers, author's collection.

more generally. Its aggressive caricature, in voice, make-up, costuming, gesture, and characterization, took hold of the public imagination in ways that no one could have predicted (Figure 5.6). This kind of entertainment was, arguably, the single most popular in North America during the second half of the nineteenth century and well into the twentieth, disseminating an image of "blackness" that affected race relations in ways that we are all still negotiating.

Although blackface performance was suppressed for many years in mass media, where old movies and television shows and musical recordings that made use of this form were not shown, it has never disappeared from local culture. There were minstrel shows, with full blackface, still being performed in Canada in the 1990s; and we still see it, from time to time, spread through social media, often at Halloween. In Toronto in the early 1840s, there was an attempt to stop something that has since had a significant effect on our cultural practice.

Bibliography and Further Reading

Careless, J.M.S. 1990. "The Cultural Setting: Ontario Society to 1914." In *Early Stages: Theatre in Ontario 1800–1914*, edited by Ann Saddlemyer, 18–51. Toronto: University of Toronto Press.

Chindahl, George. 1959. *A History of the Circus in America*. Caldwell, OH: The Caxton Printers.

Cockrell, Dale. 1997. *Demons of Disorder: Early Blackface Minstrels and Their World*. New York: Cambridge University Press.

Johnson, Stephen. 1999. "Uncle Tom and the Minstrels: Seeing Black and White on Stage in Canada West prior to the American Civil War." In *(Post)Colonial Stages: Critical and Creative Views on Drama, Theatre and Performance*, edited by Helen Gilbert, 55–63. Hebden Bridge, West Yorkshire, UK: Dangaroo Press.

———. 2017. "'Shield Us from This Base Ridicule': The Petitions to Censor Blackface Circus Clowns, 1840–43." In *Canadian Performance Histories and Historiographies*, edited by Heather Davis-Fisch, 254–79. Toronto: Playwrights Canada Press, 2017.

Johnson, Stephen, ed. 2012. *Burnt Cork: Traditions and Legacies of Blackface Minstrelsy*. Amherst: University of Massachusetts Press.

Lhamon, W.T., Jr. 1998. *Raising Cain: Blackface Performance from Jim Crow to Hip Hop*. Cambridge, MA: Harvard University Press.

———. 2003. *Jump Jim Crow: Lost Plays, Lyrics and Street Prose of the First Atlantic Popular Culture*. Cambridge, MA: Harvard University Press.

Lott, Eric. 1993. *Love and Theft: Blackface Minstrelsy and the American Working Class*. New York: Oxford University Press.

Mahar, William J. 1999. *Behind the Burnt Cork Mask: Early Blackface Minstrelsy and Antebellum American Popular Culture*. Urbana: University of Illinois Press.

Moy, James S. 1980. "The First Circus in Eastern Canada." *Theatre Research in Canada* 1 (1): 12–23.

Nathan, Hans. 1977. *Dan Emmett and the Rise of Early Negro Minstrelsy*. 1962. Reprint. Norman: University of Oklahoma Press.

Railton, Stephen. *Uncle Tom's Cabin and American Culture* (A multimedia archive). http://utc.iath.virginia.edu.

Rehin, George F. 1975. "Harlequin Jim Crow: Continuity and Convergence in Blackface Clowning." *Journal of Popular Culture*, no. 9, 682–701.

Toll, Robert C. 1974. *Blacking Up: The Minstrel Show in Nineteenth-Century America*. New York: Oxford University Press.

Winans, Robert B. 1984. "Early Minstrel Show Music, 1843–1852." In *Musical Theatre in America*, edited by Glenn Loney, 71–98. Westport, CT: Greenwood Press.

Winks, Robin W. 1971. *The Blacks in Canada: A History*. Montreal: McGill-Queen's University Press.

Wittmann, Matthew. 2012. *Circus and the City: New York, 1793–2010*. New Haven, CT: Yale University Press; New York: Bard Graduate Centre.

Transcripts of Petitions

Transcript 1

Petition No. 1:

July 20, 1840

To his Worship the Mayor and the Corporation of Toronto
The Subscribers of this humble petition represent to his Worship the Mayor,
and the Corporation that they have remarked with sorrow that the American
Actors, who from time to time visit this city, invariably select for performance
plays and characters which, by turning into ridicule and holding up to contempt
the coloured population, cause them much heart-burning and lead occasionally to violence. They therefore respectfully entreat His Worship, and all those
to whom the right pertains, to forbid in future the performance of plays likely
to produce a breach of the public peace.

Your petitioners are, in all dutiful respect to you, Her Majesty's devoted
and loyal subjects.

Transcript 2

Transcript of 'ByLaw No. 50':
ByLaw No. 50
An Act
To Regulate Theatrical Performances
and other Exhibitions
passed August 17th 1840

Whereas it is expedient and necessary to regulate and provide for the licensing
of all Theatres, Menageries, Exhibitions, Common Showmen, Mountebanks,
Circus riders, Jugglers, and other persons exhibiting any idle acts or feats for
gain or profit, in the City of Toronto and the Liberties thereof

Be it therefore enacted by The Mayor, Aldermen and Commonality of the City
of Toronto in Common Council assembled as follows:

Section 1
That from and after the passing of this Act it shall not be lawful for any person
or persons, to open a Theatre, or other place for the purpose of exhibiting any
Dramatic or other performance, or for the purpose of exhibiting any

Menagerie or any feats of Rope-dancing, Wiredancing, Juggling, Circus riding, Puppet Show, Common Show, or other idle acts or feats, generally performed or practised in such places, for gain or profit, in the City of Toronto or the Liberties thereof, or to exhibit any such Acts or Feats without having first obtained a License therefore [sic], in manner hereinafter provided.

Section 2
That all Licenses for the exhibition of any performance at the Theatre, or for the opening of any place for the exhibition of any Menagerie, or of any Circus-riding, Juggling, Puppet Show, Common Show, Robe dancing, or other idle acts or feats as aforesaid, shall be granted by the Mayor under the Seal of the City, signed by the Mayor and Chamberlain, and the person requiring such License shall say therefore, to the Chamberlain of the City, to and for the uses thereof, pay a sum of not more than five pounds, nor less than five shillings, for each day that the same shall be used, the rate in each case to be determined by the Mayor and not less than the other Magistrates.

Section 3
That all persons found aiding and assisting [?] in any performance as a Theatre or other place as aforesaid or as any exhibition of a Menagerie or of any Circus riding, Juggling, Puppet Show, Common Show, Rope dancing, or other idle Acts or Feats as aforesaid, where a License shall not have been first obtained, as aforesaid, shall be liable to a penalty for each day, or part of a day, which such person or persons respectively shall so exhibit or perform, of a sum not exceeding five pounds in the discretion of the Mayor or Alderman before whom such person or persons respectively shall be convicted, on the Oath of one or more credible witnesses, of having so performed or exhibited, without having first obtained a license so to do as aforesaid, which said fine shall be recovered by distress and sale of the offenders goods and chattels, and shall be paid into the hands of the Chamberlain of the City, to and for the public uses thereof.

[Section 4 is not in the final copy]

Section 5
That in default of goods and chattels to liquidate any fine imposed under the Authority of this Act, together with the Costs of prosecution, the offender or offenders respectively shall be committed to the Common Jail in this City for a period not exceeding Thirty days, or until the said fine and costs shall be paid.

Council Chambers
August 17 1840

John Birch, Mayor
[???], Chamberlain

Transcript 3

Petition No. 4:
April 21, 1843

To His Honor the Mayor, the Aldermen, and Councilmen of the City of Toronto

We Her Majesty's colored subjects, residents of the City of Toronto, having found by reference to an act passed in 1834 that your honorable body have the right to license or refuse the request for the exhibition of shows etc in this City—and we also find that your body have the power to make such laws, as will tend to the peace, welfare, and safety of the inhabitants of this city. And as the season for the exhibitions of plays, shows, etc is now approaching, we anticipate that our city will as usual be visited by such persons and certain acts, and songs, such as Jim Crow and what they call other Negro Characters, performed by them has heretofore been productive of many broils and suits between the white and colord [*sic*] inhabitants of this city. We your humble petitioners pray that your honorable body will act as have been done by the authorities of Kingston, to wit, refuse to license such exhibitions, unless the exhibitions pledge themselves under a penalty, not to exhibit such songs or plays. Your petitioners are well aware that other persons are [taken?] of[f] in those plays, but they are also aware that these take off [*sic*] and go no farther, which is not the case with us. They serve to degrade us as well as involve us in difficulties.

Respectfully Yrs

6 : Shipboard Performances (1851)

The Royal Arctic Theatre and the Search for the Franklin Expedition

HEATHER DAVIS-FISCH

OFFICERS AND SAILORS are crammed onto the upper deck of the HMS *Assistance*, trapped in pack ice in the Arctic. It is January 9, 1851: two months have passed since the men saw daylight. The squadron was dispatched to search for the Franklin Expedition, which had disappeared in the central Arctic six years earlier. A thick awning covers the deck, but high winds make it almost impossible to hear what's happening; steam rising from the men's bodies makes it difficult to see as well. Despite the harsh weather and uncomfortable conditions, the group eagerly anticipates the evening's entertainment: the world premiere of *Zero, or Harlequin Light*, a pantomime written by assistant surgeon Charles Ede.

The Franklin Expedition left England on May 19, 1845, tasked with completing the elusive Northwest Passage. The two ships under Sir John Franklin's command, *Erebus* and *Terror*, met British whalers in Baffin Bay in late July 1845: the whalers were the last Europeans to see them alive. The ships wintered off the coast of King William Island in 1846-47. The expedition remained trapped in the ice there until spring 1848, when 105 officers and men abandoned their ships.[1] Graves, skeletons, and personal items strewn along the shoreline suggest that the survivors ultimately made their way south, with the final few likely reaching the mouth of the Back River on the mainland of Nunavut.[2]

From 1848 to 1869, dozens of search expeditions were dispatched, peaking between 1850 and 1854. Searches were conducted overland in the fall and spring, when officers and crew were divided into small teams, each assigned a specific area to search. These were arduous undertakings: because the British Navy did not use dog teams, the men hauled sledges averaging 250 pounds per man over rough terrain covered in deep, wet snow and slush. On a good day, their pace was one mile an hour.

During the winter of 1850-51, the men and officers of the *Assistance* and the three other ships in its squadron staged an evening of theatre every two weeks. Theatre was a very popular pastime on ships wintering in the Arctic throughout the nineteenth century, encouraged by the navy because it maintained morale and prevented boredom. Moreover, theatre reinforced shipboard authority, naturalizing discipline as a beneficial part of theatrical production. Each winter, a theatre committee was established, usually led by a senior officer who acted as manager. He oversaw the production of two plays at a time, one performed by officers and one by men. The repertoire was selected from available scripts, typically comedies and lighter drama. Actors attended a handful of rehearsals, and sets and costumes were adapted from items in the ship's stores and from stock brought expressly for theatrical purposes. Plays were usually staged on the upper deck, which was decorated with symbols of imperial and naval authority (such as flags, coats of arms, or snow sculptures). Guests from nearby vessels often attended, and men were seated on trunks, with the captain and dignitaries sitting in a "royal box."

By mirroring naval authority structures and reinforcing divisions between ranks, providing the accountability of time-sensitive rehearsal and production tasks, drawing from a repertoire of "feel-good" fare, and encouraging collaboration and creative problem solving, theatre not only maintained but arguably improved shipboard discipline. This was of particular importance on ships searching for Franklin's expedition. Overland searches required a different form of management from day-to-day shipboard activities: without constant surveillance from a commanding officer, the structure of shipboard life, or the (meagre) physical comforts of the ship, search parties had to internalize their obligations, finding meaning and purpose in what could have been perceived as a pointless search. The experience of rehearsal resembled sledge travel: men had to work closely together, artistically "keeping step" in preparation for literally keeping step when hauling sledges. They had to think on their feet, adapting to changing circumstances. And they had to respect conventions, even when the consequences for disobedience were minor.

The script of *Zero, or Harlequin Light* demonstrates how theatre could shape perceptions of the Arctic and of the search. In the play's opening, for example, the officer is a model of benevolent authority and the men demonstrate how a positive attitude could overcome the dangers of climate and illness. *Zero* is an exceptional text, not only because it is the only surviving, original play written during this period of Arctic exploration,[3] but also because it reveals much about the emotional climate on the ship, providing insights into the anxieties and fixations that arose during the search for Franklin and how men and officers addressed internal and external threats to the expedition's success.

The first document (Excerpt 1) is a commentary on the play, written by Clements Markham, a midshipman on HMS *Assistance*.[4] In this excerpt from *Franklin's Footsteps*, Markham describes what the theatre on the *Assistance* looked like, highlighting how British emblems and symbols reminded men of home and emphasizing how the ship functioned as an extension of the British Empire. Markham notes, "the pantomime of fun and frolic…kept the whole party in a roar of laughter from beginning to end," indicating how audiences responded to the play. Markham provides a sense of the repertoire performed on British ships in the Arctic—farces, dramas, and comedies popular in England—and of the difficulties that theatre practitioners overcame to produce entertainments.

3. At least two other original plays were staged during the search for Franklin; however, neither script apparently survives. Patrick O'Neill lists the other plays: *Pantomime*, performed January 30, 1851, on the American search vessel *Advance*, and *King Glumpus*, performed February 1, 1853, on HMS *Resolute* (O'Neill 1990, 44). O'Neill identifies these three plays based on what appears to have been an exhaustive survey of published narratives and diaries and of unpublished personal papers and journals, playbills, and shipboard newspapers held at the Scott Polar Research Institute at Cambridge, the British Library, and the National Maritime Museum at Greenwich.

4. A midshipman was a junior officer.

The next document is an excerpt from the script (Excerpt 2). Its author, Charles Ede, entered the navy in 1845 and served in the Pacific before being appointed assistant surgeon on HMS *Assistance*. Ede's 1912 obituary notes that he was an "author, artist and wood carver of considerable ability" ("The Franklin Expedition" 1912); while it does not appear that Ede wrote any other plays, *Zero*'s adherence to generic conventions suggests that Ede was familiar with popular theatre.

Pantomime was a spectacular genre that rose to popularity in the late eighteenth century and remained popular through the nineteenth. Loosely derived from Commedia dell'Arte, pantomime follows a three-part structure. The opening, drawn from mythology or fairy tale, introduces a father figure and his servant, as well as a marriageable young woman and her preferred suitor, who is disapproved of by the father. The patriarch attempts to keep the couple apart, but as he verges on success, a "benevolent spirit, usually female, brings the opening to an end by...transforming [the lovers] into Harlequin and Columbine, while father and servant become Pantaloon and Clown" (Booth 1991, 198). The transformation marks the beginning of the harlequinade, in which Pantaloon pursues Harlequin and Columbine through a parade of shifting locales. The pantomime concludes with the characters' reconciliation and a celebration of the "triumph of true love" (198).

Zero follows this three-part structure, with a few significant changes that respond to the all-male context of Arctic exploration. The opening concerns the adventures of an ostensibly fictional search party seeking missing countrymen lost in the Arctic.[5] They are opposed by Zero and his servants, who are determined to foil their search attempts, and protected by the benevolent spirit Daylight, who counters Zero's plots. The opening reaches a crisis when Zero enters the sailors' tent, planning to freeze them to death. At this moment, Harlequin appears and sets the transformation sequence in motion, turning Daylight into Columbine and Zero and his Bear into Pantaloon and two Clowns. The harlequinade that follows includes a number of entertaining episodes, such as a pas de deux danced by Harlequin and Columbine, pranks and one-liners delivered by Pantaloon and Clowns, and a sentimental, nostalgic song sung by the North Polar Star. The script concludes with one Clown encouraging audience members to do their duty during the spring sledge searches in which they soon would participate.

This excerpt also includes *Zero*'s cast list: men and officers searching for a missing expedition and the good and bad spirits who represent explorers' hopes and fears during an Arctic winter. The cast list suggests iconic costumes for each character. The play's opening sequence allows us to imagine how Zero introduced the scenario to audience members (who were presumably delighted to see their own situation represented theatrically), including his plan to thwart the mission.

The following two documents are images that provide a sample of the extent and nature of theatre culture aboard Arctic search ships. The playbill

FIGURE 6.1: *Playbill for
Zero, or Harlequin Light.*

Item s0363, © National Maritime

Museum, Greenwich, London.

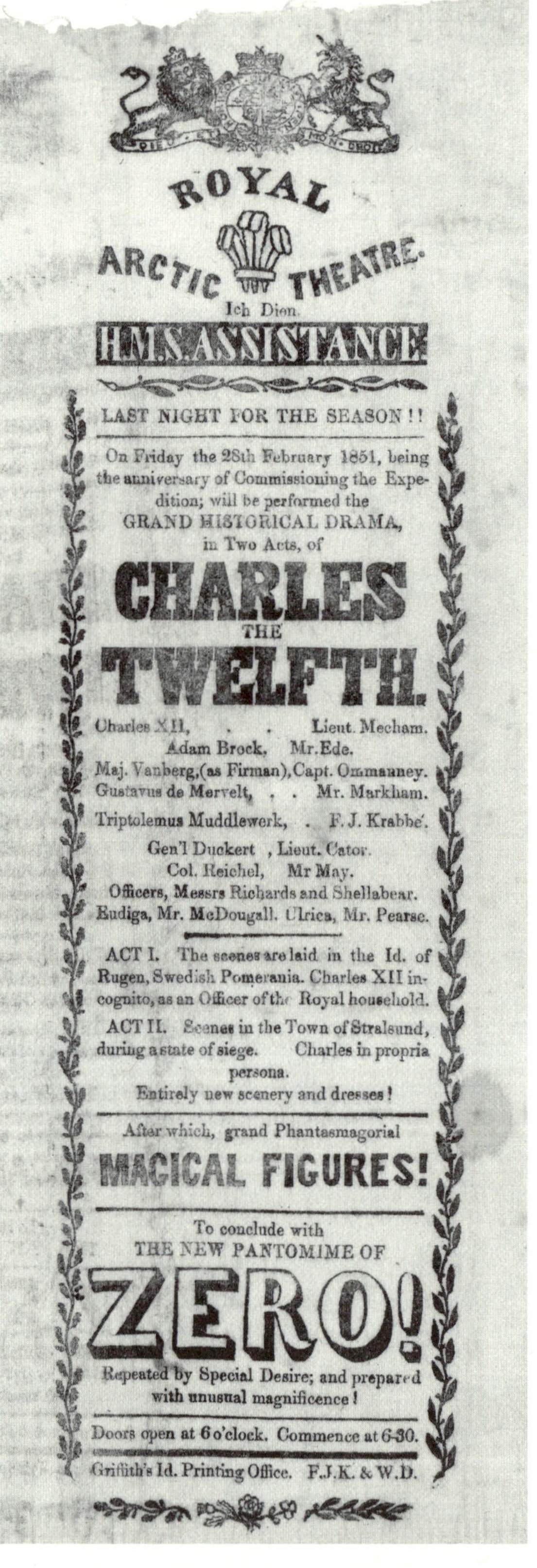
ROYAL
ARCTIC THEATRE.
Ich Dien.
H.M.S. ASSISTANCE

LAST NIGHT FOR THE SEASON!!

On Friday the 28th February 1851, being
the anniversary of Commissioning the Expe-
dition; will be performed the
GRAND HISTORICAL DRAMA,
in Two Acts, of
CHARLES
THE
TWELFTH.

Charles XII,   .   .   Lieut. Mecham.
          Adam Brock.   Mr. Ede.
Maj. Vanberg, (as Firman), Capt. Ommanney.
Gustavus de Mervelt,   .   .   Mr. Markham.

Triptolemus Muddlewerk,   .   F. J. Krabbe.

          Gen'l Duckert , Lieut. Cator.
          Col. Reichel,   Mr May.
Officers, Messrs Richards and Shellabear.
Eudiga, Mr. McDougall. Ulrica, Mr. Pearse.

ACT I.   The scenes are laid in the Id. of
Rugen, Swedish Pomerania. Charles XII in-
cognito, as an Officer of the Royal household.

ACT II.   Scenes in the Town of Stralsund,
during a state of siege.   Charles in propria
                    persona.
Entirely new scenery and dresses!

After which, grand Phantasmagorial
MAGICAL FIGURES!

To conclude with
THE NEW PANTOMIME OF
ZERO!

Repeated by Special Desire; and prepared
with unusual magnificence!

Doors open at 6 o'clock. Commence at 6-30.

Griffith's Id. Printing Office.   F.J.K. & W.D.

FIGURE 6.2: *Illustration of scene in* Zero, *in* Illustrated Arctic News. *Item number 2952796, c-028289, Illustrated Books, Albums and Scrapbooks, Libraries and Archives Canada.*

6. Most ships would have travelled north with a printing press; it would not have been uncommon to have more than one printing press within a squadron of ships, as there was no guarantee that they would remain together during their voyage.

(Figure 6.1) was printed on a printing press aboard the *Assistance* and would have built anticipation for the performance. The artist's image of the performance (Figure 6.2) was published in the *Illustrated Arctic News*, a paper printed aboard the *Resolute* and distributed to other ships when men visited one another.[6] The image represents a moment that did not actually occur in the play (as the Bear is transformed into a Clown), perhaps serving as an example of the playfulness of the performance and the impression it left on the audience, rather than an attempt at literal representation of the event.

A second excerpt from the play (Excerpt 3) includes stage directions outlining how the transformation sequence was executed, a sample of the Clown's and Pantaloon's antics, and—most notably—the transformation of a Fox into E. York, the ship's Inuk navigator and interpreter. This excerpt is followed by an artist's portrait of E. York (Figure 6.3), whose real name was Qalasirssuaq. Dubbed Erasmus York—after Erasmus Ommaney, the captain of HMS *Resolute* and Cape York, Greenland, the place where he came aboard— Qalasirssuaq was approximately sixteen years old in 1851. He was, by British accounts, a good-humoured, friendly member of the crew, apparently eager to learn English and British customs. He went to England with the *Assistance* in 1851 and attended the Missionary College at Canterbury, was baptized in 1853, and deployed as a missionary to Newfoundland in 1855, where he died soon after his arrival.

FIGURE 6.3: *Portrait of Qallisirsuaq, "Qalasirssuaq (Erasmus Augustine Kallihirua),*
ca. 1832/5–1856." Item BHC-2813. © National Maritime Museum, Greenwich, London.

The final two documents (Figure 6.3 and Excerpt 3), taken together, provide
an additional compelling reason why theatre, in particular a play like *Zero*,
was produced on search ships. In his analysis of pantomime, David Mayer uses
the term "visual simile" to describe Harlequin's transformations, arguing that
when Harlequin slaps his bat to transform objects, characters, or settings, he
changes them into "something which, in some hitherto unnoticed way, [they]
resemble[d]...disclosing that one thing has a hidden likeness to another" (1969,
39). In the play, Qalasirssuaq is transformed from Fox, a mischievous character
who has prowled around the men's campsite, into a human. In the context of
the play and the expedition, this visual simile can be interpreted in several
contradictory ways: as an invocation of genocide (through the Clown's line
about dead foxes); as a suggestion that the British saw Inuit as animal-like
rather than fully human; as a representation of how British perceptions of
Qalasirssuaq transformed over the course of the winter; or as a moment when
Qalasirssuaq demonstrated his level of understanding of British culture in a
sly, humorous manner.

There is no record of how audience members responded to Qalasirssuaq's
transformation. Personal accounts and articles in shipboard newspapers
suggest contradictory attitudes toward racial difference, unstable understandings of the difference between "civilized" and "savage" peoples, and
confusion over how to reconcile Qalasirssuaq as an individual with popular

constructions of Inuit. While the 1851 audience may not have recognized the plural and potentially political meanings of the transformation sequence, as a visual simile the scene demonstrates the complex nature of British understandings of racial difference during this period of contact with Indigenous Peoples. That this working-through of racial and cultural difference is preserved in the script of *Zero, or Harlequin Light* demonstrates how popular performance practices allowed the British to navigate the boundaries of their culture in a foreign and (to them) threatening climate.

Bibliography and Further Reading

Arctic Miscellanies. Souvenir of the Late Polar Search. By the Officers and Seamen of the Expedition. 1852. Collected and reprinted issues of *Aurora Borealis*, the onboard newspaper. London: Colburn and Co. Canadian Institute for Historical Microreproductions (CIHM/ICMH) microfiche series, no. 37229.

Beattie, Owen. 1988. *Frozen in Time: Unlocking the Secrets of the Franklin Expedition.* Saskatoon, SK: Western Producer Prairie Books.

Booth, Michael R. 1991. *Theatre in the Victorian Age.* Cambridge: Cambridge University Press.

Davis-Fisch, Heather. 2012. *Loss and Cultural Remains in Performance: The Ghosts of the Franklin Expedition.* New York: Palgrave.

Eber, Dorothy. 2008. *Encounters on the Passage: Inuit Meet the Explorers.* Toronto: University of Toronto Press.

Facsimile of the Illustrated Arctic News, Published on Board H.M.S. Resolute: Captn. Horatio T. Austin, C.B., in Search of the Expedition under Sir John Franklin. 1852. London: Ackermann & Co. CIHM/ICMH microfiche series, no. 42416.

"The Franklin Expedition Recalled. Death of Mr. C. Ede." 1912. *Surrey Times* (Surrey, UK), August 31, 1912.

Hill, Jen. 2008. *White Horizon: The Arctic in the Nineteenth-Century British Imagination.* Albany, NY: SUNY Press.

Markham, Clements. 1853. *Franklin's Footsteps: A Sketch of Greenland, along with the Shores of Which His Expedition Passed, and of the Parry Isles, Where the Last Traces of It Were Found.* London: Chapman and Hall.

Mayer, David. 1969. *Harlequin in his Element: The English Pantomime, 1806–1836.* Cambridge, MA: Harvard University Press.

Murray, Thomas Boyles. 1856. *Kalli: The Esquimaux Christian, A Memoir.* London: Society for Promoting Christian Knowledge.

O'Neill, Patrick. 1990. "Zero and the Arctic Dramatic Tradition." *Canadian Drama* 16 (1): 42–48.

———. 1994. "Theatre in the North: Staging Practices of the British Navy in the Canadian Arctic." *Dalhousie Review* 74 (3): 356–84.

Osborn, Sherard. 1852. *Stray Leaves from an Arctic Journal; or, Eighteen Months in the Polar Regions, in Search of Sir John Franklin's Expedition, in the Years 1850–51.* London: Longman, Brown, Green and Longmans.

Pearson, Mike. 2004. "'No Joke in Petticoats': British Polar Expeditions and Their Theatrical Presentations." *TDR / The Drama Review* 48 (1): 48–59.

Potter, Russell A. 2007. *Arctic Spectacles: The Frozen North in Visual Culture, 1818–1875.*
Montreal and Kingston: McGill-Queen's University Press.
Taylor, Millie. 2007. *British Pantomime Performance.* Bristol, UK: Intellect Books.

Excerpts from Shipboard Performances

1. Excerpt from Clements
    Markham, *Franklin's Footsteps:
    A Sketch of Greenland, along
    with the Shores of Which
    His Expedition Passed, and
    of the Parry Isles, Where the
    Last Traces of It Were Found*
    (London: Chapman and Hall,
    1853), 76–78.

2. Excerpt from Charles Ede,
    Zero, or Harlequin Light, in
    Franklin's Footsteps by Clements
    Markham, 131–33.

Excerpt 1: Commentary on the Play by Clements Markham[1]

This commentary, by midshipman Clements Markham, describes the theatre on the *Assistance*, highlights features of how shipboard theatre was presented, and provides a sense of how audiences responded to *Zero*.

A theatre was erected on board the Assistance, on a scale of magnificence which, considering the small means at the disposal of the Expedition, was truly marvelous. In spite of all the difficulties the manager had to encounter, the brilliant and artistic scenery of the "Royal Arctic Theatre" was displayed, to the admiration and delight of the whole Expedition, for the first time on the 9th of November. The stage was erected on the upper deck, and the front was made of painted canvas. Doric columns with vases of fruit and flowers were painted on each side of the curtain, and two snow statues of the Prince of Wales and the Princess Royal, were placed on either side of the orchestra. The first two nights were confined to farces and songs; but on the 9th of January, the famous extravaganza of "Bombastes Furioso" was brought on the boards with great applause; and on February 28th, the last night of the season, the historical drama of "Charles the Twelfth," and a pantomime written expressly for the occasion, were brought forward, which produced the greatest mirth and amusement. The pantomime was entitled "Zero, or Harlequin Light"; turning all the dangers and inconveniences to which we were exposed in these inhospitable climes, into evil spirits that were leagued against us. It supposes them continually watching every opportunity to surprise an unfortunate traveling party, till at length their power is destroyed by the appearance of the more puissant good spirits Sun and Daylight. Then the metamorphose takes place. The good spirit Daylight turns into Harlequin; Columbine jumps through an oil-skin sun, which had risen behind the back scene; and frosty old Zero, who has all along been the leader of the evil spirits, is turned into first Clown; a bear, which had been for some time prowling about, was then fired at, and out tumbled Pantaloon and second Clown. Then commenced the pantomime of fun and frolic, which kept the whole party in a roar of laughter from beginning to end.

Excerpt 2: Introductory Material and Opening Scene of *Zero, or Harlequin Light*[2]

The introductory material of the pantomime includes the list of characters, outlines key features of their iconic costumes, and provides a description of what the opening moments looked and sounded like. This excerpt also demonstrates how Ede introduced the "Evil Spirits" of the Arctic to his audience: with presentational entrances and verse rich with inside jokes about shipboard life.

ZERO, OR
HARLEQUIN LIGHT.

CHARACTERS
THE SUN, Good Spirits.
DAYLIGHT
ZERO, Evil Spirits in the shape of Arctic horrors.
BEAR
FROSTBITE
ICEBERG
HUNGER
SCORBUTUS
FOX

Tracking and Travelling Party of Four.

DRESSES.
ZERO: Full frosted wig, surmounted by a fanciful crown; long flowing beard; loose white robes with large sleeves, icicles hanging from different parts. Large thermometer with slide at Zero, and 50 marked on it in large letters.
FROSTBITE: Tight dress; upper third of body and limbs white; middle red; lower blue; passing into black; long frosted wig.
HUNGER: Long thin mask face, pale dress, loose and scanty.
SCORBUTUS: Tight white dress, covered with purple and reddish-brown spots; mask pale, with bluish-red and blotched mouth.
GOOD SPIRIT: Clothed in white, with chaplet and fancy wand.

Scene in the Arctic Regions. One of the ships in a perilous situation, nipped by ice; icebergs and moving floes drifting past. Strong blue light thrown across the stage. Drums, whistles, and all sorts of discord by Band. ZERO *enters, and walks majestically up and down the stage, one or two of his Imps pass quickly across the stage at the back.*

ZERO *advances to the front.*

ZERO. Old Christmas has almost usurp'd our rights,
    Frighten'd me! *Zero!* with his roaring nights;
    But ah! I'll be revenged, when on the floe
    These boisterous Tars shall find it all no go.

3.   Melville Bay is on the coast of northwest Greenland, and Cape York, where Qalasirssuaq came aboard, is at its northeast end.

4.   "Mr. Penny, who commanded the mercantile expedition." Note included in original text.

5.   "Floes and hummocks— masses of ice." Note included in original text.

6.   Two games that men would have likely played to entertain themselves. "Quoits" involves throwing rings made of iron, rope, or rubber at a peg in the ground while "rounders" is a variation on baseball.

7.   "The ice quarter-masters: old seamen who received £7 a month. Hence the nickname." Note included in original text.

8.   Evening parties or social gatherings.

9.   Masked ball. Newspapers, plays, parties, magic lantern performance, and masked balls all would have helped occupy men and officers during winters aboard Arctic vessels.

10.   "The Intrepid." Note included in original text.

11.   Likely a misspelling of gas.

12.   One reason why Arctic ships carried printing presses was to print out messages that could be distributed via unmanned hot air balloon. At the end of the play, balloon gear is brought on stage; this was likely actual equipment and not simply a prop.

13.   Vincenzo Bellini and Giuseppe Verdi were both popular Italian opera composers.

14.   This line seems to be loosely derived from an English Morris dance song called "Such a Getting Upstairs." The variant spelling ("sich") suggests that the variation of the song directly referenced here is actually "Sich a Getting Up Stairs," an American minstrel song dating to approximately the 1830s.

15.   The reference to side-scenes suggests either small wings to the sides of the stage, at

In Melville Bay[3] he's sought to use his might,
When lo! they blast and cut out of his sight.
And there they found a Penny[4] that would pass,
Made of good metal, not of spurious brass.
Their progress once or twice I did arrest,
By closing floes and hummocks[5] thickly press'd;
They laughed, and took to playing quoits and rounders[6]
Captains, officers, and seven-pounders;[7]
But I am formed for action, and word
Shortens the time and makes revenge absurd;
I'll summon Frostbite, for by education
He laughs at feelings and destroys sensation;
With papers, plays, and *soirées*[8] they defy,
Up to this moment my supremacy;
With magic-lantern and the *bal masqué*,[9]
They think to cheat me,—don't I wish they may!
They've turn'd a steamer[10] into a saloon,
And tried to *gase*[11] me with a news balloon.[12] (*Calls* FROSTBITE.)
Frostbite, you idle rogue, quick, quick appear!

Enter FROSTBITE.

FROST. Master, your pale and rigid slave is here.
ZERO. Wait! I am in humour for reflection,
   Of which beware you freeze not in connection.
   Dark Winter too his course doth quickly run,
   Hasten'd by their good fellowship and fun;
   My imps of horror they have laugh'd to scorn,
   Two dreaded, still remain, a hope forlorn. (*Calls in a loud tone.*)
   Scorbutus, hither come, and Hunger fierce!
   They well, I know, can any bosom pierce.

Enter SCORBUTUS *and* HUNGER.

SCOR. *and* HUN. What would our gracious liege that we should do?
ZERO. Try when within your grasp if they be true.
   Begone, and loiter not! Away! be quick!
   My spirits falter, I must have music;
   I love operas, Bellini's or a Verdi,[13]
   Play "Sich a getting' upstairs I never did see."[14]

Band plays the air: ZERO *walks majestically up and down, keeping time with his thermometer, then looks out at the side-scenes.*[15]

minimum a usable space behind the proscenium arch.

16. Excerpt from Charles Ede, *Zero, or Harlequin Light*, in *Franklin's Footsteps* by Clements Markham, 138–43.

17. "Mr. Dean, the ingenious carpenter, who made a bear for the pantomime." Note included in original.

18. "An oiled-silk sun which rises at the back scene." Note included in original. The sun was likely a star trap: a trick set piece that included a hole covered in fabric with a slit that made it appear closed but allowed people or objects to pass through.

Excerpt 3: The Transformation, Harlequinade, and Finale of the Pantomime[16]

The ending of the pantomime includes many characteristic features of the genre, such as transformations executed through stage magic, entertaining one-liners and slapstick humour, and a sentimental ending that reaffirms social norms. This excerpt also includes the transformation of a prowling fox into Qalasirssuaq, the expedition's Inuk translator and navigator, a moment which seems to have been unremarkable in 1851 but is rich for interpretation today.

ZERO. Bravo, my fox! go fetch Dean's[17] model bear;
   The morning dawns, now I for work prepare.
   If I don't freeze them as they lie asleep,
   May I no other promise ever keep!
   Ah! now some pleasures have come indeed at last:
   How sound they sleep; I have them "hard and fast."

ZERO *enters tent; his imps leave the stage;* HARLEQUIN *leaps through the Sun,*[18] *and changes (the Good Spirit)* DAYLIGHT *into* COLUMBINE; *they dance a pas de deux.*
BEAR *enters and prowls round the tent;* HARLEQUIN *slaps the ground near the tent, which disappears, leaving the* CLOWN *grinning and making faces; he sees the* BEAR, *becomes dreadfully alarmed, and makes off for a gun; returns, snaps the gun, which refuses to go off; the* BEAR *approaches, when he succeeds in firing at it;* BEAR *falls, and out roll* 2ND CLOWN *and* PANTALOON, HARLEQUIN *slapping the ground near the* BEAR. HARLEQUIN *and* COLUMBINE *retire;* CLOWNS *commence tumbling and fooling with* PANTALOON.

1ST CLOWN (*to* PANTALOON). Why, what animal are you?
PANT. A man.
1ST CLOWN. How can that be, when you were got by a bullet out of a bear? Ho! ho! ho! you fool!
PANT. Give us an account of your late proceedings.
1ST CLOWN. Well, here goes.

   I'm fond of sport, that is of fun:
   I saw a bear, and took my gun;
   Away I went, at a great pace,
   My foot it slipp'd in the wrong place,
   So down I fell, when in a trice
   I popp'd through a thin young crust of ice.
      Tol, lol, idi, idi, idi, idi, aido.

19. Likely a joke referencing that no corsets would have been necessary for an expedition comprised of only men.

20. Likely a tall landmark constructed to help men find their way back to the ships from the ice or, perhaps, an observation tower. Nelson's Column was constructed in Trafalgar Square between 1840 and 1843 to commemorate Horatio Nelson, who died at the Battle of Trafalgar in 1805. There is also a Nelson Monument in Edinburgh, constructed between 1807 and 1815.

21. "The Observatory: a snow edifice, which, on its completion, was to have had a house warming at the expense of Mr. Cheyne, the learned astronomer; but from some reason the promised entertainment never took place." Note included in original.

I crusty grew: it was not fair:
To get a wet I couldn't a bear;
I dragged myself upon the floe,
The bear came near; oh! what a go!
I pulled the trigger, but the cap
Quite finished me, by one false snap.
    Tol, lol, etc.

My legs they shook; my heart, pit pat,
Hit my backbone a loud rat-tat.
He snuffed in me a morning meal,
And thought to fix on me his *seal;*
When lo! I thought of boys who put
Their head 'tween legs when bulls would butt.
    Tol, lol, etc.

Place caps in mouth, and horrid shout,
The bulls they go to the right about;
I tried the dodge, when, bless my eyes!
The bear stood still, quite in surprise:
I gave a shout, he show'd his heels,
Oh, lor! says I, much better I feels.
    Tol, lol, etc.

2ND CLOWN (*to* PANTALOON). What foxes are easiest to shoot?

PANT. Sleeping foxes?

2ND CLOWN. No, not so bad either.

PANT. Running? walking? etc.

2ND CLOWN. Tame ones, to be sure.

1ST CLOWN. What house in this neighbourhood is the coldest?

2ND CLOWN. Mrs. Corset's?[19]

1ST CLOWN. No.

2ND CLOWN. What then?

1ST CLOWN. Why, the transit observatory, to be sure, first turning past Nelson's Monument.[20]

2ND CLOWN. How so?

1ST CLOWN. Because no one ever "heard" of its having had a warming.[21] Ha! Ha!

2ND CLOWN. Then, I'd chain up the builder.

1ST CLOWN. What good would that do, stupid? Well, why would you?

2ND CLOWN. Because he ought to have known no house can stand there unless it's had a wet.

22. "The Esquimaux we had on board." Note included in original.

23. "One of the whalers' names for an Esquimaux." Note included in original. The joke is ostensibly a pun based on two meanings of the word "husky": it referred to the voice of a person with a cold and was whaler's slang for Inuit based on a mispronunciation of "Eskimo." By 1852, a third meaning had also entered usage: the word referred to the dog breed. The ability to use the word husky to refer to both Inuit and their dogs suggests that the transformation signaled the philosophical, anthropological, and linguistic conflation of Inuit and animals.

24. A major fruit and vegetable market in central London, close to the Theatre Royal, Covent Garden.

25. "The decorations of the front." Note included in original.

26. A screw steamer was a type of steamship driven by a propeller, in contrast to a paddle steamer.

27. A drop scene was the painted curtain let down between acts of a play to close off the stage from the audience's view.

28. A chair carried by poles, often with a roof and walls.

29. To bonnet was to pull a person's hat over their eyes.

30. The tune "Ivy Green" would have immediately evoked home for audience members familiar with the ballad by Henry Russell, based on lyrics from Charles Dickens's *Pickwick Papers*.

1ST CLOWN fetches in a fox-trap, and places it at back of stage. All run off and watch it. White fox enters, and the trap falls. Enter CLOWNS, *who open the trap.* HARLEQUIN *slaps the trap, and out comes E. York.*[22]

1ST CLOWN. Why, a real native! Why is he like a man with a bad cold?

2ND CLOWN. Answer it yourself.

1ST CLOWN. Isn't he a little H(Uskey)?[23]

2ND CLOWN. Why is the Royal Arctic Theatre like Covent Garden Market?[24]

1ST CLOWN. Because it's often filled with the fresh and spicy?

2ND CLOWN. No. Because it's supported by flowers and fruit.[25]

1ST CLOWN. Why would you like to join the tenders?

2ND CLOWN. I should have a chance of keeping the steam up, and going ahead when I was screwed.[26]

2ND CLOWN. It's my turn now for guessing the last. Here you are: why do all actors think the drop scene[27] like a tyrant?

1ST CLOWN. Not being one, could not possibly say.

2ND CLOWN. Well then, because they are released and rejoiced at its fall.

Enter people coming from a masquerade, walk about the stage, CLOWNS *joking them.*

Sedan chair[28] *enters with a masked female in costume.* CLOWNS *run and bonnet chairmen,*[29] *and open the door, drag out the female, one lugging one way, the other the opposite.* HARLEQUIN *enters; they put her back into the chair, and commence to fight.* HARLEQUIN *passes quickly; slaps the back of the chair.*

1ST CLOWN, *having knocked down* 2ND CLOWN, *goes to the chair, opens the door, when out steps North Polar Star in rough dress, treads on* CLOWN'S *toe, advances to the front, and sings.*

AIR—Ivy Green.[30]

A noble soul has that man, I ween,
　Who braveth these regions cold:
No dangers that threaten his life are seen
　When he seeketh the brave and bold.
Oh! the heart must be hard and bad indeed,
　Or ruled by a coward's whim,
If it bounds not to think of the friendly deed
　Perform'd in these lands by him.
　　Seeking where the lost have been,
　　A gallant band may yet be seen.

 The final two lines of the
Clown's advice cite Nelson's
famous signal command,
issued immediately before
the Battle of Trafalgar began.
These lines were often
referenced in relation to Arctic
exploration.

Through ages long past, the British name
   Has been known in every clime,
And all must trust that the well-earn'd fame
   Will endure to the end of time.
To rescue from death the friend, or foe,
   Was ever the sailor's boast;
And now, 'mid the terrors of frost and snow,
   His course is needed most.
      Seeking, etc.

Soon night will be past, and spring draweth nigh,
   To gladden us all again,
When we'll seek around, with a watchful eye,
   Nor at any toil complain.
They await us in England, the beauteous, the fair,
   When our dangerous task is o'er,
And who would not greatest hardships dare
   To be prized by them once more?
      Seeking, etc., etc,

Exeunt OMNES. *Enter* HARLEQUIN *and* COLUMBINE, *who dance a pas de deux.*
CLOWNS *and* PANTALOON *enter, followed by men bringing in balloon gear. The*
CLOWNS *drive off the men, and inflate balloon, which, when full, takes up 1st*
CLOWN, *who exclaims, Oh! aint I Green! After a short time he descends without*
balloon, and advancing to the front with a slip of paper in his hands, reads news from
home. All well! And a happy new year to you! Now for my advice:

A fool may sometimes wisdom speak,
   Though wanting youth and beauty;
     So let me say,
     In Nelson's way,
England expects that every man
   This spring will do his duty.[31]

FINALE — GRAND TABLEAU.

7 : Canadian Fancy Dress Balls
(1876–1898)

Transcending Dress, Self, and Community

CYNTHIA COOPER

IN THE SECOND HALF OF THE NINETEENTH CENTURY, balls and parties where guests dressed up in costume, or "fancy dress," were a popular form of entertainment in Europe and North America. These events ranged from parlour pastimes, such as tableaux vivants and amateur theatrical performances, to ticketed public gatherings, to large private balls and parties with hundreds of guests. Their commemoration in photographs and souvenir publications, which is far disproportionate to that of other forms of social entertainment, foregrounds their strong hold on participants' imaginations. Dressing up in costume offered the extraordinary experience of transcending the limitations of fashionable dress and one's public self. Such socially acceptable escapism stood in stark contrast to the strict Victorian-era etiquette of both dress and behaviour.

While many nineteenth-century Canadians may have had the occasion to attend a variety of costumed entertainments in their lifetimes, particularly the skating carnivals that were a favourite winter pastime, the most widely publicized and meticulously recorded fancy dress events were four large balls held under the patronage of the governors general. These balls stood out for their magnitude and magnificence, but also for their intent to further political aims.[1] In 1876 the Earl of Dufferin[2] hosted a ball to raise the profile of the new Canadian capital of Ottawa, showing the world not a rough colonial backwater, but rather a seat of society with a stately residence where a British peer held court over a glittering season.[3] Two decades later, when viceregal agendas were more ardently imperialist, fancy dress balls again emerged as the society entertainment of choice. The Countess of Aberdeen[4] conceived of her parties as instructive pageantry, steering perceptions away from the frivolities of elite entertainment. In 1896, at the Historical Fancy Dress Ball in Ottawa, her guests represented figures from Canadian history. Her Victorian Era Ball in Toronto the following year celebrated the benefits of Canada's place in the British Empire with guests representing British colonies and cultural and scientific contributions. In 1898 another Historical Fancy Dress Ball—this one organized by the Ladies' Branch of the Antiquarian and Numismatic Society in Montreal with the Earl and Countess of Aberdeen as guests of honour—borrowed from her historical theme of two years earlier.[5]

1. The stories of these balls are told in detail in Cooper 1997.

2. Frederick Temple Hamilton-Temple-Blackwood, 1st Marquess of Dufferin and Ava. As Earl of Dufferin, he served as Canada's third governor general from 1872 to 1878.

3. In 1857 Queen Victoria made the controversial choice of the rough lumbering town of Ottawa as capital of Canada. Only after the completion of the Parliament buildings in 1866 and Confederation in 1867 did Canadian politicians reluctantly accept their seat of government. The city gradually became more sophisticated in the years that followed.

4. Ishbel Maria Marjoribanks Hamilton-Gordon was the wife of John Campbell Hamilton-Gordon, 1st Marquess of Aberdeen and Temair. As Earl of Aberdeen, he served as Canada's seventh governor general from 1893 to 1898.

5. The Antiquarian and Numismatic Society, founded in 1862, brought together Montrealers with an interest in preserving many facets of the city's heritage. In 1896 it established a Ladies' Branch to assist in furthering the mission of its new museum housed in the Château Ramezay. Lady Aberdeen was the society's first honorary president.

FIGURE 7.1: *Dr. Robert Wilson as "Samuel de Champlain" at the Historical Fancy Dress Ball, Montreal, 1898.* Wm Notman & Son. Item 11-123117. ©McCord Museum, Montreal.

FIGURE 7.2: *Lady Aberdeen as "Constance de la Tour" at the Historical Fancy Dress Ball, Montreal, 1898.* Wm Notman & Son. Item 11-123824. ©McCord Museum, Montreal.

6. Dr. Robert Wilson was a physician trained at McGill University who specialized in electrotherapy and radiotherapy.

7. Samuel de Champlain played a major role in founding New France from 1603 to 1635.

8. Lady Aberdeen believed her maternal grandmother was a descendant of the wife of Charles de St. Étienne, Sieur de la Tour, Governor of Acadia, whom she incorrectly named Constance.

FIGURE 7.3: *Lady Marjorie Gordon as "Forests of Canada," at the Victorian Era Ball, Toronto, 1897.* W.J. Topley. Item number 8423777, PA-027919, accession number 1936-270 NPC, Topley Studio fonds, Library and Archives Canada.

Guests, mostly drawn from local elites, anticipated these events for weeks. They put effort into researching characters and planning attire, in some cases incurring significant expense. The balls were widely reported in the press with long lists of guests, their characters and costumes, as well as descriptions of ballroom decor, dance programs, and menus. Minute details of the events reached a much wider audience than those in attendance.

The overtly nationalistic intent of the Aberdeen fancy dress balls insinuated itself on many levels. For one, it resulted in a particularly colonial twist on the usual popular sources of inspiration for characters. While attendees often favoured historical costumes that allowed them to reimagine themselves in a glamourized past, for these balls, they mined Canadian history to find suitable characters to portray. Dr. Wilson[6] as "Samuel de Champlain"[7] was singled out as well cast (Figure 7.1). The one time that Lady Aberdeen impersonated a historical character, it was an ostensible Acadian ancestor (Figure 7.2).[8] Another popular character type for women was an allegory of a concept or even a nation, typically rendered with imaginative trim added to a dress of

9. Marjorie Adeline Gordon, daughter of the Earl and Countess of Aberdeen, aged seventeen at the time of this event.

10. James Forman Smellie, an Osgoode Hall law graduate called to the bar in 1894.

11. Julius Gareché Lay, United States Vice and Deputy Consul General in Ottawa from 1893 to 1896.

12. Hayter Reed, whose career with the federal Department of Indian Affairs ran from 1881 to 1897, and who at the time of the ball was deputy superintendent of Indian Affairs, lent Indigenous garments to several guests. They are now in the collection of the McCord Museum.

13. William James Topley enjoyed a lengthy career as a prominent Ottawa photographer. His studio's extensive archives are held at Library and Archives Canada.

14. William Notman was Montreal's most prominent photographer and the first in the country to receive international recognition. His studio's extensive archives are held by the McCord Museum.

fashionable style. When Lady Aberdeen's daughter, Lady Marjorie Gordon,[9] attended the Victorian Era Ball as the "Forests of Canada," she sported a white satin gown with painted fir trees and a stuffed chipmunk on her shoulder (Figure 7.3).

Characters inspired by fictions of exotic "Others" were fixtures at most fancy dress events. At these Canadian balls, such portrayals took the form of stereotyped representations of Indigenous Peoples, rooted in settler colonial assumptions of racial superiority. James Smellie[10] and Julius Lay[11] donned articles of Indigenous dress incongruously and irreverently (Figure 7.4). Their attire comprises elements recognizable as Plains dress, confirming that they and several others at this ball were outfitted by collectors, often individuals who had had sustained contact with Indigenous Peoples through their roles in government.[12] Their mockery was evident not just in the manner of wearing: Lay facetiously stated that his moccasins had been made of human scalps, and his headdress of polar bear claws. If Smellie and Lay's claim to portray Mi'kmaq men betrays their utter lack of knowledge or regard for that culture's dress traditions, their posturing shows their intent to reproduce an essentializing fiction of Indigeneity that settlers had rendered pervasive to justify colonialism.

The nationalistic intent of the balls also played out in their structured programs. The two historical balls featured guests in dance sets whose themes, beginning with the discovery of North America by the Norsemen and ending with the United Empire Loyalists, set forth a chronological narrative of imperialist historiography. Each set performed a dance in keeping with the period and culture they represented. If the sets emphasized French colonial origins and acknowledged an Indigenous past as part of Canada's unique character, the expressive media of costumes and danced performances of historical periods ensured that these aspects of the past appeared amusing and caricatured. The Victorian Era Ball in Toronto also featured structured dance sets, with characterizations of Canadian natural resources placed at the forefront amongst guests representing British colonies. Sets that followed made up a dancing inventory of cultural and scientific achievements representative of the broader British cultural traditions from which Canadians presumably benefitted. In the guise of innocuous sources of amusement, these balls reinforced core myths of Canadian history and identity that persist to this day.

Self-presentation in fancy dress required careful negotiation, as the desired result was an enhanced version of one's true self. With the encouragement of local photographers, many guests satisfied with their choice of character and dress created a personal memento of the experience by having a portrait taken in costume. Ottawa photographer William James Topley[13] and his former employer, Montreal photographer William Notman,[14] were well known to privileged classes within their respective communities. Both have left meticulously kept sitter books and numbered negatives that are invaluable records of typical portrait photography of the time. Within their bodies

FIGURE 7.4: *Jim Smellie and Julius Lay as "Micmac Chief" and "Micmac Medicine Man" at the Historical Fancy Dress Ball, Ottawa, 1896.* W.J. Topley. Item number 3520050, PA-189665, accession number 1936-270 NPC, Topley Studio fonds, Library and Archives Canada.

FIGURE 7.5: *Maggie Jones as a "Bonnie Fishwife of Newhaven," at the Earl of Dufferin's Fancy Dress Ball, Ottawa, 1876.* W.J. Topley. Item number 3477370, e011091718, accession number 1936-270 NPC, Topley Studio fonds, Library and Archives Canada.

FIGURE 7.6: *Agar Adamson as the painting "Napoleon on Board the Bellerophon" by W.Q. Orchardson at the Victorian Era Ball, Toronto, 1897.* W.J Topley. *Item number 3200066, PA-138384, accession number 1936-270 NPC, Topley Studio fonds, Library and Archives Canada.*

FIGURE 7.7: *William Campbell as "Jester," at the Earl of Dufferin's Fancy Dress Ball, Ottawa, 1876.* W.J. Topley. *Item number 3421124, e011082823, accession number 1936-270 NPC, Topley Studio fonds, Library and Archives Canada.*

15. Nothing more is known about Miss Maggie Jones than her predilection for the main character of a one-act farce titled *The Bonnie Fishwife* by Charles Selby.

16. Agar Adamson had a military career. He attended the ball with his soon-to-be wife, Toronto heiress Mabel Cawthra, as "Josephine."

17. William Campbell, private secretary to the Earl of Dufferin.

18. John Fitzwilliam Stairs, Halifax-based industrialist, financier, and politician, and his second wife Helen Eliza Gaherty, née Bell.

FIGURE 7.8: *John Fitzwilliam and Helen Stairs as "Sir Edmund and Lady Andros" at the Historical Fancy Dress Ball, Ottawa, 1896.* W.J. Topley. Item number 4447410, PA-141071, accession number 1936-270 NPC, Topley Studio fonds, Library and Archives Canada.

of work, their fancy dress portraits stand out as exceptional because of the range of facial expressions and poses they capture. Images of ball guests in fancy dress reveal how they reimagined themselves in character. Many sitters attempted to convey a sense of character through performance, drawing on the photographer's props and perhaps his advice as well. Maggie Jones as "A Bonnie Fishwife of New Haven"[15] (Figure 7.5) illustrates the liberties allowed in both dress and pose. Outside the setting of a fancy dress ball, skirts covered the legs to the ankles, and portraits never showed a stance with the legs apart; otherwise only a professional actress dressed for a role would ever flout conventions of femininity in this way. Agar Adamson[16] as "Napoleon" (Figure 7.6) also took a theatrical approach to his portrait.

Portraits in character also reveal the state of the art of photographic technique. The unretouched 1876 image of William Campbell[17] as "Jester" reveals the stands employed in photographic studios to overcome the technical challenges of creating a dynamic pose at a time of long exposures (Figure 7.7). By 1896 no such devices were required when Mr. and Mrs. Stairs[18] were captured

FIGURE 7.9: *Composite photograph of the Earl of Dufferin's Fancy Dress Ball, Ottawa, February 23, 1876.* W.J. Topley. Item number 3260601, C-006865, accession number 1966-094 NPC, William Topley, Canadian Intellectual Property fonds, Library and Archives Canada.

FIGURE 7.10: *The "Voyages of the Norsemen to Northeastern North America" set at the Historical Fancy Dress Ball, Ottawa, 1896.* W.J. Topley. Item number 3524830, PA-137981, accession number 1936-270 NPC, Topley Studio fonds, Library and Archives Canada.

19. A *bourrée* is a French dance associated with the Barqoue period. Other such dances performed at the ball included a *gavotte* and a *pavane*. Many of these dances were choreographed by Professor Frank H. Norman of Montreal.

20. Chateau Ramezay collection, accession no. 1996.1075.1–139.

assuming a dance pose from their choreographed *bourrée*[19] at the Historical Fancy Dress Ball (Figure 7.8).

These portraits also functioned in wider-reaching commemorative projects. In 1876 Topley immortalized the Earl of Dufferin's fancy dress ball in a composite photograph, a re-photographed paste-up of many individual portraits, which was displayed at his studio with copies available for purchase (Figure 7.9). Twenty years later, following the Historical Fancy Dress Ball of 1896, Topley photographed each of the dance sets, albeit in the ideal conditions of his studio, for a souvenir publication (Figure 7.10, Bourinot 1896). After the Victorian Era Ball, Canadian artists sketched guests in costume, at least some working from group or individual portrait photographs. Their work resulted in a large published souvenir book (Mavor 1898). Subsequent to the historical ball in Montreal, Notman presented the organizers with an album of portraits identified with guests' names and their characters.[20]

These fancy dress balls were extraordinary events in participants' lifetimes. Meticulously orchestrated photographs suggest a personal desire to commemorate a moment of extraordinary departure from convention and re-actualize at will the sensation of the costumed presentation of the self in character.

Bibliography and Further Reading

Bourinot, Sir John George. 1896. *Illustrations of the Historical Ball Given by Their Excellencies the Earl and Countess of Aberdeen: Ottawa, 17th February, 1896*. Ottawa: Durie.

Cooper, Cynthia. 1997. *Magnificent Entertainments: Fancy Dress Balls of Canada's Governors General, 1876–1898*. Fredericton, NB: Goose Lane Editions; Gatineau, QC: Canadian Museum of Civilization.

———. 2004. "Dressing Up: A Consuming Passion." In *Fashion: A Canadian Perspective*, edited by Alexandra Palmer, 41–67. Toronto: University of Toronto Press.

Cooper, Cynthia, and Linda Welters. 1995. "Brilliant and Instructive Spectacles: Canada's Fancy Dress Balls, 1876–1898." *Dress* 22 (1): 3–21.

Mavor, James. 1898. *Book of the Victorian Era Ball: Given at Toronto on the Twenty Eighth of December MDCCCXCVII*. With a facsimile letter from the Ishbel Gordon, Countess of Aberdeen and Temair. Toronto: Rowsell & Hutchison.

8 *The Sweet Girl Graduate* (1882)

Suffrage and Sexuality on the Stage

KYM BIRD

1. The only known woman writing plays in Canada before Curzon is Eliza Lanesford Cushing.

2. The first entry for Robert Curzon in the *City of Toronto Directory* is 1864. See Edgar 1899 and Morgan 1898.

SARAH ANNE CURZON is among the earliest of Canadian women playwrights.[1] She was the first to declare herself a feminist and to use playwriting as a vehicle to support women's rights. Her two plays, *Laura Secord, The Heroine of 1812* (1887) and *The Sweet Girl Graduate* (1882), have earned more scholarly consideration than any other plays by women of the period.

Born Sarah Vincent in 1833 in Birmingham, England, Curzon was the daughter of glass manufacturer George Philips Vincent. Solidly middle class, Curzon was given a ladies-school education and privately tutored in languages and music. Sometime between 1862 and 1864 she emigrated from England to Toronto with her husband, Robert Curzon (of Norfolk), and son, Robert Jr. In Canada, she gave birth to three more sons and one daughter.[2]

Curzon was a conservative in politics but a liberal in her feminist orientation, making her among the most progressive women thinkers of her age. In 1891 she announced, "for twenty years I have been upholding the doctrine of the equal rights of woman as a human being" (Curzon 1892). She was an originating member of Canada's first feminist organization, the Toronto Women's Literary Club, and one of the earliest and most effective supporters of women in higher education: her daughter was among the first women to benefit from her mother's hard-fought campaigning when she graduated from the University of Toronto in the 1890s. Curzon was also instrumental in reforming the Toronto Women's Literary Club into the Toronto Suffrage Association and in restructuring it as the Dominion Women's Enfranchisement Association of Canada, a national body, for which she was recording secretary.

In her activism and in her literary work, Curzon argued for women's political and social equality with men. This notion of equality did not preclude her similarly strong belief in women's fundamental maternity and the virtues of sacrifice, care, protection, and succour for children, which she elaborated into a civil responsibility for the nation. As associate editor of the Toronto temperance weekly *The Canada Citizen*, her "Women's Page" was the first in the country to report upon a whole range of first-wave feminist issues, including women's emancipation and access to university education. She was also an advocate of Imperial Federation, an organization that endeavoured to create alliances between member states of the British Empire, especially through the production of histories that impressed a feeling of British identity on

Canadian nationals. Her play *Laura Secord* is inspired by this politics (Berger 1970, 3).

In Curzon's hands, the recovery of Canadian history was also a feminist strategy: a way to write women into public discourse by making their participation in war, particularly the War of 1812, part of a national and nationalist narrative.[3] Curzon makes this clear in her preface to the play in which she states that the purpose of the play is "to set [Laura Secord] on…a pedestal of equality [and] to inspire other hearts with loyal bravery such as hers." Curzon wrote for the *Canadian Monthly*, *The Evangelical Churchman*, and *The Canadian Magazine*. She reported in *The Week* and *Dominion Illustrated* on the activities of the Wentworth, Lundy's Lane, and Niagara Historical Societies; she gave lectures for them and read her poetry, but she could not be a member because she was a woman.[4] It was this peripheral status that caused her and fellow author Mary Agnes FitzGibbon to establish the Women's Canadian Historical Society of Toronto in 1895. Curzon was its first president.

Three short years later, in 1898, Curzon died of Bright's disease while living with her daughter on Harbord Street in Toronto. She was sixty-five years old.[5]

The Sweet Girl Graduate is a short, one-act comedy that in its use of cross-dressing and talk of "queer" dating has a particular appeal for a contemporary audience interested in issues of gender construction, sexuality, and subjectivity. The play was a satirical verse drama of a kind largely written by men and published in magazines such as *The Canadian Illustrated News*, *Grinchuckle*, *The Scribbler*, *The New Brunswick Courier*, and the *British Colonist*. *Grip*'s editor, the liberal-minded John Wilson Bengough, asked Curzon to write a play about the hotly debated issue of women and university education for his new "Summer Annual": *Grip-Sack* (Plant 1987).[6] The play's feminist views no doubt came as little surprise to Bengough, as Curzon's work in the Literary Club at this time was to a great extent focused on women's post-secondary access. But its parting scene—an invitation to the audience to support the club's 1882 petition to the provincial legislature urging lawmakers to admit women to the University of Toronto—was not just progressive, it was politically provocative: some might even have said radical (Ford 1985, 12).

The play begins with Kate Bloggs's mock-heroic lament to the gods as she rails against "Toronto University," which has refused her admission because of her sex.[7] Recalcitrant in the face of denial, Kate disguises herself as a man, and after so convincingly fooling her girlfriend Orphea into thinking she *is* a man, she decides to retain the costume and enroll in university classes.[8] Two letters gloss the two years Kate spends as the undergraduate student "Mr. Christopher," giving the reader a sense of "his" intellectual achievements and romantic exploits. The play ends with Mr. Christopher's graduation party: as he is celebrated for his superior accomplishments—he graduates gold medalist—he slips offstage only to reappear in Cinderella-like raiment, the very epitome of the nineteenth-century lady.

---

3. This strategy is used extensively in Curzon's play, *Laura Secord, The Heroine of 1812*, in which the events of the play are centred on women in general and Laura Secord in particular and stand in for Canadian loyalist history.

4. Curzon signed her articles S.A.C., S.A. Curzon, and Sarah Anne Curzon variously.

5. Her husband had died in 1894.

6. These Canadian periodicals had a substantial tradition of printing social and political satire and included, among other works, *The Charrivarri* (*The Scribbler* 1823), *The Triumph of Intrigue* (*New Brunswick Courier* 1833), *The Provincial Drama Called the Family Compact* (*British Colonist* 1839), *The Queen's Oak* (*The Literary Garland* 1850), William Henry Fuller's *The Unspecific Scandal* (*Canadian Illustrated News* 1874), *The Female Consistory of Brockville* (Caroli Candidus 1856), *Dolorsolatio* and *King of the Beavers* (Sam Scribble 1865). More extensive closet dramas were also popular during the nineteenth and early twentieth centuries, among which were not only Curzon's *Laura Secord*, but also Eliza Lanesford Cushing's ten plays including *Esther* (1838) and *The Fatal Ring* (1840), Charles Mair's *Tecumseh* (1886), Charles Heavysege's *Saul* (1857) and *Count Filippo* (1859), Thomas Bush's *Santiago* (1866), John Hunter-Duvar's *De Roberval* (1888) and Wilfred Campbell's *Mordred* (1895), *Hildebrand* (1895), *Daulac* (1908), and *Morning* (1908), to name only the most well known.

7. According to Peter Curzon (1992), Sarah's grandson, Kate was probably modelled on Augusta Stowe-Gullen, a friend of Sarah's daughter Edith. Stowe-Gullen was the daughter of Curzon's activist colleague Emily Stowe (the first female physician to practice medicine in Canada)

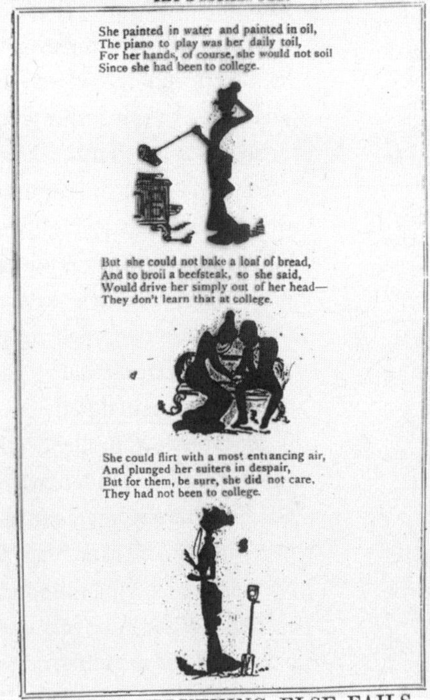

Clockwise from top left:

FIGURE 8.1: *The anti-educational stance of this tongue-in-cheek, visual rejoinder that follows the play ironically announces that higher learning produces no propitious effect on women's intelligence whatsoever, and in fact only detracts from their principal roles as wives and mothers.* Originally published July 1882 in The Grip-Sack: A Receptacle of Light Literature, Fun and Fancy, 60.

FIGURE 8.2: *Continuation of cartoon series from Figure 8.1.* Originally published July 1882 in The Grip-Sack: A Receptacle of Light Literature, Fun and Fancy, 61.

FIGURE 8.3: *Continuation of cartoon series from Figure 8.2.* Originally published July 1882 in The Grip-Sack: A Receptacle of Light Literature, Fun and Fancy, 62.

and the first woman to be admitted to the medical school at Victoria College.

8. Curzon's play may have inspired Emma Stanton Mellish to apply to Trinity College under a male appellation half a year after its publication. See Bird 2004, 48.

9. The play associates Kate's act with famous figures from history and literature, like Joan of Arc and Shakespeare's Portia, both of whom wore men's clothes for social and political liberty.

10. See Prentice et al. 1988, 158–59. Mrs. Bloggs's view was prevalent among nineteenth-century critics of women's education. Arguing in completely contradictory ways, on the one hand, they held women to be too delicate for a university education and not physically "constituted to handle the rigours of the academic life." It was even charged that their education might cause the birth rate to decline. On the other hand, some feared that academic life would unsex women and make them more masculine. In 1872 the *Christian Guardian* wrote, "very intellectual women are seldom beautiful; their features, and particularly their foreheads, are more or less masculine."

Like *Laura Secord*, *The Sweet Girl* is a closet drama. As is common to many dramatic works post-Shakespeare, characters of the elevated class often speak in iambic pentameter, even if here it is stilted and somewhat pretentious for comic effect. But *The Sweet Girl Graduate* also uses nursery rhyme, rhythm, and metre to help indicate Mrs. Bloggs's lack of education and simple prose to denote that we should take a character, like Kate herself or her father, entirely seriously. Despite its closet tropes of letters and lapses of time, the play nevertheless has theatrical influences and elements. It adapts the stage tradition of female-to-male cross-dressing, traditionally for the pleasure of men, into poetry that expresses the social and political power of women.[9] Neither was the play designed solely for private entertainment. Although clearly written to be read, it nevertheless had a distinctly political intent while allowing its author to remain quietly out of sight and above the political fray.

The Sweet Girl Graduate is liberal feminist in its ideological orientation: the character of the student occupies a social and intellectual position beyond gender where women and men are equals. Through the character of Kate's parents, Mr. and Mrs. Bloggs, the play embodies conservative, upper-class opinions respecting the education debate, underpinned by a belief in women's essential difference from men. Both mother and father hold that women's primary roles are wife and mother. Mrs. Bloggs is, not surprisingly, less educated than her husband, but informed and engaged by the debate nonetheless. She agrees with those who assert that women should be educated in domestic subjects, suitable to their sphere; but, fearful of problems posed by women's unconstrained sexual power, they must be instructed in facilities that are separate from those for men.[10] Mr. Bloggs is more passive but also more liberal: he would prefer Kate get married and "be done with it," but will support her financially if she manages to be accepted. The play is loaded in favour of liberalism, as Kate is always superior in logic and argumentation to her parents, and in the end proves to all the world that women are the intellectual peers of men. As in *Laura Secord*, though, the play's liberalism is tempered with a maternal feminism that permits Kate to find common ground with her mother and to maintain that "the more educated a woman is, the better she can fulfil her home duties."

Bibliography and Further Reading

"Achilles." n.d. Greekmythology.com. Accessed October 6, 2018. https://www.greekmythology.com/Myths/Heroes/Achilles/achilles.html.

Berger, Carl. 1970. *The Sense of Power: Studies in the Ideas of Canadian Imperialism 1897–1914*. Toronto: University of Toronto Press.

Bird, Kym. 1996. "Leaping into the Breeches: Liberal Feminism and Cross Dressing in Sarah Ann Curzon's The Sweet Girl Graduate." *Australasian Drama Studies* 29 (October): 168–79.

———. 2004. *Redressing the Past: The Politics of Early, English-Canadian Women's Drama 1880–1920*. Montreal and Kingston: McGill-Queen's University Press.

Brown, Robert Craig. 2015. "National Policy." In *The Canadian Encyclopedia*. Last edited March 4, 2015. https://www.thecanadianencyclopedia.ca/en/article/national-policy.

City of Toronto. n.d. "An Infectious Idea: Clean Water and Sewage Treatment." Accessed October 7, 2018. www.toronto.ca/city-government/accountability-operations-customer-service/access-city-information-or-records/city-of-toronto-archives/whats-online/web-exhibits/an-infectious-idea-125-years-of-public-health-in-toronto/an-infectious-idea-clean-water-and-sewage-treatment/.

Coe, Charles. 2003. "Lady Godiva: The Naked Truth." *Harvard Magazine*, July–August 2003. https://harvardmagazine.com/2003/07/lady-godiva-the-naked-tr.html.

Curzon, Peter. 1992. Interview with the author. March 11, 1992.

Curzon, Sarah Anne. 1882. "A Sweet Girl Graduate." *Grip-Sack: A Receptacle of Light Literature, Fun and Fancy*, July, 43–55.

———. 1887. *Laura Secord, The Heroine of 1812: A Drama and Other Poems*. Toronto: Blackett Robinson.

———. 1899. *The Battle of Queenston Heights, October 13th, 1812. Deeds speak.* Women's Canadian Historical Society of Toronto. Transaction No. 2. Toronto: n.p.

———. 1892. "A Paper Read before the Wentworth Historical Society, November 18, 1891." *Journal and Transactions*, no. 1, 106–14. CIHM A02075.

Cushing, Eliza Lanesford, ed. 1978. "The Fatal Ring." In *Women Pioneers*, vol. 2 of *Canada's Lost Plays*, edited by Anton Wagner, 140–54. Toronto: Canadian Theatre Review Publications.

Department of Agriculture (Ontario). 1887. *Annual Report*. Accessed December 29, 2010. Google Books.

Derksen, Céleste. 1994. "Out of the Closet: Dramatic Works by Sarah Anne Curzon Part Two: Re-dressing Gender Inequality: *The Sweet Girl Graduate*." *Theatre Research in Canada / Recherches théâtrales au Canada* 15 (2): 123–35.

Edgar, Lady. 1899. "Sketch of Mrs. Curzon's Life and Work." In *The Battle of Queenston Heights, October 13th, 1812*. Edited by Sarah Anne Curzon, 3–4. Toronto: n.p.

"First Woman Graduates from a New Zealand University—11 July 1877." n.d. *New Zealand History*. Accessed August 7, 2021. https://nzhistory.govt.nz/first-woman-graduates-from-new-zealand-university.

Ford, Anne Rochon. 1985. *A Path Not Strewn with Roses: One Hundred Years of Women at the University of Toronto 1884–1984*. Toronto: University of Toronto Press.

Friedland, Martin L. 2002. *The University of Toronto: A History*. Toronto: University of Toronto Press.

Indian Medical Gazette: A Monthly Record of Medicine, Surgery, Obstetrics, Hygiene, Jurisprudence and the Collateral Sciences; and of General Medical Intelligence, Indian and European. 1880. 15, no. 4 (April 1). Accessed October 1, 2018. https://www.ncbi.nlm.nih.gov/pmc/articles/PMC5144313/pdf/indmedgaz70731-0029b.pdf.

Johndougtaylor. 2019. "Historic Greenhouses in Allan Gardens—Toronto." *Historic Toronto*, February 16, 2019. https://tayloronhistory.com/2019/02/16/historic-greenhouses-in-allan-gardens-toronto/.

Marks, Patricia. 1990. *Bicycles, Bangs, and Bloomers: The New Woman in the Popular Press*. Lexington: University Press of Kentucky.

Mathur, Om Prakash. 1978. *The Closet Drama of the Romantic Revival*. Salzburg: Institut für Englische Sprache und Literatur, Universität Salzburg.

Morgan, Henry James, ed. 1898. *Canadian Men and Women of the Time*. Toronto: W. Briggs.

Morrell, Vivienne. 2015. "The 'New Zealander' Contemplates the Ruins of London."
    Vivienne Morrell (blog), August 8, 2015. https://viviennemorrell.wordpress.
    com/2015/08/08/the-new-zealander-contemplates-the-ruins-of-london.

Plant, Richard. 1987. "Drama in English." In *The Oxford Companion to English-Canadian
    Theatre*, edited by Eugene Benson and L.W. Conolly, 148–69. Toronto: Oxford
    University Press.

Prentice, Alison, Paula Bourne, Gail Cuthbert Brandt, Beth Light, Wendy Mitchinson,
    Naomi Black. 1988. *Canadian Women: A History*. Toronto: Harcourt.

Squair, John. 1924. "Admission of Women to the University of Toronto." *University of
    Toronto Monthly*, no. 24, 212.

University College (University of Toronto). n.d. "Our History." Accessed December 29,
    2018. https://www.uc.utoronto.ca/about-uc-our-story-our-history.

University of Canterbury. n.d. "History and Chronology" Accessed August 7, 2021.
    https://www.canterbury.ac.nz/about/history/chronology/.

Williamson, Mary F. 2009. "For Wedding *Déjeuners* to *Recherché Repasts*: The Webb Family
    Bakers, Confectioners, Caterers, Restauranteurs by Appointment to Victorian
    Toronto." In *The Edible City: Toronto's Food from Farm to Fork*, edited by Christina
    Palassio and Alana Wilcox, 66–71. Toronto: Coach House.

The Sweet Girl Graduate

SARAH ANNE CURZON

1. Bloggs and Blaggs are like the American surname "Doe" and act as stand-ins for the everywoman.
2. A township in Durham, south-central Ontario, Canada.
3. See Ford 1985, 7. Matriculation examinations were open to women at the University of Toronto in 1877. In theory, any student who passed these exams was qualified to undertake university studies. Women, however, were not allowed to attend classes until 1882.
4. "Mount Parnassus," a mountain in Greece associated with literary and poetic inspiration and writing.
5. A type of skirt.
6. A wise man, sage.

CHARACTERS

KATE BLOGGS (a.k.a. MR. TOM CHRISTOPHER)[1]

ORPHEA BLAGGS

MR. BLOGGS

MRS. BLOGGS

NURSE

MR. BIGGS

ACT I

SCENE ONE

Scugog.[2] The breakfast-room in the house of Bloggs, a wealthy Scugog merchant. At the table, KATE, his daughter, reading a letter.

KATE. (*In much indignation.*) Refused! I knew it!
    The crass ingratitude of haughty man,
    Vested in all the pride of place and power,
    Brooks not the aspirations of my sex,
    However just. Is't that he fears to yield,
    Lest from his laurelled brow the wreath should fall
    And light on ours? We may matriculate,
       And graduate—if we can, but he excludes
    Us from the beaten path he takes himself.[3]
    The sun-lit heights of steep Parnassus[4]
    Reach past the clouds, and we below must stay;
    Not that our alpen-stocks are weak, or that
    Our breath comes short, but that, forsooth, we wear
    The Petticoat.[5] Out on such trash!

Enter MR. BLOGGS.

MR. BLOGGS. Why, what's the matter, Kate?
KATE. Not much, papa, only I am refused
    Admission to the college. *Sapient*[6] says
    The Council have considered my request,
    And find it inconsistent with the rules
    Of discipline and order to admit
    Women within their walls.

MR. BLOGGS. I thought they'd say so. Now be satisfied;
    You've studied hard. Have made your mark upon
    The honour list. Have passed your second year.
    Let that suffice. You know enough to wed,
    And Gilmour there would give his very head
    To have you. Get married, Kate.

KATE. Papa, you vex me; Gilmour has no chance
    And that I'll let him know. Nor have I spent
    My youth in studious sort to give up now.

MR. BLOGGS. What will you do? They will not let you in,
    For fear you'd turn the heads of all the boys.
    And quite right, too. I wouldn't have the care
    And worry of a lot of lively girls
    For all I'm worth. (*He kisses her.*)

KATE. P'raps[7] not, papa. But yet I mean to have
    The prize I emulate.
       If I obtain
    The honours hung so tantalizingly
    Before us by the University,
    Will you defray the cost, as hitherto
    You've done, like my own kind papa? (*She kisses him.*)

MR. BLOGGS. I guess I'll have to: they won't send the bills to you.

KATE. Ah, dear papa! I'll make you proud of me
    As if I were a son.

Enter MRS. BLOGGS. *Exit* MR. BLOGGS.

MRS. BLOGGS: My dearest Kate,
    How very late
      You keep the breakfast things!

KATE. My dear mamma,
    I had papa
      To tell of lots of things.

MRS. BLOGGS: Your secret, pray,
    If so I may
      Be let into it also.

KATE. Oh, it was just this letter, mamma, from Mr. Sapient, telling me that the Council won't let me go to University College[8] to share the education that can only be had there at a reasonable cost, because the young men would be demoralized by my presence.

MRS. BLOGGS: Kate, I am astonished at you! Have I not always said that women do not need so much education as men, and ought to keep themselves to themselves, and not put themselves forward like impudent minxes?[9] What'll men think of you if you go sittin' down on the same

10. Inexperienced or naïve.

11. Annual commemoration of the founding of the Canadian nation on July 1, 1867. Its name was changed to "Canada Day" in 1982.

12. Probably a reference to Toronto's Allan Gardens, a five-acre plot of land bounded by Carlton, Sherbourne, Gerrard, and Jarvis Streets and one of Toronto's oldest parks. Allan Gardens was donated to the Toronto Horticultural Society on September 11, 1860, by George William Allan, two-time president of the society, financier, eleventh mayor of Toronto, and speaker of the Senate. Johndougtaylor 2019.

13. Daniel Wilson, president of the University of Toronto, continually delayed women's admission as he hoped the province would build a separate, affiliated women's institution. See Squair 1924.

benches at the colleges, and studyin' off of the same desk, and, like enough—for there are girls bold enough for that—out of the same books? And what must the professors think women are comin' to when they want to learn mathyphysics and metamatics and classical history, and such stuff as unfits a woman for her place, and makes her as ignorant of household work, managin' servants, bringin' up children, and such like, as the green-horns[10] that some people take from the emigrant sheds, though I wouldn't be bothered with such ignoramuses, spoilin' the knives, and burnin' the bread, for anythin'?

KATE. Now, mamma, you know we have gone all over this before, and shall never agree, because I think that the better educated a woman is, the better she can fulfil her home duties, especially in the care and management of the health of her family, and the proper training of her sons and daughters as good citizens.

MRS. BLOGGS: You put me out of all patience, Kate! For goodness' sake get married and be done with it. And that reminds me that Harry Gilmour wants you to go to the picnic with him on Dominion Day,[11] and to the concert at the Gardens at night;[12] and he said you had snubbed him so at Mrs. Gale's that he didn't like to speak about it to you without I thought he might. Now, that's what I call a real shame, the way you do treat that young man. A risin' young lawyer as he is, with no end of lots in Winnipeg, and all the money his father made for him up there; comes of a good old family, and has the best connections; as may be a member yet, perhaps senator some day, and you treat him as if he was quite beneath you. I do hope you'll just show a little common sense and accept his invitations.

KATE. Well, mamma, I think the real shame, as you call it, is that you, and other ladies, will allow your daughters to go about to picnics, parties, balls, theatres or anywhere else, with any man who happens to ask them, and without even so much as a girl-companion, and yet you see nothing but impropriety in my desire to attend college, where all the opportunity of associating with the other sex is limited to a few lectures delivered by grave and reverend Professors, under conditions of strict discipline, and at which the whole attention of the students must necessarily be concentrated on the subject. As for unlimited opportunities for flirting, there are none; and the necessities of college life compel each student to attend to his duties while within the halls, and then go home; wherever that may be.

MRS. BLOGGS: It's no use talking, Kate, you won't alter my opinion. If they'd build another college specially for ladies, as I hear the Council is willin' to do, and put it under charge of a lady who would look after the girls, I wouldn't object so much, though, as I always say, I don't see the need of so much learnin' for women.[13]

KATE. Well, mamma, how much would be gained by a separate building? The Council, it is true, offer a piece of ground, within a few minutes' walk of the college, for a ladies' college, and promise to deliver lectures specially "altered to suit the female capacity." But if there was an intention of giddiness and flirtation on the part of the lady students, how much hindrance do you think the separate college would be? And if we can't understand the same lectures as our brothers, it is evident we can't understand the same books.—Rather a hard nut to crack, isn't it?

MRS. BLOGGS: How rude you are, Kate! I am ashamed of you.

Exit MRS. BLOGGS in a rage.

KATE. Poor mamma, she thinks her only child a very *enfant terrible*.[14]

SCENE TWO

A lady's bedroom. KATE BLOGGS and her cousin, ORPHEA BLAGGS, in conversation.

ORPHEA. What will you do, dear?
KATE. A deed without a name!
    A deed will waken me at dead of night!
    A deed whose stony face will stare at me
    With vile grimace, and freeze my curdling blood!
    Will make me quake before the eye of day;
    Shrink from the sun, and welcome fearsome night!
    A deed will chase my trembling steps by ways
    Unknown, through lonely streets, into dark haunts!—
    Will make me tremble if a child observes
    Me close; and quake, if, in a public crowd,
    One glances at me twice!
    A deed I'll blush for, yet I'll do't; and charge
    Its ugliness on those who forced me to't—
    In short, I'll wear the breeks.[15]
ORPHEA. Oh, Katie! You?
KATE. Yes, me, dear coz.
ORPHEA. But then your hair, and voice!
KATE. I'll train my voice to mouth out short, thick words,
    As Bosh! Trash! Fudge! Rot! And I'll cultivate
    An Abernethian,[16] self-assertive style,
    That men may think there is a deal more in
    My solid head than e'er comes out.
    My hair I'll cut short off.

She looses down her abundant brown hair, and passes her hands through it caressingly.

17. See Coe 2003. Lady Godiva was an eleventh-century English noblewoman who, in an endeavour to have her husband repeal the onerous tax he imposed upon his tenants, rode naked through the streets of Coventry, England, cloaked only by her long and abundant hair.

18. Canterbury College, New Zealand, was founded in 1873 and permitted women's admission from its inception (University of Canterbury, n.d.). Kate Edger was the first woman to graduate from a New Zealand university in 1877 ("First Woman," n.d.).

19. Headdress associated with university graduation.

20. A popular nineteenth-century British historian, writer, and politician, Sir Thomas James Babington Macaulay, Baron of Rothley. According to Morrell (2015), he wrote of "the New Zealander" on three separate occasions. Curzon was likely thinking of his 1840 review of Leopold Von Ranke's *History of the Popes,* where he constructs the Maori New Zealanders as uncivilized in the context of the "organised European settlement of New Zealand beginning in that year."

21. A college tutor, usually associated with British universities.

KATE. Ah, woman's simple pride! these tresses brown
　　Must all be shorn. Like to Godiva fair,[17]
　　Whose heart, so true, forgot itself, to serve
　　Her suffering kind; I, too, must make
　　My hair an offering to my sex; a protest strong
　　'Gainst man's oppression.
　　Oh, wavy locks, that won my father's praise,
　　I must be satisfied to cut ye off,
　　And keep ye in a drawer 'till happier times,
　　When I again may wear ye as a crown:
　　Perchance a bang.
ORPHEA. 'Twould, perhaps, be best to wear some as moustache.
KATE. The very thing! Then whiskers won't be missed.
ORPHEA. But oh, your mannish garb! How dreadful, Kate!
KATE. True; but it must be done, and you must help.

Exeunt.

SCENE THREE

The same room. Evening. KATE *alone.*

KATE. Not let me in! We'll see. I'll beat 'em yet.
　　To think that down in Canterbury, girls,
　　Like my poor self, have had the badge bestowed
　　That I so fondly covet.[18] To think that they
　　Enjoy the rights I ask, and have received
　　The Cambridge University degree, B.A.
　　Not only wear the gown and cap
　　As college students, but the hood. The hood![19]
　　And shall Macaulay's proud New Zealander[20]
　　Thus sit on me? Not if I know it. No!
　　I'll don the dreadful clothes, and cheat the Dons.[21] (*She goes to the window.*)
　　The blinds are down, the shutters closed, the slats
　　As well, surely no one can see.

She takes up a man's coat and looks at it, then the vest, then the pants.

　　I'll do't!

Invests[22] *herself in the masculine apparel. A knock at the door: She starts and turns pale.*

A VOICE. Katie, dear!

22. To dress.

23. No doubt an ironic reference to the sorry, social outcast of song and verse, Tom o' Bedlam, who most famously appears in Shakespeare's *King Lear*.

24. American-style, rounded bowler hat.

25. Traditional academic head-wear, comprised of a cap, a stiff, square top, and a tassel.

26. French heroine and martyr who helped repel an English invasion during the Hundred Years' War.

27. Dressed as a man, she takes on the role of apprentice in Shakespeare's *Merchant of Venice* to the lawyer Balthazar and saves the life of Antonio in court.

28. One of the main character's in Shakespeare's *As You Like It*, she disguises herself as a man to travel through the Forest of Arden and escape the tyranny of Duke Frederick.

29. Achilles, hero of the Trojan War, is thought to have worn female garb and lived part of his life as a girl; "Achilles," n.d.

KATE. Pshaw! 'tis only Orphea! (*She unlocks the door. In masculine tones.*) Come in, dear coz.

Attempts to kiss her, but receives a slap in the face.

ORPHEA. How dare you, sir! Oh! let me out.
KATE. In natural voice. Orphea, you goose!
ORPHEA. Oh, Kate, you did so scare me!
KATE. And is it then a good disguise?
ORPHEA. 'Tis poor old Tom again.[23]
KATE. But how essay it in the street and hall?
ORPHEA. Well, there's the gown to help. 'Twill cover all.
KATE. And then the cap? But that I do not mind;
    My Derby hat[24] has used me to a style
    A trifle jaunty, and a hard stiff crown;
    So if my hair prove not too trying
    I yet may like to wear the "mortar-board,"[25]
    If still they wear such things.
ORPHEA. Oh, Kate, it is an awful risk!
KATE. Awful, my dear; but poor mamma
    Thinks I'm an awful girl.
    If she but knew—
    Yet might I plead that men and women oft
    Have done the same before; poor Joan of Arc;[26]
    Portia;[27] and Rosalind.[28] And I have heard
    That once Achilles donned the woman's garb:[29]
    Then why not I the student's cap and gown?

ACT II

SCENE ONE

A bedroom in a Toronto boarding-house. KATE BLOGGS *in bed. Enter boarding-house mistress.*

KATE. Yes, nursey, I'll be quick, but mind your words
    And looks, and do not make mistakes.
NURSE. Oh no, Miss Kate—or Mr. Christopher,
    As that's the name you've chose, I'll not mistake.
KATE. And always mind and keep my room,
    My time and liberty, intact, and so
    You'll make it easier for me to obtain
    By surreptitious means, the rights I should
    Enjoy in happier sort.
NURSE. I'll do my best, Miss Kate.

30. Lady Florence Harberton
(and Emily King) established
the London-based Rational
Dress Society in 1881 and,
after American Amelia Jenks
Bloomer, constructed the
divided skirt. See Marks 1990,
160.

31. Trousers.

32. To recoil from or flinch.

33. Metaphorically, to wrap or
envelop.

34. A personification of the moon.

35. A hot toddy is sweetened alcoholic drink.

36. The abstinence from alcoholic
beverages.

37. Likely a reference to the
Toronto newspaper, *The Globe
and Mail*, founded in 1844 by
George Brown.

38. Figuratively, the unsteady
steps of someone who is
inebriated. No doubt also a
reference to the buried Taddle
Creek, the southeasterly
course of which flows through
the University of Toronto.

39. An adaptation of the English
proverb, "When in Rome, do
as the Romans," meaning that
when in a foreign land, behave
as the people of that land.

40. A character in Charles
Dickens's novel *David
Copperfield* (1850), famed for
his saccharin humility.

Exit NURSE.

KATE. (*In masculine attire, about to descend to the breakfast table, turns once more
to the mirror.*) Oh, Harberton,[30]
  Hadst thou but taught the world
  The beauty of thy new divided skirt[31]
  Ere I was born, this had not now been thus.
  This blush, that burns my cheek, had long been past;
  These trembling limbs, that blench[32] so from the light,
  Had gotten strength to bear me manfully.
  Oh for the mantling[33] night, when city fa-
  Thers save the gas, and Luna[34] draws her veil! (*She sits down on a box.*)
  Away, weak tears!
  I must be brave and show myself a man,
  Nay, more, a student, rollicking and gay.
  Would I could feel so! (*Sniffs at the air.*) Somebody smokes,
  And before breakfast; pah, the nasty things!
  Would I could smoke! They say some women do;
  Drink toddy,[35] too; and I do neither:
  That's not like a man; I'll have to learn.
  But no! my soul revolts; I'll risk it.
  Surely there are among a studious band
  Some who love temperance[36] and godly life.
  That's the crowd I'll join. They will not plunge into
  Those dreadful orgies that the *Globe*[37] describes,
  Of men half-tight with lager and old rye,
  Who waylay freshmen and immerse them in
  The flowing wave of Taddle.[38]
  Horrors! Why, I shall be a freshman!
  If they touch me I'll scream! ah-ha, I'll scream!
  Scream, and betray my sex? No, that won't do;
  At Rome I'll have to be a Roman;[39]
  And, to escape that dread ordeal, I
  Shall cringe and crawl, and in the presence of
  A fourth year man step soft and bow,
  And smile if he but condescend to nod.
  Oh, yes, I'll do't. In tableaux once I played
  Uriah Heep,[40] and made the character
  So "'umble" and so crawly, that for days
  I loathed my hands, and slapped my fingers well
  For having knuckles.
  Thus will I to the tyrant play the slave.
  An old antithesis. (*Someone calls at the door.*)
  Yes, yes, I'm coming, Hannah.

Now for that dreaded step yclept[41] the first,
Pray Heaven it may cost most; but that I doubt.

Descends to the breakfast table.

ACT III

SCENE ONE

The same as Scene Two, Act I. MISS ORPHEA BLAGGS *solus,*[42] *reading a letter.*

ORPHEA. (*Reading.*) "My Dearest Orphea—Congratulate me! me, your cousin, Tom Christopher, M.A., Gold Medallist.—Mathematics, and also Natural Sciences; Honours in Classics, and Prizeman in German again. You cannot think how queer I feel with all my blushing honours thick upon me, and more to come. Tuesday! my dear Orphea, Tuesday! Only think of it, Master of Arts, or more correctly Mistress of Arts! Now let the New Zealanders boast, and the Cambridge girls bite their tongues, Canada has caught them up! Ah, my dear Orphea, that is the drop of gall[43] in the cup of your successful cousin—the Canterbury Antipodeans[44] got their honours first. It reminds me of the saying that the nearer to church the farther from heaven, since it is evidently the nearer to the centre of civilization the farther from a University Degree, so far as we unfortunate women are concerned."

"But never mind! I've proved that Canadian girls are equal in mental power with Canadian boys, and I am only impatient to let the Dons know it."

"And now, my love, for the conclusion of the two years' farce. It has cost me a whole week's sleep to sketch a plan by which to declare my sex in the most becoming manner to my fellow students."

"Do you know, dear, when I look back upon the pleasures of the past two years—how soon we forget the pain!—I am not inclined to regret the step rendered necessary by my devotion to my sex, for use has made me quite at home in the—ah—divided skirt! How many lovely girls have I danced with through the rosy hours who will never more smile on me as they were wont to smile! How many flowers of rhetoric have been wasted on me by the irony of fate! How many billets-doux,[45] so perfumed and pretty, lie in my desk addressed to my nether garment! And how many mammas have encouraged Mr. Christopher, who will forever taboo[46] Miss Bloggs! And then the parties and the picnics! Ah, my dear Orphea, what do I not sacrifice on the altar of my sex. But a truce to regrets."

47. Fine, lacy, delicate.

48. A small triangular scarf.

49. A type of lace.

50. Nineteenth-century French for "tablecloth."

51. "Toronto's Webb family [were] highly respected bakers, caterers, confectioners, and restaurant owners throughout much of Queen Victoria's reign….There is no doubt that, for fashionable Torontonians, the Webbs were the preferred choice for wedding déjeuners banquets, club-dinners, late-night suppers, or any kind of recherché repast when no expense was spared and the food, service, presentation and decoration had to be the best" (Williamson 2009, 66).

52. Ontario's Department of Agriculture's 1887 *Annual Report* identifies "H. SELLS & Son" as exhibiting a cider mill and press.

53. "Thought to be beneficial for intellectual thought," Zoedone was "a phosphate iron beverage" that claimed to be "invaluable to everyone engaged in the professional, literary scientific, commercial, athletic, or other pursuits involving the wear and tear of MENTAL or PHYSICAL strain." See the *Indian Medical Gazette* 1880.

54. Pure water in Curzon's time was associated with prohibition and moral purity, both of which were supported by women's rights organizations for which Curzon laboured. Practically speaking, pure water was also a luxury. In Toronto, the quality of public water was tested beginning only in 1883, eleven years after its first public water system was constructed. As described in "An Infectious Idea: Clean Water and Sewage Treatment," drinking water came directly from Lake Ontario "not far from…a cesspool of city runoff, industrial pollution and human waste. When the pipe that brought cleaner water

"I am longing to see the elegant costume in which I shall appear before the astonished eyes of the multitude as Miss Bloggs, M.A."

"You know my style, the latest out, which I find by the fashion books is Mignonette[47] trimmed with Chinese Pheasant. Buttons up the back of the sleeves, with rubies and amethysts. Let the fichu[48] be Eidelweiss;[49] trim the fan and slippers with the same, and use dandelions and calla lilies for the bouquets. Not a button less than forty on the gloves, and don't forget my hair."

"Get yourself up to match by contrast, and come and help me make a sensation."

"The dinner is on the *tapis*.[50] Webb will be caterer,[51] Sells will supply the cider;[52] Shapter and Jeffery the Zoedone,[53] and I have entered into a contract with the Toronto Water Works for pure water on this occasion only.[54] I have bought up every flower in Toronto, so that if the tariff does not prevent it, other folks will have to import their own roses;[55] and I have engaged every boy in the public schools who has nothing better to do next Saturday to go to Lorne Park[56] and bring back as many maiden-hairs as he can find. Ferns are my craze, as you know, and I am quite a crank on maiden-hair,[57] which I mean to adopt for my crest with 'If she will, she will,' as a motto. Ever your own, 'KATE.'"

A merry letter truly.
I'll to the dressmaker.

ACT IV

SCENE ONE

A boarding-house dining-room richly decorated with flowers and plants. Twenty gentlemen, among whom is MR. TOM CHRISTOPHER, *each accompanying a lady, one of whom is* ORPHEA. *The cloth is drawn, and dessert is on the table.*

MR. BIGGS, B.A. (Tor. Univer.): (*On his feet.*)
Ah—ladies and gentlemen, here's to our host,
And rising, as thus, to propose him a toast,
   I think of the days which together
In shade, and in sunshine, as chums we have passed,
In love, and esteem, that forever must last,
   Let happen what will to the weather.

In short, ladies and gentlemen, I have to propose the everlasting health and welfare of our host, who should have been our honoured guest but for from south of Toronto Island through the bay cracked or broke, as it did several times in the 1890s and 1900s, the entire municipal water supply became contaminated" (City of Toronto, n.d.).

55. Although intended as a joke, the protectionist "National Policy" of the John A. MacDonald government was a serious, central, and long-standing plank in the Conservative platform that levied tariffs on imported goods, largely from the United States. It endured from 1878 to the Second World War (Brown 2015).

56. A nineteenth-century holiday resort in contemporary Mississauga, Ontario.

57. A type of fern.

58. Oil for heating or lighting processed from coal.

that persistent pertinacity he exhibited in the matter, and which he does himself the injustice to call womanish. But I am sure, ladies and gentlemen, no one but himself ever accused our esteemed host of being womanish, and when we look upon the high standing he has achieved in our University, the honour he confers on his Alma Mater by his scholarly attainments and the gentlemanly character he has won among all sorts of students, I am sure, ladies and gentlemen, we should be doing great injustice to you all were we for one moment to admit that he could be other than he is, an honour to Toronto University, and a credit to his sex. I am quite sure the ladies are at this moment envying the happy woman whom he will at no distant date probably distinguish with his regard, and it must be satisfactory to ourselves, gentlemen, to know that it lies in our power, as the incumbents of academic honours, to be able to bestow that reversion of them on those who, having all the world at their feet, need not sigh for the fugitive conquests that demand unceasing toil and an unlimited amount of gas or coal-oil.[58] Ladies and gentlemen, I call upon you to fill your sparkling glasses to the honour of our host and college chum, Mr. Tom Christopher. And here's with a hip, hip, hooray! and hands all round!

ALL. Hip, hip! Hurrah!

Tremendous cheering and clinking of glasses. Several are broken, and the excitement consequently subsides.

MR. TOM CHRISTOPHER. Ladies and gentlemen, I thank you much.
 For these your loving words. A third year man,
 I came upon you fresh from nowhere;
 This in itself a warranty for cold
 And hard suspicion; but you received
 Me with some warmth, and made me one of you,
 Chaffed me, and sat on me, and lent me books,
 And offered pipes, and made inquiries kind
 About my sisters; and Time, who takes
 Men kindly by the hand, made us warm friends,
 And knit us in a love all brotherly.
MANY VOICES. Yes, brothers! Brothers! We are brothers all!
A VOICE. And sisters!
MR. TOM. I would say sisters too, but that I fear
 My lady guests would think I did presume;
 But yet I know, and knowing it am proud,
 That most men here to-night would welcome all
 The sweet girl-graduates that would fill the list
 Did but the College Council set aside
 A foolish prejudice, and let them in.
 And now, I know a girl who long has worked

To pass the exams, take the proud degree

I hold to-day, and yet her petticoat

Forbade.

SEVERAL VOICES. Name! Name! A toast! A toast!

MR. TOM. I will not name her, gentlemen, but bring

Her to your presence, if you so incline;

First begging that you will not let surprise

Oust self-possession, for my friend's a girl

Of timid temper, though she's bold to act

If duty calls.

MANY VOICES. Your friend! Your friend!

MR. TOM. I go to fetch her, gentlemen; dear ladies all,

I beg your suffrages of gentle eyes

And kindly smile to greet my guest.

Exit MR. TOM CHRISTOPHER.

SCENE TWO

The same. Enter MISS KATE BLOGGS in full dinner toilet of Reseda[59] silk, and carrying a dandelion and lily bouquet.

ORPHEA. My cousin! Oh, my cousin!

Rushes excitedly forward and falls into hysterics on KATE'S neck. The company gather round in great surprise.

KATE. Dear Orphea! Orphea, my dear! Oh, water, gentlemen! Lay her upon the couch. See! See! She gasps! Orphea, dear girl!

The ladies are much alarmed, but ORPHEA soon gives signs of recovery, and sits up.

ORPHEA. (*In tears.*) Oh, Kate! It struck me so to see you once again as you were wont to be; those nasty ugly pants forever gone, and you a girl again.

KATE. Dear friends, you look surprised.

Pray Heaven you'll not look worse when you know all.

I am indeed a girl, though you have known

Me hitherto as Thomas Christopher.

Four years ago I passed the exams, for

Us women, at your University.

Once more I passed. But when again I would,

I stumbled for the teaching that is chained—

Like ancient scripture to the reading desk—

Within your College walls. No word of mine

60. Hard or stubborn.

61. "Teachers." Refers to Paul's teacher mentioned in Acts 22:3.

62. "Courage."

63. The play immortalizes the "1882 Toronto Literary Club petition to the provincial legislature to admit women to the University of Toronto" (Bird 2004, 48).

64. The Toronto Women's Literary Club, of which Curzon was a founding member.

65. "Numerous."

Could move the flinty[60] heads of College Council.
Order and discipline forbade, they said,
That women should sit side by side with men
Within their walls. At church, or concert, or
At theatre, or ball, no separation's made
Of sexes. And so I, being a girl
Of firm and independent mind, resolved
To do as many a one beside has done
For lesser prize, and, as a man, sat at
The feet of our Gamaliels[61] until I got
The learning that I love. That I may now
Look you all in the face without a blush, save that
Which naturally comes at having thus
To avow my hardihood,[62] is praise, I trow,
You will not think unworthy; and to me
It forms a soft remembrance that will ever dwell
Within my grateful heart.
Can you forgive me?

MANY VOICES. We do, we must. All honour to the brave!
Speak for us, Biggs.

MR. BIGGS. I cannot speak, except to ask the lady's pardon
For our rough ways.

KATE. No; pardon me.

MANY VOICES. No! no! we ask your pardon.

KATE. If that, indeed, as I must need believe
From all your looks, you do not blame me much,
Endue me with a favour. It is this:—
Let every man and woman here to-night
Look out for those petitions[63] that will soon
Be placed in many a store by those our friends
Who in this city form a ladies' club,[64]
And each one sign. Nay more, to show you mean
What I, with swelling heart have often heard
You strongly urge, the rights of women to
The College privileges, get all your friends
To sign. Do what your judgment charges you
To help so good a cause, and let the lists
Of 1883 have no more names
Set by themselves as women. Let us go
In numbrous[65] strength before the Parliament,
And ask our rights in such a stirring sort,
They shall be yielded. Then I shall know
Your brotherly and pleasant words mean faith,
And shall no more regret a daring act

That else will fail of reason.
May I thus trust?

ALL. You may! You may.

KATE. Then hands all round, my friends, till break of day.

9 : *A Red Girl's Reasoning* (1892)

Reassessing the Performance History of Tekahionwake

SASHA KOVACS

1. For more on Johnson's early work in amateur theatricals, specifically with the Garrick Club in Hamilton, Ontario, see E. Johnson 2009, 46.

2. For more on Johnson's performance itinerary and schedule, see Kovacs 2016.

3. For more on the construction of Johnson as a celebrity, see York 2002.

My Forest Brave, My Redskin love—farewell;
We may not meet to-morrow—who can tell
What mighty ills befall our little band,
Or what you'll suffer from the white man's Hand?
    —E. PAULINE JOHNSON, *"A Cry from an Indian Wife"*

ON JANUARY 16, 1892, in the Art School Gallery venue in Toronto, Ontario, for the Young Men's Liberal Club "Evening with Canadian Authors," E. Pauline Johnson took centre stage to recite the opening lines from her poem, cited above, titled "A Cry from an Indian Wife." One of the only women to present material at this event, and the only Indigenous voice included in the schedule, Johnson was also the single contributor to earn an encore. While Johnson's poetic reputation afforded her the opportunity to perform at such a prestigious evening, it was her performance skills, honed through her earlier experience working in amateur theatricals, that secured her critical praise.[1] While Johnson's audience expected to see an author read her work on that January evening, they left having witnessed a recital by a multifaceted artist who would become recognized as having "one of the most successful careers in Canadian entertainment history" (Francis 1992, 111). Indeed, Johnson's contributions to theatre culture at the turn of the century were prolific—in the fall and winter of 1892 alone she gave no less than 125 recitals throughout Canada ("Miss E. Pauline" 1893). By the end of her career, Johnson had performed to great accolade in Massey Hall (in Toronto), Steinway Hall (in London, UK), in churches and community halls across Canada, and at canoe club and community meetings in New York, Boston, and other American cities.[2] She is acknowledged as one of Canada's first celebrities (York 2007) and even called "Canada's first performance artist" (Gray 2017).[3] This chapter first introduces readers to the complex performance practice of E. Pauline Johnson Tekahionwake. Next, the chapter questions how a historian might reconstruct and interpret the performances of Johnson without access to any scripts of her performance. In the process, the chapter advocates for a renewed approach to the available evidence related to Johnson's theatre history that can reconcile the politics of her performance with her activist commitments and therefore

"]

produce a more multifaceted appreciation of one of Canada's most significant early theatre artists.

E. Pauline Johnson was born on March 10, 1861, at the Six Nations Reserve near Ohsweken, Ontario (near present-day Brantford). Johnson was the youngest daughter of hereditary Mohawk (Kanien'kehá:ka) Chief George Henry Martin Johnson and Emily Howells (born in Bristol, England). Johnson's early life was spent at the family's estate home, built by her father and called Chiefswood (now a Canadian National Historic Site). After the death of her father in 1884, Johnson moved to Brantford, Ontario, and began publishing her poetry and other writings (for magazines and newspapers). By early 1892, Frank Yeigh, a friend of Johnson's, invited her to perform at the Young Men's Liberal Club "Evening of Canadian Authors." Following the success of that presentation, she was booked for a busy season of recital performance in Southern Ontario. By September of that same year, she added costuming as an element to her already lively and theatrical approach, and a few months later she also solidified her collaboration with her first stage partner, Owen Smily.[4] This alliance offered her the flexibility to engage in the presentation of more dramatic work. With Smily, she performed short sketches, duologues, and dramatic renditions of her short stories.

In 1893 Johnson travelled with Smily to perform in the northeastern United States and the Canadian West. By spring of 1894, she embarked upon her first solo transatlantic journey to London, England. There she performed in parlours and drawing rooms, billing herself by a new adopted stage name "Tekahionwake" (translated as "double wampum"—her great-grandfather's surname). After returning to Canada and touring the northeastern United States with Smily, Johnson recruited a new stage partner, Walter McRaye. He became Johnson's "friend and fellow artist for many happy years" (McRaye 1947, ix). Johnson travelled back to London, England, with McRaye in 1906, and together they performed in Steinway Hall. There, the duo also "saw many fine plays" (McRaye 1947, 107) that would inform the material they selected for performances upon their return to Canada. By 1907 Johnson and McRaye toured across the Midwestern United States as tent Chautauqua performers for the Slayton Lyceum Bureau of Chicago (McRaye 1947, 114).[5] It enabled them to access the Chautauqua circuit, which had performance stops across America.

Soon after the end of this tour, Johnson's health deteriorated. In 1909 she was diagnosed with breast cancer, and though she continued to produce literary work, her performance career came to an end. E. Pauline Johnson Tekahionwake died on March 7, 1913, in Vancouver, British Columbia. To acknowledge Johnson's contributions to the City of Vancouver's cultural life, a memorial was organized on March 10, 1913. A procession starting from her place of death at the Bute Street Hospital and ending at the Christ Church Cathedral drew a crowd of thousands and saw Chief Matthias, son of Chief Joe Capilano, follow Johnson's casket (Mobbs 2013). That same day was also

6. Though Johnson's recited poetry can be referenced in collections of her work, her scripts have not survived in archives. Indeed, the history of Johnson's archive is itself quite mysterious and dramatic. Charlotte Gray, in *Flint and Feather*, suggests that "after Pauline's death, Evelyn [Johnson—Pauline Johnson's sister] burnt as many of her sister's papers as she could lay her hands on. Letters, unpublished verses, journals, receipts, performance schedules—they all went up in smoke" (2003, 395). For a more critical consideration of the complex history of Pauline Johnson's archive, see Strong-Boag and Gerson 2000, 10; and Kovacs 2017, 45.

FIGURE 9.1: *Photograph of E. Pauline Johnson wearing a gown.* Box 10, file 21, E. Pauline Johnson fonds. Courtesy of the William Ready Division of Archives and Research Collections, McMaster University Library.

declared a civic holiday. Johnson's ashes are interred in Vancouver's Stanley Park (Gray 2003, 393).

Surprisingly, and in spite of the evidence that foregrounds Johnson's local, national, and international theatrical celebrity, her contributions to theatre culture at the turn of the century are undervalued. Canadian theatre historian Heather Davis-Fisch writes that this is a "disappointing oversight" (2017, 2). There are two explanations for the lack of scholarly attention towards Johnson's theatre history. The first proposes that the absence of scripted materials pertaining to Johnson's performance history makes the study of her performance open to criticisms of inference.[6] The second reason is perhaps more complex—and centred around assumptions regarding the semiotics of Johnson's costuming strategies. By late 1892, Johnson decided to make costuming an integral part of her approach to live performance. At

FIGURE 9.2: *Photograph of E. Pauline Johnson wearing her performance costume.*
Box 6, file 6, E. Pauline Johnson fonds. Courtesy of the William Ready Division of Archives and Research Collections, McMaster University Library.

this time, she reached out to her artistic acquaintances to ask for assistance in developing an "Indian dress to recite in" (Strong-Boag and Gerson 2000, 110).[7] Typically, after performing a number of selections in this two-piece dress, described as a "polyglot costume" (Francis 1992, 115), she would change into a boating costume or an embellished Victorian ballgown; one review of her performance describes her gown made of "cream Henrietta cloth with an orange girdle and set off by a boa of white fluffy stuff" ("The Indian Maiden" 1892). The two images of Johnson included here (Figures 9.1 and 9.2) emphasize the shifting identities that were integral to Johnson's act (she called her work "costume performance") in her early career.

By more contemporary standards, the politics of Johnson's costume changes are often interpreted as an upsetting or disappointing aspect of her performance. For example, biographer Charlotte Gray deciphers the costuming strategy as follows: "[Johnson's] stage act inadvertently implied that an Indigenous woman could be effortlessly assimilated into the dominant society. If she could switch seamlessly from Indigenous to European dress codes, couldn't the rest of the First Nations smoothly accept a European-origin way-of-life, as official 'Indian Affairs' policy required? If Johnson could walk away from the fur trade brooches, wampum belt, and angry memories of early encounters with colonizers, couldn't the rest of the 'Indian race' do the same?" (Gray 2017). Johnson's use of costumes, when viewed in this interpretive framework, functions as a dramatic visualization of assimilation. Why Johnson took this approach in performance, when she proclaimed elsewhere her commitment to "singing the glories of [her] own people" (Seaton 1913),[8] is hard for critics to reconcile. Given that the semiotic readings of Johnson's costuming strategies do not seem to align with the Indigenous politics Johnson advocated in her prose work, Johnson's theatrical approaches have required some justification. As such, scholarship that addresses Johnson's performance history mainly argues that the economic pressures of popular performance forced Johnson to give into the "demands of a White audience" (Francis 1992, 120) and "conform to the [Indian] princess stereotype" (Francis 1992, 122).

So long as Johnson's theatrical work is evaluated in this framework, her performance is a site that puts at risk her historicization and reputation as a sophisticated Indigenous poet, essayist, and critic. The documents included in this chapter respond to this paradox, suggesting that a nuanced discussion of Johnson's performance history does not threaten the legitimacy of her literary accomplishments or activist commitments. Rather, the documents here reveal the ways in which her performance career shaped her literary career and provided a platform for intercultural conversation. Johnson surely made concessions to her audience throughout her theatrical career, but her performance is not a site that should be viewed, necessarily, as compromising her commitment to Indigenous activism.

The first document included here is a program detailing the specific repertoire of Johnson's performance on December 20, 1892 (Figures 9.3 and 9.4). The program indicates that first she recited a set of "lyrics" that included "Wave-Won," "The Happy Hunting Grounds," and "Shadow River": imagistic numbers that personify varied Canadian landscapes. Next, she performed her standard "A Cry from an Indian Wife," made popular at her Young Men's Liberal Club performance. Following, and for "Part II" of the evening, she performed "As Red Men Die," a haunting account of the bravery of a "Mohawk chief" taken captive by a Huron warrior. After that came "The Song My Paddle Sings," one of her canoe poems. Finally, and to conclude the evening's entertainments, she performed "A Red Girl's Reasoning" with Owen Smily. This

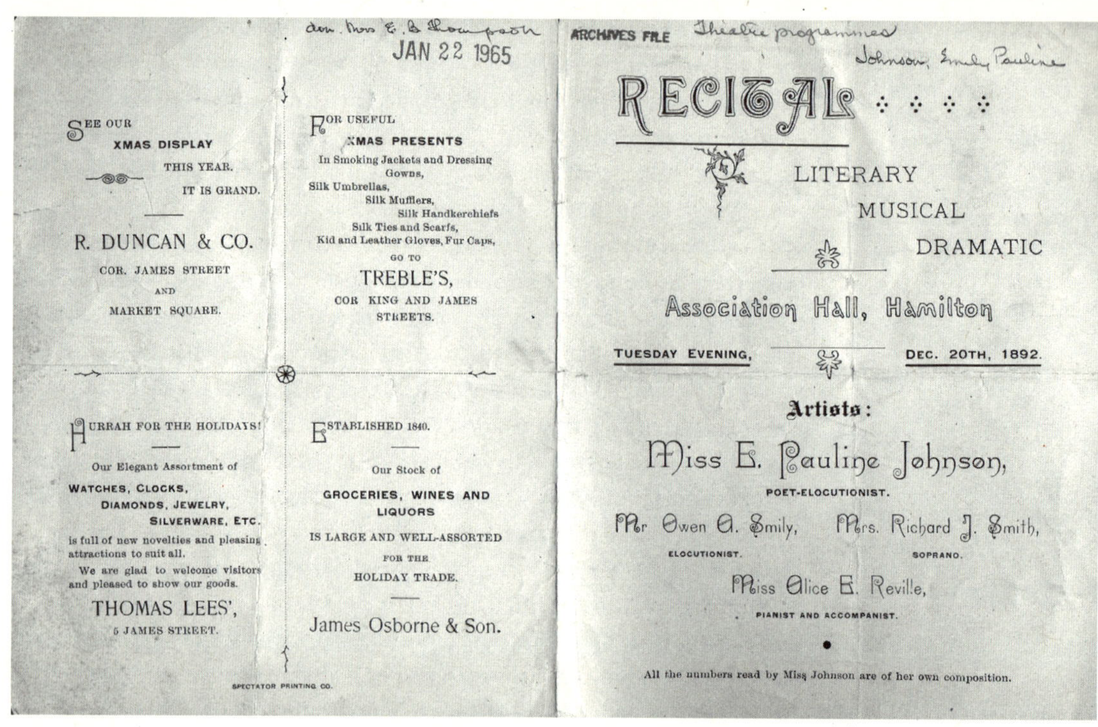

FIGURE 9.3: *Front and back cover, Pauline Johnson recital program, Hamilton, Association Hall, December 20, 1892.* Courtesy of Hamilton Public Library.

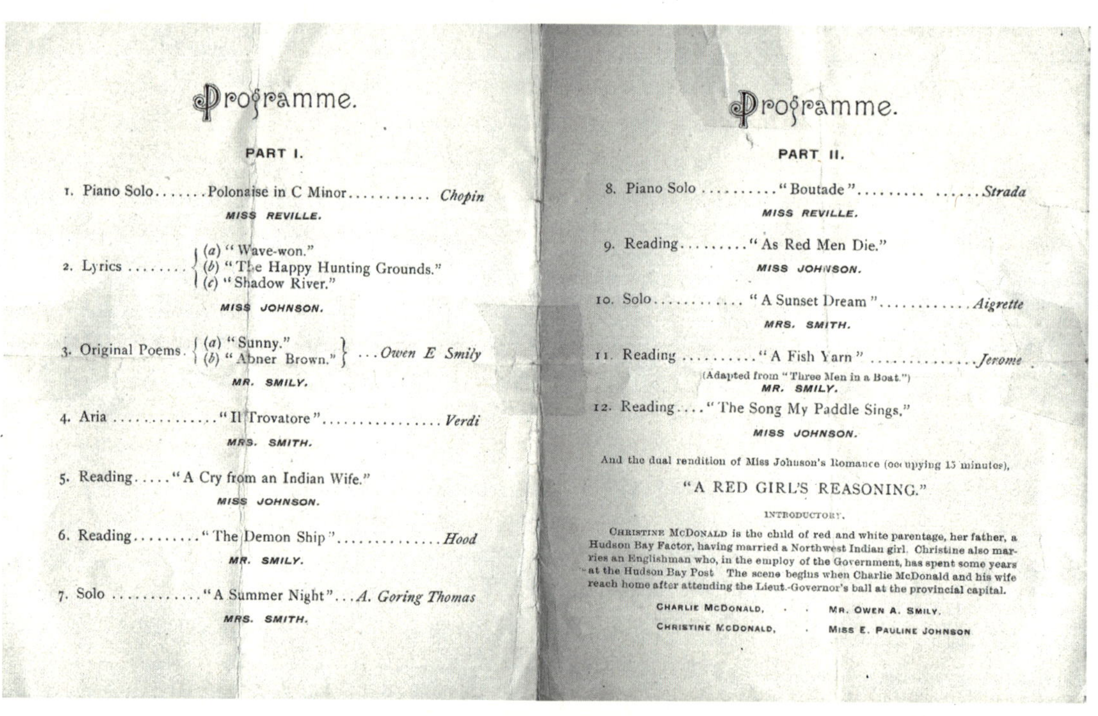

FIGURE 9.4: *Interior, Pauline Johnson recital program, Hamilton, Association Hall, December 20, 1892.* Courtesy of Hamilton Public Library.

9. For more on the relationship between "A Red Girl's Reasoning" and turn-of-the-twentieth-century politics related to Indigenous marriage ceremonies, see Van Kirk 2002.

10. Jacky Bratton's notion of "intertheatricality" is a useful lens with which one might engage in an analysis of the way Johnson's short story carries the memory of its performative history. See Bratton 2000. Johnson's poetic oeuvre also includes other poems, like "Curtain," that are informed by her theatrical history. See Gerson and Strong-Boag 2002, 106.

choice marked a shift in the performance to a more dramatic format. All these selections, save for the last title, can be referenced with ease by consulting Carole Gerson and Veronica Strong-Boag's *E. Pauline Johnson Tekahionwake: Collected Poems and Selected Prose*.

The final piece, described in the program as a "dual rendition of Miss Johnson's Romance (occupying 15 minutes)" and titled *A Red Girl's Reasoning*, is more difficult to access. There is no script yet found that can resolve precisely what was performed for this fifteen-minute playlet. This situation is especially unfortunate because, based on the billing, it seems as though this "dual rendition" was the most theatrical contribution to the evening's entertainment. The program indicates that Johnson portrays the character Christine McDonald, a "child of red and white parentage" who is returning home "after attending the Lieut-Governor's Ball at the provincial capital." These small details provided in the program's "introductory" allow a researcher to presume that Johnson, by the time she had gotten to this final selection, had changed into a gown or formal dress for her presentation of Christine McDonald. But what was she performing in that gown? How can we access and assess this performance if no script of it exists? If no photographic records are available to consult? If there are few reviews of this performance?

Johnson's short story, published under the same title (i.e., "A Red Girl's Reasoning"), begins to resolve some of these queries and challenges the perspectives which assume Johnson's costume was a visualization of "effortless assimilation" (Gray 2017). Published in the February 1893 edition of *The Dominion Illustrated Monthly* (only a few months after the performance of this "duologue" by the same title), "A Red Girl's Reasoning" is a gripping work of Indigenous activism. The story traces the experiences of its heroine, Christine McDonald, who navigates with power and resilience the social pressures she encounters in an elite Canadian society that asks her to forget her Indigenous culture in the wake of her marriage to a white husband, Charlie McDonald.[9] The short story's climax resonates in content almost precisely with the "introductory" to the "dual rendition," as written in the performance program. If the content of this short story's climax is in any way related to her performance (and one can fairly assume some overlap, based on the resonances between the program's description and the short story's content), then it is in this ballgown that Johnson was directly engaged in the portrayal of a strong and determined Indigenous woman, resolutely proud of her history and nationhood, and committed to sustaining allegiance to her nationality. This source thus prompts a reconsideration of the prevailing interpretations regarding Johnson's costume choices.

A reassessment of the short story in light of its performance histories also underscores the impact theatrical culture played in shaping the literary work that Johnson later published. Indeed, the story's theatrical intertexts point to the influence of performance culture on Johnson's literary contributions.[10] The short story evokes one of the most groundbreaking performances of the

11. George Bernard Shaw, in his *Quintessence of Ibsenism*, argues that Ibsen's use of the "discussion scene" in *A Doll's House* "signaled a change in the function of theatre"—shifting the structures of dramatic work away from the formulaic storytelling design of the well-made play, and towards a format that offered a "forum for discussion of ideas, with the events of the plot serving mainly as a pretext for debate" (Shaw 1955, 138; see also Christian 2016, 61).

12. Scholar Michelle La Flamme (Metis/Creek) suggests that the "history and historiography of Aboriginal theatre in Canada is contentious and fraught with complexities" (2017, 93), but acknowledges that the "usual historical narrative" situates the growth of an "indigenized" Canadian theatre history between 1967 and 1986 (95). Monique Mojica and Ric Knowles, in their introduction to *Staging Coyote's Dream: An Anthology of First Nations Drama in English*, likewise suggest that "in Canada, Native theatre artists only began taking control over their own representation on stage in the late 1970s and 1980s" (2003, vii), but affirm that the works generated in these contexts are entwined with the history of Pauline Johnson (vii).

late-nineteenth-century theatre: Henrik Ibsen's *A Doll's House* (1879). The reverberations between Johnson's short story and Ibsen's play are threefold: first, the central aspect of Johnson's story, like Ibsen's play, concerns marital disillusionment; second, Johnson's story concludes with a heroine, Christine McDonald, much like Ibsen's Nora Helmer, leaving her husband (never to return); and third, if Johnson's performance version of *A Red Girl's Reasoning* began at the point when the couple returns home (as the program introductory specifies), then the entire dramatic piece resembles the very dramatic device—the discussion scene—that Ibsen is credited for conceiving in *A Doll's House*.[11] These resonances clarify how Johnson's circulation in theatrical contexts may have influenced her literary approaches.

Johnson's spectacular two-piece buckskin dress was bequeathed to the Museum of Vancouver in 1913 and is now celebrated as a critical object in Canadian cultural history (Gray 2004, 482). Given that Johnson did not leave behind any scripts of her performances, it is to Johnson's costumes that critics have turned to understand the performer's approaches and legacy. However, these spectacular materials need to be considered in relation to the playbills and other textual materials that recuperate her performance history with more clarity. The documents and images included in this chapter hopefully highlight the immense contributions made to early Canadian theatrical culture by a fascinating, complex, and multifaceted Indigenous artist who worked across and between disciplines and nations. A more attentive consideration of Johnson's performance history also has implications for Canadian theatre historiography more broadly: it asks historians to trace the emergence of Indigenous voices in Canadian theatre back before the late twentieth century,[12] and it resists broader macro-narratives that characterize late nineteenth-century popular Canadian theatre as "annex[ed]" (Sandwell 1996) by American influence. Johnson's performance work, when assessed through a method that reflects the interdisciplinarity of the artist's own approaches, is a crucible for conversations about Canadian theatre's pasts, and its possible futures.

Bibliography and Further Reading

Bratton, Jacky. 2000. "Reading the Intertheatrical, or, the Mysterious Disappearance of Susanna Centlivre." In *Women, Theatre and Performance: New Histories, New Historiographies*, edited by Maggie B. Gale and Viv Gardner, 7–24. Manchester: Manchester University Press.

Braun, Marta, and Charlie Keil. 2001. "'Sounding Canadian': Early Sound Practices and Nationalism in Toronto-Based Exhibition." In *Sound and Early Cinema*, edited by Richard Abel and Rick Altman, 198–204. Bloomington: Indiana University Press.

Canning, Charlotte. 2005. *The Most American Thing in America: Circuit Chautauqua as Performance*. Iowa City: University of Iowa Press.

Christian, Mary. 2016. "Performing Marriage: *A Doll's House* and Its Reconstructions in Fin-de-Siècle London." *Theatre Survey* 57 (1): 44–62.

Davis-Fisch, Heather. 2017. "Double Lives and Disappearing Acts." In *Canadian Performance Histories and Historiographies*, edited by Heather Davis-Fisch, 1–27. Toronto: Playwrights Canada Press.

"Delightful Programme Presented by Miss E. Pauline Johnson and Mr. W. McRaye." 1903. *The Daily Examiner Peterborough*, May 20, 1903. File 8, box 4, Pauline Johnson Archive, McMaster University.

Francis, Daniel. 1992. *The Imaginary Indian*. Vancouver: Arsenal Pulp Press.

Gerson, Carole, and Veronica Strong-Boag, eds. 2002. *E. Pauline Johnson Tekahionwake: Collected Poems and Selected Prose*. Toronto: University of Toronto Press.

Gray, Charlotte. 2003. *Flint and Feather: The Life and Times of E. Pauline Johnson Tekahionwake*. Toronto: HarperCollins.

———. 2004. *The Museum Called Canada: 25 Rooms of Wonder*. Toronto: Random House.

———. 2017. "The True Story of Pauline Johnson: Poet, Provocateur and Champion of Indigenous Rights." *Canadian Geographic*. March 8, 2017. https://www.canadiangeographic.ca/article/true-story-pauline-johnson-poet-provocateur-and-champion-indigenous-rights.

Howarth, Jean. 1956. "Pauline Johnson—They Defied Her Last Wishes. WILL REVEALED." *The Province*, December 12, 1956. File 4, Pauline Johnson Materials, Vancouver City Archives.

"The Indian Maiden at St. John's Hall." 1892. *The Ottawa Journal*, November 3, 1892, 3.

Johnson, Evelyn H.C. 2009. *Memoirs*. Chiefswood, ON: Chiefswood Board of Trustees.

Johnson, Pauline. 1893. "A Red Girl's Reasoning." *The Dominion Illustrated Monthly* 2 (1): 19–28. *Canadiana Online*. Accessed August 31, 2021.

———. 1895. "A Cry from an Indian Wife." In *The White Wampum*, 16–18. Toronto: Copp Clark Co.

———. 2002. "The Iroquois Women of Canada." In *E. Pauline Johnson Tekahionwake: Collected Poems and Selected Prose*, edited by Carol Gerson and Veronica Strong-Boag, 203–05. Toronto: University of Toronto Press.

———. 2002. "Mothers of a Great Red Race." In *E. Pauline Johnson Tekahionwake: Collected Poems and Selected Prose*, edited by Carol Gerson and Veronica Strong-Boag, 223–27. Toronto: University of Toronto Press.

———. 2002. "A Strong Race Opinion: On the Indian Girl in Modern Fiction." In *E. Pauline Johnson Tekahionwake: Collected Poems and Selected Prose*, edited by Carol Gerson and Veronica Strong-Boag, 177–83. Toronto: University of Toronto Press.

Kovacs, Alexandra. 2016. "'I may act till the world grows wild and tense': The Performances of E. Pauline Johnson Tekahionwake." PhD diss., University of Toronto.

———. 2017. "Beyond Shame and Blame in Pauline Johnson's Performance Histories." In *Canadian Performance Histories and Historiographies*, edited by Heather Davis-Fisch, 31–51. Toronto: Playwrights Canada Press.

La Flamme, Michelle. 2017. "BC Aboriginal Theatre History in the Making: Talking with Margo Kane about the History of Full Circle and the Talking Stick." In *Canadian Performance Histories and Historiographies*, 93–114. Toronto: Playwrights Canada Press.

McRaye, Walter. 1947. *Pauline Johnson and Her Friends*. Toronto: Ryerson Press.

"Miss E. Pauline Johnson." 1893. *The Globe (1844-1936)*, September 23, 1893, 2. ProQuest Historical Newspapers: The Globe and Mail (1844-2011).

Mobbs, Leslie. 2013. "E Pauline Johnson (Tekahionwake), 1861–1913." *AuthentiCity: The City of Vancouver Archives Blog*, March 7, 2013. https://www.vancouverarchives.ca/2013/03/07/epaulinejohnson/.

Mojica, Monique, and Ric Knowles. 2003. "Introduction to Staging Coyote's Dream." In *Staging Coyote's Dream: An Anthology of First Nations Drama in English*, edited by Monique Mojica and Ric Knowles, iii–ix. Toronto: Playwrights Canada Press.

Sandwell, Bernard K. 1996. "The Annexation of Our Stage." In *Canadian Theatre History: Selected Readings*, edited by Don Rubin, 16–20. Toronto: Copp Clark.

Seton, Ernest Thompson. 1913. Introduction to *The Shagganappi*, by E. Pauline Johnson, 4–7. Toronto: William Briggs.

Shaw, George Bernard. 1955. "The Quintessence of Ibsenism." In *Major Critical Essays*, 1–150. London: Constable.

Strong-Boag, Veronica, and Carole Gerson, eds. 2000. *Paddling Her Own Canoe: The Times and Texts of E. Pauline Johnson Tekahionwake.* Toronto: University of Toronto Press.

"To Appear Here. One Night Only." 1896. *The Fort Wayne Sentinel* (Fort Wayne, Indiana), November 23, 1896, 4. http://www.newspapers.com/image/29297831/?terms=tekahionwake.

Van Kirk, Sylvia. 2002. "From 'Marrying-In' to 'Marrying-Out': Changing Patterns of Aboriginal/Non-Aboriginal Marriage in Colonial Canada." *Frontiers: A Journal of Women's Studies* 23 (3): 1–11.

York, Lorraine. 2002. "'Your Star': Pauline Johnson and the Tensions of Celebrity Discourse." *Canadian Poetry: Studies, Documents, Reviews* 51 (Fall): 8–17.

———. 2007. *Literary Celebrity in Canada.* Toronto: University of Toronto Press.

A Red Girl's Reasoning[1]

E. PAULINE JOHNSON (TEKAHIONWAKE)

1. Text transcribed from the February 1893 printing in *The Dominion Illustrated*. Text also published as "A Sweet Wild Flower" in the *Evening Star* (Toronto), February 18, 1893.

"Be pretty good to her, Charlie, my boy, or she'll balk sure as shooting."—

That was what old Jimmy Robinson said to his brand new son-in-law, while they waited for the bride to reappear.

"Oh! you bet, there's no danger of much else. I'll be good to her, help me Heaven," replied Charlie McDonald, brightly.

"Yes, of course you will," answered the old man, "but don't you forget, there's a good big bit of her mother in her, and—" closing his left eye significantly, "you don't understand these Indians as I do."

"But I'm just as fond of them, Mr. Robinson," Charlie said assertively, "and I get on with them too, now, don't I?"

"Yes, pretty well for a town boy; but when you have lived forty years among these people, as I have done; when you have had your wife as long as I have had mine—for there's no getting over it, Christine's disposition is as native as her mother's—every bit, and perhaps when you've owned for eighteen years a daughter as dutiful, as loving, as fearless, and, alas! as obstinate as that little piece you are stealing away from me to-day—I tell you, youngster, you'll know more than you know now. It is kindness for kindness, bullet for bullet, blood for blood. Remember, what you are, she will be," and the old Hudson Bay trader scrutinized Charlie McDonald's face like a detective.

It was a happy, fair face, good to look at, with a certain ripple of dimples somewhere about the mouth, and eyes that laughed out the very sunniness of their owner's soul. There was not a severe nor yet a weak line anywhere. He was a well-meaning young fellow, happily dispositioned, and a great favorite with the tribe at Robinson's Post, whither he had gone in the service of the Department of Agriculture, to assist the local agent through the tedium of a long census taking.

As a boy he had had the Indian relic-hunting craze, as a youth he had studied Indian archaeology and folk-lore, as a man he consummated his predilections for Indianology by loving, winning and marrying the quiet little daughter of the English trader, who himself had married a native woman twenty years ago. The country was all back-woods, and the Post miles and miles from even the semblance of civilization, and the lonely young Englishman's heart went out to the girl who, apart from speaking a very few words of English, was utterly uncivilized, and uncultured, but had withal that marvellously innate refinement so universally possessed by the higher tribes of North American Indians.

Like all her race, observant, intuitive, having a horror of ridicule, consequently quick at acquirement and teachable in mental and social habits, she

2. Tuberculosis, which, before the advent of modern antibiotics, was a frequently fatal disease.

3. "Gim" = "smart," so "smart cracks."

4. Very simple, light, four-wheeled, horse-drawn vehicle.

had developed from absolute Pagan indifference into a sweet, elderly Christian woman, whose broken English, quiet manner, and still handsome copper-colored face, were the joy of old Robinson's declining years.

He had given their daughter Christine all the advantages of his own learning—which if truthfully told was not universal, but the girl had a fair common education, and the native adaptability to progress.

She belonged to neither, and still to both types of the cultured Indian. The solemn, silent, almost heavy manner of the one so commingled with the gesticulating Frenchiness and vivacity of the other, that one unfamiliar with native Canadian life would find it difficult to determine her nationality.

She looked very pretty to Charles McDonald's loving eyes, as she re-appeared in the doorway, holding her mother's hand and saying some happy words of farewell. Personally she looked much the same as her sisters, all Canada through, who are the offspring of red and white parentage, olive complexioned, grey eyed, black haired, with figure slight and delicate, and the wistful, unfathomable expression in her whole face that turns one so heartsick as they glance at the young Indians of to-day—it is the forerunner too frequently of "The Whiteman's disease"—consumption[2]—but McDonald was pathetically in love, and thought her the most beautiful woman he had ever seen in his life.

There had not been much of a wedding ceremony. The priest had cantered through the service in Latin—pronounced the benediction in English, and congratulated the "happy couple" in Indian as a compliment to the assembled tribe in the little amateur structure that did service at the post as a sanctuary.

But the knot was tied as firmly and indissolubly as if all Charlie McDonald's swell city friends had crushed themselves up against the chancel to congratulate him, and in his heart he was deeply thankful to escape the flower pelting, white gloves, rice-throwing, and ponderous stupidity of a breakfast, and indeed all the regulation gim-cracks[3] of the usual marriage celebrations, and it was with a hand trembling with absolute happiness that he assisted his little Indian wife into the old muddy buck-board,[4] that, hitched to an under-bred looking pony, was to convey them over the first stages of their journey. Then came more adieus, some hand-clasping, old Jimmy Robinson looking very serious just at the last, Mrs. Jimmy, stout, stolid, betraying nothing of visible emotion, and then the pony, roughshod and shaggy, trudged on, while mutual hand waves were kept up until the old Hudson Bay Post dropped out of sight, and the buck-board with its lightsome load of hearts deliriously happy, jogged on over the uneven trail.

She was "all the rage" that winter at the Provincial Capital. The men called her a "deuced fine little woman." The ladies said she was "just the sweetest wildflower—" Whereas she was really but an ordinary, pale dark girl who spoke slowly and with a strong accent, who danced fairly well, sang acceptably, and never stirred outside the door without her husband.

Charlie was proud of her; he was proud that she had "taken" so well among his friends, proud that she bore herself so complacently in the drawing-rooms of the wives of pompous Government officials, but doubly proud of her almost abject devotion to him. If ever human being was worshipped that being was Charlie McDonald; it could scarcely have been otherwise, for the almost Godlike strength of his passion for that little wife of his would have mastered and melted a far more invincible citadel than an already affectionate woman's heart.

Favorites socially, McDonald and his wife went everywhere. In fashionable circles she was "new"—a potent charm to acquire popularity, and the little velvet-clad figure was always the centre of interest among all the women in the room. She always dressed in velvet. No woman in Canada, has she but the faintest dash of native blood in her veins, but loves velvets and silks. As beef to the Englishman, wine to the Frenchman, fads to the Yankee, so are velvet and silk to the Indian girl, be she wild as prairie grass, be she on the borders of civilization, or having stepped within its boundary, mounted the steps of culture even under its superficial heights.

"Such a 'dolling little appil' blossom," said the wife of a local M.P., who brushed up her etiquette and English once a year at Ottawa. "Does she always laugh so sweetly, and gobble you up with those great big grey eyes of hers, when you are togetheah at home, Mr. McDonald? If so I should think youah pooah brothah would feel himself terribly de trop."

He laughed lightly—"yes, Mrs. Stuart, there are not two of Christie, she is the same at home and abroad, and as for Joe, he doesn't mind us a bit, he's no end fond of her."

"I'm very glad he is. I always fancied he did not careh for her, d'you know."

If ever a blunt woman existed it was Mrs. Stuart. She really meant nothing, but her remark bothered Charlie. He was fond of his brother, and jealous for Christie's popularity. So that night when he and Joe were having a pipe, he said:

"I've never asked you yet what you thought of her, Joe." A brief pause, then Joe spoke. "I'm glad she loves you."

"Why?"

"Because that girl has but two possibilities regarding humanity—love or hate."

"Humph!—Does she love or hate *you*?"

"Ask her."

"You talk bosh. If she hated you, you'd get out. If she loved you I'd *make* you get out." Joe McDonald whistled a little, then laughed.

"Now that we are on the subject, I might as well ask—honestly old man, wouldn't you and Christie prefer keeping house alone to having me always around?"

"Nonsense, sheer nonsense. Why, thunder, man, Christie's no end fond of you, and as for me—you surely don't want assurances from me?"

"No, but I often think a young couple—"

"Young couple be blowed! After a while when they want you and your old surveying chains, and spindle-legged tripod telescope kick-shaws, further west, I venture to say the little woman will cry her eyes out—won't you, Christie?" This last in a higher tone, as through clouds of tobacco smoke he caught sight of his wife passing the door-way.

She entered. "Oh! no, I would not cry, I never do cry, but I would be heart-sore to lose you, Joe, and apart from that"—a little wickedly—"you may come in handy for an exchange some day, as Charlie does always say when he hoards up duplicate relics."

"Are Charlie and I duplicates?"

"Well—I—not exactly"—her head a little to one side, and eyeing them both merrily, while she slipped softly on to the arm of her husband's chair, "but, in the event of Charlie's failing me"—everyone laughed then. The "some day" that she spoke of was nearer than they thought. It came about in this wise.

There was a dance at the Lieut.-Governor's, and the world and his wife were there. The nobs[5] were in great feather that night, particularly the women, who flaunted about in new gowns and much splendor. Christie McDonald had a new gown also, but wore it with the utmost unconcern, and if she heard any of the flattering remarks made about her she at least appeared to disregard them.

"I never dreamed you could wear blue so splendidly," said Capt. Logan as they sat out a dance together.

"Indeed she can though," interposed Mrs. Stuart, halting in one of her gracious sweeps down the room with her husband's private secretary.

"Don't shout so, Captain. I can hear every sentence you uttah—of course Mrs. McDonald can wear blue—she has a morning gown of cadet blue that she is a picture in."

"You are both very kind," said Christie—"I like blue, it is the color of all the Hudson's Bay Posts, and the factor's residence is always decorated in blue."

"Is it really? How interesting—do tell us some more of your old home, Mrs. McDonald, you so seldom speak of your life at the Post, and we fellows so often wish to hear of it all," said Logan eagerly.

"Why do you not ask me of it, then?"

"Well—er, I'm sure I don't know, I'm fully interested in the Ind—in your people—your mother's people, I mean, but it always seems so personal I suppose; and—a—a—"

"Perhaps you are like all other white people, afraid to mention my nationality to me."

The Captain winced, and Mrs. Stuart laughed uneasily. Joe McDonald was not far off and he was listening, and chuckling, and saying to himself, "That's you, Christie, lay 'em out, it won't hurt 'em to know how they appear once in a while."

"Well, Captain Logan," she was saying, "what is it you would like to hear—of my people, or my parents, or myself?"

"All, all, my dear," cried Mrs. Stuart clamorously. "I'll speak for him—tell us of yourself and your mother—your father is delightful I am sure—but then he is only an ordinary Englishman, not half as interesting as a foreigner, or—or, perhaps I should say, a native."

Christie laughed. "Yes," she said, "my father often teases my mother now about how *very* native she was when he married her; then how could she have been otherwise, she did not know a word of English, and there was not another English speaking person besides my father and his two companions within sixty miles."

"Two companions, eh? one a Catholic priest and the other a wine merchant I suppose, and with your father in the Hudson Bay, they were good representatives of the pioneers in the New World," remarked Logan, waggishly.

"Oh, no, they were all Hudson Bay men. There were no rumsellers, and no missionaries in that part of the country then."

Mrs. Stuart looked puzzled, "No *missionaries*," she repeated with an odd intonation.

Christie's insight was quick. There was a peculiar expression of interrogation in the eyes of her listeners, and the girl's blood leapt angrily up into her temples as she said hurriedly, "I know what you mean, I know what you are thinking. You were wondering how my parents were married—."

"Well—er, my dear, it seems peculiar—if there was no priest, and no magistrate, why—a—." Mrs. Stuart paused awkwardly. "The marriage was performed by Indian rites," said Christie.

"Oh, do tell me about it; is the ceremony very interesting, and quaint—are your chieftains anything like Buddhist priests?" It was Logan who spoke.

"Why, no," said the girl in amazement at that gentleman's ignorance. "There is no ceremony at all save a feast. The two people just agree to live only with, and for each other, and the man takes his wife to his home just as you do. There is no ritual to bind them, they need none, an Indian's word was his law in those days you know."

Mrs. Stuart stepped backwards. "Ah!" was all she said. Logan removed his eyeglass and stared blankly at Christie. "And did McDonald marry you in this singular fashion?" he questioned.

"Oh! no, we were married by Father O'Leary, why do you ask?"

"Because if he had, I'd have blown his brain out to-morrow."

Mrs. Stuart's partner, who had hitherto been silent, coughed, and began to twirl his cuff stud nervously, but nobody took any notice of him. Christie had risen, slowly, ominously—risen, with the dignity and pride of an empress.

"Captain Logan," she said, "What do you dare to say to me? what do you dare to mean? do you presume to think it would not have been lawful for Charlie to marry me according to my people's rites? do you for one instant dare to question that my parents were not as legally—."

"Don't, dear, don't," interrupted Mrs. Stuart hurriedly, "it is bad enough now, goodness knows—don't make—" Then she broke off blindly. Christie's eyes glared at the mumbling woman, at her uneasy partner, at the horrified Captain, then they rested on the McDonald brothers, who stood within earshot, Joe's face scarlet, her husband's white as ashes, with something in his eyes she had never seen before. It was Joe who saved the situation, stepping quickly across towards his sister-in-law, he offered her his arm, saying, "The next dance is ours, I think, Christie."

Then Logan pulled himself together, and attempted to carry Mrs. Stuart off for the waltz, but for once in her life that lady had lost her head. "It is shocking!" she said, "outrageously shocking!—I wonder if they told Mr. McDonald before he married her!" Then looking hurriedly round, she too saw the young husband's face—and knew that they had not.

"Humph, deuced nice kettle of fish—and poor old Charlie has always thought so much of honorable birth."

Logan thought he spoke in an undertone, but "poor old Charlie" heard him. He followed his wife and brother across the room. "Joe," he said, "will you see that a trap is called?" Then to Christie, "Joe will see that you get home all right," he wheeled on his heel then and left the ball-room.

Joe *did* see.

He tucked a poor shivering, pallid little woman into a cab, and wound her bare throat up in the scarlet velvet cloak that was hanging uselessly over her arm. She crouched down beside him, saying: "I am so cold, Joe, I am so cold," but she did not seem to know enough to wrap herself up. Joe felt all through this long drive that nothing this side of Heaven would be so good as to die, and he was glad when the little voice at his elbow said, "What is he so angry at, Joe?"

"I don't know exactly, dear," he said gently, "but I think it was what you said about this Indian marriage."

"But why should I not have said it? is there anything wrong about it?" she asked pitifully.

"Nothing, that I can see—there was no other way—but Charlie is very angry, and you must be brave and forgiving with him, Christie, dear."

"But I did never see him like that before, did you?"

"Once."

"When?"

"Oh! at college, one day, a boy tore his prayer book in half, and threw it into the grate, just to be mean, you know. Our mother had given it to him at his confirmation."

"And did he look so?"

"About, but it all blew over in a day—Charlie's tempers are short and brisk. Just don't take any notice of him, run off to bed, and he'll have forgotten it by the morning."

They reached home at last, Christie said goodnight, quietly, going directly to her room. Joe went to his room also, filled a pipe and smoked for an hour. Across the passage he could hear her slippered feet pacing up and down, up and down the length of her apartment. There was something panther-like in those restless footfalls, a meaning velvetyness that made him shiver, and again he wished he were dead—or elsewhere.

After a time the hall door opened, and someone came upstairs, along the passage, and to the little woman's room. As he entered, she turned and faced him—

"Christie," he said harshly, "do you know what you have done?"

"Yes,"—taking a step nearer him—her whole soul springing up into her eyes, "I have angered you, Charlie, and—"

"Angered me? You have disgraced me, and moreover you have disgraced yourself and both your parents."

"*Disgraced*?"

"Yes, *disgraced*, you have literally declared to the whole city that your father and mother were never married—and that you are the child of—what shall we call it—love? certainly not legality."

Across the hallway sat Joe McDonald—his blood freezing—but it leapt into every vein like fire, at the awful anguish in the little voice that cried simply,— "Oh! Charlie!"

"How could you do it, how could you do it Christie, without shame either for yourself or for me, let alone your parents?"

The voice was like an angry demon's—not a trace was there in it of the yellow-haired, blue-eyed, laughing-lipped boy who had driven away so gaily to the dance five hours before.

"Shame? Why should I be ashamed of the rites of my people any more than you should be ashamed of the customs of yours—of a marriage more sacred and holy than half of your white man's mockeries?"

It was the voice of another nature in the girl—the love and the pleading were dead in it—

"Do you mean to tell me, Charlie—you who have studied my race and their laws for years—do you mean to tell me that, because there was no priest and no magistrate, my mother was not married? Do you mean to say that all my forefathers, for hundreds of years back, have been illegally born? If so, you blacken my ancestry beyond—beyond—beyond all reason."

"No, Christie, I would not be so brutal as that, but your father and mother live in more civilized times. Father O'Leary has been at the Post for nearly twenty years, why was not your father straight enough to have the ceremony performed when he *did* get the chance?"

The girl turned upon him with the face of a fury. "Do you suppose," she almost hissed, "that my mother would be married according to your *white* rites after she had been five years a wife, and I had been born in the meantime?

No, a thousand times I say, *no*. When the priest came with his notions of
Christianizing, and talked to them of re-marriage by the Church, my mother
arose and said, 'Never—never—I have never had but this one husband; he has
had none but me for wife, and to have you remarry us would be to say as much
to the whole world as that we had never been married before.[6] You go away, *I*
do not ask that *your* people be re-married, talk not so to me. I *am* married, and
you or Church cannot do or undo it.'"

"Your father was a fool not to insist upon the law, and so was the priest."

"Law? *My* people have *no* priest, and my nation cringes not to law. Our
priest is purity, and our law is honor. Priest? Was there a *priest* at the most holy
marriage known to humanity? That stainless marriage whose offspring is the
God you white men told my Pagan mother of?"

"Christie—you are *worse* than blasphemous, such a profane remark shows
how little you understand the sanctity of the Christian faith—"

"I know what I *do* understand, it is that you are hating me because I told
some of the beautiful customs of my people to Mrs. Stuart and those men."

"Pooh! who cares for them? It is not them, the trouble is they won't keep
their mouths shut. Logan's a cad and will toss the whole tale about at the club
to-morrow night, and as for the Stuart woman, I'd like to know how I'm going
to take you to Ottawa for presentation and the opening, while she is blabbing
the whole miserable scandal in every drawing-room, and I'll be pointed out as
a romantic fool, and you— as worse; I *can't* understand why your father didn't
tell me before we were married, I at least might have warned you to never
mention it." Something of recklessness rang up through his voice, just as the
panther-likeness crept up from her footsteps and couched herself in hers. She
spoke in tones quiet, soft, deadly.

"Before we were married! Oh! Charlie, would it have—made—any—
difference?"

"God knows" he said, throwing himself into a chair, his blonde hair
rumpled and wet. It was the only boyish thing about him now.

She walked towards him, then halted in the centre of the room. "Charlie
McDonald," she said, and it was as if a stone had spoken, "look up." He raised
his head, startled by her tone. There was a threat in her eyes that, had his rage
been less courageous, his pride less bitterly wounded, would have cowed him.

"There was no such time as that before our marriage, for we *are not married
now*. Stop," she said, outstretching her palms against him as he sprang to his
feet, "I tell you we are not married. Why should I recognize the rites of your
nation when you do not acknowledge the rites of mine? According to your own
words my parents should have gone through your church ceremony as well
as through an Indian contract, according to *my* words, *we* should go through
an Indian contract as well as through a church marriage. If their union is
illegal so is ours. If you think my father is living in dishonor with my mother,
my people will think I am living in dishonor with you—how do I know when
another nation will come and conquer you as you white men conquered

us, and they will have another marriage rite to perform and they will tell us another truth, that you are not my husband, that you are but disgracing and dishonoring me—that you are keeping me here, not as your wife, but as your—your—*squaw*."

The terrible word had never passed her lips before, and the blood stained her face to her very temples; she snatched off her wedding ring and tossed it across the room, saying scornfully, "That thing is as empty to me as the Indian rites to you."

He caught her by the wrists, his small white teeth were locked tightly, his blue eyes blazed into hers.

"Christine, do you dare doubt my honor towards you? *you*, whom I should have died for, do you *dare* to think I have kept you here, not as my wife, but—"

"Oh! God. You are hurting me, you are breaking my arm," she gasped.

The door was flung open, and Joe McDonald's sinewy hands clinched like vices on his brother's shoulders.

"Charlie, you're mad, mad as the devil, let go of her this minute."

The girl staggered backwards as the iron fingers loosed her wrists. "Oh! Joe," she cried,—"I am not his wife, and he says I am born—nameless."

"Here," said Joe, shoving his brother towards the door, "Go downstairs 'till you can collect your senses. If ever a being acted like an infernal fool, you're the man."

The young husband looked from one to the other, dazed by his wife's insult, abandoned to a fit of ridiculously childish temper; blind as he was with passion, he remembered long afterwards seeing them standing there, his brother's face darkened with a scowl of anger—his wife, clad in the mockery of her ball dress, her scarlet velvet cloak half covering her bare brown neck and arms, her eyes like flames of fire, her face like a piece of sculptured grey-stone.

Without a word he flung himself furiously from the room, and immediately afterwards they heard the heavy hall door bang behind him.

"Can I do anything for you, Christie?" asked her brother-in-law calmly.

"No, thank you—unless, I think I would like a drink of water, please."

He brought her up a goblet filled with wine, her hand did not even tremble as she took it; as for Joe—a demon arose in his soul as he noticed she kept her wrists covered. "Do you think he will come back?" she said.

"Oh! yes, of course; he'll be all right in the morning, now go to bed like a good little girl, and—and, I say, Christie, you can call me if you want anything, I'll be right here, you know."

"Thank you, Joe, you are kind—and good."

He returned then to his apartment, his pipe was out, but he picked up a newspaper instead, threw himself into an armchair, and in a half-hour was in the land of dreams.

When Charlie came home in the morning, after a six-mile walk into the country and back again, his foolish anger was dead and buried. Logan's "Poor old Charlie" did not ring so distinctly in his ears. Mrs. Stuart's horrified expression had faded considerably from his recollection, he thought only of that surprisingly tall, dark girl, whose eyes looked like coals, whose voice pierced him like a flint-tipped arrow—Ah, well, they would never quarrel again like that, he told himself. She loved him so, and would forgive him after he had talked quietly to her, and told her what an ass he was. She was simple-minded and awfully ignorant to pitch those old Indian laws at him in her fury, but he could not blame her, oh! no, he could not for one moment blame her, he had been terribly severe, and unreasonable, and the horrid McDonald temper had got the better of him, and he loved her so. Oh! he loved her so, she would surely feel that, and forgive him, and— He went straight to his wife's room. The blue velvet evening dress lay on the chair into which he had thrown himself when he doomed his life's happiness by those two words, "God knows." A bunch of dead daffodils and her slippers were on the floor, every-thing—but Christie.

He went to his brother's bedroom door.

"Joe," he called, rapping nervously thereon—"Joe, wake up, where's Christie, d'you know?"

"Good Lord, no," gasped that youth, springing out of his armchair, and opening the door. As he did so, a note fell from off the handle. Charlie's face blanched to his very hair, while Joe read aloud, his voice weakening at every word:—

"DEAR OLD JOE.—I went into your room at daylight to get that picture of the Post on your bookshelves. I hope you do not mind, but I kissed your hair while your slept, it was so curly, and yellow, and soft, just like his. Good-bye, Joe. CHRISTIE."

And when Joe looked into his brother's face and saw the anguish settle in those laughing blue eyes, the despair that drove the dimples away from that almost girlish mouth; when he realized that this boy was but four and twenty years old, and that all his future was perhaps darkened and shadowed for ever, a great, deep sorrow arose in his heart, and he forgot all things, all but the agony that rang up through the voice of the fair handsome lad, as he staggered forward, crying, "Oh! Joe—what shall I do—what shall I do?"

It was months and months before he found her, but during all that time he had never known a hopeless moment; discouraged he often was, but despon-dent, never. The sunniness of his ever-boyish heart radiated with a warmth that would have flooded a much deeper gloom than that which settled within his eager young life. Suffer? ah! yes, he suffered, not with locked teeth and stony stoicism, not with the masterful self-command, the reserve, the conquered bitterness of the still-water sort of nature, that is supposed to run to such depths; he tried to be bright, and his sweet old boyish self. He would laugh sometimes in a pitiful, pathetic fashion, he took to petting dogs, looking into their large solemn eyes with his wistful, questioning blue ones, he would kiss them, as women sometimes do, and call them "dear old fellow," in tones that had tears, and once in the course of his travels, while at a little

way-station, he discovered a huge St. Bernard imprisoned by some mischance
in an empty freightcar; the animal was nearly dead from starvation, and
it seemed to salve his own sick heart to rescue back the dog's life. Nobody
claimed the big starving creature, the train hands knew nothing of its owner,
and gladly handed it over to its deliverer. "Hudson" he called it, and afterwards
when Joe McDonald would relate the story of his brother's life he invariably
terminated it with, "And I really believe that big lumbering brute saved him."
From what, he was never known to say.

But all things end, and he heard of her at last. She had never returned to the
Post as he at first thought she would, but had gone to the little town of B—, in
Ontario, where she was making her living at embroidery and plain sewing.

The September sun had set redly when at last he reached the outskirts of
the town, opened up the wicket gate, and walked up the weedy, unkept path
leading to the cottage where she lodged.

Even through the twilight, he could see her there, leaning on the rail of the
verandah—oddly enough she had about her shoulders the scarlet velvet cloak
she wore when he had flung himself so madly from the room that night.

The moment the lad saw her his heart swelled with a sudden heat, burning
moisture leapt into his eyes, and clogged his long, boyish lashes. He bounded
up the steps— "Christie," he said, and the word scorched his lips like audible
flame.

She turned to him, and for a second stood magnetized by his passionately
wistful face; her peculiar greyish eyes seemed to drink the very life of his
unquenchable love, though the tears that suddenly sprang into his seemed to
absorb every pulse in his body through those hungry, pleading eyes of his that
had, oh! so often been blinded by her kisses when once her whole world lay in
their blue depths.

"You will come back to me, Christie, my wife? My wife, you will let me love
you again?"

She gave a singular little gasp, and shook her head. "Don't, oh! don't," he
cried piteously. "You will come to me, dear? it is all such a bitter mistake—I did
not understand. Oh! Christie, I did not understand, and you'll forgive me, and
love me again, won't you—won't you?"

"No," said the girl with quick, indrawn breath.

He dashed the back of his hand across his wet eyelids, his lips were growing
numb, and he bungled over the monosyllable "Why?"

"I do not like you," she answered quietly.

"God! Oh! God, what is there left?"

She did not appear to hear the heart break in his voice, she stood like one
wrapped in sombre thought, no blaze, no tear, nothing in her eyes, no hardness, no tenderness about her mouth. The wind was blowing her cloak aside,
and the only visible human life in her whole body was once when he spoke the
muscles of her brown arm seemed to contract.

"But, darling, you are mine—*mine*, we are husband and wife, oh, Heaven, you *must* love me, you *must* come to me again."

"You cannot *make* me come," said the icy voice, "neither church, nor law, nor even"—and the vice softened—"nor even love can make a slave of a red girl."

"Heaven forbid it," he faltered. "No, Christie, I will never claim you without your love, what reunion would that be? But, but oh! Christie, you are lying to me, you are lying to yourself, you are lying to Heaven."

She did not move. If only he could touch her he felt as sure of her yielding, as he felt sure there was a hereafter. The memory of the times when he had but to lay his hand on her hair to call a most passionate response from her filled his heart with a torture that choked all words before they reached his lips; at the thought of those days he forgot she was unapproachable, forgot how forbidding were her eyes, how stony her lips. Flinging himself forward, his knee on the chair at her side, his face pressed hardly in the folds of the cloak on her shoulder, he clasped his arms about her with a boyish petulance, saying, "Christie, Christie, my little girl wife, I love you, I love you, and you are killing me."

She quivered from head to foot as his fair, wavy hair brushed her neck, his despairing face sank lower until his cheek, hot as fire, rested on the cool, olive flesh of her arm. A warm moisture oozed up through her skin, and as he felt its glow he looked up, her teeth white and cold were locked over her under lip, and her eyes were as gray stones.

Not murderers alone know the agony of a death sentence.

"Is it all useless? all useless, dear?" he said, with lips starving for hers.

"All useless," she repeated. "I have no love for you now, you forfeited me and my heart months ago, when you said *those two words*."

His arms fell away from her wearily, he arose mechanically, he placed his little grey checked cap on the back of his yellow curls, the old-time laughter was dead in the blue eyes that now looked scared and haunted, the boyishness and the dimples crept away for ever from the lips that quivered like a child's; he turned from her, but she had looked once into his face as the Law Giver must have looked at the Land of Canaan[7] outspread at his feet. She watched him go down the long path and through the picket gate, she watched the big yellowish dog that had waited for him, lumber up on to its feet—stretch—then follow him. She was conscious of but two things, the vengeful lie in her soul, and a little space on her arm that his wet lashes had brushed.

It was hours afterwards when he reached his room. He had said nothing, done nothing—what use were words or deeds? Old Jimmy Robinson was right, she had "balked" sure enough.

What a bare hotelish room it was! he tossed off his coat and sat for ten minutes looking blankly at the sputtering gas jet. Then his whole life, desolate as a desert, loomed up before him with appalling distinctness. Throwing himself on the floor beside his bed, with clasped hands and arms outstretched on the white counterpane, he sobbed. "Oh! God, dear God, I thought you loved me, I thought you'd let me have her again, but you must be tired of me, tired of loving me too; I've nothing left now, nothing, it doesn't seem that I even have you to-night."

He lifted his face then, for his dog, big and clumsy, and yellow, was licking at his sleeve.

10 : Walker Theatre, Winnipeg
(1905–1907)

An Outpost of New York?

ANTHONY J. VICKERY

1. A combination company was a theatrical touring company that travelled via railroad with a full acting company, main crew members, and all sets and costumes required for one or more productions.

BEFORE THE GROWTH of professional theatre companies based in Canada (after the Second World War), the majority of professional theatre seen by Canadian audiences came from the United States (or the United Kingdom via the United States). After the 1870s, most of the travelling companies originated in New York City and toured via the growing rail networks that covered the entirety of the United States and many parts of Canada. Winnipeg benefitted from an early connection to the United States rail network when a line was built directly north from Minneapolis/St. Paul in 1878, making it a natural stop on the intercontinental touring routes. This chapter examines the business operations of the chief theatre in Winnipeg for New York touring companies, first the Winnipeg and later the Walker Theatre, operated by Corliss Powers Walker in the first decade of the twentieth century.

As Walker's daughter, Ruth Harvey, recalls, it was not easy for her father to interest theatre managers in Winnipeg:

> *Papa never forgot the first time he had gone to New York and suggested to a manager there that he send his company to Winnipeg.*
>
> *"Winnipeg!" The manager said it with disbelief and derision. "How do they get there—by dog sled? What do they play in—an igloo?" (Harvey 1949, 291)*

While Winnipeg was a major stop on the touring route, it was still regarded by New York producers as a remote location (Harvey does not provide any details to the identity of this "manager").

Walker was originally from the United States and came to Winnipeg in 1897 supposedly on the advice of railroad baron James J. Hill, who was an advocate for the commercial potential of the city (Harvey 1949, 52). Walker had already operated theatres hosting combination companies[1] in Crookston and Brainerd, Minnesota, as well as Fargo and Grand Forks, North Dakota, before moving to Winnipeg. However, his theatre in Winnipeg became the centrepiece of his theatrical empire. Later, his circuit included additional stops in Alberta and Saskatchewan. Walker continued to operate his theatre in Winnipeg until the 1930s, and died on December 23, 1942 ("C.P. Walker" 1942).

2. First-class touring was defined as a company that included the largest cities in their route (such as Chicago or San Francisco) and charged a ticket price that was equivalent or higher than ticket prices on Broadway.

3. Correspondence involving Small's and Cort's circuits can be found at the Shubert Archives in New York City.

4. No major circuit existed east of Quebec.

During the period covered by the correspondence in this chapter (1905–1907), Walker built his new theatre and had a booking agreement with the New York firm of Marc Klaw and Abraham Erlanger (part of the Theatrical Syndicate, which was the dominant booking agent for first-class touring[2] in the United States and Canada). While local conditions particular to Winnipeg impacted Walker's operations in the 1905 to 1908 period, many of the day-to-day details of running his theatre circuit were typical of circuits in the United States and Canada in their interactions with New York booking agents and producers. Walker and the Klaw and Erlanger office wrote each other often, sometimes multiple times in a week. While most of their correspondence covered the scheduling of acts into Walker's theatres, there were also many letters from Walker to New York detailing local theatrical opportunities and business conditions. While technically a transnational enterprise, Klaw and Erlanger treated Walker's Winnipeg stop as if it was just another stop in the United States rather than in a foreign country, with no changes made to the companies and their plays when performing for Canadian audiences.

The documents in this chapter provide a number of technical details about touring and demonstrate how closely the New York producers controlled activity on the commercial road in this era. They also give some indication of the amount of administrative time that Walker had to spend on routing the companies over his small network of theatres. Similar volumes of correspondence (with very similar themes) exist for Ambrose Small's circuit of theatres in Ontario and Quebec, and John Cort's circuit covering coastal British Columbia (primarily Victoria and Vancouver).[3] In fact, the same companies that played Winnipeg in a particular year would likely have also already played in Quebec and Ontario and would probably go on to play in British Columbia afterwards (or vice versa, if moving from west to east rather than east to west).

Because of the dominance of New York producers over the entirety of the road, there would be a consistency to what audiences experienced in Montreal, Toronto, Winnipeg, and Vancouver in any particular season.[4] These documents demonstrate that for the entrepreneurial theatre owner, day-to-day work was more about the commerce of theatre and less about creation or the artistic side of performances. The examples included in this chapter clearly demonstrate that the local theatre owners, for the most part, had to take whatever productions were sent to them by the New York producers unless they could not come to a financial agreement about the individual act. If they could not agree, the theatre sat empty or a local booking could be substituted.

The producers in New York City created the theatrical companies who were then booked by agents all over the United States and Canada. These agents had booking agreements with circuit owners (like Walker) who either owned or leased theatres in discrete areas of the two countries (or, in Walker's case, both countries). While the producers and booking agents owned (or directly controlled) theatres in the large cities (such as Chicago, Boston, or San

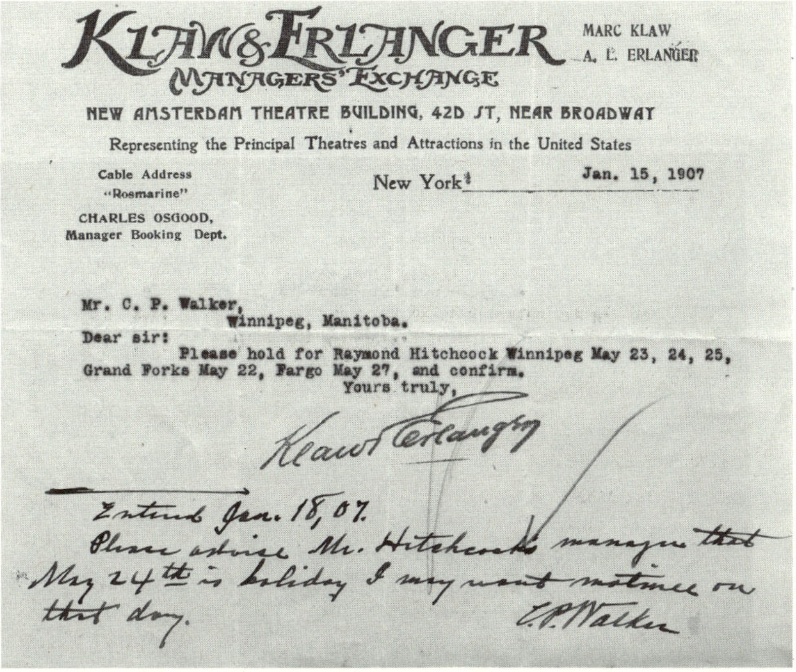

KLAW & ERLANGER
MANAGERS' EXCHANGE
MARC KLAW
A. L. ERLANGER

NEW AMSTERDAM THEATRE BUILDING, 42D ST, NEAR BROADWAY

Representing the Principal Theatres and Attractions in the United States

Cable Address
"Rosmarine"

New York,   Jan. 15, 1907

CHARLES OSGOOD,
Manager Booking Dept.

Mr. C. P. Walker,
          Winnipeg, Manitoba.
Dear sir:
          Please hold for Raymond Hitchcock Winnipeg May 23, 24, 25,
Grand Forks May 22, Fargo May 27, and confirm.
          Yours truly,

          Klaw & Erlanger

Entered Jan. 18, 07.
Please advise Mr. Hitchcock's manager that
May 24th is holiday I may want matinee on
that day.
          C. P. Walker

FIGURE 10.1: *Letter from Klaw and Erlanger to C.P. Walker, January 15, 1907.*

Shubert Archives, New York.

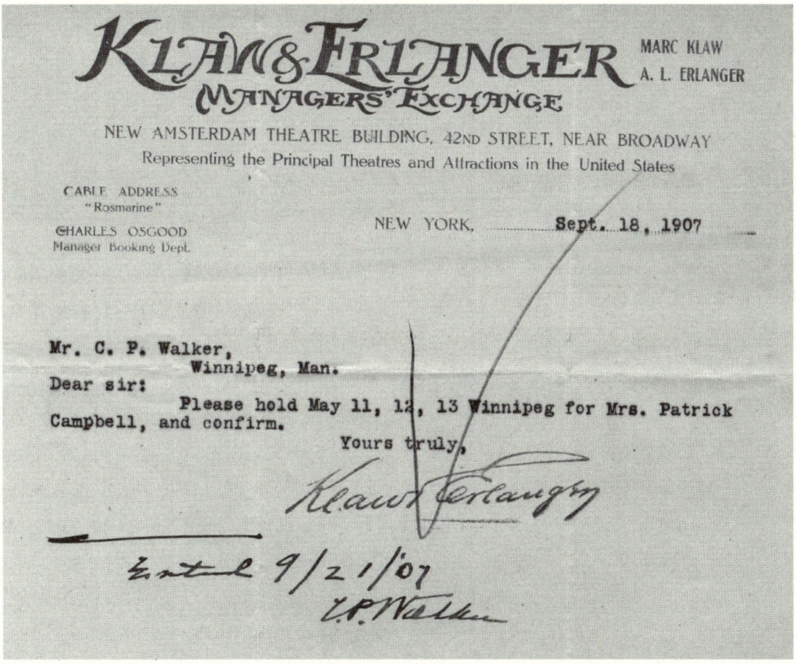

KLAW & ERLANGER
MANAGERS' EXCHANGE
MARC KLAW
A. L. ERLANGER

NEW AMSTERDAM THEATRE BUILDING, 42ND STREET, NEAR BROADWAY

Representing the Principal Theatres and Attractions in the United States

CABLE ADDRESS
"Rosmarine"

NEW YORK,   Sept. 18, 1907

CHARLES OSGOOD
Manager Booking Dept.

Mr. C. P. Walker,
          Winnipeg, Man.
Dear sir:
          Please hold May 11, 12, 13 Winnipeg for Mrs. Patrick
Campbell, and confirm.
          Yours truly,

          Klaw & Erlanger

Entered 9/21/07
          C. P. Walker

FIGURE 10.2: *Letter from Klaw and Erlanger to C.P. Walker, September 18, 1907.*

Shubert Archives, New York.

WINNIPEG

GRAND FORKS

FARGO

CROOKSTON

BRAINERD

WALKER THEATRE CO.
LESSEE

FOR TIME AND TERMS ADDRESS

C. P. WALKER

P. O. DRAWER 1242

WINNIPEG, MANITOBA

WINNIPEG THEATRE
WINNIPEG, MAN.

METROPOLITAN THEATRE
GRAND FORKS, N. D.

FARGO OPERA HOUSE
FARGO, N. D.

CROOKSTON OPERA HOUSE
CROOKSTON, MINN.

BRAINERD OPERA HOUSE
BRAINERD, MINN.

Winnipeg Man. february 16, 1905.

Klaw and Erlanger,
   New York.
  Gentlemen:-
    Please mark off the following time for the Marks Repertoire
company: Winnipeg, Feb 28 to Mar. II, Grand Forks, week Mar. 20,
Crookston, week Mar. 27, Fargo, Week Apr. 3, Brainerd, week Apr IO.
My contract with them allows me to lay the company off one night
each week should anything turn up and you desire the time. Can lay
them off two nights in Winnipeg.

          Yours very truly

              C. P. Walker

FIGURE 10.3: *Letter from C.P. Walker to Klaw and Erlanger, February 16, 1905.*
Shubert Archives, New York.

Francisco), they only had contractual arrangements to book theatres in smaller cities. However, these smaller cities were important because the cost of transporting companies was a key expense for producers, and they needed to minimize train travel between engagements to less than a day to allow the companies to spend the maximum amount of time playing engagements rather than travelling. The small stops between the large cities provided the revenue to keep the companies moving on the road. Walker was not a business partner of the New York producers (in fact, his agreement with them explicitly stated that they were not partners), so as an independent business under contract, he had to play the attractions the New York producers sent him.

The documents in this chapter are drawn from the Klaw and Erlanger Collection housed at the Shubert Archives in New York City. The letters collected here are either on typical Klaw and Erlanger letterhead and authored by Charles Osgood (or his office) or from Walker to the Klaw and Erlanger offices. Osgood was the long-time manager of Klaw and Erlanger's booking department and conducted most of the day-to-day operations in their office.

Klaw and Erlanger had an exclusive booking arrangement with Walker that gave the New York agents full control over Walker's schedule. This was the standard arrangement between the New York producers and all of the local theatre managers across the United States and Canada, not just with Walker. The New York producers needed full control of all the schedules so they could route hundreds of companies over the complete network of circuits efficiently from New York. Figures 10.1 and 10.2 reflect the measure of control the New York producers had over Walker's schedule and demonstrate the typical pattern of booking correspondence from New York to Walker. Klaw and Erlanger would send a list of dates with locations (since Walker controlled a number of theatres) and the name of the production. At this point, no financial details for the booking were indicated as these would be worked out later, usually between the particular act and Walker. Klaw and Erlanger often would not participate in the financial negotiations unless they were the producers themselves or there was a difficulty (as seen particularly in Figure 10.4).

If Walker wanted to book a local company or minor act into his theatre, he had to ask Klaw and Erlanger if the time was available (Figure 10.3 is a request for time from the notable Marks Brothers, a group of Canadian touring companies all linked by family ties that toured mostly secondary cities (see Marks and Croft 1958). Walker's acknowledging the booking and returning a copy of the original request back to Klaw and Erlanger completed the process in the case of the correspondence in Figures 10.1 and 10.2. Walker's reply to the letter in Figure 10.1 was typical of many occurrences in the correspondence: Walker giving some indication of local conditions (in this case May 24, Victoria Day, celebrating Queen Victoria's actual birthday—a holiday not celebrated in the United States). Walker's circuit was fully integrated into the Klaw and Erlanger overall route with companies entering or departing the circuit from Minneapolis/St. Paul to the east and likely Bismarck, North Dakota, to the west.

For the touring industry that Walker was a part of, the main measure of success was financial profit, with artistic success as only a secondary concern. Therefore, a great deal of Walker's managerial correspondence concerned financial negotiations. Figure 10.4 gives a number of pieces of information about the financial arrangements of touring. This letter is addressed to Osgood and is predominantly about arranging the financial terms of a number of companies. In the opening paragraph, Walker presents the two main financial configurations used when booking acts. In his negotiations with John Cort (a producer and circuit owner originally based in Seattle who later moved to New York) for the engagement of Max Figman, Walker wrote, "I have offered him $2,000 or sixty percent" in response to a higher demand put forth by Cort. The first figure represents a guarantee and the second a sharing arrangement. A guarantee was a set amount of cash that a theatre manager would pay to the company with the entirety of the box office take[5] being retained by the theatre. When the acting company manager or producer set their guarantee amount, they would include all of their expenses plus an appropriate amount of profit in the total. The company received this fee regardless of box office performance; therefore, all of the risk was borne by the local theatre owner. If the company proved to be a hit, the local theatre owner could capture significant revenue (from which they paid all of their expenses—usually front-of-house staff, local crews, a proportion of advertising, and cost of venue). The amount of the guarantee was the contentious item in this negotiation, with Cort demanding $2,500 for the three-day engagement and Walker offering $2,000.

WINNIPEG
GRAND FORKS
FARGO
CROOKSTON
BRAINERD

DIRECTION
KLAW & ERLANGER

FOR TIME AND TERMS ADDRESS
C. P. WALKER
P. O. DRAWER 1242
WINNIPEG, MANITOBA

WINNIPEG THEATRE
WINNIPEG, MAN.

METROPOLITAN THEATRE
GRAND FORKS, N. D.

FARGO OPERA HOUSE
FARGO, N. D.

CROOKSTON OPERA HOUSE
CROOKSTON, MINN.

BRAINERD OPERA HOUSE
BRAINERD, MINN.

Winnipeg, Man., Dec.11, 1906.

Mr. Charles Osgood,
New York City, N.Y.

My dear Mr. Osgood:--

I have yours of 4th inst.   Have been dickering with Cort by wire. He demands $2500 for Figman's three days here, which is ridiculous.   I have offered him $2000 or sixty percent.   If I don't get any more encouragement from others than from John I will put stock in the house and get the benefit of the improved conditions brought about because of my large investment.

The thing figures out about this way:--by investing $300,000 I have made it possible and probable that the gross business of attractions playing the combination house here will be increased y by $75,000 per season. This outlay has increased my expenses fully $25,000 per year.   Now if I must play attractions at the same terms as in the old house my share of the increased business will be no more than my increased expenses.   Therefore company managers are the only ones who will profit by my investment, they doing so to the extent of $50,000. This is figuring that I get on an average one-third of the gross.   , which is probably rather more than I do get. So, you see, if I am to get no increase in sharing terms I have made a very foolish investment.

I figured that by building a theatre which would be perfect-ly satisfactory to my patrons (the old house was far from being satis-factory to the better class of theatregoers) with a money capacity fully fifty per cent greater than the old house, I would have no difficulty in getting from 5 to 10% better sharing terms.   Was I wrong in figuring this way?   Why should not companies playing the old house at 70% prefer to play the new one at 60%? They will certainly get a whole lot more money in the new house at the lower tersm than in the old house at the higher per cent.   Only by get-ting an increase in percentages can I participate in the advantages. my investment has made possible. In fact, with my largely increased expenses, I cannot break even at the old terms.

There is no doubt in my mind but that I am entitled , because of improved conditions here, to an increase in terms. And as stated before I must have the increase in order to make my invest-ment profitable to me.   You state "it would be a pretty action on your part to inform attractions that you would not play them on a percentage basis."   I have no wish to employ harsh or arbitrary methods, but I am afraid nothing else will bring about the desired result.   I don't want to hold anyone up, but do want what I am entitled to.   And it's a gamble that in some instances I will not get it unless I do use harsh methods.   For example, take John Cort's position in regard to Figman terms.   He claims he is en-titled to two-thirds of the gross (has sent his contract at 70-30%) or $2500 certainty.   You know and I know that he is not entitled o to either of these propositions.   Then there is Louis White. He writes that he should have even better terms than in the old house for "The Heir to the Hoorah" because the show costs $150 per week more than it cost last season.   My expenses are fxxkyxx increased over last season fully four times that amount.   So you see these fax fellows don't advance, in most cases at least, any sound arguments to uphold the position they take.   With such people harsh methods will have to be used, I reckon

I shall probably accept Mr. Slocum's certainty proposition for "The Yankee Consul". Will advise you soon. Will also send you "Peggy from Paris" contracts with certainty clause for Winnipeg

which I think will be equitable.   Will also write you soon about certainty for "The County Chairman".   I will give every one of these attractions money enough to make them a handsome profit----- at the rate of at least $1000 a week.

Shall open the house next Monday with the Pollards. It will not be complete in every detail, but will be usable alright.

As soon as I can get some photos of the interior you shall have one.

Sincerely yours,

C. P. Walker

FIGURE 10.4: *Letter from C.P. Walker to Charles Osgood, December 11, 1906.*

Shubert Archives, New York.

6. Over six hundred people died in the fire (the actual total is not known, as many bodies were removed from the scene before the final count was made). "Over 500 Die" 1903; see also Everett 1904.

7. The Winnipeg Theatre did burn down on December 23, 1926, injuring and killing a number of firemen ("Three Firemen Die" 1926).

The second set of terms, for sharing, was a method of splitting the gross box office with the percentage named (60 per cent) going to the acting company and the remainder being retained by the theatre owner with some expenses, such as advertising or extra crew, if necessary, shared proportionally. In this era, both of these deal configurations were relatively straightforward. The letter also discloses the costs Walker had just incurred to construct his new theatre and his rationale for trying to increase his share of the box office take. He notes that the old house (the Winnipeg Theatre) "was far from being satisfactory to the better class of theatregoers." In the wake of the deadly Iroquois Theatre fire in Chicago in 1903,[6] all wooden, second-floor theatres were regarded with some suspicion due to the increased attention paid to fire safety, and the Winnipeg Theatre was no exception.[7]

The remainder of the correspondence collected here deals with particular aspects of theatre on Walker's circuit. Figure 10.5 advises complete omission of Grand Forks as a touring stop. This advice turns up in a number of Walker's letters as Grand Forks (and Brainerd) often returned poor box office results. The most interesting part of this letter, though, is the "quiet tip" Walker details for Osgood. Instead of forwarding advertising paper directly to Winnipeg, Walker advises Osgood to send the paper to Grand Forks where Walker's man would forward it on to Winnipeg. Walker asks Osgood to keep the matter "confidential." By smuggling the advertising across the border, the duty on theatrical paper of fifteen cents per pound would be avoided ("Canadian Tariff" 1899). The letter in Figure 10.6 details unusual weather conditions that could occur during the winter. While train service was usually quite regular and dependable, heavy snow, reminiscent of sentiments in the opening quote, could occur and delay or cancel performances even though Walker notes that such occurrences were rare.

While the New York producers dominated business decisions regarding routing, not surprisingly, the local theatre owner had a better sense of their audience. Figure 10.7 provides a fascinating insight into the Winnipeg audience at the time. The letter reads,

April 7, 1907.

Dear Mr. Osgood:
    I fear I am making a mistake in playing "Mrs. Warren's Profession" at Winnipeg.
    My patrons are very prudish, and I believe they and the newspapers will severely criticize me for offering the play.
    Just at this time such criticism would be very harmful.
    I wish you would cancel the Winnipeg dates for this attraction. If you will do so please advise.

Sincerely yours,
C.P. Walker

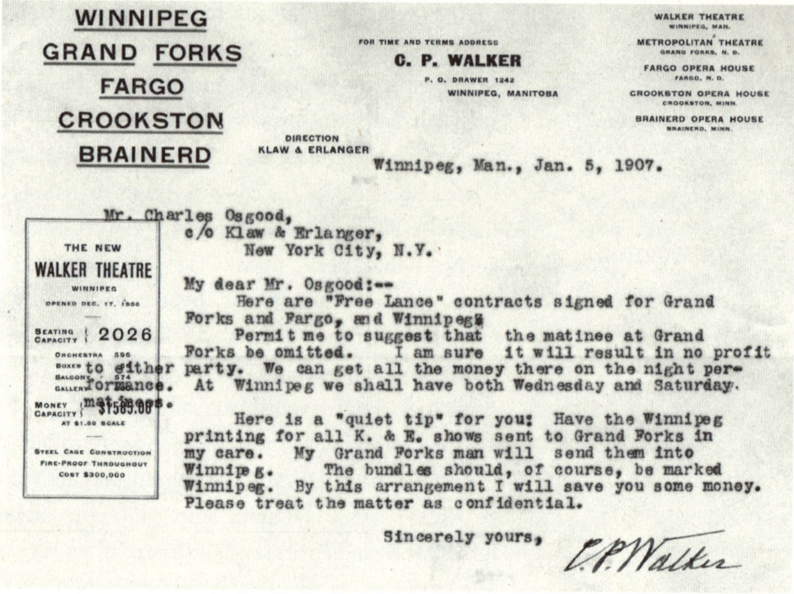

WINNIPEG
GRAND FORKS
FARGO
CROOKSTON
BRAINERD

FOR TIME AND TERMS ADDRESS
C. P. WALKER
P. O. DRAWER 1242
WINNIPEG, MANITOBA

WALKER THEATRE
WINNIPEG, MAN.
METROPOLITAN THEATRE
GRAND FORKS, N. D.
FARGO OPERA HOUSE
FARGO, N. D.
CROOKSTON OPERA HOUSE
CROOKSTON, MINN.
BRAINERD OPERA HOUSE
BRAINERD, MINN.

DIRECTION
KLAW & ERLANGER

Winnipeg, Man., Jan. 5, 1907.

THE NEW
WALKER THEATRE
WINNIPEG
OPENED DEC. 17, 1906

SEATING CAPACITY 2026
ORCHESTRA 596
BOXES 56
BALCONY 574
GALLERY 800
MONEY CAPACITY $1585.00
AT $1.50 SCALE

STEEL CAGE CONSTRUCTION
FIRE-PROOF THROUGHOUT
COST $300,000

Mr. Charles Osgood,
c/o Klaw & Erlanger,
New York City, N.Y.

My dear Mr. Osgood:--
Here are "Free Lance" contracts signed for Grand
Forks and Fargo, and Winnipeg.
Permit me to suggest that the matinee at Grand
Forks be omitted. I am sure it will result in no profit
to either party. We can get all the money there on the night per-
formance. At Winnipeg we shall have both Wednesday and Saturday.
matinees.

Here is a "quiet tip" for you: Have the Winnipeg
printing for all K. & E. shows sent to Grand Forks in
my care. My Grand Forks man will send them into
Winnipeg. The bundles should, of course, be marked
Winnipeg. By this arrangement I will save you some money.
Please treat the matter as confidential.

Sincerely yours,
C.P. Walker

FIGURE 10.5: *Letter from C.P. Walker to Charles Osgood, January 5, 1907.*

Shubert Archives, New York.

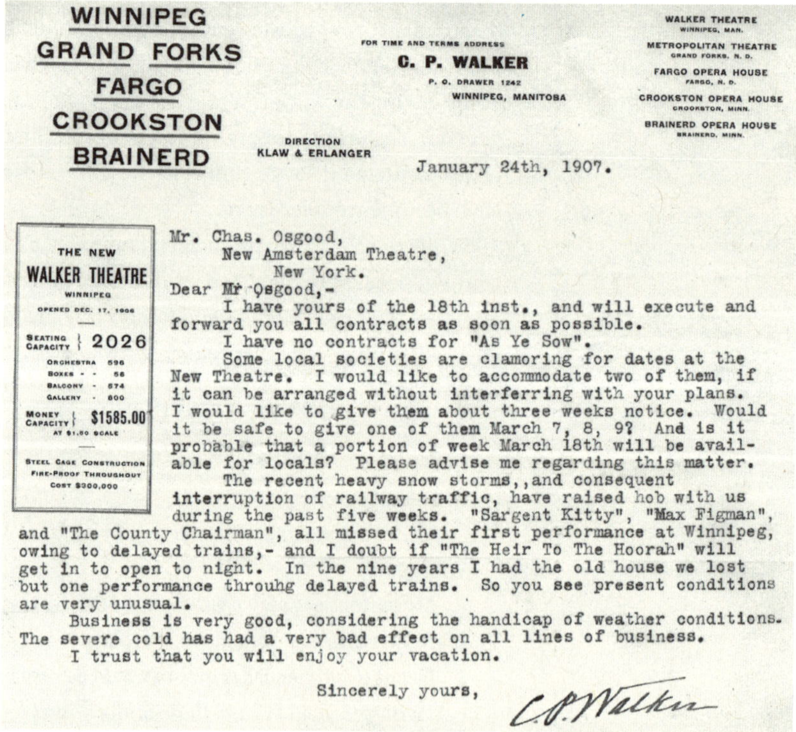

WINNIPEG
GRAND FORKS
FARGO
CROOKSTON
BRAINERD

FOR TIME AND TERMS ADDRESS
C. P. WALKER
P. O. DRAWER 1242
WINNIPEG, MANITOBA

WALKER THEATRE
WINNIPEG, MAN.
METROPOLITAN THEATRE
GRAND FORKS, N. D.
FARGO OPERA HOUSE
FARGO, N. D.
CROOKSTON OPERA HOUSE
CROOKSTON, MINN.
BRAINERD OPERA HOUSE
BRAINERD, MINN.

DIRECTION
KLAW & ERLANGER

January 24th, 1907.

THE NEW
WALKER THEATRE
WINNIPEG
OPENED DEC. 17, 1906

SEATING CAPACITY 2026
ORCHESTRA 596
BOXES 56
BALCONY 574
GALLERY 800
MONEY CAPACITY $1585.00
AT $1.50 SCALE

STEEL CAGE CONSTRUCTION
FIRE-PROOF THROUGHOUT
COST $300,000

Mr. Chas. Osgood,
New Amsterdam Theatre,
New York.
Dear Mr Osgood,-
I have yours of the 18th inst., and will execute and
forward you all contracts as soon as possible.
I have no contracts for "As Ye Sow".
Some local societies are clamoring for dates at the
New Theatre. I would like to accommodate two of them, if
it can be arranged without interferring with your plans.
I would like to give them about three weeks notice. Would
it be safe to give one of them March 7, 8, 9? And is it
probable that a portion of week March 18th will be available for locals? Please advise me regarding this matter.
The recent heavy snow storms,,and consequent
interruption of railway traffic, have raised hob with us
during the past five weeks. "Sargent Kitty", "Max Figman",
and "The County Chairman", all missed their first performance at Winnipeg,
owing to delayed trains,- and I doubt if "The Heir To The Hoorah" will
get in to open to night. In the nine years I had the old house we lost
but one performance throuhg delayed trains. So you see present conditions
are very unusual.
Business is very good, considering the handicap of weather conditions.
The severe cold has had a very bad effect on all lines of business.
I trust that you will enjoy your vacation.

Sincerely yours,
C.P. Walker

FIGURE 10.6: *Letter from C.P. Walker to Charles Osgood, January 24, 1907.*

Shubert Archives, New York.

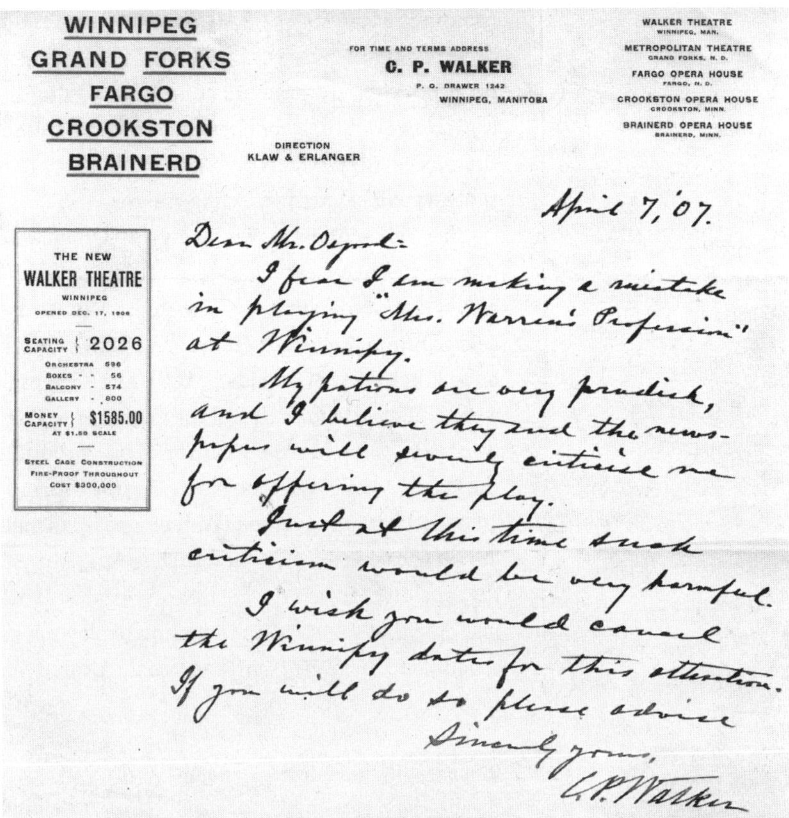

FIGURE 10.7: *Letter from C.P. Walker to Charles Osgood, April 7, 1907.*
Shubert Archives, New York.

George Bernard Shaw's *Mrs. Warren's Profession* had run into legal trouble in a number of the locations it played after its debut in 1902. Walker noted that he felt it would be a mistake to host the play in Winnipeg, as his "patrons are very prudish" and he believed the newspapers would be very critical. The production still played Winnipeg on April 30, 1907. His worries were somewhat justified, as on May 1 the reviewer in the *Free Press* wrote, "No more unwholesome nor repulsive play has ever been seen in Winnipeg than George Bernard Shaw's 'Mrs. Warren's Profession' produced at the Walker Theatre last night. It has not one redeeming feature. True, there are one or two smart lines and a certain sort of brilliancy which one has learned to term Shawian [*sic*], but the bitter sewerlike flavor one carries away in the mouth is not compensated for by a false and meretricious glitter." No lawsuits emerged from the performance in Winnipeg, but this issue does show that Walker definitely knew the tenor of local sentiment better than his New York agents. The overall issue of the appropriateness or quality of productions was often discussed in Walker's letters. What was deemed appropriate for large cities in the United States was not necessarily well received in a city such as Winnipeg. The courts examined *Mrs. Warren's Profession* on first presentation in New York City the previous year for indecency ("The Court" 1906). While the justices called the play "not pleasant" and full of "repellant things," they did not declare it indecent. However, the producers had sunk costs into mounting a production and therefore had to send it out on the road to try to recover those costs despite the protests of local managers like Walker.

The Walker Theatre was an active performance venue in Winnipeg during the early years of the twentieth century. Due to the exclusive booking arrangement the theatre had with the New York office of Klaw and Erlanger, a large number of productions were performed in the city before carrying on to other parts of Canada or the United States. While Walker's theatre was a prominent site for cultural activity in the city, the majority of productions were programmed from New York City with little regard for the tastes of the local audience. For the most part, the touring fare offered at the Walker Theatre was well accepted (Walker was financially successful for many years), but on occasion a production such as *Mrs. Warren's Profession* would reveal the tension between the desires of a local audience and the needs of a touring machine that required a production to play a specified route on a particular schedule to move efficiently across the United States and Canada.

Bibliography and Further Reading

Brown, Mary. 1982. "Ambrose Small: A Ghost in Spite of Himself." In *Theatrical Touring and Founding in North America*, edited by L.W. Conolly, 77–88. Westport, CT: Greenwood Press.

"A Canadian Tariff Amendment." 1899. *The New York Dramatic Mirror*, August 12, 1899, 16.

"The Court Approves Bernard Shaw's Play." 1906. *The New York Times*, July 7, 1906, 7.

"C.P. Walker Dies at 89 on Wednesday." 1942. *Winnipeg Free Press*, December 23, 1942, 1.

Davis, Peter A. 1991. "The Syndicate/Shubert War." In *Inventing Times Square: Commerce and Culture at the Crossroads of the World*, edited by William R. Taylor, 147–57. Baltimore: Johns Hopkins University Press.

Evans, Chad. 1983. *Frontier Theatre: A History of Nineteenth-Century Theatrical Entertainment in the Canadian Far West and Alaska*. Victoria, BC: Sono Nis Press.

Everett, Marshall. 1904. *The Great Chicago Theater Disaster*. Chicago: Protestant Bible House.

Hartman, James B. 2002. "On Stage: Theatre and Theatres in Early Winnipeg." *Manitoba History* 43 (Spring/Summer).

Harvey, Ruth. 1949. *Curtain Time*. Boston: Houghton Mifflin Company.

Marks, Kitty, and Frank Croft. 1958. "My Life with the Original Marks Brothers." *Maclean's*, June 21, 1958, 58.

"Music and Drama." 1907. *Winnipeg Free Press*, May 1, 1907, 8.

"Over 500 Die in Chicago Theatre." 1903. *The New York Times*, December 31, 1903, 1.

Schweitzer, Marlis. 2017. "Aggressive, Beleaguered, Commercial, Defiant: Marc Klaw and Abraham Erlanger." In *The Palgrave Handbook of Musical Theatre Producers*, edited by Laura MacDonald and William A. Everett, 59–68. New York: Palgrave Macmillan.

Skene, Reg. 1990. "C.P. Walker and the Business of Theatre: Merchandizing
    Entertainment in a Continental Context." In *The Political Economy of Manitoba*,
    edited by James Silver and Jeremy Hall, 128–50. Regina: Canadian Plains Research
    Center.

Stuart, E. Ross. 1984. *The History of Prairie Theatre: The Development of Theatre in Alberta,
    Manitoba and Saskatchewan, 1833–1982*. Toronto: Simon & Pierre.

"Three Firemen Die and Nine Injured as Wall Collapses." 1926. *The Globe and Mail*,
    December 24, 1926, 1.

Vickery, Anthony. 2010. "Two Patterns of Theatrical Touring in Canada, 1896–1921."
    Theatre Research in Canada 31 (1): 1–19.

11 : Cantonese Theatre in Vancouver
(1916–1936)

Glimpses into the World of Chinatown Theatre

WING CHUNG NG

1. For a brief biographical sketch of Yip Sang, see Stanley 2005. Nancy Rao notes the building of the venue in the Shanghai Alley (2017, 136). See also the recollection of J.S. Matthews (1947) on his visit to the theatre in the winter of 1898: the writing was prompted by the theatre's destruction in a fire the preceding week.

FROM THE 1920S TO THE LATE 1930S, Vancouver was a major hub of Chinese theatrical activities in the western hemisphere. Commonly referred to as the "Saltwater City" throughout the Chinese diaspora, Vancouver was a principal gateway for incoming and departing opera performers and musicians who crossed the Pacific. In conjunction with San Francisco and New York City, Vancouver was one of the three major hubs that anchored a transnational circuit for the dissemination of opera theatre across Canada and the United States, with offshoots reaching some neighbouring countries in Latin America and the Caribbean (Ng 2015, 161-64).

After Chinese migrants had settled in Victoria in the latter part of the nineteenth century, Chinese opera troupes based in California (first appearing in San Francisco as early as 1852) soon made their way up the Pacific Northwest and performed for their countrymen in this city, the site of the earliest Canadian Chinatown (Sebryk 1995). By the turn of the twentieth century, Vancouver had also joined this regional circuit with its first known Chinese theatre built by the prominent merchant Yip Sang in 1898. The venue was located in the Shanghai Alley and remained in use for theatrical entertainment over extended periods of time until it burned down in 1947.[1] In the 1910s, after Vancouver's Chinese settlement had grown into the largest in Canada, its theatrical scene developed into a vibrant component of the community. Two additional theatres were built in close proximity within the ethnic neighbourhood in 1913-14.

Since Chinese migrants in North America were overwhelmingly Cantonese natives hailing from the Pearl River Delta of Guangdong in South China, the theatrical fares they enjoyed belonged to the genre known as Cantonese opera. In its original habitat, this native theatre catered initially to the village communities across the Pearl River estuary and was performed by itinerant companies as part of communal celebration of local deities and seasonal festivals. By the late nineteenth century, Cantonese opera had entered the regional metropolises of Guangzhou (the provincial capital of Guangdong) and Hong Kong (the nearby British Crown Colony), and thrived as commercial entertainment in the twin cities' playhouses as well (Ng 2015, see especially Part I). No wonder Cantonese opera was immensely popular among Chinese migrants in North America. Indeed, the sojourn overseas only deepened a desire for

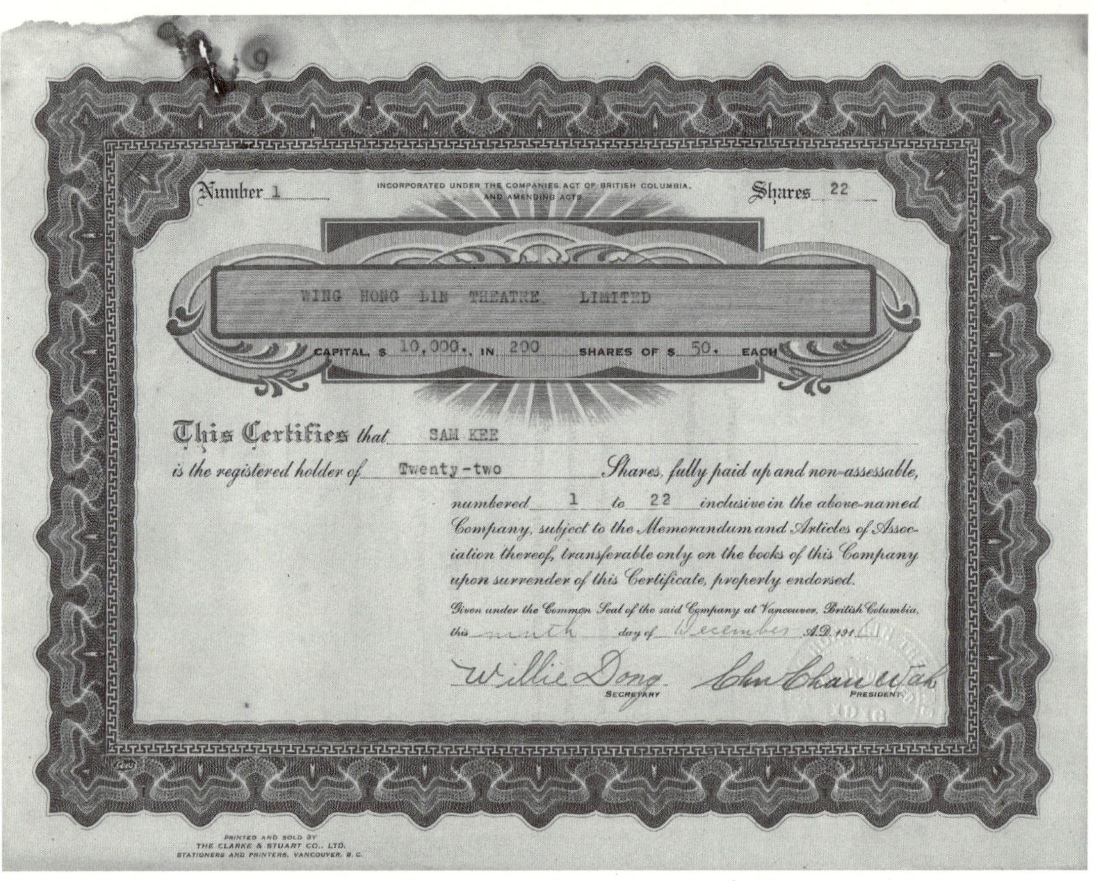

FIGURE 11.1: *Wing Hong Lin Theatre Limited, Certificate of shares owned by Sam Kee, December 1916.* MSS 571, 566-G-4, file 2, Sam Kee Papers, City of Vancouver Archives.

heartwarming entertainment from home. As we shall see in this chapter, the theatre was deeply woven into the social and cultural fabrics of Chinatown life, even as the theatrical entertainment was facilitated by, if not dependent on, the migrant community's long-distance contacts and ocean-spanning activities. The following discussion seeks to unveil the local as well as transnational dynamics of the theatre world by drawing on some untapped sources: archives left by Chinatown businesses involved in the promotion of the theatre and available in the City of Vancouver Archives and the Special Collections at the University of British Columbia Library; theatre advertisements and various reports in the Chinatown daily newspaper the *Chinese Times* (*Dahan Gongbao*); and finally, a small number of photographs taken in the late 1930s deposited in the photographic collection of the Vancouver Public Library.

Though theatre entrepreneurs seldom physically ascended the stage, they played a pivotal role in the theatre world. In Vancouver, one of the earliest instigators was the Wing Hong Lin Theatre Company, which was established by a group of Chinese merchants in December 1916 to engage troupes directly

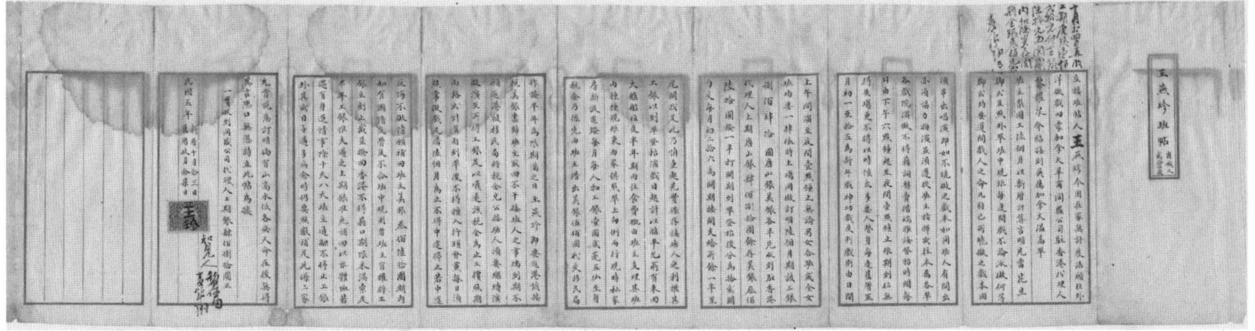

FIGURE 11.2: *An actress's contract, October 1916.*

Add. MSS 571, 566-G-4, file 12, Sam Kee Papers, City of Vancouver Archives.

from China for performance abroad. The principal partner was Chang Toy, better known to his business associates and non-Chinese counterparts by the name of his firm, Sam Kee. As Paul Yee (1986) points out, Sam Kee was no small shopkeeper, but an influential figure with wide-ranging business interests inside and outside of Chinatown. Figure 11.1 shows the very first copy of Wing Hong Lin's share certificate issued to none other than Sam Kee. Of the initial capital of $10,000, Sam Kee invested $1,100, making him the largest shareholder. Other items in Wing Hong Lin's extant business archives further confirm Sam Kee's prominent role. According to company minutes, board meetings were held at his business premises on 111 East Pender Street, and he was the landlord of the Sing Ping Theatre on Columbia Street, where the company's troupes performed for two seasons of about six to seven months each between December 1916 and May 1918 ("Wing Hong Lin").

The several notarized performance contracts in the Wing Hong Lin collection are among the earliest extant copies of such documents signed by Cantonese opera actors for overseas engagement in the early twentieth century. Figure 11.2 shows a contract for an actress Wang Yanzhen, aged twenty-five and a native of Guangzhou, signed in Hong Kong in October 1916. Wang Yanzhen was engaged to play the female lead role of *huadan*,[2] with the understanding that she might be assigned other role types because overseas troupes were typically much smaller than those in South China, and itinerant performers had to be versatile and flexible. A local agent in Hong Kong signed the contract on behalf of the Wing Hong Lin Company. Apparently, North American–based theatre entrepreneurs relied on their distant business associates in Hong Kong (and also Guangzhou) for recruitment of actors as well as for shipment of performance paraphernalia and other stage supplies. The contract also details compensation, travel arrangements, and other terms of employment. One particular item pertains to the payment of the $500 bond required by the Canadian immigration authorities for actors seeking entrance into the country. Since actors were not deemed labourers and therefore not liable to the payment of the infamous head tax, they were subject to

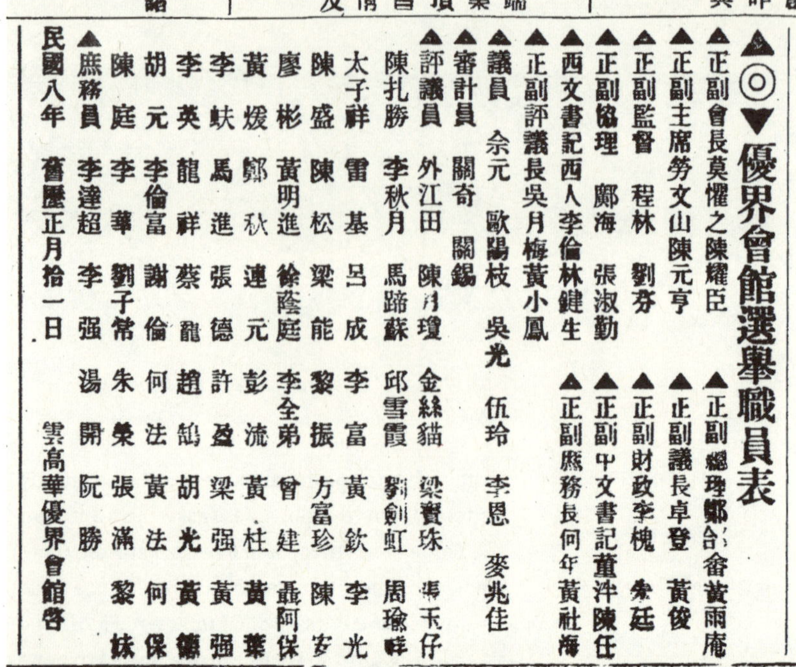

優界會館選舉職員表

▲正副會長　莫懼之　陳耀臣
▲正副總理　鄭合畲　黃雨庵
▲正副主席　勞文山　陳元亨
▲正副議長　卓登　黃俊
▲正副監督　程林　劉芬
▲正副財政　李槐　余廷
▲正副協理　鄭海　張淑勤
▲正副中文書記　董沊　陳任
▲正副庶務長　何年　黃社海
▲西文書記西人　李倫林　健生
▲正副評議長　吳月梅　黃小鳳
▲議員　佘元　歐陽枝　吳光　伍玲　李恩　麥兆佳
▲審計員　關奇　關錫
▲評議員　外江田　陳月瓊　金絲貓　梁寶珠　尋玉仔
陳扎勝　李秋月　馬蹄蘇　邱雪霞　劉劍虹　周瑜啤
太子祥　雷基　呂成　李富　黃欽　李光
陳盛　陳松　梁能　黎振　方富珍　陳安
廖彬　黃明進　徐蔭庭　李全弟　曾建　聶阿保
黃煥　鄧秋　連元　彭流　黃柱　黃葉
李蚨　馬進　張德元　許盈　梁強　黃強
李英　龍祥　蔡龍　趙鵠　胡光　黃德
胡元　李倫富　謝倫　何法　黃法　何保
陳庭　李華　劉子常　朱榮　張滿　黎妹
▲庶務員　李達超　李子強

民國八年　舊曆正月拾一日
雲高華優界會館啟

FIGURE 11.3: *List of officers and members of the Actor's Guild, 1919.* First published on February 13, 1919, in the Chinese Times (Vancouver). UBC Asian Library.

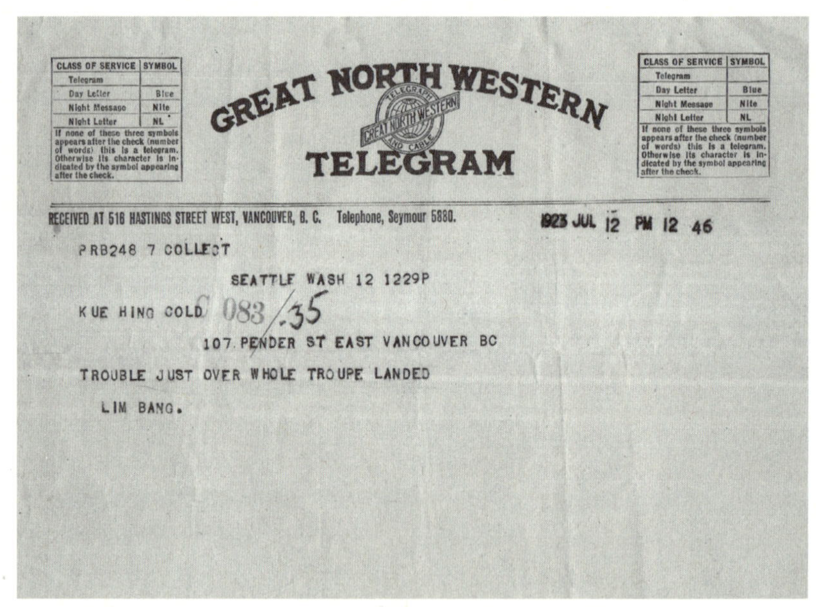

GREAT NORTH WESTERN TELEGRAM

GREAT NORTH WESTERN NO CABLE

CLASS OF SERVICE | SYMBOL
Telegram
Day Letter | Blue
Night Message | Nite
Night Letter | NL
If none of these three symbols appears after the check (number of words) this is a telegram. Otherwise its character is indicated by the symbol appearing after the check.

RECEIVED AT 516 HASTINGS STREET WEST, VANCOUVER, B. C.　Telephone, Seymour 5880.

1923 JUL 12 PM 12 46

PRB248 7 COLLECT

SEATTLE WASH 12 1229P

KUE HING COLD　083/.35

107 PENDER ST EAST VANCOUVER BC

TROUBLE JUST OVER WHOLE TROUPE LANDED

LIM BANG.

FIGURE 11.4: *Telegram from Lim Bang to Kue Hing Company, July 12, 1923.*

Add. MSS 1108, 612-F-7, file 1, Yip Family and Yip Sang Ltd. fonds, City of Vancouver Archives.

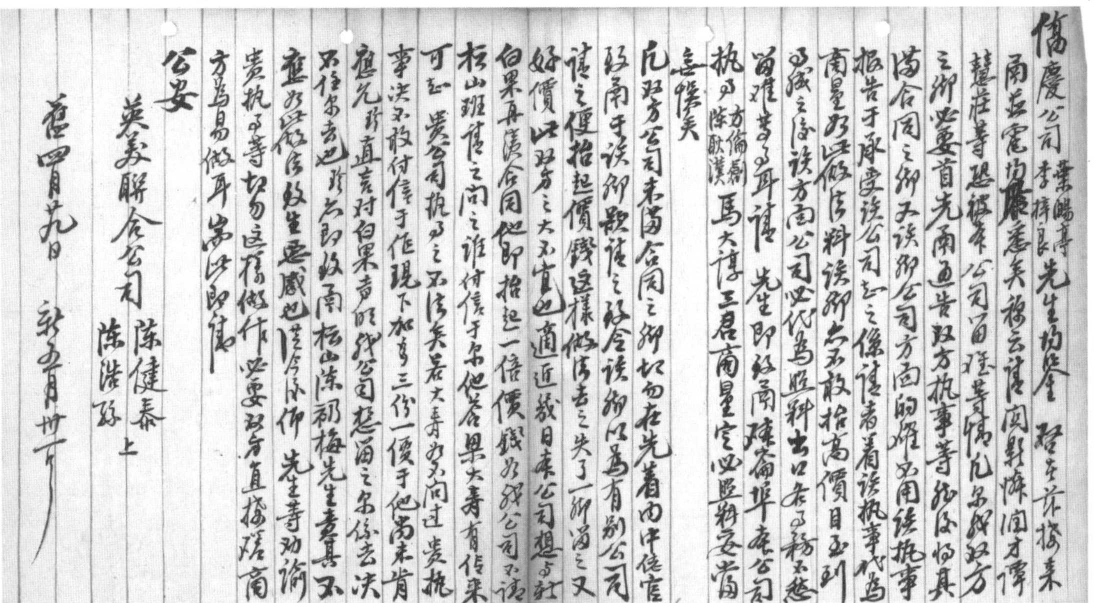

FIGURE 11.5: *Letter from the Anglo-American Joint Company (San Francisco) to Kue Hing Company, May 31, 1924.* Folder 0018, file 3, Yip Sang Family Series, Chung Collection, Rare Books and Special Collections, UBC Library.

the payment of a bond in return for a six-month entry permit renewable up to three years.

A stipulation on the contract explicitly disallows actors from joining any guild or occupational group, fearing that such involvement would foster an uncooperative spirit and acts of intransigence at the expense of the theatre company. In light of the overt disapproval of collective action, it is interesting to see in Figure 11.3 the announcement of a full slate of officers and the general membership of an actors' guild printed in the *Chinese Times* in April 1919. We do not have much information on this group except that some ninety-two individuals had agreed to take part in the public expression of solidarity and even defiance. Actors were transient figures and quintessential sojourners, making any organized activities hard to initiate and even harder to sustain. On this membership roll are noticeably less than a dozen actresses, which is indicative of traditional opera as a male-dominated performance space. More will be said below about the exceptional importance of female entertainers in an immigrant community of primarily adult males.

Although Wing Hong Lin ended up folding after two seasons, others followed in its footsteps. In January 1923 the Kue Hing Company was established by a group of Chinese merchants in British Columbia. Their business plans hinged on the successful sponsorship of an acting troupe to perform locally and then in the United States, beginning with Hawai'i and followed by potential theatres back on the continent. Conceived as a

3. The Kue Hing material is deposited in two separate locations. See "Theatre Management," n.d. and "Kue Hing Company," n.d.

4. The case of Kue Hing cannot be contained as a Canadian story. Whereas its business record in Canada ended abruptly in the spring of 1924, Rao has been able to trace some remnant of its business activities in Hawai'i on and off until 1929. Indeed, Rao's use of US government immigration files, Chinese American newspapers, and other research collections is most instructive in placing Chinese immigrant theatre on a transnational canvas (see Rao 2017, 297–303).

transnational operation, the company had to deal with numerous logistical, financial, and legal obstacles. Its archives consist almost entirely of internal correspondence, and one particular segment details an excruciating effort in summer 1923 to rescue the troupe detained by United States immigration authorities at the Seattle port of entry.[3] Lim Bang, a bilingual board member from Victoria, was dispatched immediately, and after twenty days of forceful and repeated representation, and having obtained paid assistance by immigration attorneys in Seattle as well as Washington, DC, the troupe was released and granted entry. Included in the telegraphic correspondence was a six-word telegram sent by a triumphant Lim Bang: "Trouble just over whole troupe landed" (Figure 11.4).

Unfortunately, trouble was not quite over for Kue Hing, rendering this moment of self-congratulations and exuberance ephemeral at best. As it turned out, the ensuing Hawaiian adventure failed to yield positive results, and subsequent planning to bring the troupe back to criss-cross the continent was grounded to a halt for unspecified reasons.[4] Indeed, aside from confronting a hostile immigration bureaucracy (both in Canada and the United States) armed with racial prejudice and assumption of fraud on the part of any and all Chinese, the theatre business was very competitive. Rivals fought over a range of issues, including favourable ruling by the immigration authorities (especially in the United States, where theatres lobbied for quotas regarding the numbers of actors they could sponsor), access to preferred venues, the scheduling of seasons, and, of course, the booking of actors and actresses of choice at one another's expense. Figure 11.5 shows a letter penned by two directors of the Anglo-American company based in San Francisco (with its headquarters in the Great China Theater; together with the Mandarin Theater, the two were regarded as powerhouses) in which they accused Kue Hing of malpractice. According to this letter, the two US and Canadian companies had swapped actors between them before, but by then Kue Hing had approached several famed performers still under contract with its San Francisco counterpart without the latter's consent. The unwarranted overture emboldened these individuals to bargain for more expensive contracts, the letter writers complained.

Commercial entertainment thrives on publicity, and Chinatown theatre was no different. In Vancouver, the first time a visiting troupe took out a daily advertisement in the Chinatown newspaper was in late 1918, trumpeting the presence of Cantonese opera as an increasingly regular part of Chinatown's public life.[5] Some advertisements give considerable details, especially when both the performers and the plays were unfamiliar to the audience. The majority of them are more modest than the one in Figure 11.6, in which the title of the play and the lead actor can be identified in bold font on the right. Equally noteworthy is an announcement to the left that the evening program would feature a special appreciation for a husband-and-wife team. Jinshan Bing and his spouse, Xin Guifei, were veteran performers on the North American circuit.

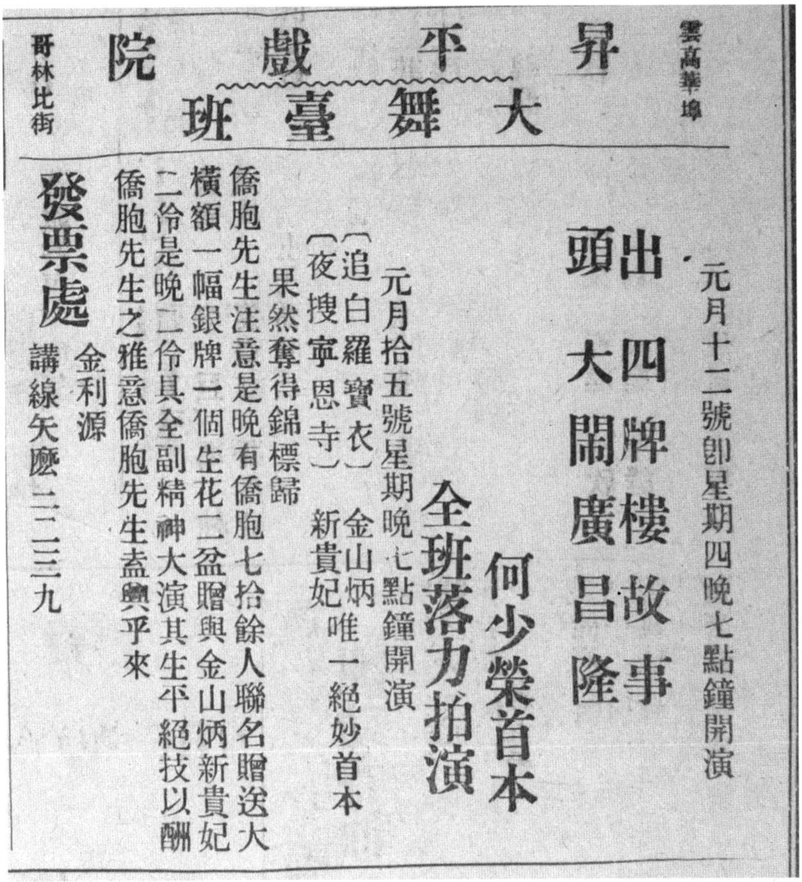

雲高華埠　哥林比街

昇平舞臺　大戲院班

元月十二號即星期四晚七點鐘開演

出四牌樓故事
頭大鬧廣昌隆　何少榮首本

全班落力拍演

元月拾五號星期晚七點鐘開演

〔追白羅寶衣〕金山炳
〔夜搜寧恩寺〕新貴妃　唯一絕妙首本

果然奪得錦標歸

僑胞先生注意是晚有僑胞七拾餘人聯名贈送大
橫額一幅銀牌一個生花二盆贈與金山炳新貴妃
二伶是晚二伶其全副精神大演其生平絕技以酬
僑胞先生之雅意僑胞先生盡與乎來

發票處　金利源　講線矢廳二三三九

FIGURE 11.6: *Theatre advertisement and a special notice on the farewell appreciation for a performing couple, 1928.* First published on January 12, 1928, in the Chinese Times (Vancouver). UBC Asian Library.

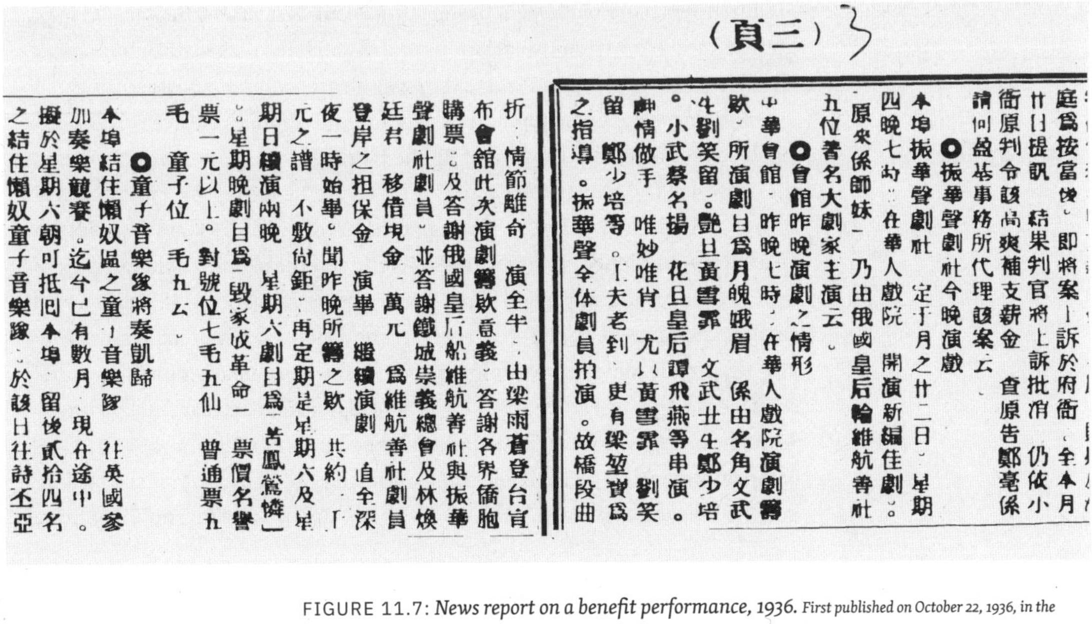

（頁三）

庭爲按當後，即將案一訴於府衙，全本月
廿日提訊，結果判官將上訴批消，仍依小
衙原判令該尚爽補支薪金，查原告鄭毫係
請何盈基事務所代理該案云。

●振華聲劇社今晚演戲

本埠振華聲劇社，定于月之廿二日，星期
四晚七點：在華人戲院開演新編佳劇，
原來係師妹，乃由俄國皇后輪維善社
九位著名大劇家主演云。

●會館昨晚演劇之情形

中華會館，昨晚七時：在華人戲院演劇警
所演劇目爲月魄娥眉，係由名角文武
生劉笑留。艷旦黃雪霏，文武丑鄭少培
小武蔡名揚，花旦皇后譚飛燕等串演。
腳情做手唯妙唯肖，尤以黃雪霏劉笑
留鄭少培等。工夫老到、更有梁垫寶爲
之指導。振華聲全体劇員拍演。故橋段曲
折：情節離奇，演全牛、由梁雨蒼登台官
布會舘此次演劇響欵意義、答謝各界僑胞
購票：及答謝俄國皇后船維善社與振華
聲劇社劇員、並答謝鐵城崇義總會及林煥
廷君，移借埠金一萬元，爲維航善社劇員
登岸之担保金演畢，繼續演劇，直全深
夜一時始畢。聞昨晚所響之欵，共約二千
元之譜，不數尚鉅：再定期是星期六及星
期日續演兩晚，星期六劇目爲「苦鳳鶯憐」
星期晚劇目爲「毀家成革命」，票價名譽
票一元以上。對號位七毛九仙，普通票九
毛，童子位。毛九仝。

●童子音樂隊將奏凱歸

本埠結住懶奴區之童，音樂隊，往英國家
加奏樂競賽。迄今已有數月、現在途中。
擬於星期六朝可抵回本埠，留後貳拾四名
之結住懶奴童子音樂隊，於該日往詩丕亞

FIGURE 11.7: *News report on a benefit performance, 1936.* First published on October 22, 1936, in the Chinese Times (Vancouver). UBC Asian Library.

5. See *Chinese Times*, September 5, 1918 to April 12, 1919.

6. Ng (2015, 146 and 164) recounts the couple's itinerary; see also pp. 177–80 for a discussion of sociocultural significance of such "rite of affection."

7. After the overthrow of the Qing imperial government in 1912, Sun Yat-sen reorganized his revolutionary base into a formal political party called the Guomindang, hoping it would capture power and guide China toward republicanism. However, the country stayed mired in factional politics for over a decade under rival warlords and contending parties. Even after the Guomindang became the ruling party in 1928, partisan politics lingered in Chinese communities abroad.

They had spent considerable time on the San Francisco stage before a five-month stint in Vancouver. The evening was toward the end of the couple's Canadian tour (after which they were New York bound), and over seventy people had signed up to present the two with a silk banner, a silver trophy, and two flower brocades. At the height of Chinatown theatre, such expression of affection added an element of festivity and heartfelt warmth to an immigrant community that suffered harshly under exclusion laws.[6]

What endeared Cantonese opera to the Chinese audience then was not simply a matter of its alluring artistry, the sonic resonance of the music, and the emotional intimacy aroused by their favourite plots. Opera performance was part entertainment and part social and communal ritual. The theatre was often a focal point of public celebration and collective solidarity. Figure 11.7 offers another excellent example in a report printed in the *Chinese Times*. In the fall of 1936, the Chinese Benevolent Association that acted as the community's spokesperson and an umbrella organization for all the Chinatown groups, was in financial straits. Jin Wah Sing, a musical society of opera enthusiasts and amateur musicians, joined a small group of professional actors in a three-night fundraiser. The second half of the report (on the left) draws attention to the generosity of a Chinese community leader who advanced $10,000 as bond money so that the professional group from the Canadian Pacific ocean liner the *Empress of Russia* could perform onshore for the occasion. The theatre was at once a site for the display of public leadership, non-partisanship, and a spirit of charity.

The local organizers and boosters were keen to tap into the existing social networks and organizational affiliations for marketing purposes. Figure 11.8 is an undated photograph taken at a reception hosted by another musical society, Ching Won, in Vancouver (probably in the late 1930s). The flag indicates that the society was pro-Guomindang (Chinese Nationalist Party)[7] in the politics of Chinatown. Upon arrival, a performing group was often chaperoned to pay their respects to various associations and dignitaries before its debut onstage. Needless to say, the common courtesy was also a sound business strategy.

Photographs of Chinatown theatre before the Pacific War are rare, and the small collection in the Vancouver Public Library were most likely taken inside the old Sing Ping Theatre on Columbia Street in the late 1930s. Figures 11.9 and 11.10 shed light on the theatre through the lens of gender. Figure 11.9 captures an attentive audience of all males: a reflection of the skewed demographics of the Chinese immigrant population. Hence actresses were exceedingly popular as the main draw of a delightful spectacle and as an object of male fantasy on and offstage. Female companionship and family were not completely inconceivable though, as Figure 11.10 shows an unidentified actress fully gowned with her headgear and make-up adoring a toddler (possibly hers) with a male companion (perhaps a spouse). Using Vancouver's Chinatown as the backdrop in their respective novels, both Dennis Chong (1994) and Wayson Choy (1999)

FIGURE 11.8: *Tea reception hosted by a Chinatown musical society for a newly arriving acting group, late 1930s.* Photograph # 50481, Vancouver Public Library.

FIGURE 11.9: *Audience inside a theatre, late 1930s.* Photograph #48412, Vancouver Public Library.

FIGURE 11.10: *In the Green Room, late 1930s.* Photograph #48421, Vancouver Public Library.

depict the commonplace presence of women and children among audiences on the eve of the Pacific War.

Compared to many other components of the Canadian mosaic encompassed in this anthology, the history of Chinese Canadian theatre has yet to receive much scholarly attention and take its place in the relevant literature. The brief discussion of select documents in this chapter clearly indicates that extant sources in text and image alone are wide-ranging, not to mention the plentiful material artifacts preserved (Liu 2019). Moreover, preliminary work has been done to pave the way for further inquiry to acquaint us with both the Cantonese stage that enchanted an early generation of Chinese migrants and the trans-Pacific world they lived in.

Bibliography and Further Reading

Chong, Dennis. 1994. *The Concubine's Children: Portrait of a Family Divided*. Toronto: Penguin Canada.

Choy, Wayson. 1999. *Paper Shadows: A Memoir of a Past Lost and Found*. New York: Penguin.

Johnson, Elizabeth. 1996. "Cantonese Opera in its Canadian Context: The Contemporary Vitality of an Old Tradition." *Theatre Research in Canada* 17 (1): 24–45.

———. 2005–06. "Evidence of an Ephemeral Art: Cantonese Opera in Vancouver's Chinatown." *BC Studies* 148 (Winter): 55–91.

"Kue Hing Company File Regarding a Chinese Acting Troupe." n.d. Yip Sang Family Series, folder 0018, file 3, Chung Collection, Rare Books and Special Collections, UBC Library.

Liu, April. 2019. *Divine Threads: The Visual and Material Culture of Cantonese Opera.* Vancouver: Museum of Anthropology at UBC.

Matthews, J.S. 1947. "Chinese Theatre." December 4, 1947. AM 54, vol. 13, 506-C-5, file 6, City of Vancouver Archives.

Ng, Wing Chung. 2015. *The Rise of Cantonese Opera.* Urbana: University of Illinois Press; Hong Kong: HKU Press.

Rao, Nancy. 2017. *Chinatown Opera Theater in North America.* Urbana: University of Illinois Press.

Sebryk, Karrie M. 1995. "A History of Chinese Theatre in Victoria." MA thesis, University of Victoria.

Stanley, Timothy. 2005. "Yip Sang." In *Dictionary of Canadian Biography*, vol. 15. Toronto: University of Toronto / Université Laval, 2003–. Accessed October 18, 2018. http:// www.biographi.ca/en/bio/yip_sang_15E.html.

"Theatre Management—Kue Hing Co. Ltd." n.d. Yi Family and Yip Sang Ltd. fonds, Add. MSS 1108, 612-F-7, City of Vancouver Archives.

"Wing Hong Lin Theatre Records." n.d. Sam Kee Papers, Add. MSS 571, 566-G-4, City of Vancouver Archives.

Yee, Paul. 1986. "Sam Kee: A Chinese Business in Early Vancouver." *BC Studies*, no. 69–70, 70–96.

12 : *The Man Who Went* (1916)

Well-Made in Canada

ANTHONY J. VICKERY

WILLIAM ANDREW TREMAYNE was born in 1864 in Portland, Maine, while his Canadian parents were on vacation there. While few details about his life are known, he seems to have grown up and lived his entire life in Montreal. *Lovell's Montreal Directory* lists him from 1890 through 1938 at a number of addresses in and around Westmount with his various professions noted as clerk for the Grand Trunk Railway, editor, journalist, author, and, in 1937–38, shortly before his death in 1939, stage director. His first produced play was titled *The Notary* (1893), but his later plays—specifically, *A Secret Warrant* (1897) and *The Dagger and the Cross* (1899) for the American actor-manager Robert Bruce Mantell—brought him his greatest successes (Edwards 1982). In his obituary, an anonymous speaker is quoted as saying that Tremayne was the "most popular and energetic of all producers of amateur organizations and must have produced over a thousand shows" in Montreal ("W.A. Tremayne" 1939). This number of productions is probably hyperbole, but at the time of his death he was remembered as an active member of the amateur theatre community in Montreal. Tremayne was a prolific playwright, with fourteen plays copyrighted in the United States and twenty other extant plays that were mostly one-acts.

The Man Who Went, which Tremayne wrote in 1916, concerns the intrigues of a number of spies in England shortly before the outbreak of the First World War in 1914.[1] The action centres on the delivery of a sensitive message to Vienna. Jack Thornton is a King's Messenger entrusted with couriering this message to the British Ambassador in Austria-Hungary at the extremely tense moment just before the outbreak of warfare. Jack is seduced and drugged by the Countess Wanda von Holtzberg, an Austrian spy who steals the message and plans to deliver it to two other spies: the Baron von Arnheim and his henchman Hogue. However, another young Englishman, Dick Kent, appears and, though seeming to be a foolish individual, is actually a sophisticated spy in the service of the British government à la James Bond who ultimately thwarts the plotting of the Baron, Countess, and Hogue. Woven into the plot is a love story involving Jack's sister, Evelyn Thornton, and Dick Kent, who had previously met in Canada and who are a couple by the conclusion of the play.

The first performance of *The Man Who Went* took place in Toronto in September 1916, approximately two years after the events depicted in the narrative. The war would be foremost in the minds of the audience, as news

1. The play was initially titled *The Black Feather*, but was copyrighted and published in the United States as *The Man Who Went* in 1918.

FIGURE 12.1: *Grand Opera House, Adelaide St. W., Toronto. Site of the first performance of* The Man Who Went. *Item 26, fonds 1478, City of Toronto Archives.*

and casualty reports were published every day in the Toronto newspapers. The audience would also be aware that, while Dick's mission in the play was a success, war had not been averted. Since the war had been raging for just over two years with Germany and Austria-Hungary, the audience would be predisposed to root for the British and Canadian characters and be against "the three sinister figures of the German spies," as detailed by the reviewer from *The Globe*.

Although Tremayne did not necessarily try to establish himself as a "Canadian" playwright in his career, setting his plays mostly abroad in Europe, *The Man Who Went* is marked by its many references to Canada and the colonies as well as having a Canadian, Evelyn Thornton, as a primary character. The play often contrasts the Old and New Worlds. There are frequent references to colonies and colonials (mostly meaning Canadians) as less sophisticated or civilized than their European counterparts. However, the main character, Dick Kent, greatly admires Canada, especially as personified by the character of Evelyn, who is "modern" and unrestrained, particularly in comparison to Lady Caxton and the Countess. There are Canadian details mentioned in the play such as long-distance train travel and cities such as Winnipeg and Edmonton. Tremayne was writing for Canadian and American audiences who would find humour in quaint, Old-World (and in the case of Lady Caxton, Victorian) attitudes. Theatre scholar Murray Edwards notes that much of the Canadian content was merely window dressing, including the scene where Evelyn gives Dick a flower and "he stands looking after her in admiration, and then, lifting the flower to his lips says, 'Made in Canada.' This, of course, would have impressed the Canadian audience for it was a direct reference to a government-sponsored drive to make the citizens conscious of their duty to buy Canadian goods" (Edwards 1968, 163).

This play was typical commercial fare similar to other plays mounted on Broadway during the early twentieth century and much like those that toured extensively across both the United States and Canada. The production that preceded this play at the Grand Opera House was the light opera *The Bohemian Girl* by Michael W. Balfe and Alfred Bunn (first produced in New York in 1844, but then later on Broadway as recently as 1911). It was followed by *Twin Beds* by Salisbury Field and Margaret Mayo (originally produced on Broadway in 1914), which the reviewer in *The Globe* summed up as very funny but "there is no 'plot'" (Parkhurst 1916b). At the Royal Alexandra (the main rival to the Grand Opera House) was a touring production of a melodramatic courtroom drama *On Trial*, the first play written by Elmer Rice (which first appeared on Broadway in 1914) (Parkhurst 1916a).[2] None of the productions mentioned, including *The Man Who Went*, contained challenging subject matter. At the same time that *The Man Who Went* was opening, the most popular cinema attraction was D.W. Griffith's *The Birth of a Nation* (1915), which achieved its hundredth showing at Massey Hall. Other than *The Man Who Went*, all of the performances detailed above were American in origin. However, editorial treatment of Tremayne's play in *The Globe* (other than mentioning that Tremayne was from Montreal) was no different from the other plays mounted at the two theatres.

The play adheres closely to the well-made play structure established by Eugène Scribe and developed by Victorien Sardou in the nineteenth century right down to the plot hinging on the importance of a scrap of paper: a dramaturgical feature that echoes Sardou's *A Scrap of Paper* (1861). Both plays rely on information known to the audience, but not to all characters, as well as information that would be interpreted differently by different characters. A particular example in *The Man Who Went* is the "Beware of Dog" poster. In Act I, scene 2, the audience hears Dick on the telephone receiving intelligence about where the Baron will meet with his henchman Hogue: "near a poster, with the words 'beware of the guard dog' written on it." In Act II, scene 1, the Baron is waiting in front of this poster and interacts with Hogue; Dick is ostensibly hidden nearby, as shortly afterwards he emerges from the bushes. The Baron thinks this spot is secure, but Dick knows that this is where the critical interaction between the spies will take place. Later, Dick makes a joke about the poster:

SIR GEORGE. *Dropped off?*

DICK. *Yes, off to sleep—and I had such a jolly rum dream—I thought that*
after all there was a dog here, you know, but he wasn't a watch dog.

SIR GEORGE. *No?*

LADY CAXTON. *What kind of a dog was he?*

DICK. *A German poodle—and one of the trickiest little devils you ever saw. I*
was trying to catch him when somebody woke me up by talking excitedly.

The action gradually grows more intense until the climax in Act III, scene
1, when Dick recovers the papers stolen from Jack by the Baroness and delivers
them to Vienna. Act IV is typical of a well-made play where all is revealed and
society is rebalanced, allowing the spectator to leave the theatre, in Scribe's
parlance, *bien content* (or happy), with no unresolved plot points; in the case
of this play, Dick reveals that he is a master spy, the day (and Jack) is saved,
and the romance between Dick and Evelyn can continue. For this sourcebook, only an excerpt of the play (the final scene) is included in order to give a
sense of the written qualities of the overall play. Due to the length of the play
and its predictable well-made play construction, which dictates that all of the
machinations that take place during the play must be resolved and explained
in the final scene, this decision will allow readers to focus on the thematic
and stylistic elements discussed in this introduction. A synopsis of the play
precedes the excerpt.

After the debut of this play in 1916, Tremayne began to fade from sight as
an active playwright (Edwards 1982, 45). He continued to write plays, but after
the First World War, theatrical tastes changed and his type of play was seen
as old-fashioned. His plays depended on the actor-manager system of theatre,
which dominated the nineteenth and early twentieth centuries and fell out
of favour after the war (Edwards 1982, 45). The star system in the theatre with
the actor-manager at its head transferred to the film industry, and producers
in the commercial theatre took the place of actor-managers as the driving
force behind the creation of new productions. As well, touring theatre, which
provided a great deal of opportunity for Tremayne's plays, almost entirely
disappeared in the 1920s, as most Canadian live-performance venues switched
to the more popular and much less expensive film. Tremayne's last years
in Montreal were very difficult as he was impoverished. He died just a few
months after the beginning of the Second World War.

Most well-made plays by Scribe and Sardou contained an element of
social criticism. Scribe's plays were often set in the past, but commented on
the contemporary situation in France. Sometimes, as in the case of Sardou's
Let's Get a Divorce (co-written with Emile de Najac in 1880 and dealing with
proposals to legalize divorce in France that were introduced in the 1870s, but
not passed until 1881), a play could comment on events then taking place.
Politicized commentary is present in this play in the antiquated attitudes
of the German and Austrian spies, as well as in the older generation of

English characters whose archaic ways rooted in the world of the nineteenth century led to the calamity of the First World War. Conservative attitudes are expressed by Evelyn's guardians, Sir George and Lady Caxton, who make negative comments about the unsophisticated nature of colonials and, in particular for Lady Caxton, the scandalous behaviour of Evelyn, as she is caught alone in an entirely innocent situation with Dick, a male who is not a relative. Tremayne's play in some ways calls to mind attitudes expressed over sixty years later in John Gray's *Billy Bishop Goes to War*. The parallel with the most resonance is between Lady Caxton and Lady St. Helier. The two characters express very similar opinions of colonials, which both playwrights use to point out the condescending attitudes of British imperialists.

Three of Tremayne's plays were produced on Broadway, and there was the possibility that he could have had a successful career as a dramatist there,[3] but by all indications he worked in Canada for his entire career and was heavily engaged in amateur theatre in Montreal until a few years before his death. His obituary states that he had stayed in Montreal during his life to take care of relatives rather than seeking out fame in New York ("W.A. Tremayne" 1939). At the time, the perception was that to be successful in the professional theatre, you had to leave Canada for the United States (or Great Britain). While there was a great deal of professional theatrical activity in Canada during Tremayne's lifetime, it was seen as either of secondary importance to foreign companies (local stock companies were only used by theatre owners when touring companies were not available) or merely facilitating the performances of those foreign companies. This feeling reflected the perception that Canada was as much a cultural colony of the United States as an actual colony of Great Britain. This colonialism is reflected in the play itself in the attitudes expressed by some characters about Canada, as noted above. The initial production of this play took place a year before the Battle of Vimy Ridge during the First World War. During the battle, the units of the Canadian Army fought together for the first time, and many historians mark this battle as the moment Canada started to move out from under the shadow of Great Britain and onto the world stage. However, cultural colonialism lingers to this day. In the cultural sector, this is usually expressed when artists feel they need to be acknowledged abroad to be successful or when audiences assume that Canadian plays, movies, or television productions in general are inferior to American ones.

When Great Britain declared war on Germany on August 4, 1914, Canada, which did not have control of its own foreign policy, was automatically at war as well and contributed troops to fight in France under the control of the British Army. The structure and plot of *The Man Who Went* reflects the effect of the imperial connection as a former colony of Great Britain in its positive portrayal of the actions of the British government of the time and the approval of the Canadian aspects of Evelyn by the English secret agent, Dick Kent.

Bibliography and Further Reading

Benson, Eugene, and L.W. Conolly. 1987. *English-Canadian Theatre*. Toronto: Oxford University Press.

Bulliet, C.J. 1918. *Robert Mantell's Romance*. Boston: John W. Luce and Company.

Cardwell, Douglas. 1983. "The Well-Made Play of Eugène Scribe." *The French Review* 56 (6): 876–84.

Edwards, Murray D. 1968. *A Stage in Our Past: English-Language Theatre in Eastern Canada from the 1790's to 1914*. Toronto: University of Toronto Press.

———. 1982. "A Playwright from the Canadian Past: W.A. Tremayne (1864–1939)." *Theatre Research in Canada* 3 (1): 43–50.

Lovell's Montreal Directory for 1891–92: Containing an Alphabetical Directory of the Citizens, a Street Directory, an Advertisers Classified Business Directory, and a Miscellaneous Directory...Corrected to 25th June, 1891. Montreal: Lovell, 1891. CIHM/ICMH microfiche series, no. 37066. https://www.canadiana.ca/view/oocihm.37066.

"Mr. Hilliard at Hoyt's." 1895. *New York Times*, September 3, 1895, 3.

Parkhurst, E.R. 1916a. "Music and the Drama," *The Globe*, September 5, 1916, 6.

———. 1916b. "Music and the Drama." *The Globe*, September 19, 1916, 8.

"W.A. Tremayne, Actor, Dies." 1939. *Montreal Star*, December 4, 1939, 17.

"W.A. Tremayne." n.d. Internet Broadway Database. Accessed May 17, 2018. https://www.ibdb.com/broadway-cast-staff/w-a-tremayne-399652.

The Man Who Went[1]

WILLIAM ANDREW TREMAYNE

1. The play was published in Boston by Walter H. Baker and Co. in 1918.

Originally Produced as THE BLACK FEATHER

CHARACTERS

BARON VON ARNHEIM, *in the German Secret Service*

JACK THORNTON, *a King's Messenger*

EVELYN THORNTON, *Jack's sister*

SIR GEORGE CAXTON, *in the British Foreign Office*

LADY VENETIA CAXTON, *his wife*

DICK KENT, *in the English Secret Service*

HOGUE, *a German spy*

COUNTESS WANDA VON HOLTZBERG, *in the Austrian Secret Service*

BARNES, *a chauffeur*

PATTON, *a keeper*

The Action of the play takes place in the early summer of 1914.

SUMMARY

ACT I, SCENE ONE

Setting: Jack Thornton's Apartments, No. 7, Portman Square, London, Early evening.

The scene opens with Jack Thornton and the Baron von Arnheim getting ready to go out in the evening to a party. Their conversation turns to the Countess Wanda von Holtzberg, who is a beautiful young widow. Jack is a confidential courier for the British Government and, unknown to Jack, the Baron and the Countess are German and Austrian spies, respectively, tasked with intercepting any correspondence that Jack may carry. Jack's sister, Evelyn Thornton, arrives and reveals that she and Jack were raised in Canada. Evelyn disapproves of Jack's friendship with the Baron and the Countess. Lady Venetia Caxton and Sir George Caxton, Evelyn and Jack's aunt and uncle and Evelyn's guardians, arrive and put forth conservative views reminiscent of the Victorian era, now in the past by approximately fifteen years. Evelyn states that she has some "business to talk over" with Jack, but she will wait until after the party. The Baron is invited to the Caxton estate the next week and all depart for the party, but not before the Baron makes a last-minute phone call to the Countess asking her to delay Jack at the party that evening.

Setting: The same as Scene One, 11 p.m.

The scene opens with Dick Kent talking on the phone in French; he makes a note about "beware of dog," a statement whose meaning will become apparent in the next scene as the place the spies are to meet. Evelyn enters and we quickly learn that while Dick and Evelyn do not formally know each other, they have met before. Evelyn questions why Dick is in her brother's apartment and he relates a story that he was given the key to No. 7 Portman Square by a friend of his. However, we learn there is a No 7. East and a No. 7 West—the key Dick was given fit the lock here by chance, or so he states. Lady Caxton and Sir George enter and are shocked to find Evelyn with a strange man. Evelyn clarifies for them that they met on a train in Canada some years before when Dick loaned her a blue mackintosh during an unexpected stop of the train in the rain, but she did not actually learn his name back then. Shortly after more formal intro-ductions, we find out that a great deal is expected of Dick because he is the son of a famous British diplomat, but he has to date a reputation as an idle man. Jack and the Baron enter and all that has transpired in the scene since Evelyn arrived is retold. The Baron thinks he recognizes Dick but cannot remember from where. Evelyn and Dick begin a gentle courtship. Dick finds an envelope with the Countess Wanda Von Holtzberg's crest on it, an iron hand holding a single black eagle's feather, which he asks for and is granted permission to keep. Soon after, the gathering breaks up and we learn that all of them, without Dick, of course, are to meet at the Caxton estate in the next few days.

Setting: A corner of Sir George Caxton's estate at Thorncliffe, during the day. The Baron's henchman Hogue is introduced. We learn that there is a crisis in Serbia (the crisis that would eventually lead to the outbreak of the First World War—a fact which would not be lost on the original audience of the play). Hogue is dismissed to return later to courier some stolen documents to Vienna. The Countess Wanda Von Hotlzberg is introduced and we find she is a reluctant spy, but has agreed to seduce Jack and steal his confidential letters, which the Baron will then pass on to Hogue. The Countess is to recognize Hogue when he gives her an envelope containing an item from the Countess's family crest—a black feather. Lady Caxton and Sir George enter and we find out that the Countess must return to London and she and the Baron exit. Dick emerges from the bushes where he has been for some time and points out the sign with "beware of dog" written on it—the meeting place for the Baron and Hogue that Dick was told about at the top of Act I, Scene Two. Evelyn and Jack enter and we find out that Jack must meet his supervisor, Lord Royallieu, and possibly courier documents to Vienna that evening. Evelyn and Dick continue their courtship from the previous scene. The scene ends with Evelyn giving some flowers to Dick, which he presses to his lips saying "made in Canada!"

ACT II, SCENE TWO

Setting: The same as Act II, Scene One, night lit by moonlight.

Dick is onstage at open and is talking to an armed servant. Then, Dick hides
and the Baron and Hogue enter. The Baron gives a letter to Hogue to be given
to the Countess identifying him as the courier who will take the documents
she is stealing from Jack. The Baron exits and Dick emerges from hiding. Dick
takes the letter from Hogue, creates a disturbance and has Hogue arrested by
Sir George. Dick drives off to London with his servant.

ACT III, SCENE ONE

Setting: Jack Thornton's Apartments, No. 7, Portman Square, London, night.
Jack and the Countess are together on stage at the opening of the scene. Jack
has secret state documents in his possession (instructions for the British
Ambassador in Vienna on the eve of the Serbian Crisis). The Countess drugs
Jack and steals the documents without Jack's knowledge. Dick, pretending
to be Hogue and using a letter with a black feather in it, gets the documents
from the Countess and hides. Jack awakens and departs. Dick comes back out,
still posing as Hogue, and Evelyn enters. She inadvertently reveals that Dick
is not Hogue. At that moment, Sir George also arrives and wants to arrest
Dick for the disturbance he caused at his estate in the last scene. Dick eventually dodges Sir George's servant and escapes to Charing Cross Station, Jack's
destination.

ACT IV, SCENE ONE

JACK THORNTON'S Apartments, No. 7, Portman Square, London.[2]
Time, about four days after the start of the play.
Afternoon.
*The curtain rises on an empty stage; the door—bell rings; EVELYN enters from door
L. and crossing to door C.[3] opens it; SIR GEORGE and LADY CAXTON enter; LADY
CAXTON casts a look of disapproval at EVELYN, and, without a word, sweeps down
to sofa R. and sits.*

EVELYN. Good-afternoon, Aunty. (*LADY CAXTON. pays no attention to her;
     EVELYN goes up to SIR GEORGE. and kisses him.*) How are you, Uncle
     George?

SIR GEORGE. *clears his throat in a rather embarrassed fashion, glancing at LADY
CAXTON.*

SIR GEORGE. Ahem! My dear Evelyn, your aunt and I have called to have a
     serious talk with you.
EVELYN. (*With a look of comical horror.*) Again? On the same subject?
SIR GEORGE. (*Nodding rather resignedly.*) Yes.

EVELYN. Don't you think we thrashed all that out thoroughly the last time?

LADY CAXTON. I do not know what you and your uncle have thrashed out, I only know that I have a last word to say on the subject.

EVELYN. Another?

LADY CAXTON. And then the matter is closed forever.

EVELYN. (*With a relieved expression.*) Oh, well, let's get it over then.

LADY CAXTON. Am I to understand that you still persist in your intention of occupying these rooms—alone?

EVELYN. My brother's rooms? Yes—till his return.

LADY CAXTON. And are you aware that another man besides your brother has a key to these rooms?

EVELYN. Yes—that is exactly the reason I am stopping.

LADY CAXTON. (*In a tone of horror.*) Evelyn!

EVELYN. After the strange happenings of last Monday—you'll allow they were strange.

SIR GEORGE. Strange! Good Heavens! They were weird.

EVELYN. I agree with you. Well, after the weird happenings of last Monday, without seeing or speaking to any of us, the Baron packed up his belongings, sent you a hastily scribbled note that he had been called away on important business, and departed.

LADY CAXTON. I can quite understand why.

EVELYN. Can you?

LADY CAXTON. Yes. He had no doubt heard from his friend, Mr. Hogue, of the extraordinary events which had taken place, and not wishing to be further connected with anything so unpleasant, he, with a delicacy which is characteristic of him, took the quietest way out of the dilemma. I think he was very wise.

EVELYN. I am not questioning his wisdom; but why did he not return his latch-key?

LADY CAXTON. Perhaps he forgot it.

EVELYN. At the time of his departure?—perhaps; for more than three days since, it seems hardly possible; however, that is my reason for wishing to remain here, and till Jack comes back or the key is returned—here I stay.

SIR GEORGE. My dear Evelyn—

LADY CAXTON. Have you no respect for the family honor?

EVELYN. A great deal—that's why I'm stopping. I am afraid it may be in danger—but not through me.

LADY CAXTON. What do you mean?

EVELYN. I do not trust the Baron.

LADY CAXTON. Nonsense! The Baron is the soul of courtesy and good breeding. If you want to distrust any one, distrust your friend, Mr. Kent, who, by the way, has also a latch-key to these apartments. If the family honor has an enemy, mark my words, he is the man.

SIR GEORGE. Now look here, Evelyn—once and for all—

4. Finely ground tobacco meant to be inhaled.

EVELYN. (*Raising her hand to stop him.*) Once and for all, Uncle George, it's no use to argue. Till I was twenty-one you were my guardian—you are still my father's trustee and my honored friend and adviser, but I am a free agent, and when it comes to a case of duty, I shall act according to my own reason.

LADY CAXTON. Very well then, George, I shall speak my final word. If Evelyn persists in this highly improper conduct, from now on I wash my hands of her.

EVELYN. Very well, Aunty, consider the washing done, the towel supplied, and your fingers dried and "comfy"—and let us get on to more interesting matters. (*LADY CAXTON stares at EVELYN, speechless with indignation, takes salts bottle from her bag and sniffs it at intervals.*) Have you heard any news of Jack?

SIR GEORGE. Not a word. In spite of my warning, the police let that fellow Kent slip through their fingers. I laid a complaint at headquarters, but they seemed quite indifferent; then I appealed to Lord Royallieu, told him of my anxiety about Jack, and asked for news; he shook his head enigmatically, said there was no very definite news of Jack, but not to worry—and that he would investigate the police affair. Then he took a pinch of snuff[4] and told me to be calm!

LADY CAXTON. And very good advice, too—that is what I am always telling you, George.

SIR GEORGE. (*In a burst of indignation.*) Confound you and Lord Royallieu both—mind your own business. I'm an Englishman with a Constitutional right to the use of my own temper within the limits of the law, and I'm d--d if I'll keep calm if I don't want to!

He rises and crosses angrily down to L.; the door C. is suddenly opened, and JACK *appears at it; his dress is disordered and untidy, his face unshaven and haggard; he pauses in the door, looking around wildly; the others all turn to him,* LADY CAXTON *and* EVELYN *rising, and exclaim, together "Jack" Then* EVELYN *and* SIR GEORGE *go up to him.*

EVELYN. Jack, dear, what has happened?

SIR GEORGE. Jack, my boy— (*JACK comes down with uncertain steps to chair R. of table and sinks into it as if exhausted.* EVELYN *follows him down;* SIR GEORGE *goes down L. of table;* LADY CAXTON *R.C.*) Jack, you have come from Vienna?

JACK. Yes.

SIR GEORGE. And the papers—you took them there in safety?

JACK. I thought so.

SIR GEORGE. Thought so?

JACK. I took the package Lord Royallieu gave me and which never, to my knowledge, was out of my possession from the time I left Thorncliffe till I

placed it in the hands of our Ambassador at Vienna; but when he opened
the package, the papers were—blank.

EVELYN.

LADY CAXTON.} Blank!

SIR GEORGE.

SIR GEORGE sinks into a chair L. of table; LADY CAXTON sinks on sofa R.C.
EVELYN stands behind JACK's chair, a look of horror on her face.

SIR GEORGE. Good God! You came straight from Thorncliffe here?

JACK. Yes.

SIR GEORGE. You spoke to no one on the train?

JACK. To no one.

SIR GEORGE. You can swear to that?

JACK. Yes; there was only one man in the compartment with me—a laborer—
and he left at the first station beyond Thorncliffe; after that I was alone.

SIR GEORGE. From Victoria you drove straight to these rooms?

JACK. Yes.

EVELYN. When you arrived, was the Countess here?

JACK. (*Looking up at her with a startled expression.*) No.

EVELYN. When did she come?

JACK. How do you know—

EVELYN. Never mind how—we know that she was here. How did she come?

JACK. (*Reluctantly.*) A few minutes after—when I was packing my valise.

EVELYN. Why?

JACK. (*With an effort.*) She wanted to say good-bye. At Thorncliffe she had
asked me to call on her before I left London, but afraid of delay, I refused—
so she came to me.

SIR GEORGE. She was here with you—alone?

JACK. Yes. (*LADY CAXTON exhibits consternation.*)

EVELYN. You are quite sure that she could not have tampered with the
papers?

JACK. Good God! What are you thinking of? Of course not. I tell you they never
left the inside pocket of my vest or the despatch case from Thorncliffe to
Vienna.

SIR GEORGE. You are sure of that?

There is a pause; JACK seems to struggle with himself, and then speaks with an effort.

JACK. Quite sure.

EVELYN. Why did you hesitate?

JACK. Because I wanted to make certain I was telling the truth. (*Turning
quickly to SIR GEORGE as if to change the subject.*) You are sure the papers
given me at Thorncliffe were the genuine thing?

SIR GEORGE. Do you think Royallieu is in his dotage to send you on a fool's errand like that?

JACK. But—how—how —

SIR GEORGE. How—how? Some one must have taken them; you must have slept.

JACK. I never closed my eyes between Charing Cross and Vienna.

SIR GEORGE. But how the devil did it happen? Papers don't change without the aid of human hands.

JACK. I don't know—I don't know; I've thought and thought till I've almost gone mad, but I can't understand. (*A pause.*)

SIR GEORGE. (*Slowly.*) What did they say over there?

JACK. Not much—it's not their way. They questioned me closely, and then dismissed me to another room. I stayed there two hours—suffering torments. Then they sent for me. They told me to take the next train for London and report the loss to Lord Royallieu, and see if I could get any trace of the papers.

SIR GEORGE. That's d--d funny; you'd have thought they'd have kept you for investigation.

JACK. (*Eagerly, as if catching at a straw.*) Yes, but they didn't; they let me go— that showed they still trusted me, don't you think so?

SIR GEORGE. I don't know what to think; it's an infernal muddle—my head's in a whirl.

EVELYN. Have you been to Lord Royallieu?

JACK. Not yet—I—I came here first.

EVELYN. Why?

JACK. Because—I—I can't tell why. I was hoping against hope—I thought—oh, I don't know what I thought, only that here—

EVELYN. Here is the only place the papers could possibly have changed hands. Jack, you're keeping something back.

JACK. I'm not—what do you mean? Oh, for God's sake don't torture me. (*He rises and makes a move toward door C. then stops.*) I'm going to Royallieu now. Where's the Baron?

SIR GEORGE. Called away on important business—packed up and left the morning after you went.

EVELYN. And took his latch-key with him. Since then I've been stopping here.

JACK. You?

LADY CAXTON. Yes, contrary to the advice of her friends and relatives, and in defiance of all known laws of propriety.

JACK. And why did you do this?

EVELYN. In case some one of importance might call and find you out.

JACK. (*Eagerly.*) There—there—has been no one here?

EVELYN. No one. (*Looking at him earnestly.*) Were you expecting some one?

JACK. No, no—I only asked. (*He goes up to door C.*)

LADY CAXTON. One moment. Evelyn and Sir George are strangely forgetful of important facts. Have you seen anything of Mr. Kent?

JACK. (*Puzzled.*) Kent—Kent—(*As if he had forgotten the name.*) Oh, that silly ass—(*As if remembering.*) No.

SIR GEORGE. And you didn't see him here—in this room, before you left for Vienna?

JACK. (*Down a little C.*) Certainly not. What on earth should he be doing here?

LADY CAXTON. He might have made another mistake in the numbers.

SIR GEORGE. We have reason to suspect Mr. Kent of being a foreign spy.

JACK. What rot! He hasn't got brains enough.

EVELYN. I'm not sure that he hasn't got more brains than you think, but I don't believe he is a spy.

JACK. Well, it's no use talking. I haven't set eyes on him since the day at Thorncliffe. I'm off to Royallieu's.

He moves dejectedly to door C.; EVELYN *follows him and lays her hands on his shoulders, looking earnestly up into his face.*

EVELYN. And then?

JACK. God knows. It's ruin and disgrace anyway—a bullet in my head would be the best end of it all.

EVELYN. No, Jack, not that—(*With deep emotion, but very quietly.*) That would be a coward's way out of it—and you're not a coward. Promise me, not that. (*A pause.*) Your word of honor, Jack.

JACK. Very well—it doesn't much matter;—I promise.

EVELYN. God bless you, dear. (*She throws her arms around his neck and kisses him, then speaks to him almost in a whisper.*) Don't give up hope—after the night comes morning.

JACK *exits quickly at door C.*

SIR GEORGE. (*Sinking in chair L. of table.*) Well, I'll be—

LADY CAXTON. George!

SIR GEORGE. Well, it's enough to make a saint swear—and I'm no saint!

LADY CAXTON. (*With an air of gentle resignation.*) No.

SIR GEORGE. What the devil can have become of those papers!

LADY CAXTON. The explanation is very simple.

SIR GEORGE. (*Staring at her, with a gasp.*) Oh, is it? Then perhaps you'll kindly enlighten my ignorance.

LADY CAXTON. Certainly. (*With an air of finality.*) Mr. Kent.

EVELYN. (*Coming C.*) What do you mean?

LADY CAXTON. He took them.

EVELYN. But how?

LADY CAXTON. My dear Evelyn, I am not versed in the ways of crime, nor do I
pretend to understand the workings of the criminal mind; I am not dealing
in theories, I am merely stating facts.

SIR GEORGE. Facts? Good Lord! Facts! Why, you haven't got a fact that couldn't
be torn to pieces in a minute in any court.

LADY CAXTON. (*Looking him over, contemptuously.*) My dear George, for a
diplomatist you are singularly lacking in intelligence, which unfortunately
I am powerless to supply.

SIR GEORGE stares at her in speechless indignation, unable to express his feelings.

EVELYN. Well, I'm not a diplomatist, and I have no facts or theories—only a
woman's instinct, sharpened by the danger of those she loves—and I tell
you the Countess and the Baron are at the bottom of this.

LADY CAXTON. Preposterous! Except for her indiscretion in visiting Jack's
rooms, the Countess is one of the most charming women I ever met; as for
the Baron—well—(*She shrugs her shoulders with a hopeless gesture, as if it
were impossible to make them understand.*) Oh, what's the use of talking?

SIR GEORGE. My dear Evelyn, you are altogether wrong. I know I objected
to Jack's intimacy with them, but that was merely a matter of policy on
account of his position. Why, the Count Von Szalras, the Countess's uncle,
is one of the most prominent men in the Austrian Embassy, and the Baron
came to us with unimpeachable letters of introduction. These people are
not the stuff spies are made of.

EVELYN. That's just where I differ with you—I think they are. The Baron
laughs at you for being afraid of the British bogey of the foreign spy, and
he is right—because you are frightened only at the bogey, and pursue the
shadow. You waste time looking for the spy of romance with a slouch hat
and a dark lantern, while all the while the real article sits at your dinner
tables, dances at your balls, smiles in your face, wins your confidence, and
then betrays you.

SIR GEORGE. And what about your Mr. Kent—who poses one moment as an
English fop,[5] and the next as a Frenchman? Doesn't that look rather fishy?

EVELYN. I am holding no brief[6] for my Mr. Kent, as you call him, only, again—
my woman's instinct tells me to trust him.

*A ring at door-bell C.; EVELYN goes to door and opens it and discovers DICK
standing in the hall, smiling; SIR GEORGE and LADY CAXTON glare at him; LADY
CAXTON turns her back on him; SIR GEORGE rises and goes a little L.*

DICK. (*In a cheerful tone.*) Halloa, everybody.

SIR GEORGE. (*In a low grumbling tone.*) Talk of the devil —

He goes up to fireplace; DICK advances into room.

7. A restaurant in the Savoy
    Hotel in London, famous for its
    inventive chefs.

8. In 1605 conspirators planned to
    destroy the English Parliament
    by setting off explosives in the
    basement of the building. Also
    meant to denote treasonous
    doings.

DICK. Jolly lucky to find you all here. Just got back and dropped in on chance; thought we might fix up that little dinner at the Savoy.[7]

SIR GEORGE. Confound it, sir, do you remember what happened the last time we met?

DICK. Oh, rather—beastly muddle, wasn't it? Everybody at cross purposes and ragging everybody else unmercifully. Awfully sorry I hadn't time to explain things, but now —

SIR GEORGE. Damn your impudence! Do you know you're liable to arrest for assault and battery?

DICK. Oh, by Jove, yes—that was too bad. That poor Johnny of a servant—hope I didn't hurt him much; but it was his own fault—would get in my way, you know, and I had to catch that train.

SIR GEORGE. Lucky for you, sir, the police didn't catch you.

DICK. I should say so. Awfully fine force, the police, you know—but slow.

SIR GEORGE. Perhaps it may not be too late yet.

DICK. Oh, but it's all right now. When you hear my explanation you won't want to arrest me.

SIR GEORGE. I'm not so sure of that.

DICK. Oh, but I am. I'm going to give you the surprise of your life.

LADY CAXTON. George, this atmosphere of intrigue is getting on my nerves. I feel myself breathing in conspiracy and gunpowder plots.[8] I need fresh air—I will await you in the motor below.

She moves toward door C.; DICK very politely holds the door open for her, bowing; she draws aside her skirts as if unwilling to touch him, and sweeps past and out into the hall; DICK closes the door behind her and comes back into C. of room.

SIR GEORGE. Well, sir?

DICK. Well—er—let's sit down; it's so much more sociable. (*EVELYN sits on sofa R.C. with an air of suppressed excitement; SIR GEORGE with an air of indignant resignation L. of table; DICK sits R. of table.*) Right, oh! Now in the first place, where is Thornton?

SIR GEORGE. What the devil has he got to do with your explanations?

DICK. Oh, lots. He's, as it were, the pivot of the whole concern.

EVELYN. (*Excited.*) Jack?

DICK. Of course—he's the storm centre, so to speak, of our little tempest.

SIR GEORGE. Say, do you know what you are talking about?

DICK. Oh, rather.

SIR GEORGE. Well, I don't.

DICK. Not now, but you will by and by, if you'll only be patient and keep calm.

SIR GEORGE. (*With a growl of fury.*) Hell! (*He rises and walks angrily up to fireplace.*)

DICK. Well, to come back to the starting point, where's Thornton?

SIR GEORGE. What business is that of yours?

EVELYN. Oh, Uncle, why waste time? What difference does it make? (*To* DICK.) He's gone to Lord Royallieu's.

DICK. Too bad—hoped I'd catch him first. It would have made it so much easier.

SIR GEORGE. Made what easier?—who easier?—oh, good Lord, I'm going crazy! (*He paces up and down excitedly.*)

DICK. Made him easier, if you like—easier in his mind, you know. He must be awfully worried about those papers.

EVELYN. What papers?

DICK. The papers he was to have taken to Vienna, but didn't, you know.

SIR GEORGE. (*To* EVELYN, *in a triumphant tone.*) What did I tell you? What did I tell you?

DICK. Well, what did you tell her? Something interesting?

SIR GEORGE. I said you knew all about those papers.

DICK. Why, of course—that's what I'm here for.

SIR GEORGE. (*Sitting opposite* DICK L. *of table.*) Then, sir, since you are such a well of information, where are the papers now?

DICK. In Vienna.

SIR GEORGE. Who has them?

DICK. Our Ambassador. He got them in plenty of time to cram for his interview with the Austrian Johnny, and it went off splendidly—and there you are.

Complacently, as if the matter were now quite settled.

SIR GEORGE. Who took the papers to Vienna?

DICK. I did.

SIR GEORGE. Where did you get them?

DICK. From the Countess.

EVELYN. Ah, what did I tell you?

SIR GEORGE. And where the devil did she get them?

DICK. Ah, thereby hangs a tale, the details of which you must get from my young friend Thornton. I never pry into a lady's private affairs. And, by the way, talking of Thornton, don't you think you might run your motor over to Royallieu's? Even though things are all right, the poor boy must be having a pretty hard time—and you might comfort him and soothe Royallieu.

SIR GEORGE. But what the devil am I to say?

DICK. Oh, just tell Royallieu you've been talking to me.

SIR GEORGE. To you! Young man, in the name of all that's infernal, who and what are you? For years every one has looked on you as an idler who never did a stroke of work in his life—as a fool who never had an idea in his head; and now—

DICK. You're beginning to think I'm not such a fool as I look? My dear Sir George, haven't you lived long enough in the diplomatic world to know that it pays to play the fool sometimes—that he is often used as a bait to catch wiser men? For years I have been serving my country as a "fool," while the world has known me only as "my father's son." The Secret Service discovered my capacity for being a "fool" and paid me for using it. Think it over, Sir George, while you are driving to Lord Royallieu's.

SIR GEORGE. sits staring at him dumb founded, and then rises in a dazed manner.

SIR GEORGE. I give it up. In my young days diplomacy was a profession; it is nothing now but a d--d melodrama. (*He crosses slowly up to door C. DICK and EVELYN rise; DICK crosses down L.*) Coming, Eve?

DICK. Oh, I say, Sir George—I must ask you to leave Miss Thornton here for a little while longer.

SIR GEORGE. With you?

DICK. Yes.

SIR GEORGE. Alone! My wife will have a fit.

DICK. Lady Caxton will have to control her feelings. She mustn't interfere with my stage management.

SIR GEORGE. Stage management! What are you going to do now?

DICK. Play the last act of the melodrama; I haven't squelched the villain yet.

SIR GEORGE. But what do you want her for?

DICK. The role of heroine. It's a short act—you can come for her in less than half an hour.

SIR GEORGE. Have it your own way. I'm through with diplomacy. I'll take to country life and raising prize vegetables.

He exits, door C. DICK crosses to door and calls after him.

DICK. You might tell Thornton I'd like to see him some time soon, will you?

The outside door slams; DICK comes back into room; he and EVELYN stand looking at each other; then she goes to him, C., half shyly, and stands with downcast eyes.

EVELYN. Mr. Kent.

DICK. You called me Dick the other night, you know.

EVELYN. Well, then, Dick—speaking of vegetables, I—I think the potato is sprouting wonderfully.

DICK. (*DICK looks at her with admiration.*) By Jove, you know, you really are one of the nicest girls I ever met.

EVELYN. And I want to thank you with all my heart for what you've done for Jack; I can never repay you.

DICK. Oh, yes you can, right now—more than repay me. Er—will you kiss me? (*EVELYN hesitates a moment, and then raises her face to his; he bends down and kisses her.*) Thank you! You know you really are the very nicest—

EVELYN. (*Interrupting.*) Dick—

DICK. Yes?

EVELYN. Last Monday night, when things looked so black for you—being what you are, and knowing what you did, why didn't you clear yourself then?

DICK. Let's sit down and be sociable. (*He takes her by the hand and leads her to sofa R.C. and they sit.*) In the first place; I didn't want to give Jack away and make matters appear any worse than they were; and he had been a bit of a fool, you know, made so, like many a wiser man before him, by a bad woman; and in the second place, I didn't want to give myself away and show the Baron and Countess my trump cards till I could catch them red-handed and before witnesses; and that's what I think I'm going to do now.

EVELYN. Now?

DICK. I told Sir George I wanted you for the heroine of my little drama. Are you willing to play the part?

EVELYN. Yes, Dick, if you think I can.

DICK. Rather.

EVELYN. I'm ready then.

DICK. Even if it should involve some danger?

EVELYN. I like a spice of danger. I was brought up that way.

DICK. (*In admiration.*) Were you? Really, you know, you are the very nicest— Would you again? (*She holds up her face and he kisses her.*) Thank you. And now to give you stage directions. If any one rings the bell, go at once into that room. (*Pointing to door L.*) Take this notebook and pencil with you (*Taking book and pencil from his pocket and handing them to her.*) and make notes of all you hear.

EVELYN. Is that all?

DICK. No, one thing more. No matter what happens—in whatever danger I may be—you must not come out or speak till I tell you. Do you promise?

EVELYN. (*After a pause, holding out her hand.*) Yes.

He stands holding her hand and looking at her admiringly, then he leaves her and goes quickly to window R.C. and looks out, keeping well behind the curtain.

DICK. Just as I thought—my friends have been watching me; now they are going to act. You needn't wait for the bell—get into the room now. (EVELYN *moves up to door L.*) Evelyn. (*She stops; he goes to her and bends toward her.*) Before you go—would you again? (*She lifts her face and he kisses her.*) Thank you.

She exits quickly, door L.; he smiles as if well pleased; he crosses to window R.C. again, and keeping well behind the curtain, looks out; then he comes down to sideboard, takes a cigarette and lights it; doorbell C. rings; he goes up to door C. and opens it; the COUNTESS *enters; on seeing* DICK, *she stops with pretended surprise.*

COUNTESS. I beg your pardon—is Miss Thornton in?

DICK. No.

COUNTESS. No? (*With an inflection of surprise.*) I met Lady Caxton in her motor, and she informed me that she had left her here.

DICK. So she did, with Sir George; but he is gone, and knowing the Caxton sense of propriety, you didn't suppose they would leave her here with me—alone.

COUNTESS. Well, to be perfectly candid, I didn't think they'd leave you here alone either with or without her. You were scarcely in their good books last Monday.

DICK. By Jove, I should say not; but I'm all right now—they've changed their minds about me.

COUNTESS. Indeed!

DICK. Absolutely.

COUNTESS. How nice for you. Well, my visit to Miss Thornton was from a selfish motive. I forgot to give some important directions to my dressmaker, and I wanted to use the 'phone. Though she is out, may I still trespass on her kindness?

DICK. I'm sure she'd be delighted—the 'phone is at your service, Countess.

COUNTESS. Thank you. (*As she crosses to table L. she casts a swift watchful glance around the room, sits at desk and takes up the receiver.* DICK *strolls up to fireplace L.C., and stands with his back to it, regarding her closely, and smoking—a curious expression on his face.*) Give me Regent 1560. Are you there—is that you, Madame? Countess Von Holtzberg speaking—that dress of mine I spoke of—it is ready—yes—now—send for it at once—you understand. Thank you—good afternoon. (*She hangs up receiver and turns toward door C.*) I am much obliged

DICK. Don't mention it, Countess.

She pauses halfway to the door and faces DICK.

COUNTESS. Did you have a pleasant trip to Vienna?

DICK. Ripping.

COUNTESS. And you delivered your papers in safety?

DICK. Oh, rather. I kept my word to you to the letter, and placed them in the hands of those for whom they were intended, and I am taking a reply back to those for whom it is intended. I should have been on my way now if it hadn't been for your charming and unexpected visit.

A look of triumph comes into the COUNTESS*'s face for a moment, but she controls herself at once and speaks carelessly.*

COUNTESS. Really. (*A pause.*) You played a clever game that night, Mr.—

DICK. Kent. Awfully good of you to say so—but I think you flatter me.

COUNTESS. I assure you I am perfectly sincere. I admired your skill so much (*She draws nearer to door C.*) that I hope some day we may play against each other again.

DICK. Oh, I'm sure we shall—some day. (*The outer door slams.*) And I shouldn't be surprised if it were very soon—and this time, I think, it will be four-handed—or three—and a dummy. (*A key is heard turning in lock, door C.; the* COUNTESS *steps quickly to door C. and opens it; the* BARON *enters, followed by* HOGUE; *he casts a quick glance at the* COUNTESS, *who nods her head.*) Four handed. (*He comes down L.C.*) How are you, Baron; awfully glad to see you and Mr.—what's the latest—eh? Lenoir, drop in in this friendly manner. Thornton's out, but I'll try my best to do the honors.

BARON. Mr. Kent, I am here for a purpose.

DICK. You don't say so? How awfully jolly. Being a purposeless Johnny myself, I always appreciate that sort of thing in other people—tremendously.

BARON. I have several things to say to you. Sit down.

DICK. My idea exactly—so much more sociable.

BARON. Hogue, guard the door.

The COUNTESS *sits on sofa R.C.*

DICK. (*Sitting L. of table.*) Make a better job of it than Patton did, won't you, Hogue? (*HOGUE casts a look of hatred at* DICK, *but is evidently worried. To* BARON.) Fire away.

BARON. Those papers which you have just left at Vienna, and which you obtained possession of by underhand trickery—

DICK. Oh, I say, you know, isn't that rather like the pot calling the kettle black?

BARON. Will you please listen to me—I am in earnest, and I am in a hurry.

DICK. All right, old chap—sorry I interrupted.

BARON. Those papers were of the greatest importance to the government of my country and the government of Austria. The Countess, Hogue and myself were commissioned to obtain possession of them; we had almost succeeded when —

DICK. When I took a hand and trumped your long suit. Awfully sorry, but those papers were of importance to my government too.

BARON. We risked our liberty—perhaps our lives—for nothing, and we lost prestige with those who trusted us.

DICK. So no one can blame you for feeling peevish, can they?

BARON. However, all is not lost yet.

DICK. No—really?

BARON. There is a reply to those papers—more important, perhaps, even than they were. If we can hand copies of that to the ministers at Berlin and Vienna, we shall be restored to favor.

DICK. And do you think you can do it?

BARON. I think so.

DICK. How ripping!

BARON. Our agents have followed you ever since you left Vienna. (*With a sudden change of tone.*) Those papers are in your possession. (*DICK makes a half start, as if taken unawares, and then appears to recover himself with an effort; there is a pause.*) Do you deny it?

DICK, embarrassed, remains silent.

COUNTESS. It would be foolish to do so, since Mr. Kent has already confided in me that he has them. (*A pause.*)

BARON. Well?

DICK. Not much good lying after that, is there?—Besides, I'm such a truthful Johnny anyhow, I'd be sure to make a mess of it. Yes—I have the answer.

BARON. Then will you kindly hand it over to me? (*DICK remains motionless.*) At once.

DICK. And if I refuse?

BARON. (*Whipping a revolver from his pocket and covering DICK.*) I'll play the game you threatened to play on Hogue—shoot you first, and take the papers afterward. Hogue, lock that door.

Without taking his eyes from DICK, he takes latchkey from his pocket and gives it to HOGUE, who locks door C.

DICK. Now don't you think, Baron, that that would be rather foolish? The shot might rouse the neighbors, and I'm too well known to disappear easily. The people who are waiting for these papers would ask questions. (*He touches his hand to his breast involuntarily and the BARON'S eyes gleam with anticipation.*) And together you might get yourself into a very unpleasant position, because in England we hang for murder, and we don't waste much time at the trial, either.

BARON. When it comes to—what the Americans call a "show down"—I am used to taking desperate chances. The papers—or I shoot.—

DICK. All right—you've got me. I agree; only before I give up may I ask one question?

BARON. Yes, if you'll be quick—

DICK. I'll be quicker if you'll point that damned thing at the ceiling—it's getting on my nerves. (*The BARON elevates the barrel of the revolver slightly.*) *Thanks.* In asking me to hand over to you these papers you are fully aware that they are of strictly private nature, addressed to the Minister of Foreign Affairs, and that I am in the service of the British Government?

BARON. Fully.

DICK. Yet you still force me, with threats of violence, to betray my trust and give them up to you?

BARON. Yes, and you'll find the threat a reality if you don't give them up at once.

A slight pause; DICK *gives a sort of helpless look round the room and speaks in a dejected tone.*

DICK. All right—you win.

He takes a large envelope from his pocket, sealed with three seals, and hands it to the BARON; *then he rises and walks dejectedly to fireplace at back; the* BARON *drops his revolver on the table beside him, and with nervous fingers begins tearing open the envelope.*

BARON. (*To the* COUNTESS.) The code-book—quick. (*The* COUNTESS *takes book from her dress and hands it to him; she stands beside him leaning over his shoulder;* HOGUE *steps down a little from the door, eager to see what is happening, all of them for a time oblivious of* DICK, *who quietly draws a revolver and covers them; the* BARON *takes papers from, envelope and hastily turns them over; as he does so, a blank expression comes into his face and that of the* COUNTESS, *which changes to one of baffled rage.*) These papers are blank— (*He turns on* DICK *to find himself covered by the revolver.*) What the devil does this mean?

DICK. That the Countess taught me the game, and I am an apt pupil—what? I placed the real papers in Lord Royallieu's hands two hours ago. (*The* BARON *makes a move to pick up his revolver;* HOGUE *shrinks in terror against the door.*) No, don't touch that, please—I'll take it. (*He advances covering the* BARON *with his revolver, and picks up the other one.*) To paraphrase the saying of some philosophical Johnny—"two revolvers are better than one";—also the code-book, please. (*Holding out his hand.*) You won't have any further use for it. (*The* BARON *takes code-book from the* COUNTESS *and reluctantly hands it over.*) Thank you.

COUNTESS. But why—why—

DICK. Why did I let you go to the trouble of forcing me to give you an envelope containing—nothing? Because I wanted to catch you in a trap. The night you drugged and robbed the man who loved you I was powerless, because I had no witnesses to your guilt; but now, every word you have said has been recorded against you—and your own tongues have declared that you are spies and traitors. Miss Thornton—(EVELYN *enters from door L., pale and excited, but controlling herself admirably, notebook and pencil in hand.*) There is my witness. I think, Countess, I take the odd trick.[9] (*There is a tap heard at door C.;* DICK *turns his revolver on* HOGUE.) Open that door, please. (HOGUE *unlocks the door, and a* DETECTIVE *and a* POLICEMAN *are seen standing in the hall;* DICK *points to* HOGUE *and the* BARON.) Your prisoners. (*The* DETECTIVE *and* POLICEMAN *arrest* HOGUE *and the* BARON, *and slip handcuffs on them; then they move toward door C.*) Baron. (*They stop a moment.*) The night you first met me here you thought you knew my face; you were right. I met you years ago when I was a lad with my father in Vienna and Berlin. The smooth-faced boy meant nothing to you—he was beneath your notice; but he wasn't quite the angel child he looked—even then he had begun to learn your record. The knowledge has since proved useful—and let this affair teach you the truth of two proverbs: "Never judge by appearances"—and a man "is not always such a fool as he looks." Good-night.

The BARON and HOGUE are led out, HOGUE in terror, the BARON sullen and defiant, and the door is closed; the COUNTESS stands looking at DICK in a sullen, defiant manner, and then speaks.

COUNTESS. What is to be my fate?
DICK. (*A pause, DICK regarding her curiously.*) Countess, we Englishmen have a foolish prejudice against crushing a woman, if we can help it; besides, I don't want to hurt the feelings of your worthy uncle, the Count Von Szalras—only I advise you that your visits to him cease. I feel sure the air of Vienna is much more healthy to you. Leave England tonight—others may not prove so lenient.

The COUNTESS moves slowly up to door C.; EVELYN goes up and sits in chair by fire-place L.C., gazing into fire.

COUNTESS. Mr. Kent—you are generous. We would not have shown the same mercy.
DICK. (*Cheerfully.*) Of course not—but then you're—well, different.
COUNTESS. Yes, we're different—and I sometimes wonder if—but there—it's too late to learn a new code of life. I must stick to the old one—my country first and above all, and for her all things are lawful. There is not one action of the past that I regret, except—Jack.
DICK. (*Softly.*) Ah!
COUNTESS. Even to serve one's country one should not betray an honest love or break a true heart; and it's dangerous to play with edged tools—you cut your own hands. I—I am sorry, and in the future—"always alone"—I shall be sorrier still. (*A pause.*) Couldn't you tell him that?
DICK. Don't you think it would be better to say nothing? To let him learn to despise and forget—the follies of youth?

She looks at him for a moment, and then slowly bows her head.

COUNTESS. Perhaps you are right. (*She goes slowly out at door C.; EVELYN sighs.*)
EVELYN. Poor Countess.
DICK. You pity her?
EVELYN. Yes.

DICK. Well, I'm not sure that I don't pity her myself. Married to an old
reprobate and brought up under the shadow of that bally black feather and
that morbid motto—it doesn't seem as if she'd had half a chance, does it?
EVELYN. (*Shaking her head sadly.*) No.
DICK. (*In a meditative manner.*) "Always Alone." Do you know, there are more
people in the world than you'd think possible who are always, or mostly
always, alone? I've been a lonely sort of Johnny myself in the past.

EVELYN. *rises, comes down behind him and lays her hand on his shoulder, speaking
a little shyly.*

EVELYN. But you won't be in the future—will you, Dick?
DICK. (*DICK turns to her quickly.*) You mean that—(*EVELYN gives a quick nod
of her head, and then turns away shyly; he takes her in his arms.*) Really, you
know, you are the very nicest—(*Slam of door outside is heard, and then the
handle of the inside door turns; DICK releases EVELYN and she moves down L.C.*)
Oh, damn!

*The door opens, and JACK rushes into the room; he seizes DICK by the hand and
shakes it enthusiastically.*

JACK. My dear Kent, I—I don't know what to say to you.
DICK. Then don't say it, old chap.
JACK. I owe it to you that I am not a disgraced and ruined man. Oh, Eve—he's
just splendid. (*Crossing to her L.C.*) Don't you think so?
EVELYN. (*Smiling up in his face.*) I do indeed, Jack, just splendid. (*She turns up to
fireplace L.; DICK crosses down to R.C. in a fidgety manner.*)
JACK. (*Crossing over to him.*) Why, Lord Royallieu hardly said a thing to me—
just a bit of a lecture and a reprimand;—and I thought my career was over.
DICK. Not a bit of it, dear boy—only they may remove you to another branch
of the service; you are a bit too susceptible for a King's Messenger.
JACK. And it's all your doing—you needn't deny it. Oh, I can never repay you.

*DICK seizes him by the arm, and after a hasty glance over his shoulder at EVELYN,
speaks in a low voice.*

DICK. Yes you can, if you want to, right now.
JACK. How—how? Anything in the world—
DICK. (*Leading him to door R.*) Go into that room and for heaven's sake stay
there till I call you.
JACK. (*Looking at him.*) You—you don't mean—
DICK. Yes I do. Get out!
JACK. (*Wringing DICK's hand.*) God bless you.

He hurries out through door R., closing it behind him; DICK *turns toward* EVELYN *with an assumption of ease; she comes down to him C.*

EVELYN. Dick—do you like me as a heroine?
DICK. Rather! Do you like potatoes?
EVELYN. Rather. I'm a confirmed vegetarian.
DICK. Really, you know, you are the very nicest girl—

Taking her in his arms and kissing her; enter SIR GEORGE, *door C. He pauses and gazes at* EVELYN *and* DICK *dumbfounded.*

SIR GEORGE. What the devil do you think you're doing now?
DICK. (*Drawing* EVELYN *closer to him and kissing her.*) Tightening the bonds of the Empire.

Curtain

13 : Little Theatre Scenography (1919–1937)

A New Vision on the Canadian Stage

PAUL J. STOESSER

1. The author acknowledges with thanks Nazli Akhtari and Khadijah Salawu for the excellence of their research assistance on this project. My thanks also to the editors for their firm guidance and redoubtable patience.

2. Roy Mitchell hosted William Butler Yeats at Hart House Theatre (January 1920) and earlier worked at the Garrick Theatre (1916) in New York City, coincident with Théâtre du Vieux-Colombier's tenure there. See Stoesser 2007, 47, 243, and 259. Members of the Montreal Repertory Theatre who worked with American companies include founder Martha Allan at Pasadena and early director Rupert Caplan at Provincetown. See Booth 1989, 13–15

3. "Scenography" should be understood to encompass all physical features necessary for the production of a play. Historically the concept derives its theoretical basis from the Aristotelian term *opsis* ("spectacle"): one of the elements of tragedy discussed in his *Poetics*. See Aristotle 1907, 126.

4. In this introduction, the term "Art Theatres" (such as the Moscow Art Theatre) refers to the European progenitors of the Canadian Little Theatres (such as Hart House).

5. For example, Carol Nesbitt's thesis on the Vancouver Little Theatre Association notes that the idea for the

IN THE WAVE OF NATIONALISM following the First World War, the Little Theatre Movement, which had its genesis in Europe in the late nineteenth century, took firm root in Canada.[1] Canadian Little Theatres drew inspiration from the reputations of companies such as the Moscow Art Theatre, André Antoine's Théâtre-Libre in France, J.T. Grein's Independent Theatre in Great Britain, as well as from the demonstrated successes of other theatres, including the Provincetown Players and Pasadena Community Playhouse in the United States, and even more specifically the North American exposures to Dublin's Abbey Theatre and Jacques Copeau's Théâtre du Vieux-Colombier.[2] There is neither a single cause for the growth of Little Theatres in Canada, nor a single date for the beginning of the movement. Nevertheless, and in spite of little formal coordination between the theatres, in a few cities like Toronto and Ottawa, Little Theatres came into existence prior to the First World War (Toronto's Arts and Letters Club, inaugurated in 1908, is one such example), yet the "golden age" of the Little Theatre Movement in Canada flourished between the First and Second World Wars. The Little Theatres discussed in this chapter share three significant attributes: a similar repertoire of plays, an intimate and communal experience of the drama enhanced by the architecture and equipment of the theatres, and the use of innovative scenography.[3]

A number of influences motivated the rise of these theatres throughout the country. There was a desire among the participants in these companies to emulate the Art Theatres mentioned above, and to produce plays not likely to be presented by touring or professional stock companies.[4] The Little Theatres considered in this chapter also shared the desire (often not achieved) to mount plays written by Canadians. They championed Canadian playwrights because touring companies and the few existing professional stock companies were unlikely to produce these plays, which had uncertain chances of profitability. Another cause for the rise of Little Theatres was the desire for Canadians across the country to participate in the creation of theatre.[5]

The six case studies examined here include Hart House Theatre in Toronto (1919): the gold standard of theatre buildings that other Little Theatres strove to emulate (Denison 1923d, 61–63). Hart House Theatre's first artistic director, Roy Mitchell, specified several superior production systems for the well-

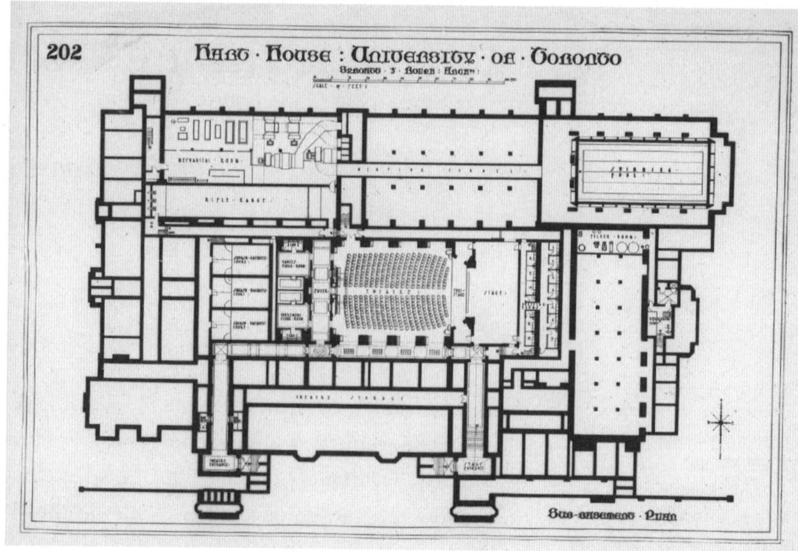

FIGURE 13.1: *Plan of the Hart House Theatre. First published in* Hart House Theatre, Toronto; A Description of the Theatre and the Record of Its First Nine Seasons, 1919–1928. *Courtesy of the University of Toronto Archives.*

company started with two couples in 1921, but after their first production was mounted in 1921, the company was so popular that they had to limit the number of full members of the theatre to two hundred. They created two other classes of members, associates and subscribers, who would be eligible for full membership depending on their participation in the company's operations. By 1930 total membership in the association (all classes) stood at 1,500 (Nesbitt 1992, 21–28).

6. This theatre would remain its home for over fifty years. They renovated the building in 1939–40 and renamed it "The York." It was renovated again in 2013, reopening as a live performance venue (see Figure 13.3).

7. The Community Players performed at the "Winnipeg Little Theatre" until 1931 when the performing company changed its name to match the theatre. See "UM Digital Collections," n.d.; "Winnipeg Little Theatre Collection," 1921–58.

8. The Theatre Guild was initially dedicated to serving those authors whom commercial— that is, Broadway—managers would not produce.

equipped stage plan, which included extensive wing space representing almost half the stage area, dedicated backstage production workshops, and modest rigging possibilities. Merrill Denison noted that the lighting system was "truly extraordinary," and that "there are only two or three theatres in America with as complete or as large a stage switchboard" (1923d, 61). The Ottawa Little Theatre (founded in 1913 as the Ottawa Drama League) operated alternately out of the Russell Theatre on Queen Street (1914–1915, 1916–1923) and the Auditorium of the Victoria Memorial Museum (1915–1916, 1923–1928) until they purchased and converted a church on King Edward Avenue for its centralized production and performance needs: a space they fittingly named The Little Theatre (1928). While the Vancouver Little Theatre Association (1921) started its existence in a rented facility, within two years it purchased the Alcazar/Palace Theatre (originally constructed in 1913), which they renamed the Vancouver Little Theatre.[6] The Community Players of Winnipeg (founded 1921) changed its name to Winnipeg Little Theatre in 1931. After mounting 60 full-length plays and 137 one-act productions in the Dominion Theatre (a converted movie theatre at Selkirk and Main called the Winnipeg Little Theatre from 1922, which the group purchased in 1927), the Winnipeg Little Theatre disbanded in 1937 (Stuart 1997, 89–94).[7] The company was revived in the 1950s and later absorbed into the Manitoba Theatre Centre. The Montreal Repertory Theatre mounted its first production in 1930 as the Montreal Theatre Guild to align it closely with the ideals of New York's Theatre Guild. It remained an active producer of English-language theatre in Montreal until the 1960s.[8] The company used a number of venues during this period, often

9. For instance, Shakespeare's plays are notably absent from the Vancouver Little Theatre's seasons during the 1920s and 1930s.

10. Hart House Theatre was a particular champion of these authors. Detailed production histories are available: for Hart House Theatre, see "HHT Production History" 2012; for the Montreal Repertory Theatre, see Booth 1989, 195–214; for the Vancouver Little Theatre, see Nesbitt 1992, Appendix B; for the Community Players of Winnipeg, see "UM Digital Collections," n.d.; for the Ottawa Drama League/Little Theatre, see "Ottawa Little Theatre," n.d.

overlapping, including Moyse Hall, McGill University (1929–1934); Victoria Hall, Westmount (1931, 1933–1937); Salle Académique, Collège Ste. Marie (1933); MRT Studio, Union St. (studio productions, 1933–1937); and the Ritz Carlton Hotel (1934–1937). In Halifax, the still-operational Theatre Arts Guild (founded in 1931) did not have a permanent theatre until the 1960s, but it used a number of venues including the Garrick Theatre (1931, currently used by Neptune Theatre) and rented space from Navy League at Barrington and South Streets (1935–1939).

Canadian Little Theatres, wherever they were located, tended to mount similar plays. The most popular playwright was George Bernard Shaw followed closely by William Shakespeare, although his plays were not mounted at all theatres.[9] Playwrights from the Abbey Theatre—particularly J.M. Synge, W.B. Yeats, and Lady Gregory—were also popular. Other authors including Somerset Maugham, John Galsworthy, A.A. Milne, and W.B. Priestley commonly appeared in seasons across the country. American playwrights Eugene O'Neill, Maxwell Anderson, and Elmer Rice received multiple productions at various theatres. Non-English-language European writers such as Luigi Pirandello, Maurice Maeterlinck, Leonid Andreyev, and Luigi Chiarelli were produced in translation in several communities. Notably, Czech playwright Karel Čapek's *R.U.R.* received performances at almost all of the Little Theatres examined. Most of the theatres mounted plays of varying length by Canadian writers such as Merrill Denison, Mazo de la Roche, and Carroll Aikins, but the proportion of Canadian works within the overall number of plays produced remained low.[10]

The Little Theatres in Canada developed a surprisingly similar architectural vocabulary that enhanced the intimate relationship of the stage and audience. Among the features common to many of the theatres were limited audience capacity, similar house-to-stage ratios, and the proportion of wing to stage area.

The seating capacity of most Little Theatre venues was less than 500 seats arranged in similar configurations incorporating proscenium arches or modified end stages with seating on a single main floor. The smallest of these, the MRT Studio, used by the Montreal Repertory Theatre, was a modestly sized house that accommodated only 172 seats, including two rows on a small balcony. Other venues used by the group were slightly larger, such as Moyse Hall at 400 seats. In Winnipeg, the Dominion Theatre accommodated approximately 400 patrons, as did the Garrick Theatre in Halifax. The auditoria of both the Ottawa Little Theatre and Hart House accommodated slightly fewer than 500 patrons, with seating divided into 20 rows.

When opened in 1913, Vancouver Little Theatre featured the largest seating capacity noted as 675, including the balcony; however, while larger overall, the limited main floor capacity with seating for 417 patrons ensured that the intimacy of the audience-performer relationship was retained, like in other Little Theatre venues. In addition, the overall length of the Vancouver Little Theatre was only 81 feet (24.7 metres), making the back wall of the audience only 57

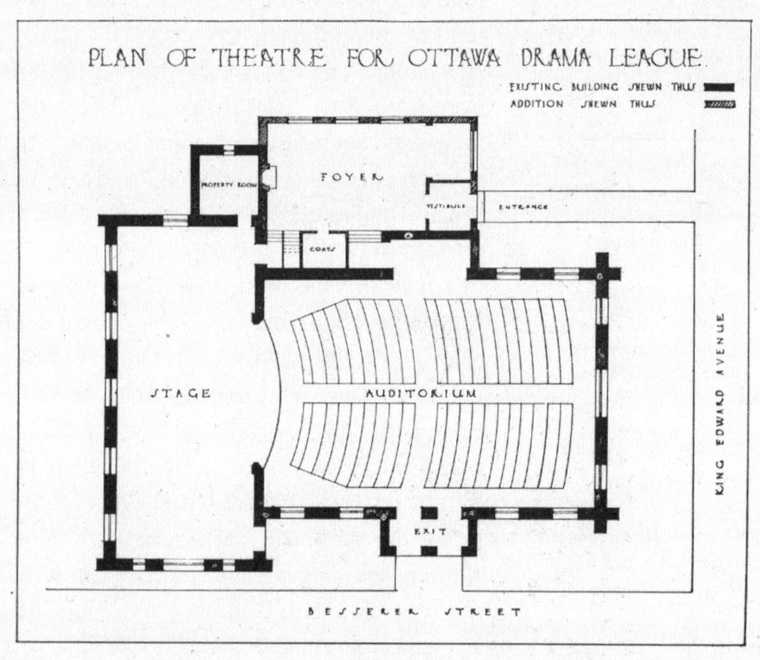

FIGURE 13.2: *Detail of a ground plan for the Ottawa Little Theatre, 1927.* Item MG569, CA026034. *Courtesy of the City of Ottawa Archives.*

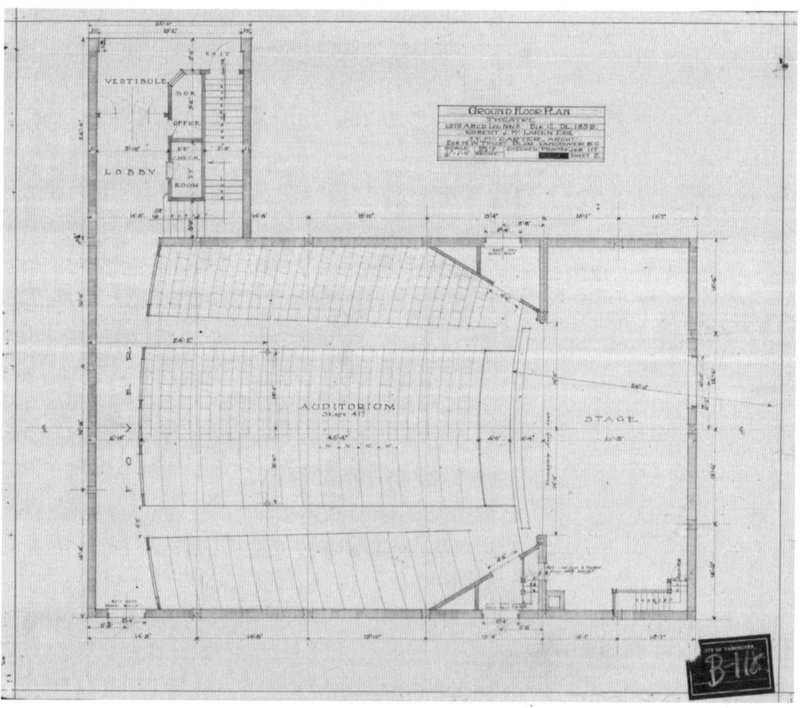

FIGURE 13.3: *Ground plan of the Alcazar Theatre, later known as the Vancouver Little Theatre and finally the York Theatre in 1940. Architect J.Y. McCarter.*

Item COV-S393-1-AP 292-8. *Courtesy of the City of Vancouver Archives.*

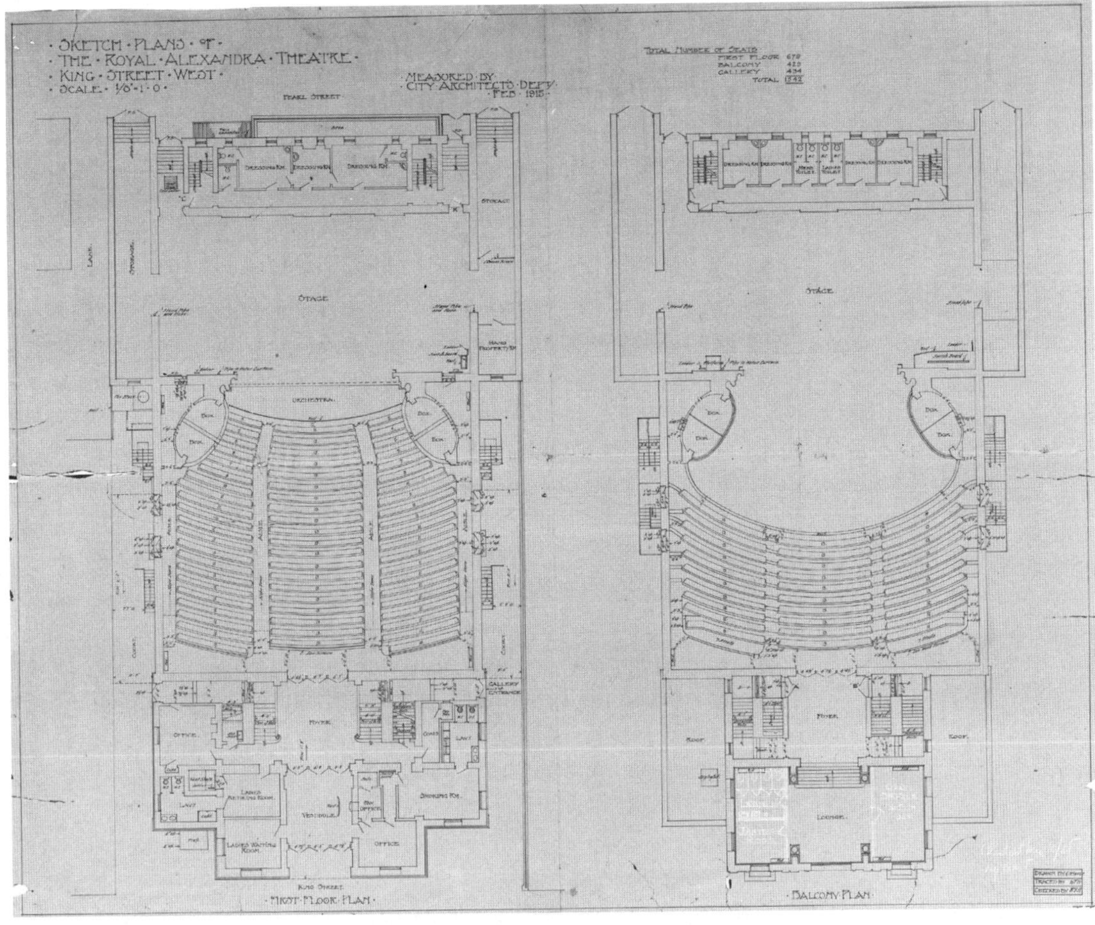

FIGURE 13.4: *Plan of the Royal Alexandra Theatre, Toronto, 1915 (re-dated 1938 in pencil).*
138.3 from B308238, RG 56-10, folder "Toronto-Royal Alexandra." Courtesy of the Archives of Ontario.

feet (17.4 metres) from the edge of the stage, which guaranteed that even the most distant audience member was less than 60 feet from centre stage.

The Little Theatres' emphasis on a lower audience capacity was a deliberate reaction against the large theatres used by professional companies, which often held more than a thousand spectators. The larger number of spectators maximized profits on commercial investments. The enormity of the professional theatres necessitated glaring and relatively undifferentiated white lighting merely for visibility, while at the same time their settings required overt and extreme embellishment typical of the pictorial scenic style that prevailed in the commercial houses, such as the Walker in Winnipeg or the Royal Alexandra in Toronto (see Figure 13.4: "Plan of the Royal Alexandra"). The Little Theatre Movement embraced the smaller scale in this reimagined actor-audience relationship and capitalized on the resultant intimacy it afforded, which differentiated the Little Theatre artistry further from the professional companies.

Considering the physical layout of the stage itself, there are clear similarities between the Ottawa Little Theatre and Hart House. Their wing-to-stage ratio was similar across the Little Theatres. The ground plan of the remodelled Ottawa theatre from 1927 (Figure 13.2) shows the relatively wide wing space of the stage in relation to its depth,[11] creating an approximately two-to-one ratio. Similarly, the depth of the stage at Hart House Theatre (Figure 13.1) from front edge of the playing area to upstage wall was likewise approximately half its overall width, including wing space. A greater sense of depth in the settings was achieved through the combined use of the cyclorama and illumination provided by the advanced lighting system. The production photograph of the setting for *Alcestis* from the second season at Hart House (Figure 13.5) was taken from near the back of the auditorium and reveals both the relationship between the setting and the cyclorama as well as the intimate nature of the theatre. This image also clearly shows the deliberate restraint in the architectural decoration of the auditorium typical of Art Theatres in order not to draw attention away from the stage. The main difference between the stage plans of these two theatres is the inclusion of a forestage in Toronto, thus providing more overall stage area than at Ottawa.

The approximate two-to-one ratio of wing space-to-stage depth of Hart House and the Ottawa Little Theatre was also evident at the Vancouver Little Theatre, which was noted as 50 feet (15.2 metres) wide and 24 feet (7.3 metres) deep (Figure 13.3). The stage also featured a proscenium arch 28 feet (8.5 metres) wide and 20 feet (6.1 metres) high ("Alcazar Theatre" 1913). Thus, as in Ottawa and Toronto, as well as the Dominion Theatre in Winnipeg, the stage width at the Vancouver Little Theatre was over twice its depth, due again to considerable wing space on both sides of the stage. The consistency of the physical layout of these theatres—including both reduced audience size and high wing space-to-stage depth ratios—combined with the shared similar repertoire of plays meant that a comparable scenography developed among Little Theatres across the country.

Originating in the visionary and revolutionary theories of Adolphe Appia and other contemporary continental practitioners, the Canadian Little Theatres, for both artistic as well as economic reasons, used the new style of theatre scenography, which emphasized simplicity, suggestion, and stylization, all combined in a synthetic form of presentation. These innovations concentrated on sets and lighting.

When examining the physical production facilities of these theatres through the accompanying photographic evidence from 1919 to 1937, the scenographic record reflects two distinct design styles. The design of many of the plays was clearly in the manner of the New Stagecraft inspired by Adolphe Appia, proselytized by Edward Gordon Craig, and notably applied with such conviction and imagination by American designers Lee Simonson and Robert Edmond Jones. The experimentation and use of New Stagecraft techniques produced a wide range of attempts and successes yet varied greatly in its

FIGURE 13.5: *The set of* Alcestis *at Hart House Theatre, Toronto, 1921.* Item A1973-0039/001 (03). Courtesy of the University of Toronto Archives.

FIGURE 13.6: *Scene from* The Bad Man, *Vancouver Little Theatre, 1927.* Item AM41 1971-054.1, 500-F-04 fld 08. Courtesy of the City of Vancouver Archives.

FIGURE 13.7: *Scene from* She Stoops to Conquer, *Theatre Arts Guild, Halifax, 1932.*
Courtesy of the Theatre Arts Guild fonds (MS-3-4), Dalhousie University Archives, Halifax, Nova Scotia.

application across the country. Another more pervasive design style employed at this time consisted of static box sets with a preponderance of scenic detail supporting the many realistic plays mounted. Nevertheless, even with this stylistic solution, the new theatre movement sought "to avoid the dull literalism that so often characterizes the treatment of realistic plays" and so turned frequently to the new-found expressiveness in sets and lighting (Rubin 1996, 82).

The many box-type settings encountered in the collections of production photographs from these Little Theatres usually featured three walls upstage of the proscenium arch with the so-called invisible fourth wall so that the audience peered, as it were, into the setting. Often, with the exception of furniture and other properties, the sets themselves did not change during the performance. Realistic details proliferate in the production photographs of box sets presented here. Figure 13.6 is a photograph from the 1927 Vancouver Little Theatre Association production of *The Bad Man*. Note the simply decorated three walls and even a ceiling in this set. A solid ceiling, as this one appears to be, would not allow for the use of over-the-stage lighting, nor do the walls at the edge of the stage allow for side lighting of any sort. This set is an excellent example of removing a fourth wall to gaze into the world of this play. And yet, the perspective of the walls had to be modified to give an even greater illusion of depth than the stage physically allowed (see Figure 13.3). Figure 13.7

FIGURE 13.8: *Scene from* The Tragedy of Nan, *Winnipeg Little Theatre, 1926.*

Image 12, "The Tragedy of Nan," December 1926, P7825/3, N32361, Winnipeg Little Theatre Collection, Archives of Manitoba.

FIGURE 13.9: *Scene from* See Naples and Die, *Ottawa Little Theatre, 1934.*

Photograph by Yousuf Karsh, accession 1987-054 NPC, e010678964, Yousuf Karsh fonds, Library and Archives Canada.

12.   Shallow drapes rigged above the stage to mask the lighting instruments and other production equipment from the audience.

13.   Compare the *Alcestis* setting with Figure 13.10: Appia's design for *Orpheus* (Gluck's opera *Orfeo ed Euridice*, which is listed in the Bibliothèque du Genève as "Hellerau, théâtre: décor d'Orphée par Adolphe Appia"), staged at Hellerau in 1912–13 but not published until five years after the Hart House production.

14.   Several European practitioners, among them Mariano Fortuny, a protégé of Appia's, experimented with curved, plaster covered "*kuppelhorizont*" walls and various other materials such as silks, linens, and canvas to achieve with lighting these illusions of greater depth.

15.   Further study of Little Theatre lighting systems during this period should include Carroll Aikins's Home Theatre established in Naramata, BC, the year after Hart House opened and which benefitted from the consultations and recommendations of Lee Simonson, a leading Appia proponent who knew of Mitchell's pioneering work in Toronto and New York.

is an image of *She Stoops to Conquer* from the Theatre Arts Guild in Halifax in 1932. This set is also composed of walls that cover the entire stage from left to right with painted—as opposed to three-dimensional—detail. In this photograph, the painted panelling and the cornice work are plainly evident where the flat and the ceiling piece converge on stage left. Note also the shadows on the ceiling resulting from the use of footlights, a technique associated with larger commercial theatres and, due to their distraction, typically avoided in new stagecraft practice. The set for *The Tragedy of Nan* at the Winnipeg Little Theatre in 1926 (Figure 13.8) has few details on the walls but is similar in structure and execution to the previous two examples.

Sometimes the settings were not continuous walls or were located outside, as in the setting for *See Naples and Die* at the Ottawa Little Theatre in 1934 (Figure 13.9), which nevertheless provided a static scene with a great amount of realistic detail. This particular setting differs slightly from the other examples given that the back wall of the stage, which appears to be a cyclorama, is visible and quite likely used in conjunction with lighting effects. Also, instead of a ceiling, at least two borders[12] are visible that allow the use of overhead stage lighting without the instruments being seen by the audience.

Reliance on lighting as a major scenographic component was characteristic of the Art Theatre principles of New Stagecraft espoused at Hart House and emulated widely in the Little Theatre Movement. More abstract settings were the hallmark of this new scenography, which typically used suggestion reinforced by lighting to indicate location and feeling. The 1921 set for *Alcestis* from Hart House (Figure 13.5) was the epitome of New Stagecraft design at the time, with only a staircase and "the symmetrical repetition of the six vertical elements that rose up out of view as well as from the suggestion of the off-stage continuation of the colonnade they formed" (Stoesser 2007, 205). The Appian influence is unassailable.[13] The production photograph of the setting for *Alcestis* (Figure 13.5) was taken in an obviously empty theatre with house lights on, and so it can only hint at the possible effectiveness of the lighting facilities. Due to the technical limitations of both cameras and stage lighting at the time, it is only the rare, skilled photographer who could create a faithful representation of theatrical lighting effects prior to the second half of the twentieth century. The lighting instruments Mitchell specified included the latest developments in condensed lamp-filament technology in order to deliver the most intense beams to the stage. At Hart House, Mitchell also used a retractable roller cyclorama, which was a state-of-the-art lighting component necessary for achieving great sense of depth, especially in the confinement of the smaller stage area.[14] Complementing the different types of lighting instruments was the heart of the lighting system: a sixty-channel dimming switchboard that allowed the designer to connect any configuration of lights and control them by colour, direction, and, above all, intensity, providing limitless nuanced possibilities for lighting both the setting and the acting area.[15]

FIGURE 13.10: *Adolphe Appia's set for* Orpheus *at Hellerau, 1912.*

Item ijd b 1 3 p 01. Courtesy of the Bibliothèque de Genève.

FIGURE 13.11: *Scene from* Night, *Vancouver Little Theatre, 1925.*

Item AM 41 1971-054.2, 500-F-04 fld 08. Courtesy of the City of Vancouver Archives.

FIGURE 13.12: *Scene from R.U.R., Montreal Repertory Theatre, 1931.*

Envelope 19, Production Photographs, Theatre Collection, Toronto Public Library.

FIGURE 13.13: *Scene from* Street Scene *at the Ottawa Little Theatre, 1937.*

Photograph by Yousef Karsh, accession 1987-054 NPC, PA-165893, Yousef Karsh fonds, Library and Archives Canada.

16. For the outstanding lighting design of his 1932 production of *Earth Song* at the Sarnia Little Theatre, Herman Voaden required as many as seven lighting operators and several additional technicians for the installation of the equipment.

In the 1925 production of *Night* from the Vancouver Little Theatre Association (Figure 13.11), the combination of lighting and scenic items silhouetted against the cyclorama evoked the outdoor setting. Stage directions in this Symbolist script indicate the main characters "appear in silhouette before a lighted blue screen upon a simple mound that suggests a hilltop" (Oppenheim 1994, 155). The cut-out trees on stage left and rudimentary furniture provide a vivid indication of the setting without engaging in painted detail. A similar design treatment was employed in their 1927 production of *Arms and the Man*, which was supported with some realistic detailing.

Many plays written at the end of the nineteenth century and in the early years of the twentieth called for non-realistic settings. Figure 13.12 is a 1931 production photograph of Karel Čapek's *R.U.R.* from the Montreal Repertory Theatre. While effectively a box set with three walls containing exits to left and right and a window centre stage, its simplicity of decoration and its mere suggestion of an interior locates this design within the New Stagecraft style rather than with box settings. In the case of this production, as in *Night*, the lighting, dominated by the central backlit window, functions less for depicting reality and more for indicating mood and emotion. Some settings were a sophisticated mixture of new scenography and realism, such as *Street Scene* at the Ottawa Little Theatre in 1937 (Figure 13.13). This design combined painted detail with a staircase centre stage, which was one of the recurring elements in many new scenography designs. The repetition of rhythmic massing in the window frames and masonry in the building walls added visual interest to this dynamic setting. The unique work of Herman Voaden is unequivocally part of the new scenography, with its dependence on abstract settings and extensive lighting effects.[16]

There is an unmistakeable pan-national similarity of experience evident in the Little Theatres represented in this chapter, which demonstrates the level of sophistication that the designers in the Canadian Little Theatres achieved. They incorporated the latest ideas and techniques on scenic design from Europe and the United States. They established superb technical facilities and developed the expertise to accomplish striking effects. That so many of these amateur companies continued to thrive, often for decades, indicates how well established they were, both in their respective communities and in their common production ethos. Having for the most part embraced the Art Theatre's synthetic values of simplicity, suggestion, and stylization and adapting them to their specific needs and tastes, the Canadian Little Theatre Movement remains an important cultural expression of our local and, indeed, national identities.

Bibliography and Further Reading

"Alcazar Theatre." 1913. *The Daily News-Advertiser* (Vancouver), November 2, 1913, 28–29.

Aristotle. 1907. *Aristotle's Theory of Poetry and Fine Art, with a Critical Text and Translation of the Poetics*, 4th ed. Translated by S.H. Butcher. London: Macmillan.

Benson, Eugene, and L.W. Conolly. 1987. *English-Canadian Theatre*. Toronto: Oxford University Press.

Booth, Philip. 1989. "The Montreal Repertory Theatre: 1930–1961." M A thesis, McGill University.

Canada West: Performance Culture in Southern Ontario. 2008. Web-based database of popular performance culture. https://canadawest.library.utoronto.ca/.

Chansky, Dorothy. 2005. *Composing Ourselves: The Little Theatre Movement and the American Audience*. Carbondale: Southern Illinois University Press.

Denison, Merrill. 1923a. "The Theatre in Canada." *Canadian Bookman*, January, 8.

———. 1923b. "The Arts and Letters Players." *Canadian Bookman*, February, 31–32.

———. 1923c. "The Little Theatres." *Canadian Bookman*, February, 32.

———. 1923d. "Hart House Theatre." *Canadian Bookman*, March, 61–63.

Dominion Drama Festival. 1929. *The Curtain Call* 5, no. 1 (Nov.). Toronto: M.H. Coxwell.

Hesson, Hilda. 1923. "The Community Players of Winnipeg." *Canadian Bookman*, May 1923, 121.

"H H T Production History." 2012. Hart House website. Accessed June 21, 2018. http://harthouse.ca/wp-content/uploads/2012/07/HHT-Production-History4.pdf.

Lee, Betty. 1982. *Love and Whisky: The Story of the Dominion Drama Festival and the Early Years of Theatre in Canada, 1606–1972*. Canadian Theatre History. Toronto: Simon & Pierre.

Mann, Martha, and Rex Southgate. 1997. "Amateur Theatre." In *Later Stages: Essays in Ontario Theatre from the First World War to the 1970s*, edited by Ann Saddlemeyer and Richard Plant, 260–304. Toronto: University of Toronto Press.

McNicoll, Susan. 2011. *The Opening Act: Canadian Theatre History, 1945–1953*. Vancouver: Ronsdale Press.

Mitchell, Roy. 1929. *Creative Theatre*. New York: Day.

Nesbitt, Carol Dell. 1992. "The History of the Vancouver Little Theatre Association." M A thesis, University of British Columbia.

Oppenheim, James. 1994. "Night." In *The Provincetown Players: A Choice of the Shorter Works*, edited by Barbara Ozieblo, 155–65. Sheffield: Sheffield Academic Press.

"Ottawa Little Theatre—Past Productions." n.d. Ottawa Little Theatre website. Accessed August 19, 2021. http://www.ottawalittletheatre.com/ProductionHistory/Main.php.

Rubin, Don. 1996. *Canadian Theatre History: Selected Readings*. Mississauga, ON: Copp Clark.

Saddlemeyer, Ann. 1990. *Early Stages: Theatre in Ontario, 1800–1914*. Toronto: University of Toronto Press.

Simonson, Lee. 1963. *The Stage Is Set*. 1932. Tab Paperbook, No. 8. Rev. and amended ed. New York: Theatre Art Books.

Smillie, E Arma. 1923. "Ottawa Drama League—Early History." *Canadian Bookman*, June 1923, 151–52.

Stoesser, Paul J. 2007. "Hart House and the International Art Theatre." P H D diss., University of Toronto.

Stuart, E. Ross. 1997. *The History of Prairie Theatre*. Toronto: Simon & Pierre.

U M Digital Collections, Community Players of Winnipeg fonds, Amateur Dramatics in Winnipeg. n.d. University of Manitoba Libraries Digital Collections. Accessed June 21, 2018. https://digitalcollections.lib.umanitoba.ca/islandora/object/uofm%3Acpow.

"Winnipeg Little Theatre Collection." 1921–1958. Archives of Manitoba. Accessed December 9, 2019. http://pam.minisisinc.com/scripts/mwimain.dll/144/PAM_DESCRIPTION/WEB_DESC_DET_REP/REFD%20%2219867%22?SESSIONSEARCH.

Winston, Iris. 1997. *Staging a Legend: A History of Ottawa Little Theatre*. Carp, ON: Creative Bound.

The Wood Carver's Wife (1919)

"Will the light hold until they come for me?"

MOIRA DAY

LIKE E. PAULINE JOHNSON, whose work she admired (Keller 1981, 98, 205), Marjorie Pickthall was one of the few pre–First World War Canadian women writers and poets who achieved a national and international literary reputation. Both women flourished in late Victorian homes suffused with artistic, musical, and literary richness before making the difficult transition in their late twenties to full-time literary careers. However, where Johnson quickly overcame her shyness to become a noted public speaker and performer, Pickthall rejected a similar invitation to stage public recitals with a pert "not on your tintype" (M. Pickthall 1908c). Shortly before her death, she informed an American publicist seeking "exciting material" about her life that "there isn't any" (M. Pickthall 1922). Nonetheless, both women wrestled with the profound personal, physical, and professional compromises demanded of them as the price for succeeding as career women in a male-dominated publishing and entertainment industry. And while Johnson, by race, upbringing, and temperament, may have been better situated, as Pickthall herself suggested, to deliver more influential, sympathetic portrayals of Indigenous life and culture to the national and international audiences of her time (Keller 1981, 198), both women were also undeniably shaped by a more romantic, "universalist" kind of post-Confederation and early twentieth-century nationalism that was judged as increasingly dated and sexist as the century progressed. It is only recently that they have started to be re-examined as more complex women and artists than they may have appeared either in their own lifetimes or during the decades when their work was in eclipse.

In 1919, the same year that Pickthall completed *The Wood Carver's Wife*, she wrote the following to a friend: "To me the trying part is being a woman at all. I've come to the ultimate conclusion that I'm a misfit of the worst kind, in spite of all superficial femininity—Emotion with a foreknowledge of impermanence, a daring mind with only a tongue as an outlet, a greed for experience, plus a slavery to convention—what the deuce are you to make of that as a woman? As a man you could go ahead and stir up things *fine*" (M. Pickthall 1919b). While marked by Pickthall's characteristic wry, self-deprecating humour, her comment was an acknowledgement that the graceful, melancholy, "Celtic twilight" world of wholeness, harmony, and grace perpetuated in her poetry—and in her public persona, at least in Canada, as an ethereal pre-Raphaelite

 In a letter to her American publicist, Miss Wilson, she commented that there was virtually no Canadian coverage of "her years of hard work for London and New York publications" as a prose writer, because "Canada has always persisted in regarding me as a verse-writer only" (M. Pickthall 1922). The news that she had successfully acquired lucrative serial rights and was in the midst of negotiating film rights for her novel *The Bridge* was also largely confined to her letters (M. Pickthall 1921c).

FIGURE 14.1: *Marjorie Pickthall, 1916.*

Courtesy of Marjorie Pickthall fonds, Victoria University Library (Toronto).

poet—was increasingly at odds with a sense of self, fragmented by the contradictory and polarizing currents of modern life and experience.[1]

Born in England in 1883, Pickthall moved to Ontario when she was six; she sold her first short story to the Toronto *Globe* when she was only fifteen, and between 1898 and 1910, her literary career flourished first in Toronto newspapers, journals, and publications for young people, then in prestigious American journals such as *Century, Atlantic, Scribner's, Harper's,* and *McClure's.* The death of her mother in 1910 precipitated a major health breakdown, and in 1912, still wrestling with chronic health problems and depression, she quit her job as a librarian at Victoria College in Toronto to return to England. Between 1912 and 1919, she continued to publish poetry, short stories, and a novel while contributing to the war effort as an ambulance driver, farm labourer, and library clerk. In 1919 she returned briefly to Toronto, before retreating to coastal British Columbia in 1920 to concentrate on her writing. At the time of her sudden death in 1922, she had published some five hundred pieces, including numerous short stories and articles, one hundred poems, two novels—and one late, enigmatic play. Written in 1919, shortly before her return to Canada, *The Wood Carver's Wife* first appeared in *University Magazine* in Toronto in 1920 and then featured more prominently in the 1922 posthumous collection, *The Wood Carver's Wife and Other Poems*. It has continued to puzzle and intrigue readers, critics, and theatre producers.

While the play, which is set on the outskirts of a settlement in New France, could be seen as continuing an older tradition of verse drama celebrating the history of the new Dominion, the wilderness surrounding Pickthall's characters is much more a psychic than a physical or historical one. The wood carver's seemingly simple devotional action of completing a pietà for the colony's church using his young wife as a model for the Virgin becomes complicated by the wife's guilty passion for a secret lover and by the carver's equally consuming passion for his muse. Ultimately, the tightening knot of sexual, religious, and artistic obsession is violently severed with horrifying and tragic results.

Contemporaries like Pickthall's biographer Lorne Pierce felt that the "magic sound of the words" (Pierce 1925, 196) carried the piece to a realm of "sombre beauty" (114) transcendent of genre. However, later critics, such as W.E. Collin, felt its beauties did not wholly excuse its "shortcomings [as] a hybrid form," and that in aspiring "first and foremost" to be poetry, it failed as drama (Collin 1932, 375).[2] As historical verse drama, it was deemed as falling short because its New France was as static and picturesque as a "historical tableau" (Collin 1932, 377) and was so unspecific that "it might have been placed in Fiesole as in Quebec" (Pratt 1933, 335);[3] even as poetic drama, its action seemed blunted in verse that was more aesthetic than dramatic in its impact (Pratt 1933, 335). Nor did it measure up well against the gritty realism of new schools of playwriting centred on characters driven by psychology, heredity, and environment. Collin (375–78) and E.J. Pratt (335), among others, criticized Pickthall's characters as more symbolic than psychological in realization, while Northrop Frye dismissed the play as a "melodrama with a lot of Browning in it" (Frye 1958, 450).[4] While not without validity—Pickthall had a Victorian aversion for Ibsen, dismissing him as "deadly dull" with "a warped and distorted" view of life (M. Pickthall 1908b)—such later views overlooked the fact that Pickthall was nonetheless a knowledgeable theatregoer[5] who shared the disappointment of the Montreal and Toronto theatre critics that her work, as first performed in 1921 by the Montreal Community Players at the New Empire Theatre in Montreal and then at Hart House Theatre in Toronto, had been so inadequately realized on stage.[6]

In this regard, Patricia Badir has suggested that the acting and technical limitations of the first production were less important than the fact that the work was embraced so quickly by a new, rapidly expanding amateur art theatre movement eager to expose Canadians to new, native avant-garde or experimental theatre (Badir 2000, 235–36). Ironically, at a time when the

2. W.E. (William Edwin) Collin was a Canadian literary critic and writer whose 1936 collection of essays *The White Savannahs* is considered the first major, full-length, modernist analysis of Canadian poetry from the nineteenth century to the 1930s.

3. "Fiesole" is a reference to the setting of Robert Browning's 1855 dramatic monologue "Andrea del Sarto." E.J. (Edwin John) Pratt, who, as a student, met Pickthall when she was working as an assistant librarian at Victoria College and who was influenced by her poetry, is considered one of the foremost Canadian poets of the first half of the twentieth century.

4. Northrop Frye was a Canadian literary critic and theorist whose 1957 book *Anatomy of Criticism* is considered one of the most important works of literary theory in the twentieth century.

5. While she admired W.B. Yeats enormously as a poet, ironically she dismissed his plays as "thin, limp, unreal fare after Shakespeare" (M. Pickthall 1908a). By contrast, she loved Lord Dunsany (Edward Plunkett, eighteenth Baron of Dunsany), who may have been a greater model for the play's brooding sense of darkness and menace than Browning (M. Pickthall 1920c).

6. For a thorough summary of the critical response to the original Montreal and Toronto productions, as well as Pickthall's own response as recorded in her correspondence, see Badir 2000.

7.   While Badir has suggested that other local productions would likely surface "in a dedicated search of Canadian amateur theatre archives" (2000, 219), she has confirmed specific stage productions of the play in Winnipeg (1921–1922), Saskatoon (1934), Kingston (1934), and Calgary (1947); radio productions in Regina (1928) and Winnipeg (1932); and an opera adaptation in 1960 (Badir 2000, 218–19).

literary reputation of the "play as poetry" had started to decline along with Pickthall's own pre–First World War eminence as a poet, the play's new stature as an intriguing, distinctively Canadian experiment in symbolic drama led to a string of radio and community theatre productions across the country that paradoxically established Pickthall as one of the most frequently produced female playwrights of the amateur art theatre until the 1950s.[7] Undoubtedly, as a synthesis of art, imagery, and musicality, *The Wood Carver's Wife* has more in common with the symphonic expressionism of Herman Voaden's *Rocks* than the Marxist agitprop of Oscar Ryan's *Unity*; Badir has also suggested that both Voaden and Pickthall were influenced, in turn, by the expressionism of the Group of Seven; significantly, one of its artists, J.E.H. MacDonald, did the decorations for the 1922 edition of the play (Badir 2000, 299–32).

However, it is also important to contextualize Pickthall's work within a rising feminist movement in the early twentieth century that saw an increase in the number of women writers, playwrights, musicians, and artists alike. It is seldom mentioned that the Montreal premiere of the play coincided with the first exhibition of the Beaver Hall Group (a woman-dominated group of Canadian painters influenced by the Group of Seven) or that Pickthall, who sketched, painted, and photographed, was also a trained musician whose poetry was successfully adapted to music by others. In commenting on Pickthall's writing process, Pierce noted that while Pickthall's novels were the result of constant rewriting and redrafting, her poetry was committed to paper "unchanged" as an organic, fully conceived whole (1925, 121–22). It is striking that of the four extant versions of *The Wood Carver's Wife*, there are surprisingly few changes in the text from the handwritten copy of 1919 through to the final published version of 1922—and even the handwritten copy has very few blots or changes. It is also telling that a large proportion of the minor revisions Pickthall introduced over the four drafts of the play relate to changes in the stage directions or "beats" in the verse—suggesting that Pickthall conceived the play as a visual and rhythmic as well as literary score.

For example, some of the "beats" in the original manuscript give the impression of a younger, more high-spirited and impulsive Louis than in the 1922 version:

> MS *(1919): Nor tie my shoe without a grant for it…*
> *That's right, you smile. You look less angel so,*
> *But match me better…I have so much time*
> *As the old priest here uses for a Pater,*

> 1922: *Nor tie my shoe without a grant for it.*
> *That's right, you smile. You look less angel so,*
> *But match me better. I have so much time*
> *As the old priest here uses for a pater,*

However, the character who changes the most through small changes in imagery and "beats" in both the text and stage instructions is Jean. His final action of violence may be the same in all four drafts, but the process by which he arrives at that action, and the point at which passion solidifies into a plan, alters subtly from draft to draft. Generally, the 1919 (handwritten manuscript (MS) and typescript (TS) add more reactive pauses, or still, silent moments in the interchanges between Jean and Dorette to suggest a greater degree of ambiguity in their relationship (earlier 1919 and 1920 additions indicated in boldface):

> *As his song ends, Jean reaches the door, and stands within it, gazing at Dorette, who remains before the Pieta. [**For a moment they neither speak nor move. Then**] (M.L.C. Pickthall [1919-20]) he enters the room, his gaze still upon her. [**After a time,**] (M.L.C. Pickthall [1919-20]; 1920) Jean seats Dorette again in the chair, where she remains quite motionless.*

In contrast to the 1922 version which sees Jean moving Dorette immediately to her chair and taking up his tools, in one case, Jean only "goes back to the Pieta" (TS), while in the other he returns but only "handles his tools" (MS). Similar delays, pauses, and hesitancies in the earlier drafts leave Jean's motives and reactions somewhat more enigmatic. Is his plan of action already set when he re-enters the cabin, or is it a reaction ultimately triggered by Dorette's calling out to Louis for help and the latter's possibly responding with force? The 1922 text makes a significant departure from the three earlier drafts, both in eliminating a number of the earlier pauses and in cutting all the earlier lines or stage directions that depict Dorette calling out to Louis for help. As a result, the final 1922 version presents a colder, harder Jean whose actions appear more callous and calculating, and who seems more capable of re-entering the room with his vengeance fully planned and, in conjunction with Shagonas, simply playing a cruel cat and mouse game until he feels the moment is ripe to spring the trap.

It is little wonder, then, that recent feminist critics, most notably Diana Relke, in addressing the play's incipient feminism as a major source of contemporary critical attention, have tended to see Pickthall's own sense of isolation and entrapment most strongly manifested in the figure of Dorette, the tormented wife brutally objectified into an male artistic idealization of pure, suffering female essence (Relke 1987, 187–200). However, noting Pickthall's own claim that the play, written near the end of her short life, was a deeply personal work that rose out of her own psychic depths with a passion and intensity that she confessed was "entirely unexpected" (M. Pickthall 1919a), one might argue with Badir that even now the enduring appeal of the work resides in its essentially expressionistic nature. All the remaining characters in the play—Jean, the obsessive artist whose drive for artistic perfection threatens to destroy what he most wants to preserve and immortalize; Louis, the impulsive romantic whose determination to live out his idealized dreams in reality carries the seeds of his own self-destruction; and Shagonas, an icon of the natural forces of creativity that can sweep the self up to liberating visions of beauty, life, and ecstasy, and downwards into depression and madness—could also be seen as aspects of Pickthall's difficult relationship not just with herself as a woman, but also with her own muse.

It is telling that Pickthall was frankly baffled by the 1921 players' decision to make Dorette the focus of the drama, when she regarded this as Jean's play (M. Pickthall 1921a). There is little doubt that her own flight, as a writer, into the solitude of a small cottage in the BC wilderness after 1919 reflected Jean's own choices more closely than Dorette's (M. Pickthall 1920a, 1920b). The wood carver's concern about "the light" holding up long enough to finish the work may also have come to preoccupy his own "carver" over the final year of her life. Pickthall's writing was interrupted by another serious breakdown over the summer and fall of 1921 (M. Pickthall 1921b). A nurse tending to Pickthall at that time noted that Pickthall's doctor, alarmed at the toll the writing seemed to be taking on her mental and physical health, recommended that at the age of thirty-eight she consider relinquishing her career and settling into a more conventional domestic happiness. Pickthall was adamant that neither was possible: she had "never yet met the man who [would] consent to my keeping on with it after marriage" and the only way to deal with the psychic/physical pain and pressure was to write: "I *must* write these stories. They are all in my head...and they *must* be written" (Place, n.d.).

In an effort to gain more time, she agreed to back surgery in spring 1922 to alleviate chronic health problems. Instead, her sudden death from a surgery-related embolism on April 19, 1922, brought all choices, all pain, and all stories abruptly to an end, and only Pickthall's complex, enigmatic, tormented play was left to speak for her.

Bibliography and Further Reading

Badir, Patricia L. 2000. "'So Entirely Unexpected': The Modernist Dramaturgy of Marjorie Pickthall's *The Wood Carver's Wife*." *Modern Drama* 43 (2): 216–45.

Collin, W.E. 1932. "Marjorie Pickthall: 1883–1933." *University of Toronto Quarterly* 1 (3): 352–80.

Frye, Northrop. 1958. "Poetry." In "Letters in Canada: 1957." *University of Toronto Quarterly* 27 (4): 434–50.

Keller, Betty. 1981. *Pauline: A Biography of Pauline Johnson*. Vancouver and Toronto: Douglas & McIntyre.

Pickthall, Marjorie. 1908a. Letter to Helen Coleman, July 5, 1908. Box 2, file 13, Marjorie Pickthall Collection, E.J. Pratt Library, Victoria University, Toronto, ON.

———. 1908b. Letter to Helen Coleman, July 19, 1908. Box 2, file 13, Pratt Library.

———. 1908c. Letter to Helen Coleman, December 25, 1908. Box 2, file 13, Pratt Library.

———. 1919a. Letter to Arthur C. Pickthall, October. In *Marjorie Pickthall: A Book of Remembrance*, by Lorne Pierce, 103. Toronto: Ryerson, 1925.

———. 1919b. Letter to Helen Coleman, December 29, 1919. Box 2, file 20, Pratt Library.

———. 1920a. Letter to Nina Gale, June 22, 1920. Box 2, file 23, Pratt Library.

———. 1920b. Letter to Auntie Emily, July 8, 1920. Box 2, file 20, Pratt Library.

———. 1920c. Letter to Helen Coleman, October 21, 1920. Box 2, file 21, Pratt Library.

———. 1921a. Letter to Alfred Gordon, May 5 and 19, 1921. In *Marjorie Pickthall: A Book of Remembrance*, by Lorne Pierce, 131-32. Toronto: Ryerson, 1925.

———. [1921b]. Letter to Nina Gale, n.d. [Fall]. Box 2, file 23, Pratt Library.

———. 1921c. Letter to Helen Coleman, December 26, 1921. Box 2, file 21, Pratt Library.

———. 1922. Letter to Miss Wilson, January 19, 1922. Box 2, file 24, Pratt Library.

Pickthall, Marjorie L.C. (Lowry Christie). [ca. 1919-20]. "The Wood-Carver's Wife." MS. Last MS book, box 61, file 09, Lorne Pierce Papers, Queen's University Archives, Kingston, ON.

———. [1919]. "The Wood-Carver's Wife." TS. [with inscription: "With every good wish to H.C. Christmas, 1919"]. Box 1, file 07, Pratt Library.

———. 1920. "The Wood-Carver's Wife." *University Magazine* 19 (2): 218-36.

———. 1922. *The Wood Carver's Wife and Later Poems*, with decorations by J.E.H. Macdonald. Toronto: McClelland.

Pierce, Lorne. 1925. *Marjorie Pickthall: A Book of Remembrance*. Toronto: Ryerson.

Place, Mrs. Ethel G. n.d. "Notes Regarding Miss Pickthall." [May 13, 1926 or March 15, 1927.] Box 69, file 04, Lorne Pierce Papers, Queen's University Archives, Kingston, ON.

Pratt, E.J. 1933. "Marjorie Pickthall." *Canadian Forum*, no. 13, June, 334-35.

Relke, Diana. 1987. "Killed into Art: Marjorie Pickthall and *The Wood Carver's Wife*." *Canadian Drama* 13 (2): 187-200.

The Wood Carver's Wife[1]

MARJORIE PICKTHALL

1. There are four extant drafts of the play. A handwritten manuscript (MS) and a typescript (TS) both from 1919, the first published version in a 1920 issue of *University Magazine* (UM), and the final 1922 version published in the volume, *The Wood Carver's Wife and Later Poems*. This edition uses the 1922 text, but notes any significant variations from earlier drafts that may provide additional insights into the way Pickthall approached character, plot, and imagery during the process.

2. Lotbinière in the MS and TS. It is possible that Louis and his great cousin, the Intendant, are based on the historic de Lotbinière family. René-Louis Chartier de Lotbinière immigrated with his family to Quebec when he was ten, becoming the first Seigneur de Lotbinière in 1672. However, since the family remained active in Quebec politics until well into the nineteenth century, the play's action is not definitely tied to that date.

3. Pickthall was apparently dismayed by the decision of the 1921 production to "prettify" Shagonas into "a sugary child" by casting a woman in the role. She saw Shagonas as being about sixteen years old and genuinely menacing (M. Pickthall 1921a).

4. Note that on June 22, 1920, Pickthall mentioned to her friend Nina Gale that she was living "in a little pine-board shanty in a clearing" in British Columbia. About a week later, July 8, 1920, she wrote to "Auntie Emily" that she hoped she could persuade a neighbour to build "a little

CHARACTERS

JEAN MARCHANT, *the wood-carver.*
DORETTE, *his wife.*
LOUIS DE LOTBINIERE.[2]
SHAGONAS, *an Indian lad.*[3]

The scene is a log-built room. There is a door; and a narrow window, both open. Outside can be seen fields of ripe corn, a palisade, and the corner of a loopholed block-house; beyond is the forest; all is silent and deserted in the sun.

The walls of the room are hung with skins,[4] and here and there with things Jean has carved,—masks, two crucifixes, pipes, a panel showing a faun dancing to the piping of an Indian girl; there are guns also,[5] rods and nets, a long French spade, and a shelf with a few books.

The bare floor is strewn with fine wood-shavings. Jean is carving a Pieta[6] for the new church, in high relief on panels of red[7] cedar wood. Opposite him, facing the door, is DORETTE, *in a rough chair covered with a fur rug; she is sitting to him for the face of the Madonna. In the doorway sits* SHAGONAS, *mending a snare.*

JEAN. (*Singing.*) Hard in the frost and the snow,
    The cedar must have known
    In his red, deep-fibred heart,
    A hundred winters ago,
    I should love and carve you so.
    And the knowledge must have beat
    From his root to his height like the mid-March heat
    When the wild geese cry from the cloud and the sleet,
    And the black-birch buds are grown.

    Then, were you then a part
    Of the vast slow life of the tree?
    Did you rise with the sap of his spring?
    Did you stoop like a star to his boughs?
    Did you nest in his soul and sing,
    A silver thrush in a shadowy house,[8]
    As now, beloved, to me?
DORETTE. Not I. I have not sung.

log-house" for her "on a bit of cleared land," preferably "with deerskins on the walls."

5. The first three drafts also add "hunting knives" to the list. Only the 1922 draft leaves them out, perhaps to heighten the shock effect of Shagonas suddenly producing his knife in his initial scene with Dorette.

6. It remains one of the mysteries of the play why Jean would choose to represent his presumably young and beautiful wife as the older Madonna who has lost her only child, rather than the younger and more popular Madonna and child of the Nativity. The absence of children—or at least surviving children—in a time, place, and culture where offspring would not only be valued but perceived as the primary social, religious, and personal raison d'être for marriage adds yet another potential level of tension to the couple's relationship. It also further complicates Jean's reasons for choosing to portray Dorette as the barren, now-childless manifestation of the Virgin, especially if the couple has been married for a time. The absence of an actual son may not only complicate Jean's own relationship with the presumably adolescent Shagonas, but possibly Dorette's with Louis—especially if the latter is not significantly older than Shagonas, and his romantic impetuousness is more the result of youth than aristocratic gallantry.

7. While all previous drafts specify that the pietà be in relief on cedar panels, this is the first one that specifies that it should be "red" cedar wood, presumably to reinforce the red/blood imagery elsewhere in the play.

8. One of the first of many allusions to Dorette as a thrush (or songbird) nesting in the tree. Significantly, her

JEAN. The sight of you
    Sings to the eyes. A little lower down,—
    Lean but a little lower that fair head,
    The head of Mary o'er her murdered Christ,
    The head I kiss in darkness all night long,—
    Lord! and the delicate hollow of the cheek
    Defeats the tool. There's no blade fine enough,
    Unless a strand of cobweb steeled in frost,
    Or Time's own graver.
DORETTE. Hush. I'll not grow old.
JEAN. Grow old? I shall grow old along with you.
DORETTE. Together? No, old age is solitary.
    A little stretching out of hands, a little
    Breathing on ashes, and even regret is gone.
    I tell you, I have seen old people here
    As not in Picardy. The milk-dry woman
    Crouching above her death-fire in the snow,
    The old man biting on a salted skin,—
    Their patience and the forest—O, I fear
    Age more than anything.
JEAN. You are yet too young,
    Beloved, for my Mary.
DORETTE. What do I lack?
JEAN. Why, the cold barren look on nothingness,
    The grief that cannot weep, for if it could
    It would be less grief. The inconsolable
    Dumb apprehension, the doubt that asks for ever
    "Is it so?" of Love and hears the answer "Yea,"
    For ever...
        I would grieve you if I could
    To make my Mary perfect.
DORETTE. You are hard.
    You love your cold woods more than loveliness
    Of look and touch.
JEAN. Why, only as Lord God
    Might love the delicate dust He made you from,
    You and great trees, rivers and clouds, the plain
    Of ripened grasses running into flowers,
    And all that breathes in the world.[9]
        There, you have moved!
DORETTE. I only moved a little way to look.
    You have carved Our Lady's hair in Indian braids.
JEAN. Why not?

response, "Not I. I have not sung," marks not only her resistance to Jean's suggestion that she may be the eternal Muse of Nature, now singing specifically for him, but also to his more conventional romanticization of her as a contented love/soulmate "nesting" happily with him here as a "beloved."

9. One of several places where Jean's approach to religion and art suggests pantheism: a belief that all of reality is suffused with the divine, or that all of the material world, including nature, is a manifestation of an all-encompassing, immanent deity. While the term "pantheism" was not coined in Europe until 1697 and is now more associated with the Romantic movement of the nineteenth century, pantheistic thought gained ground over the seventeenth and early eighteenth centuries mostly through the influence of philosophers Baruch Spinoza (1632–1677) and Giordano Bruno (1548–1600). Pantheism was also seen as a dangerous heresy by the Catholic Church, and Bruno, among others, was condemned and burned for it. Jean's unorthodox views may account for at least some of the reasons that he left France for the Canadian wilderness despite his obvious talents. It may also explain some of Dorette's subsequent nervousness about any unorthodoxy in his art, like "Our Lady's hair in Indian Braids," that may strike the religious or civic authorities the wrong way.

10. In the previous three drafts: "the small church." Perhaps Pickthall regarded "dark" as more evocative of mood.

11. Jean seems to argue that the Intendant is too focused on practical matters to be overly concerned with small irregularities of art in a small, dark church in a distant colony. Also, if the success of

DORETTE. And laid the Lord on cedar boughs,
    Wrapping His body in a beaded skin.
JEAN. Why not? He would have walked in our New France
    Greatly as there, and died for these as well.
DORETTE. He is half-Indian. The Intendant will not like it.
JEAN. The Intendant will not see in the dark[10] church.
    Old Father Peter has a new lace cope,
    And even his dark-skinned servers will go fine.[11]
DORETTE. Ah, the dark people! How I fear them too.
SHAGONAS. The lady should not fear. Their hearts are open
    Even as Shagonas's heart. Shagonas knows
    Only the ways of stream and wood a little,
    And whence to bring the lady snake-root,[12] whence
    White waterlilies,[13] whence sweet sassafras,[14]
    And berries in the moon of Falling Leaves.[15]
DORETTE. Not you, Shagonas. I've no fear of you.
SHAGONAS. The young dog-foxes running in the fern,
    The bittern[16] and the arrow-dropping kite,[17]
    The tall deer with five summers on his head, —
    These were Shagonas' brothers. Now he comes
    With broidered nut-bags and a little snare[18]
    To catch a musk-rat for the lady's sake.
    Is it well made?
JEAN. Well made and strong, Shagonas,
    You sleek wolf apt to catch the herd-dog's bark.[19]
    The musk-rat ate our pansies[20] out of France
    And vexed the lady.
SHAGONAS. She must not be vexed.
    Shagonas dreamed the lady had two shadows.[21]
    If but the following darkness touches her,
    Or strikes at her, Shagonas will strike too.
    So!
DORETTE. O, the knife, the knife!
JEAN. Put up, Shagonas.
    We love it not, the steel in a red hand,
    Who have seen too much. But what did the boy mean?
    Beloved, how you cried!
DORETTE. It was the sunlight
    On the bare blade. I did not guess he wore it.
JEAN. They always have a claw beneath the pelt.
    I know them well.
DORETTE. When do you go to see
    The place preparing for your altar-piece?
JEAN. Why, any hour. But I can't leave her yet.

the colony is partially judged
by the success of the Church in
attracting Indigenous converts,
then the colony's Church
will take care to include its
Indigenous converts and allies
as well as its priests in its
public displays of religious
finery. If that is the case, then
why would a carving that is
also partially reflective of
the Church's "dark-skinned
servers" not also have a place
of honour at the altar?

12. An ordinarily toxic plant tradi-
    tionally used by Indigenous
    Peoples to produce medic-
    inal tea and poultices for
    snakebites.

13. While traditionally used
    for medicine and food by
    Indigenous Peoples, water
    lilies can also symbolize
    rebirth, fertility, and regener-
    ation after a dry season. White
    water lilies are further asso-
    ciated with purity, peace, and
    spiritual enlightenment.

14. A tree valued by settlers for its
    aromatic and culinary prop-
    erties, but also traditionally
    used by Indigenous Peoples for
    healing wounds and creating
    medicines.

15. The sense here is of bringing
    wild berries, many of which
    ripen in late summer or early
    fall, as a gift of medicine or
    food. However, additional
    meanings associated with
    death or passion are also intro-
    duced as the play evolves.

16. A large marsh bird of the
    heron family. Part of the water
    imagery of the play.

17. A large bird of prey often asso-
    ciated in myth with death and
    predation.

18. A trap, usually made of a noose
    of wire or cord, used to catch
    small birds and animals.

19. Presumably Jean sees
    himself as the protective
    watchdog who was not quick
    or wary enough to prevent
    an unexpected predator
    from stealing or destroying
    something precious he had
    brought from France. Jean's
    appreciation of "the wolf"

Look, how the long hand grows from grain to flesh!
Did not the bosom lift? Here at her throat's
The beating of a vein. O, if she came
From her imprisoning dead cedar wood,[22]
   'Gemma decens, rosa recens,
    Castitatis lilium,'[23]—
You, or the Mother of God? I do not know.
I should have two breathing lilies in my room,
Two queens, two heavenly roses,
O, donum Dei![24] And yet...the face, the face!
Beautiful. But there's no despair in her.
That makes despair in me. Look you my girl,
Suffer it with her. Think. She only knows
The dead weight of the Saviour on her knees
As it were a little child's.[25] She's woman. There
Is her dead heaven, her babe, her God, her all,
Unrisen. The grave yet holds Him.
   Why, you weep.

DORETTE. I am tired and cold.

JEAN. Well,...Rest you, little heart.
   I would not have you greater. Dry your tears.
   She has dried hers long ago.

DORETTE. I have sat too long.
   Will you go now to the church?

JEAN. Yes, yes, and see
   The shrine prepared to put my Lady in.
   You or the Virgin Mother? You, I think.
   They'll see you there between the candle flames
   A hundred years. The lads will worship you
   And maids with innocent eyes will wonder at you.
   Your beauty will lift many souls to God.
   Come, boy.

SHAGONAS. The lady must not be afraid
   Of any shadow.

JEAN. Fare you well, my rose.

*JEAN kisses her, takes his sword and broad hat, and goes out, followed by
SHAGONAS. DORETTE watches them through the open door as they cross the corn-
fields towards the blockhouse. When they are out of sight she shuts the door, crosses
the room, and kneels before the Pieta, her face hidden in her hands.*

DORETTE. If you have lain in the night
   And felt the old tears run
   In their channels worn on the heart,

moving in silently and
efficiently to anticipate and
eliminate any perceived threat
to his interests may motivate
Shagonas's next disturbing
speech to Dorette.

20. The word "pansy" is derived
from the French word *penseé,*
or "thought." While also
symbolic of "free-thinking,"
the flower was particularly
seen as inspiring romantic
thought, either as a part of
love magic or potions (as in
Midsummer Night's Dream) or
as simply reminding the lover
to think of or remember the
beloved (as in *Hamlet*). In the
Victorian era, it could also
signal constancy and passion
in a love that had to remain
quiet or hidden for a reason.
While Jean may assume
Dorette was vexed because the
muskrat destroyed flowers
planted as a symbol of their
shared love, Dorette is revealed
as having more complex
reasons to fear nature's
thoughtless devouring or
destruction of French flowers
that evoke deeper levels of
meaning, passion, and remembrance for her.

21. Shagonas's reference to
Dorette having "two shadows"
is most obviously a veiled
warning to her that he knows
about Louis's shadow joining
hers in the forest, and that
she has an additional hidden
shadow "self" at odds with the
image she casts before Jean.
Many of Shagonas's gifts to
her, including the snare, have
ambivalent images of death
and healing attached to them;
he seems to suggest here that,
if the threat posed by the
internal or external "darkness"
of her "shadows" becomes too
great, he will not hesitate to
kill what "vexes" or disturbs in
order to effect a cure.

22. On one level, Jean seems
to be referencing medieval
mysticism, where statues
of the Virgin and the saints
were believed to momentarily
take on life or aspects of life

Pity me, Mary.

If you have dreaded the light
And turned from the warmth of the sun
Like a blind child groping apart,
Pity me, Mary.

If you have risen from sleep
To the shadow of death, and the moon
White as one slain for your sake,[26]
Pity me, Mary.

If you have longed for the deep
Close dark in the fulness of noon
When the eyes of the forest awake,
Pity me, Mary.

O, you who went folded in wings
Of Godhead, the maiden of God,
First star of the morning He made,
Pity me, Mary.

No bird of the meadow that sings,
No bud that shines up from the sod
But pierces me too with its blade.
Pity me, Mary.

Ah Christ! but will she pity, being pure?
You also, yet you pitied. Have compassion.
You stilled the wild seas at Gennesaret.[27]
Stretch out Your hand and still me. I am torn
With tempest, and the deep goes over me.

He does not stir. He is dead. O, Louis, Louis![28]

*There is a soft knocking at the door, but she does not hear. She remains motionless
before the Virgin. The door opens,* DE LOTBINIERE *enters and shuts it behind him.
Seeing her, he uncovers, steals across the room and kneels beside her. Presently she
lifts her head and looks him in the face.*

DORETTE. Louis!

DE LOTBINIERE. O loveliest, join me to your prayer.

DORETTE. Louis!

DE LOTBINIERE. I too will kneel to Christ and weep

(moving, shedding tears or blood) and to work miracles through the power of faith. On another level, he seems to be referencing the Greek myth of Pygmalion, who fell in love with Galatea, his ivory carving of the ideal woman. In the end, the Greek goddess of love, Aphrodite, took pity on him and changed the statue into a real woman so he could marry and bear children with her.

23. "Graceful bud, fresh rose, lily of chastity," from *Omni die dic Mariae*," a twelfth-century Gregorian chant ascribed to Bernard of Cluny.

24. O, gift of God!

25. One of several places where Jean strikingly conflates the imagery of the younger Madonna of the Nativity with the older one of the pietà.

26. A suggestion that the second "shadow" that Shagonas sees attending Dorette is the shadow of death and that she has at least a foreboding of a loss that unites her in sympathy with the woman, Mary, in ways unknown to Jean.

27. The Sea of Galilee.

28. The first of several images connecting the dead Christ on Mary's knees in the carving with Louis and his possible fate.

29. Throughout this scene, Dorette and Louis play with the interface between medieval Marian devotion to Our Lady and the courtly love ideal of the knight devoting himself wholly to the service of His Lady. While Louis finds it easy to conflate and elide over the differences between the human woman and the divine and artistic manifestations of the Virgin as realized in his idyllic liaison with Dorette, she is far more concerned about the potential chasms between them.

30. Louis combines religious and courtly love imagery again. He refers to Dorette as a dove—a symbol of the Holy Spirit and of transcendent purity

That anything so beautiful as love
   Should have such sorrow on it.
DORETTE. O my dear,
   I think I knew. But you are mad to come here,
   Here in broad day.
DE LOTBINIERE. I am growing tired of darkness,
   Dark hours, dark deeds, and little darkling ways,
   A dirty smoke across the flame of love.
   I had rather meet your Jeannot face to face
   With sunshine and clean air.
      Clean hands, clean heart,
   They would be his. He's welcome.
      Does he know?
DORETTE. You have not kissed me yet.
DE LOTBINIERE. Come to my heart.
   Now answer me.
DORETTE. The boy Shagonas knows,
   Not yet my husband.
DE LOTBINIERE. I almost wish he knew...
DORETTE. O, Louis, Louis, if you're in haste for that,
   Content you. He will learn it very soon.
   The sharp-tongued grasses that I trod towards you
   Will whisper him, the winds will tell him, Here,
   The dews will lie at noontime to betray me,
   The dawn come out of hour, the dark boughs sigh,
   There, there the foul thing passed.
DE LOTBINIERE. O, my Dorette!
DORETTE. That's right. I'll stand and let you kneel to me.
   Will you kneel gladly?
DE LOTBINIERE. As I would to her,
   God's Mother, looking earthward with your face.[29]
DORETTE. There's not a chisel-stroke he used to brand
   My likeness there, but casts me farther out
   From God's forgiveness.
DE LOTBINIERE. Alas, my pretty dove.[30]
   You make me hate myself, my love, my choice
   That so hath caged you, for you flew so cheerly
   Between the kind leaves and the little clouds.
   Gold were your feathers and your wings of silver,
   And now you feel the mire.
DORETTE. Nay, you have loosed me
   A flight above the stars. God pity us.
   We were not made for sin. I love you, Louis.
DE LOTBINIERE. Why, so I came to hear.

and spiritual ecstasy—but by modifying the image with the word "pretty" or, a little later on, "wild," he simultaneously evokes imagery more associated with sexual passion.

31. *Pater Noster*: Latin version of the traditional Christian prayer, "Our Father."

32. Reflects the mystic ideal, reflected in Jean's earlier speeches, of the mortal being completely subsumed by and united with the divine in an act of mystical love. However, consistent with courtly love, Louis suggests that it is Dorette who is the divinity that he worships and serves.

33. Another image that combines both religious and sexual imagery, evoking the Catholic sacrament of the Eucharist and the mystical transformation of bread and wine into the divine presence. At the same time, Louis's appeal to Dorette as the wine that fills his chalice also references sexual passion.

34. Red lilies, unlike the white ones that both Shagonas and Jean evoke, signify intensity, heat, desire, and passionate love. The colour also connects both Dorette and Louis to the image of blood, another double-edged symbol of passion and death.

35. A herb or plant with striking blue or violet flowers. Blue is a colour traditionally associated with the Virgin, while violet is associated with love or passion.

36. Dorette seems to suggest that if only her own soul, "that storm-driven bird," could ascend to seek solace and repose in the cradling, compassionate hands of the Mother, the eternal feminine essence of the maternal, then perhaps her own oppressive "heaviness" of pain, guilt, and mortal fragility would pass.

37. Dorette—who earlier confesses that her greatest fear is old age and death, especially as it manifests itself in this fierce, wintery

DORETTE. You are in haste?

DE LOTBINIERE. So bound to my great cousin the Intendant
    I may not breathe without his lordship's leave
    Nor tie my shoe without a grant for it.
    That's right, you smile. You look less angel so,
    But match me better. I have so much time
    As the old priest here uses for a pater,[31]
    No more, no less.

DORETTE. But that's enough for love.

DE LOTBINIERE. Why, love's timed by the heart beat or the slow
    Century's half. I have no thought but you,
    No care, no pride, no hope, no anything.
    I am not myself but you. My very flesh
    Has taken your tender likeness on. I see,
    Speak, breathe, hear, hunger but as you, Dorette.
    Smile on your servant.[32]

DORETTE. I smiled upon you once,
    Out in the forest when you talked to me.
    It seemed no sin among the idle leaves.
    But here the very windows are sealed up
    With watchfulness, the doorsill seems aware
    Who lately crossed it. Louis, I cannot smile.
    I fear for you, beloved. Will you go?

DE LOTBINIERE. What, go so soon? I have scarcely looked at you,
    Nor touched your hair, nor lifted your sweet hands.
    My chalice has gone drained of you its wine
    These three days.[33] Love, I cannot leave you yet.

DORETTE. But if he comes…

DE LOTBINIERE. When will you to the forest,
    My dear wild dove? I saw red lilies[34] there
    Burning in sun-bleached grass, and gentians[35] spread
    Beside a little pool, less blue than he,
    The great kingfisher poised on the dead bough.
    Black squirrels chirred against the quarrelling jays,
    There came a flight of emerald hummingbirds,
    While through the wind-swayed walls of reed and vine
    Laced the quick dragonflies. Sweet, will you come?

DORETTE. I am yours, my heart, wherever I may be.
    Let it content you.

DE LOTBINIERE. I am not content.

She leaves him, goes to the Pieta, and standing before it, speaks.

DORETTE. O Mother, tell him I cannot go.

wilderness—personally confronts the question of her own mortality and where she feels her own "being" may endure beyond the grave. The thought that the essence of her "storm-driven bird" of a soul may be dispersed and absorbed into a larger transcendent Nature that does not exclude her sometimes flying to and sheltering in the hands of the Mother reflects more than a little of the pantheism of Jean's first speech. Tellingly, though, she does not see her soul as mystically inhabiting Jean's "cold woods" and imbuing the carving with immortal aesthetic/religious life. And it is not her love for Jean that would pull her up from the roots of the tree to nest and sing. Instead, she claims that it would be her love for Louis that would drive her, despite herself, to rise upwards every spring to look for him.

38. Earlier reference to Dorette as his "wine," combined with suggestion of "deep" or dark red roses, makes the grapes another symbol of salvation through passion come to full fruition in its proper season.

39. Earlier unpublished drafts suggest a stronger, more visceral maternal image linking Dorette, the Virgin as Mother, and Louis. After the line, "Are with us, and the strong bird fledged to fly," Pickthall originally wrote, "/ And the meek nest he sprang from" rather than "/ Forgetful of the nest." Far from implying that he is the young bird who has outgrown the nest and is strong enough to fly on his own with whatever risks that brings, in the earlier versions, Louis implies that, at least spiritually/sensually, Dorette is the "meek nest" that he, the nestling, has "sprang from," and that even as the "strong bird fledged to fly" he continues to need her protective love and nurturing. Jean returns to the same

DE LOTBINIERE. Dorette.

DORETTE. O Mother, hold me fast against his voice.

DE LOTBINIERE. Dorette.

DORETTE. O Mother, hide me from his eyes.

>   Build from your sorrowing hands a little ark
>   Where that storm-driven bird, my soul, may rest
>   Till all its heaviness is overpast.[36]
>   Where will that be? In the grave? I think not there.
>   Though my slight bones had lain for centuries
>   Bound over with the prisoning forest roots,
>   And had no other feasting than the rain,
>   And known no other music than the wind,
>   I should yet go climbing upward every spring,
>   When the whitethroat came and burgeoning grains put out
>   To look for him...[37]
>   See, Louis, she will not hear me.
>   She is not Our Lady, for she has my face...
> What was that noise?

DE LOTBINIERE. I heard none.

DORETTE. It was like

>   The sound of a stretched bow this side the river.
>   Beyond the fields. It had a sound of death.

DE LOTBINIERE. Loveliest, what frights you? Life is all for us.

>   The fulness and fruition of the year
>   Are on our side, deep rose and darkening grape[38]
>   Are with us, and the strong bird fledged to fly
>   Forgetful of the nest.[39]
>   In those deep woods
>   I found white flowers beside a little stream
>   With three waxed petals round a core of gold.
>   I would have brought them to you, but I thought
>   To crown you with them there,[40] where balsam boughs
>   Strain the sweet sun, and every hour is stayed
>   On silence, and but the stream runs into song.

DORETTE. If you owe me any favour, any grace,

>   Of a promise I once kept, I pray you go.

DE LOTBINIERE. Are you tired of loving me?

DORETTE. I tired? O Christ!

>   I would lay my body for your feet to walk on,
>   And make a carpet of my hair for you,
>   Be the unsensed[41] wood, the stone, the dust you trod,
>   So that you trod safety.[42]

DE LOTBINIERE. Dear, I'll go,

>   But kiss me first.

metaphor in a more chilling context later in the play.

40. Here, as elsewhere, Louis combines images of Marian devotion and courtly love, associating Dorette with flower colours associated with passion (red, violet) and with Mary: blue, white, and gold. The three petals also evoke the image of the Holy Trinity. Louis also draws upon the popular medieval image of the Assumption: of the Virgin ascending body and soul into Heaven upon her death, where she is triumphantly crowned as the Queen of Heaven. However, Louis makes it clear that it is Dorette that he wishes to crown and serve as the queen of their own incarnate "heaven on earth." Louis's implicit vision of her as the new Eve, who has transformed the wilderness into an Eden for him, contrasts sharply with Jean's later image of Dorette as the frail piece of clay who has cost him Paradise.

41. Dorette, picking up on her earlier contemplation on being absorbed into nature as an escape from the trap of her mortal flesh, seems to suggest that she would prefer to be an inanimate part of nature with no feelings, or to have him notice her no more than if she were a part of nature, than put his life or safety at risk.

42. In the other three drafts, the wording is slightly altered to give a more urgent sense of Dorette wanting Louis to leave an immediate area of danger so that he will be safe.

43. An important city in northern France. It boasts the tallest complete cathedral in France. While the main structure was built during the thirteenth century, subsequent additions and repairs, including some made during the seventeenth century, would have made it an attractive centre for a talented carver or sculptor such as Jean to seek work.

DORETTE. O Louis, I will seal you
    With a charm of sevenfold kisses against wrong,
    Here, here, and here, on hands, cheeks, lips, and head.
    When first I saw you, back in Amiens,[43]
    Go riding with the great folk past our door,
    I thought that head a king's.
DE LOTBINIERE. Sweet, losing you
    I should go unkinged for ever, since my kingdom[44]
    Rests but in this.
DORETTE. You need not fear to lose me,
    Save as the strong tree loses the dead leaf
    Or the full tide one star.[45] Though I should die
    Soon,[46] and be set behind you like a song
    Heard once between the midnight and the dawn,
    And then forgotten, yet all I was, looked, said,
    Should still be yours, warm night be full of me,
    And morning come for ever with my face,
    Who have given you your first love.
DE LOTBINIERE. First love, and last.
DORETTE. And last...and last...Go now.
    O Christ, too late.
DE LOTBINIERE. Too late?
DORETTE. They are coming upward from the river,
    Jean and his Indian boy.
DE LOTBINIERE. So soon returned?
DORETTE. He is walking very fast. I think he knows.
DE LOTBINIERE. Does he, at last?
DORETTE. Perhaps Shagonas told him,
    Perhaps the dumb earth lightened into speech,
    As often times to flowers, or the blank air
    Took colour in our likeness...Why, you wait!
    O, I am going mad. Have you no limbs,
    No breath, no natural motion? Would you bide
    Thus, thus the loosening rock, the falling tree,
    Fingering a sword?
DE LOTBINIERE. Is your Jean not[47] so much?
    Let him find me here beside you.
DORETTE. If he does
    I shall go mad indeed. Have I no claim?
    Have you no pity for me? Is your love
    Of such a bitter substance that my tears
    Can wring no answer from it, nor my hands
    Avail against your pride? See, see I'll kneel,
    Nay, stretch my length before you, in the dust

44. Both Jean and Louis make reference to Dorette being their "kingdom" and either being "kinged" or "unkinged" in reference to her.

45. Starfish. The shifting of the tides that inevitably bring hardship and death to some creatures in the tide pools also bring new life and sustenance to others with every cycle. While earlier acknowledging that the consummation of her love for Louis has loosed her to "a flight above the stars," she suggests that he will possess and keep the essence of her longer, better, and more safely if he looks for her in the regenerative cycles and tides of nature than in the flawed, mortal woman.

46. A sense of urgency increased in earlier three drafts by using "Now" instead of "Soon," suggesting that she fears that she too may not long survive Jean's discovery of their affair.

47. Quite possibly a typo that inadvertently alters meaning. All the earlier drafts give the line as "Is your Jeannot so much?" That is, "Is your husband such an overwhelming threat that I need fear an honest confrontation with him?" As worded here, the sense seems to be "Do you think so little of your husband that you feel he does not deserve the dignity of being confronted and told the truth by a worthy rival?"

48. An elderberry thicket: an ambiguous symbol of life and death. While elderflowers and ripe cooked berries are frequently turned into food, beverages, and medicines, other parts of the plant, including the uncooked berries, are poisonous.

49. It is established here that Louis will hide in the elderberry thicket until Jean has entered and the door has shut, indicating that it is safe for him to slip away.

50. In all versions, these stage directions set up two important plot devices: the

Darken the hair you praise, with very death
Entreat, beseech you, only that you go.

DE LOTBINIERE. There, lest my heart break. There, poor child, I'll go!

DORETTE. Now? Now?

DE LOTBINIERE. Now, now. Why, you will make me laugh
At these so tender terrors. I will slip
Into the berried elder-brake[48] that throws
Shade on your sill, and wait till he's within,
And the door shut.[49]

DORETTE. Go, go.

DE LOTBINIERE slips from the door which he leaves open and hides in the thicket which has thrown leaf shadows upon it through the afternoon.[50] DORETTE again kneels before the Pieta.

DORETTE. Keep open door,
O Saviour, of your mercy. Blot him out
In soft leaf-shadows like a little death.
Shut thou his eyes with webs, his breath with buds,
Prison his hands with branches. Strew Thou me
Dust on the wind to blind them so they see not,
Nor hear[51]...Ah!

JEAN is heard singing as he approaches the house.

JEAN. (*Singing.*) Three kings rode to Bethlehem
By the sand and the foam.
Three kings rode to Bethlehem.
Only two rode home.

O, he hath stayed to watch her face
And make his prayer thereto,
And to lay down for his soul's grace
The straw beneath her shoe.

O, he hath sold the golden rings
That linked his camel-reins,
And the low song a mother sings
Is all his sorrow gains.

Two rode home by the foam and the sand,
Between the night and the day,
But one has stayed in Holy Land
And cast his crown away.[52]

leaves as indicative of Louis's hiding place outdoors, and the open door as his cue that it is not yet safe to leave. Unfortunately, and despite Dorette's best efforts, she is not able to shut the door at any time during the upcoming scene.

51. This is one of the passages where Pickthall revised the language and imagery in subtle ways across all four drafts. The 1922 version is the only one where Dorette explicitly refers to herself as "Dust on the wind," continuing her prayer that not only does Louis become subsumed enough into nature and the tree to escape detection, but also that she can become blowing dust to hide him and any trace of the guilty ecstasy ("little death") they have shared.

52. This is another place in the play where the traditional Madonna of the Nativity is introduced as a counterpart to the Madonna of the pietà. However, while there is an implication that Jean sees himself as one of the kings who came to worship both the mother and the miraculous, redemptive child, he has ended up throwing all away in a foreign land for an empty or forlorn hope.

53. "Irised" means iridescent, or having the colours like those of the rainbow; in this context, Jean may suggest that she is beautiful, but shifting and inconstant. However, his reference to "iris" may also refer to the eye and Jean's preoccupation with reading Dorette's eyes and face for meaning for the rest of the play. Referencing the Creation story in Genesis, Jean also seems to suggest that he too has also fallen into the sin of idolatry through mistaking a frail, fallen, mortal creature made of clay for an embodied spirit of the divine. However, as a sculptor, he is also aware that the same fire that tempers

As his song ends, JEAN *reaches the door and stands within it, gazing at* DORETTE, *who remains before the Pieta. Presently he enters the room, his gaze still upon her.*

JEAN. Do you pray there to yourself?

DORETTE. Rather to God.

JEAN. Why, that's a better prayer.
 You should not pray to yourself. You are too tender,
 You irised bubble of the clay,[53] to bear
 The weight of worship. Prayer must not be made
 To the weak dust the wind cards presently
 About the world.[54] Why, even your shadow, she,
 Madonna of the reddening cedar wood,
 Hath but a troubled momentary power,
 A doubtful consolation, and a look
 As though the wind would rend her and the fire[55]
 Eat to swift ash. No comfort there for sinners.
 But you're no sinner, need no comforting
 Other than mine,—as this, and this, and this.

DORETTE. You hurt me.

JEAN. I? What, hurt you with a kiss?
 Shall I go kiss her so?

DORETTE. It were a sin.

JEAN. Here is too much of sin and sin and sin.
 Go, get you to that chair.

DORETTE. Why do you look
 So strangely on me?

JEAN. Is my look so strange?

DORETTE. Yea, sure, as if you found me dead but now
 And saw my face.

JEAN. I see a kind of death there.
 Go, sit you in your chair.

DORETTE. Where is Shagonas?

JEAN. Lingering to shoot at crows with his great bow
 More fit for war. He has fledged an arrow thrice
 In carrion hearts, until the feather dripped
 Blood, blood, and blood again. You shrink? By blood
 Was the world saved, and what's as red as it
 Only by blood is turned wool-white again.
 What's that to you, white rose? Go, sit you there.
 I would make you more Madonna.

DORETTE. Jean, not now.
 I am sick. I am weary.

JEAN. Do you pray to me?
 You should not. You're Our Lady. You will taste

steel transforms soft clay into something permanent, unchanging, and enduring—provided the vessel does not hold a hidden flaw or "bubble" before it is fired. Jean seems to suggest there may yet be a way to "test," salvage, and redeem the "weak clay" of his wife.

54. Jean's comparison of Dorette to dust exists in sharp contrast to Dorette's own vision of herself as dust as an expression of love, abnegation, and caring. In an earlier speech, Jean claims that he loves his wood only in the same way that the "Lord God / Might love the delicate dust He made you from." Here he suggests that what comes from dust will dissolve and return to dust and be blown away, even as Dorette's "shadow" of wood can be rent by wind and eaten to "swift ash" by fire. It is also evocative of the phrase "Ashes to ashes, dust to dust" in the Anglican funeral service in the Book of Common Prayer.

55. Jean appears to be playing with the ambivalent image of fire as an apocalyptic force that consumes whole worlds and plunges lost souls into a perpetual inferno of torment and as a Pentecostal fire which refines and purifies the spirit towards redemption, which through candles and incense lifts the contemplative soul closer to God.

56. *Stella Maris* (Latin for "star of the sea") is a widespread honorific for the Virgin dating back to the early medieval period and is meant to convey both her role as a guiding "star" to her son and her special protection for those on the sea. While with Louis, Dorette interprets her own role as a "star" in the sea quite differently.

57. A very loaded image, at once sexually and religiously suggestive of a lover, while also referring to the infant of the Nativity and the dead grown

The year-long incense and the holy heat
Of candles. They will hail you mystic rose,
The tower of ivory, the golden house,
Sea-star[56] and vase of honour. Sit you there.

DORETTE. I cannot.

JEAN. Go.

DORETTE. You are very harsh with me.

JEAN. 'Tis you are hard to please. I kiss; you tremble,
I speak; you are in tears.

DORETTE. Where is Shagonas?

JEAN. Without, without.

DORETTE. I have an errand for him.

JEAN. He will come soon…Fie, what a withered look,
How your heart beats. You are fevered. Sit, Dorette.
Lift your face to the light,—a little forward,—
So, now,—and dream you hold across your knees
What's dearest of your world, and slain for you
That blood may wash out sin.[57]

DORETTE. O, Christ!

JEAN. Of course.
Who else but Christ? That suits me. Hold your peace.

While they are speaking, DORETTE *has seated herself again in the chair facing towards the door, upon which the lightly-stirred shadows of elder leaves come and go.* JEAN *takes up his tools.*[58]

JEAN. 'Tis a fine blade,[59] this one. Do you remember?
I sold its fellow when we were in France
To buy you a ring.

DORETTE. I had forgotten.

JEAN. Turn
Your face this way. Look towards me, not the door.
What see you? There is only sun outside,
Harsh elder drops,[60] ripe fields and ripening hours,
Soft birth of wings among the woven shadows,
And a Southward-crying thrush.[61] Do you remember?
They built and sang what time we built this house.
I left the elder thicket for their sake,
Who also built for love.

DORETTE. Shagonas…where?

JEAN. What do you say? Are you sick? You speak so low.

DORETTE. O, sick of heart! Jean, Jean, I cannot bear it.

JEAN. If you move more, I will bind you to the chair
As the Indians bind a prisoner to the stake

son of the pietà resting "across your knees."

58. In the MS version, the stage directions again more explicitly connect the images of the leaves, shadows, furs, and the open door. By touching rather than taking up his tools, Jean also again signals hesitation over how to read the situation or act on it. Contrasting text from the 1919 MS edition indicated in boldface: "*While they are speaking Dorette has seated herself [once more] in [the fur-covered] chair facing the open door, upon which [the shadows of] lightly-stirred elder leaves come and go. Jean [has gone to the unfinished Pieta and touched his tools].*"

59. Jean draws a sobering parallel between the hunting knife, which can protect, sustain, defend, and destroy at the will of its owner, and the chisel, which can do the same.

60. Jean refers to the ambivalent image of the elder bush as a source of both death and life. The image seems to suggest that the berries have already ripened, dropped from the trees, and been wasted. This image exists in sharp contrast to Louis's earlier image of the ripening grapes of autumn; he evokes the clustering fruit on the vine as a sign that life and love are both similarly growing to fullness and fruition for the lovers.

61. By drawing Dorette's attention to the departing song of the southward-migrating thrushes, Jean reminds her again of the spring season of their early love that had seen the building of the cabin and his sparing of the elder thicket for the songbirds to sing and nest in as well. By doing so, he returns to the theme of the nestling, which he can choose to love and protect or destroy. His veiled warning that he already suspects what the elder thicket is currently hiding or sheltering resonates

---

Lest they miss one shuddering nerve, one eyelids droop
Before the lifting fires...Your pardon, wife.
Was I so fierce? There's fire in me to-day
Would close a burning grip on the whole earth
And break it into ash...Your face, your face.
That's beautiful. Why, almost here's the look
I crave to lend Our Lady, yet too quick
With life and dread. Will you not mend your eyes
That yet lay hold on Love, and teach your lips
Too eager for that cup, and school your heart
That yet strains after him the way he went
That he returns no more? O, two rode home, —
   'Two rode home by the foam and the sand[62]
   Between the night and the day,
   But one has stayed in Holy Land,' —
One always stays, one always stays behind
Where the heart made Holy Land. This king of song
Was worshipful, just, and mighty,[63] His great place
Knew him no more. He cast it all away, —
The pity of it! — so he might serve till death
God's Mother. But she did not wear your face.

DORETTE. This heat...I am dying.

JEAN. What is it you say?
   If I should gash this sacred brow I smoothe
   Would you break blood? If I should pierce your heart
   Would she of the sevenfold sorrows[64] leap and cry?
   I cannot part you. O the grief of it,
   That Mary should sit there with you, and you
   Climb heaven with her. I am grown old with grief
   In a short hour. To work, to work, — your face.

DORETTE. Call, call Shagonas.

JEAN. Has he the art to heal you?
   What do you fear? I would not have you fear.
   I would have you like poor Mary here, who passed
   Beyond it, of a Friday.[65]

DORETTE. O my heart.

JEAN. Broken like mine? And so you had a heart,
   As well as those round limbs, those prosperous lips,
   The bloom of bosom and hair? O, he hath stayed, —
      O, he hath stayed to watch her face[66]
      And make his prayer thereto,
      And to lay down for her soul's grace
      His life beneath her shoe, —
Why, I have changed the song. What's come to it?

ominously not only with Jean's own opening references to Dorette as a nesting songbird, but also with Dorette and Louis's earlier image of the young man as a nestling having grown to maturity and first flight under Dorette's care. Equally ominously, Jean also mentions that the hopeful spring has now yielded to a silent autumn of ripening and harvesting.

62. Earlier two drafts indicate that this line and the two that follow are to be sung, strengthening the analogy to Jean as the "king of song."

63. The three earlier drafts use "holy" instead of "mighty," a less authoritarian image.

64. The devotion of the Seven Sorrows of Mary dates back to the early thirteenth century and revolves around seven key moments of profound grief in her life as the mother of Christ, culminating in his passion, death, removal from the cross, and burial.

65. Reference to Good Friday, the day of Eastertide commemorating the crucifixion and death of Christ.

66. The MS and TS clearly indicate that this line and the four that follow should be sung.

67. In the TS and 1920 magazine version, the phrase becomes "bind the wound" rather than "heal the wound," suggesting that Jean may act physically to contain or constrain her.

68. Again, Jean's vindictiveness is somewhat softened in the earlier three versions of the script, which essentially follow the MS in allowing Jean to express more grief over what has been lost than rage over his injury. Wording of 1919 MS indicated in boldface: "And his, the high / Clear laughter on the threshold of renown, / [**Courage most like an old song on the lips, / Stilled,**] stilled. [**But**] I could weep for him [/] and you, / Weep all my [**life**] away."

An ill song for the Mother o' God to hear.
Well, well, your pardon. Keep your face to me.
DORETTE. Pity, O Saviour.
JEAN. I am saving you,
    Your soul alive, a brand in a great burning
    Here in my breast. I saw where you will sit
    Years in the little forest-scented church,
    And lives like peaceful waves will break in foam
    Of praise before you. Then I turned me home.
    I saw—I saw—O, God, the chisel slipt
    And I have scarred you! I will heal[67] the wound,
    Thus, thus. Be still. I am saving you. Now, Shagonas!

JEAN has crossed the room, caught her to her feet, and stands holding her and her face to the door. Suddenly the note of a drawn bowstring is heard outside, something flashes past, there is a silence. Then among the shaken shadows of elder leaves on the door is seen for one moment the shadow of a man, erect, with tossed arms, and pierced through with a long arrow. Comes the sound of a fall, or broken branches. Then again silence, and the shadows of the leaves are still. JEAN seats DORETTE again in the chair, where she remains quite motionless; he returns to the Pieta and takes his tools.

JEAN. Your face again. Why, now you are fulfilled.
    You will make my Mary perfect yet, your eyes
    Now, now the barren houses of despair,
    Of the passion that is none, of dread that feels
    No dread for ever, of love that has no love,
    Of death in all but death. O beautiful,
    Stretched, stamped and imaged in the mask of death,
    The crown of such sweet life! Your looks, your ways,
    Your touches, your slow smiles, your delicate mirth,
    All leading up to this! And his, the high
    Clear laughter on the threshold of renown,
    Stilled! I could almost weep for him and you,
    Weep all my wrong away.[68] My queen, my rose
    Rent with strange swords, my woman of light worth,
    Behold, you have brought forth death.[69]

SHAGONAS enters, carrying DE LOTBINIERE's sword, which, obeying a gesture of JEAN's, he lays across the knees of DORETTE. She looks down upon it as though blind.

JEAN. Your only fruit[70]
    Destruction and the severing steel, the heat

69. This constitutes the play's final, chilling, and definitive conflation of the image of the Madonna of the Nativity and the Madonna of the pietà.

70. Ironic reference to the traditional Catholic prayer, the "Hail Mary": "Blessed art though amongst all women, and blessed is the fruit of thy womb, Jesus."

71. In all the earlier versions, Pickthall repeats the word "Wait." The substitution of "Stay" makes it unclear whether Jean is speaking to himself or asking Shagonas to "stay," only to change his mind a moment later.

72. O Lady of Sorrows!

73. Hail, holy Queen, Mother of mercy,
Our light, our sweetness, our hope, hail.
O clement, O loving, O sweet Virgin Mary.
Excerpts from the "Salve Regina," a twelfth-century Marian chant often recited at the end of the rosary.

Of tears unshed, the ache of day and day
  Monotonous in want, inevitable,
  The dry-rot of the soul. Have you no words?
DORETTE. He said—he said there were flowers in the forest,
  White flowers by a blue pool, Our Lady's colours.
  May I go look for them? All white, he said,
  White as the Virgin's hands. But you have made her
  Out of red wood with a light of fire upon it.
  Perhaps the flowers turned red.
SHAGONAS. There is no fear
  In the forest shadows now for the fair lady.
JEAN. Fear's slain with that it fed on. To your wilds,
  You wolf that watched the flock. I will wait here with her,—
  Stay,[71] hearing a certain crying from the ground,
  The faint innumerable mouthing leaves,
  The clamour of the grass, the expectant thunder
  Of a berry's fall. Go you, go you. But first
  Turn me her head a little to the shoulder
  So the light takes the cheek, raise the calm hand
  Clasping the sword, set the door wide, and go.
  Now, now my Virgin's perfect. Quick, my tools!
  O Mater Dolorosa![72] O Dorette!

All is silent save for the tinkle of a little church bell ringing for vespers, and a faint sound of chanting.

JEAN. Salve, Regina, Mater misericordiae,
  Vita, dulcedo, et spes nostra, salve.
  O clemens, O pia, O dulcis Virgo Maria.[73]

  Will the light hold until they come for me?

Curtain

AMY BOWRING

15 : Evelyn Geary and the Uptown Girls (1922–1938)

A Vaudeville Dancer's Story

1. There are many sources that describe the business model of vaudeville and the palace-like design features of its theatres. For example, see Kibler 1992; Gardner 1997, 135-50; "Vaudeville" 2002. However, not all theatres were so grandiose, and many that dotted towns between major centres were independently run and did not necessarily operate on the circuit system (Mann 1993, 58-60).

IN THE EARLY TWENTIETH CENTURY, before television was available in Canada and when film was the newest mass medium, vaudeville was a popular live entertainment choice for filling the increased leisure time people had before and following the First World War. Its success is largely due to a combination of large and glamorous venues in major cities, the cachet of a star system, a series of circuits and allied theatre networks to provide both branding and efficiency in touring, and accessible prices.[1] The career of Evelyn Geary provides an excellent case study of the joys and rigours of a vaudeville dancer's life.

The heyday of vaudeville in Canada spans roughly the period of the decade leading up to the commencement of the First World War in 1914 and culminating just after the stock market crash of 1929 and the onset of the Great Depression. It was a time when Canada was experiencing a major migration of people out of rural areas and into urban centres coinciding with growth in industrialization. Canada needed labourers and skilled workers in construction, factories, and textile mills, which also meant the growth of a white-collar labour force of managers and supervisors. The rise of these professionals led to a high demand for women to work in domestic service, which was one of the chief occupations for women by 1921 along with jobs such as teachers, nurses, telephone operators, shop clerks, and even a small percentage as owners and managers of shops or small businesses (Granatstein et al. 1990, 116-17).

The vaudeville circuits that dotted the country presented the first significant opportunity for Canadian dancers, who were primarily women, to earn a living as performers. The *Toronto Star Weekly* reported in 1930 that "Toronto, it appears, may almost begin to count dancing as one of the major professions of women. Upwards of a hundred girls earn their living by 'hoofing'" ("'Hoofing'" 1930). While their incomes were quite decent for the time, they worked long, exhausting days. They also had to contend with assumptions about the lack of morality associated with their career choice.

Geary began dance lessons in 1918 at age nine with Toronto teacher Samuel Titchener Smith. She got her first paid job in 1922 dancing with the Defoe Grand Opera Company. That same year, Geary encountered controversy when her mother asked her school principal to let Geary out of school at 2:30 p.m. each day for one week so she could perform, but the request was denied. After

FIGURE 15.1: *Evelyn Geary, ca. 1925.*

Accession number 131.2009-1-2. Courtesy of Evelyn Geary Portfolio, Dance Collection Danse.

FIGURE 15.2: *News clipping from Evelyn Geary scrapbook, ca. 1928.*

Accession number 131.2009-1-3. Courtesy of Evelyn Geary Portfolio, Dance Collection Danse.

2. The article "'Hoofing' Now Offers Girls a Profession" (1930) reveals that Aileen Parker started performing at age four and also states that dancers really needed to start their careers before age fourteen to ensure success. The Edna Liggitt Electronic Archives at Dance Collection Danse in Toronto contain several contracts for and photographs of the Liggitt sisters as child performers.

Mrs. Geary removed her daughter from school without the principal's permission, a truant officer arrived at the Geary household and threatened the family. Geary's parents argued that performing was a valid part of their daughter's education, as she showed the promise of having a career as a dancer. They threatened to take their case to court, if necessary. A statement by Mrs. Geary recorded in *The Star* (Toronto) summarizes the double standard at work against aspiring dancers: "If I had asked to have [Evelyn] stay at home to mind the baby or run a message, it would have been all right and no one would have said anything about it...She must get used to being on the stage, because the stage will probably be her career" ("Miss Evelyn's Education," n.d.). Geary fell under the regulations of the Ontario Adolescent School Attendance Act passed in 1919, which mandated that teenagers up to the age of sixteen were required to attend school unless ill health (theirs or a family member's) or employment exempted them; if exempt, they were still required to take part-time courses throughout the year (Nicolson 2018).

The Toronto Board of Education's refusal to accept Geary's employment for stage and modelling work as a legitimate reason for an exemption may be related to the perceived legitimacy of the work itself. Chief Inspector R.H. Cowley told reporters, "We are not going to have Toronto Public school children used as window dolls by any firm when they should be in school." Cowley continued, "It has come to my notice that children have been employed at the theatres in pantomime work, etc. If parents want this sort of thing for their children they will have to secure private tuition for them, and not have them under the jurisdiction of the Public school at all" ("Must Attend School," n.d.). Cowley's language certainly implies that he did not view performance work to be an adequate reason to miss school.

Geary was not alone as a child performer at this time: Aileen Parker began performing at Shea's Hippodrome at age four, and Geary's fellow Titchener Smith students, the Liggitt sisters, also performed during their childhood years.[2] Probably the most famous child performers in Canada during the First World War and in the early 1920s were the Winnipeg Kiddies. Formed in 1915 by a Winnipeg-based accountant named A.H. Smith, the Kiddies toured Canada and the United States to raise funds for First World War recruitment efforts (Hunt, n.d.). Performing songs, dances, and comedy sketches, they also received a general education from their private tutor and had access to interesting and educational sites, such as Niagara Falls, while on tour ("Winnipeg Kiddies at Niagara Falls," n.d.; "Winnipeg Kiddies Delight," n.d.). While these examples of child performers came from middle-class upbringings, the reality for Canada's poorest children in the early twentieth century was to begin working in adolescence, or younger, even in difficult and dangerous jobs such as mining and railway work (Granatstein et al. 1990, 238).

Geary continued dancing throughout her schooling and pursued this career into adulthood. Her skill at dancing *en pointe* in addition to the usual national, fancy, skirt, and partnered dances put her in high demand ("Miss

FIGURE 15.3: *News clipping from Evelyn Geary scrapbook, ca. 1921.*

Accession number 131.2009-1-3. Courtesy of Evelyn Geary Portfolio, Dance Collection Danse.

FIGURE 15.4: *The* King's Scandals *show possibly at Roxy Theatre, New York, 1927.*

Accession number 131.2009-1-2. Courtesy of Evelyn Geary Portfolio, Dance Collection Danse.

FIGURE 15.5: *Evelyn Geary's backstage pass for New York's Roxy Theatre, 1927.*
Accession number 131.2009-1-1. Courtesy of Evelyn Geary Portfolio, Dance Collection Danse.

Evelyn's," n.d.). With the help of a booking agent, she performed in vaudeville theatres across Canada and the United States.

Working conditions varied from theatre to theatre, but they were generally harsh. Dancers were responsible for arriving in correct costume and make-up, and call times did not include preparation. Most theatres did not provide adequate space for warming up; Geary once stated that the usual routine was to warm up "in the wings, up and down on your toes a few times and that was it" ("Miss Evelyn's," n.d.). She cited New York's Roxy Theatre as particularly harsh. Dancers at this theatre worked seven days a week performing shows in repertory—while one show was performed over the course of the week, the next week's show was being rehearsed. On weekdays there were four shows per day, and five on weekends and holidays. The first performance of the day was followed by a rehearsal for the next week's show, the second performance was followed by a break, the third performance was followed by more rehearsal, and the day concluded with a fourth performance. Toronto's Uptown Theatre had a similar routine to the Roxy: four performances per day with rehearsals between for the next week's show. The workday usually began at 10:00 a.m. and the last show started at 10:30 p.m., although, in contrast to the Roxy, Sunday was a free day (Warner, n.d., 24–25).

No matter how rigorous the days were, the dancers were passionate about their work. When the Uptown Girls were interviewed as a group for *Toronto Star Weekly*, they emphasized how they had no intention of giving up the stage for a man and that dancing came first in their lives ("Oh, We Love it" 1929).

Beginning in 1923, Geary kept a record of each job and its rate of pay. Venues listed include the Selkirk Dance Hall, Canadian National Exhibition Coliseum, Loew's Uptown Theatre, Shea's Hippodrome, King Edward Hotel

FIGURE 15.6: *News clipping from Evelyn Geary scrapbook,* The Toronto Star Weekly, *June 15, 1929. Accession number 131.2009-1-3. Courtesy of Evelyn Geary Portfolio, Dance Collection Danse.*

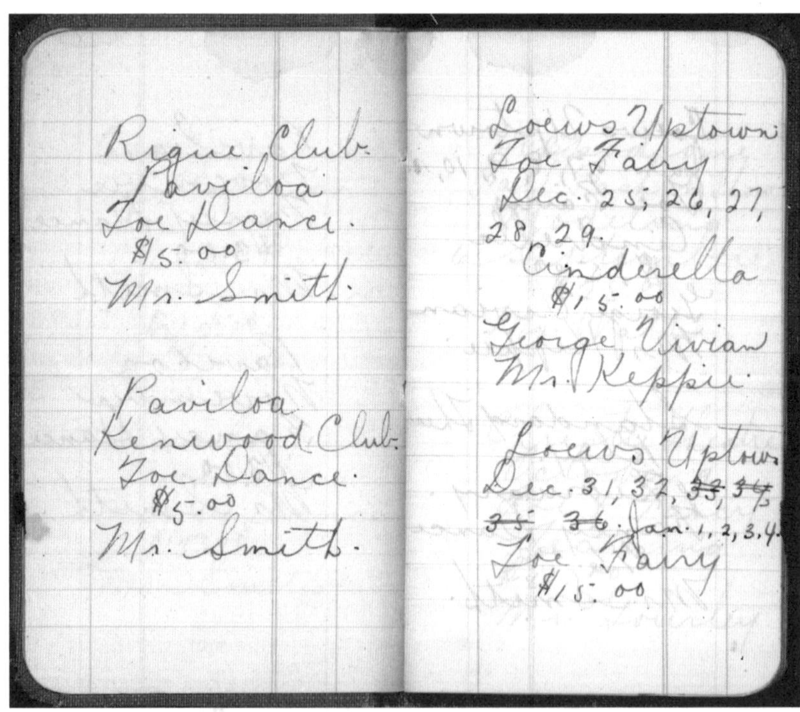

FIGURE 15.7: *Evelyn Geary's notebook, 1923–30.*

Accession number 131.2009-1-7. Courtesy of Evelyn Geary Portfolio, Dance Collection Danse.

3. Geary's $2,000 income equalled half the cost of an average house in Toronto during the vaudeville era.

FIGURE 15.8: *The cast of Captain Plunkett's tour of* Three Little Maids, *ca. 1926.*
Accession number 131.2009-1-2. Courtesy of Evelyn Geary Portfolio, Dance Collection Danse.

Crystal Ballroom, and summer performances at Scarboro Beach. The rates varied from $3 to $5 per show, or a weekly rate of $15 to $20. By the time she was working at the Uptown, Geary probably earned more than $2,000 per year, which compared favourably to the average Canadian production worker at the time, earning around $1,000 per year and a supervisory or office employee earning $1,890 annually (Statistics Canada, n.d.).[3] At the height of her vaudeville career, Geary earned more than her father who worked in management in the rag trade (Geary Moffitt 1997). It should be noted that Geary's American colleagues actually earned quite a bit more per week. The Chorus Equity Association was able to ensure that performers received a minimum weekly salary of $30 per week and $35 on tour, and some performers were known to be contracted at $40 and $50 per week (Chorus Equity 1919; Chorus Equity Sample Contracts 1920s, n.d.).

Geary's most lucrative jobs included a touring production with Captain M.W. Plunkett, founder of the famed Dumbells, and a job with the Pedro Rubin

Girls. At \$55 and \$60 per week, respectively, Geary was making an exceptional wage, but her rights as an artist were few. The Plunkett tour of 1925 began at the end of November and ran until the following April. The sixteen-year-old Geary was engaged as a specialty dancer performing toe and acrobatic dances. While her contract states that she earned \$55 per week, her personal notebook indicates that this amount applied to the first two weeks and then dropped to \$50 for the remainder of the tour (Geary, n.d.). While the tour began on November 23, 1925, rehearsals actually began on October 26 (before the contract was signed). Geary's contract plainly states that she would not be paid for the rehearsal period; unpaid rehearsals were also the norm for Chorus Equity Association contracts in the United States. Payment began with the first public performance.

Geary's notebook provides an idea of the rigorous touring schedule: two nights in Ottawa; a day of travel to Fort William,[4] three nights there; a day of travel and then a one-night stand in Kenora; the very next day, a five-night stand starts in Winnipeg; with a day of travel between each destination, the company begins a series of three-night stands in Regina, Saskatoon, Edmonton, Calgary, Vancouver, Victoria (over Christmas and Boxing Day), Vancouver again, Calgary again, and then one night in Lethbridge immediately following Calgary; then one-night stands in Medicine Hat and Swift Current, three nights in Regina, two in Moose Jaw, and three in Winnipeg with only a day of travel between each. Three days on the train are followed by five nights in Montreal, and then performances in Saint John, Moncton, New Glasgow, and Halifax. Geary then writes, "Have forgotten rest of Feb., Midland, Welland, Orillia, Woodstock, Kingston, Toronto" and she concludes with a list of about ten other small Ontario towns. But Geary was having the time of her life despite the gruelling schedule (Geary Moffitt 1997).

When the stock market crashed in 1929, live theatre was significantly affected. People had less money for entertainment, so the live acts that had preceded the movies were gradually phased out. Dancers either scrounged for work or left the business. Geary mixed her sporadic performing jobs with teaching work and she also worked more in the United States. Like many women of her generation, her career ended when she married in 1938 (Warner, n.d., 39). Unlike many women of her generation, Geary's dance career enabled her to have financial independence that was not part of many other women's lives; this financial independence also gave her agency to make decisions about her life. She did not live the scenario of most women, who moved from their father's house to their husband's house, but rather had the chance to tour Canada and to live and work in the United States when it suited her.

Vaudeville essentially represents the last heyday of live performance before competition with mass media changed the entertainment industry permanently. For female performers like Geary, it provided an opportunity for financial independence and personal agency not available to most women. But contemporary newspaper accounts and later oral histories, where these

FIGURE 15.9: *Evelyn Geary, 1925–26.*

Accession number 131.2009-1-2. Courtesy of Evelyn Geary Portfolio, Dance Collection Danse.

FIGURE 15.10: *Willie Teece, Rose Baker, May Wright, Edna Grice, Grace Rae, Violet Gore, Helen Sale, Charles Farrell, Evelyn Cloutier, Louise Burns, Jolyne Gillier, Jean Hemsworth, Marjorie Pethick, Marjorie Singer, and Evelyn Geary outside the Uptown Theatre, Toronto,* 1929. *Accession number 131.2009-A-8. Courtesy of Evelyn Geary Portfolio, Dance Collection Danse.*

dancers could reflect on their lives, reveal that it was the opportunity to dance
and perform every day that mattered most and gave them the deepest satisfaction.

Bibliography and Further Reading

Chorus Equity. 1919. PDF. Box 2, folder 12, Collection: Actors' Equity Association Records WAG.11, Tamiment Library and Wagner Labor Archives, NYU, New York.

Chorus Equity Sample Contracts 1920s. n.d. PDF. Box 2, folder 19, Collection: Actors' Equity Association Records WAG.11, Tamiment Library and Wagner Labor Archives, NYU, New York.

Gardner, David. 1997. "Variety." In *Later Stages: Essays in Ontario Theatre from the First World War to the 1970s*, edited by Anne Saddlemeyer and Richard Plant, 121–223. Toronto: University of Toronto Press.

Geary, Evelyn. n.d. Hand-written notebook. Evelyn Geary Portfolio, 131.2009-1-7, Dance Collection Danse, Toronto.

Geary Moffitt, Evelyn. 1997. Interview with Lawrence Adams and Miriam Adams, September 25, 1997. Oral History Collection, Dance Collection Danse, Toronto.

Granatstein, J.L., Irving M. Abella, T.W. Acheson, David J. Bercuson, R. Craig Brown, and H. Blair Neatby. 1990. *Nation: Canada Since Confederation*. 3rd ed. Toronto: McGraw-Hill Ryerson.

"'Hoofing' Now Offers Girls A Profession." 1930. *Toronto Star Weekly*, March 22, 1930.

Hunt, Alison. n.d. "Those Winnipeg Kiddies—First War Stage Patriots." Catherine Cummings Electronic Archives, ArticleFreePress1.jpg, Dance Collection Danse, Toronto.

Kibler, M.A. 1992. "The Keith/Albee Collection: The Vaudeville Industry, 1894–1935." *Books at Iowa*, no. 56, 7–24. https://doi.org/10.17077/0006-7474.1208.

Mann, George. 1993. *Theatre Lethbridge: A History of Theatrical Production in Lethbridge, Alberta (1885–1988)*. Calgary: Detselig Enterprises.

"Miss Evelyn's Education Not to Interfere with Art." n.d. *The Star* (Toronto). In Scrapbook 1, Evelyn Geary Portfolio, 136.2009-1-3, Dance Collection Danse, Toronto.

"Must Attend School." n.d. Clipping. In Scrapbook 1, Evelyn Geary Portfolio, 136.2009-1-3, Dance Collection Danse, Toronto.

Nicolson, Joanne. 2018. "Radical Reform: Education and Society, 1845–1945." Toronto District School Board and Virtual Museum Canada. http://www.virtualmuseum.ca/edu/.

"Oh, We Love It!" 1929. *Toronto Star Weekly*, June 15, 1929. In Scrapbook 2, Evelyn Geary Portfolio, 136.2009-1-3, Dance Collection Danse, Toronto.

Statistics Canada. n.d. "Annual Earnings in Manufacturing Industries, Production and Other Workers by Sex, Canada, 1905, 1910, and 1917 to 1975." Chart E41-48. https://www150.statcan.gc.ca/n1/pub/11-516-x/sectione/4147438-eng.htm#2.

"Vaudeville: A Dazzling Display of Heterogenous Splendor." 2002. American Studies, University of Virginia, http://xroads.virginia.edu/~ma02/easton/vaudeville/vaudevillemain.html.

Warner, Mary Jane. n.d. "Evelyn Geary: A Canadian Dancer" (unpublished essay). In Evelyn Geary Portfolio, 136.2009-1-1, 24–25, Dance Collection Danse, Toronto.

"Winnipeg Kiddies at Niagara Falls." n.d. Edna Patrick Electronic Archives, Edna Patrick 16.tif, Dance Collection Danse, Toronto.

"Winnipeg Kiddies Delight Calgary Audience Again." n.d. Edna Patrick Electronic Archives, Edna Patrick 17.tif, Dance Collection Danse, Toronto.

16 : The IODE's *Historical Pageant*
(1927)

Spectacle in the Service of Empire

ALLANA C. LINDGREN

ON THE EVENING OF JUNE 22, 1927, theatregoers filled Massey Hall in Toronto to watch *Historical Pageant*, a lavish spectacle featuring over five hundred performers interpreting scenes from Canada's history ("Progress of Canada" 1927).[1] These patrons, and those who defied the summer heat wave to wait in long lines at the box office for tickets to one of the four subsequent performances, were reportedly exhilarated with the "dramatic vividness" of *Historical Pageant*'s nine scenes and eight tableaux vivants ("People and Events" 1927; "Ontario: Toronto" 1927). Created as part of the celebrations for Canada's Diamond Jubilee, which marked sixty years of Confederation, *Historical Pageant* was written, arranged, and choreographed by Amy Sternberg, a highly respected dance teacher with her own studio in Toronto. Over three thousand people participated in the production, including many of Sternberg's students as well as performers from the Hart House Players, members of the Navy League, school children, and interested participants from the Toronto community ("Children," n.d.; "Gowns" 1927; "Toronto IODE," n.d.). The majority of the production team and performers, however, came from sixty-five chapters of the Imperial Order Daughters of the Empire (IODE).

This chapter analyzes *Historical Pageant* to determine how gender and empire intersected within the context of the IODE.[2] More precisely, *Historical Pageant* provides an opportunity to consider how the women associated with the IODE used theatre to convey the organization's aspirations "to draw women's influence to the bettering of all things connected with the Empire" (Program 1927, 5).[3]

The timing of the production is significant. In 1927 the IODE was not just celebrating Canada's Diamond Jubilee, but also promoting allegiance to the British Empire at a moment when Canada was gaining more autonomy. Canada's role in the First World War had generated national pride and a sense of national independence. Similarly, the Balfour Declaration, which emerged out of the Imperial Conference of 1926, affirmed a desire for increased self-government and anticipated the 1931 Statute of Westminster, which, in turn, granted Canada legal self-rule. A strictly hierarchical relationship between Canada and Britain was an idea losing ground among many Anglo-Canadians more attuned to a new concept: the British Commonwealth of

Nations, which had been crafted at the Imperial Conference of 1926 and meant that member states, including Britain, Canada, and other dominions, were united in their allegiance to the British Crown, yet all "equal in status" (Inter-Imperial Relations Committee 1926, 2). These steps to reconfiguring Canada's relationship to Britain facilitated a continued close association, but nevertheless were in tension with the IODE's ardent imperialist agenda. As historian Katie Pickles has written, the IODE, which was founded in 1900, actively contributed to "the construction of an Anglo-Canadian identity that celebrated all things British and advanced Canada's destiny as a part of the British Empire" (2002, 2). In so doing, this Canadian women's organization "confidently positioned itself at the centre of the British Empire, declaring itself to be the Empire's 'premier' women's patriotic organization. It was certainly the largest in membership, and, for many years, went about its work proudly advancing its patriotic intentions" (Pickles 2002, 2).

The members of the IODE, in other words, strongly believed that women had key leadership roles to play in ensuring the continuation of the British Empire, even as—or especially because—Canada was exercising more political independence. The work the IODE members proudly advanced stemmed from the maternal feminist belief that women's experiences as mothers and caregivers in the private or domestic sphere positioned them to act decisively to make vital contributions to society in the public sphere. The IODE also was aligned with the imperial feminism race-based objective to populate Canada with British immigrants or "Canadianize" non-British immigrants through assimilation. The IODE activities that demonstrated these ideological allegiances ranged from knitting for soldiers to advocating for eugenics.

Theatrical productions were also part of the IODE undertakings. Notably, the December 1926 issue of *Echoes*, the IODE's national quarterly magazine, included a list of scenes from Canadian history that were deemed appropriate for the staging of pageants to honour Canada's Diamond Jubilee ("Recommendations for Celebration" 1926, 23). Sternberg appears to have incorporated some, but not all, of the suggestions listed in the *Echoes* article. For instance, as recommended in the magazine, *Historical Pageant* began with the "Landing of the French in Canada," a scene in which French settlers were portrayed as pious and patriotic as they established and protected their settlements. A few scenes later, the production ambitiously presented a theatrical version of the Battle of the Plains of Abraham, including the onstage deaths of Generals Montcalm and Wolfe, who were identified in the program notes as "valiant leaders and honorable foes" (Program 1927, 57). The remaining scenes extolled the accomplishments of the British in Canada, characterizing them as having selfless courage and loyalty. In describing the War of 1812, the program for *Historical Pageant* stated that "the Canadas reaffirmed once more their stand for British institutions and backed this decision by the offer of their lives" (75). Similarly, in "Homesteading in the West," the penultimate scene, "colonists sought homes undismayed by danger or hardships" (78).

After an intermission, "Sixty Years of Confederation," the extravagant finale began. A procession of performers in "symbolical" costuming crossed the stage with rousing enthusiasm (Program 1927, 99). First came people attired as natural resources—silver mines, fisheries, forests, grain, and so on—that were intended to represent the provinces. They were followed by a parade of technical, cultural, and legislative advances, including telephones, electricity, art, literature, Mother's Allowance, the Workmen's Compensation Act, and the Department of Soldiers' Civil Re-Establishment. Young women representing the Air Force, Mounted Police, Navy, and Army apparently "danced prettily" ("People and Events" 1927). Next in line were IODE Standard Bearers. Finally, at the culmination of *Historical Pageant*—and of Canadian history, according to the pageant's narrative trajectory—Mrs. Vera McLean Somerville, dressed as Canada, stepped onto a dais draped with a Union Jack and sang "O Canada." She was followed by Miss Agnes Adie as Britannia who provided what one reviewer called "the climatic thrill" when she sang "Rule Britannia" ("Progress of Canada" 1927).

There are several female characters featured in *Historical Pageant*. Sternberg chose a seemingly eclectic group to highlight in *Historical Pageant*, including the Ursuline nuns, Marie-Madeleine Jarret de Verchères, the fictitious figure of Evangeline, and Laura Secord. This list might have seemed arbitrary or unusual, but each of these characters conveyed IODE values, thereby emphasizing that women were central to a prosperous society. The third tableau, "Madeleine de Verchères, 1692," depicted Verchères, a young woman who had defended her family's seigneury against a violent attack. The fourth tableau, "Ursulines Landing at Quebec," honoured the first Catholic order of nuns in New France, who, in 1639, dedicated themselves to teaching girls, including Indigenous children. Sternberg's dancers appeared in the next scene, which was an enactment of "Evangeline," Henry Wadsworth Longfellow's poem about the expulsion of the Acadians in 1755. The titular character represented unwavering faithfulness in her long search for the man she loved. Sternberg also honoured Laura Secord, the woman who, during the War of 1812, is credited with walking over thirty kilometres to warn the British of an impending attack by the Americans.

In their various scenes, these characters validated the importance of women in protecting their families, teaching children, demonstrating loyalty for loved ones, and exhibiting courage and a sense of duty to defend the British Empire. In other words, these characters disclosed the IODE's maternal feminist belief that women's supposed innate sense of caregiving positioned them to act decisively to make vital contributions to the welfare of their families, communities, and the British Empire.

Reading the program, it becomes apparent that *Historical Pageant* also subtly framed race relations in gendered terms, implicitly asserting that the British Empire was a benevolent caregiver in its dealing with Indigenous and other non-white people. A scene entitled "The First School," for instance,

The Elizabeth Ann Tea Rooms

(Formerly The Mission Tea Rooms)
82 BLOOR ST. WEST
Still Under the Same Management
Luncheon and Teas—Chicken Dinner Every Evening
These Attractive Tea Rooms are Noted for Excellent Service and
Delicious Home Cooking. Garden, Teas, Bridges, Etc., may be
Arranged.   Kingsdale 2306.

COMPLIMENTS
OF
BAKE-RITE
LIMITED

SCENE No. 9—*Continued*

CANADA .... Madame Vera McLean Somerville
BRITANNIA .... Miss Agnes Adie

Symbolical costumes designed by Miss Amy Sternberg, sketched by Miss
Muriel Lea and made and donated by Joseph & Milton.

Are You Asking Your
Grocer or Butcher

for

GRIDLAND'S
HAM or BACON **?**

Specialist in Cooked Meats

*For Afternoon
Tea . . . .*

HOVIS
The Bread of Health

Serve Hovis buttered
or made into sand-
wiches.

Hovis is temptingly dainty
delightfully different
always enjoyable.

99

MRS. CLARK MURRAY, Montreal

Founder of
The Imperial Order Daughters of the Empire

2

Clockwise from top left:

FIGURE 16.1: *Listing for Scene 9 of the pageant in*
program for the Historical Pageant, *1927, 99.*

Courtesy of Amy Sternberg Portfolio, Dance Collection Danse.

FIGURE 16.2: *Photograph of Margaret Murray in the*
program for the Historical Pageant, *1927, 2.*

Courtesy of Amy Sternberg Portfolio, Dance Collection Danse.

FIGURE 16.3: *Biographical entry for Margaret Murray*
in the program for the Historical Pageant, *1927, 3.*

Courtesy of Amy Sternberg Portfolio, Dance Collection Danse.

An Intimate Sketch

Margaret Polson Murray, as she was best known, was born in Paisley,
Scotland, in 1844. Her father was William Polson, the well known manufacturer there. Even in her young days Mrs. Murray showed signs of the
intense application that resulted later on in the wonderful success of the
Imperial Order Daughters of the Empire. While at school she was accustomed to getting up so that she could practice on the piano from five to
eight in the morning, and this, be it remembered, in the cold, dark Scotch
winter days. Her executive ability seems to have been indicated by the
fact that it was she who took her father's large family away to their summer
quarters at Innellan on the Clyde.

She married early in life Professor J. Clark Murray and he took her
back with him to Queen's University, Kingston, where they resided from
1865 until 1871, when he was transferred to McGill University. Even then
Mrs. Murray found scope for her organizing ability by being the first secretary of the Young Women's Christian Association, being associated in that
good work with the late Mrs. John McDougall.

She was also very much interested in the work of the Church of St.
Andrew and St. Paul, Montreal, at that time St. Paul's Church, and was
one of those who helped materially to work up the voluntary choir which
has since developed so splendidly.

During the South African war her sympathetic heart was evidently
touched by the thought of the graves of the Canadian and other Empire
soldiers who fell in South Africa and she founded the South African Graves
Association, the first movement in history to take care, by the loving hands
of women, of the graves of men who fell in war. It was in connection
with this work and during her frequent visits to Britain that she was struck
forcibly with the lack of knowledge, in Great Britain and the Dominions,
about other parts of the Empire, and she did a great deal to interest the
different Dominions' officials in London towards promoting Inter-Empire
education. Much of her energy was spent in enlarging the knowledge in
Canada of Empire facts and it was possibly from this idea that the under-
lying scheme for an association of women throughout the British Empire
took shape. For some years Mrs. Murray worked away quietly herself but
evidently she had struck a very sympathetic cord; for it was surprising
how quickly the idea spread, grew, and took tangible form.

While it may have seemed long to her, in reality no great time
elapsed before she saw on 13th February, 1900, her dreams become realized
into an organization which is now known as the Imperial Order Daughters
of the Empire. As probably a more central executive point Mrs. Murray
suggested that the headquarters, which had originally been in Montreal,
should be removed to Toronto.

Some years later when the Order had grown so that it became a
power in the land, Mrs. Murray gradually retired from any active participation in her work, and unfortunately her health failed, and she was more
or less forced to go into complete retirement. Her death came quite peace-
ably on 27th January, 1927, at the age of 83. The memorial service in her
own church of St. Andrew and St. Paul was a remarkable tribute not only
to herself but to the wonderful organization into which her idea has grown.

3

4. Indigenous Peoples were not the only non-white characters portrayed in the *Historical Pageant* as recipients of colonial "kindness." Under the leadership of John Graves Simcoe, the first lieutenant-governor of Upper Canada (and a character in the pageant), the Act Against Slavery was passed in 1793. In her foreword, Sternberg praised British North America for being "a haven to runaway slaves" (Program 1927, 67). The program also noted the inclusion of characters of African heritage who were almost certainly played by white members of the IODE in blackface. While the underground railway was a conduit for tens of thousands of slaves in search of freedom, the idealized version of the past presented onstage did not acknowledge the racism experienced within the British colony.

showed Indigenous and French children learning together in a classroom. Sternberg's program notes contextualized this inclusion by stating that "amid scenes of native warfare and menace and in the midst of savage customs these and many highly placed men and women from France gave their whole lives to the care of redskin and colonist alike" (Program 1927, 33).[4]

Women, in this way, were legitimizing and furthering the imperialist view that Indigenous Peoples needed to be educated and cared for by white people. In *Historical Pageant*, paternalism was more precisely exercised through actions stereotypically associated with maternalism.

The instances of personification in *Historical Pageant* similarly divulge a sense of pride in women while simultaneously promoting social initiatives. For instance, the choice to cast women in the celebratory parade personifying various objects, services, and political entities—including telephones, Mother's Allowance, and the provinces—visually conveyed the IODE view that women were integral to the prosperity of modern society.

Sternberg clearly was conversant with the standard conventions of the historical pageant genre by featuring female performers who played the personification of countries. Specifically, the choice to conclude *Historical Pageant* with the appearance of Canada and Britannia further emphasized women's role in the sustainment of the British Empire. As the curtain lowered, Canada stood patriotically beside Britannia. That both these roles were played by women visually stressed the feminine as the quintessence of nation and empire. Moreover, both performers were members of the IODE, potentially signalling the Balfour Declaration view that Canada was equal to Britain, but more likely promoting the IODE's steadfast conviction that Canada should "stand by" the British Empire.

Not only were IODE values constructed and transmitted through the female characters and onstage performance of *Historical Pageant*, but the program text also offers insight into how the spectacle promoted female agency in the name of the British Empire. Prominently displayed on page two was a photograph of Mrs. Clark Murray (Margaret Polson Murray), the founder of the IODE.

Printed on the facing page was a brief biography that outlined key moments from Murray's life. The profile implicitly stressed repeatedly that the values the IODE idealized were ably embodied by Murray. Readers were told that even in her early life, Murray was hardworking, showing evidence of the "intense application" that would subsequently enable the IODE's success (Program 1927, 3). Moreover, after she arrived in Canada as a young wife, Murray volunteered in the service of the Young Women's Christian Association and involved herself in church activities. Her energetic sense of patriotic duty provoked her to respond to the South African War (Boer War) by founding the South African Graves Association to mobilize women to tend the graves of war veterans. This experience apparently led Murray to believe that the various constituents of the British Empire were lacking in

FIGURE 16.4 (left): *Photograph of Miss R.M. Church in the program for the* Historical Pageant, *1927, 4.* Courtesy of Amy Sternberg Portfolio, Dance Collection Danse.

FIGURE 16.5 (right): *List of aims and objects for the* IODE *in the program for the* Historical Pageant, *1927, 5.* Courtesy of Amy Sternberg Portfolio, Dance Collection Danse.

understanding of each other: a situation she wanted to remedy through the promotion of educational opportunities that were facilitated, once again, by women. Her coupling of ingenuity and agency in the public sphere, which was buttressed by her commitment to the British Empire, led to the creation of the IODE.

Turning over the page, readers of the program encountered a photograph of Miss. R.M. Church, the then National President of the IODE. The choice to include the IODE motto ("One Flag. One Throne. One Empire.") along with a list of the organization's aims and objects on the page opposite to Church's photograph visually suggested that Church was the agent of IODE ambitions, including "to stimulate and give expression to the sentiment of patriotism which binds the women and children of the Empire around the throne and person of their Gracious and Beloved Sovereign" (Program 1927, 5).

FIGURE 16.6: *Amy Sternberg, ca. 1915.* Courtesy of Amy Sternberg Portfolio Dance Collection Danse.

5. While it is uncertain if
    Sternberg was a member of
    the IODE, she clearly had
    a close relationship to the
    organization. She placed
    advertisements for her school
    in *Echoes*, the IODE's official
    magazine. Her students
    stayed in the homes of IODE
    members when touring
    Ontario and, in 1915, the IODE
    was one of the main sponsors
    of *Fantastic Extravaganza*,
    another large-scale theatrical
    spectacle featuring Sternberg's
    choreography, which raised
    wartime funds for the Red
    Cross.

6. For a similar discussion, see
    Prevots 1990, 2–3.

The one image not from the program but included in this chapter is a photograph of Sternberg, the woman who was the creative force behind *Historical Pageant*. While her picture did not appear in the program, Sternberg's name was prominently displayed in the credits throughout this document. To those who knew her or knew of her, Sternberg's numerous professional activities signalled the kind of hard work and dedication that the IODE prized.[5] For example, hundreds of students enrolled in Sternberg's school every year to take a range of classes, including "classical" and "national" dance, acrobatic, tap, toe (i.e., pointe work), and ballroom dancing ("Recital" c. 1929; "Miss Sternberg Dancing" 1928–29). Sternberg regularly booked two evenings at Massey Hall for her annual recitals because of the popularity of these events. Graduates of her three-year teacher-training program became successful teachers who followed in Sternberg's footsteps. Other students found employment as performers in the Canadian National Exhibition Grandstand Show, the Vaughan Glaser Repertoire Company, and with Ruth St. Denis and Ted Shawn's Denishawn company in the United States (Warner 1995, 61; Tilley, n.d.; "Dance Teacher," n.d.).

In examining the program for *Historical Pageant*, it becomes clear that the production adhered to the goals of the historical pageant genre, which usually offered a view of a glorified past that negated the complexity of a country's history. In this way, *Historical Pageant* illustrates historian David Glassberg's suggestion that many early twentieth-century pageants were based on the assumption that "history could be made into a dramatic public ritual through which the residents of a town, by acting out the right version of their past, could bring about some kind of future social and political transformation" (1990, 4).[6] *Historical Pageant* conveyed the IODE view that Canada's past and implicitly its future were best defined by values the organization associated with women. Therefore, although the maternal and imperial feminisms underpinning *Historical Pageant* are now outmoded, the archival documentation for the production is important to study because it offers contemporary readers an opportunity to understand the compatibility of gender and empire during Canada's Diamond Jubilee while demonstrating how one theatrical spectacle sublimated ideology into art.

Bibliography and Further Reading

Buckner, Phillip. 2005. "The Long Goodbye: English Canadians and the British World." In *Rediscovering the British World*, edited by Phillip Buckner and R. Douglas Francis, 181–207. Calgary: University of Calgary Press.

"Children Take Part in Canadian Pageant." n.d. Newspaper clipping, Amy Sternberg fonds, Dance Collection Danse, Toronto.

"Dance Teacher Called by Death." n.d. Newspaper clipping, Amy Sternberg fonds, Dance Collection Danse, Toronto.

Fletcher, John. 2010. "Sympathy for the Devil: Nonprogressive Activism and the Limits of Critical Generosity." In *Theatre Historiography: Critical Interventions*, edited by Henry Bial and Scott Magelssen, 110-22. Ann Arbor: University of Michigan Press.

Gaudet, Lisa. 2001. "The Empire Is Woman's Sphere: Organised Female Imperialism in Canada, 1880s-1920s." PHD diss., Carleton University.

Glassberg, David. 1990. *American Historical Pageantry: The Uses of Tradition in the Early Twentieth Century*. Chapel Hill: University of North Carolina Press.

"Gowns a Century Old Procured for Pageant." 1927. *The Toronto Daily Star*, June 18, 1927.

Inter-Imperial Relations Committee. 1926. *Imperial Conference 1926 Inter-Imperial Relations Committee Report, Proceedings and Memoranda*. November, 1926.

Johnstone, Marjorie Winnifred. 2015. "Diverging and Contested Feminisms in Early Social Work History in Ontario (1900-1950)." PHD diss., Graduate Factor-Inwentash Faculty of Social Work.

Lindgren, Allana C. 2011. "Amy Sternberg's *Historical Pageant* (1927): The Performance of IODE Ideology during Canada's Diamond Jubilee." *Theatre Research in Canada / Recherches théâtrales au Canada* 32 (1): 1-29.

"Miss Sternberg Dancing." 1928-29. Brochure, Amy Sternberg fonds, Dance Collection Danse, Toronto.

"Ontario: Toronto." 1927. *Echoes*, October, 44.

"People and Events of Past Live Again in IODE Pageant." 1927. *The Globe*, June 23, 1927, 11.

Pickles, Katie. 2002. *Female Imperialism and National Identity: The Imperial Order Daughters of the Empire*. Manchester: Manchester University Press.

Prevots, Naima. 1990. *American Pageantry: A Movement for Art and Democracy*. Ann Arbor, MI: UMI Research.

Program for *Historical Pageant*. 1927. (June), Amy Sternberg fonds, Dance Collection Danse, Toronto.

"Progress of Canada Depicted in Pageant." 1927. *The Toronto Daily Star*, June 23, 1927.

"Recital of Classical, National and Tap Dances." c. 1929. Program, Amy Sternberg fonds, Dance Collection Danse, Toronto.

"Recommendations for Celebration of the Jubilee of Confederation." 1926. *Echoes*, December, 23.

Tilley, Jean. n.d. "Toronto's First School of Ballet—1891." Typescript, Amy Sternberg fonds, Dance Collection Danse, Toronto.

"Toronto IODE Plan Pageant for Jubilee." n.d. Newspaper clipping, Amy Sternberg fonds, Dance Collection Danse, Toronto.

Warner, Mary Jane. 1995. *Toronto Dance Teachers, 1825-1925*. Toronto: Dance Collection Danse Press/es.

HERMAN VOADEN was the most significant experimental theatre director and playwright in English Canada prior to 1950. He completed his Queen's University MA thesis on Eugene O'Neill in 1926, began directing and writing plays the following year, and edited *Six Canadian Plays* in 1930. In his introduction to that anthology, Voaden postulated that there were three main lines of advance open to the Canadian dramatist. The first was a realistic drama depicting the harsh hardships of life faced by "old pioneers in southern Ontario and new pioneers in the West and North, with fishermen on lake shore and coast, and lonely inhabitants of far-flung mining and frontier towns." The second line was romantic drama dealing with the discovery, exploration, and frontier life of Canada. The third option the playwright-director presented was his own conception of a distinct "Canadian Art of the Theatre" that was "different from the accepted pattern of both realistic and romantic plays" (Voaden 1930, xx–xxi). *Rocks: A Play of Northern Ontario* was Voaden's first attempt to create such a Canadian Art of the Theatre in a style he later came to call "symphonic expressionism." It was the most performed of Voaden's experimental plays.

Despite the historical importance of *Rocks*, the play has only been published once before in *A Vision of Canada* anthology (Simon & Pierre 1993), which has long been out of print. Voaden himself carefully reviewed the lighting, music, and movement cues for this version of the text before his death so that this performance text most closely captures his artistic vision and actual production of his critically best-received script.

In his critical writing, Voaden had championed the non-realist aesthetic and cultural nationalism of the Group of Seven painters since 1928, urging the Canadian Little Theatre Movement to follow its example (Voaden 1928). When the *Toronto Star* critic Augustus Bridle reviewed the *Rocks* premiere in 1932, he quoted the author-playwright stating that he "got the idea from studying pictures of the Group of Seven" and declared of the production that "nothing quite like it has ever been done in Canada" (Bridle 1932). Voaden himself wrote in an introduction to the play that with the non-realist multimedia production style he had developed for *Rocks*, "I was able to draw nearer, in theatre, to the achievements of the Group of Seven—reaching toward, paralleling—their deeply held belief in the North and what it held for us as a driving force in moving us toward a new belief in ourselves as a nation" (Wagner 1993, 182).

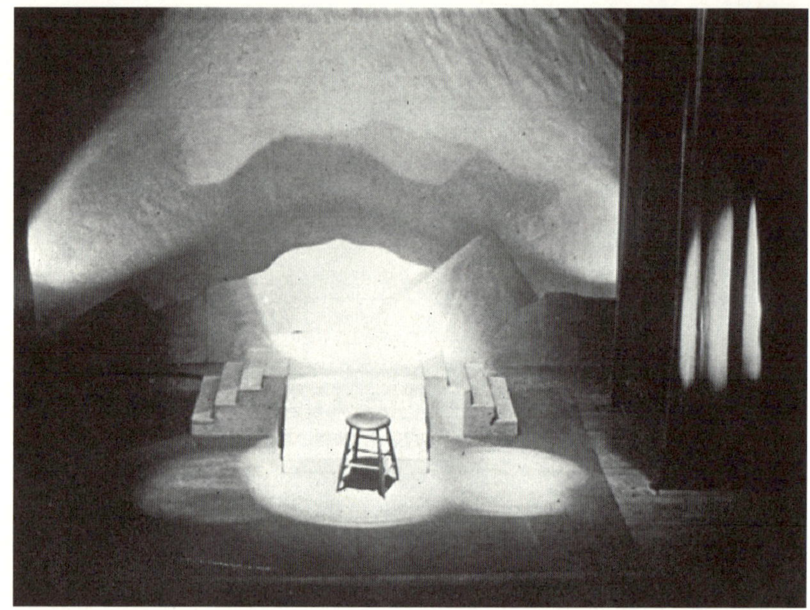

FIGURE 17.1: *The set of* Rocks, *April 22, 1932, Central High School of Commerce premiere.*
Courtesy of the Estate of Herman Voaden.

The plot of *Rocks* is simple. The play tells the story of Mary, a young school-teacher in the north country whose lover, Blake, is lost in a snowstorm. While Mary's progressive realization that Blake has perished in a blizzard is tragic, Voaden affirmed in a manifesto written at the time of the play's premiere that in recalling Blake's visions, Mary is herself spiritually transformed. "The glory of the North transcends the smaller human figures, infusing them with some-thing of its own majesty. Thus the author has used his characters as mirrors in which we may catch reflected the North in action, moulding lives" (Voaden 1932a).

Initially, Voaden envisioned *Rocks* as a realistic play entitled *Wilderness: A Play of the North*, which he wrote for George Pierce Baker's famous play-writing class at the Yale Graduate School of Drama in 1931. Baker praised the play—its plot was identical and very similar in dialogue to the later *Rocks*—as "a very promising piece of work" (Voaden 1931).[1] It was first produced at Yale on May 2, 1931, directed by the American playwright George Sklar.[2]

Voaden acknowledged the many influences that shaped *Wilderness* in his introduction to the 1980 publication of the play: the vision and idealism of the Group of Seven and the mystic, exultant vision of the British poet and painter William Blake, after whom Mary's lover is "perhaps too obviously named." The old mother, Ella Martin, is a mixture of a fearful fisherman's wife the play-wright met in Port Coldwell, Ontario, and Maurya in John Millington Synge's drama *Riders to the Sea*. Blake's death was suggested by that of François Paradis

FIGURE 17.2: *Ella Martin (Catherine M. Lynn) comforting Mary Brown (Jean Wylie) in the April 22, 1932, Central High School of Commerce premiere of* Rocks.
Courtesy of the Estate of Herman Voaden.

in Louis Hémon's novel *Maria Chapdelaine* and by a trapper Voaden met on a 1929 trip to Lake Superior (see Voaden 1980).[3]

In Canada, the play, retitled *Rocks*, was first staged by the Queen's University Players, a leading amateur theatre group, in Convocation Hall on February 2, 1932. It was directed by Professor Wilhelmina Gordon, one of Voaden's former English lecturers. Reviewing the production, Professor H.W. Alexander noted "the deep impression left upon the minds of the audience." But he nevertheless found the play "a depressing, humorless study in brown, with tragic moments, failing to scale the heights of great tragedy, however, perhaps because of its length" (Alexander 1932).

Two months later, Voaden staged *Rocks* at the Central High School of Commerce in Toronto on April 22, 1932. He "abstracted" *Wilderness* by eliminating all the realistic stage business of the play and adding music, lyric speech, stylized movement and dance, and particularly varied coloured lighting to express the themes of the transcendence of death and oneness with

4. See also Bridle 1932;
    Charlesworth 1932; Craig 1932;
    Mason 1932b; Piitulainen 1932;
    and Wodson 1932.

nature he wanted the play to convey. As he described what became his first symphonic expressionist production, "I sought to make the actors sculptured figures, in part, and to turn the realistic dialogue a little more towards ritual chanting…Then to give their movements and gestures to the dancers and their moods to the music, with the light enveloping and mingling and intermeshing with everything so that the whole thing moved on to its singing climax" (Voaden 1976, 68). In a manifesto published in the *Toronto Globe*, he declared that—particularly through the ever-changing lighting of a cyclorama— "The North is viewed as a participant in the action, an unseen actor" (Voaden 1932a).

Not all viewers applauded Voaden's playwriting and directing style. In the *Canadian Forum*, the noted amateur actor Ernest A. Dale criticized the diminished role of the actor and the lack of realistic emotional character development in the multimedia production, claiming, "The reconciliation of Mary Brown to her lover's death is so abrupt and so immediately complete as to be unreal, if not inhuman" (Dale 1932, 76).

As example of the favourable press, the dean of English Canadian theatre critics, the *Globe*'s Lawrence Mason, hailed Voaden as "the foremost figure in the Dominion's experimental theatre movement" (1932a).[4] After viewing his second symphonic expressionist production of *Rocks* on September 23, 1932, Mason declared that the playwright-director had succeeded in fusing his various art forms into an effective synthesis: "Living light and color, rhythmic intoning of lines, symbolic dancing, pulsing drum-beats, musical themes, architectural patterns, statuesque poses, and stark Greek drama are fused in a composite art which projects a tragic story with melting and yet exalting effect. A very smooth blending of all these different elements was attained, and this beholder, in common with many others, was deeply moved" (1932c).

Despite this critical and important support, *Rocks* was unsuccessful when it competed at the first Dominion Drama Festival competitions in 1933. Mason reported that at the Central Ontario Regional Dominion Drama Festival finals, the adjudicators determined that "this production must be regarded as an exhibition of advanced modern stagecraft quite outside the competition, since the marking system sent out by Ottawa made no provision for the suitable appraisal of such work" (Mason 1933).

Voaden's non-realistic, multimedia theatrical vision was too personal and technically complex to find wider audiences and artistic followers for the distinct Canadian Art of the Theatre he wished to develop. That the great majority of Canadian amateur theatres were unsubsidized and that the Dominion Drama Festival did not encourage theatre experimentation militated against the wider acceptance of production styles such as symphonic expressionism. The immense destruction and carnage of the Second World War also made Voaden's romantic vision of Canada untenable. The extensive research and theatre experimentation carried out by the playwright-director over a decade—from *Rocks* and *Earth Song: A Drama in Rhythmic Prose and Light*

(1932) to *Ascend as the Sun*, directed by Voaden at Hart House Theatre in 1942 with music by Godfrey Ridout and choreography by members of the Volkoff Ballet—would only begin to be equalled with the advent of the government-subsidized professional "alternate" theatres of the 1970s.

Bibliography and Further Reading

Alexander, H.W. 1932. "Faculty Players." *Queen's Journal*, February 5, 1932.

Bridle, Augustus. 1932. "Drama Is Presented in Lights and Colors." *Toronto Star*, April 23, 1932.

Charlesworth, Hector. 1932. "Unique Dramatics." *Saturday Night*, October 1, 1932, 8.

Craig, Thelma. 1932. "Unusual Play Given By Toronto Teacher: School of Commerce Production Employs Unique Method." *Mail and Empire*, September 24, 1932.

Dale, Ernest A. 1932. "Mr. Voaden's Rocks." *Canadian Forum*, November, 75–76.

Grace, Sherrill. 1982. "A Northern Quality: Herman Voaden's Canadian Expressionism," *Canadian Drama* 8 (1): 1–14.

———. 1989. "Herman Voaden's 'Symphonic Expressionism.'" In *Regression and Apocalypse: Studies in North American Literary Expressionism*, 117–37. Toronto: University of Toronto Press.

Mason, Lawrence. 1932a. "Introduction to Voaden's Article 'Producing Methods Defined.'" *Toronto Globe*, April 16, 1932, 15.

———. 1932b. "Modern Stagecraft: Notable Evening of Canadian Plays and New Producing Methods." *Toronto Globe*, April 25, 1932, 12.

———. 1932c. "'Rocks': Expressionist Play and Other Essays in Experimental Theatre." *Toronto Globe*, September 24, 1932, 12.

———. 1932d. "Symphonic Expressionism: Notable Recent Example in Toronto of Ultra-Modern Producing Methods—Plea for Less Persistent Use of Realism by Canadian Directors." *Toronto Globe*, April 30, 1932, 6.

———. 1933. "Drama Festival Ends." *Toronto Globe*, March 27, 1993, 10.

Piitulainen, H. 1932. "The Annual School Concert." *The Torpedo*, p. 21.

Voaden, Herman. 1928. "A National Drama League." *Canadian Forum*, no. 9, December, 105–06.

———. 1929a. "Government-Owned Theatres?" *Toronto Globe*, November 30, 1929, 12.

———. 1929b. "What Is Wrong with the Canadian Theatre?" *Toronto Globe*, June 22, 1929.

———. 1931. Letter to Violet Kilpatrick, New Haven, February 24, 1931. Herman Arthur Voaden fonds, York University Archives.

———. 1932a. "Canadian Plays and Experimental Stagecraft." *Toronto Globe*, April 23, 1932, 18.

———. 1932b. "Creed for a New Theatre: 'Symphonic Expressionism,' a Composite Blending of All Theatral Arts Explained in Detail as a Possible Stage Method for the Future." *Toronto Globe*, December 17, 1932.

———. 1932c. "Drama Festival Thoughts: A Canadian Director Urges the Importance of Recognizing Canadian Point of View, in the Adjudications—Competitors Should Not be Restricted to 'Realistic Methods' Exclusively." *Toronto Globe*, November 12, 1932.

————. 1932d. "Producing Methods Defined: Realism and Its Modern Successors Explained and Contra-Distinguished—'Symphonic Expressionism' as the Art of the Future." *Toronto Globe*, April 16, 1932, 15.

————. 1976. Ontario Historical Studies Series oral history interview.

————. 1980. "Introduction to *Wilderness*." In *The Developing Mosaic: English-Canadian Drama to Mid-century*, edited by Anton Wagner, 85–87. Toronto: Canadian Theatre Review Publications.

Voaden, Herman. ed. 1930. *Six Canadian Plays*. Toronto: Copp Clark.

Wagner, Anton. 1984. "Herman Voaden's Symphonic Expressionism." PHD diss., University of Toronto.

————. 1985. "Herman Voaden's 'New Religion.'" *Theatre History in Canada* 6 (2): 187–201.

————. 1991. "Herman Voaden and the Group of Seven: Creating a Canadian Imaginative Background in Theatre." *International Journal of Canadian Studies*, no. 4, 145–64.

Wagner, Anton, ed. 1993. *A Vision of Canada: Herman Voaden's Dramatic Works 1928–1945*. Toronto: Simon & Pierre.

Wodson, Edward W. 1932. "Not an Accent Raised, Telling Tragic Stories: Students at the Central High Stage Remarkable North Ontario Play—Symphony of Light." *Toronto Telegram*, September 24, 1932, 15.

Rocks

HERMAN VOADEN

A Play of Northern Ontario
Rocks was first produced at the Central High School of Commerce in Toronto, April 23 and 23, 1932, under the direction of the author.

CHARACTERS
MRS. MARTIN
MARY BROWN
MAXWELL, *The Station Agent.*
BILL
ED

Text of symphonic production with setting, music, movements for actors and dancers, and light-colour orchestration.

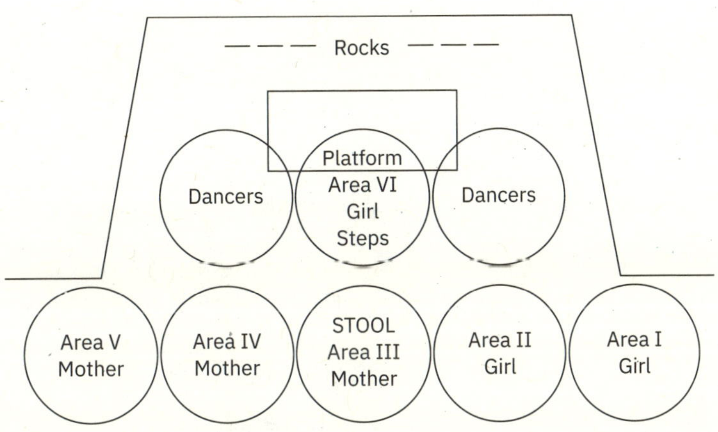

Note: Area II and IV are further upstage, in the line between the outer areas and the stool.

In the Central High School of Commerce production, areas I and II (Girl) and IV and V (Mother) were lit by spotlights in the balcony. In a normal theatre, as at Hart House Theatre, these spotlights are on the first pipe batten. Areas III and VI were lit by spotlights on the pipe batten directly overhead. Also overhead, lighting the stage and cyclorama,[1] were the traditional red and green border lights, and four flood-lights with blue screens. Red, green, amber and blue-screened floodlights were behind

*the upstage curtains to light the cyclorama—also two spotlights on the rocks, and
two diagonal spots.*

Violin and cello themes were played on the viola.

*While the spring violin theme is played the blue, red, green and amber floodlights
from the upstage corners and the red and green borders flare to full.* MARY's *light on
area I builds to full.*

MARY. It's been a wonderful spring day. I like to see the snow melting. I like to
know that everything's coming to life again. (*The light on* MARY *dims to 6/8.*)
I hope there's a letter from Blake on the train.

Blake violin theme.

I had a lovely walk after school. The sun was warm and everything was spring-
like. The spring's going to be better even than the fall.
When I came last September

the country was beautiful,

The cyclorama lights pulse in waves in a dance of colour through this sentence.

colour everywhere in the hills,

colour blazing like fire

and colour singing inside me

like music.

Mirroring her dreams of happiness, MARY's three dancers, behind her, lift heads and shoulders in delight. The MOTHER's dancers are quiet, fearful.

But Blake said, "Wait till the spring. This won't be anything compared to the spring." And I let him go.

One drum beat. MARY's dancers are checked in their eager happiness. The MOTHER's dancers are knowing and quiet. The light on MARY dims to 2/8. The amber above and upstage is dimmed out. The red cyclorama lights are lowered to 6/8, the blue and green to 2/8, making a mauve-purple glow. There are slight changes or pulsations in the cyclorama lights during MARY's protest, following the rhythms and emotional intensity of her words.

Then the long winter set in and gripped us day after day, week after week, month after month. And I've grown more and more unhappy. (*Lights on the cyclorama become grey and menacing.*) Nothing to do but teach three or four children. Nothing to look at but half a dozen unpainted shacks half-buried in white. (*MARY's dancers' heads are bowed.*) Never a road, or a farm, or a field, or a horse—no life but ten or twenty people moving through the deep snow like ghosts—and four trains a day to come and go and only make me lonelier than ever—four trains a day to break the stillness.

The light blue spotlight on the mother builds up slowly to full as MARY finishes her speech. The cyclorama lights become more agitated, building to a climax on "cold."

How I've envied the people on the trains. They look so comfortable and certain—as if they are doing something—going somewhere—while I—I've been lost here—lost in this deathly silence—lost in the monotony—in the deep, deep snow and the cold.

During the cello theme music and the MOTHER's speech, MARY's dancers are quiet, the MOTHER's mirror her passive acceptance. The red and amber above and upstage are dimmed out. The MOTHER's dancers reflect her stoic pessimism during the music and her speech.

MRS. MARTIN. Folks on the train don't look no happier than we are, if y'ask me. I guess nobody's very happy—least not for long.

One drum beat. As the theme of MARY*'s longing is played—portion of violin spring theme—the light on the* MOTHER *dims to 2/8 and* MARY*'s light builds to 4/8. The spotlights on the hills upstage build to 4/8).*

MARY. (*Impulsively.*) I want to be happy. (MRS. MARTIN*'s dancers listen, quiet and unmoved.* MARY*'s dancers are lyrical and expectant.*) The sun has just gone down. I like winter sunsets—with the snow and the dark pines—the white branches of the birches—and the black rocks jutting through.

Pause. One drum beat. Touches of colour appear and flow with mournful rhythms on the cyclorama. Through the rest of MARY*'s speech the light on her builds to full, pulsing with her longing. Her dancers are tense; they mirror her loneliness through her speech to its climax, then subside. The cyclorama is a low cold blue-green.* MRS. MARTIN*'s dancers listen, far off, as in a dream, knowing her truth.*

Look at the hills—to the west and the north and the east—nothing but grey-black hills rolling away into gloom. (*One drum beat. The light on the* MOTHER *builds slowly to full as* MARY *continues.*) If you only knew how I've been a prisoner to these hills. I've stood at the school window and looked out, day after day—looked at the snow four and five feet deep—looked at the hills—and thought about Blake, and wished he were here.

MARY *withdraws into herself; the light on her dims to 2/8. The rock lights dim out. The cyclorama blue fades out. The* MOTHER*'s dancers match her words in gesture and attitude.*

MRS. MARTIN. When you're as old as me you won't dream no more, and you won't be wishin' for nothin'.
MARY. (MARY*'s spotlight builds to full on "lonely," then falls to 2/8.*) I've been so lonely. (*Pause.*) No one my own age—missing the dances and fun we used to have back home. (*Her dancers smile sadly, remembering. The cyclorama sky is low, cold, and green.*)
MRS. MARTIN. (*Light in area V builds to full through her speech.*) We never get very close to the things we really want—there's always somethin' in our way. (*Two drum beats, then Blake's theme on both instruments.*)

MARY*'s light builds to full, the* MOTHER*'s dims to 2/8. Red is added, lighting the cyclorama which pulses with hope on her words. She moves toward the adjacent*

area II as she speaks, eagerly and hopefully. But she does not speak directly to MRS. MARTIN; *rather to herself, as in a dream. The light on area I dims out, the light on area II builds as she moves.*

MARY. It's going to be better here soon. Blake says there's a great future for the north country—that it won't be long before there'll be mines and railways and waterpower dams and roads and cities everywhere.

The hopeful red dims out from overhead and from the cyclorama border and floodlights; the cold green builds to full. The light on MRS. MARTIN *builds to full. One drum beat. Her dancers speak for her gathering bitterness and gloom.*

MRS. MARTIN. The north is full o' dreams—always was since I first come to it with Tom—(*She moves into the adjacent area IV as she speaks. The light on area V dims out, the light on area IV builds to full.* MARY's *light builds to full through the sentence.*) lurin' men on in wild goose chases that never amount to nothin'.

MARY's *dancers reflect her appeal to* MRS. MARTIN, *and her fears. The faces and attitudes of the* MOTHER's *dancers are tragic with the prescience of what is to come. The light on* MRS. MARTIN *dims to 2/8. The diagonals build to full. They and the cyclorama lights are agitated, following the rhythm and intense fears of* MARY's *speech. The light on her builds from half to full through her sentences. It, too, should pulse with her words. One drum beat.*

MARY. (*With hesitation.*) I've got to talk to someone, someone who knows him and loves him as I do. (*Turns.*) I'm worried. (MARY *is drawn, bewildered and appealing, to area II. The light flows with her, disappearing on area I and building to 4/8 on area II.*) Why haven't I heard from him? It's more than two weeks now since I've had a letter. (*Light on area II builds from 4/8 to full through her speech.*) He was to've been home by this time. I suppose the camp might have kept open after last week's snow storm. (*With sudden fear. Agitation on the cyclorama.*) Or do you think he might have got restless again and joined the long fur drive to Hudson's Bay?[2] Surely he wouldn't do that with me waiting and the winter so long. Have you had any word from him? Do you know what has happened to him? (MARY's *dancers bespeak her anguish.* MRS. MARTIN *is silent, brooding deeply. One drum beat. She shakes her head slowly.*) Have you heard from him? Tell me. (*Another pause.* MRS. MARTIN *does not reply. The diagonals are dimmed out. The light on* MARY *in area II falls to 2/8 through her speech with her quiet resolution. The red borders and amber cyclorama floods are dimmed out through the next three speeches.*) You shouldn't mind Blake and me getting married, this summer. We'll look after you well. I promise you we will.

MARY's dancers mirror her appeal, while the MOTHER's stare bitterly, dropping
their heads on "I won't be livin' long." The light on the MOTHER in area IV builds to
half on the first sentence and drops to 2/8 on the second.

MRS. MARTIN. Mighta' looked after his mother himself for a year or so. I
    won't be livin' long.
MARY. (With MARY's words her dancers reach forward in appeal.) Don't say that.
MRS. MARTIN. (As MRS. MARTIN asks her question, her dancers mirror her
    words. The light on her builds to 6/8.) Why didn't you stop him from goin' to
    the camp, this winter, if you loved him?

Her light falls to 2/8. The red and blue cyclorama lights and the area light on MARY
pulse upward with each of the impulses of hope in her words. MARY's light builds to
full, the cyclorama lights to half. The green cyclorama dims out.

MARY. I couldn't even if I tried. Besides I don't think I'd want to. (Two impulses,
    one before each of the last two sentences, then colour fades.) It's his life to be
    roaming. It's his life to be tramping the woods.

MARY's dancers dream of Blake. All the cyclorama lights fade as the MOTHER begins
to speak. Her light in area IV builds to 6/8 on "peace."

MRS. MARTIN. Ain't I always knowed it. The north's in his blood, and it'd
    give him no peace. (Her light drops to 2/8. A drum beat, low and slow at first,
    is heard. It quickens and grows louder, rising and falling with the rhythm of the
    sentences, to the climax on "Tom! Tom!" MARY's light fades to nothing through
    the next two sentences.) Reckless, like his father before him. It's gettin' dark.
    Ghosts tonight! (The dancers are tense and fearful. Through the storm sentence
    their agitation builds. The light on MRS. MARTIN and the green ghost cyclo-
    rama lights build to 6/8, pulsing with the rhythm of the sentence.) I c'n see my
    Tom standin' there as plain as can be—an' me warnin' and beggin' him not
    to go fishin'—only a year ago—an' then the storm comin' on in the night—
    an' the wind howlin' an' the waves hurlin' against the rocks fifty feet above.
    (Both MARY's light and the green cyclorama lights drop to 2/8. In the build to
    the climax to Tom's death, they increase in pulsing intensity (not colour) to full,
    along with the diagonals, the blue cyclorama lights, and the blue and green over-
    head lights. MRS. MARTIN's dancers reach up their hands in terror and appeal.
    MARY's dancers echo their movements in sympathy.) 'N me sittin' here rockin'
    and tremblin' all night long—fearin' what was happenin'—fearin' and seein'
    his body hittin' the rocks somewhere along the shore—and cryin' out Tom!
    Tom!

Blackout. Darkness for a moment. In the dark MARY and MRS. MARTIN return
to their opening positions at either end of the forestage. MARY's light builds to 2/8

*along with a low magenta sky—red and blue. MAXWELL comes up the steps and
stands on the upstage platform, area VI. The dancers stir. The light builds on MRS.
MARTIN to 2/8.*

MARY. Here's Mr. Maxwell.
MRS. MARTIN. You'd better go. There's somethin' I want to talk to him about.
MARY. All right.
MAXWELL. Hello Mrs. Martin, hello Mary.
MARY. Hello Mr. Maxwell. I hope there'll be a letter from Blake.
MAXWELL. If there is, I'll bring it up to you.
MARY. Thanks.

*The dancers watch and listen distantly as in a dream. MAXWELL descends to area
III, facing front. MARY moves diagonally upstage to centre at foot of steps. MRS.
MARTIN simultaneously moves diagonally downstage to stool at centre down forestage. The lights on areas I and V dim and build to 4/8 on the two centre areas, III
and VI. MRS. MARTIN sits on the stool facing the audience. From her upper centre
position, MARY walks up the steps in area VI, stands looking out for a moment,
and then exits offstage right. MAXWELL follows upstage to area VI and turns
before speaking. One drum beat. The red dims from the sky as the cyclorama lights
change to green. The light on MARY's dancers dims out as she leaves. They lie down,
completely out of the picture. MRS. MARTIN's dancers respond to her account of
MARY's fears and the search for Blake with attitudes that reflect their foreknowledge
of his fate.*

MAXWELL. So you haven't told her.
MRS. MARTIN. No, I thought I'd wait till you found out for sure.
MAXWELL. Doesn't she suspect anything?
MRS. MARTIN. She's worrying 'cause he promised he'd be here long before
    this. She's been expectin' a letter for a long time. (*Pause. Two drum beats.*)
    Have y' had any word of the boy?
MAXWELL. Sandy and Bert just wired from the flag station[3] near the lumber
    camp. They've been searching three days. They followed the trail from here
    right through to the camp, along the east chain of lakes. But they couldn't
    find any sign of him. (*Three drum beats.*)
MRS. MARTIN. 'N they won't neither. (*Her light in area III dims to 2/8 as the cello
    theme of loneliness is played.*) (*Bitterly.*) He mighta' stayed with me at least for
    this winter, with Tom gone.

MAXWELL. (*There is a slow, measured drum beat through MAXWELL's fatalistic
    words. MRS. MARTIN's dancers echo the tragic fear.*) Such things are bound

to happen. There's many a man goes into the woods and is never heard of again. This time of year, storms like we had last week are pretty bad. He should never have tried to make it alone—just a boy. (*MRS. MARTIN sits silently, a stolid, huddled figure.*) He was a fine lad—a little daring and queer at times.

MRS. MARTIN. There w's never no good to come of him.

As MAXWELL continues the blue overhead and cyclorama lights build to full slowly through the four sentences to "news." MRS. MARTIN's dancers do not respond to MAXWELL's hopeful suggestion. They remain passive and tragic figures as he speaks.

MAXWELL. We haven't given up hope yet. Ed and Bill Keenan were at the camp with him. When they heard he was missing they set out to follow the west chain of lakes. There was a cabin he might have made before the storm struck him. They left on Monday and planned to get here before dark today. If they come I'll send them up with the news. (*There is a pause. The blue overhead and cyclorama lights dim to 4/8.*) But don't expect much. It's more than a week now. He probably lost his way in the blizzard and gave up. (*There is a pause.*) Here's Mary coming back.

MRS. MARTIN. (*One drum beat. Green light on MRS. MARTIN builds to 6/8 through her speech and holds. Small excited drum beats reflect her anger.*) It's her fault-spurrin' him on to his crazy notions and takin' him away from me—when he's all I've got. (*Her dancers respond to her bitterness.*)

MAXWELL. You mustn't say that. She's a good girl. She's had a hard winter here teaching three or four children, with no one her own age to keep her company, and you jealous of her.

MRS. MARTIN. (*Her light builds to full with her anger. There are drum beats to a climax through the sentence.*) Marry him in the spring, would she? (*The light in area III dims to 4/8.*)

MAXWELL. (*After a pause, awkwardly.*) Well, I won't be staying. I must get the mail ready for the train. It'll be here in ten minutes. Goodbye, Mrs. Martin.

One drum beat. MAXWELL goes off right. The viola plays a gentle, hopeful violin spring theme. There is a flare of red and amber on the cyclorama, pulsing happily, as does the light on MARY on the up centre platform where she comes and stands, looking out upstage.

MARY's dancers reach up and are happy with her delight in the spring and memories of her lover. The light in area VI dims up very slowly to 1/8 before her speech.

MARY. I hope there's a letter from him. Wouldn't it be wonderful if he was on the train.

MRS. MARTIN. (*Her green light dims to 2/8 as she speaks. Her dancers complement her words. The sky lights are quiet. Darkly.*) I wouldn't expect too much if I w's you.

MARY. (*Her dancers provide a rhythmical counterpoint to her words as she dreams of Blake's return. The red has drained from the sky as the cyclorama dims to 2/8. The spotlights on the rocks dim up to 4/8.*) I suppose I shouldn't. But I think I'll get a letter just the same. (*Pause.*) Most of the red's gone from the sky now. The hills are grey and mysterious.

Through the remainder of this speech and the next six, to MARY*'s words ending "I believe in him," the overhead and upstage lights on the cyclorama play a counter-point colour rhythm, amber, red and blue, to* MARY*'s speeches and blue-green to the* MOTHER*'s. Violin theme.*

I can almost smell the trees and the wind—

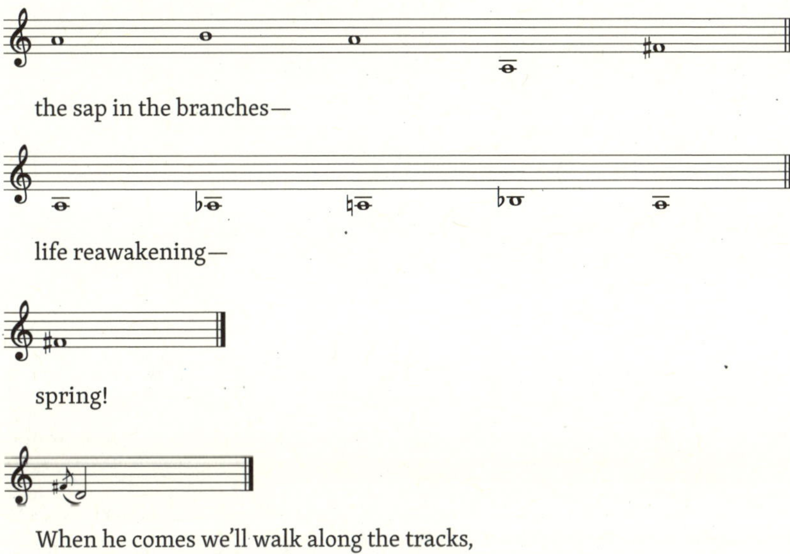

the sap in the branches—

life reawakening—

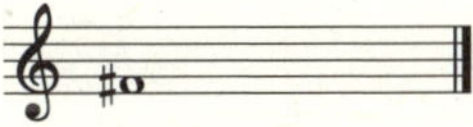

spring!

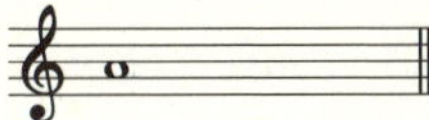

When he comes we'll walk along the tracks,

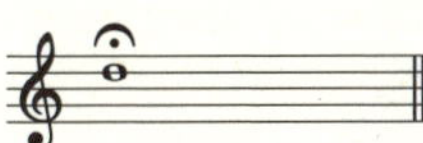

and through the woods.

We'll climb the hills like adventurers discovering a new world.

The light in area VI dims to 1/8. The viola plays a fragment of Blake's theme in the cello register as the MOTHER *remembers the strange moods of her son. Her light is at 4/8.*

MRS. MARTIN. (*As if talking to herself.*) There was always something wrong with him—mighty queer somehow. You'd almost think he saw things at times.

MRS. MARTIN's *light dims to 2/8.* MARY's *light builds to 3/8 through her speech. Both groups of dancers relive the emotions of the two women.*

MARY. I believe he did too. On the big hill I've known him to get very solemn and quiet. (*Blake theme in violin softly throughout.*) "Sometimes I'm afraid of things," he'd say.

"They seem to come flaming on me too brightly.

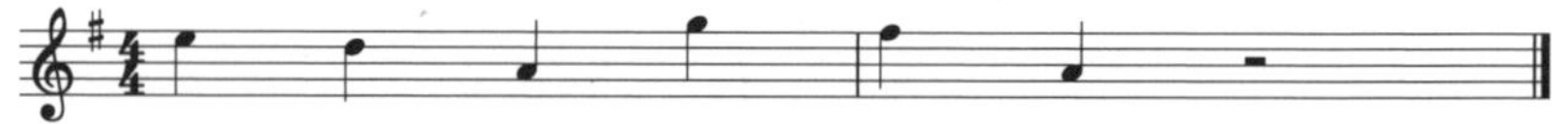

God's to be seen in the silver and gold of dawn—

in the crimson and purple of sunset,"

and he'd lift his arms as if he was worshipping.

MRS. MARTIN's *light builds to 4/8,* MARY's *drops to 2/8, as the* MOTHER *remembers her son's loneliness and strangeness. Blake theme in cello.*

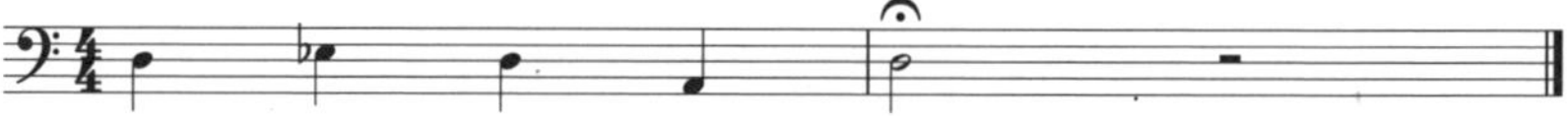

MRS. MARTIN. Too much schoolin', 'nreadin', 'npoetry, 'ndreamin'. Spendin' half his time on the hill or out on the small lake at night in his canoe—'n me wonderin' where he was. (*Her light in area III dims to 2/8.*)
MARY. (*Her light in area VI builds to 4/8 through the first sentence, then drops quickly to 2/8 and holds at "peace." Violin theme. Remembering.*) "Feel strong and hopeful about life," he'd say—"let the winds sweep through you—

Largo

let the light thrill you, warm you—

let the earth give you power and peace."

(*Pause.*) Sometimes I couldn't understand him. Sometimes he'd forget I was
with him and his eyes would be strange.

MRS. MARTIN. (*Her light builds to 4/8 as she speaks, mirroring her anger. Then it
dims to 1/8.*) You should never h've encouraged him in his wild notions. (*One
drum beat.*)

MARY. (*The light on her builds to 5/8 as she speaks, then drops to 1/8.*) I am trying
to understand him. I believe in him.

The dancers reflect MARY*'s mounting agitation and* MRS. MARTIN*'s stoic grief
and resentment as she recalls her son's strange ways. A drum beats through* MRS.
MARTIN*'s speech, building in vexation and bitter finality with the red pulsations of
light on the cyclorama and the pulsations of light on her as she speaks with sudden
bitterness and intensity. The light on area III builds to 5/8 on "not for the likes," then
dims to 2/8 on "neither."*

MRS. MARTIN. (*With this second outcry, her light builds to 6/8 on "never love
you," dropping to 3/8 on "him" and holding through the second sentence.*) He'd
never love you the way y'love him. An' the years'd only make it worse.
(*Her light flares up to 7/8 on "bush-crazy" then drops to 4/8 on "was," builds
to full on "mad" and drops to 3/8 at the end of the sentence.*) Bush-crazy he
was! Strange an' mad as them hills out there. (*Her dancers lift higher as they
remember Blake's strangeness.*) He liked the woods more'n he liked you 'r
me. (*The cyclorama lights change to a low menacing green. On the first "never've
belonged"* MRS. MARTIN*'s light builds to 5/8, dropping back to 2/8 on "us." On
the second it flares to 7/8 again, dimming to 2/8. Her dancers are less wild, but
bitter still, following the same rhythm as the lights. A slow sinister drum beat
increases to a climax on "belonged".*) He'd never've belonged to either of us.
He'd never've belonged!

*As the cello theme is played the cyclorama sky changes to a low blue. The light on the
rocks dims.* MRS. MARTIN*'s dancers are old and wise, but* MARY*'s dancers sense the
hope and belief of Blake.*

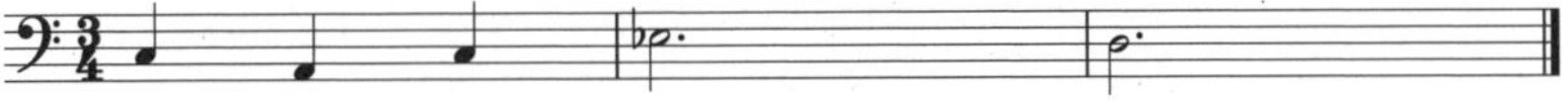

MRS. MARTIN. It's a lonely land. It's as lonely now as it was a thousand years
ago. We come and go. Only the rocks remain.

The blue sky brightens while the violin theme is played. The dancers echo the light-dark confrontation.

MARY. (*The light on her in area VI builds to 3/8.*) Blake didn't think so. (*Her light builds to 7/8 on "anything" in her declaration of faith, then dims to 5/8.*) To him anything was possible in this land. (*Her light builds to 6/8 on "fling himself," holds through the two sentences, then drops to 4/8 at the end of her speech.*) He'd fling himself out to the winds and the sunlight. He rejoiced in the gleam of the water, the strength of the rocks.

MRS. MARTIN's *light builds to 3/8 as the cello theme is played slowly.*

MRS. MARTIN. The lakes an' the hills wall us in. There's no escapin'. We go round like strangers and prisoners—trapped—hungerin' for somethin' we c'n never get. (*Her light dims to 1/8.*)
MARY. (*Her light builds slowly to 7/8 through the first sentence, the violin spring theme, and her second sentence. There are happy blue and red pulsations on the cyclorama.*) The spring will be beautiful.

I begin to understand many things he said.

Through MRS. MARTIN's *speeches there are slow mournful movements of blues and greens on the cyclorama. Her light and the green on the cyclorama slowly builds to 7/8 on "lost inside ourselves." There is a slow and quiet drum beat before she speaks, and before the cello theme is played.*

MARY *kneels quietly on the upper platform, the light in area VI at 2/8 while* MRS. MARTIN *speaks. Her dancers are quiet, listening.* MRS. MARTIN's *dancers relive her story, dancing her emotions in gesture and expression.*

MRS. MARTIN. (*Unnoticing—her voice has all the sombre remoteness of the hills outside.*) Most folks goes through life lonely—even in crowded cities an' where there's lots of people. It's worse up here where there's nothin' much but rock an' stone—water and trees. I come from England when I was a girl. There the skies was close an' friendly. Here they're so wide I been always frightened an' kind o' strange-like. I felt as if I never belonged. And our

men is part of this bigness too. They're always strangers. You can't understand 'em or hold 'em to you. Tom an' me got married and thought we was
goin' to be happy. But he went from place to place—trappin' an' lumberin'.
I followed him. Finally he come here an' took up fishin'. But he's never
been mine. Nobody really belongs in this country—we just get lost inside
ourselves. (*Her light dims to 2/8.*) Then last spring he—went—and it's all
over now. (*Quick increase in her light to 4/8. Cello theme.*)

Too much woods. (*Her light increases to 6/8.*) Too much rock.

*MARY's dancers enact her belief in Blake. The light on the rocks dims out. In ritual
dream-like fashion, as she speaks, MARY moves down the steps and stands above the
MOTHER in the centre area III. The light on her is at 2/8. The light on area VI dims out.*

MARY. Blake liked the loneliness of the country—its harshness. He was
strong—

*As she finishes, MARY and MRS. MARTIN move simultaneously from area III
through areas II and IV to their original positions, areas I and V. The light on area
III dims out. The lights on areas II and IV build to 2/8 and dim as they pass through
them. The lights on areas I and IV built to 2/8 as they enter them. They move in low
lighting, the spotlights at 2/8.*

MRS. MARTIN. It was too strong for him. The water and the woods will claim
their own.

*One drum beat. There is increasing violence on the cyclorama as MARY realizes
what has happened to her lover. There are stabbing gleams of amber at first, then red
flashes. MARY's dancers enact her violent agitation. MRS. MARTIN's dancers are
knowing and withdrawn.*

MARY. What do you mean? (*She turns quickly to the front. Her light builds to 4/8
as she speaks.*)
MRS. MARTIN. (*Her light in area V drops to 1/8. The light on the rocks has dimmed
out entirely.*) Nothin'—(*Two drum beats.*)
MARY. (*Her light in area I builds to 5/8 on the sentence.*) But I want to know.
(*Her light builds to 6/8.*) I've a right to know. (*One drum beat. The light builds
to 7/8.*) Tell me—(*She speaks more quietly. The light drops to 5/8.*) Why have
you been so quiet and gloomy? (*One drum beat. Her light builds to 6/8.*)
Everyone's hiding something from me. (*Her light drops to 3/8 as she remembers what has happened.*) Some of the men have been away for the last three
days. They said they were hunting back in the woods. (*One light drum beat.*

The light on her builds to 4/8.) What were they doing really? (*A heavier drum beat. Her light builds to 5/8.)* Is anything wrong? (*The heaviest drum beat. The light builds to 7/8.)* Has anything happened to Blake?

MRS. MARTIN *stares straight ahead.* MARY *is quiet for a moment, filled with a fear which her dancers show in frightened movements. A light drum beat. In the moment of tension the light on* MARY *dims to 3/8. During her next speech, the light rises sharply before each sentence.*

MARY. Where is he now? (*Heavier drum beat. Her light builds to 4/8.)*
You do know. (*Heavier drum beat. The light grows stronger to 5/8.)*
You do know. (*Heavier drum beat. The light increases to 6/8.)*
I can see it in your face. (*Heavier drum beat. As* MARY *pauses suspiciously, her light lowers in intensity to 5/8.)* You're hiding something from me. (*Heavier drum beat. Her light grows stronger to 7/8.)* Why hasn't he written? (*Two drum beats, stronger than before. The light on* MARY *builds to full intensity.)* Why hasn't he come?

MRS. MARTIN *does not answer. There is one drum beat before each sentence increasing in strength to the climax on "snowstorm" as* MARY *realizes the truth. Starting at 2/8 the light on her increases by 1/8 with each sentence to full on the blackout. The cyclorama flashes—blues and greens—increase in intensity in corresponding rhythms up to the blackout. The pulsations are attuned to the sentences and drum rhythms.*

MARY. I wonder—could he have tried to walk from the camp? Perhaps he started out last Wednesday before the storm. It's true! It's true! He's gone! He was lost—in that snowstorm!

MRS. MARTIN *is silent.* MARY *stands dazed and trembling. Blackout. A low blue light floods the cyclorama. The lights build to 1/8 on* MARY *and* MRS. MARTIN. MRS. MARTIN'*s dancers speak her embittered loneliness,* MARY'*s her anxious fears.*

There may be a letter. I wish he'd hurry. I can't stand waiting like this. (*Her light builds to 2/8.)* I must know! (*The light increases to 3/8.)* I must! (*Her light dims to 2/8 and holds through her speech.)* Yes—there's a letter—for one of us. He's bringing it up now. If it's for me I'll be almost afraid to open it—now.

A menacing rumble in the drums announces MAXWELL'*s approach. The blue on the cyclorama sky increases in intensity to 2/8.* MAXWELL *enters and climbs the steps to the upstage centre platform area VI. The light in the area builds to 1/8 as he moves into it.*

MAXWELL. A letter for you Mary—from the camp. It's dated more than a
week ago. Trains from the north on the branch line were held up by the
storm.

MARY. (*Her light holds at 1/8.*) I hope—I hope—it's not too bad news! (*A pause.
The facial expressions of MARY and MAXWELL and the movements of MARY's
dancers indicate or represent the giving of the letter. The blue concert flood
lighting the cyclorama from behind the back curtains builds to 6/8 through
MAXWELL's speech. The green concert flood builds slowly to 6/8 by "read your
letter," then dims sharply.*)

MAXWELL. Mrs. Martin, the conductor said they passed Ed and Bill Keenan a
quarter of a mile up the track. They'll be here in a few minutes. Apparently
they came through by the west chain of lakes and struck the tracks this
side of Horton. If there's any news, I'll ask them to let you know when they
come.

MARY. (*There is pathos in the faces and gestures of MARY's dancers. Her light is still
low at 1/8, in the mood of her intense fears.*) What news? Mr. Maxwell, has
anything happened to Blake?

MAXWELL. I—ask Mrs. Martin. I must be going.

*Diminishing drum beats accompany MAXWELL's departure. The blue sky dims out
as does the light on the platform area VI.*

MARY. Have Ed and Bill Keenan been—

MRS. MARTIN. (*Gruffly.*) Read your letter. (*In a softer voice.*) Well? What does
he say?

*On MRS. MARTIN's question, they walk slowly, as in a strange, intense dream, to
the adjacent areas. The lights on areas I and V dim out, and the lights on areas II and
IV build to 2/8 as they move. MARY does not reply until the viola plays a fragment of
the violin spring theme. 2/8 red is briefly added to the blue on the cyclorama.*

MARY. It's spring and I'm coming home. Leaving Wednesday morning and
cutting across country. I should be home by Saturday or Sunday, if I don't
hit a storm. (*One drum beat. The light on MARY in area II dims out as if she
herself is lost.*)

MRS. MARTIN. Is there anything more?

MARY. (*The light on her builds to 2/8.*) Yes, there is. (*The light grows to 4/8.*) But
I can't read it—to you. (*Her light dims to 2/8. One drum beat. Her dancers echo
her heart-broken realization of Blake's death. There is excitement on the cyclorama—the diagonals and blue greens flaring and pulsing with the story that
is now told. MARY's light dims out on "out." Fumbling for her words.*) Then he

started out—And the storm— (MRS. MARTIN *makes no reply. One drum beat.* MARY*'s light builds to 1/8.*) And Bill and Ed Keenan, and Sandy and Bert?

MRS. MARTIN. (*Her light in area IV builds to 1/8.*) Yes—they been out lookin' for him.

MARY. (*As she asks her pitiful question, she crosses to centre stage and sits on the stool down centre in area III. One drum beat.*) Why—didn't—you tell me?

MRS. MARTIN crosses to the centre area and stands behind MARY, comforting her. The lights on areas II and IV fade out as MARY and MRS. MARTIN leave them, and build on the downstage centre area as they enter it, to 2/8. The diagonals fade out. The cyclorama becomes quiet, a low blue touched with red. The dancers enact the story with great pity.

MRS. MARTIN. (*Standing above MARY, a dark cloaked figure.*) There, there, girl. There's a chance yet. Bill and Ed followed the west chain of lakes, lookin' for him. There w's a cabin he might h've reached before the storm struck him. (*One drum beat. The light on the two women remains at 2/8.*)

MARY. But they're coming back now—without him.

Her dancers lift their heads and bodies, questioning and tense. Red flares resume and grow on the cyclorama to MARY's protest "Why did you go?" MRS. MARTIN's dancers bespeak her new mood of gentleness and pity.

MRS. MARTIN. They might've found him—before it was too late—and left him back in the cabin—or up the line.

There are staccato growing drum beats to the climax in "Why did you go?", with a pause for MRS. MARTIN's speech. In face and gesture MARY's dancers enact her bitter grief, the rhythmic sweep of their bodies corresponding to the sentence rhythms and the pulsations of MARY's light and the cyclorama.

MARY. No! He's gone—he's gone—he won't come back. And you wouldn't tell me. You tried to keep it from me. You've been cruel, cruel, all of you.

MRS. MARTIN. We w's thinkin' o' yer own good.

MARY. I don't believe it. Oh Blake, Blake! Why did you leave me? Why did you go?

She cries, at first violently, then more quietly. The cyclorama is blue and still with a faint suggestion of red. The viola plays the cello theme of the MOTHER's grief and loneliness, with a pause for MARY's speech, building to "live in my heart."

MRS. MARTIN. When yer as old as me and such thin's happen you sit an' wait an' know there's no help—an' you keep on waitin' till the end. You don't mind nothin'—you jest want to rest and be quiet—an' for people to be kind to yuh. (*Her dancers are soft, patient and resigned in attitude and gesture.*)

MARY. (*Her dancers respond to* MARY's *gentleness.*) I'll be kind to you, Mrs. Martin.

MRS. MARTIN. You'll miss him a while. Then you'll make new friends, an' I'll be left alone—an' he'll only live in my heart. An' then when I'm gone—

The light in area III dims out on the last sentence. The cello theme is played.

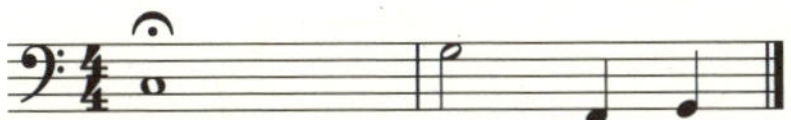

Suddenly, with MARY's *cry of faith, the mood changes. Her dancers are radiant and tender. The cyclorama lights grow and play gloriously and tenderly during her two sentences, building to "in my heart," then dropping to dark blue, then shadow. The violin Blake theme joins the lights, building to a serene climax on "heart."*

MARY. Then he'll live, as he said, in the woods and the rocks and the skies— and in my heart too. (*The viola plays while, as in a ceremony,* MARY *walks up the steps to the upper platform area VI in 2/8 light. The light on the area dims to 1/8 on "heart." The light on* MRS. MARTIN *fades out.*)

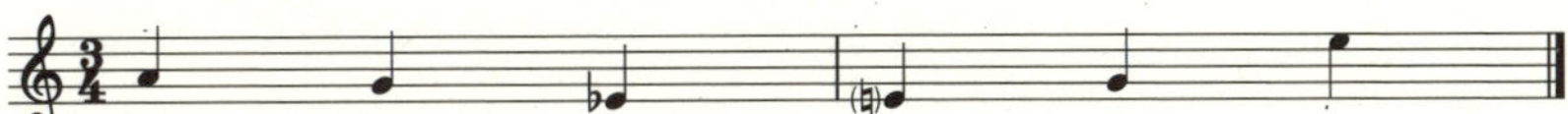

I'll keep him always in my heart. (*When the viola phrase completes the moment there is a pause.*)

(*One drum beat.*) Bill and Ed Keenan are coming up the path. (*The cyclorama lights fade to a dark blue.*)

MRS. MARTIN. (*Her light, as she sits on the stool, builds to 3/8 through her sentence.*) The water on the one hand and the woods on the other ha' been pressin' in on me all my life. (*Her light falls to 2/8 and holds, dimming to 1/8 on "I'm waitin' quiet and rested."*) Now the shadows is gatherin', an' I'm waitin' quiet and rested.

The light on the rocks has built and faded with MRS. MARTIN's *words. Now there is a change in mood. The violin sings the message of Blake's belief in the North.*

MARY. All the things he said begin to have new meaning for me. (*On the impulse of her belief* MARY's *light builds to 2/8 on "new meaning." The wave of the sentence dims back to 1/8 as it is completed. Her dancers, heads raised, shoulders back, echo her faith. Their movements join with light and music to confirm and strengthen* MARY's *declaration. Her light builds to 3/8. The violin music is under her words.*) I begin to understand his faith.

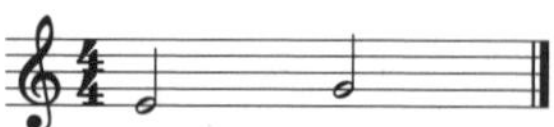

(*Her light builds to 5/8.*) It will be my faith.

(*Her light dims to 3/8.*) I'll try to have no fear.

Pause. The light on MRS. MARTIN, *sitting on the stool in area III is at 1/8.*

MRS. MARTIN. They never found Tom's body. They won't find his neither.
MARY. Hush, here they are!

As all lights fade slowly, to drumming that increases in volume, MARY *descends from the upper platform to area III and she and* MRS. MARTIN *walk to their outer areas I and V. There is a moment of silence. A colossal shadow grows out of a blue light which is dimmed up on the cyclorama in silence. The lights on* MARY *and* MRS. MARTIN *build to 1/8.*

MARY. Won't you come in? (*One drum beat.*)
BILL. (*The off-stage voices of* BILL *and* ED *are hollow and lonely.*) No thanks, we'll have to be goin'.
MRS. MARTIN. Well?
ED. We been lookin' steadily. (*One drum beat.*) No trace of him. (*Two drum beats. There is another pause.*) Let us know if there's anythin' we can do.
MRS. MARTIN. I reckon you done all you can.

The shadow disappears to slowly diminishing drum beats. The viola plays a cello theme, with broken and bitter accent.

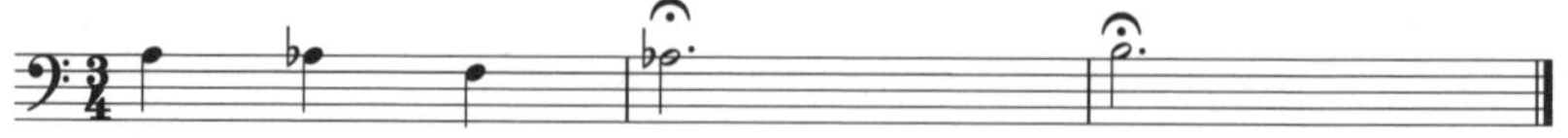

MARY and MRS. MARTIN leave their outer areas I and V and come together in the down centre area III. The lights on I and V fade as they leave them, and build and fade on areas II and IV as they pass through them. MARY goes up the steps and kneels on the upstage area VI, facing out. There is no light on the area. The light on MRS. MARTIN, sitting on the stool below her, is at 1/8.

MRS. MARTIN. Just the two o' us now—gropin' in the dark. (*Pause. MARY's dancers make a gesture of understanding. There is harmony between the two groups of dancers in their mood and attitudes at last. Throughout MRS. MARTIN's account of how her son died, the rock diagonals, with dark blue screens, pulse slowly in the rhythm of her light. They fade as the account closes on "What good was your strength to you then—against the woods?" MRS. MARTIN speaks sonorously as if chanting.*) I know what happened— (*Her light builds to 2/8.*) I've known it before. (*The light dims to 1/8 as she starts. It builds to 3/8 through the sentence.*) The snow kept gettin' deeper an' deeper an' the blizzard blinded him. (*The light dims to 2/8.*) 'N he fought on an' on till he come back on his own tracks. (*Both groups of dancers relive the story. MRS. MARTIN's light builds to 3/8.*) 'N then the darkness set in (*The light dims to 2/8.*)—'n he give up (*The light dims to 1/8.*)—'n the snow was warm. (*She cries out bitterly. Both groups of dancers echo the challenge. Her light flares to full and holds through the sentence.*) What good was your strength to you then— against the woods? (*There is a pause. The mood changes. MRS. MARTIN's dancers show her final lonely acceptance of her lot and coming death. Her light drops to 2/8. The viola plays a peaceful, resigned cello theme.*)

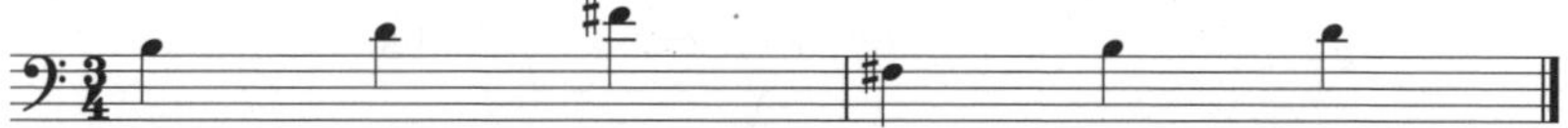

'N he's my last. (*Both groups of dancers drop down, almost crumpling, with bitter final grief—MARY's in sympathy with MRS. MARTIN's. But toward the end of MRS. MARTIN's lament MARY's dancers begin to remember Blake and MARY's belief in her lover.*) I've got nothin' more to worry over now—just to wait—until the end. (*Her light builds to 3/8 with her bitterness.*) An' it won't be long for me— (*Her light dims to 2/8, and out on her last words.*) It won't be long.

Suddenly the cyclorama is a symphony of colour, building, flashing and waving and growing rhythmically in intensity with the rhythm of MARY's words to her exultant declaration that she, too, will know the glory that her lover knew—"part of its flashing northern lights." Her dancers re-live her rapture. MRS. MARTIN's dancers follow the older woman in mood and attitude. They are quiet and withdrawn, but gentle. The violin theme merges with the Blake theme to "northern lights."

MARY. He was so young,

he didn't want to be safe about things.

Her light follows the rhythm of the sentence, building to 2/8 of "safe" and falling to 1/8 on "about things." As the new sentence begins it builds to 2/8, and 3/8 on "strong in me."

And now his words are strong in me.

(The light builds to 4/8.) They are my words.

(Her light grows to 5/8 with her transfiguring vision. The violin theme leaps up with her faith.) I too shall see banners shaking before me—

(Her light builds to 6/8 on "great white" and to 7/8 on "blinding." The music builds with it.) A great white light blinding me—

(The light builds to full on "music ringing" and holds at 8/8 through the next three sentences, to "flashing northern lights.") Music ringing in my ears.

I too shall hear the wilderness calling,

calling my life into a great adventure.

It will be my land.

I'll belong to it.

I'll be part of winds and woods and rocks—

part of its flashing northern lights.

(Her light dims to 6/8 and holds through her speech. The cyclorama lights cease pulsing as strongly and brightly and are dimmed to blue and darken after "content.") Though he's gone now

he'll still be part of it.

He'll still belong.

And he'll be content.

The violin themes die away slowly. The light on MARY *dims to 4/8.* MRS. MARTIN'S *light builds to1/8. Her dancers capture her words in motion.*

MRS. MARTIN. *(After a pause.)* Too much thinkin' an' dreamin' ain' good
for yuh.
MARY. I want to watch the night.
MRS. MARTIN. *(Her light builds to 2/8 on "both of us" and holds through her speech.)* It's been a hard country on both of us. Now it's done it's worst t' me. You better go south, where there's fields and more people. *(Her dancers stir and lift with the suggestion, thoughtful and kindly.)*
MARY. *(Her light falls to 1/8 with her quiet, tender mood. Her dancers follow her in her mystical serenity. The cyclorama remains a deep, low-level blue. The Blake*

and spring themes continue to second "I can't go.") I can't go now—never. He is
out there— (*The light in area VI builds to 5/8.*)

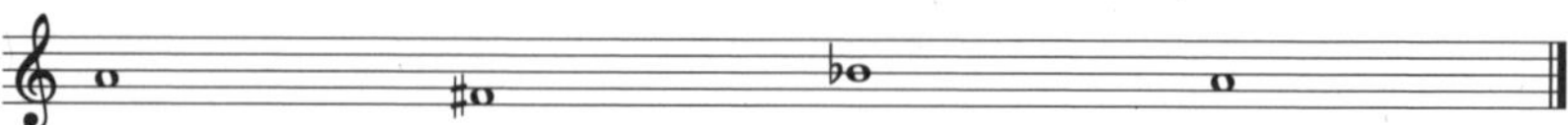

wrapped in the night

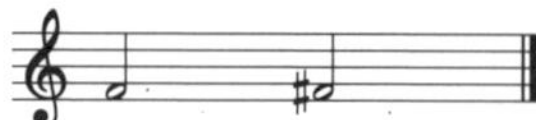

and quiet. (*Her light dims to 4/8 and to 1/8 in area III on "go."*) I can't go. (*Cello
theme to "gloom." Light in area VI dims to 2/8.*) How dark the hills are now—

like palls to his grave—reaching further than I can see—folding back and
back into mystery and gloom. (*Her light in area VI builds to 3/8 on "tender."
Her dancers lift and listen, as if they too felt the wind. The violin builds to "my
heart."*) And yet the wind on my face

is so tender

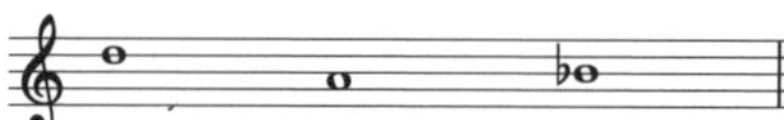

*Red builds into the cyclorama, suggesting the mystical exultation of remembered
love. It increases, with amber added, to the end of* MARY's *speech, "Blake! Blake!"
Then both colours fade out, leaving a deep blue sky for the closing moment.* MARY's
dancers relive the hunger and triumph.

as if he would speak to me. (*Her light dims to 2/8.*)

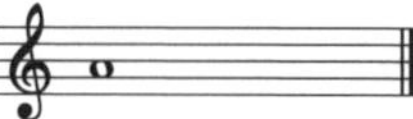

So many springs will come—

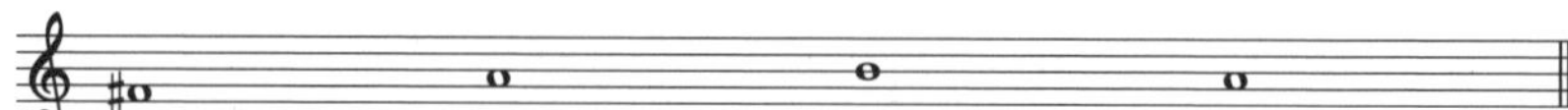

(*Her light builds to 3/8.*) And always this restlessness—

(*The light builds to 4/8.*) This hunger—

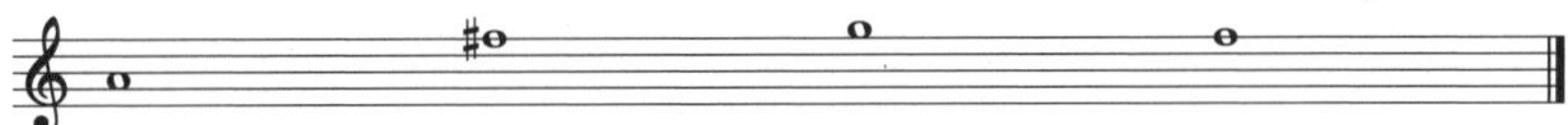

(*The light builds to 5/8.*) this triumph in my heart.

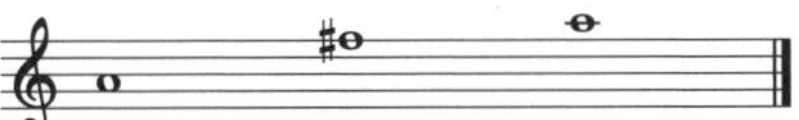

(*Her dancers lift and sway in the rhythm of her words to "Oh Blake! Blake!"* MRS. MARTIN*'s dancers stir, sensing her protest against the land.* MARY*'s light builds to 6/8 on the first "Blake," to full on the second.*) Oh Blake! Blake!

Her light dims to 1/8. In a pause, the viola plays a lonely, tender strain.

MRS. MARTIN. (*Her dancers make her final protest against what the North has done to her. Her light in area III is 2/8.*) Too much woods—too much rock.

There is a pause before the closing moment. MARY *stands above* MRS. MARTIN, *with longing and belief. The movements and gestures of both groups of dancers are similar as they dance the thoughts and feelings of the two women. Their heads are flung back, their arms outstretched—but* MRS. MARTIN*'s in despair,* MARY*'s in exultation. The violin and cello themes play together resolving at last into a final statement of serenity.*

MRS. MARTIN. (*She sits motionless—a still huddled lonely figure. Her light, with a climaxing drum roll, builds to full as she cries out. She is forlorn and bitter, and her cry has great finality.*) Rocks!

MARY. (*She speaks as if whispering a magic charm. Her light builds to full with a more restrained drum roll.*) Rocks!

A violin phrase proclaims MARY*'s love.*

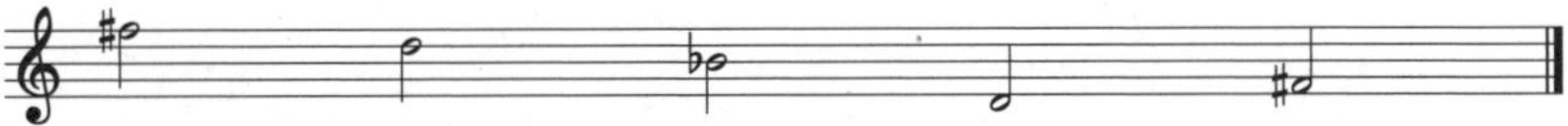

The lights fade, diminishing with each firm, dull, slow beat of the drum.
At last there is silence and darkness.

18 ⋮ *Unity* (1933)

Enacting Revolution

ALAN FILEWOD

UNITY is one of the few Canadian examples of the revolutionary agitprops produced during the 1930s in the Workers' Theatre Movement, a loose alliance of left-wing theatre troupes affiliated with the Moscow-based Communist International (commonly known as the Comintern). Its author, Oscar Ryan (born Oscar Weinstein), was a leading activist in the underground Communist Party of Canada (CPC) in the 1930s. He grew up in Montreal and Winnipeg and after high school joined the Young Communist League as a full-time party activist. With an idiomatic and forceful proletarian writing style, he became a writer for the Communist Party's *Daily Worker* and its successors, the *Daily Clarion* and the *Canadian Tribune*.

In the CPC, Ryan was an early supporter of Tim Buck, who took over the party in 1929 when communist parties around the world assumed a more radical militant stance in answer to Stalin's call for revolutionary class war. Under Buck, Ryan became a leading figure in the party's propaganda wing, as a cultural organizer, publicity director of the Canadian Labour Defence League, and the author of numerous pamphlets. In 1932 he founded the Toronto Progressive Arts Club and was co-editor of its magazine, *Masses*. He was also instrumental as a writer and director in the club's theatre wing, the Workers' Experimental Theatre (WET), where he met his future wife, Toby Gordon. At Ryan's initiative, WET produced the first major Canadian documentary play, *Eight Men Speak*, in December 1933; Ryan was one of four co-authors. The play was closed by the Toronto Police and banned by the federal government in one of the most notorious censorship cases in Canadian history.[1]

Oscar Ryan's published work includes *Unity* (1933), *Eight Men Speak*, the novel *Soon to be Born* (1980), and a partisan propaganda biography of Tim Buck. Under the alias Martin Stone, he was a theatre critic for the *Canadian Tribune* from 1955 to 1988.

Unity was produced by WET, which Ryan and Toby Gordon had founded in 1932 to stage agitprops[2] in parks, factories, and rallies. The play premiered on May 1, 1933, in Toronto's Hygeia Hall, as part of a program celebrating May Day, the annual day of solidarity and protest for the international labour movement. The political atmosphere was heated; the federal government had outlawed the CPC in 1931 and at the time of the performance, the CPC's senior leadership was incarcerated in Kingston Penitentiary. The troupe encountered frequent harassment from the Toronto Police's "Red Squad"; two members

1. For a full account and historical documentation of the suppression of *Eight Men Speak*, see the editorial introduction to the text in Ryan et al. 2013.

2. A portmanteau that combines "agitation" and "propaganda" to convey the terse telegraphic efficiencies of early Soviet bureaucratic rhetoric. In the theatre, agitprop developed in the USSR and Germany as a mobile form of exhortative revolutionary theatre designed for quick outdoor performance. It was adaptive to location, audience, and cast, and suited the sightlines and acoustics of outdoor performance in found spaces. Short phrases, heavy cadence, and repetition allowed performance to project through noisy and unruly audiences

FIGURE 18.1: *Members of The Workers' Theatre that produced* Unity, *ca. 1932. As marked on the back of the photograph: "from left: Izzy Levine, Jim Watts, Percy Matthews, JP Smith, Toby Gordon, Avrom Yanovsky."* Item xz1 ms a012000. Courtesy of the Toby Gordon Ryan Collection, Archival and Special Collections, University of Guelph Library.

of the cast of *Unity* were arrested on the day of the performance but were released just in time to make it to the show.

The text of *Unity* survives in two editions. It originally appeared in *Masses* in 1933, shortly after its first performance, and was republished in 1976 in *Eight Men Speak and Other Plays from the Canadian Workers' Theatre*, edited by Robin Endres, who worked closely with Oscar Ryan in selecting and editing the plays. There are no eyewitness accounts of the performance, and although Endres writes that *Unity* "subsequently became one of the more popular agit-props throughout the country" (1976, xxvi), no actual documentary evidence of those performances has turned up. It is possible that she relied on Oscar Ryan's anecdotal knowledge as her source. We can safely surmise that the text as it appears here was what the audience saw in that original performance. If there ever was a cast list or program, they have not survived.

With its broad, cartoonish satire, *Unity* is typical of the international agitprop form. Communist theory of the day argued that this new combative theatre was a truly working-class and international art form that stood in opposition to the realist and national traditions of the capitalist classes. As described in *Masses*, "All that is required is a platform, players, ideas and audience. Scenery and properties, beyond the most elementary suggestion of atmosphere are only necessary for a bourgeois audience which is too mentally enervated by the stupid wasteful routine of its daily life to think or have ideas of its own" (Cowan 1932). Reflecting on *Unity* almost fifty years later, Ryan wrote that the agitprops "introduced some innovations to Canada—the use of mass chants, of stylized motion, of satire and caricature, and even the uniform group costume, as well as living tableaux, and even a kind of choreographed movement, sometimes exaggerated, sometimes supple and direct—but never above the heads of the audience" (quoted in T. Ryan 1981, 42).

Unity draws on two common techniques that were particularly effective in outdoor venues. The first is the cartoon iconography of the one-dimensional characters. The Capitalists appear as rotund businessmen wearing top hats, spats, gloves, and canes; they are immediately familiar as a popular icon, made famous by the logo of the board game Monopoly (which first appeared in 1932). The Workers are dressed in the Workers' Theatre uniform of black shirt and trousers with a red neck-scarf. The physicality of the performance, with the Capitalists in their drunken kick line and the accusative Workers opposing them, offers an immediate image of the play's political argument. The use of risers to establish levels was not just an effective device to control sightlines in outdoor venues; it also added another visual layer of political symbolism as the working class literally rises up to defeat the leaders of capitalism.

The second technique is the use of the choral mass chant, perhaps the most innovative agitprop technique and the one that most clearly modelled the aesthetics of revolutionary modernism. It combines the cadence and oratory of nineteenth-century recitations with the staccato rhythms, segues, and transitions of radio. At its most effective, it was drilled and choreographic; in *Unity* the discipline of the Workers when speaking in chorus is a political rebuke of the unruly drunkenness of the Capitalists. The mass chant was, in effect, an enactment of revolutionary dynamism.

As a work of political theatre, *Unity* marks a major moment of transformation in Communist revolutionary strategy. In 1933 the Comintern responded to the victory of Nazism in Germany by realigning its politics away from class war in favour of a strategy of broad political alliance to combat fascism. In this shift to what was called the Popular Front, the workers' theatres moved away from divisive revolutionary rhetoric; plays like *Unity* were devised to communicate the new political message of co-operation to party members and supporters.

Historically, *Unity* stands as both the high point and the final stage of agit-prop in the Workers' Theatre Movement in Canada. Over the ensuing year the movement effectively phased itself out, subsumed by a new Popular Front professionalism that advocated socialist realism and national cultural traditions, and which produced a revisionist critique that denounced agitprops like *Unity* as crude and inartistic propaganda. Despite this disavowal, agitprop saw a major revival in the guerrilla street theatre of the 1960s, and it remains popular today as an accessible, affordable, and mobile form of theatre that can respond and adapt quickly to political events.

Bibliography and Further Reading

Cowan, Andrew Gillespie. 1932. "Red Theatre." *Masses* 1, no. 3 (June): 3.

Endres, Robin. 1976. Introduction to *Eight Men Speak and Other Plays from the Canadian Workers' Theatre*, edited by Richard Wright and Robin Endres, xi–xxxvi. Toronto: New Hogtown Press.

Filewod, Alan. 2011. *Committing Theatre: Theatre Radicalism and Political Intervention in Canada*. Toronto: Between the Lines.

Ryan, Oscar. 1976. "Unity." In *Eight Men Speak and Other Plays from the Canadian Workers' Theatre*, edited by Richard Wright and Robin Endres, 97–107. Toronto: New Hogtown Press.

Ryan, Oscar, et al. 2013. *Eight Men Speak*. Edited by Alan Filewod. Ottawa: University of Ottawa Press.

Ryan, Toby Gordon. 1981. *Stage Left: Canadian Theatre in the Thirties: A Memoir*. Toronto: Canadian Theatre Review Publications.

Unity

OSCAR RYAN

1. Cloth or canvas cover for the upper part of a shoe, seen as a sign of snobbish refinement.
2. The Workers' Experimental Theatre in Toronto adopted a basic stage "uniform" of black shirt and trousers and red neck-scarf.
3. In 1933, when *Unity* was written, the worldwide Great Depression was in its fourth year; it lasted until 1939.
4. Early twentieth-century slang meaning "excellent."

CHARACTERS

> 4 CAPITALISTS, *each with identical white spats,*[1] *cane, silk hat, white gloves, bow ties and black workers' theatre uniform.*[2]
> 4 WORKERS, *in workers' theatre uniform.*
> *Crowd of workers of about 10 or if the group is small there can be less.*

Plain back drop; three levels, bench, chair, table suggested.

1ST CAP. (*Enters from right rapidly walking to and fro.*) I can't stand it any longer! (*To audience.*) I say I can't! (*Walking.*) I can't! I CAN'T! I CAN'T! (*To audience.*) Is it my fault if they're out of work and broke? (*Walking.*) I'm not to blame: It's the fault of International conditions. (*To audience.*) We've all got to tighten up our belts. We all suffer. Is it my fault? (*Turns to walk, but stops.*) I know what's wrong: It's the gold standard! It's inflation! (*Pause: Faster and faster.*) It's deflation! It's high tariffs! Low tariffs! High taxes! Low taxes! It's—(*Walks quickly.*) I know what's wrong, I know what's wrong, I know what's wrong! It's in-ter-nat-ion-al conditions. (*To audience.*) Just a little, Just a Teenie, Weenie little depression![3] (*Walking.*) If only I could convince my workers, If only I could get them to understand, that if we pull together, we'll muddle through—somehow. If only I could get them to believe that they and I should work together to fight Old Man Depression, then, we'd all be jake.[4] At least I would. (*In ecstasy.*) Then, Ah then! The coins would flow in faster; My profits (*Steps up.*) Would go up (*Higher.*) And Up (*Highest level.*) And UP! (*Stands.*) And I'd be on top of the world again! (*Sad.*) But now...Everything, Everything (*Steps down.*) Seems to be going Down (*Down.*) And DOWN (*On floor.*) And (*Quickly.*) DOWN. (*Sits on bench.*) Down. (*Holds head in hands.*)

2ND CAP. (*Enters from left, slowly thinking.*) It can't go on...They won't listen to me any more...(*To audience.*) Ladies, gentlemen: Can't I get any sympathy from you? Did the last war kill all your patriotism? Don't you realize that the cause of all our troubles (*Slowly.*) Is Russia? (*Bitterly.*) Russia...(1ST CAP. *looks up.*) If only we got her out of the way, we'd have prosperity again! Russia is a threat to our civilization, to you, (*Loudly.*) to ME! (1ST CAP. *climbs to second level, happier.*) Don't pay any attention to Moscow agents: They say there's no unemployment there. (*Hysterically.*) Lies, LIES, LIES, LIES! They shoot off all their unemployed! (*Pleading.*) There's no equal opportunity for all in Russia. If I went there, what chance would I stand? These agitators who tell you our Canadian factories are closing down, while

Russia builds huge industries—They're just plain liars! (*1ST CAP. stands on top level, arms flung out. Cynically.*) New power stations?

1ST CAP. New power stations?

2ND CAP. Metal plants?

1ST CAP. Metal plants?

2ND CAP. Tractor factories?

1ST CAP. Tractor factories?

2ND CAP. Auto shops?

1ST CAP. Auto shops?

2ND CAP. There's no such places.

1ST CAP. There's no such places.

2ND CAP. They're only made.

1ST CAP. They're only made.

2ND CAP. To show off to the tourists!

1ST CAP. To show off to the tourists!

2ND CAP. looks around at audience to see what impression he made.

2ND CAP. (*Walking back and forth.*) I don't seem to be convincing them...

1ST CAP. (*Drops arms, dejected.*) But Russia does...

2ND CAP. (*Feeling happier.*) I wonder whether I can get them hot by raking up (*Rubbing hands.*) Some tall tales of Soviet dumping?...(*To audience.*) May I appeal to you: Dear ladies! Dear gentlemen! Do you know (*Demagogically.*) That Russia's dumping goods? That's why we have a depression. Do you know that some of our best Canadians are being buried in coffins made of SOVIET lumber? That every time you chew a toothpick, you may be chewing SOVIET lumber? That every time you light a match you may be unpatriotic, by lighting up a RED flare, instead of encouraging home industries such as Mr. Bennett's Eddy match?[5] (*Looks to see impression on audience. Walks back and forth nervously.*) Hm...They won't budge...Don't seem to care very much for Mr. Bennett or his matches. Maybe they've all got lighters.

1ST CAP. sits in top level dejected again.

2ND CAP. (*Sits on bench.*) Once, I thought, they would eat up my words, like I eat up profits...Once, it seemed to me, they would follow me through hell. Now, they seem too anxious to send me there, Alone...all, all Alone...

1ST CAP. Alone...

3RD CAP. (*Enters from the right, blusteringly, laughing.*) No need for that, boys! (*Stands between both capitalists, behind them.*) Listen: You're out of date. You're played out. You've got one foot in the grave. But there's still hope. What you need is monkey glands,[6] and I'm the guy that's going to show you how. I'm going to jazz things up. I'm going to make you feel young again. Say! You're going to have a good time again. Here! Have a drink! (*All drink.*)

You're going to have a spree. They're all doing it. Look what handsome Adolph's done for Germany[7] —Boy! And Mussolini[8] for Italy! —Hotcha![9] And Pilsudski for Poland![10]—Whoopee! (*Walks away, left.*) Those fellows know the trick. Shay! C'mere! (*All go into corner.*) Thass wha' we need right here in Can'da. We'll force 'em tu ferget the dep-dep-dep-rezzion.

2ND CAP. I gottit! I gottit! Less make a law puviding death for ad aj-tators who talk 'bout de-de-prezzion!

1ST CAP. I gotta better one: Less say 'sall the fault of the Jews.

3RD CAP. And the Indians!

2ND CAP. And of course the Reds. (*Prancing.*) The Jews; the Indians; And of course the Reds. (*Prancing.*) The Reds; the Indians; And of course the Jews. (*Dancing into left front stage in a straight line with canes and feet raised, in ecstasy.*) The Indians; the Jews; and of course the Reds! (*Takes hats off on last word and stand for a second in a grotesque pose.*)

1ST CAP. But suppose some finicky people raise hell about DEMOCRACY?

2ND CAP. Aw nerts![11] They won't miss it that much. They have almost forgotten what it's like in Canada.

3RD CAP. And if they don't like it, and if they start spreading atrocity stories about us, we'll torture the dogs to death!

ALL THREE. (*Gaily strutting across to right side of stage, front.*) We'll torture the dogs to death!

4TH CAP. (*Runs in, grabs outside man by arm and is very nervous.*) Please, please, listen: Not the Jews, Not the Indians—Only the Reds!

FIRST THREE CAP. (*Other three capitalists ignore him and pull him along, reciting gaily.*) The Indians, the Jews and the Reds!

Enter 4 WORKERS left, each coming in with their "Well" very militant

1ST WORKER. Well?...

2ND WORKER. Well?...

3RD WORKER. WELL?...

4TH WORKER. WELL?...

ALL 4 WORKERS. (*Taking step forward.*) WELL?

1ST WORKER. We heard you...

2ND WORKER. We know what you want.

3RD WORKER. And we're going to put an end to you!

4TH WORKER. All our existence has been

ALL 4 WORKERS. In your hands!

4TH WORKER. Too long!

3RD WORKER. All our thinking has been trained

ALL 4 WORKERS. In your interests!

3RD WORKER. Too long!

2ND WORKER. All our toil, all our strength, all our striving have poured profits into your pockets!

12. Section 98 of the Canadian Criminal Code, introduced in 1919 as an instrument to suppress communism, gave the government arbitrary powers to arrest anyone suspected of belonging to a criminal organization. It was used in 1931 to imprison senior leaders of the Communist Party; they were found guilty in trial and as a consequence the Communist Party was declared illegal. Section 98 was repealed in 1936 after massive national protest.

13. The biblical patriarch who, according to the Book of Genesis, lived to the age of 969.

2ND WORKER. Far too long!

1ST WORKER. And we're going to put an end,

2ND WORKER. An end,

3RD WORKER. An end,

4TH WORKER. An end,

ALL 4 WORKERS. (*Taking a step forward, while* ALL 4 CAPITALISTS *retreat.*) An end to you!

ALL 4 CAPITALISTS. (*Imploring.*) Wait!

1ST CAP. (*Warning.*) It's against the law!

2ND CAP. (*In awe.*) It's sedition!

3RD CAP. (*Angrily.*) It's Section 98![12]

4TH CAP. (*In fear.*) It's force and violence to put an end to us.

1ST WORKER. And it's law and order to shoot down hungry workers!

2ND WORKER. And justice to jail working class leaders!

1ST CAP. So long as we're the state, the law will take care of you and your kind.

2ND CAP. To deport.

3RD CAP. To jail.

4TH CAP. And to shoot at you!

1ST CAP. And we'll do it all through our laws, to show you that democracy cannot be tampered with by a lot of trouble makers.

2ND CAP. And if that doesn't stop you, we, the people, will find other ways.

1ST WORKER. (*Stepping forward.*) Hitler's Way!

2ND WORKER. (*Stepping forward.*) Pilsudski's way!

3RD WORKER. (*Stepping forward.*) Mussolini's way!

4TH WORKER. (*Stepping forward.*) Fascism!

1ST WORKER. And we say:

ALL 4 WORKERS. (*Stepping forward.*) DOWN WITH FASCISM!

3RD CAPITALIST. (*Stepping forward, other 3* CAPITALISTS *follow.*) You'll never put an end to us, we're too strong, (*Piously.*) and history has willed that—

ALL 4 CAP. We will live forever!

1ST WORKER. (*Coolly.*) Even Methuselah[13] died.

2ND WORKER. (*Ironically.*) And we would not for anything allow you to spoil Mr. Methuselah's reputation.

2ND CAP. It's in your own interests that we hold you in check, discipline you, teach you your place in the order of things. It's all for the best, and it hurts us—

3RD WORKER. (*Sneering.*) Yes, more than it hurts us.

4TH WORKER. Enough! We have no time nor patience for such discussions. We have an object that clamours for attainment.

3RD CAP. Never!

1ST CAP. (*Nervously.*) N-n-never!

ALL 4 CAP. NEVER!

4 CAPITALISTS advance, canes raised threateningly. At that moment the crowd enters from the left side holding banners, "UNITY," "STRUGGLE." All group, banners raised, behind 4 WORKERS, while CAPITALISTS stand rooted, drop canes.

1ST WORKER. I'm a trade unionist.

2ND WORKER. I—a socialist worker.

3RD WORKER. And I'm a communist.

4TH WORKER. I'm an unorganized worker.

Workers step forward with each slogan.

WHOLE CROWD. We're the working class!

1ST VOICE IN CROWD. We're from the Pacific Coast!

2ND VOICE. From the East!

3RD VOICE. From the Northlands!

4TH VOICE. And the South!

WHOLE CROWD. From all Canada! And we are UNITED!

1ST VOICE. We're from our brothers and sisters, our comrades, in GERMANY!

2ND VOICE. In GREAT BRITAIN!

3RD VOICE. In CHINA!

CROWD. In the SOVIET UNION!

CAPITALISTS turn to flee right, 4 WORKERS simultaneously kick them out and take up positions on the three levels. Banners are handed up to them, while crowd forms single file in front, slanting down towards right stage front, with the tallest at the head of the line and the smallest at the bottom. They all stand in position in order to be able to point towards banner with "UNITY" on it which should be held by 4TH WORKER.

1ST WORKER. (*On lower level.*) Comrades! We must remember the deeds and the hopes, and the struggles of all those who have fought for the cause of the working class!

WHOLE CROWD. (*Clenching fists.*) Our cause!

2ND WORKER. (*Higher level.*) Comrades! We must pledge ourselves to greater struggles, to carry on the fight against the system that has stained with blood and sweat our whole existence.

CROWD. (*Raising fists higher.*) We struggle!

3RD WORKER. (*Higher level.*) Against hunger, Against terror, Against war!

CROWD. (*Lunging forward with fists pointing down.*) Against fascism! (*They remain forward.*)

4TH WORKER. (*Highest level.*) And we shall defeat them, All our enemies, All, Through UNITY!

CROWD. (*With clenched fists.*) Through united struggle!

4TH WORKER. Strong as steel, We must build our UNITY!

4 WORKERS. (*On levels.*) UNITY
CROWD. (*With clenched fists toward banner "UNITY."*) UNITY! UNITY!

CURTAIN OR BLACKOUT

19 : *Cocktail* (1935)

Women in Early Modern Quebec Drama

CHRISTL VERDUYN

CHRISTL VERDUYN

YVETTE OLLIVIER MERCIER-GOUIN was born in Quebec City to Héloïse Roy and Quebec Liberal MP Nazaire-Nicolas Ollivier. The Ollivier family valued education and had the means to provide it for their daughter. Yvette studied with the Ursulines[1] and at the Conservatoire français du Québec—opportunities that reflected her family's comfortable economic and social circumstances and that provided the foundation for a life in the arts. Education and family support led Yvette to theatre, first as an actor and then as a playwright. She wrote numerous texts for stage as well as for radio. Despite the fragile state of theatre in 1930s Quebec,[2] two of Mercier-Gouin's plays, *Cocktail* (1935) and *Le Jeune Dieu* (1937), saw their way to publication[3] and to stages across Quebec in a significant boost to the development of theatre in Quebec. For many years, Gratien Gélinas[4] has been allocated the honour of inaugurating the Quebec theatrical tradition with his 1948 play *Tit-Coq*. Reconsideration of *Cocktail* suggests that it was a woman—Yvette Mercier-Gouin—who deserves this recognition.

Cocktail was an enormous success. Newspapers hailed it as the first "Canadian" play, which in the Quebec context of the time meant that it was not the work of a playwright from France. Theatre was not the only genre in search of a Quebec voice at the time; Quebec literature in general was in the process of establishing itself as distinct from its French headwaters. Against this backdrop, *Cocktail* was proclaimed the best play ever written in Canada (*Le Droit*, May 21, 1935, 12), a *tour de force* (*La Presse*, May 19, 1936, 8), and Canada's first great play by a woman (*La Presse*, May 16, 1936, 27). It was especially noteworthy that these distinctions were accorded to a play not only written in Quebec but also by a woman. Culturally dominated by France,[5] 1930s Quebec was also socially dominated by a conservative ideology of preservation of its past as a rural, religious society. The Quiet Revolution of the 1960s had yet to dislodge values and views by which women were expected to be wives and mothers, not writers. Women who did pursue writing—Gabrielle Roy, Anne Hébert, Rina Lasnier, Eva Senécal, Jovette-Alice Bernier, and Marie-Claire Daveluy among them—typically took the more private paths of poetry and the novel. By contrast, Mercier-Gouin sustained a writing career in the public space of theatre and at a time when the genre was seriously underdeveloped in Quebec. Favourable family circumstances notwithstanding, Mercier-Gouin raised four children as she carried on her work for theatre in Quebec. Then,

---

1. The Ursuline nuns came to Canada in 1739 under the leadership of Marie de l'Incarnation and, among other initiatives, established the oldest educational institution for women in North America. Le Conservatoire français du Québec aimed to *"former les élèves à la diction française"* [train students in French elocution] (Lemay 2009, 12), a goal toward which student theatre activities played a significant role.

2. See Chartier (2000, 251–53) and Lemay (2009, 10) for a discussion of *"le théâtre en crise"* at the time, due to a lack of Quebec playwrights, professional critics, and resources; the genre's status as "secondary" to poetry and fiction; and lingering clerical condemnation of theatre for its threat to moral probity.

3. This was exceptional at the time, as Lemay explains (2009, 10). Published by les Éditions Albert Lévesque, established in 1926, *Cocktail* benefitted from the publishing house's goal to bring new Quebec authors into print, and from the fact that the director of the press's theatre series was Marie-Claire Daveluy, herself a playwright as well as a journalist and librarian at the Bibliothèque de Montréal.

4. Gratien Gélinas's triumphantly successful play *Tit-Coq* (1948) has long been regarded as the beginning of Quebec theatre. The play's popular protagonist developed out of Gélinas's early career sketches, the

FIGURE 19.1: *Yvette Mercier-Gouin, Studio Harcourt, Paris, n.d.*
P764,S7, D4_01 Famille Mercier-Gouin fonds. Courtesy of Bibliothèque et Archives nationales du Québec.

as now, her accomplishments and the success of her plays—*Cocktail* in particular—appear remarkable.

Cocktail premiered in Montreal's Théâtre Stella on April 22, 1935. It
moved on to Quebec City's Palais Montcalm for May 22–23 and to Ottawa's
Little Theatre on May 29. The following year the play was produced at the
Monument National in Montreal on May 18, 1936, and then at the city's La
Palestre Nationale on December 8, 1937. The newspaper *Le Soleil* enthused that
all Quebec—perhaps more accurately an emerging urban, educated bourgeois class—applauded the play (May 23, 1935, 3). *Cocktail* offered a glimpse
at a new and different Quebec, where neither church and religion nor rural
views and values were key concerns.[6] The focus of the play was a woman's
story: that of the forty-year-old recently widowed Montrealer Nicole Beaudry.
Urban and gender dimensions make *Cocktail* as compelling today as it was
groundbreaking in 1935. This relevance is reinforced by the play's thematic
exploration of love, friendship, female desire, and changing social attitudes, as
well as its exploration of language.

Cocktail confronts the enduring theme of love but transcends the exploration of traditional romantic relationship between a man and woman to

examine relationships and love between mother and daughter, between daughter and father, and between friends. In Nicole's hesitation to remarry, the play portrays changing social attitudes about love and marriage. Women "want to live," Nicole insists, and to be loved and desired as individuals, a view echoed by her daughter Geneviève. The play's language fuels these themes. Nicole tells her suitor, François, that he takes her for granted, overlooks her for who she is, and indeed loves her poorly. "My love is impassioned by all the ideals which yours lacks," she observes: "Your love has never inspired the least bit of sacrifice for me. You take everything I do for you for granted…I love you with all your faults, your masculine egoism, your cowardice which allows me to say these things to you without you rebelling. I love you for loving me so poorly." Mercier-Gouin's protagonist presents a complex, nuanced character whose insights do not preclude instances of weakness and drama. But where Nicole collapses in the face of love betrayed, she stands firm on friendship and its values. She resists François's attempt to control her acquaintances. When François queries, "Your friends…Your friends…Do you really believe them… your friends…and that they are really that open-minded?" Nicole's reply is short and strong: "Yes, I believe them. I believe in *my* friends." Nicole's belief deepens in meaning with the unveiling of François's perfidious manipulation of their relationship at the end of the play.

While Nicole loves her father, she is also critical of his control in choosing her former husband for her: "I might have had my own tastes, desires, personality, but his strength of will crushed me…I was twenty years old. You had chosen him for me…You had me trained never to hold an opinion different from yours." Even though Nicole is ultimately thwarted in her efforts to live and be loved on her own terms, the play puts into words winds of change in 1930s Quebec.

Language is a critical theme in the play, where words often fail to facilitate effective communication. *Cocktail* explores the theme of language to greater depths than the superficial but striking use of an English word as the title for a French play. Mercier-Gouin probes men's and women's differing relationships to language. Nicole strives to communicate her understanding of love, friendship, and family relationships. In one of my earlier feminist readings of the play (1990), I note that Nicole's struggles reflect women's efforts to articulate female experience in the language of their fathers or husbands. "I used to catch your way of expressing yourself coming out of my mouth," Nicole observes to her father, "I saw the world through your eyes." Alas, Nicole's insight—and her defence of both her own and her daughter's aspirations to live as they desire—do not spare her the all-too-familiar fate of silence, madness, or death assigned to many female characters in Quebec literature. Nevertheless, *Cocktail* announces that change is coming for men and women in Quebec. Change can already be seen in the evolving cultural "cocktail mix" of immigrant Montreal, evoked by the drinks served at Nicole's party. The powerful social concoction of immigration will unleash in full force with the impact of the Second World War and Quebec's Quiet Revolution during the 1960s.

Despite its stellar debut in 1935, *Cocktail* fell into obscurity, eclipsed by the literary establishment's love of Gélinas's orphan soldier Tit-Coq. However, Mercier-Gouin's play has garnered renewed attention in recent years. My 1989 article "La prose féminine québécoise des années 1930" called for closer study of the play as a work that marked a bold departure from the dominant conservative social discourse of the era. My 1990 article "Une voix précoce" undertook that work with a feminist examination of the play. A decade later, Daniel Chartier included a chapter about Mercier-Gouin's work in *L'émergence des classiques: La réception de la littérature québécoise des années 1930* (2000). Two further studies appeared in 2009: Lucie Robert's article "Yvette Mercier-Gouin ou Le désir du théâtre" and Dominique Lemay's MA thesis "L'œuvre drama-turgique d'Yvette Ollivier Mercier-Gouin: Un parcours aux frontières de l'institution littéraire québécoise." These investigations provide more detailed information about the context of the play's creation, including Mercier-Gouin's social and class background, the role of literary institutions and journalism, and the advent of cinema and other competing forms of entertainment during the 1930s. While acknowledging her talent as a writer, Chartier and Lemay discuss Mercier-Gouin's bourgeois background as key to her career and success as a playwright. Robert joins Chartier and Lemay in considering the larger literary context of *Cocktail*'s production, including an active practice of journalism and a nascent literary criticism in 1930s Quebec. In this context, the popularity of the actors, the impact of the stage set, even the rate of ticket sales are as determinant of a play's success as the actual quality of the text (Chartier 2000, 101). Layering complexity to the story of *Cocktail* was the advent of cinema and the attraction of other forms of entertainment, such as circuses or other shows and spectacles that the public might choose over a play. Last but not least was the war (1939–1945) to turn all attention away from a middle-aged, middle-class woman's worries and woes to matters of greater international import. Gélinas's 1948 *Tit-Coq* was credited with the birth of a national theatre in Quebec, and Marcel Dubé's 1950s plays were recognized for their examination of Quebec bourgeois society. The translation into English of Yvette Ollivier Mercier-Gouin's 1935 stage-hit *Cocktail* is a welcome step toward renewed attention to its vital place in the story of Quebec theatre.

Bibliography and Further Reading

Chartier, Daniel. 2000. "Le théâtre d'Yvette Ollivier Mercier-Gouin: égarement et désorganisation du système de réception." In *L'émergence des classiques: La réception de la littérature québécoises des années 1930*, 241–79. Montréal: Éditions Fides.
Cunningham, Joyce. 1977. "L'ancien théâtre Stella (1930–1936)." *Jeu*, no. 6, 62–79.
Larrue, Jean-Marc. 1998. "Le théâtre au Québec entre 1930 et 1950: Les années charnières." *L'Annuaire théâtral*, no. 23, 19–37.

Lemay, Dominique. 2009. "L'œuvre dramaturgique d'Yvette Ollivier Mercier-Gouin." MA thesis, Université de Sherbrooke.

Mercier-Gouin, Yvette Ollivier. 1935. *Cocktail*. Montréal: Éditions Albert Lévesque.

———. 1937. *Le Jeune Dieu, Les œuvres d'aujourd'hui*. Vol. 1, 99–174. Montréal: Éditions de l'Action canadienne-française.

Robert, Lucie. 2009. "Yvette Mercier-Gouin ou Le désir du théâtre." *L'Annuaire théâtral* 46 (Fall): 117–37.

Verduyn, Christl. 1989. "La prose féminine/féministe québécoise des années 1930." *Quebec Studies* 8 (Spring): 43–58.

———. 1990. "Une voix féminine précoce au théâtre québécois: *Cocktail* (1935) d'Yvette Ollivier Mercier-Gouin." *Histoire du théâtre au Canada* 11 (1): 48–58. Reprinted in *L'autre lecture: La critique au féminin et les textes québécois*. 1992. Tome I. Edited by Lori Saint-Martin, 73–85. Montréal: XYZ.

Cocktail, a Comedy in Three Acts[1]

YVETTE O. MERCIER-GOUIN
Translation by GLEN F. NICHOLS

1. Published with permission from the estate of Yvette O. Mercier-Gouin.

2. A significant port city on France's southern, Mediterranean coast.

Cocktail was first performed at the Théâtre Stella in Montreal on March 22, 1935, under the direction of Henri Letondal, with collaboration by Antoine Godeau and Ferdinand Biondi for technical direction. The production was designed by [Wilfrid] Boissonnière and stage machinery by J[oseph] Paquette.

CHARACTERS

FRANÇOIS NORMAND

MONSIEUR ARDOUIN

CHARLES BLACK

JACK LYNCH

DANIEL RAYMOND

PIERRE LEGENDRE

SOSTHÈNE, *butler*

NICOLE BEAUDRY

MADGE ROBSON

GENEVIEVE BEAUDRY

FRANCINE BEAUDRY

LOUISE RAYMOND

BERTHE LEGENDRE

ROSE MARIE, *housemaid*

ACT ONE

The play takes place in Montreal in the spring. The modern living room of NICOLE BEAUDRY. *The housemaid,* ROSE, *is arranging flowers in a vase on a table* US *of the divan, her back is to the door of the apartment. She is whistling a popular tune. The butler,* SOSTHÈNE, *enters carrying a basket of flowers. He stops when he sees* ROSE, *sets down his basket and tiptoes towards her, kissing her on the neck.*

ROSE. (*Jumping. Hint of a slight Marseille[2] accent.*) Hey! You gave me a fright!
SOSTHÈNE. (*Strong Marseille accent.*) It that my only effect on you?
ROSE. (*Smiling.*) Idiot! Go on with ya.
SOSTHÈNE. Fortunately...around you...that's the word for...fondness...
ROSE. (*Mocking.*) Why not "love," while you're at it...
SOSTHÈNE. (*Laughing.*) Who knows...
ROSE. You smug...
SOSTHÈNE. Sssh! Or I'll kiss you again.
ROSE. Just try it.

SOSTHÈNE. Oh, would you like that?

ROSE. No. Listen…stop joking around, Sosthène. If the mistress catches us, it won't be pretty.

SOSTHÈNE. As if that should offend the mistress…what, with her "François"…

ROSE. Will you be quiet! If anyone overheard us…

SOSTHÈNE. Do you know what the mistress and François talk about, when they're alone?

ROSE. You eavesdrop on them?

SOSTHÈNE. Call it a fringe benefit of being the butler.

ROSE. Oh, you've got all the answers.

SOSTHÈNE. Listening to everything…learning everything…understanding everything…and never repeating a word…

ROSE. Well you got the first parts down all right…the ideal butler.

SOSTHÈNE. But…(*Picking up the basket.*)

ROSE. As for the rest of it, well if you can't say something nice about someone…

SOSTHÈNE. What do you mean?

ROSE. (*Mocking.*) Let's see…"never repeating a word"…hmmm…

SOSTHÈNE. To you…only to you…and you, well you are me.

ROSE. Thanks all the same. I think I prefer to be just me; I don't want to be you.

SOSTHÈNE. Idiot…

ROSE. And is that fondness?

SOSTHÈNE. No…love…true love.

ROSE. Oh, love Marseille-style…in other words, love for a day…

SOSTHÈNE. No. Love Marseille-style…is love for the night…

ROSE. Get back to work, will ya.

SOSTHÈNE. (*Indicating the basket.*) And this mini-garden…should I put it here? (*Going to set the basket on the table SR.*)

ROSE. No. Not there. We need to keep that table clear.

SOSTHÈNE. What for?

ROSE. The tutor. He gives his English lessons to the girls at that table.

SOSTHÈNE. That's right. I forgot.

ROSE. You always forget.

SOSTHÈNE. No not always. But the tutor, I forget. He's a quiet one.

ROSE. Not like you then.

SOSTHÈNE. No idea what you mean. So as I was saying…the tutor is a quiet type: polished, aloof, and in love.

ROSE. In love?

SOSTHÈNE. Oh yes. Y'know…in love with the mistress. You haven't seen anything then? Heard anything?

ROSE. I don't eavesdrop.

SOSTHÈNE. You don't need to, do you? You hear all the mistress's secrets anyway.

ROSE. Well after ten years as maid here, that's normal.

SOSTHÈNE. She adores you.

ROSE. You're jealous.

SOSTHÈNE. Yes. Like that Englishman.

ROSE. Englishman?

SOSTHÈNE. The girls' tutor.

ROSE. You really think he loves the mistress?

SOSTHÈNE. It's pretty obvious. And the fact he hates the doctor...

ROSE. Gossipmonger.

SOSTHÈNE. Because the mistress loves the doctor.

ROSE. The mistress is a widow. She may very well fall in love again.

SOSTHÈNE. Was he nice, the mistress's first husband?

ROSE. Oh my, yes! Everyone loved him.

SOSTHÈNE. Even the mistress's father, the old grump, did he love him too?

ROSE. First of all, Mr. Ardouin is not an old grump; he is a wonderful man, who loves the mistress to bits.

SOSTHÈNE. Don't you find everyone in this house loves the mistress to bits?

ROSE. When you've been here a few months, you'll also love her to bits.

SOSTHÈNE. And with you around that'll be a drama.

ROSE. You better believe it.

SOSTHÈNE. Even a tragedy, more or less...

ROSE. How's that?

SOSTHÈNE. (*Mysterious and dramatic. Approaching* ROSE.) Can't you just see, one day, the mistress's two lovers fighting a duel?

ROSE. (*Laughing.*) A duel? You're in Canada, remember, not Marseille.

SOSTHÈNE. (*Waxing poetic.*) When I am alone with you, feeling romantic and hearing you speak, then...(*Sighing.*) I am back in Marseille...

ROSE. And while you spout foolishness, the dining room table is still not dressed.

SOSTHÈNE. (*Admiring.*) The table still not dressed, is it?...that's wonderful... you see, just what I was saying...when you speak like that, there is only Marseille...

ROSE. If you keep wasting time, the mistress will be sending you back there.

SOSTHÈNE. I'm not worried. You will always find a way to keep me here.

ROSE. (*Furious.*) Listen to that...shameless!

SOSTHÈNE. So why then...if you don't love me...did you convince the mistress to take me on.

ROSE. I would never see a man from the Midi on his uppers.

SOSTHÈNE. I was not on my uppers.

ROSE. No. That's right. You were loaded.

SOSTHÈNE. I was fixing up a bouillabaisse.[3]

ROSE. Without any fish.

SOSTHÈNE. Is it my fault the fish of Marseille don't want to come to Canada?

ROSE. They told you that?

SOSTHÈNE. Possibly. The fish back home are so smart that if they don't like
  something, they keep quiet about it.
ROSE. Or maybe the Marseillais just don't give you the time of day.
SOSTHÈNE. Smarty-pants! Don't you find my bouillabaisse to be excellent?
ROSE. (*Laughing.*) I've never swallowed a second bite; the fishbones in the first
  bite always choke me.
SOSTHÈNE. But the first bite is to die for, no?
ROSE. Is that what you're serving the guests tonight, a bouillabaisse?
SOSTHÈNE. Never! What a sacrilege! Bouillabaisse...to people who don't
  recognize a good wine and don't know how to use garlic.
ROSE. What do you expect? Maybe they would like garlic, but just don't like
  bad breath!
SOSTHÈNE. Hmph. What funny people!
ROSE. No accounting for taste, huh.
SOSTHÈNE. In Montreal, you know, you don't find bouillabaisse in soup bowls
  but around the table.
ROSE. What do you mean?
SOSTHÈNE. French, English, Irish, Scottish...you see...every sort of fish...
ROSE. I hear someone.... Hurry up, let's get out of here. It might be the
  mistress. (*They leave.*)

FRANCINE enters. She stops at the door. The others are still off stage.

FRANCINE. Mr. Black...Genevieve...hurry up and see all the flowers.

GENEVIEVE appears, followed by CHARLES.

GENEVIEVE. I'm just glad I'm not forty years old and getting a bunch of
  flowers.
CHARLES. Genevieve, don't talk like that. It would hurt your mother's feel-
  ings.
FRANCINE. So, Mr. Black, do we have to have our English lesson today?
CHARLES. What's special about today?
FRANCINE. It's mama's birthday.
GENEVIEVE. And what if, on this special occasion, you spoke French with us?
FRANCINE. Oh yes! Speak to us in French.
CHARLES. Does speaking English bother you that much?
GENEVIEVE. Does speaking French bother you?
CHARLES. When I speak French, my words can't keep up with my thoughts.
GENEVIEVE. So, think in English but speak in French.
CHARLES. That's an idea.
FRANCINE. It's agreed then...no English lesson?
GENEVIEVE. We must do our bit for the big celebration!
FRANCINE. Where is mama anyway?

4. Mount Royal, the dominant geological feature of the city of Montreal.

CHARLES. (*Looking at his watch.*) She's still out riding.

GENEVIEVE. (*Cutting.*) With the doctor?

CHARLES. They should be back any minute now.

FRANCINE. (*Happily.*) Mama will be so happy to see all these flowers.

CHARLES. If both of you were really nice, you'd read me a few lines from tomorrow's lesson.

GENEVIEVE. My reader is so boring!

*The three take their places at the table...*FRANCINE *takes her book.*

FRANCINE. What are you complaining about...at least there are love stories in yours. Mine all talk about birds and flowers. (*She opens the book.*) Listen: "The bird landed right beside the little girl..." What did I tell you?

CHARLES. Do you mind reading silently, Francine. I want Genevieve to start.

GENEVIEVE. When mama comes, the lesson will be over, right?

CHARLES. Well then we better get started, hadn't we?

GENEVIEVE. "It had now been seventeen years since the count and countess had been united."

CHARLES. Now translate it...

GENEVIEVE. Il y avait maintenant dix-sept ans que le comte et la comtesse étaient unis.

NICOLE enters, along with FRANÇOIS NORMAND. *Both are wearing riding clothes, their cheeks flushed and with an air of pleasure about them. The girls look at each other with glee and toss their books on the table.*

NICOLE. Whew! What a ride! I'm beat. But it was worth it. (*She drops into the divan.*)

FRANÇOIS. My dear, I think we are interrupting the English lesson.

NICOLE. Mr. Black is used to my noisy entrances. Anyway, the lesson should be over. Come here my darling girls, give me a hug, then and go find grand-papa in the garden. I think he is working on a surprise for you. Opps! And I promised not to say anything. (FRANCINE *kisses her mother tenderly.* GENEVIEVE *does the same but without enthusiasm.*)

NICOLE. Say hello to our friend, François. (FRANCINE *furrows her brow.*)

GENEVIEVE. (*Dry and curt.*) Good day, doctor. (*The girls slip away.*)

CHARLES. I take it the ride was a success.

NICOLE. The light was marvelous. I've never seen the mountain[4] so beautiful. I felt like I was twenty again.

FRANÇOIS. You're not even that old yet.

NICOLE. Flatterer! Go on.

CHARLES. Madame Beaudry, would it bother you if I dined with my friends this evening?

NICOLE. Oh no! You can't do that to me. I have guests coming this evening,
and in particular a charming young Scottish girl that I have in mind for
you.
CHARLES. Oh that's different then. If you need me "pour l'équilibre de la
table," as you say in French, then I will stay here, with pleasure.
FRANÇOIS. (*Mocking.*) "Pour l'équilibre de la table" or to meet the young lady?
CHARLES. (*Somewhat dry.*) Perhaps both. And now, if you will excuse me,
I should let my friends know whom I shall be dining with this evening.
(*Nodding to NICOLE.*) Good-bye, doctor.

CHARLES exits.

NICOLE. François, you are incorrigible. You never miss an opportunity to
provoke poor Mr. Black.
FRANÇOIS. Between you and me, I sense your tutor never falls for it. Not
really.

*NICOLE takes a peek out the door, listening carefully, then assured they are alone,
opens her arms to FRANÇOIS.*

NICOLE. My dear! (*They kiss. There's a noise and they pull apart.*) Quick! Wipe
your cheek...there's a bit of lipstick...
FRANÇOIS. Where?
NICOLE. There! (*The noise stops. She kisses him again.*) There...now you have
some on both cheeks. How about some port? I think it would do us good.
(*She rings.*) What time shall we go out tomorrow?
FRANÇOIS. Not before 5:00. I do have to make a living. And besides, I have to
keep a clear head all day.
NICOLE. Charming.
FRANÇOIS. I have two very serious operations to perform. I need to focus.
NICOLE. Are you saying I distract you?
FRANÇOIS. And how!
NICOLE. Really?
FRANÇOIS. I adore you!
NICOLE. Say it again.

ROSE enters with the port and cookies.

NICOLE. Rose, will you get my red dress ready for this evening? I think it's
missing a hook.
ROSE. Of course, Madame.

ROSE exits

NICOLE. Do you remember...that's the hook that popped off when we were
dancing at the Ritz.

FRANÇOIS. Oh yes. I squeezed you so hard it made the hook pop right off.

NICOLE. Ah! No...that's enough. No more jokes...keep them for this evening.

FRANÇOIS. And which imbeciles will be keeping us apart this time?

NICOLE. That's a nice way to talk about my guests.

FRANÇOIS. What do you expect? I don't like your friends, most of them
anyway. They all seem to have it in for me, the men especially.

NICOLE. Well that makes sense. Before you came on the scene, they were
indispensable for my existence. And now I rarely invite them anymore.
They feel that my affections for you have come at their expense somehow.
They're confused. Where will they go this evening? Where will they get
their cocktails? And they're right, you know, to resent you.... And I'm in the
wrong for neglecting them.

FRANÇOIS. And then there's that English tutor you have staying here. That's
pretty foolish, you know...

NICOLE. Foolish? How so?

FRANÇOIS. You're a widow...He's young...people talk.

NICOLE. Oh come on, François, don't talk nonsense. All my friends know very
well that Mr. Black, besides coming from an excellent family, only became a
tutor for the girls because he had no choice. He had to do whatever he could
to save himself from penury.

FRANÇOIS. My poor Nicole! Your kind heart makes you do the silliest things.

NICOLE. Cripes! Drat! Triple drat! You drive me crazy. You can't be jealous of
Mr. Black, surely.

FRANÇOIS. Jealous? Me? Of that cold English beanpole, who talks to you like
you were his mother!

NICOLE. That's his way of showing his appreciation, and making it clear to my
friends that he is nothing but the tutor here.

FRANÇOIS. Your friends....Your friends...Do you really believe them...your
friends...and that they are really that open-minded?

NICOLE. Yes, I believe them. I believe in *my* friends.

FRANÇOIS. Fine. Your naiveté will drive me round the bend yet.

NICOLE. And your scepticism offends me.

FRANÇOIS. Listen, Nicole, we're going to end up saying things we regret. And
all because of a bunch of bores, whose disapproval is getting in the way of
our marriage plans.

NICOLE. No François, you're wrong. That is not the real reason for my hesitation. I love you enough to sacrifice all my society friends, without regret.

FRANÇOIS. So then what's stopping you?

NICOLE. I don't know. It's more delicate, complicated. You wouldn't
understand.

FRANÇOIS. And once more, you're treating me like an imbecile.

NICOLE. Great. This is how it starts all over again. I beg you, don't get touchy at every little thing I say.

FRANÇOIS. I'm getting tired of waiting for you.

NICOLE. You don't have much patience. We've known each other for ten months. That might seem like a long time, but ten months to consider the rest of one's life…is very short.

FRANÇOIS. So then…what's wrong with me?

NICOLE. What's wrong with you? Nothing. Or rather…what's wrong with you…is just simply you.

FRANÇOIS. Explain.

NICOLE. You are so hard to understand. You say you love me, but your love has never inspired the least bit of sacrifice for me. You take everything I do for you for granted. In talking about our future together, you never say, for example, "Let's find an apartment in the part of town you like….Let's go to the play you were talking about…" No. You always say, "When we get married, we'll see that show by my favourite author." Or "I've always dreamed about an apartment in Outremont.[5] We'll find something over there." Or even, "We'll get rid of your sedan and get a roadster.[6] They're much nicer." You overlook the fact that at forty, I get chilly easily.

FRANÇOIS. In other words, I'm a selfish egoist.

NICOLE. Maybe not. You're just a man. And I expect too much. I admit I'm a bit reserved in our relationship.

FRANÇOIS. We just don't have the same way of expressing our love, that's all. You're a romantic; while I've never been one to spend a long time digging up my emotions.

NICOLE. I don't have to dig up my emotions; I simply experience them. My poor François, it's your heart you need to dig up.

FRANÇOIS. That's a nice thing to say. Jolly opinion you have of me.

NICOLE. Admit that it's a little bit your own fault. It would be so easy for you to pay me some attention, to think of me other than to invite me to dinner downtown or go riding.

FRANÇOIS. Ok, come on, where are you going with all this?

NICOLE. Do you know why I'm having a party tonight?

FRANÇOIS. No.

NICOLE. Do you know why there are so many flowers in here?

FRANÇOIS. Your house is always full of them.

NICOLE. Not this many.

FRANÇOIS. (*Blanching.*) It's your birthday!

NICOLE. Bingo.

FRANÇOIS. I'm a triple idiot! Listen, Nicole, I'm devastated! I should have made a note of the date. This is unforgiveable. (*Taking out his agenda book and flipping through.*) And the stupidest thing is, look! I do have it written down.

NICOLE. (*Taking the agenda book.*) What is unforgiveable, it that you had to write it down at all. (*She reads from the agenda book.*) Dinner at Nicole's... and a little further down..."It's working; there's progress"...What is that all about?

FRANÇOIS. (*Troubled.*) Let me see that. (*Searching for an answer.*) Ah...that's a note about one of my patients. (*Suddenly recovering.*) You know...little Jarry...the boy whose foot I operated on. He's walking; there is progress.

NICOLE. (*Looking at* FRANÇOIS, *sadly. Shaking her head, she extends her arms to him.*) Come here! Hold me close. (*They hug. She pulls away, still holding both his hands.*) Look at me with those adorable eyes. They are so sweet, so tender, so open. Why isn't your heart made of the same stuff?

FRANÇOIS. If I seem to you to be so weak, so vain, why do you love me?

NICOLE. Do you know why people fall in love? My love is stronger because it doesn't rely on anything else. I love you with all your faults, your masculine egoism, your cowardice which allows me to say these things to you without you rebelling. I love you for loving me so poorly. Perhaps I'd love you less if I could always believe in you.

FRANÇOIS. What a strange woman you are! My plain, simple soul just can't compete with all your passion.

NICOLE. But my love is impassioned by all the ideals which yours lacks. I suspect that I will suffer because of you and, for you, I accept that suffering.

FRANÇOIS. But not to the point of marrying me.

NICOLE. That's different. For that, I'm not the only one I have to think about. There's my father.

FRANÇOIS. He doesn't like me, I'm sure of that. But don't forget, he's seventy years old.

NICOLE. Exactly. And ill at heart, with sorrow, worry...

FRANÇOIS. Nevertheless, you can't sacrifice your love, your life...for him.

NICOLE. No, but I can wait. I owe him my life, so I would prolong his. And that's not all. There are the girls.

FRANÇOIS. Well, of course. I'll be their father. They will learn to love me.

NICOLE. Francine, ok. That's already the case. But Genevieve, I'm not so sure.

FRANÇOIS. We'll make her change her mind.

NICOLE. You see. A second ago you said "they will learn to love me." And now you say "We'll make her change her mind." You sound like a step-father already.

FRANÇOIS. Sorry, Nicole! If Genevieve is an obstacle, then let's marry her off.

NICOLE. At eighteen?! She hasn't come out yet.[7] No. Believe me. We just have to be patient a little longer. Work on winning Genevieve over; the same goes for my father. Let's not rush anything. Your charms that have worked on me will perhaps also work on them. Nothing is hopeless. My life has been so sweet since I fell in love with you. Ok, let's not talk about serious things anymore. Let's talk about you.

FRANÇOIS. Thanks.

NICOLE. Because after all, you are the only one that counts in our love.

FRANÇOIS. (*Looking at his watch.*) Oh, look at the time. It's already 7:00 and dinner is at 9:00. I have just enough time to jump in my car and change into my dinner jacket.

NICOLE. You live two steps away.

FRANÇOIS. Yes, except I have to take my car back.

NICOLE. Kiss me.

FRANÇOIS. (*Holding her close.*) You're wicked. This evening you will make me suffer even more.

NICOLE. (*Looking at him, passionately.*) Yes, to feel you love me all the more.

FRANÇOIS. Till later, my torturer. (*Exit, throwing* NICOLE *a kiss.* NICOLE *rings.*)

NICOLE. (*When the housemaid enters.*) Would you tell Mr. Black that I'd like to speak with him?

NICOLE *arranges some cushions, fixes the flowers a bit, looks over the girls' English homework, and eventually sits on the divan with a book.* CHARLES *enters, remaining a respectable distance* US *of the divan.*

CHARLES. Madame Beaudry...

NICOLE. Mr. Black...(*She doesn't turn.*) I have something very difficult to talk to you about.

CHARLES. Is there something I can help you with?

NICOLE. Possibly...

CHARLES. May I sit?

NICOLE. No. Be a dear. Don't move. Stay where you are. I would rather speak to you without looking at you.

CHARLES. Madame, you are worrying me. Is the subject indeed so troubling?

NICOLE. What I have to tell you is very serious. The happiness of my life is at stake.

CHARLES. In that case, I am all ears.

NICOLE. Ask me questions.

CHARLES. You want I should act as your confessor?

NICOLE. Yes.

CHARLES. I'm not in the habit...

NICOLE. There's a first time for everything.

CHARLES. Am I responsible in any way for the situation?

NICOLE. Not at all. But you have the power to help me.

CHARLES. Is it about...your father?

NICOLE. No.

CHARLES. ...about Genevieve?

NICOLE. Yes.

CHARLES. (*Stiffly.*) So, you want to talk to me about...her attitude towards Dr. Normand?

NICOLE. (*Turning.*) How did you guess that so easily?

CHARLES. I have lived closely with the girls for several months. I have learned
to love them.... They have shared with me their joys and their problems.

NICOLE. Genevieve has no problems. The way she acts with Dr. Normand is a
result of her selfishness. That child has always been difficult to understand,
she is so close-minded.

CHARLES. Genevieve is remarkably intelligent. She is a delightful girl, with a
strong personality. And anyway, she's not a child. She is a young woman. A
mother so easily forgets the age of her children, especially a young mother.

NICOLE. (*Somewhat stung.*) Mr. Black. Since you have come to live with us,
I have always treated you as one of the family; however, that does not, I
think, give you the right to tell me how to raise my girls.

CHARLES. Excuse me, madam. I didn't mean to hurt you. (*Smiling.*) I was only
playing my role as confessor a tad too seriously.

NICOLE. (*Gesturing for* CHARLES *to sit next to her.*) Don't joke about it. I am so
unhappy.

CHARLES. (*Crossing to sit.*) I am at your disposal. I will do anything in my
power to help you. You do know how fond I am of you.

NICOLE. Yes, Charles...I may call you Charles?

CHARLES. That would make me happy.

NICOLE. Charles, I don't know anyone else in the world who is more devoted
to me than you are.

CHARLES. You have done so much for me.

NICOLE. Please. Don't mention that.

CHARLES. (*Remembering.*) I was alone...hopeless...ruined...abandoned...

NICOLE. You had known such luxury...comforts. You were powerless, faced
with such a struggle.

CHARLES. You didn't even ask who I was.

NICOLE. Women have an infallible instinct. I knew right away that you were
worthy of my support. But...back to Genevieve. What would happen if I
were to marry Dr. Normand?

CHARLES. Genevieve would no doubt try hard to appreciate the man whom
her mother has chosen.

NICOLE. Would she love him?

CHARLES. I doubt it.

NICOLE. Then in that case, I cannot marry François.

CHARLES. That depends on one's perspective...whether Genevieve's happiness
is more important to you than your love.

NICOLE. My daughter's happiness will not be up to me for much longer. My
love is my life.

CHARLES. How you have changed, Madame Beaudry.

NICOLE. What makes you say that?

CHARLES. When I came to this house, only your father and your daughters
mattered to you. You were so selfless.

NICOLE. And now...

CHARLES. Now you are a little more like every other woman...love has made you more human...and that's a shame.

NICOLE. Charles! Charles, help me. Understand me. If you only knew how much I love him. And despite everything, he is worthy of my love...I am the only one who recognizes what he is. Oh no...I cannot give him up. No, I cannot. I don't want to. (*Struggling with invisible conflicts.*) Life would be so sad. His cheerfulness, his wit...that is my life! When he is around, I feel like I am young again. And he loves me too, in his own way...I swear he does love me...(*Nearly crying.*) Even he doesn't know himself how much he loves me!

CHARLES. The lady seemeth to protest too much. One would think you were trying to convince yourself.

NICOLE. My father, Genevieve, you...you, my best friend...you are all against me: I know it. I can feel it. Your attitude will end up separating us, tearing us apart. What will become of me if he should leave?

CHARLES. You still have your father.

NICOLE. He won't be here forever.

CHARLES. And the girls.

NICOLE. They'll get married.

CHARLES. I will never be far away.

NICOLE. You will also get married.

CHARLES. Never!

NICOLE. Oh...and why would that be?

CHARLES. The woman I love is in love with someone else.

NICOLE. She might change her mind, and her love?

CHARLES. I doubt it. And even if she did, I could never tell her how I feel.

NICOLE. Because...

CHARLES. ...unless one day I were to become rich again. In that case...

NICOLE. (*Imploring. Not seeming to have heard* CHARLES*'s last sentence.*) This evening, at dinner, will you be nice to François? I so want the two of you to be friends.

CHARLES. Would that really make you happy?

NICOLE. More than anything.

CHARLES. I will try.... You know, Madame Beaudry, to make you happy I would do anything, no matter how difficult. I'll even speak to Genevieve. It's possible everything will work out in the end.

NICOLE. (*Taking both his hands.*) Thank you, Charles, you're the best. I feel I can count on you. (*Looking at the time.*) But I have to run. I have just enough time to get ready before my guests arrive.

GENEVIEVE *and* FRANCINE *enter.* FRANCINE *in pajamas.*

NICOLE. (*Exiting.*) Good evening, my darlings. Now, good night. Mama is in a hurry.

8. The Imperial Theatre opened in 1913 and operated as a mixed vaudeville and movie house until 1936 when it was acquired by Consolidated Theatres of Montreal. It still operates as a cinema today. The Piccolis was the name of several musical and performing troupes, including possible puppetry companies in the 1930s.

CHARLES. (*Welcoming the girls, smiling.*) Was your mother happy about this morning's surprise?

FRANCINE. Mother said the idea of the flowers must have been yours.

GENEVIEVE. And when I told her it was grandfather's, she seemed disappointed.

CHARLES. Genevieve, you shouldn't let your imagination run away with you.

GENEVIEVE. I believe I'm old enough to guess what mama's thinking.

CHARLES. Good night, children. (*He exits.*)

FRANCINE. (*Picking up a scribbler and pencil, she sits on the floor to draw.*) Why did you say that to Mr. Black?

GENEVIEVE. So that he will have more confidence in himself. I want him to ask mama out.

FRANCINE. But since mama loves our friend François...

GENEVIEVE. First of all, don't call him "our friend, François." He's *your* friend, not mine.

FRANCINE. Oh. I like him. Mama is so cheerful when he's around. And besides, he's fun; he draws me things, sings me songs...

GENEVIEVE. (*Impatient.*) You were too young when papa died.

FRANCINE. So what?

GENEVIEVE. You wouldn't understand.

FRANCINE. Yes I would.

GENEVIEVE. Just do your drawing.

FRANCINE. Listen, Genevieve, I am not a baby anymore. I can feel something is going on around here. Tell me...

GENEVIEVE. No.

FRANCINE. Mama is different. Some days she's sad. Other days she's too cheerful. Grandpa just stays inside all day. He hardly speaks to mama and doesn't go anywhere with her anymore.

GENEVIEVE. Mama is always out with the doctor.

FRANCINE. Mr. Black is very funny. He cuts our lessons short. And remember...the other day his eyes filled up with tears.

GENEVIEVE. When was that?

FRANCINE. I was talking about the Piccoli show at the Imperial.[8]

GENEVIEVE. The one you saw with mama and the doctor.

FRANCINE. Yeah. But I don't see why that would make Mr. Black so sad. And what's more, he talks to us so gently, as if you and I were unhappy.

GENEVIEVE. (*Straightening up.*) No more!

FRANCINE. (*Affectionately, putting her arms around GENEVIEVE's neck.*) So tell me, dear sister, tell me...what's going on? I'm scared.

GENEVIEVE. Go play.

FRANCINE. I don't feel like it anymore. Why are you so mean to everyone?

GENEVIEVE. That's just the way I am.

FRANCINE. No it's not.

GENEVIEVE. You and grandpa are the only ones who understand me.

FRANCINE. And Mr. Black?

GENEVIEVE. Oh, he likes me because I hate the doctor.

FRANCINE. But what has the doctor ever done to you and everyone else?

GENEVIEVE. You can't understand.

FRANCINE. Try me.

GENEVIEVE. Mama loves him.

FRANCINE. So what? Mama loves lots of people: grandpa, Mr. Black, Aunt Berthe, cousin Jean...

GENEVIEVE. That's not the same thing.

FRANCINE. Why?

GENEVIEVE. There are two kinds of love. The ordinary, everyday sort...and the other one...that one that makes you selfish, blind...blind enough to drive other people crazy; the one that...that makes little girls cry...

FRANCINE. I still don't understand.

GENEVIEVE. I told you. You're too little.

FRANCINE. Then mama is right. You read too much; it's turned your head.

GENEVIEVE. Mama doesn't see that I'm grown up. She doesn't want me to grow up.

FRANCINE. No way. She's always filling you with tonics.

GENEVIEVE. Yes, and English lessons, and diction lessons, painting...I am done with my studies: they bore me. Don't you see, Francine, a mama who is young and pretty is too much for everyone else and not enough for her children.

FRANCINE. Well I like it that mama is pretty. I think she is beautiful.

GENEVIEVE. You're not old enough to be a young woman; you don't know what it feels like to want to be someone in the house, someone just as pretty...to have friends who don't speak to you like a child: "What a big girl for such a young mother!" or even worse, with a tone of regret, "She doesn't look at all like her mother." Oh, one day, I will surprise all those handsome fellows. They will see that one can be pretty without looking like mama. Tell me, Francine, am I really so ugly?

FRANCINE. I don't think so....And anyway, you're beautiful in my heart because I love you...

The two hug. Then, hearing a noise from the hall, they pull apart suddenly. Mr. ARDOUIN appears.

FRANCINE. Oh, it's only grandpa! (*They run into his arms.*)

ARDOUIN. Hey, my little rascals...a bit of respect for your elders. (*They drag him to the divan.*)

FRANCINE. Being respectful is so exhausting! And anyway, you know, grandpa I've never been afraid of you, even when I was really little and you used to make mean faces and talk with a gruff voice.

ARDOUIN. All the same, back in those days everyone was scared of me.

FRANCINE. Oh yes...you were a very important man, a banker. You could make or unmake fortunes.

ARDOUIN. I also bailed out lots of people.

GENEVIEVE. I could have guessed that; in your heart you were always very kind and good.

FRANCINE. (*Laying her head on her grandfather's shoulder.*) He just couldn't let anyone know.

ARDOUIN. You don't win business deals by being nice.

FRANCINE. So you were especially nice to us to make up for all the effort of making yourself seem severe and cold to others.

GENEVIEVE. You never scolded us, and you used to spoil us in secret so mama didn't know.

ARDOUIN. And your mother wasn't any more afraid of me than you were. She used to rake me over the coals whenever she found out I had, as she put it, compromised her education system.

FRANCINE. Do you remember the day I stuffed your ears with balls of tin foil from your cigarette packages?

GENEVIEVE. Mama was right to be furious. That was dangerous.

ARDOUIN. The danger never occurred to me. It was so funny to see the little bundle of pink and white sitting on the arm of the big chair, laughing so adorably through her missing teeth, and saying in that way she used to talk...gampa, need 'nother box.... Nomo papper, your ea's too big.

FRANCINE. Good thing the diction lessons have made a difference.

GENEVIEVE. Oh baby Francine's language was unforgettable. Do you remember, grandpa, the time she fell down the stairs, her eyes full of tears and her tragi-comic voice..."I ouch me...Fwancin too wittle t'up stair"

FRANCINE. What did that mean?

ARDOUIN. You meant "Francine is too little to climb the stairs."

FRANCINE. You must have really loved me to be able to understand that.

GENEVIEVE. Oh yes, everyone loved you. Used to love watching you stuff yourself with cake...just to see your little face all covered in cream.

FRANCINE. (*Falling asleep.*) You gave me an upset tummy.

GENEVIEVE. Those were good times. We used to cuddle up all together.

ARDOUIN. Those weren't good times for everyone. Mama dressed in black and felt very sad.

GENEVIEVE. (*Nearly in tears.*) I was also very sad. I missed papa so much. But feeling sad together and for the same reason, helps make it feel less bad.

ARDOUIN. Oh you little psychologist!

FRANCINE seems to have fallen asleep. ARDOUIN shushes GENEVIEVE and picks FRANCINE up in his arms.

GENEVIEVE. You know she's faking, right?

ARDOUIN *crossing the stage with his precious armload, serious, emotional.*

ARDOUIN. As long as she is small enough my old arms can still carry her to
bed, I only hope she'll fake it every night.

CURTAIN

ACT TWO

Same setting. Small bar US. Discovered onstage: NICOLE, CHARLES, FRANÇOIS,
ARDOUIN, PIERRE *and* BERTHE LEGENDRE, *and* LOUISE *and* DANIEL
RAYMOND. *The guests are drinking cocktails.* FRANÇOIS *raises his glass, stopping
the others.*

FRANÇOIS. My friends, let's raise our glasses to Nicole's twentieth birthday.
NICOLE. (*Very gay.*) You've aged me.
FRANÇOIS. Twenty years of wit and twenty years of beauty; that still just
makes for twenty years.
EVERYONE. (*Cheering and drinking.*) To Nicole! To being young!
NICOLE. Thank you, my friends. Thank you, François. You are as good a friend
as you are a bad mathematician.
CHARLES. It's not that I'm curious or anything, Madame Beaudry, but I don't
see the charming Scottish girl you mentioned earlier.
NICOLE. Oh don't lose hope. She will be here soon. Your friend Jack is bringing
her.
CHARLES. Jack Lynch? No. Really? I haven't seen him in ages.
ARDOUIN. Is that your Irish friend?
LOUISE. Whatever became of him?
CHARLES. He went on a business trip to Winnipeg and I haven't heard a word
from him since last summer.
FRANÇOIS. Doesn't your family live in Winnipeg?
CHARLES. Once upon a time, many years ago. My father lives in Montreal
now.
BERTHE. And what's this young Scottish girl to Jack?
NICOLE. I understand she's a guest of his mother's. I believe they met in
Winnipeg. In any case, on the telephone Jack seemed very enthusiastic
about how beautiful Miss..., oh I didn't even catch her name.
DANIEL. Wedding bells in the air, perhaps?
FRANÇOIS. Tell us, Charles, did you know many pretty women out West?
CHARLES. (*Pensive.*) A few. Yes.
LOUISE. (*A spoiled child.*) Who are more beautiful? Us or the English girls in
the West?
CHARLES. They are different...more...how should I say it...more dazzling, but
with less charm.
PIERRE. Hey, you might even know Jack's pretty little friend?

CHARLES. It's unlikely. Winnipeg has dozens of beautiful women...and besides, it's been five years since I left the West. My friends must be married by now...or old maids. (*Shaking off the memory.*) All that was a long time ago. Let's have another cocktail. What do you say?

NICOLE. (*Drinking.*) It's so good to have friends like all of you. I am so happy this evening. I almost forget that I am at home.

LOUISE. For the mistress of the house, the feeling is relaxing.

ARDOUIN. Maybe it's that your friends are giving you the impression it's their house.

FRANÇOIS. Is that a complaint?

NICOLE. No, just a wisecrack. You all know how papa likes to joke around.

The doorbell rings.

DANIEL. That must be Jack.

EVERYONE. It's them!

General excitement. Everyone waits, eyes on the doorway. JACK and MADGE enter. She is extremely pretty. NICOLE crosses to greet them. JACK makes the introductions. When MADGE appears in the door, CHARLES is visibly surprised.

JACK. Mrs. Beaudry, my friend, Miss Marjorie Robson, from Winnipeg.

NICOLE. Welcome to my home, Miss Robson.

MADGE. Jack has told me so much about you, Madame Beaudry. I am thrilled to finally meet you.

NICOLE. What pretty French you speak.

MADGE. I studied in Paris.

NICOLE. Allow me to introduce my friends...my father...

MADGE. (*Nodding.*) Monsieur!

NICOLE. Dr. Normand.

MADGE. A pleasure, doctor.

NICOLE. Mr. and Mrs. Legendre. (*MADGE nods.*) Mr. and Mrs. Raymond.

Seeing CHARLES, MADGE takes a slight step back. He extends his hand to her but seems very ill at ease.

CHARLES. How are you, Miss Robson?

NICOLE. Oh! I see you know each other.

MADGE. A little, yes. But it is a surprise to find us both here.

CHARLES. (*Nervous.*) Jack never told me you were his friend.

MADGE. Our friendship is quite recent.

FRANÇOIS. (*Very gallantly.*) A cocktail, Miss Robson?

MADGE. You bet.

ARDOUIN. (*Crossing to MADGE.*) Are you enjoying Montreal?

MADGE. Totally.

FRANÇOIS. Have you been here before?

MADGE. No. Never. It's silly, really. I know the States, Europe...but hardly know my own country.

FRANÇOIS. That's not surprising. As a Francophone from France, I have often noticed that Eastern Canada is quite ignorant of Western Canada, and vice versa...

MADGE. It's a question of race, of language, perhaps?

ARDOUIN. I don't think so. It's simply that we tend to look far away, among strangers, to find what is often right under our noses close to home.

MADGE. In any case, springtime in Montreal puts sunshine in one's soul.

FRANÇOIS. Being near you, Miss Robson, must be like having springtime all year round.

EVERYONE. Hey hey! Did you hear that?

JACK. The doctor is right, especially when Madge laughs and sings all day long.

MADGE. Are you complaining, my dear?

JACK. Oh, no! On the contrary, I am delighted. You have a marvelous voice.

NICOLE. Is that true? Well then, after dinner you will have to sing something for us.

MADGE. Sadly, I don't know how to accompany myself.

NICOLE. No problem. My banker father is a musician.

LOUISE. No? Really?

PIERRE. You have kept your talent hidden, Mr. Ardouin.

ARDOUIN. (*Laughing.*) I missed my calling. I would have liked to have been an artist.

FRANÇOIS. But nevertheless you chose the best path to get there.

ARDOUIN. How's that?

FRANÇOIS. Well, these days good business is music to our ears!

EVERYONE. Oh! Hahaha! Not bad...

LOUISE. François, you're awful.

FRANÇOIS. But always in tune.

NICOLE. (*Wagging her finger at him.*) François!...François! You promised you'd stop with the puns.

FRANÇOIS. I forgot. (*Serious.*) Forgive me, Madame. (*Dramatic.*) I swear!

ARDOUIN. Until the next time.

LOUISE. By the way, Nicole, I thought your cousin Julie was going to dine with us tonight.

FRANÇOIS. Cousin Julie...at a cocktail party...that'll be the day.

ARDOUIN. Why not? She is gay...she has heart.

FRANÇOIS. Heart burn more like.

LOUISE. François, you are horrid.

BERTHE. Not very kind to the cousin. What has she ever done to you?

FRANÇOIS. Nothing. She is too perfect. One gets the feeling that that woman has never known a weakness in her life.

9. The treaty formally ended
the First World War, but it
imposed heavy penalties on
Germany. By the time of this
play, Germany had broken
several tenets of the treaty.

MADGE. But that's wonderful, isn't it?

FRANÇOIS. No, it's annoying. I loath perfect people.

ARDOUIN. Not up your alley, eh?

NICOLE. François doesn't believe anything he's saying. And the proof that he doesn't hate cousin Julie is that he saw her this morning at the clinic.

EVERYONE. The clinic! Is she unwell?

NICOLE. Yes. They have to operate on her left eye.

FRANÇOIS. (*Mocking.*) Yes, my friends, this woman who has never turned a blind eye, may end up with an eye that's blind.

EVERYONE. Oh! Hahaha...Enough!

LOUISE. Nicole, give him a bone and put him in the basement.

NICOLE. Your promises are as reliable as the Treaty of Versailles,[9] my poor François.

PIERRE. It's the fault of the cocktails.

BERTHE. It's true. Your cocktails are a pure marvel, Nicole! They make us forget all our promises.

FRANÇOIS. And cousin Julie especially. (*He drinks.*)

JACK. Can we know the recipe for your famous cocktail, Madame Beaudry?

NICOLE. Ask Louise; she's the barmaid.

LOUISE crosses to the bar where she starts to mix another cocktail. The guests gather around her. General enthusiasm. MADGE and CHARLES are the only ones not sharing in everyone's gaiety. They look at each other surreptitiously. Meanwhile, FRANÇOIS is dazzled with MADGE's beauty.

DANIEL. (*Watching the preparation of the cocktail.*) Please, Louise, don't make it too strong. When we get home, you'll drag out of me what little money I have left.

JACK. (*To LOUISE.*) What do you call this cocktail?

LOUISE. I have a whole series of them. (*Thumbing through a book of recipes and stopping at a page, she looks at FRANÇOIS.*) Would you like a..."Bolt of lightning"?

DANIEL. (*Not making the connection.*) No! too much gin.

LOUISE. (*Turning the page.*) How about an "Inside stroke"? It uses cognac.

NICOLE. No. There are eggs in that one. It's too complicated.

During this time, FRANÇOIS speaks tenderly to MADGE. The look on his face reminds one of a cat with a bowl of cream. ARDOUIN watches the goings-on, and then turns to NICOLE.)

ARDOUIN. What about an "Eye-opener"?

BERTHE. What! Mr. Ardouin...do you know about cocktails too?

ARDOUIN. I know my psychology.

NICOLE. Oh, papa is an expert. I saw him perusing my book of recipes just a
while ago.

EVERYONE: Oh! Hahaha.

ARDOUIN. (*Caught out.*) I was studying the enemy before the battle.

LOUISE. Ok then. Shall I make an "Eye-opener"?

NICOLE. (*NICOLE notices that FRANÇOIS is still in admiring conversation with
MADGE; she is under no illusions.*) Perhaps a "Leave-him-to-me" would be
better.

LOUISE. That one has gin again. And Daniel loathes gin.

BERTHE. Oh, as if!

LOUISE. Someone decide!

CHARLES. (*Irritated, calling on FRANÇOIS.*) Why doesn't the doctor decide?

FRANÇOIS. (*Coming back to earth.*) Decide what?

JACK. Mix the drinks…It's your turn to do some work, François.

FRANÇOIS. All right! If you like…(*He takes LOUISE's place at the bar, and with a
pose of comic importance, raises his arm.*) May I have proper silence please…
to allow my brain to invent for you the nectar which will cascade rivulets of
joy and floods of enthusiasm through your veins.

ARDOUIN. Careful you don't drown!

BERTHE: Less talk and more action.

FRANÇOIS. (*Touching his forehead.*) Shhh! Quiet! This minute is sacred! (*A brief
silence.*) Eureka! I have it. (*He turns to the bottles.*)

BERTHE. What's the name of this one?

FRANÇOIS. "Cheery love."

PIERRE. I know it…splendid!

EVERYONE. Oh yes. Smashing…Delicious. Very good! A marvel!

BERTHE. Rather strong! I know something about that!

PIERRE. (*To BERTHE.*) Me too…do you remember?

FRANÇOIS. After this cocktail, I'm warning you'll be walking on your heads.

ARDOUIN. As if you need any more!

FRANÇOIS. (*Bragging.*) Don't worry, good man. I'll be walking on the others.

NICOLE. The recipe…hurry up…the recipe…

EVERYONE. The recipe!

ARDOUIN. How thoughtful.

FRANÇOIS. (*To ARDOUIN.*) How trusting!

LOUISE. (*To ARDOUIN.*) Since you aren't drinking any!

ARDOUIN. No, but I live here.

JACK. (*Imploring FRANÇOIS.*) I'm thirsty. Make it snappy.

FRANÇOIS. (*Serious, mixing the drink while pretending to consult the recipe book.*)
Put a few grains of French malice into a beaker. Pour fifteen drops of very
golden Scottish syrup (*Looking at MADGE.*), two large glasses of Canadian
generosity (*An eye on NICOLE.*), three teaspoons of Irish humour (*Looking
towards JACK.*), and a smidge of English bitters (*Looking at CHARLES.*).

NICOLE. (*Protesting.*) François…

10. The name of a demon made famous in Christopher Marlowe's play *Doctor Faustus*, but who appears in many works of literature.

11. A famous nineteenth-century novel by Alexandre Dumas *fils*, which was adapted into a stage play and is the source of *La traviata*, an opera by Giuseppe Verdi.

12. Joseph Ponton Costumes was established in Montreal in 1865 and was still operating in 2018.

FRANÇOIS. Beat the mixture very carefully, and somewhat longer than usual because the ingredients don't marry together very well.

CHARLES. Use lots of ice. I understand such a concoction can be explosive.

FRANÇOIS shaking the shaker, then pouring into glasses. EVERYONE *helps themselves.*

NICOLE. (*Raising her glass.*) To Miss Robson, our charming new friend.

JACK. To her long stay in Montreal!

MADGE. Thank you, Madame Beaudry. I am very touched. Thank you, Jack.

EVERYONE. (*Drinking and cheering.*) Wonderful...Delicious...What aroma... Whew! Strong!

NICOLE. (*Turning back to* CHARLES.) The English bitters give its special flavour. Oh, by the way...who's going to the masked ball on Thursday?

EVERYONE. I am! We are...

DANIEL. I'm going as Romeo.

LOUISE. That's good, 'cause I'm going as Juliet.

BERTHE. I'm going as Marguerite.

PIERRE. And me...Mephistopheles![10]

ARDOUIN. And you, Charles?

CHARLES. Oh, I'm not going. I'm dining with my father that evening.

FRANÇOIS. I'll be disguised as a gentleman.

ARDOUIN. No one will recognize you for sure.

FRANÇOIS. Thanks!

BERTHE. What about you, Nicole?

NICOLE. I'll be wearing an 1830s dress.

PIERRE. Is it pretty?

NICOLE. Very.

FRANÇOIS. And I'll be accompanying Nicole in a suit from 1825.

BERTHE. That's not very chivalrous; you will appear younger than Nicole.

FRANÇOIS. Not at all...1825 is five years earlier than 1830.

LOUISE. He's right.

DANIEL. Well, from today's perspective, that's true.

JACK. Let's go to the ball, Madge.

MADGE. We don't have any costumes.

BERTHE. I can lend you a dress from la Dame aux Camelias.[11]

JACK. And I can rent something from Ponton's.[12]

MADGE. (*Serious.*) I know the story of Marguerite Gautier.

PIERRE. A scholar of French literature.

DANIEL. Did you learn that at the convent in Paris?

MADGE. (*Serious.*) No, later on...much later. Marguerite Gautier died because she was abandoned by her lover.

CHARLES. (*Nervous.*) But these days, women don't die of love.

MADGE. You're wrong, Mr. Black. These days, women are just as foolishly
romantic as they were back in 1830.

CHARLES. (*Provoking.*) I don't believe you.

MADGE. Wrong again. And I can just about prove it. A few years ago, one of
my friends...my best friend...(*She stops.*)

EVERYONE. A story...a story...

MADGE. (*Back-pedalling.*) It's not a happy story, I'm warning you.

FRANÇOIS. Have another cocktail, and tell us your story of love.

PIERRE. Yes...have another drink. Hurry up!

FRANÇOIS. I can't wait to learn how a woman can die of love for us.

ARDOUIN. Do you really need a long story to be convinced of your own
personal worth?

FRANÇOIS. (*To himself.*) Here we go again.

EVERYONE. The story...the story...tell us the story...

JACK. (*Begging her.*) For god's sake, Madge, don't tell that story here!

MADGE. (*Looking at* CHARLES.) Why? This is just the right place for my story.

JACK. It's not the right time.

MADGE. (*A little tipsy.*) At least it's drinking time. (*She takes a drink.*)

JACK. (*Trying to take her glass.*) You know you'll regret it.

MADGE. Who's the boss?

ARDOUIN. The woman, always.

PIERRE. Jack, don't be a party-pooper.

JACK. Madge is upset this evening. I would prefer she didn't tell that story.

BERTHE. Let us be the judge of that.

EVERYONE. Go on...please...for pity's sake...the story!

During this time, CHARLES *holds himself very still near* NICOLE, *who is observing
his attitude.*

PIERRE and LOUISE. We're waiting!

MADGE *takes another sip of her cocktail, looking fixedly at* CHARLES *who leans on
the fireplace, facing* US. *Only the line of his shoulders, first by shrinking, then by
bending, bit by bit, show first his tension, his nervousness, then growing humiliation
as the story proceeds. He and* MADGE *are the centre of focus.* JACK *watches* MADGE
anxiously, while NICOLE *follows* CHARLES*'s expression with a look of tender pity.
We can follow* CHARLES*'s feelings by watching* NICOLE*'s face as she is facing him.
The other party-goers listen without realizing the meaning of the story.*

MADGE. The friend I'm talking about lived in Winnipeg. Let's call her June.
She was rich, very rich, beautiful and elegant. Men were crazy about her.
Maybe because she used to tease them royally. She held court, made them
adore her, adulate her, then broke their hearts: those were her favourite
games.

FRANÇOIS. Fascinating!

NICOLE. Hardly. As interesting as a heroine in a cheap novel!

MADGE. Wait. My friend has a defence; a secret...a very sad secret.

LOUISE. (*To* NICOLE.) The plot thickens, my dear!

JACK. For god's sake, Madge, drop the subject!

MADGE. (*Provoking.*) Make me!

JACK. I'm warning you...(*She shrugs her shoulders.*)

EVERYONE. Go on...go on...continue...

MADGE. (*Continuing the story.*) At the age of eighteen, June fell head-over-heels in love with a young lawyer whom she trusted completely.

DANIEL. Never trust one of those...

MADGE. He was the son of a millionaire. So, June knew very well he didn't want her for her money. They exchanged very serious promises. Their love, so she thought, was a marvellous thing.

FRANÇOIS. (*Slightly mocking.*) Even death couldn't separate them.

PIERRE. (*Quietly, to* FRANÇOIS.) Shut it.

MADGE. (*Looking at* CHARLES.) That's what June thought. Her friend's father was a broker.

DANIEL. Ah. Bad news. Very bad.

FRANÇOIS. The crash...the crash...

MADGE. (*To* FRANÇOIS.) Do you want to tell this story for me?

FRANÇOIS. My lips are buttoned.

MADGE. You guessed it anyway. In 1929 the young man's father was wiped out and after the collapse of his business, his reputation became a matter for discussion before a tribunal.

FRANÇOIS. A dishonest man is most often only an unlucky businessman.

BERTHE. Rather!

EVERYONE. Go on! What happened next?

MADGE. It was so painful for the family they left Winnipeg and no one heard a word from any of them ever again.

BERTHE. What? Even June's lover disappeared?

CHARLES. (*Still not moving.*) Miss Robson, I would greatly appreciate it if you would stop your story now.

JACK. Charles is right, Madge, this is not appropriate for a cocktail party.

MADGE. (*Tipsy.*) What? Not a story for a cocktail party? Au contraire... consider what happened next: love, money, life...death!

EVERYONE. Go on. Continue...(*General excitement builds.*)

JACK. (*Aside.*) Madge, I beg you, come to your senses.

MADGE. So then, why did you bring me here?

JACK. I wanted to know if you still loved him.

MADGE. No danger of that! But I am looking for revenge.

JACK. That is unworthy of you.

MADGE. Maybe...but it feels great.

13. An early brand name for the
     sleep aid, barbital, sold in
     the first half of the twentieth
     century.

BERTHE. Mr. Ardouin, settle them down. I don't understand what all the fuss is about. We just want to hear the end of the story.

MADGE. And you will hear it...Now, where was I?

CHARLES makes a move to leave the room but NICOLE takes his hand.

NICOLE. (*Whispering to CHARLES.*) Courage, Charles! I'm here.

MADGE goes to have a drink. This time JACK takes her glass away. FRANÇOIS gives her his. MADGE drinks. The atmosphere is charged.

MADGE. Where was I?

CHARLES. (*Shifting his attitude more provoking.*) The son of the broker left Winnipeg.

MADGE. (*She is surprised by his remark, seems to hesitate, but then recovers and starts again in a low voice, no sparkle. From this point onward the story is not interrupted. We can hear a pin drop.*) Thank you, Mr. Black. The broker's son left Winnipeg without a word of good-bye. For days, weeks, months, June waited, hoping for a letter, a sign, a word of explanation...of love. Nothing. Silence. She couldn't forget, couldn't stop loving him. She did everything she could to find him, wrote to friends in other cities, travelled: not to distract herself but in the hope that by chance it might bring her back the man that was her life. But he was nowhere and no one knew what happened to him. One night after hours of nightmare, of pain: not being able to take it any longer, she got up, turned on the light and contemplated her reflection in the mirror for a long time. A strange phantom suddenly met her gaze, a shadow of herself. Her eye swollen with tears, her cheeks pale and sunken...wrinkles making her smile a pathetic little expression... What had become of that beautiful, triumphant woman of yesterday? The days of waiting and profound despair had extinguished her youth. Suddenly an irresistible desire for oblivion, for sleep, overwhelmed her. She reached out and grabbed a bottle of Veronal.[13] She slowly swallowed the whole bottle, repeating quietly to herself...sleep...sleep...sleep. Then she started to laugh...to laugh! What a joke! A joke she was going to play on this stupid life. It was so easy to stop the suffering, so easy just to go to sleep forever. But would he ever know? Would he care? Feeling the world spinning around her, she lay back, her head on the pillow, in that awful silence of the mute night, abandoned by God and by men, she heard the thunder of her beating heart. Then she was afraid; she tried to cry out, to scream! But no sound passed her lips. A dark blindfold covered her eyes, a great stone on her chest, her arms so heavy...she struggled against invisible enemies, then sunk into a sleep with no dreams.

BERTHE. (*Whispering.*) Did she die?

MADGE. No.

EVERYONE. (*Breathing.*) Whew!

FRANÇOIS. You gave me a fright.

LOUISE. I have goosebumps.

MADGE. June slept for hours...days. They saved her and slowly youth was victorious. But two things had died in her.

PIERRE. What things?

MADGE. Love. And faith. Since death had not wanted her, she grabbed onto life...there was no choice. She grabbed onto life, but very differently... In her heart she hated men...men in general. She swore she'd make them all pay for the infamy of the one. (*Artificially gay.*) Laughing and singing, she harvested as many hearts as she could...crushing them in her fragile fingers became her nasty game. From then on, she was a social success...the flirting...the cocktail parties...

Sighs of relief.

LOUISE. I'm glad the story ended happily.

FRANÇOIS. Not for the poor sods whose hearts she crushed.

BERTHE. Mr. Ardouin, you have lots of life experience...what do you think? What should we make of the lover's behaviour?

ARDOUIN. We shouldn't judge him too harshly. I rather think the fault lies with...(*He hesitates, looking at* MADGE.)

EVERYONE. With...

ARDOUIN. With...June.

FRANÇOIS and OTHERS. (*Protesting.*) Explain that! What do you mean?

ARDOUIN. It's all very normal.

EVERYONE. Come on!...How can you say that?

ARDOUIN. The young man, realizing he could no longer marry the beautiful heiress, had the courage to leave, but not enough to say good-bye.

NICOLE. (*Looking at* CHARLES.) In other words, he had no choice.

MADGE. (*Rattled.*) Perhaps...

FRANÇOIS. I don't share your opinion, Nicole, I would take great pleasure in meeting this young man, so I could smash his face.

CHARLES. (*Aggressive.*) And what would you have done if you were in his shoes?

FRANÇOIS. I would not have abandoned my love.

CHARLES. (*Fiercely.*) It's true...running away would have meant giving up the young girl's fortune.

FRANÇOIS. My dear friend, you make such a defence of this young man, one would almost think we'd found the hero of this lovers' tragedy.

CHARLES. And so you have! Go on...smash my face!

FRANÇOIS *turns pale and doesn't move. General embarrassed silence.*

CHARLES. (*Shrugging his shoulders.*) So brave...in words...

MADGE. (*Trying to save the situation.*) This is all completely ridiculous. Mr. Black never even knew my friend June. And what's more, Jack was right; this story wasn't right for this occasion.

ARDOUIN. (*Interrupting.*) Perhaps it is not a cocktail party story. In any case, we are under the spell of cocktails.

EVERYONE. What do you mean? What? How so?

ARDOUIN. At a cocktail party, even the smallest incidents can turn into a tragedy. A story of the past, about people you don't even know, sets you all one against the other and almost brought Charles and François to the point of fighting a duel.

SEVERAL. Mr. Ardouin is right. He's right.

DANIEL. We are being ridiculous.

ARDOUIN. You are children taking yourselves too seriously.

NICOLE. (*Still trembling from her fright.*) Papa is right, the cocktails have turned our heads. We're acting like kids playing at being adults.

The conversation returns to general. NICOLE wipes her eyes.

CHARLES. (*Aside, to NICOLE.*) Are you crying?

NICOLE. (*Aside, to CHARLES.*) When one's a kid, one cries easily.

CHARLES. I'm sorry, Nicole.

NICOLE. You shouldn't have humiliated François.

CHARLES. (*Aside, to NICOLE.*) I lost my head. I shouldn't have done it. But all the same, what was he doing cozying up to Miss Robson like that?

NICOLE. He's always like that. The presence of a beautiful woman intoxicates him. In the end, it doesn't mean anything; I'm getting used to it.

CHARLES. (*Making up his mind.*) Nicole!

NICOLE. What?

CHARLES. Let's play a trick on François.

NICOLE. How?

CHARLES. Let's you and me give him a taste of his own medicine.

NICOLE. He wouldn't even notice.

CHARLES. I have an idea.

NICOLE. You're scaring me.

CHARLES. I'm going to announce our engagement.

NICOLE. That isn't funny.

CHARLES. We'll soon see.

NICOLE. (*Holding him back.*) Charles...no! Don't do that. Don't do it.

CHARLES. (*Breaking away from NICOLE.*) Let me go. (*Turning to the other guests.*) My dear friends, Nicole and I have a surprise for you all.

LOUISE. Marvellous! Finally something cheery.

NICOLE. (*Protesting.*) Charles! Charles...you've got it all wrong.

CHARLES. Nicole and I have decided to get married.

FRANÇOIS. (*With a cry.*) Nicole!

EVERYONE. No! Oh! Really? Are you serious?

FRANÇOIS. (*Hard.*) Nicole, I want to hear this news from your own lips.

NICOLE. François, it was just a joke.

CHARLES. (*Seeing the joke has turned sour.*) Yes of course...it was just a joke...

FRANÇOIS. (*Nasty.*) A stupid joke.

ARDOUIN. Perhaps not as stupid as it seems.

PIERRE. How's that?

ARDOUIN. Some people need a shock to see the truth.

LOUISE. (*Looking at* FRANÇOIS.) A cry from the heart.

CHARLES. Or of fear.

FRANÇOIS. (*Exploding.*) I have really had enough of your stories, enough of your thinly disguised malicious remarks. Maybe you think I don't see anything, don't hear anything, that I don't feel anything? Perhaps, Mr. Ardouin, you think your kindnesses touch me, that I will thank you for the hurtful comments you make at my expense? And you, Mr. Black, the family tutor, not only managing the children but, and maybe especially, Nicole too: I have had enough of your disapproving airs, your silences that are even more cutting than your slurs. You are the serious man, and I only the light friend. Ah well, marry Nicole...marry her...you will make her happy: you're made for one other. After all, your "joke" was full of good sense. In fact, I bet Nicole was the instigator.

CHARLES. No. I am the only one to blame.

NICOLE. (*Furious at* FRANÇOIS*'s attitude.*) François is right. The idea of the stupid joke was mine.

CHARLES. Nicole, you know that's not true. Why are you saying that?

FRANÇOIS. (*Very bitter.*) Oh this just gets better and better. Nicole takes the blame for you. Only love could inspire such devotion. (*Mocking and mean.*) Allow me...(*With a grand bow to* CHARLES.) She's all yours...sir...good evening!

He leaves. General shock. Nicole is distraught.

LOUISE. (*To* DANIEL.) Charming cocktail party.

ARDOUIN. ...Off to a great start.

DANIEL. Poor Nicole.

BERTHE. Some birthday.

MADGE. (*Approaching* NICOLE.) I am so sorry, Madame Beaudry. I feel responsible. I am sorry, Charles, I should never have...

BERTHE. (*Approaching Nicole.*) He'll be back. He loves you.

NICOLE is motionless, like a statue.

CHARLES. (*To* NICOLE.) Do you want me to go after him? Bring him back? I could explain…(*Reacting to* NICOLE'*s despair.*) I could apologize…(NICOLE *shakes her head. Her face is painfully tense.*)

SOSTHÈNE. Dinner is served.

ARDOUIN. Come along, Nicole, let's go in.

NICOLE. (*On the verge of tears.*) Go ahead without me. I can't.

PIERRE. It will cheer you up.

NICOLE. (*Her lips quivering.*) Give me five minutes. Just five minutes, my friends. I promise to join you. Please, I will come find you right away. Papa, you are the master of the house, offer your arm to Louise…Louise take my place.

JACK. (*Offering his arm to* MADGE, *aside.*) Madge, I cannot help but feel happy.

MADGE. I don't understand.

JACK. You did not so much as frown when Charles announced his engagement.

MADGE. But isn't that awfully sad?

JACK. Sad?

MADGE. (*They talk as they exit.*) Yes, to think that love can be extinguished so quickly.

Everyone exits except NICOLE *and* CHARLES.

CHARLES. (*Goes towards the door, but returns.*) Will you ever forgive me?

NICOLE. (*Throwing herself on the divan.*) I am so unhappy.

CHARLES. If only I could undo it.

NICOLE. And you even promised to be nice to François tonight.

CHARLES. He was being so ungentlemanly towards you.

NICOLE. I wasn't jealous.

CHARLES. Nicole, don't you see, don't you get it that François is not worthy of your love?

NICOLE. (*Stopping him.*) Be quiet, Charles…not you too, not you…François is worthy of the most marvelous of loves.

CHARLES. (*Bowing his head.*) Do you want to go in now?

NICOLE. No. Go on alone. Tell them on my behalf to have a good time, enjoy themselves. I will be there in a few minutes…You will see, you will see: I will be brave…I don't want to spoil the evening.

CHARLES. As you wish. (*He exits regretfully.*)

NICOLE *remains prostrate for several minutes. She looks at her watch. Making a sudden decision, she rushes to the telephone, then changes her mind and backs away. She goes back, then after a moment, dials a number.*

NICOLE. (*On the phone.*) Hello…The doctor, please…He's not there?…He doesn't want to be disturbed?…But if…this is an emergency…very urgent…

Yes I understand...but please...I have to speak with him...(*She waits a few seconds...then a muffled cry.*) François!...You...finally...No, don't hang up, please!...no...listen...Let me explain...One minute only...No, they've all left. They're eating...I couldn't...I wasn't able...François, my François... Don't speak to me with that tone...Every word is like a knife in my heart... I'm asking you to forgive me...on my knees...if you want...(*She slides to the floor.*) if you could see me...I don't care...it's all the same to me...except you...François...Forgive me, I lost my head...(*In a very small voice.*) You don't want to hear my apologies?...You don't want any?...I am ashamed...You are right...I love without dignity...I simply love...for me there is only love... for you...It's so strong...so big...so complete...That there is no nuance in its place...no...not even dignity...(*Begging.*) Will you come back?...(*Horrified.*) Never?...You said "Never"? You can't do that...You can't do that to me... François, not this evening...if you want...but tomorrow, or the day after... no? The evening of the ball, then? Don't say that...be quiet...But François I will die...Listen...No, don't hang up...Listen to me carefully...I will not call you again...I will not write to you...Thursday evening, I will put on my dress for the ball, even if I don't hear anything from you...I will wait for you; I will wait for you all night...You will come...you will come...If you don't come...(*Her tragic expression evokes an idea of death.*) But you will come...I know you will come...(*She hangs up, infinitely weary and with a sob, as the curtain falls.*) You will come.

CURTAIN

ACT THREE

A few days later. The sitting room. 9:00 in the evening. MR. ARDOUIN *and* GENEVIEVE *are playing Rummy near the lamp. If necessary this act could be played on the same set as the first two.*

ARDOUIN. If only the Jack of Hearts would turn up.
GENEVIEVE. (*Glancing towards the door.*) Oh, don't worry, he'll be here soon. It's about time.
ARDOUIN. What do you mean?
GENEVIEVE. The Jack of Hearts...the doctor, of course.
ARDOUIN. (*Indulging her.*) My little Genevieve, you're just making it harder on yourself.
GENEVIEVE. No more than you.
ARDOUIN. But I am old, the pain can't hurt me much longer.
GENEVIEVE. Grandpa! Stop it! You are young and strong. What would I do without you?
ARDOUIN. It's really special you know, my Genevieve, to be your best friend.
GENEVIEVE. (*On an impulse.*) You are my mama!

ARDOUIN. Don't say that. Your mother loves you very much. You will find her
    again.

GENEVIEVE. Will you bring her back to me?

ARDOUIN. I don't know.

GENEVIEVE. I hate him...I hate him.

ARDOUIN. That's bad...Very bad...

GENEVIEVE. Are you saying you like him? I dare you to say it...(*ARDOUIN
    lowers his head.*) You see...(*Silence.*) Grandpa, does the doctor know that
    mama only has the money that you give her?

ARDOUIN. (*Embarrassed.*) What are you getting at?

GENEVIEVE. I think the doctor only wants to marry mama because we are
    rich.

ARDOUIN. But he has a good job.

GENEVIEVE. I heard Mr. Black tell his friend Jack that the doctor has a lot of
    debts.

ARDOUIN. You mustn't be unfair, Genevieve. I think Dr. Normand loves your
    mother as much as he is capable of loving.

GENEVIEVE. Which is not likely very much. Why do you always take the
    doctor's side against me? I know inside you are just as unhappy as I am.

NICOLE. (*Off.*) Rose, bring the needle and thread into the sitting room. The
    mirror is higher here and the light is better.

ARDOUIN *puts his finger on his mouth. He and Genevieve look engrossed in their
game.* NICOLE *enters like a whirlwind. She is wearing the 1830s dress. She stops,
surprised.* ROSE *follows her carrying some artificial flowers.*

NICOLE. Oh! You're both in here.

ARDOUIN. You are beautiful!

NICOLE. Do you like it?

ARDOUIN. The dress makes you look twenty again.

NICOLE. You are kind, papa. I want to be beautiful this evening. I must be
    beautiful; I have to make a perfect impression.

GENEVIEVE. (*Drily.*) When don't you?

NICOLE. Does your mother's success bother you so much?

GENEVIEVE. At what age does a mother get over this craze for success?

ARDOUIN. Genevieve!

GENEVIEVE. (*More and more sullen.*) And at what age is a young woman
    allowed to start her own success?

NICOLE. When the young woman learns to be nice, she can have success very
    young.

GENEVIEVE. Then there are some mothers who are annoyed by the success of
    their daughters.

NICOLE. Genevieve, I have had enough of your spiteful comments. Go to your
    room. For months now you have done your best to spoil everything. This

evening I don't have the time to tell you what I think, but you will lose
nothing in waiting. Go up and join Francine.
GENEVIEVE. Grandpa, will you come up and see us?
ARDOUIN. (*Very sad.*) I'll be up. Go on...

GENEVIEVE *exits.*

NICOLE. (*Taking the flowers, the needle and the thread from* ROSE.) You can go,
Rose, I'll sew the flowers on myself.
ROSE. Should I wait up for you, Madame?
NICOLE. No, I'll be back very late.
ROSE. Should I leave the night light on?
NICOLE. Yes, please.
ROSE. Very well, Madame. (*She exits.*)
NICOLE. I swear, papa, I can't take much more. If Genevieve were younger, I'd
send her to boarding school.
ARDOUIN. As if that would help. (*Pause.*) I thought François...
NICOLE. What?! What did you think...?
ARDOUIN. Nothing.
NICOLE. (*Worried.*) You don't think he's coming, do you.
ARDOUIN. Well?! After what happened on Monday night...
NICOLE. But papa...he can't do that to me...Everyone just lost their head.
ARDOUIN. And you think three days are enough for him to find his again?
NICOLE. Papa, don't be so cynical. If you knew how much I'm suffering.
ARDOUIN. My poor Nicole.
NICOLE. He just can't not come back to me...He can't abandon me...He'll come,
I know he will come.
ARDOUIN. Have you heard anything from him?
NICOLE. (*Lowering her head.*) No.
ARDOUIN. So...
NICOLE. That doesn't mean anything. I feel he will come. I cannot doubt it. I
refuse to.
ARDOUIN. And Genevieve...what are you going to do?
NICOLE. If I marry François, life will be more bearable here.
ARDOUIN. So you're still thinking of marrying him?
NICOLE. Of course, papa. I love him.
ARDOUIN. And him?
NICOLE. What do you mean...and him?
ARDOUIN. Does he love you?
NICOLE. Why wouldn't he marry me? Am I not young enough? Not pretty
enough to be loved?
ARDOUIN. To be loved by some men, it's not enough to be young and pretty.
One has to be sure of staying that way for a long time.
NICOLE. But François is not that young himself.

ARDOUIN. A man ages more slowly than a woman.

NICOLE. You know very well that I don't look forty.

ARDOUIN. A pain, or even just the absence of happiness, gives away your age very quickly.

NICOLE. But love has made me young again.

ARDOUIN. And its reality will age you. You know that François has lived a full life. He will be demanding.

NICOLE. Never enough. If you knew how much love I have in store for him.

ARDOUIN. You misunderstand me.

NICOLE. No. You mean that François has known many beautiful, young, and hot-blooded women, and that compared to him I am like a child without experience, without passion. You think he will leave me.

ARDOUIN. It's in the cards.

NICOLE. No, and no! I will be whatever he wants me to be. He will teach me, awaken me. You can't understand. I have never known what love is.

ARDOUIN. But you loved your husband. You were happy with him.

NICOLE. A happiness born of ignorance. And that happiness, now that I love François, seems to me like something so dull, that I am frightened by all the time I've lost.

ARDOUIN. Nicole, you shock me. Jacques didn't make you happy?

NICOLE. Think back. I was only a little girl to him.

ARDOUIN. A little girl whom he adored.

NICOLE. He was too intelligent, too strong for me. He always commanded, organized, decided. I might have had my own tastes, desires, personality, but his strength of will crushed me.

ARDOUIN. All the same, you loved him when you married him.

NICOLE. I don't know anymore. I was twenty years old. You had chosen him for me. He was your best manager. I adored you. Anything you gave me had to be the best. After all, before living through Jacques's mind, I had gotten used to living through yours. You had me trained never to hold an opinion different from you. I saw the world through your eyes. I used to catch your way of expressing yourself coming out of my mouth.

ARDOUIN. You raised your children with Jacques.

NICOLE. The tutors, even the maids, were chosen by you and Jacques.

ARDOUIN. We just wanted to spare you those little nuisances.

NICOLE. More like you didn't take me seriously.

ARDOUIN. It was our joy to see you gay and relaxed. We wanted you to be elegant.

NICOLE. Like a doll! You never talked to me about your business. Your interminable conversations about the bank drove me crazy. That domain was off limits to me.

ARDOUIN. We were of the old school. Your mother would never have thought to be interested in anything other than children and the house.

NICOLE. And love? Do you think Jacques fulfilled me in that area?

ARDOUIN. He was young. He maybe didn't have the experience of a François Normand.

NICOLE. He loved numbers too much to waste his time studying the sentimental nature of a woman. Love played the same part in his daily routine as his morning hygiene.

ARDOUIN. You didn't seem to suffer.

NICOLE. There are disappointments one doesn't share with one's father, or even admit to oneself. One settles for a very small box of joy but then one day, facing the dazzle of true happiness, one understands the miserable emptiness of the past.

ARDOUIN. How you have changed, my poor Nicole!

NICOLE. I'm forty years old. For the first, and perhaps last time, love and happiness are within my grasp. No, you will not separate me from François. I want to live. Perhaps he will be able to teach me everything that life hasn't taught me. He will give me back myself. He will give me back my personality.

ARDOUIN. Personality? What do you call having a personality? Acting like queen bee surrounded by a bunch of friends who don't have any? Drinking cocktails...Smoking cigarettes...coming in at all hours...?

NICOLE. I'm not doing anything wrong. I'm having fun.

ARDOUIN. Believe me, Nicole, this life will very quickly leave you empty.

NICOLE. When I marry François, I will give up all these distractions. I will be happy, quiet: just him, my children, and you.

ARDOUIN. You don't really believe in that blissful happiness, my poor Nicole.

NICOLE. So, what am I supposed to do?

ARDOUIN. Give up François.

NICOLE. I've tried.

ARDOUIN. Not hard enough. You haven't really applied your whole will to it.

NICOLE. In love, there is no such thing as will.

ARDOUIN. But since you are so sure of not being happy with François...

NICOLE. I'd rather suffer with him, than be miserable without him.

ARDOUIN. My poor little girl, you are more smitten than I realized. I don't know what more to say to you. Marry him. Genevieve and I will go live together somewhere else.

NICOLE. No. Never. You will not abandon me.

ARDOUIN. It's you who are abandoning us.

***Appendix I insert here

ROSE. (*Appearing.*) Madame, the doctor has arrived.

NICOLE. (*A cry of joy.*) OH! He has come...I don't want him to see me like this... Papa, will you take care of him? I am too upset...I have to be beautiful... Rose...go show the doctor up.

ROSE. Yes ma'am. (*She exits.*)

NICOLE. Papa, I beg you, don't hurt him.

ARDOUIN. Don't worry...go...

NICOLE exits. FRANÇOIS enters. He is wearing a grand cape that covers his suit; he is holding his hat and gloves.

***

FRANÇOIS. Good evening, Mr. Ardouin. Nicole isn't here?

ARDOUIN. She's putting the finishing touches to her costume. It looks great though. And you?

FRANÇOIS. (*Taking off his cape and putting on his top hat.*) Voilà...1825...

ARDOUIN. Very dapper! Some port?

FRANÇOIS. A Scotch if you have it. I've had a terrible day. I am dead with exhaustion.

ARDOUIN. Demanding patients?

FRANÇOIS. Surgery in particular takes a lot out of one's nerves.

ARDOUIN. You did a lot of operations?

FRANÇOIS. Quite a few. This morning a case of mastoiditis.[14] The patient died on the operating table. So you can imagine: telling the family, the paperwork, the upset nurses...all that sets your nerves on edge.

ARDOUIN. A child?

FRANÇOIS. A young girl. Genevieve's age, and an only child.

ARDOUIN. I can understand that it must be upsetting, and the idea of the ball might not bring much of a smile to your face.

FRANÇOIS. (*Pouring a Scotch.*) On the contrary, it will clear my mind. If I turned my life upside down every time a patient was unhappy, it would be rather a nuisance.

ARDOUIN. So your patients' problems don't follow you home?

FRANÇOIS. Happily, no. When I **leave** work, I leave all the worries of the job, along with my gloves, in the change room.

ARDOUIN. (*Pointing to his gloves.*) This evening you seem to have forgotten to leave them behind.

FRANÇOIS. Maybe that's why I told you about my surgery today. But what can Nicole be doing?

ARDOUIN. It always seems to take ladies a long time to get ready. A cigar?

FRANÇOIS. Thank you! (*They seem to be bored.*) I have never understood how it can take a woman so long to get dressed. I can transform in a jiffy.

ARDOUIN. Professional practice?

FRANÇOIS. Oh no. I never get excited when a patient calls. Patients always think they are about to die.

ARDOUIN. In other words, you take life pretty easily.

FRANÇOIS. Is that wrong?

15. A brand of cigarettes produced by a Quebec company in the 1930s.

ARDOUIN. Maybe not. In my day, we took our actions more seriously. We carried around a certain...idealism.

FRANÇOIS. How cumbersome.

ARDOUIN. No, productive.

FRANÇOIS. You didn't know how to have fun.

ARDOUIN. Oh yes...in other ways...not with cocktails.

FRANÇOIS. Or Scotch?

ARDOUIN. I'm not saying a little shot from time to time is to be sneered at. We preferred our pleasures, the way you like your drinks, straight up.

FRANÇOIS. I'm afraid, Mr. Ardouin, that we have two very different ways of thinking; there is a chasm between our two generations.

CHARLES *enters. He stops at the doorway, hesitating.*

CHARLES. Oh. Excuse me. I am sorry to bother you, Mr. Ardouin. I thought you were alone.

FRANÇOIS. (*Extending his hand to* CHARLES.) Come in, please. I am very happy that you found us. I suppose I have kind of an apology to make to you. I rather lost my head on Monday night.

CHARLES. (*Relieved.*) Weren't we all a bit ridiculous?

ARDOUIN. Cocktails, my friends, cocktails...Didn't I predict what would happen? The smallest incident can become a tragedy.

FRANÇOIS. Happily, everything goes back to normal when the effect of the cocktails wears off.

ARDOUIN. My friends, I feel that in one area at least we can all be in agreement.

CHARLES. What is that?

ARDOUIN. Nicole's happiness.

FRANÇOIS. You're right, there, Mr. Ardouin. Nicole deserves to be happy. And I am totally aware of what a lucky man I am.

ARDOUIN. Nicole's love is so different, so selfless.

CHARLES. (*Uneasy.*) I have forgotten my cigarettes. Will you allow me to go back up to my room?

FRANÇOIS. Here, have one of mine.

CHARLES. No, thank-you. I'm used to my Grads.[15] If you'll permit, I will go get my cigarette case...but I will return.

ARDOUIN. I thought you were meeting your father this evening.

CHARLES. We had dinner together. (*Turning to the doctor.*) If I'm not back before you leave, let me wish you the most pleasant of evenings.

FRANÇOIS. (*Looking at the time.*) I'm afraid we're going to be late for the ball. See you another time. (CHARLES *exits.*)

ARDOUIN. What a fine fellow Charles is. His judgement, intelligence, heart in the right place...our girls adore him.

FRANÇOIS. He bugs me a little. He's too perfect. Anyway, like most English,
    his coldness chills my blood.
ARDOUIN. You have to get to know them. Their cold exterior almost always
    hides a very great tenderness.

*NICOLE and GENEVIEVE enter. GENEVIEVE is wearing the 1830s dress. She is
stunning and radiant. NICOLE, her eyes red, is wearing a simple night dress. Her
hair, stripped of its party curls, is tied up with a tight headband. She looks ten years
older. ARDOUIN and FRANÇOIS exclaim in surprise.*

ARDOUIN. Nicole, what does this mean?
FRANÇOIS. (*At almost the same time.*) Adorable.
NICOLE. (*A bit sad.*) Isn't my daughter pretty?
ARDOUIN. Will you tell us...
NICOLE. (*Speaking to FRANÇOIS, who never takes his eyes off GENEVIEVE.*)
    I have a dreadful migraine. I simply couldn't go...
FRANÇOIS. (*Without sincerity.*) What a shame!
NICOLE. I thought...so you wouldn't have to miss the ball...that I could entrust
    Genevieve to you.
FRANÇOIS. But what will all your friends say? (*Gesture of indifference from
    NICOLE.*) Especially after the incident on Monday.
NICOLE. Assuming of course that the point here is indeed concern about what
    my friends think. In any case, with Genevieve by your side, the gossips will
    be silenced.
ARDOUIN. You've thought of everything.
NICOLE. I even called Louise; I asked her to apologize to the others on my
    behalf and told her to keep an eye on Genevieve.
FRANÇOIS. A chaperon?
ARDOUIN. Trust reigns.
NICOLE. Don't talk such foolishness. I only want François not to have to worry
    too much about Genevieve. Remember she has never been out in society. Go
    on. It's time to go.
FRANÇOIS. Really, Nicole, are you really that tired? (*Without conviction.*) We
    can go to the ball later, or simply spend the evening here, quietly.

GENEVIEVE makes a face as a sign of her disappointment.

ARDOUIN. (*To GENEVIEVE.*) Does going to the ball mean that much to you,
    Genevieve?
GENEVIEVE. Oh yes, grandpa...dancing...the costumes...the music...my début.
NICOLE. Don't worry, Genevieve, François has no intention of staying here.
    Moreover, he will be pleased to accompany you. Isn't that right, François?
FRANÇOIS. One would have to be heartless to deprive Genevieve of a pleasure
    that she seems to have placed such importance on.

ARDOUIN. And to top it all, the ball will please you as well young man.

FRANÇOIS. To make my happiness complete, I would be joined by both mother and daughter.

ARDOUIN. A family night out…

NICOLE. It's getting late. Hurry up you two. François, I'm trusting her to you. Don't leave her alone too often. She knows hardly anyone.

GENEVIEVE. (*Putting an evening cape on over her shoulders.*) When they realize I am your daughter they will want to meet me.

FRANÇOIS. You are pretty too, Genevieve, they will introduce themselves without having to know who you are.

GENEVIEVE. For myself? Do you think so? I am happy…so happy…(*She gives her grandpa a hug, nearly knocking him over with her crinoline.*) Grandpa, I am crazy with joy. (*Then she kisses her mother.*) Thank you, mama!

FRANÇOIS who has put on his cape and gloves, ceremoniously offers her his arm. She makes an 1830s-style curtsey and takes his arm. The two cross slowly to the door.

GENEVIEVE. (*At the door, turning back to the others.*) You know, mama, the two of us will talk about nothing except you. (*They exit.*)

ARDOUIN. It's a good thing you have done here, Nicole.

NICOLE looks at herself in the mirror, noticing her wrinkles, smooths her headbands. She sighs.

ARDOUIN. I'm going to say good-night to Francine and take a stroll in the garden before retiring. Do you want to come?

NICOLE. No. I'll stay here. Don't worry about me.

ARDOUIN. You're not going to wait for them, are you?

NICOLE. Maybe. I don't know.

ARDOUIN. Goodnight, Nicole.

NICOLE. Goodnight, papa.

ARDOUIN starts to say something but changes his mind and exits. NICOLE lights a cigarette, crosses to the little desk, picks up a photo of FRANÇOIS and looks at it a long time. Then she goes over to the divan where she sits with her head in her hands. CHARLES enters.

CHARLES. What, Madame Beaudry, you are not at the ball? (*NICOLE cannot speak but shakes her head.*) But what happened? (*Looking at NICOLE.*) You've been crying. Has someone hurt you?

NICOLE. I had a rather heated discussion with Genevieve.

CHARLES. On the subject of Dr. Normand.

NICOLE. Yes, about François.

CHARLES. But that doesn't explain why you aren't at the ball.

NICOLE. I couldn't go. I was too upset.

CHARLES. And François?

NICOLE. He went all the same.

CHARLES. Alone?

NICOLE. No. With Genevieve.

CHARLES. Genevieve? I don't understand.

NICOLE. It's a long story.

CHARLES. Nicole, tell me.

***Appendix II insert here

NICOLE. After a painful conversation with my father, I ran up to my room because I didn't want François to see me, my eyes still red with tears.

CHARLES. Oh...and then...

NICOLE. There I found Genevieve crying hysterically.

CHARLES. The poor thing.

NICOLE. It was a shock.

CHARLES. And nothing had happened before that?

NICOLE. Yes. After dinner, she spoke to me so insolently. To punish her I sent her to her room.

CHARLES. Her heart was so full...it broke.

NICOLE. I chose my moment badly. I was in such a state that her tears really hit a nerve. I felt so mean: I accused her of stealing my happiness; I scolded her for her attitude towards François and her selfish lack of understanding my situation.

CHARLES. And what did she say?

NICOLE. Not a word, not a sound. Tight-lipped, she stood up, her skin a deathly pale against the dark colour of her dress. Her eyes fixed on me with frightening hardness.

CHARLES. I'm *so* sorry!

NICOLE. I couldn't take that look any more. I cried. I screamed, almost hysterical. Talk to me...Talk to me...but don't look at me like that...don't stare at me with those eyes.

CHARLES. And then...

NICOLE. She still didn't move. It was terrible! I crumpled at her feet not knowing what I was going to do. My strength drained out of me. I clasped her legs; I trembled. Miserably, I begged her...Genevieve, my life, my happiness is in your hands. One word, just one word and you can make me the happiest woman alive. One word, just one word and you can break my heart in your fingers.

CHARLES. (*Kneeling.*) Poor...poor, Nicole!

NICOLE. Her heart melted. She slid to her knees on the floor beside me and started to cry softly..."Mama...mama...We are so unhappy! I don't want you to be miserable! I don't want you to cry." Then, hiding her face in her hands, "But I can't stand the idea of that Dr. Normand in this house, with you...always...your husband...I love you, mama, I love you too much. I am jealous...I hate him. He has stolen our mother from us! Help me...have pity on me. I feel I am wrong. I am ashamed of being so selfish. Mama...Oh! Mama...Can't we still love each other like we did before...like we did before he came?

CHARLES. What a situation!

NICOLE. And then she went on If at least I had some friends...if I was out in the world, if I had my début, maybe if my spirits were distracted by something else, I wouldn't be so haunted by this horrible marriage."

CHARLES. That would be a solution, though not radical.

NICOLE. That was when the idea came to me of sending Genevieve in my place to the ball, with François.

***

CHARLES. What a strange idea!

NICOLE. Who knows? A few hours spent together in an atmosphere of gaiety, of pleasure...perhaps it would bring them together?

CHARLES. And how did Genevieve take this idea?

NICOLE. At first she was revolted.

CHARLES. I'm not surprised.

NICOLE. Then I described all the pleasures of a grand ball...the lights, the music, the dancing...I promised her she'd be a success and assured her that she would be ravishing in my dress.

CHARLES. You tempted her.

NICOLE. With every word I could think of. She is young and the dream was magnificent. She weakened and was won over. Voilà...that's why I'm not at the ball.

CHARLES. (*Lowering his head.*) I see again the woman I used to know.

NICOLE. (*Dreaming.*) You should have seen how lovely she was in the 1830s dress. Her cheeks still damp with tears, she studied her image in the mirror. She reminded me of my own youth...my youth was there smiling back at me in the mirror, reaching towards me across the gulf of years past. Her happiness brought my daughter back to me.

CHARLES. I wish I were there.

NICOLE. Then my daughter gave me back my happiness.

CHARLES. Your hands are like ice.

NICOLE. My whole life is in the balance.

CHARLES. You are playing a dangerous game.

NICOLE. The reward is worth the risk.

CHARLES. You love him that much?

NICOLE. More than that.

CHARLES. Love hurts.

NICOLE. (*Suddenly looking at him.*) You're shaking...

CHARLES. Your distress is too much for me.

NICOLE. What a marvelous friend you are, Charles! If I marry François, will you leave?

CHARLES. It's for the better.

NICOLE. You too? Oh...so I'm sacrificing all of you for him...my father, my daughter, and you...you...it's horrible! (*She puts her head in her hands and cries.*)

CHARLES. Nicole!...(*He hesitates.*) I have something to tell you.

NICOLE. Nothing sad, please...I couldn't take it.

CHARLES. Earlier this evening, I had dinner with my father.

NICOLE. Is he ok?

CHARLES. Yes, very well, thank-you. Business is picking up. He wants to make me a partner.

NICOLE. I am very happy for you, Charles. But that means you really must leave.

CHARLES. I'm afraid so.

NICOLE. What will become of me?

CHARLES. You have François.

NICOLE. But what if I don't marry him?

CHARLES. I will never be far away.

NICOLE. (*Suddenly remembering.*) But in fact, since you will be independent again, nothing can stop you from marrying Miss Robson.

CHARLES. She doesn't love me anymore.

NICOLE. And you?

CHARLES. (*Suddenly making a decision.*) I love you, Nicole. I will never love any other woman.

NICOLE. Charles! My poor Charles!

CHARLES. I would never have told you, but this is our last evening. I leave tomorrow. I should have gone several weeks ago, but I didn't have the courage. My father doesn't want to wait any longer.

NICOLE. Oh, Charles, I will miss you so much! I have been so blind...forgive me. It must have been hard for you.

CHARLES. I have known every emotion in this house...hell as much as heaven.

NICOLE. And I took you as a confidante about my love troubles.

CHARLES. My own suffering helped me to understand yours and sympathize with you.

NICOLE. And when François was around?

CHARLES. It was torture.

NICOLE. And I saw nothing...guessed nothing.

CHARLES. We English often carry the heaviest burdens with a smile...it's pride perhaps.

NICOLE. No...courage.

CHARLES. Even if I cannot see you again, I am not totally unhappy: you have
my secret and that is a weight lifted from my heart.

NICOLE. You will suffer.

CHARLES. Perhaps...when the dream is really over. Nevertheless, I am not
going away empty-handed. I am so much richer than I was the day I first
met you. Love has taught me a marvellous lesson: the memories of an
infinite sweetness will be with me forever. I will remember the blue dress
you were wearing that April morning, the little tulle hat crowning your
golden hair, the sparkles of sunlight cast on your cheeks through the
fringe of your parasol. I will especially remember the white dress you were
wearing the unforgettable evening of your birthday party...

NICOLE. After you leave, I will be very sad.

CHARLES. You only have to call me and I will return.

NICOLE. Charles, do not sacrifice your life; I am not worth the pain. One day
you must marry.

CHARLES. I will never love any other woman.

NICOLE. Even if I didn't love François, we couldn't marry.

CHARLES. Why not?

NICOLE. You're Protestant.

CHARLES. Anglican. Our religions are not so different. In any case, you would
never have heard a word from me on the subject.

NICOLE. Oh, I know. You are so good, so considerate. Your wife, Charles, will
be very happy.

CHARLES. (Rising.) Good night, Nicole. From time to time think about the poor
devil of a tutor who will have nothing in life other than the memory of you.

NICOLE. You will come back...tell me you will come back.

CHARLES. Not if you are happy...I want so much for you to be happy.

NICOLE. I am losing a great friend in you.

CHARLES. Confessing my love for you was the death of our friendship.

NICOLE. Before we part, do you want to kiss me?...I think that would make me
happy.

*CHARLES crosses to her to kiss her on the cheek, but feeling her body next to his own,
he cannot help himself and presses her close to him, kissing her passionately. She
pulls away, shocked. He bows his head, ashamed, all hope gone.*

CHARLES. (Fleeing.) It's best I never return.

NICOLE. (Left alone.) My god. Life is terrible!

*Completely dazed, she rubs her forehead, turns off the lamps, leaving only one
shaded lamp lit. She sits in the large soft chair facing the fireplace and starts to
dream, to wait.*

The curtain falls to indicate that several hours pass. The curtain rises, slowly.
NICOLE *is asleep. The audience can see her in profile. A gray dawn is visible through*
the window whose curtains were not pulled closed. For a moment the room is silent.
Then GENEVIEVE *and* FRANÇOIS *enter on tip-toe. The chair is positioned so they*
cannot see NICOLE.

GENEVIEVE. Shhh!...Don't wake up the whole house!
FRANÇOIS. (*Somewhat too merry.*) Are you happy?
GENEVIEVE. (*Excited.*) It was the most wonderful night of my life.

At this moment, NICOLE *opens her eyes, but doesn't move.*

FRANÇOIS. The most beautiful morning.
GENEVIEVE. But you shouldn't have come up.
FRANÇOIS. I forgot my cigarette case.
GENEVIEVE. Here it is.
FRANÇOIS. Let me look at you. Tomorrow you will no longer be a little girl.
GENEVIEVE. Yes. I will struggle. Good-bye to a child's life. No more English
    lessons, no more boarding school dresses. I want to live my life. I'm
    eighteen years old.
FRANÇOIS. Shhh...Not so loud! (*He crosses to the table and pours himself a glass*
    of Scotch.)
GENEVIEVE. Tough. What's more...to prove to you my decisions are serious...a
    cigarette...
FRANÇOIS. You've been smoking all night. You'll make yourself sick.
GENEVIEVE. So what? It won't be the first time. I will soon get used to it.
    (*Looking at the bottle of Scotch.*) What if I tried a little Scotch...
FRANÇOIS. Ahh! No. Not that. Let's not lose our heads.
GENEVIEVE. Mama drinks enough of it.
FRANÇOIS. That's not the same thing. And anyway, you drank lots of punch,
    that's enough. You're starting to frighten me. What are you turning into,
    little Genevieve? You're not tipsy I hope?
GENEVIEVE. Yes. Tipsy with joy, with hope. I learned a marvellous lesson
    tonight.
FRANÇOIS. (*Amused.*) Oh, what was that?
GENEVIEVE. That I am pretty.
FRANÇOIS. You had doubts?
GENEVIEVE. Of course. I wasn't pretty until someone told me.
FRANÇOIS. My child!
GENEVIEVE. (*Putting her finger on his mouth.*) Shhh...that word is forbidden.
FRANÇOIS. (*Holding her hand, looking at it, turning it over.*) Oh, the lovely hand
    of a woman. And who courted you this evening?

GENEVIEVE. Everyone who danced with me, especially mama's lovers. Poor mama! If she could have heard them...the comparison wasn't always in her favour. People can be nasty.

FRANÇOIS. And me?

GENEVIEVE. Oh, it wasn't pretty. You came awfully close to losing own your head too.

FRANÇOIS. (*Protesting, but not vigorously.*) Please!

GENEVIEVE. During the final tango.

FRANÇOIS. I was so sad that it was the last one.

GENEVIEVE. You held me very close to you.

FRANÇOIS. Only in order to lead you better. The tango can be difficult when one isn't practiced.

GENEVIEVE. And the words you whispered to me...were they some sort of Spanish song?

FRANÇOIS. You heard me...?

GENEVIEVE. (*Closing her eyes and remembering.*) You said, "I am crazy with happiness...Tell me that you don't hate me anymore..."

FRANÇOIS. And what was your answer?

GENEVIEVE. I started to fall in love with you.

FRANÇOIS. For real? Do you really mean that, Genevieve?

GENEVIEVE. (*The sound of her voice is false and her look gives the lie to her words.*) Of course it's true, my friend, François.

FRANÇOIS. What wonderful words on lips so fresh!

GENEVIEVE. Are they less pleasing on forty-year-old lips?

FRANÇOIS. Touché! Don't remind me. Who knows what tomorrow will bring?

GENEVIEVE. I don't care about tomorrow. Tomorrow, like today, I will be a young girl, a beautiful young girl whom others will pay attention to. (*She spins around and curtsies to* FRANÇOIS.) Kiss my hand, sir.

Suddenly FRANÇOIS *draws her to him and kisses her on the mouth.* GENEVIEVE *pulls back.* NICOLE *stands up.*

NICOLE. (*With a cry. Shocked by the two others.*) François, what are you doing?

GENEVIEVE. Mama!

NICOLE. (*To* GENEVIEVE, *with an icy voice.*) Go to your room.

GENEVIEVE. (*Imploring.*) Mama!...Mama...You don't understand...

NICOLE. Your room! Now!

GENEVIEVE. (*Devastated.*) Mama...will you come and tuck me in?

NICOLE. (*Very harsh.*) No! (GENEVIEVE *exits, crying.*)

FRANÇOIS. Please, Nicole, it's my fault.

NICOLE. You!...You!...oh...such loving words to my daughter!...your man's lips on her "fresh" lips...(*Disgusted.*) And to think...to think...I was going to make you her father! (*She laughs madly.*) You...(*Then, changing her tone, as if defeated.*) Oh...it hurts...it hurts so much...(*She starts to cry.*)

16. Nicole is alluding to the "Sisters of Charity," a term used by many benevolent religious orders.

FRANÇOIS. Don't cry, Nicole. Forgive me; I'm an idiot.

NICOLE. You...François...my life...my whole life...(*She cries, overcome.*)

FRANÇOIS. Despise, me, but don't chase me away. I will simply be your friend. I don't deserve anything else...(*Very humbly.*) Just your friend.

NICOLE. My friend?...But do you even know what it means to be a friend? A friend is someone you can always count on, someone you can tell anything to...who will never embarrass you over a daft idea...someone who understands you better through your silences then through your words... someone who accepts your tears and dries them...who makes you smile... someone who loves you despite your wrinkles, despite your gray hair... despite the aging that is coming...A friend? That's someone who does everything to make you happy...someone who suffers with you, cries with you...laughs with you...A friend is all of those things!

FRANÇOIS. You can teach me. Oh, forgive me, Nicole, forgive me!

NICOLE. And to think it was only last night I finally decided to marry you. Nestled in my corner by the fire, waiting for you and Genevieve to return... waiting patiently; I wasn't anxious; I knew that you were going to come up. My house would be yours. I waited for you until morning...(*She opens the window.*) And waiting like that I began to feel a little like your wife. I wasn't angry with you...having fun out there without me for so long...I loved you for the taste of pleasure that is you. I would have had the patience to wait my whole life...I was that sure of you. It would have felt so good to always forgive you for your neglect...to never complain to you, to always be understanding...and to tell myself that maybe in the world there is only one woman capable of loving you the way you are. And the older you'd get, the closer you'd get to me, for none of the women you would have left me for would forgive you for your next dalliance.

You would have loved all of them, and so never really loved any of them. I would be the only one who would never reproach you, because my love would have been profound, vast; it would have flourished...survived regardless of your behaviour, even of your thoughts. And that is what you have broken, what you have stopped from becoming real. There was only one woman whom you did not have the right to choose as a rival. And that woman is my daughter...the mirror of myself against whom I have no defence. This rival is stronger than me; she is young, beautiful, and I love her. She is the only one whom I fear because in loving her it is my own past that you love. Do you have any understanding of how you have hurt me and which you cannot undo? Do you have any idea especially of the wrong you have done to me, any concept that from this moment this house is closed to you?

FRANÇOIS. Nicole...don't chase me away. I need you...I need this house...Your love would have transformed me.

NICOLE. I can no longer be a sister of charity.[16]

FRANÇOIS. I might have eventually loved you the way you wanted me to.

NICOLE. It's too late.

FRANÇOIS. I don't want to leave forever. Ask me to do anything. I have no other home but yours; I want to stay…I want to stay, under any terms.

NICOLE. (*Cynical.*) Under any terms? So, then if my daughter loved you? You would perhaps ask me for her hand…?

FRANÇOIS. (*Firmly.*) Your daughter does love me.

NICOLE. No. Be quiet!

FRANÇOIS. And I am asking you for her hand.

NICOLE cries out like a wounded animal. She crumples into the chair. GENEVIEVE, who has heard everything, enters and kneels at her mother's feet.

GENEVIEVE. Forgive me, mama, I never knew you loved me so much.

NICOLE. (*Pushing GENEVIEVE away.*) Go away!

FRANÇOIS. Come here, Genevieve!

GENEVIEVE. (*Standing.*) Get out, mister! Leave! Mama…mama…You don't understand. I never loved this man…I hate him…I hate him…It was you who asked me to be nice to him, and then…I wanted to see his true face… (*Kneeling again and speaking as if to someone ill.*) Today you are angry with me, but later…perhaps much later, you will thank me. We would have been so unhappy!

NICOLE. (*Gently pushes GENEVIEVE aside. GENEVIEVE crosses US. NICOLE, lost and in despair, no longer hearing anything.*) François, my love…my poor love…I loved you…I knew all your weaknesses, your shortfalls…It will be so difficult to no longer suffer for you. (*More sweetly, tenderly, without revulsion.*) Go away…go away and don't look at me…don't speak to me… remember how we parted, every evening…Remember me the way I was yesterday, fresh, young, still pretty…Do not look at this poor haggard face, don't stare at the lines your leaving has etched there…Take with you your light heart that I adored…leave me only that beautiful lie your voice lulled me with…Go…and don't let me even hear the noise of your footsteps on the carpet…I will believe that you have never left…

At this point, FRANÇOIS is at the door he backed over to, heartbroken. He is about to leave, but the following sentence immobilizes him.

NICOLE. Remember the evening when I watched you sleeping in the big chair by the fireplace. Every evening I will watch you sleep…Go…Go, my poor love, I don't understand why you're still here. (*Then with infinite sweetness, passionate and painful.*) Go! I want to be alone to think of you!

CURTAIN

ARDOUIN. It is you who are abandoning us.

GENEVIEVE*'s head appears in the doorway* SR.

GENEVIEVE. Grandpa, aren't you coming?
ARDOUIN. Of course, in a few minutes. You can see I'm talking with your
  mother.
GENEVIEVE. Francine is crying.
ARDOUIN. Francine? Why?
GENEVIEVE. I hurt her. And you're the only one who can make her feel better.
ARDOUIN. I understand. I'll go up right away.
NICOLE. And you, Genevieve, stay here. I have something to talk to you about.

GENEVIEVE *enters, but reluctantly.*

ARDOUIN. See you in a few minutes, Nicole. (*He exits.*)
GENEVIEVE. I would rather go with grandpa.
NICOLE. I don't doubt it. (*Drily.*) What did you do to make Francine cry?
GENEVIEVE. We were arguing...
NICOLE. What about...?
GENEVIEVE. Dr. Normand.
NICOLE. Again? And what did you say to her to make her cry?
GENEVIEVE. (*Hesitating.*) I told her...I told her that you don't love us
  anymore...that you only care about him.
NICOLE. Genevieve, enough! For months now you have cast a shadow over all
  my joys. Until now I have put up with your wounding comments without a
  word of reproach. I was hoping for a change in your attitude. I was patient.
  But I can't be anymore. I only have a moment to talk to you; it's not the best
  time. This evening I have to think about other things besides you.
GENEVIEVE. You're always thinking about other things besides me.
NICOLE. Ungrateful! Have I not loved you enough? Have I not spoiled you
  enough? For years I have sacrificed my youth for you. When you were little,
  I didn't have any friends so I could spend more time with you. Remember
  when you had scarlet fever; I hardly slept, hardly changed my clothes...
  And when the doctor said one night that he didn't have any more hope, I
  held you in my arms until morning. I kept you warm with my own body
  and if you didn't die during those hours it was because I breathed for you.
  Remember...remember...
GENEVIEVE. (*Hard.*) Only too well.
NICOLE. And...
GENEVIEVE. You loved me...you loved me too much!
NICOLE. I still love you.

GENEVIEVE. No.

NICOLE. Be quiet. You are being so unfair. I have a right to happiness; it's my turn.

GENEVIEVE. Your happiness is built on our suffering.

NICOLE. Be quiet! Be quiet. Your attitude is disgusting. You are nothing but a selfish brat. You have no idea what love is. You are stealing my happiness, sucking the life out of me. (*GENEVIEVE is rigid, immobile like a statue, her face hard, tight-lipped.*) Genevieve!...Genevieve!...in the name of all I've done for you in the past, answer me. (*NICOLE throws herself to the ground, wraps her arms around GENEVIEVE's knees and cries in begging her.*) My little girl... my Genevieve, have pity on me...My fate is in your hands...one word, a single word and you can make me the happiest woman alive; one word, a single word and you can break my heart with your fingers.

During these final words, GENEVIEVE's face softens. Her heart melts. She slides to her knees beside her mother, laying her cheek on that of her mother.

GENEVIEVE. Mama...mama...We are so unhappy! I don't want you to be miserable! I don't want you to cry...(*Then hiding her face in her hands.*) But I cannot stand the idea of that Dr Normand in this house...with us... for always...your husband! I love you, mama...I love you too much...I am jealous...I hate him...He has stolen our mother from us. Help me...have pity on me! I feel I am wrong. I am ashamed for being selfish...Mama...oh... mama. Can't we go back to loving each other like we did before...before he came? If only I had some friends at least...if I was out in the world, if I had my début...Maybe then I would think of something besides this horrible nightmare.

NICOLE. (*Rocking GENEVIEVE.*) Maybe that's a solution...listen, Genevieve, tomorrow would you like to go riding in my place...with...the doctor?

GENEVIEVE. Oh no! Not with him!

NICOLE. You hate him as much as that?

GENEVIEVE. (*Reflecting.*) Maybe not. If you didn't love him, I could think differently about him.

NICOLE. Would you like to go out with us sometimes, to get used to him?

GENEVIEVE. If you like. I will try not to be jealous. I do so want you to be happy.

NICOLE. Thank you, Genevieve! I think we are going to start to all be happy again.

GENEVIEVE. (*Sadly.*) Perhaps.

ROSE. (*Enters.*) Madame, the doctor is here.

NICOLE. Oh! He came...I don't want him to see me like this...I am too upset. Come here, Genevieve...(*To the maid.*) Rose, ask Mr. Ardouin to take care of the doctor.

GENEVIEVE. I'll go warn grandpa; he's with Francine.

NICOLE. If you like. (*Tenderly.*) But come back up to my room.
GENEVIEVE. Right away, mama. (*She throws a kiss at her mother and exits.*)
NICOLE. Rose, show the doctor up.
ROSE. Yes, ma'am. (*ROSE and NICOLE exit.*)

The stage remains empty for a few seconds. FRANÇOIS *enters, wearing his grand cape which covers his 1825 suit. He is holding his hat and gloves.* ROSE *follows him.*

ROSE. Mr. Ardouin and Madam will be here in a moment, sir.
FRANÇOIS. Thank you, Rose. (*ROSE exits.* FRANÇOIS *lights a cigarette.*)
ARDOUIN. (*Entering.*) Good evening, doctor.
FRANÇOIS. Good evening, Mr. Ardouin. Isn't Nicole here?

APPENDIX II

CHARLES. Nicole, tell me.
NICOLE. After dinner, Genevieve was particularly insolent.
CHARLES. About what?
NICOLE. About my going to the ball.
CHARLES. Ahhh.
NICOLE. A few minutes later, alone with her, I couldn't help but scold her for her attitude towards François. All the words I'd held back for months came pouring out, rather harsh words I think.
CHARLES. Poor Genevieve!
NICOLE. Protestations, tears, hurtful accusations; it was a terrible scene...
CHARLES. I'm understanding less and less why Genevieve went to the ball.
NICOLE. Just wait. When our nerves were a bit calmer, our chat ended with a bit of rapprochement. Together we talked about finding ways to get past our suffering. And that was the moment when François arrived. Genevieve and I had already both decided to each do our best: she to be nicer to the doctor and me to go out more often with my daughters and father.
CHARLES. But...the ball...
NICOLE. I'm coming to that. While my father entertained François, I was still with Genevieve, touching up my make-up. The whole scene had shattered me. I had a pounding migraine. I was afraid of my poor tired face. Beside me, reflected in the mirror was the slight figure of my daughter. I suddenly understood the whole reality of my 40 years next to her youth. I was so weary...the thought of facing all the guests at the ball filled me with dread. And then I had this fantastic idea...to send Genevieve there, to the ball...in my place...with François...
CHARLES. What a strange idea!

The Winnipeg Ballet Club (1939)

A Happy and Glorious *Debut*

ERIN JOELLE MCCURDY

THE ROYAL WINNIPEG BALLET (RWB), founded by Gweneth Lloyd and Betty Hey (later Farrally), was the first professional ballet company established in Canada. From its humble beginnings as an amateur local ballet club, the RWB has flourished, developing its own distinct aesthetic and earning a renowned reputation at home and abroad. Overcoming its share of internal turmoil and close brushes with bankruptcy, the company has been lauded for its innovativeness, perseverance, and grit—qualities that have sustained the RWB as North America's oldest continually operating ballet company. For these reasons, the 1939 debut of the Winnipeg Ballet Club, which would become the RWB, is a notable moment in Canadian dance history. As part of the *Happy and Glorious* pageant staged for the 1939 Royal Tour, however, this inaugural performance also sheds light on the broader socio-historical circumstances surrounding King George VI and Queen Elizabeth's cross-Canada visit.

Although traces of the Winnipeg Ballet Club's debut are scant, the pageant program (see Figure 20.1), photographs, and newspaper clippings that survive offer insight into the two original ballets produced by Lloyd and Hey for scenes in the *Happy and Glorious* pageant. Titled *Grain* (scene 8) and *Kilowatt Magic* (scene 10), the ballets expressed local identity, portraying "Winnipeg's debt of gratitude to wheat and cheap electrical power" ("Ballets Tell Story" 1939). When analyzed within the context of the pageant as a whole and the Royal Tour more broadly, the Winnipeg Ballet Club's debut also reveals insight into how the arts in Canada were used to promote nationalism and strengthen colonial loyalties as the Second World War loomed on the horizon.

Prior to the Royal Tour, Canada had been growing increasingly independent from Britain. This newfound autonomy was partially cultivated in response to the sacrifices made on behalf of Britain during the First World War and the subsequent hardships of the Great Depression. Throughout the 1920s, Canada had begun asserting its autonomy through foreign policy, and in 1931 Britain passed the Statute of Westminster, conceding its legal authority over Canada and the other Commonwealth nations, except in areas of voluntary subordination. In response to these shifting legislative ties, the Royal Tour aimed to galvanize emotional and symbolic ones (Rayner 2011, 73).

Initially proposed by Canadian Prime Minister William Lyon Mackenzie King in 1937 as a visit to Ottawa, the trip grew into a month-long cross-country

FIGURE 20.1: *Front cover,* Happy and Glorious Program, *May 20–27, 1939.*
Courtesy of Dance Collection Danse.

tour, with four days spent south of the border (Rayner 2011, 73). As plans for the trip evolved, so did its circumstances. Tensions overseas were rising and, with them, the threat of another world war. For Britain, the tour thus had the crucial purpose of strengthening Canadian and American allegiances. If Britain were to go to war, it would need its former colonies to follow.

The tour marked the first time any reigning British monarch set foot on North American soil (Rayner 2011, 73), and each stop drew substantial crowds hoping to catch a glimpse of the King and Queen. In addition to the royal appearances, popular attractions were produced to entertain the throngs of Canadians and Americans who descended on hosting cities (MacDonnell 1989, 125). For the occasion, Winnipeg produced the pageant *Happy and Glorious: A Cavalcade of Welcome.* This pageant applauded the city's cosmopolitanism, while showcasing its popular Little Theatre scene. Under the direction of pageant master John Craig, and assistant pageant master Irene Craig,[1] the pageant captured the themes of the tour, which celebrated Canada as a diverse nation united under the Crown. The mixed program featured choral singing, orchestral interludes, tableaux, dramas, social and traditional dances, and a sing-along. It also included the new ballets produced by Lloyd and Hey, two recent British transplants.

Lloyd and Hey arrived in Winnipeg less than a year before the Royal Tour. Prior to this, Lloyd had been the co-founder of a successful dance school in Leeds, UK. Hey, fourteen years her junior, had been a student at the school before joining the ranks of the teaching staff. After operating the school for over a decade, Lloyd was ready for a change, and following a trip to visit friends in Winnipeg, she decided to try her luck establishing a ballet school across the Atlantic. When Hey learned of her plans, she eagerly joined her (Wyman 1978, 17).

Once in Winnipeg, the pair rented a modest studio in the heart of the city and founded the Canadian School of Ballet. Initial enrolment was low, but Lloyd and Hey took strategic steps to increase public interest and support. They approached private girls' schools with offers to teach revived Greek dance, citing its popularity in London, and found employment instructing the daughters of the city's elite (Wyman 1978, 21). Monthly, they also welcomed prominent locals into their studio for lecture-demonstrations about ballet (Wyman 1978, 23). Their most notable strategy, however, was to establish the Winnipeg Ballet Club. At the time, professional dance performances in Winnipeg were limited to international touring companies; there were no local opportunities for serious technical training, and few throughout the country (Wyman 1978, 20). Under the unpaid leadership of Lloyd and Hey, the amateur club aimed to increase local interest in ballet through quality performances, which would, in turn, improve enrolment at the school (Smith 2004, 200). With the promise of free training to anyone who successfully auditioned (Wyman 1978, 21)—an appealing offer at the tail end of the Great Depression—they attracted some of the strongest home-grown talent from existing dance schools, much to the chagrin of local teachers (Adams 1999, 13).

The Winnipeg Ballet Club had not yet performed publicly when the pair was approached by city officials to contribute two short ballets to the *Happy and Glorious* pageant program. Lloyd and Hey's networking had proved effective (Wyman 1978, 25).[2] Together, their complementary abilities created a powerful partnership: Lloyd acted as artistic director and choreographer, while Hey, a disciplined teacher, assumed the role of ballet mistress. The requested ballets were to be around five minutes each, feature "plenty of leg," and embody the local themes of grain and hydroelectric power. Presumably, on account of their British citizenship, teaching experience, and growing society connections, Lloyd and Hey were also tasked with coaching city officials and their spouses on how to bow or curtsey to the royal couple (Wyman 1978, 26).

1. Husband-and-wife team John and Irene Craig were well-known figures in the city's amateur theatre scene. In 1930 John Craig became the first professional director of the Winnipeg Little Theatre. For six years he managed the theatre with Irene, who led workshops and was in charge of costumes, props, and sets. Under their leadership, the theatre was a critical and popular success, serving as a model within the Canadian Little Theatre Movement. The couple also had previous experience producing large-scale civic pageants. With Irene assisting, John had directed pageants honouring the coronation of King George (1937) and La Vérendrye (1938) (Stuart 1984, 89, 92–93). The latter, held during the bicentennial of the French Canadian fur trader's arrival at the confluence of the Assiniboine and Red Rivers, endorsed a colonialist narrative of the "discovery and development of Western Canada" ("La Verendrye Pageant" 1938).

2. The school, however, would take a while to turn a profit. Lloyd and Hey were forced to live frugally and were aided by a yearly stipend from Lloyd's grandmother (Wyman 1978, 25).

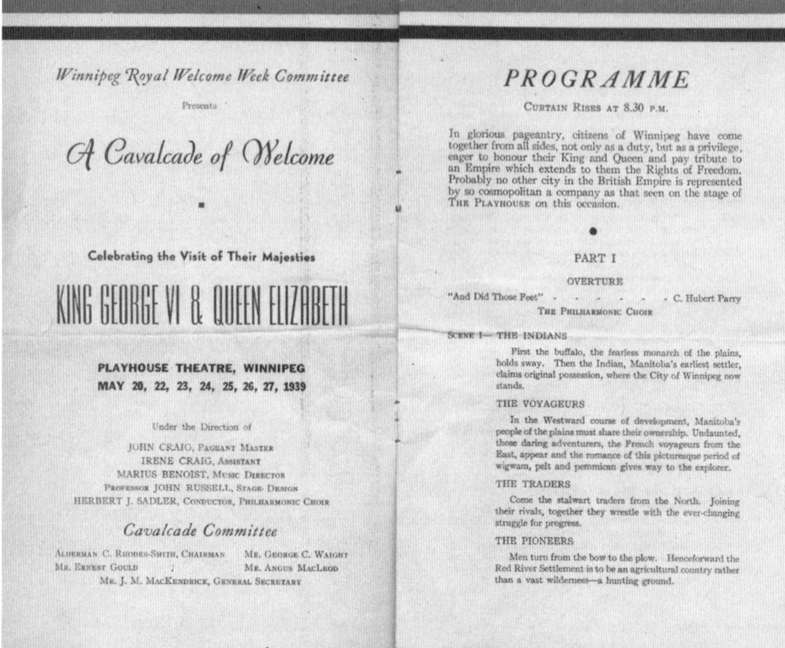

FIGURE 20.2: *Pages 2 and 3, Happy and Glorious Program, May 20–27, 1939.*

Courtesy of Dance Collection Danse.

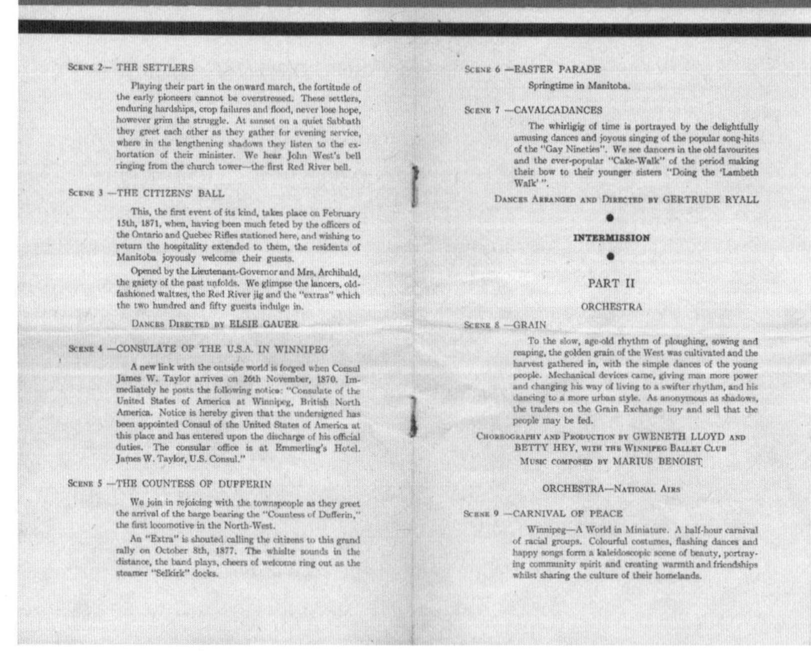

FIGURE 20.3: *Pages 4 and 5, Happy and Glorious Program, May 20–27, 1939.*

Courtesy of Dance Collection Danse.

The opening night of the week-long pageant received a rave review in the local newspaper. The headline of the *Tribune* declared that the "Civic Pageant Wins Triumph at Opening" and reported on its "enthusiastic" reception ("Civic Pageant" 1939). The pageant "blithely" depicted "Manitoba's colorful history" as a "saga of 200 years" through thirteen short scenes, two of which consisted of the new ballets ("Civic Pageant" 1939). Overall, the format of the pageant was not novel. While the ballets were entirely new additions to the program, *Happy and Glorious* was modelled after two previous local pageants staged by John and Irene Craig, and it featured many of the same cast members. Nevertheless, the press decided that *Happy and Glorious* outshone its predecessors: "Its pace was faster, its scenes briefer, the whole show was shorter and it had more vivid action and comedy than its forerunners" ("Civic Pageant" 1939).

To an extent, the cast of the pageant reflected the city's diversity, with "400 artists representing twenty-one of the nationalities mingled in Winnipeg's cosmopolitan population" ("Civic Pageant" 1939). In the 1930s, Winnipeg was the fourth largest city in Canada, and its railway access attracted a large immigrant population. Reviews of the pageant frequently mentioned scene nine, the "Carnival of Peace," which featured members of Winnipeg's different "racial groups...sharing the culture of their homelands" in a colourful "kaleidoscopic scene of beauty" that incorporated costume, song, and dance (Program 1939; see Figure 20.3). Yet, Indigenous Peoples were significantly absent from this celebration of diversity. In fact, Indigenous representation appears to have been limited to the pageant's first half, which recounted Winnipeg's settlement and development from a colonizer's perspective (see Figures 20.2 and 20.3). In this partial narrative, six thousand years of First Peoples' histories were reduced to a "picturesque period of wigwam, pelt and pemmican" that quickly yielded to French explorers and the perceived imperative of westward development. Far from problematizing colonialism, the pageant applauded courageous voyageurs, traders, and pioneers and the "onward march" of progress that transformed the Red River Settlement from "vast wilderness" to "agricultural country" (Program 1939). It also failed to acknowledge Indigenous agricultural practices predating colonial contact.

The pageant finale, "The Royal Salute," was described in the newspaper as a "magnificently regal" tribute ("Civic Pageant" 1939) in which "Winnipeg, the Gateway of the West joins with Canada in saluting the Crown, Symbol of Our Freedom" (Program 1939; see Figure 20.4). It would appear as though the pageant celebrated diversity as long as Winnipeggers ultimately united in their loyalty to the British Empire. This sentiment was reinforced by Manitoba Premier John Bracken when he publicly addressed the King and Queen, extending "the assurance" of Manitobans' "deepest loyalty and respect." In the speech, broadcast nationally by CBC radio, Bracken declared that Manitobans, "now of many racial origins," were "united" in their "common citizenship," "proud to be members of the Commonwealth of British nations and prouder

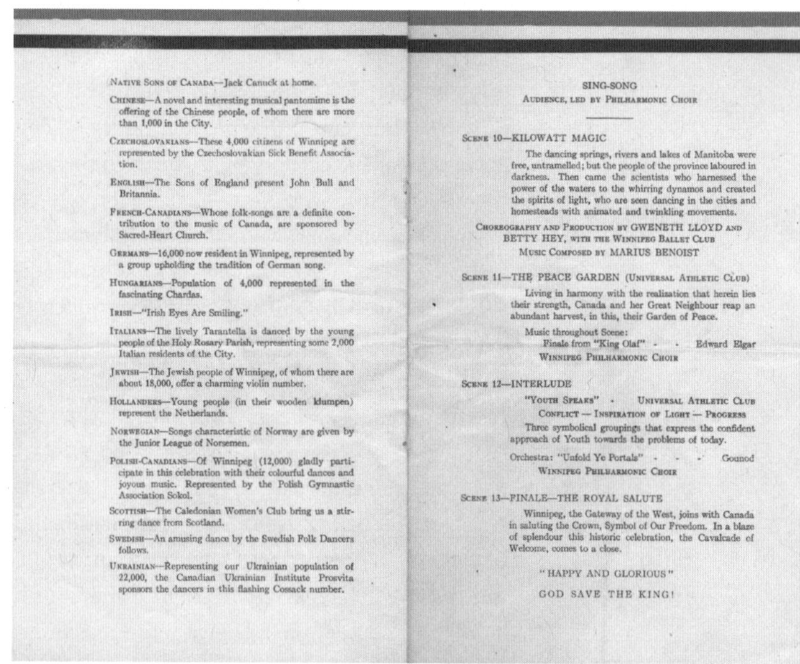

NATIVE SONS OF CANADA—Jack Canuck at home.

CHINESE—A novel and interesting musical pantomime is the offering of the Chinese people, of whom there are more than 1,000 in the City.

CZECHOSLOVAKIANS—These 4,000 citizens of Winnipeg are represented by the Czechoslovakian Sick Benefit Association.

ENGLISH—The Sons of England present John Bull and Britannia.

FRENCH-CANADIANS—Whose folk-songs are a definite contribution to the music of Canada, are sponsored by Sacred-Heart Church.

GERMANS—16,000 now resident in Winnipeg, represented by a group upholding the tradition of German song.

HUNGARIANS—Population of 4,000 represented in the fascinating Chardas.

IRISH—"Irish Eyes Are Smiling."

ITALIANS—The lively Tarantella is danced by the young people of the Holy Rosary Parish, representing some 2,000 Italian residents of the City.

JEWISH—The Jewish people of Winnipeg, of whom there are about 18,000, offer a charming violin number.

HOLLANDERS—Young people (in their wooden klumpen) represent the Netherlands.

NORWEGIAN—Songs characteristic of Norway are given by the Junior League of Norsemen.

POLISH-CANADIANS—Of Winnipeg (12,000) gladly participate in this celebration with their colourful dances and joyous music. Represented by the Polish Gymnastic Association Sokol.

SCOTTISH—The Caledonian Women's Club bring us a stirring dance from Scotland.

SWEDISH—An amusing dance by the Swedish Folk Dancers follows.

UKRAINIAN—Representing our Ukrainian population of 22,000, the Canadian Ukrainian Institute Prosvita sponsors the dancers in this flashing Cossack number.

SING-SONG
AUDIENCE, LED BY PHILHARMONIC CHOIR

SCENE 10—KILOWATT MAGIC

The dancing springs, rivers and lakes of Manitoba were free, untramelled; but the people of the province laboured in darkness. Then came the scientists who harnessed the power of the waters to the whirring dynamos and created the spirits of light, who are seen dancing in the cities and homesteads with animated and twinkling movements.

CHOREOGRAPHY AND PRODUCTION BY GWENETH LLOYD AND BETTY HEY, WITH THE WINNIPEG BALLET CLUB
MUSIC COMPOSED BY MARIUS BENOIST

SCENE 11—THE PEACE GARDEN (UNIVERSAL ATHLETIC CLUB)

Living in harmony with the realization that herein lies their strength, Canada and her Great Neighbour reap an abundant harvest, in this, their Garden of Peace.

Music throughout Scene:
Finale from "King Olaf" - - Edward Elgar
WINNIPEG PHILHARMONIC CHOIR

SCENE 12—INTERLUDE

"YOUTH SPEAKS" - UNIVERSAL ATHLETIC CLUB
CONFLICT — INSPIRATION OF LIGHT — PROGRESS
Three symbolical groupings that express the confident approach of Youth towards the problems of today.

Orchestra: "Unfold Ye Portals" - - - Gounod
WINNIPEG PHILHARMONIC CHOIR

SCENE 13—FINALE—THE ROYAL SALUTE

Winnipeg, the Gateway of the West, joins with Canada in saluting the Crown, Symbol of Our Freedom. In a blaze of splendour this historic celebration, the Cavalcade of Welcome, comes to a close.

"HAPPY AND GLORIOUS"

GOD SAVE THE KING!

FIGURE 20.4: *Pages 6 and 7*, Happy and Glorious Program, *May 20–27, 1939.*

Courtesy of Dance Collection Danse.

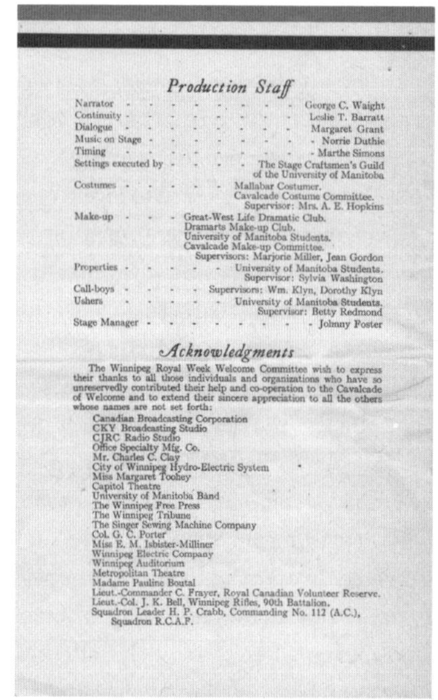

Production Staff

Narrator - - - - - - - - George C. Waight
Continuity - - - - - - - - Leslie T. Barratt
Dialogue - - - - - - - - Margaret Grant
Music on Stage - - - - - - - - Norrie Duthie
Timing - - - - - - - - - Marthe Simons
Settings executed by - - - - The Stage Craftsmen's Guild of the University of Manitoba
Costumes - - - - - Mallabar Costumer. Cavalcade Costume Committee. Supervisor: Mrs. A. E. Hopkins
Make-up - - - Great-West Life Dramatic Club. Dramarts Make-up Club. University of Manitoba Students. Cavalcade Make-up Committee. Supervisors: Marjorie Miller, Jean Gordon
Properties - - - - - University of Manitoba Students. Supervisor: Sylvia Washington
Call-boys - - - - Supervisors: Wm. Klyn, Dorothy Klyn
Ushers - - - - University of Manitoba Students. Supervisor: Betty Redmond
Stage Manager - - - - - - - - Johnny Foster

Acknowledgments

The Winnipeg Royal Week Welcome Committee wish to express their thanks to all those individuals and organizations who have so unreservedly contributed their help and co-operation to the Cavalcade of Welcome and to extend their sincere appreciation to all the others whose names are not set forth:

Canadian Broadcasting Corporation
CKY Broadcasting Studio
CJRC Radio Studio
Office Specialty Mfg. Co.
Mr. Charles C. Clay
City of Winnipeg Hydro-Electric System
Miss Margaret Toohey
Capitol Theatre
University of Manitoba Band
The Winnipeg Free Press
The Winnipeg Tribune
The Singer Sewing Machine Company
Col. G. C. Porter
Miss E. M. Isbister-Milliner
Winnipeg Electric Company
Winnipeg Auditorium
Metropolitan Theatre
Madame Pauline Boutal
Lieut.-Commander C. Frayer, Royal Canadian Volunteer Reserve.
Lieut.-Col. J. K. Bell, Winnipeg Rifles, 90th Battalion.
Squadron Leader H. P. Crabb, Commanding No. 112 (A.C.), Squadron R.C.A.F.

FIGURE 20.5: *Back cover,* Happy and Glorious Program, *May 20–27, 1939.*

Courtesy of Dance Collection Danse.

still of the traditions of the British Crown and of the British parliamentary institutions" (Bracken 1939).

In contrast to "The Royal Salute," the two ballets produced by Lloyd and Hey, which were set to music composed by Marius Benoist ("Ballets Tell Story" 1939), celebrated sources of local pride. Comprising scenes 8 and 10 in the pageant's second half, the ballets reportedly involved sixty participants ("Welcome Week" 1939) and bookended the "Carnival of Peace." Scene 8, the ballet *Grain*, was inspired by—and titled after—Winnipeg's chief export (although, leading up to the performance, the work was poetically titled *Sheaves of Gold*) ("Ballets Tell Story" 1939). The program description suggests that *Grain* featured a rhythmic progression from the "slow, age-old rhythm" of manual labour to the "swifter rhythm" of modern machinery, which seemed to parallel an evolution from the "simple dances of the young people" to a "more urban style" (Program 1939; see Figure 20.3). A rehearsal photograph printed in the *Winnipeg Tribune* shows a group of dancers "whirling in the colourful ballet" ("Cavalcade of Pageantry" 1939). With the women in bonnets and aprons and the men in plaid shirts with rolled sleeves and trousers, the image appears to capture the "simple dances" of the harvest. An article in the *Winnipeg Free Press*, released a few weeks before the pageant's opening, reveals that the ballet originally concluded with "the business man co-operating with the farmer, creating harmony and happiness all moving together with simplicity and a common aim—the providing of grain for the people" ("Ballets Tell Story" 1939). Interestingly, the narrative provided in the program concludes with the "anonymous shadows" of the Grain Exchange traders, who "buy and sell that the people may be fed" (Program 1939). While this revised ending is less idyllic, it seems to hint at farmers' dissatisfaction with the Winnipeg Grain Exchange and their mistrust of the railways, marketing companies, and private traders that had possessed disproportionate control over wheat prices.[3]

Scene 10, the ballet *Kilowatt Magic*, depicted the hydroelectric power produced by the Winnipeg River, which was among the most affordable in the world (Wyman 1978, 26). This second ballet was also evocatively described in the program, but unlike *Grain*, its narrative structure varied minimally from the earlier account in the *Winnipeg Free Press*. Also featuring an arc of technological advancement, the narrative begins by representing the "free, untrammelled" dancing waters of Manitoba (see Figure 20.4). When channelled by the scientists, these waters set the "whirring dynamos" in motion, producing "the spirits of light, who are seen dancing in the cities and homesteads with animated and twinkling movements" (Program 1939). Two photographs from the production reveal additional details about the work. The first image captures Paddy Stone and Edith Jamieson, two of the rwb's earliest stars, in *Kilowatt Magic* (see Figure 20.6). Presumably abstractions of electric power, the pair assume dynamic poses, wearing ultramodern, androgynous costumes. The second image, of Doris Swain, seemingly represents a "spirit of light," with her skirt overlaid in what appears to be a twinkling layer of cellophane (see Figure 20.7). According to one attendee, the material featured prominently in the ballet; they recalled "a great deal of cellophane and some earnest young men flailing their arms in symbolism of the wheels of industry" (quoted in Wyman 1978, 26).

Interpreted in context, the ballets functioned as pre-war propaganda, championing resources essential to the war effort while overlooking the broader implications of their subject matter. As the Second World War unfolded, the Wartime Information Board would promote hydroelectric power as the source of Canada's manufacturing strength, and wartime measures would result in expanded power generation and conservation strategies (Evenden 2009, 847, 853). In the long term, however, hydroelectric development in Manitoba, and throughout Canada, would have detrimental effects, adversely affecting water levels and quality. Like agricultural development, it also displaced Indigenous Peoples, disrupting hunting, trapping, and transportation, and impacting cultures, communities, and daily lives.

Wheat quite literally had a history of fuelling the Allied powers; their reliance on the Canadian staple during the previous world war had stimulated a wheat boom. To meet demand, farmers went into debt acquiring equipment and land. With the global market collapse of the Great Depression and droughts of the 1930s, wheat farmers were hit especially hard (Easterbrook and Aitken 1988, 489–93). With the exception of a shadowy depiction of the Grain Exchange traders, these social, economic, and environmental impacts of industrial and agricultural expansion seem to have been largely overlooked by both the ballets.

Unlike the pageant's light-hearted depiction of imperialism, 1930s Winnipeg did have its share of politically engaged theatre. The Workers' Theatre, which was part of the Winnipeg branch of the Communist-led Progressive Arts Club, revolted against the status quo through agitprop readings, plays, and satire (Stuart 1984, 94). Elsewhere at this time, socially conscious dancers were working alongside leftist theatre groups to achieve similar political ends. In New York City, the Workers' Dance League (renamed the New Dance League) supported the development of politicized, anti-balletic dance as a weapon of revolutionary class struggle (Graff 1997, 7–8).

In June 1940 the Winnipeg Ballet Club would return to the Playhouse Theatre with its first full-length program. This two-day run took place in a different political climate: the Second World War had become a reality. The previous September, following Hitler's invasion of Poland, Britain declared war on Germany. Less than a week later, Canada followed suit, confirming the allegiances portrayed in the regal finale of *Happy and Glorious*. In this context, the club's performance was promoted as a "courageous" display in which Winnipeg would "carry on the tradition of ballet now interrupted in Europe" ("Ballet in Winnipeg" 1940). In this spirit of "carrying on" in the face of war, the ballet promised "to show mankind the ideal" while navigating

FIGURE 20.6: *Paddy Stone and Edith Jamieson in Kilowatt Magic, 1939.*
Courtesy of the Royal Winnipeg Ballet Archives.

FIGURE 20.7: *Doris Swain in Kilowatt Magic, 1939.*
Courtesy of the Royal Winnipeg Ballet Archives.

"the realms of beauty in movement, color and music" ("Ballet in Winnipeg" 1940). As a popular diversion and colonial tradition, the ballet was framed as a celebration of human achievement during a period of mass destruction.

The mixed program, which included an eighteenth-century comedy and a series of romantic vignettes, culminated with an extended version of *Kilowatt Magic*, which one reviewer described as a "so-called futuristic ballet" ("Ballet Thrills" 1940). In the *National Monthly*, Ray Darby applauded the extended work as a "startlingly modern dramatization of the development of electric power, in which…lighting, make-up and vigorous movement combined to hold the audience spellbound" (quoted in Adams 1999, 14).

Although the *Happy and Glorious* pageant commemorated the Royal Tour, the King and Queen did not attend the performance. In 1951, however, the Winnipeg Ballet, which had become a full-fledged company, performed for their daughter Princess Elizabeth and her husband the Duke of Edinburgh on their tour of Canada (Wyman 1978, 80). The following year, the princess ascended to the throne, and in 1953, under her rule as Queen Elizabeth II, the Winnipeg Ballet was granted its "Royal" status. At the time, the RWB was only the third ballet company in the world—and the only one outside of Europe—to receive the royal designation (Wyman 1978, 83). Throughout the twentieth century and into the twenty-first, the RWB would go on to garner international recognition, acting as "an unofficial, but highly celebrated, ambassador" for Canada (Lindgren 2004, 8), while still maintaining its own unique Winnipeg style.

Bibliography and Further Reading

Adams, Lawrence. 1999. "Sifting through the First Decade of the RWB." *Dance Collection Danse Magazine*, no. 48, 1, 7, 10, 13, 15.

"Ballet in Winnipeg." 1940. *Winnipeg Tribune*, June 10, 1940, 6.

"Ballet Thrills Large Audience." 1940. *Winnipeg Tribune*, June 12, 1940, 10.

"Ballets Tell Story of Farm and Power Development." 1939. *Winnipeg Free Press*, May 3, 1939, 6.

Bracken, John. 1939. "1939 Royal Tour Rolls through Winnipeg." Recorded May 24, 1939. *CBC Digital Archives*. http://www.cbc.ca/archives/entry/royal-tour-rolls-through-winnipeg.

"Cavalcade of Pageantry." 1939. *Winnipeg Tribune*, May 19, 1939, 5.

"Civic Pageant Wins Triumph at Opening." 1939. *Winnipeg Tribune*, May 22, 1939, 5.

Easterbrook, W.T., and Hugh G.J. Aitken. 1988. *Canadian Economic History*. Toronto: University of Toronto Press.

Evenden, Matthew. 2009. "Mobilizing Rivers: Hydro-Electricity, the State, and World War II in Canada." *Annals of the Association of American Geographers* 99 (5): 845–55. doi: 10.1080/00045600903245847.

Graff, Ellen. 1997. *Stepping Left: Dance and Politics in New York City, 1928–1942*. Durham, NC: Duke University Press.

Lindgren, Allana. 2004. "Why Winnipeg?" *Dance Collection Danse Magazine*, no. 57, 6–10.

MacDonnell, Tom. 1989. *Daylight upon Magic: The Royal Tour of Canada - 1939*. Toronto: Macmillan of Canada.

Program for *Happy and Glorious: A Cavalcade of Welcome*. 1939. Box 1, folder 3, David Adams fonds, Dance Collection Danse, Toronto.

Rayner, William. 2011. *Canada on the Doorstep: 1939*. Toronto: Dundurn.

Smith, Cheryl. 2004. "Stepping Out: A New Look at Canada's Early Ballet Companies, 1939 to 1960." In *Canadian Dance: Visions and Stories*, edited by Selma Landen Odom and Mary Jane Warner, 197–223. Toronto: Dance Collection Danse Press/es.

Stuart, E. Ross. 1984. *The History of Prairie Theatre: The Development of Theatre in Alberta, Manitoba and Saskatchewan, 1833–1982*. Toronto: Simon & Pierre.

"La Verendrye Pageant Holds Capacity Crowd." 1938. *Winnipeg Tribune*, September 5, 1938, 3.

"Welcome Week Pageant Will Open Saturday Evening." 1939. *Winnipeg Tribune*, May 19, 1939, 8.

Wyman, Max. 1978. *The Royal Winnipeg Ballet: The First Forty Years*. Toronto: Doubleday.

21 : *William Tell* (ca. 1943–1945)

Theatre in Captivity

CODY POULTON & JORDAN STANGER-ROSS

INTERNED BY THE CANADIAN GOVERNMENT during the Second World War, Japanese Canadians turned to theatre as part of their efforts to rebuild their cultural and creative lives in a context of unjust incarceration (Read and the Landscapes of Injustice Collective 2016). Friedrich Schiller's *William Tell*, in a Japanese adaptation by John Nihei, a young man who lived and produced theatre in the 1940s at the Tashme internment camp, is one of several manuscripts of Japanese playtexts donated to the Nikkei (Japanese Canadian) National Museum in Burnaby, British Columbia.

In the decades prior to the Second World War, Japanese Canadians built vibrant communities, predominantly in British Columbia, despite racist immigration policies and laws that prohibited or limited the licensing of businesses, the practice of certain professions like law, service in the armed forces, and the right to vote. Nonetheless, Japanese Canadians created diverse and successful lives throughout Pacific Canada. They excelled as fishers and farmers, and also established urban commercial hubs, most notably along Vancouver's Powell Street (Adachi 1976, 142–53). By the 1930s, they owned (and worked in) lumberyards, laboured in mines, cooked meals, ran groceries, gardened, shaved beards, and ran small businesses in locales throughout coastal British Columbia (Sumida 1935; Adachi 1976; Takata 1983; Ayukawa 2008; Fukawa and Fukawa 2009; Switzer and Switzer 2012). Japanese Canadians founded schools, baseball teams, churches, temples, and communal associations.

In 1942, along with some 22,000 other Japanese Canadians, John Kumaji Nihei was evicted from his home in coastal British Columbia. That February, less than two months after Japan's attack on Pearl Harbor, the Canadian government used the authority of the War Measures Act to uproot and intern Canadians of Japanese ancestry living on the West Coast of Canada.[1] More than 12,000 people were sent to live in purpose-built camps and ghost towns in the interior of British Columbia, while some 4,000 others were shipped to beet farms in Alberta and Manitoba. Another 1,000 moved to "self-supporting camps" where, by special permission, internees arranged their own housing and sustenance. Many able-bodied men were sent to work in labour camps; those who resisted the uprooting and family break-ups were incarcerated in prisoner-of-war (POW) camps in Ontario. Once Japanese Canadians were interned, the government sold everything they had been forced to leave behind, without consent of the owners. Homes, farms, businesses, and innumerable personal belongings were lost forever: the proceeds of the sales used to support their basic needs during years of internment. In 1946, after Japan's surrender, almost 4,000 (most of them Canadian-born and naturalized Canadians) were deported to Japan, a country that many of them had never seen before. The remainder were banned from returning to the Pacific Coast and denied full rights of citizenship until 1949.

Entertainment in the internment camps, as it had been in the Japanese Canadian communities prior to the war, was divided along generational, linguistic, and cultural lines. Members of the first generation adapted the theatre, dance, and music of traditional Japan to their circumstances in Canada, while the younger generations of English-speaking Japanese Canadians eagerly adopted the popular culture of their contemporaries across North America. Their recitals of jazz and big band music and mixed dancing were frowned upon by many of their conservative elders. Like music and dance, theatrical performances were generally light-hearted attempts to provide some amusement and distraction from the tedium and privation of living in tarpaper shacks in the depths of cold winters in the British Columbia interior. Never far from their minds, however, was an awareness of their own predicament. Jean Kamimura, the daughter of John Nihei, recalls that one of the most popular songs sung by Nikkei young people was the Bing Crosby–Andrews Sisters's hit "Don't Fence Me In." Some interned Japanese Canadians, like Nihei, produced theatre, including this adapted version of Schiller's *William Tell*.

Nihei's love of theatre had been encouraged by his father, Yūjirō Nihei. A native of Fukushima Prefecture, Yūjirō had performed as an actor in provincial theatrical troupes in Japan before coming to Canada in 1907. In that year, the Asian Exclusion League sparked a riot in the Chinese Canadian and Japanese Canadian neighbourhoods of East Vancouver. Amidst the mayhem and destruction, Yūjirō was forced to flee and hide amongst fishing nets in nearby Steveston, an experience that convinced him to abandon Vancouver and to relocate north to smaller communities (Atkinson 2016). Like many Japanese Canadians along British Columbia's central coast, he worked in forestry and fishing canneries. His granddaughter, Jean Kamimura, recalls that "doing *shibai* (theatre) was my grandfather's hobby and passion" (interview 2017). He would entertain Japanese Canadians in towns along British Columbia's central coast like Essington, Prince Rupert, and Ocean Falls during the winter, when the mostly male communities had time off from work. All his savings were poured into buying props and costumes.

Yūjirō returned to Japan in 1924 upon the death of his wife, who was not allowed to accompany him to Canada. His son, John Nihei, continued to produce theatre in British Columbia. Born in Japan, John had immigrated to Canada in 1919 when he was sixteen. He boarded for the first three years with prominent socialite and activist Jessie Hall, at Killarney, her family mansion in Point Grey, Vancouver. Like his father, John made several trips back and forth

FIGURE 21.1: *The Engeiza (Performing Arts Troupe) in a kabuki production in Ocean Falls, 1931. Image courtesy of Jean Kamimura and the Nikkei National Museum.*

Figure 21.2: *Mrs. Tanaka and Mrs. Murakami playing Omiya and Kan'ichi in a 1935 production of Konjiki Yasha (Demon gold) in Ocean Falls. Though kabuki was typically a male-only performance genre, sometimes plays were performed by women in all the roles, as seen here with the heroine and hero of Ōzaki Kōyō's best-selling 1902 novel, which was adapted to stage and screen numerous times. Courtesy of Jean Kamimura and the Nikkei National Museum.*

between Canada and Japan to visit family; his wife and child were not allowed to immigrate until 1940. In addition to sharing his father's passion for theatre, John had a love of literature, art, history, music, and sports, and was active in the cultural life of Japanese communities.

When his family was uprooted from Ocean Falls in 1942, John Nihei spent the better part of the following year forced into roadwork, building the Yellowhead Highway; he was later reunited with his family in Tashme, the largest internment camp for Japanese Canadians, near Hope, British Columbia, where they lived until July 1945. There he organized concerts and other performances for the camp's entertainment committee. He continued to contribute to the social and cultural life of his community when they were moved to another camp in East Lillooet in the last month of the war; there they would remain until 1951. While in Lillooet, he engaged another of his passions, coaching the camp's baseball team. Because of the efforts of people like Nihei, the cultural lives of Japanese Canadians continued, despite the severe disruption of their material lives and civic belonging.

After he and his family were uprooted and interned, Nihei used theatre to both escape and express the hardship of the era. For *Issei* (first-generation Japanese immigrants) the model for theatre was kabuki, Japan's most popular performance art from the seventeenth century to modern times, but a few of Nihei's plays were also adaptations of puppet theatre and contemporary cinema. Not all of his plays were simple distractions from the troubles of daily life. One, *The Umbrella of Leaving a Child* (*Kowakaregasa*), was an adaptation of a 1933 film script by popular playwright and novelist Matsutarō Kawaguchi. This sentimental tragedy about a family torn apart must have resonated with audiences in the camps that were only too familiar with separation from loved ones.

Theatre-making in the internment camps remains a fairly undocumented aspect of the daily lives of the Japanese Canadian community during the Second World War. Tom Matsui, who was a teenager at the time, managed to smuggle in a camera with which he was able to create a precious archive of photographs of his family's time in Lillooet. The photograph in Figure 21.3 shows Nihei in one of the plays he staged in 1946 in the camp he and his family transferred to after Tashme, but Matsui's caption does not identify which play it was. Outside of these photographs and the text of this play, historians have found little record of these remarkable productions.

Despite some of the uncertainties of the history of Nihei's theatrical activities, we know that it was during the 1940s, in one of the camps—probably the Tashme camp where he and his family spent most of the decade—that his Japanese adaptation of Schiller's *William Tell* was staged. Translated back to English from John's script, a scene from the play is presented here as an example of this obscure but important moment in Canadian theatre history.

FIGURE 21.3: *John Nihei (with rifle) in a performance at East Lillooet, BC, 1946.*
Courtesy of the Japanese Canadian Cultural Centre.

William Tell concerns the legendary hero of the Swiss Confederacy who
assassinated the governor, Albrecht Gessler. Schiller's play had its first
production in Weimar in 1804 under the direction of his friend, the great
poet and dramatist Johann Wolfgang von Goethe. One of the cardinal texts
of German Romanticism, the play lauds the efforts of the common people
of Switzerland to slough off the shackles of their Habsburg overlords.
Undoubtedly, the Germans of Schiller's generation saw in this tale an object
lesson for their own efforts at liberation from Napoleon's expanding empire.
We know from his granddaughter that Nihei loved Gioachino Rossini's
famous overture for an opera based on this play. Translated here from Nihei's
adaptation is the most famous scene, from Act III, scene 3, in which the hero
is dared, on pain of death by the governor, to shoot an apple off his son's head.
Pitting virtue against evil and love against inhuman law, this is a dilemma
perfect for melodrama—or, for that matter, kabuki, a theatrical form that
revels in heroic spectacle, wicked villains, and decisive moral choices in which
"virtue is rewarded and vice punished" (*kanzen chōaku*). One of the prevailing
features in early modern Japanese theatre was the dramatization of a moral
dilemma between reason, or social obligation (*giri*), and passion, or personal
inclination (*ninjō*). Usually, tragedy ensues regardless of which wins over the

other, but occasionally (as in *William Tell*, or in many kabuki history plays) good triumphs over evil. No doubt an adaptation of Schiller's revolutionary play about liberation from despotism, in a mountainous land not unlike the British Columbia's interior, *William Tell* struck a chord with Nikkei audiences. It was an indictment of the shameful treatment that a supposed democracy meted out to an innocent minority in a time of racial prejudice and hostility.

Bibliography and Further Reading

Adachi, Ken. 1976. *The Enemy that Never Was.* Toronto: McClelland & Stewart.

Atkinson, David. 2016. "Out of One Borderland, Many: The 1907 Anti-Asian Riots and the Spatial Dimensions of Race and Migration in the Canadian-U.S. Pacific Borderlands." In *Entangling Migration History: Borderlands and Transnationalism in the United States and Canada*, edited by Benjamin Bryce and Alexander Freund. Oxford University Press Scholarship Online. doi: 10.5744/florida/9780813060736.001.0001.

Ayukawa, Michiko. 2008. *Hiroshima Immigrants in Canada, 1891–1941.* Vancouver: UBC Press.

Fukawa, Masako, and Stanley. 2009. *Spirit of the Nikkei Fleet: BC's Japanese Canadian Fishermen.* Madeira Park, BC: Harbour Publishing.

Kamimura, Jean. 2017. Interview with Cody Poulton. July 26, 2017.

Read, Heather, and the Landscapes of Injustice Collective. 2016. "The Legacy of a Hidden Camera: Acts of Making in Japanese-Canadian Internment Camps during the Second World War, as Depicted in Tom Matsui's Photograph Collection." *Material Culture Review / Revue de la culture matérielle* 84 (Fall): 26–47.

Robinson, Greg. 2009. *A Tragedy of Democracy: Japanese Confinement in North America.* New York: Columbia University Press.

Sumida, Rigenda. 1935. *Japanese in British Columbia.* MA thesis, University of British Columbia.

Switzer, Ann-Lee, and Gordon Switzer. 2012. *Gateway to Promise: Canada's First Japanese Community.* Victoria, BC: Ti-Jean Press.

Takata, Toyo. 1983. *Nikkei Legacy.* Toronto: NC Press.

William Tell[1]

FRIEDRICH SCHILLER

1. This is the entirety of the adaptation by Nihei as submitted by his family to the Nikkei National Museum and Cultural Centre. Selection reproduced here (Act III, scene 3) was translated from the Japanese by Matsuki Masutani. This selection is the only part of Schiller's play that is extant in the donated manuscripts. Published with permission from Nikkei National Museum.

2. The play was not published and performed until 1804, so Nihei is incorrect about the date here.

3. The overture to Gioachino Rossini's opera *William Tell* premiered in 1829 and is one of the composer's most famous pieces.

ACT III, SCENE THREE, in a Japanese rendering by John Nihei
Translation from the Japanese by Matsuki Masutani

(A Note by John Nihei)

This play was written in 1759 [*sic*],[2] about 180 years ago by a German, [Friedrich] Schiller. The play depicts the act of a heroic hunter who saved people from oppression. He risked his life for those who suffered under oppressive rulers, and in the end, vanquished them.

The play was translated all over the world and the story gave courage to those who suffered under undue political oppression. Schiller is considered the founder of today's peaceful Swiss Republic and his play inspired the work of many artists, poets and sculptors. We also recall that a composer wrote the "William Tell Overture" inspired by Schiller's work.[3]

Beside a lake in the foothills of the Alps, amid green pastures, forests and the sound of sheep bells, outwardly everything seemed peaceful, but in fact people were suffering and oppressed by the heavy taxes imposed by their Governor, a man named Gessler.

One day Governor Gessler erected a pole in the town square and placed his hat on top of it. He ordered people to respectfully salute the hat before crossing the square. People took detours to avoid having to do this. Therefore, the square, which used to be a vibrant market at year's end, became a deserted and desolate place.

Tell came to cross this square while on a visit to see his father, whom he hadn't seen for some time. This is the beginning of the famous scene with the apple.

Two guards are guarding the pole:

GUARD 1. What a laugh standing with a serious face and guarding a hat. It's ridiculous having to salute a hat.
GUARD 2. It's easier saluting an empty hat. We have to salute an empty head.

Tell, holding a bow, appears with a child. He doesn't notice the hat and walks in front of it, to stand at the front of the stage.

TELL. Hey, my child, look at those mountains and snow! You can see a pure white ridge.
WALTER. Oh, that's the glacier that causes thunderous avalanches.

TELL. Without the forest up there, this village would long ago lie under
   avalanches.
WALTER. Dad, are there any countries without mountains?
TELL. If you descend this mountain and follow the stream you will encounter
   beautiful fields with bountiful crops. They look like flower gardens.
WALTER. In that case, why aren't people heading to that beautiful country?
TELL. Yes, it is good land, but the people who work in the fields can't dispose
   of the crops as they wish. The fields belong to the bishop and to the king.
WALTER. But can they go to the forest and hunt at will?
TELL. The animals, birds, fish and everything else all belong to the king. The
   ocean with its salt and all the rivers also belong to the king.
WALTER. In that case, it is not so nice a country.
TELL. That's right. It is better to have the glacier behind you than wicked men.
WALTER. Look, dad! There's a hat placed at the top of that pole.
TELL. Never mind with the hat, let's go.

The two of them try to pass through the square.

GUARD 1: (*Holding up his spear.*) By order of the king, stop!
TELL. Why can't we pass?
GUARD 2: Anyone who doesn't salute the hat must be thrown into jail. Come!
WALTER. They are throwing my father in jail. Please help! Please someone
   come! Everyone please come! They are taking my dad away!

Many villagers appear.

VILLAGER. What? Taking William Tell away?
VILLAGER. Don't let them take William away just because he didn't salute the
   hat.
VILLAGER. There are more people than guards. Let's not lose against them.
GUARD 1, 2. Revolt! Uprising! Help!
GUARD. (*Entering.*) Here comes the Governor! (*GOVERNOR GESSLER comes out
   with his armed retainers.*)
GESSLER. What a fuss! Who called for help?
GUARD 2: Because this man refused to salute the hat we arrested him. Then
   the fuss started.
GESSLER. If you are disrespectful of the Governor you must be disrespectful
   of the king as well.
TELL. I just didn't notice it. Please forgive me.
GESSLER. Well, Tell, I heard you're a master of the bow.
WALTER. Yes, Governor! My father could shoot an apple from a tree at a
   hundred paces.

GESSLER. Well, I'd like to see such skill. Prepare your bow. Put an apple on the head of your boy and shoot it down with one try. If you miss, your head will be off.

TELL. Governor! It's too cruel to order such a thing! It is out of the question to put an apple on my own child's head and shoot it off with an arrow. It must be a mistake on your part to impose such an onerous task on the father of a young child.

GESSLER. Well, the choice is to shoot or die with your child. (*He picked an apple from a tree.*) Here is an apple. Clear the place. I will decrease the distance to 80 paces. Bind the boy to that tree.

WALTER. I don't want to be bound. I'll be as quiet as a sheep.

RETAINER 1. I will blindfold you at least.

WALTER. I don't need to be blindfolded. I won't even blink my eyes. Well dad, let's show how good you are to these people.

A retainer took the boy under the tree and placed an apple on his head.

TELL. (*Puts an arrow in the bow as if he's made up his mind.*) Please step aside and clear the space. (*He puts down the bow.*) I can't do it. My hand is trembling and my eyes are glazed.

TELL. (*To the Governor.*) Please save me from doing this. Please kill me with your spear.

GESSLER. I am not interested in killing you. I want to see your skill.

Tell is in anguish. He suddenly takes another arrow from the quiver and inserts it in his belt.

WALTER. Dad! Please shoot. I'm not afraid.

Tell takes aim and gathers the courage to shoot.

PEOPLE'S VOICES. Look! The apple has dropped. The boy is safe. He hit the apple!

WALTER. (*Brings the apple pierced by the arrow. He approaches his dad.*) My dad would never hit me. I knew that from the beginning.

Tell embraces the boy and falls to the ground.

PEOPLE. Hurrah! What an expert marksman!

TELL. Well, let's go home. (*Tell braces himself and tries to head home.*)

GESSLER. Wait, Tell! Why did you insert another arrow in your belt?

TELL. That is a convention among hunters.

GESSLER. Don't lie to me. Confess like a real man. I will promise not to kill you.

TELL. In that case, I'll confess. If I hit my child by mistake, I would have shot
you with this arrow.
GESSLER. All right! I won't kill you, but I don't feel safe unless you are in jail.
Take him away.

Retainers hold Tell and take him away.

WALTER. Dad! My father!

He runs after his dad and the curtain falls.

They took William Tell away. Crossing a lake, a huge storm came up and Tell
managed to escape his captors and reach the lakeshore. He awaited Gessler
at a rugged mountain pass and shot him dead. William Tell thereby released
the people from suffering under the evil Governor and built a foundation of
freedom for the people of Switzerland.

Gay/Queer and Trans Performances and Cultures in Toronto (1946–1965)

Dragging at the Margins

J. PAUL HALFERTY

1. I employ the terms "queer" and "gay" in this article historically, as these were the most commonly used terms in this period. "Queer" was most often a term of abuse used by the broader world, while "gay" was an emergent and more loosely defined term that some used to represent their gender and sexual differences from heterosexual norms.

THIS CHAPTER EXPLORES the interrelated nature of identity, community, and drag performance through engagement with two historical documents: "John Herbert's Memories of Carol Desmond," a series of photos of Herbert dressed as his feminine alter ego "Carol Desmond" in the 1940s and 1950s, and "A Look at Tracy Roberts," a profile of a drag queen published in Toronto's *Two* magazine in the mid-1960s. In this short introduction, I will focus on contextualizing these documents and suggest that they reveal the powerful role that drag performance has played for both individuals expressing their own gender identities and for the city's gay/queer[1] communities from the mid-1940s through to the mid-1960s. What emerges from this discussion is the truly trans nature of sartorial practices in this period, as clothing and body styling were used by individuals and groups to move across and subvert the highly restrictive and heteronormative lines of gender current in this period.

"Drag" is a simple term that represents complex practices—"complex" because, as an embodied action, drag can be performed with a variety of intents and in diverse and differently framed contexts, prompting various interpretations and a range of social and cultural effects. Drag is also complex because, like all theatrical performances, it holds an ambivalent relationship to lived realities: Can even the most overtly *theatrical* of theatrical performances— a performance of Shakespeare at the Stratford Festival, for example—ever be completely separated and bracketed off from the imaginative and material circumstances of its production? From the identities of the players and the roles they play? From the various realities of our social lives, with which the theatrical performance might resonate? Anthropologists and performance studies scholars Erving Goffman, Victor Turner, Richard Schechner, and Rebecca Schneider, among others, explore the often-blurred boundaries between theatricalized performances and everyday life and have produced a number of theories that elaborate on how performance, play, ritual, and re-enactment undergird and structure our lived realities. Countless theatre, performance, and, indeed, drag artists have engaged in actions and performances that criss-cross the conventional boundaries of performance and reality, while others have highlighted their imbrication. And in her foundational work, *Gender Trouble: Feminism and the Subversion of Identity*,

FIGURE 22.1: John Herbert's Memories of Carol Desmond, 1946. GA305, *John Herbert fonds, Special Collections and Archives, University of Waterloo. Courtesy of University of Waterloo Library.*

feminist philosopher and gender theorist Judith Butler famously used drag, as well as other forms of gender performance, as a metaphor to clarify the performative nature of our gendered lives: "The notion of an original or primary gender identity is often parodied within the cultural practices of drag, cross-dressing, and the sexual stylization of butch/femme identities" (1990, 137).[2] In these contexts, the terms "drag" or "cross-dressing" seem like a misnomer because all our social and theatrical roles are, arguably, performative; as the world's most famous drag queen, RuPaul Charles has suggested, "You're born naked and the rest is drag."

In the 1940s and 1950s, gay/queer subcultures in Toronto were small, marginal, and segregated from the mainstream along the lines of class, sex, gender performance, and race. In bars and taverns, men and women—in segregated drinking rooms—found spaces to meet, flirt, and talk. Unlike today, these spaces were not exclusively "gay," "lesbian," "queer," or "trans," nor were they overtly queer-owned, as laws still prohibited both same-sex sexual relations and "cross-dressing." Rather, bars and taverns catered to straight, gay, and lesbian clienteles, whose gender and sexual identities and dissidence were differently coded and read, enacted, and received, depending mostly on the class affiliation of the establishment. Located mostly in the city's downtown, among the bars that gay men frequented and colonized for their own queer purposes were the King Edward and Ford Hotels, the Municipal Tavern and the Union House hotel—affectionately called "the Corners," since they were located on the southeast and southwest corners of Queen and Bay (Egan and McLeod 1998, 72–73), and lesbians were known to patronize the Continental Hotel bar in Chinatown. Especially for gay men, the more upscale the bar, the more conservative and "straight"-looking were its patrons; this was not the case for lesbians in Toronto in the 1950s as "the Continental was considered the only thing going" (Chenier 2004, 86).

The more marginal the bar or tavern, the more likely transgressive sexual and gender behaviours might be tolerated. In these establishments, hustlers and other sex workers met their clients (Churchill 2004, 835), some queer/ trans people dressed in drag or expressed their gender identity non-conforming ways, and lesbian women effected butch and femme gender styles.[3] Jim Egan, an early gay activist in the city, remembers two trans women and sex workers, Frances and Geraldine, who "were mirror opposites of each other": both were over two hundred pounds and wore a great deal of makeup, but Frances was Black and Geraldine was white (Egan and McLeod 1998, 72). That Frances and Geraldine lived most of their public lives as women is suggested by the fact that Egan, who describes being "great friends with them both," cannot recall if he "ever knew their real [sic] names," and also by the following statement: "Frances and Geraldine could pass, especially back then, because the average straight man meeting them really wouldn't question that they were women" (Egan and McLeod 1998, 72–73).

Like Frances and Geraldine, John Herbert, who would go on to write the highly successful play *Fortune and Men's Eyes*, regularly dressed in drag in this period (see Figures 22.1 to 22.4), and would continue to do so until his death in 2001. In his unpublished memoirs, Herbert recalls that he and his friends would spend all the money they earned at their day jobs on dresses, gloves, hats, and make-up to wear out on the town in the evenings (Herbert 1995, 4). He was influenced by the stars of the day: contemporary feminine icons such as Joan Crawford, Bette Davis, and Rita Hayworth, "Gypsy Rose Lee" (Figure 22.2), and Marlene Dietrich (Figure 22.2). In Figure 22.1, Herbert notes that the ensemble Carol is wearing was first worn in 1946 for the Halloween party

FIGURE 22.2: John Herbert's Memories of Carol Desmond, *"In Paris after Midnight, Model Shows Tour, 1953."* GA305, *John Herbert fonds, Special Collections and Archives, University of Waterloo. Courtesy of University of Waterloo Library.*

in "Letros." Letros Nile Room was a bar on King Street that hosted annual Halloween balls from the late 1940s until 1969 (Sismondo 2017, 102–03), but Herbert did not only dress and pass as a woman at Halloween. He would often dress in women's clothing and go with friends to the Devon Restaurant, which was located until 2004 at the intersection of Church and Wellesley Streets, the current epicentre of Toronto's queer communities, or to one of the bars where other queers socialized (Herbert 1995, 1–3).

As a man who acted femininely and also dressed in women's clothing, Herbert's life in Toronto was impinged upon in very serious ways by a number

FIGURE 22.3: John Herbert's Memories of Carol Desmond, *"Model Shows, 1953."* GA305, John Herbert fonds, Special Collections and Archives, University of Waterloo. Courtesy of University of Waterloo Library.

of run-ins with the police, which included casual harassment, assault, and finally arrest and incarceration. As he suggests, "The rouged and mascaraed queens were beaten up frequently. [They were] taken to the police station and beaten up! Taken up alleyways and beaten up" (Wagner 2013). Herbert was arrested for the first time in the autumn of 1947 when two youths attempted to rob him. Herbert thought he might be saved when the police happened upon the scene, but the boys claimed that he had solicited sex from them and testified to this effect in court. As a result, Herbert was convicted of two counts of gross indecency and sentenced to eight months in the Guelph reformatory. After

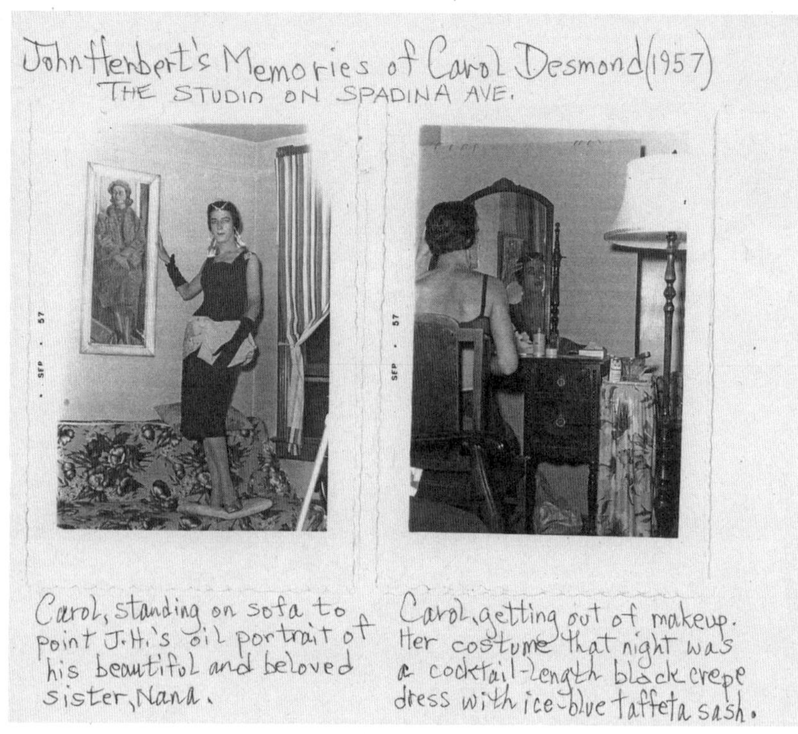

FIGURE 22.4: *John Herbert's Memories of Carol Desmond, "The Studio on Spadina Avenue, 1957."* GA305, *John Herbert fonds, Special Collections and Archives, University of Waterloo. Courtesy of University of Waterloo Library.*

discharge from Guelph, Herbert was arrested once again in February 1948 (Wagner 2021). This time, Herbert was dressed in women's clothing and was arrested in a parked car in Toronto's Rosedale neighbourhood with a man who had picked him up on Church Street. In his unpublished memoirs, he describes how they were pulled from the car by two plain-clothed officers of the morality squad (Herbert 1995, 14). Herbert was charged and eventually sent to the reformatory in Mimico.

Leaving Mimico, Herbert was an ex-con and had very few options left open to him, especially in terms of employment. He took odd jobs in a number of cities and towns in Canada, working in northern Manitoba and Montreal, and also living and working in Chicago for a short time. In 1953 he travelled across Canada as a female impersonator in a burlesque show called "Paris after Midnight," performing and living as "Carol Desmond"—the images of which collected here document this time in Herbert's life. Herbert got the job through his friend Alan Maloney, whom he met while incarcerated at the Guelph reformatory. Maloney was an early Toronto drag queen called "Brandy," and the character Queenie from *Fortune and Men's Eyes* is based on him. While on tour, Herbert and Maloney lived as women onstage and off. Herbert recalls, "After being a while with the show we had quite long hair.

4. For more on how Herbert effected femininity in his personal gender performance, see Herbert 1978.

5. The Music Room was located upstairs at 575 Yonge Street (Egan and McLeod 1998, 86) and the Melody Room was located at 457 Church Street (Egan and McLeod 1998, 114n7).

We kept ourselves absolutely hairless…our bodies. We were young and it's easier to appear feminine when you're young, and we got away with it. That was, I think, when something inside me said, 'God it's good to just be oneself'" (Wagner 2013).

In the images included here, Herbert refers to "street clothes" and "stage costume," documenting the looks effected for the stage and for *her* everyday life on the street as Carol Desmond. I use the feminine pronoun here because when Herbert was dressed in women's clothing and living life as a woman, *she was not being theatrical*; rather, as stated above, Herbert was being "oneself." The lack of gendered pronouns in this statement is important and truthful because Herbert criss-crossed the lines of gender, living as an effeminate gay man and as a rather glamorous woman, expressing his and her own queer, androgynous, masculine, and feminine identities onstage and off.[4] While Herbert lived most of the rest of his life as a gay man, Carol Desmond was a lived part of his identity until his death. Onstage or off, wearing women's clothes was not "cross-dressing," it was not always theatrical, it was not always an act: for Herbert/Desmond, the clothing they wore was a personal form of what we would characterize today as transgender expression.

In the 1960s, social interest around homosexuality increased, and social mores and laws liberalized, though, as Tom Warner notes, the "liberalization of mainstream attitudes…still relegated homosexuals to a secondary status in [Canadian] society. They were to be treated with compassion and pity, but such attitudes continued to perpetuate their underclass existence" (2002, 25). In Toronto, gay/queer magazines, bars, and clubs, owned and operated by gay men and lesbians, began to emerge in this period. Like the bars that existed before them, these venues provided spaces for the performance of various gender and sexual identities; however, as gay/queer-owned and -operated spaces and magazines, they were also important arenas for political organization and as the building blocks and markers for queer existence and community. "A Look at Tracy Roberts" is a manifestation of these developments: a profile of a drag queen published in *Two* (a "homosexual" magazine published in Toronto) that details her act at the Music Room and Melody Room, which were two unlicensed gay clubs operated by Richard Kerr, a gay man, and by Sarah Ellen Dunlop, a lesbian (Egan and McLeod 1998, 86).[5]

Two was a magazine that, in its own words, expressed "The Homosexual Viewpoint in Canada." It was published from 1964 to 1967 and, in almost every issue, there is a section called "Cameo" in which a local drag queen is profiled. This focus on local queens was at least partially the case because the magazine, published first by Gayboy and then by Kamp Publishing, was run out of the Melody Room at 457 Church Street and likely published by Kerr. About half of each issue of *Two* is dedicated to the "Two Physique Section": pictures of scantily clad, athletic young men, some of which were photographed by Kerr himself. In addition to these sections, the magazine includes articles on a variety of topics relevant to gay men and also, occasionally, lesbian women.

The announcement of the name Tracy Roberts, from any stage, in any gay club in Toronto is the signal for spontaneous, enthusiastic applause.

Tracy is the only colored boy working as a female impersonator in Toronto and it is interesting that as the representative of one minority group, he is eminently successful and completely accepted by another.

Tracy started his stage career as a male dancer in the U.S.A. After a few ups and downs, Tracy arrived in Toronto. His first experience with mime theatre was at the Music Room where he wowed audiences with his interpretation of Jonny Mathis.

Surrounded by female impersonators Tracy wondered if he could ever convince an audience that he was a girl.

The Christmas Review that year was Tracy's first try at female impersonation. Audiences were a little stunned to see the transformation. From the voice of Jonny Mathis to Ertha kitt, doing Santa Baby. From sweater and slacks to a but gorgeous evening gown. The over all effect was so stunning the audience drowned out the first part of the song with their applause.

A new 'feminine', star was born and Tracy has never looked back since.

Popular off stage as he is on (something rare among female impersonators) Tracy enjoys a fast social whirl and is never at a loss for handsome escorts.

Tracy is a tall boy and in high heels and bouffant wig, he is to say the least, a striking figure in any crowd. While he rarely appears in public as a girl, when he does he passes muster with many an admiring glance from the men and not a few envious ones from the girls.

However it is on stage that Tracy is really at home. Moving with the inherent grace of the colored people he casts the spell of reality over the audience.

Lip sync, the latest "discovery" of the Loyd Thaxton show has been around the gay clubs for many years, and Tracy Roberts is a past master. So perfect is Tracy's syncronisation that onlookers, who are

FIGURE 22.5: *Pages from "Cameo: A Look at Tracy Roberts," Two, Toronto, 1965.*

Courtesy of The ArQuives: Canada's LGBTQ2+ Archives, Toronto.

not aware of the possibilities of lip sync, are loath to believe that he is not, in fact, singing. Inspite of the fact that Tracy mimes he has an excellent singing voice, and is presently experimenting, and contemplating "going live".

Tracy's success as a female impersonator has not prevented him from pinch hitting in male roles, when a show requires a "butch". In fact, on occassions we have seen Tracy do both at once quite convincingly, which is quite a trick even for a female impersonator, ...but then doing tricks is a daily occurrence for Toronto's one and only Mr. Tracy Roberts.

One of the biggest obstacles in mime theatre is finding suitable recordings or tapes. Comedy material is especially difficult to come by and is always in demand. For those who are interested RAE BOURBON has a new recording out with the camp title "A trick ain't always a treat". According to the advertising this album is for "elderly delinquents and for those preparing to become one- and especially for people who like to laugh." Personally we think it is more likely to be tailor made and just right for Femme Imps. on the mime theatre circuit.

FIGURE 22.6: *Pages from "Cameo: A Look at Tracy Roberts," Two, Toronto, 1965.*

Courtesy of The ArQuives: Canada's LGBTQ2+ Archives, Toronto.

For example, it printed an article about what to do if you were arrested "on a charge of a sex-oriented nature" called "What to Do When Arrested or What Now My Love"; another, written by an unnamed author, who describes himself as "homosexual and an ex-con," addresses homosexuality and the prison system ("The Homosexual" 1966); and a tongue-in-cheek article called "What Is a Downtown Butch?" provided a lionizing account of the character of butch lesbians in Toronto at the time.

In "John Herbert's Memories of Carol Desmond," we see a personal documentation of a single individual expressing their own gender identity onstage and off. In the profiles published in *Two*, of which "A Look at Tracy Roberts" is but one example (Figures 22.5 and 22.6), we see photos and articles that represent a collective of people performing publicly in drag as entertainment within early gay/queer spaces. The article belies the casual racism of the time, referring to the African American Roberts as "coloured," and quickly containing the issues faced by racialized people when it suggests that "it is interesting that as the [only] representative of one minority group, he is eminently successful and completely accepted by another"; one wonders if Roberts would characterize their experience in this way. And yet, this profile is a testament to the kinds of diversity that existed within the city's queer communities, and to the cross-border as well as other forms of migration that allowed people like Roberts and Herbert to find queer places to exist.[6]

In each issue of *Two*, the Music Room and the Melody Room are advertised in the following manner: "Toronto's original after-hours gay clubs. Offering you a complete range of facilities from the quiet intimacy of our TV lounge to lively floorshows featuring Toronto's finest Female Impersonators" (quoted in Egan and McLeod 1998, 87). In this advertising and in the Cameo profiles published in *Two*, the "female impersonators" are characterized as entertainment; but these performers were also engaged in performances that worked in concert with audiences of gays, lesbians, and trans people to performatively and collectively produce the space they inhabited as affirmative to their identities. As I've argued elsewhere, the proprietors and patrons of queer bars and clubs performatively construct these spaces as particularly sexualized and gendered through their statements, actions, and presence: by the ways they talk about and promote, move through and interact within these spaces.[7] The Cameo profiles and advertising in *Two*—as well as the performances of queens like Tracy Roberts—hailed and interpellated individuals within the discursive and performative possibilities created and enacted within the Music Room and Melody Room. As these people danced, talked, and flirted, and as they watched the drag performers sing or lip-sync songs like "Just an Old Fashioned Girl" by Eartha Kitt, or "Somewhere Over the Rainbow" by Judy Garland, they imagined and created for themselves new queer worlds and possibilities for living their lives. Through drag and a variety of other performance modes,

6. Another important example of both cross-border traversals and Black trans and queer performance in Toronto is African American singer Little Jackie Shane. Shane was a soul singer from Nashville, Tennessee, who performed in straight music clubs such as the Sapphire and the Blue Note in Toronto in the 1960s, and whose song "Any Other Way" charted at number two on the local CHUM radio chart. Onstage and off, Shane wore make-up, dressed femininely, and made many remarks in her songs and on stage that were coded gay slang—for example, her song "A New Way of Lovin'." Shane disappeared from Toronto music scene in the early 1970s and she now lives as a woman in her native Nashville. For more on Shane, see Maynard 2017.

7. Following the lead of Jonathan Bollen, who employs the theory of Michel de Certeau to conduct a performance analysis of "Sleaze Ball 1994," a party produced as part of the Sydney Lesbian and Gay Mardi Gras, I analyzed the ways in which two bars, Bar Le Stud in Montreal and Goodhandy's in Toronto, were gendered and sexualized through the statements and actions of their proprietors and the patrons who inhabited their spaces. See Halferty 2008 and Bollen 1996.

on stage and off, the people gathered in these spaces formed early and visible examples of gay/queer and trans communities in Toronto.

Bibliography and Further Reading

Aizura, Aren Z., and Susan Stryker. 2013. *The Transgender Studies Reader 2*. New York: Routledge.

Bollen, Jonathan. 1996. "Sexing the Dance at Sleaze Ball 1994." *TDR / The Drama Review* 40 (3): 166–91.

Butler, Judith. 1990. *Gender Trouble: Feminism and the Subversion of Identity*. New York: Routledge.

———. 1993. *Bodies That Matter: On the Discursive Limits of Sex*. New York: Routledge.

Chenier, Elise. 2004. "Rethinking Class in Lesbian Bar Culture. Living 'the Gay Life' in Toronto, 1955–1965." *Left History* 9 (2): 85–118.

Churchill, David S. 2004. "Mother Goose's Map: Tabloid Geographies and Gay Male Experience in 1950s Toronto." *Journal of Urban History* 30 (6): 826–52.

Egan, Jim, and Donald W. McLeod. 1998. *Challenging the Conspiracy of Silence: My Life as a Canadian Gay Activist*. Toronto: Canadian Lesbian and Gay Archives.

FitzGerald, Maureen, and Scott Rayter. 2012. *Queerly Canadian: An Introductory Reader in Sexuality Studies*. Toronto: Canadian Scholars Press.

Halferty, J. Paul. 2008. "Performing the Construction of Queer Spaces." *Canadian Theatre Review* 134 (Summer): 18–26.

Herbert, John. 1978. "The Sissy." In *Stage Voices: Twelve Canadian Playwrights Talk about Their Lives and Work*, edited by Geraldine Anthony, 186–95. Toronto: Doubleday.

———. 1995. "Writing in the Sand: Material for a Memoir by John Herbert—1995." John Herbert fonds, accession no. GA305, Series 7 Biographical, file 149, University of Waterloo Archives, Special Collections, Dana Porter Library.

"The Homosexual and the Prison System." 1966. *Two*, July–August, 5–6.

Irving, Dan, and Rupert Raj. 2014. *Trans Activism in Canada : A Reader*. Toronto: Canadian Scholars Press.

"A Look at Tracy Roberts." 1965. *Two*, no. 6, n.p.

Maynard, Steven. 2017. "'A New Way of Lovin'': Queer Toronto Gets Schooled by Jackie Shane." In *Any Other Way: How Toronto Got Queer*, edited by Stephanie Chambers et. al., 11–20. Toronto: Coach House Books.

Namaste, Viviane K. 2000. *Invisible Lives: The Erasure of Transsexual and Transgendered People*. Chicago: University of Chicago Press.

———. 2005. *C'était du spectacle!: L'histoire des artistes transsexuelles à Montréal, 1955–1985*. Montreal and Kingston: McGill-Queen's University Press.

———. 2011. *Sex Change, Social Change: Reflections on Identity, Institutions and Imperialism*. Toronto: Women's Press.

Newton, Esther. 1972. *Mother Camp: Female Impersonators in America*. Englewood Cliffs, NJ: Prentice-Hall.

RuPaul. 1995. *Lettin It All Hang Out: An Autobiography*. New York: Hyperion.

Senelick, Laurence. 2000. *The Changing Room: Sex, Drag and Theatre*. New York: Routledge.

Sismondo, Christine. 2017. "Halloween Balls: From Letros to the St. Charles." In *Any Other Way: How Toronto Got Queer*, edited by Stephanie Chambers et al., 102–04. Toronto: Coach House Books.

Stryker, Susan, and Stephen Whittle. 2006. *The Transgender Studies Reader*. New York: Routledge.

Wagner, Anton. 2021. "Herbert, John." In *Canadian Theatre Encyclopedia*. Athabasca University Press. Last updated January 24, 2021. http://www.canadiantheatre.com.

———. 2013. *John Herbert: Fortune and Men's Eyes*. YouTube. https://www.youtube.com/watch?v=_5okzdZA-OM.

Warner, Tom. 2002. *Never Going Back: A History of Queer Activism in Canada*. Toronto: University of Toronto Press.

"What Is a Downtown Butch?" 1966. *Two*, July–August, n.p.

"What to Do When Arrested or What Now My Love." 1964. *Two*, no. 3, 17–19.

CLAUDE GAUVREAU was still in his teens when he was encouraged by his brother Pierre, a painter, to join a group of young people inspired by the teacher and established artist Paul-Émile Borduas. The group, who were first identified as the Montreal Surrealists, were later dubbed "les automatistes" by journalists because of their call for a new spontaneity in art, as well as in life. The Automatist painters were developing techniques begun by movements such as Futurism, Dadaism, and Surrealism to subvert traditional processes and intentions in art, to question the dominance of rational control, to liberate the unconscious, and to go beyond naturalism and realism into the realm of dreams and fantasy. In painting, especially in North America, those experiments moved in the direction of non-representational art that was concerned more with the gesture of painting than with the need to depict an object or a scene. And just as his painter friends were concentrating on the act of applying colours to a surface with no preconceived idea of what they would represent, Gauvreau began experimenting with theatrical language that would not necessarily tell a story, not necessarily imitate familiar emotions or actions, and not necessarily make obvious sense, either logically or linguistically. Words, syllables, and sounds became the raw material to which the audience would respond, just as viewers can respond to colours in a painting without necessarily having to recognize a figure.

The Montreal Automatists were an eclectic group of men and women comprising dancer-choreographers, theatre people, designers, and photographers, as well as painters and writers. Convinced their experiments could have a social as well as artistic impact, they organized exhibitions, performances, and public forums while writing for local and student newspapers. But their most famous act was the publication of a manifesto entitled *Refus global* in August 1948. This was an unbound, cheaply produced pamphlet of about ninety pages with photographs of Automatist artwork and a variety of texts by five people, including three short plays by Gauvreau, one of which was *Bien-être* (The Good Life). *Refus global* caused a scandal among church and government officials, essentially because of its lead manifesto, written by Borduas and signed by fifteen others, which was seen as anticlerical and demeaning in its portrait of the people of Quebec as timid and repressed. The manifesto is now regarded as

FIGURE 23.1: *The Woman: My womb, cradle of life and consecrated urn. Spheres affiliated in the arch of aged autumn. Powder of kisses in the damp ditches of white gardens. Maurice Perron, Bien-Être, July 1948. Collection du Musée national des beaux-arts du Québec © Maurice Perron fonds, P35.S87.P6. With kind permission of Line-Sylvie Perron.*

a major document in Quebec's Quiet Revolution, but at the time, a strong negative public reaction destroyed Borduas's professional and family life.

The Good Life was one of a series of twenty-six pieces written by Gauvreau between 1944 and 1946, to which he gave the general title of *Les entrailles* (Entrails). He called them "dramatic objects" because, though most had titles, stage directions, and identified characters, they were, to say the least, not conventional plays. Some of them recall experiments by symbolist and absurdist dramatists in France such as Paul Claudel,[1] Guillaume Apollinaire,[2] Alfred Jarry,[3] or even Samuel Beckett.[4] But Gauvreau's texts were actually more intransigent, especially on the level of language play. For example, one "object" was only a half-page long, entirely made up of lines such as "*Keulessa Kyrien Cobliéniz Jaboir*" (never mind consulting your French dictionary). *The Good Life* was certainly not the most daring of the *Entrailles*, with its hint of domestic drama involving tennis-playing newlyweds at home, but it was alien enough to startle the audience when first performed at the Congress Hall in Montreal on May 20, 1947, by some future signatories of *Refus global*

5. Gauvreau described four types
    of surrational image in a 1950
    letter to Jean-Claude Dussault
    (see translated excerpts in *The
    Lucid Clusters: Poetics of Claude
    Gauvreau*, 2011).

6. In a public reading of this
    English translation during
    a Playwright's Workshop
    in Montreal in 1988, it was
    decided to perform the final
    crescendo mutely, with the
    actor miming screams.

and their friends. Here is Gauvreau's description of the event from his 1969 retrospective article *"L'épopée automatiste vue par un cyclope"* (The Automatist Epic as Seen by a Cyclops):

> *I had asked Pierre Gauvreau to do the set and costumes for "Bien-être"; he did the set himself and asked Madeleine Arbour to do the costumes. Madeleine Lalonde agreed to play the insistent five-note theme on the piano. This was the first time anyone in the general public had ever heard a single creative line by me; we were absolutely new and there was certainly no prejudice against us... The presence of Murielle Guilbault, who was a well-known actress, no doubt was partly responsible for the fact that our audience was a cultural elite (though most were relatively conservative). I knew they were in for a terrible shock...*
>
> *[Right at the beginning] Pierre's set, which was made of newspaper, gave out and we had to repair it. The audience started to clap, impatient for the curtain to go up. At last, Muriel and I appeared on stage, dressed as newlyweds. The play begins with a monologue by the husband, and I spoke: "Hands in the abyss making leaves. That's a wedding." Starting with those words, which don't seem very offensive nowadays (especially if you compare them with what I've written more recently), the entire audience burst into outrageous and uncontrollably hysterical laughter. The more complex verbal fusions I write today still provoke laughter, but it's chickenshit compared to the astonifying hilarity of those hunchbacks in a trance. The hyperthunderous claps of laughter never stopped through the entire play...maybe just a little for the man's final monologue. (Gauvreau 1996a, 50)*

In this play, spoken words do not always relate clearly to the action, as if they had a life of their own—as if statements by the characters are independent clusters of images meant to have their own impact, whether related or not to what is happening on stage. And those images don't necessarily follow the common rules of logical description: "Peace, silken-eared snake in the damp laundry of noon."[5] By the same token, the various actions on and offstage seem to lack causal or logical connection. The bride sinks down dead while the groom seems controlled by a five-note theme, played on a piano, eventually rising to a crescendo. There are no explanations offered, and no denouement.[6]

Undaunted by the reaction to this first performance of one of his plays, Gauvreau believed the public would eventually understand that, as he wrote later, in 1970, in his "Réflexions d'un dramaturge débutant," "the avant-garde must begin in the non-figurative and go beyond" (Gauvreau 1972, 47). He insisted that, however enjoyable the work of popular dramatists like Gratien Gélinas might be, "if Quebec is incapable of producing anything else, dramatically or verbally, then we are in our senile second-childhood" (48). In fact, during the twenty years following his death, Gauvreau gradually became a sort of cult figure in Quebec, seen as a *"poète maudit"* doomed to madness and early death,

FIGURE 23.2: *A piano is heard, languidly playing a five-note theme. The man, who now moves with jerky motions, bends to pick up the ball of string. Maurice Perron, Bien-Être, July 1948.*
Collection du Musée national des beaux-arts du Québec © Maurice Perron fonds, P35.S87.PD. With kind permission of Line-Sylvie Perron.

often equated with Antonin Artaud, the poet and drama theorist associated with French Surrealism who is famous for his meditations on *The Theatre of Cruelty*. Artaud was known to insert passages of glossolalia in his poetry, but not in his dramatic works, whereas Gauvreau used what he called "explorational language" even in his more accessible, longer plays.

Gauvreau was a prolific poet, critic, and playwright. Several of his shorter plays were produced on radio and others were destined for television. But he is best known for two long plays written near the end of his life: *La charge de l'orignal épormyable* (The Charge of the Expormidable Moose) and *Les oranges sont vertes* (The Oranges Are Green). These are generally less experimental than *The Good Life*, but still extravagant in their plots. And the plays' characters occasionally break into passages of "explorien," a complex fusion of syllables and sounds that Gauvreau insisted would defy traditional analysis. Nonetheless, these plays are now considered classics of Quebec theatre, acknowledged by younger dramatists such as Robert Lepage[7] and performed on the major stages of Montreal and Quebec City. Other productions of Gauvreau's work include an opera using his libretto, *Le vampire et la nymphomane* (The Vampire and the Nymphomaniac); a play based on his novel, *Beauté baroque*; two other full-length dramas, *La reprise* (The Revival) and *L'asile de la pureté* (Asylum of Purity); and even musical acts based on his poetry. Since the 1990s there have been at least three major stage productions in Quebec of *La charge de l'orignal épormyable*, as well as an excellent version for television. Lorraine Pintal—who was for many years the director of Montreal's prestigious Théâtre du Nouveau Monde—was a great champion of Gauvreau's work and was responsible for productions of his major plays as well as the vampire opera.

The Charge of the Expormidable Moose was actually performed in Toronto at the Tarragon Extra Space by One Little Goat theatre company, directed by Adam Seelig in May 2013 (see Seelig 2013–14). This was the first and only production to date of Gauvreau's work in English by a professional company. Although that production was certainly well received, Claude Gauvreau has not been accepted in English Canada as readily as other Quebec dramatists such as Michel Tremblay, probably because the poetic extravagance of his plays is disconcerting for theatre companies and audiences who are used to the more naturalist traditions of English-Canadian drama.

Bibliography and Further Reading

Les Automatistes. 1969. Special number. *La Barre du Jour* 17–20 (janvier-août).

Borduas, Paul-Émile, et al. 2009. *Total Refusal / Refus global*. Translated by Ray Ellenwood. Toronto: Exile Editions.

Bourassa, André-G. 1984. *Surrealism and Québec Literature*. Translated by Mark Czarnecki. Toronto: University of Toronto Press.

Ellenwood, Ray. 1992. *Egregore: A History of the Montréal Automatist Movement*. Toronto: Exile Editions.

———. 2014. *Ègrègore, Une histoire du mouvement automatiste de Montréal*. Augmented edition, translated by Jean Antonin Billard. Montréal: Kétoupa Édition.

Gauvreau, Claude. 1972. "Réflexions d'un dramaturge débutant." Translated by Ray Ellenwood as "Reflections of a Young Dramatist." *Exile* 1 (2): 45–52.

———. 1977. *Oeuvres créatrices complètes*. Montréal: Éditions Parti Pris.

———. 1991. *Entrails*. Translated by Ray Ellenwood. Toronto: Exile Editions.

———. 1996a. *The Charge of the Expormidable Moose*. Translated by Ray Ellenwood. Toronto: Exile Editions.

———. 1996b. *Écrits sur l'art*. Edited by Gille Lapointe. Montréal: Éditions de l'Hexagone.

———. 2002. *Lettres à Paul-Émile Borduas*. Montréal: Les Presses de l'Université de Montréal.

———. 2011. *The Lucid Clusters, Poetics of Claude Gauvreau*. Texts selected and translated by Ray Ellenwood. Calgary: No Press.

Gauvreau, Claude, and Jean-Claude Dussault. 1993. *Correspondance, 1949–1950*. Montréal: Éditions de l'Hexagone.

Marchand, Jacques. 1979. *Claude Gauvreau, poète et mythocrate*. Montréal: VLB Éditeur.

Saint-Denis, Janou. 1978. *Claude Gauvreau, le cygne*. Montréal: Les Presses de l'Université du Québec.

Seelig, Adam. 2013–14. "Flexible Impossibilities: On *The Charge of the Expormidable moose*, Director's Statement." *Rampike* 22 (2): 16–19.

The Good Life

CLAUDE GAUVREAU
Translation by RAY ELLENWOOD

*The interior of a house, at once slightly austere and slightly weird in proportions.
To the left, almost in the center, a closed door that leads to another room of the house.
A* MAN *and a* WOMAN *enter, both wearing wedding clothes.* THE MAN *wears
black gloves.*

THE MAN. Hands in the abyss making leaves. That's a wedding. The cup
    running over with love like seaweed on the porch.
  A stream of clouds dives into the hearts: king-fisher.
  Wreaths in cheeks, peace sculpted in the worried profiles of existence.
  Sugar Woman. Hebrew.
  Hebraic joy in the convoy of symbolic orange.
  Spread wings in the conjugated marbles.
  I see the furrows, I notice the wound of the roots. The poet who came into
    our souls by the keyhole.
  The buds make faces in the acidic lake, but the chattering of the Turkish
    tooth floats up in the shady catacombs. Superior life! Acid delirium!
    Parallel cones set on the spherical circle and moss of foam like mercury,
    the amber-coloured sponge.
  Apollo's desire. Spontaneous springs. Keys to bliss. Keys to blisses.
  Reflection smiling on my beloved's steel breasts.
  I feel the clenched repentance of solitude. Clear voices, mauve-scented
    soup-tureens. Ideal! Idea. Ideal: Pure Zeal.
THE WOMAN. My womb, cradle of life and consecrated urn. Spheres affiliated
  in the arch of aged autumn. Powder of kisses in the damp ditches of white
  gardens. Versicoloured hysteria.
  The sublime fraction of golden Armenian curls.
  Entrance and procession of children.
  Arbitrary farandole in the yellow brick paths.

THE MAN *and* THE WOMAN *sit on a sofa, kissing tenderly. The lights go out. After
a moment, only a beam of whitish light reappears, not enough to show the back of
the stage, giving the impression of being suspended in mid-air.* THE MAN, *dressed in
a white leotard and still wearing his black gloves, is standing up, and at his feet is a
conical ball of white string.*

THE MAN. I am dreaming.

A piano is heard, languidly playing a five-note theme. The man, who now moves with jerky motions, bends to pick up the ball of string. But each time he is about to grasp it, another note of the theme is heard and the ball of string jumps out of his reach. This occurs with all five notes. Then, the beam of whitish light disappears and the stage is dark. The five notes of the theme are heard once again in the darkness, then the lighting returns to normal. THE MAN, dressed normally, is sitting alone on a sofa and he rubs his eyes with his gloved hands.

THE MAN. I dreamt.

The lights go out. In the darkness, the five notes of the theme are heard. The lights come on again. THE MAN, standing on a chair, hangs a picture on the wall. THE WOMAN, in a dressing gown, is sitting on the sofa.

THE MAN. The lights like malevolent dreams. The backs of shadows forever
    lost to the ashes of humanity.
  I see the ropes that encircle mankind. I see bodies mutilated by remorse.
  I understand the ropes pinned in memory.
  Woman with chocolate nails, with eyelashes of armistice, you are mine.
  I am the seal that has plunged into streams of syrup. Battered raincoat
    chopped like the notes of a flute.
  The walls like grey deserts levelling their faces long as anticipations.
  Beloved raspberry in the secret valley and the complicit silence.
  Bronzed butterfly wings.
  Obsession. Love.
  I rock myself in my arms and harmony comes out my ears: decayed tooth in
    the spiral.

From the next room the five-note theme is heard, played on the piano.

THE WOMAN. My sister. My twin sister is playing the piano. She is there.
THE MAN. Your twin sister?
THE WOMAN. Fingers at the door of dimensions sucking white arms that
  wave against a black background and compete in speed.

The lights go out. In the dark, the five notes of the theme are heard. The lights come on. THE MAN and WOMAN, wearing tennis togs, stand kissing.

THE MAN. Peace, silken-eared snake in the damp laundry of noon.
  I torqued your body in the space suspended between two facing mirrors;
    and your image forever climbs the rungs of an infinity of numbers.
  Woman's ear and skin of a pink pig.
  Ah! I'm having fun.
  The man's skin like an ox horn in the influence of icy rose-window skies.

Autumn is hatching summer.
Tonight I shall lie on your body in the black redemption that slips from
stones dreamed nonetheless.

From the next room, the five-note theme is heard on the piano. THE MAN *listens,*
dreaming.

THE WOMAN. Dressed in white on hesitant foot-bridges we are soap bubbles.
Throats of madness in basins full of perspiration.
Ahoy! Clowns of beggary, shout yourselves hoarse in centenarian cassocks!
Shell the seeds make the sculptures urinate! Death to tapestry! I've got my
man.
The sipping whispers in the aerial grass.
School is out! Breast-plates are nailed!
THE MAN. I believe it.

The lights go out. The five notes of the theme are heard in the dark. The theme lingers
on and is still heard when the lights come on. THE MAN, *in street clothes, wearing*
his black gloves, stands next to the door, musing. The theme is still heard. THE
MAN *walks towards the door, bends down and looks through the keyhole, but he*
immediately jerks back, covering his eye with both hands.

THE MAN. The pain in my eye!
Nothing! There is nothing to see! Frothy peaks of green vapour thicker than
bearskins!
My lowly eye. My diminished eye. My wounded eye. The pain in my eye!
Light that blinds!

The lights go out. The five notes of the theme are heard in the dark. The lights come
on. THE MAN *and* THE WOMAN, *wearing street clothes, stand facing one another.*
The man is holding a newspaper in his right hand.

THE MAN. The quilted captainries have absurdly abased themselves.
Let's be serious.
If I found a reed with its root in a nickel cupboard, I would run to wash
myself and I would listen, anxious.
The throbbing parade in an olive capital which is made of plums.
Let's discuss that!
Judases come to scratch the dirt of our lawns, pricks in the air. Absurdity
truer than bearded mounds.
Critical swelling. I discuss it canonically. Voices of nuggets brewed in rusty
woodcutter hands.
You have your ladies, all is well, don't go fishing under the crescent moon.
The death of captives in pools of tomato juice. Perplexed.

So in that way cancers grow like oysters on the inside of a jar.
Juice of palisades. Effort hernia completion.
We are not the kind who labour in flashes of mud.
Parasol to shade us from half-breed insinuations.
Serbian misconduct and medieval remonstrance. Let us think of children
     covered with green vines.
The day bathes in gloom laid flat by the scythe.
Proud panoply.

The first four notes of the theme are heard from the next room. THE MAN *listens.
The fifth note does not come.* THE MAN, *frozen in expectation of the fifth note, is as
unfeeling as a lead statue. Nothing happens.* THE WOMAN *totters several times and
then finally sinks down, turning on herself as in a whirlpool.* THE MAN *does not
budge. Eventually, the fifth note is heard very faintly, and then* THE MAN *rushes to*
THE WOMAN. *He bends over her.*

THE MAN. She is dead.

*He draws himself up mechanically and turns to the door which he stares at, dreamily.
He waits, he does not move. Then he takes off his black gloves and walks towards
the door. He stops, then opens the door. Nothing comes from the room but a thick,
clammy, inexhaustible green light. It seems that there is nothing in the next room but
that light, covering everything. The green light strikes the man's face and he jumps
back, covering his eyes with his hands.*

THE MAN. Ah! My eyes! It gnaws my eyes!

*He quickly pulls himself together and enters the room. We can no longer see him. He
comes back after a moment, his eyelids tightly clenched with pain. He has put on the
black gloves again. The door closes.*

THE MAN. She died beside her piano.
   I see the windowless cellars in the light of the sun.
   Drunkenness intoxicates and falls like sick leaves.
   Nothing. Nothing. The desert. The sign in the filthy weights.
   At last, the soul has hushed its dawn.
   Black snakes slip through the dusty hay.
   Adamic treachery. The dead in the bloods of oxen.
   Reddened slate. Headless poplar.
   The mimes catch fire.
   Cut-off. Leprous mug more emotional than acid contritions. Barrier. Scarf
      of the innate veins.
   The fox-terriers plunged in orthodox marriage contracts.
   Cossack boot in the devastated plains. Conclusion. Initiation.
   I see the cellars, the cellars, the cellars.

Then the five notes of the theme are heard from the next room. THE MAN *turns towards the door and stares at it, perplexed and frightened. The lights go down and out. In the darkness we hear the five notes of the theme trailing after each other while the light returns, and they continue once the light is back to normal. The man is still in the same position with the same expression on his face, but he has wrinkles on his forehead and grey hair at his temples. The woman is gone. The theme finally stops.*

    THE MAN. Steaming pies. I boil more than the intelligence of a calamitous
       man.
    I live the universe of landings without stairs.
    The makers of umbrellas for sheep laugh in my face because we are
       brothers. We are from the same plague.

The five notes of the theme are heard. THE MAN *opens the door with a sharp blow. Instinctively, the man lifts his hands to his eyes, but he controls himself and forces himself to look at the green light.*

THE MAN. Nobody there.

The door closes. The theme is heard again, repeated many times. THE MAN *approaches the door without making a sound, bends over furtively and looks through the keyhole.*

THE MAN. Nobody there. Nobody there. And my eyes hurt.
    Ah! the assorted turds that vegetate in your patiences!
    The mature man is as flexible as a reed.

The italicized words below are sung to the five notes of the theme, without accompaniment.

I see the cellars   *The cellars*   *cellars*
                     The cellars   *cellars*

    Homeland with a hundred faces cut up into abscissae. Who will read the
       deepest truths of common sense?

The theme is heard.

    Clubs in hand. Shameful peasants. Panting Atlas.
    Minute proceedings. It's the exegesis of Spring.
    How many winds?
    Fathers! The saxophone clans in the villages.

Requisitioner of clumsy deaths.
I want to kiss maidens' legs.
Ah!
My hands! My hands! It's my hands! My hands that are playing!

He takes off his black gloves with his teeth. There are no longer any hands under the gloves, the cuffs are empty. THE MAN *looks at his cuffs close up, because his eyes are feeble. He drops his gloves on the floor. With a kick, he opens the door.*

THE MAN. Completely useless! My hands! On the piano, my hands! Those are my hands playing! I can see my hands playing the piano!

He has fully entered the room and can no longer be seen. Suddenly, he is heard howling. Finally, he reappears. The door closes.

THE MAN. I am blind.
The stations in the distance, the stations forever in the distance.

Someone knocks at another door. Two working men come in, both wearing overalls.

FIRST WORKING MAN. We are the movers.
THE MAN. Ah!
SECOND WORKING MAN. We've come to move the piano.
THE MAN. (*As in a dream.*) Ah! Just a minute.

He picks up the gloves with his teeth and goes into the room. He comes out again without the gloves. The movers, without hesitating, go into the next room and come out with the piano. The door closes. On the piano are the two hands, gloved. The movers disappear with the piano.

THE MAN. Butterfly, get up.
Valves crystallized in the seas of iodine.
The Huns with boney canes walk in the middle of lukewarm paths, they are caravans of camels in the Sahara.
Embossed in leaves too slow for life, like the Dead Sea.
Who walks like puppets in the raw autumn like the sun in centuries past.
Explosive powder under the soles of centenarian feet.
Swimming stroke faintly twisting in the mists of autumn.
Pains like the beads of a rosary.
Slow death slowly bent like the statue's head by time.
I had ten coins. In the dictatorial flame of white suns.
Yellow fell in the nostalgic forests of the mornings.
Nostalgia in the buttoned bellies, under the golden chains of almonds.
The chevaliers of Auvergne keep me company in the obedient spring.

Caressing obsession. Chain of lugubrious pier in the more vivacious smiles.

Lessons of tenderness in the blond evening.

Silver-plated mechanisms sink in supernatural stages.

The old brothers are flowing, flowing.

Adamic silk. I need tenderness in the palm fronds of my anxiety.

Anxious benediction, you who capitulate in the broadside of timid and
reckless clouds.

Don't be cheeky, oh you sincere ones, be wheedling bumpkins.

Industrious cracks in the times of human lives, it's the canal with black
boats that forget themselves in their fantasies.

We are weary. Our legs bleed. Our livers fester.

It's the Algonquin chief who does not forget the shores of creamy sands.

Noisy dogs adorn our solitary thoughts. The nuns' veil gets lost in our
stately breasts. Sad Frederick in the spiritual oils. It's the defections of
uncles who die, skeletons, in the swans' mirages.

Decked-out sweetness. Abnormal boredom in human sorrows! O, the
lullaby thoughts.

It's a man strolling in the lone house.

I am afraid among inhuman comforts.

O fiscal torment. Brutal profligacies offer themselves masked in the
countries of black wings.

I am a generation of old youth. You paid dearly for your passports, awfully
dearly.

You are the young who dreamed of chimneys with blinding metal.

We are leaving in the thorns of sparks.

Smiling hope that falls in the toenails of cutting feet.

Ah! the misty cousinry.

I signal with my arms at the haughty future like a sailor covered in cankers
of boredom.

*At that moment, the five notes of the theme are heard from the next room, played
on the piano. THE MAN shudders. He turns heavily towards the door, almost with
despair. He looks at it, and then, deliberately, he goes towards the adjoining room
and walks in. The door closes after him. Silence. We hear noises like chairs being
moved around, like hammering on the wall, like the uproar of an angry man, a
general confusion. Then the five notes of the theme are heard in a very high, thin,
piano sound. Then the theme is played on lower notes. And then everything rushes
headlong. The theme is heard played louder and louder by an orchestra. The five-note
theme is played by the orchestra in a crescendo that amplifies indefinitely.*

CURTAIN

24 : *Hilda Morgan* (1949)

Early CBC Radio Drama

JOHN JACKSON & HOWARD FINK

FROM THE EARLY 1900S TO THE LATE 1940S, radio was the principal household source of information and entertainment.[1] Families would gather around their radios after the evening meal to listen to the news of the day and enjoy comedies, dramatic presentations, and sporting events. Canadians of all ages were familiar with programming on stations across Canada and the United States. It was in this setting that Canadian Broadcasting Corporation (CBC) radio drama achieved a prominent place in Canadian entertainment, especially in the early years of public broadcasting. Radio drama was also a central driving force of English-Canadian theatre, supporting live stage theatre as both a training ground and a source of employment for writers, actors, and directors.[2] Reciprocally, radio drama was supported by live theatre, which provided scripts for adaptation, and radio drama provided alternate employment opportunities for theatre personnel. Moreover, radio plays, like *Hilda Morgan*, were often more than just entertainment; they were a venue for social and political criticism.

At the very beginning of radio broadcasting in the early 1920s, plays were broadcast over local public stations and, to a lesser extent, private radio stations. The former included a network of Canadian National Railway (CNR) stations from Vancouver (CNRV) to Halifax (CNRH). Thus, radio broadcasts were available across the country. At that point in time, trains were a preferred mode of intercity travel. For example, while travelling from Halifax to Montreal, Toronto to Winnipeg, or Edmonton to Vancouver, passengers would be treated to a radio drama as well as the latest news and perhaps a baseball or hockey game. *The Romance of Canada*, the first drama series broadcast over the CNRV network, was produced and directed by Jack Gilmour (1927). In 1932 the CNRV yielded to the Canadian Radio Broadcasting Commission which, in turn, became the CBC four years later.

The development of Canadian theatre—writing, acting, and producing[3]— was nurtured at the CBC. Despite eventual competition from television, dramatic production in the CBC continued until March 2014, which marked the end of a long and successful tradition of Canadian radio drama. The demise was principally due to a loss of audience, writers, and actors to live theatre and television.[4] Plays may be found along the full spectrum of dramatic forms: from classical to contemporary, from tragedy to romance, and comedy to irony (Fink et al., n.d.; see also Frye 1957).

---

1. A selection of scripts of plays broadcast during the 1940s and 1950s may be found in Fink and Jackson 1987. Bibliographies of radio drama scripts, many annotated by the producer prior to broadcast, may be viewed at www.concordia.ca/research/broadcasting-journalism/archives.html.

2. French-language radio drama had its origins in 1922 in the context of private radio, first appearing over station CKAC out of Montreal, the first French-language station in North America. Writers, actors, and producers were well known in Quebec radio and theatre (Legris 2004).

3. In radio drama the producer and director were the same person, thus the phrase "producer-director" is at times used or just "producer" or "director."

4. A successor to the tradition may be explored on the podcast *PlayME*, which recasts "new theatre scripts and short stories" as contemporary radio plays.

5. *The Jinker*, written by Joseph
Schull, produced by Andrew
Allan, broadcast March 20,
1955, Stage 55, CBC Trans-
Canada Network; see Fink and
Jackson 1987, 268–99. *The Pillars
of Hercules*, written by Gerald
Noxon, produced by Andrew
Allan, broadcast March 5, 1944,
CBC Trans-Canada; see Fink
and Jackson 1989, 75–91.

FIGURE 24.1: *Canadian Broadcasting Corporation Radio Production, ca. 1945–55.*
Item 2097, series 1057, Alexandra Studio fonds 1257, City of Toronto Archives.

Radio-play dramatization was—and is—a highly specialized skill in a medium that has none of the visual instruments of communication available in live theatre, but must speak through sound alone: voices, sound effects, and music. This situation is a disadvantage, perhaps, but also an opportunity: "The lack of a mimetic visual reality gives the radio play a tremendous freedom from the physical world" (Fink and Jackson 1987, xi). A radio drama may bring its audience to any location and move from one to another through the use of music and sound effects. It can take warring ships through rough seas and crashing ice flows off the coast of Newfoundland, as in *The Jinker*, or place the listener in the middle of an air raid in southeast England in 1940.[5] Indeed, before audio taping was readily available, actors sat around a table, microphone in the middle and, following several rehearsals, read their lines with confidence in a stage-like manner. Producer-directors, sound effects technicians, and musicians were located with the players in the same studio. The producer would work with the author, musicians, sound effects personnel, and the operator (the station's technician) before going to rehearsal.

In 1942 a young man, Andrew Allan, joined the CBC as national supervisor of the Radio Drama Department. Drawing from local drama departments across Canada, he developed what soon became Canada's National Theatre of the Air. The two prestige programs he created were *Stage*, which presented a series of original Canadian plays on Sunday evenings, and *Wednesday Night*, a series featuring classical and international plays. Allan recruited a group of experienced producer-directors, who worked in major centres like Montreal (Rupert Caplan) and Winnipeg (Esse W. Ljungh). Also, playwrights such as W.O. Mitchell, Lister Sinclair, Gerald Noxon, Patricia Joudry, and Len Peterson regularly contributed original scripts. Actors such as John Drainie, Alan King, Ruth Springfield, Alice Hill, Tommy Tweed, Barry Morse, William Shatner, Christopher Plummer, and Lorne Greene brought the productions to life on air.

Under Allan's supervision, productions followed two major orientations. One featured classical, international, and established Canadian productions. The other featured new Canadian plays. More than half of the *Stage* productions were highly critical with respect to social class, the economy, politics, and the condition of women. Needless to say, these plays elicited considerable criticism from audiences unprepared for a dissection of the norms of the day. Allan was well aware of the criticism directed toward many of the plays broadcast over the *Stage* series. In his biography, *A Self-Portrait*, Allan noted that "many of our plays in the early years had what was called 'social content,' this was because the writers—in fact all of us—were products of a Depression and a War. Ideas bred from these twin phenomena were inevitable, unless you put artificial curbs on them. And we had determined not to apply those curbs" (Fink and Jackson 1987, xiv).

Indeed, neither public nor private drama broadcasters shied away from controversial material; subtlety was not part of their mandate. Plays frequently stirred up social and political controversy. For example, actor Jack Bowdery created the comedy show *Millie and Lizzie*, a radio drama serial that was broadcast regularly between 1930 and 1934 over several Vancouver private stations. Millie and Lizzie were two working-class women making their way through life with difficulty during the Great Depression. Their ways of escaping the difficulties in which they found themselves from time to time were hilarious and highly critical of middle- and upper-class values and politics (Fink and Jackson 1994). *Who Killed Cock Robin?*, another socio/political play written by Alan King and produced by Andrew Allan in May 1952, was broadcast by CBC Toronto. Though some twenty years after *Millie and Lizzie*, it is another example of the social criticism common to Canadian radio drama. It is a bitter, satirical work in which Sydney Sparrow (a sparrow) is on trial for the murder of Cockford Robbins (a robin). The defence argues that the killing is acceptable because the robin was furthering socialist ideologies.

One of the most controversial plays produced during this period was *Hilda Morgan* by Lister Sinclair, which aired on CBC on May 22, 1949. It was a play about choices set in the context of the norms and values surrounding the issue of children conceived out of wedlock. While *Millie and Lizzie* was social and political in its stance and *Who Killed Cock Robin?* was political, *Hilda Morgan* was pure social criticism, given its defiance of the then accepted values and norms pertaining to unmarried mothers, marriage, and sexual relationships.

Hilda, a young woman in her twenties and a schoolteacher, announces her pregnancy to Mrs. Morgan, her mother, and Ruth, her sister. There is a reluctant acceptance, foreshadowing later arguments, since Hilda will soon be married to David, the father. This more or less satisfies Mrs. Morgan and Ruth. All is reasonably quiet until David is killed in an automobile accident. Now the threat of exposure and damaged reputation takes over. Mrs. Morgan's fear of what the neighbours will think and Ruth's worries about how the news might negatively impact her husband's job at the bank lead them to concoct a set of possible strategies to avoid shame: have the child and put it up for adoption, have an abortion, or marry Wally (an earlier boyfriend) are among the solutions offered. Nevertheless, Hilda is firm; she will have the child and rear it alone in honour of the child's father.

It is important to underscore that *Hilda Morgan* aired in 1949. The issue was not uncommon, but the mores of the day did not accept the stand taken by Hilda. Angry letters to the CBC, the prime minister, and Parliament followed the broadcast. Individuals and organizations alike expressed outrage. A rebroadcast a year later served to increase the outrage. There is the hint of an emancipatory quality in the play. A new role for women and the possibility of a single woman with children as an acceptable arrangement were there for the audience to consider (Fink and Jackson 1987, 69–70). At the time, most listeners were reluctant to accept the possibility.

Bibliography and Further Reading

BBC Sounds (Drama). www.bbc.co.uk/radio/drama.

Beatty, Bill. 1949. "'Pyramid Clubs' Sweep Toronto." *CBC News Roundup*, March 29, 1949.

Concordia Centre for Broadcasting and Journalism Studies (CCBJS) Archives. https://www.concordia.ca/research/broadcasting-journalism/archives.html.

Cusson, Marie, and Greg M. Nielsen. 2004. "Canadian Radio Satire." In *Museum of Broadcasting Communications Encyclopedia of Radio*, edited by Christopher Sterling with Michael C. Keith, 285–89. New York: Fitzroy Dearborn.

Drakakis, John, ed. 1981. *British Radio Drama*. Cambridge: Cambridge University Press.

Duffy, John. 1993. *From Humors to Medical Science: A History of American Medicine*. Urbana: University of Illinois Press.

Expect Theatre PlayME. CBC Podcasts. www.playmepodcast.com.

Fink, Howard. 2004. "English Radio Drama." In *Museum of Broadcasting Communications Encyclopedia of Radio*, edited by Christopher Sterling with Michael C. Keith, 282–85. New York: Fitzroy Dearborn.

Fink, Howard, et al., eds. n.d. *Canadian National Theatre on the Air*. A Descriptive Bibliography and Union List. 3 vols. Concordia University, Montreal: Centre for Broadcasting and Journalism Studies. https://www.concordia.ca/research/broadcasting-journalism/archives/cbc-radio-dramas.html.

Fink, Howard, and John Jackson. 1994. "Jack Bowdery/Ammon: Pioneer Leftist 'Thirties B.C. Dramatist." *Fréquence/Frequency*, no. 1–2, 59–71.

Fink, Howard, and John Jackson, eds. 1987. *All the Bright Company: Radio Drama Produced by Andrew Allan.* Kingston, ON: Quarry Press; Toronto: CBC Enterprises.

———. 1989. *The Road to Victory: Radio Plays by Gerald Noxon.* Waterloo, ON: Malcolm Lowry Review; Kingston, ON: Quarry Press.

Frye, Northrop. 1957. *Anatomy of Criticism: Four Essays.* Princeton, NJ: Princeton University Press.

Jackson, John. 1999. "Canadian Radio Research: An Introduction." *Journal of Radio Studies,* no. 6, 116–20.

———. 2002. "From Cultural Relativity to Multiculturalism: The CBC's Ways of Mankind Series, 1953." *Fréquence/Frequency,* no. 9–10, 95–107.

Knox, James Samuel. 1921. *The Science and Art of Selling.* Cleveland, OH: Knox Business Book Co.

Kuffert, Len. 2009. "'What do You Expect of This Friend?': Canadian Radio and the Intimacy of Broadcasting." *Media History* 15 (3): 303–19.

Legris, Renée. 2004. "French Radio Drama." In *Museum of Broadcasting Communications Encyclopedia of Radio,* edited by Christopher Sterling with Michael C. Keith, 280–82, New York: Fitzroy Dearborn.

MacLennan, Anne F. 2013. "Learning to Listen: Developing the Canadian Radio Audience in the 1930s." *Journal of Radio and Audio Media* 20 (2): 311–26.

Nothof, Anne. 1990. "Canadian Radio Drama in English: Prick up Your Ears." *Theatre Research in Canada / Recherches théâtrales au Canada* 11 (1) (Spring): 59–70.

Partridge, Eric. 1993. *A Dictionary of Catch Phrases.* New York: Routledge.

Vipond, Mary. 2013. "What's a New Public Broadcaster to Do?: The Canadian Radio Broadcasting Commission's Programs in Transnational Context, 1932–1936." *Journal of Radio and Audio Media* 20 (2): 295–310.

Hilda Morgan

LISTER SINCLAIR

1. Since about 1870, the monkey is used in English vulgar speech as a witty and wise figure that often offers a clever statement on something a person just said—often an elaboration of a cliché that employs scatological details (Partridge 1993, 32).
2. The bodywork of a motor vehicle.
3. In James Samuel Knox's *The Science and Art of Selling*, a salesmanship engineer is a person knowledgeable about the technique of selling who can advise other salespeople on their technique (1921, 329).
4. As with film, radio drama will carry a principal musical theme as background music communicating changing moods, questions, and conflicts. Music is crucial to the listener who must depend totally on sound—voice, sound effects, and music. The instructions here, instructions to the music director and his players, set the mood for conflicts to come.
5. A well-known radio, stage, TV, and film actress. She died November 2010.
6. An established composer, arranger, and conductor. He was a major contributor to CBC radio drama.

PRODUCTION

Producer: Andrew Allan

Music: Lucio Agostini

Sound: David Tasker

Operator: Bruce Armstrong

Announcer: Elwood Glover

Program: Stage 49, Item34

Broadcast: May 22, 1949, 10:00–11:00 pm EDT

Studio: Toronto

Network: Trans-Canada

CHARACTERS

HILDA MORGAN

MOTHER

RUTH

WALLY TURNBULL

MRS. TEMPLE

DAVID TEMPLE

POLICEMAN

WALLY. (*Familiar and loquacious.*) I had a narrow squeeze myself once, as the monkey said.[1] Even now it's enough to make a person think when you talk about Hilda Morgan. What about her, eh? These days you can't tell by the coachwork,[2] and I should know! After all, when a person's a Salesmanship Engineer[3] (on the road in the wholesale end since I was eighteen), if there's one thing: well, a person certainly gets to know the girlies. One kind's worth a million dollars, and you can't buy it; and the other, why, like we always say in the business: I can get a million for you wholesale, and you take my advice; keep 'em separate. There's the kind to settle down with, and the kind to settle up with. But sometimes you never know which you've got until it's too late. If then.

MUSIC: *a questioning phrase, rather dark and foreboding: then to background.*[4]

ANNOUNCER. Stage 49, Item 34…"Hilda Morgan," a new original play by Lister Sinclair…starring Ruth Springford[5] in the title role. Produced and directed by Andrew Allan, with a special musical score composed and conducted by Lucio Agostini[6]…Lister Sinclair's new play: "Hilda Morgan."

*MUSIC: up for a strong punctuation: down to blues-type background: out with
Wally's narration.*

WALLY. Now the lay of the land was this: Thursday and Friday I used to be
in Southwestern Ontario, up to and including London: that's as far as I
go, as the monkey said. Friday night, I'm back in Toronto; and Saturday
afternoon, I used to call on Hilda. They'd just moved near the park: 2046
Grosvenor.[7] She lived with her mother. Very lovely person, Mrs. Morgan,
we used to get on…

MUSIC: out with voice.

MRS. MORGAN. (*With a theatrical sigh.*) Wally: don't ever move. You find
out how much rubbish you've accumulated during the years, and in the
meantime, all your precious things are just smashed to pieces. Moving
simply isn't worth it: take my advice.
WALLY. I'd love to, Mrs. Morgan; but of course, I move all the time. On the
road: live in a suitcase, if you get the point! Well, it's half past three, and
still no sign of Hilda, eh?
MRS. MORGAN. (*Shaking her head.*) Honestly, Wally, I don't know! She said
she was going to take my necklace to the jewellers. I have a beautiful pearl
necklace, cultured, they say (but I can't tell the difference, and I'm sure
nobody else can); and I took it out of the case for the moving, and string
must have perished, because it all broke to pieces in my hands: pearls all
over everywhere, and I know some of them are lost, you can never get it
back the same as it was, and that's life. And Hilda said she'd take it in, and
have them look at it, but that was an hour and a half ago.
WALLY. (*Rather plaintively.*) She *knows* I always come on Saturdays.
MRS. MORGAN. (*Roguish.*) Well, I should say so!
WALLY. It's a regular date, and I brought her in some chocolates. Got 'em
wholesale.
MRS. MORGAN. Oh, Wally, really you shouldn't.
WALLY. Well, I behave here like I'm one of the family, so a little present does
no harm. I always say you can slide further on…Well, I got a four o'clock
appointment. (*Embarrassedly.*)
MRS. MORGAN. I'm sure Hilda has so much on her mind these days, I don't
know what's the matter. (*Then roguish again.*) Though I have a premonition
it may be love.
WALLY. (*Pleased.*) Now that's a possibility. What do you think, Mrs. Morgan?
MRS. MORGAN. You're the one who'd know *that*, Wally!
WALLY. A year ago, I'd have said yes. Haven't been around so much lately. (*But
he sounds pretty confident.*)
MRS. MORGAN. (*With a naughty twinkle.*) Haven't been around *here*, you
mean.

8. Yonge Street is one of the
oldest north–south streets in
Toronto. As a former part of
Ontario Highway 11, it moves
north to Newmarket and
then changes to Highway 51
proceeding north through the
province.

WALLY. (*Delighted.*) Well, if there's one thing I'm certainly sure of, all right, I'd venture to say that I pretty well know the girlies. Practice makes perfect.

MRS. MORGAN. As Hilda's mother, I shan't let you talk like that! Next thing she'll be getting jealous of me. As it is, I don't know what she'll say when she finds we've spent the afternoon alone together.

WALLY. Well, it's a good sign if they get jealous: means they're getting ready for Mr. Right, if you get the point. And anyway, it's all in the family.

SOUND: *doorbell slightly off.*

MRS. MORGAN. Doorbell! That's Hilda now! Excuse me!

WALLY. (*Raising his voice after her.*) Better late than never, as the...

MRS. MORGAN. (*Fading off a little.*) Forgotten her key again. She's either crazy or she's in love, and she certainly isn't crazy.

SOUND: *door opens off.*

RUTH. (*Off.*) Hello, Mother.

MRS. MORGAN. (*Off.*) Ruth, my dear! It's my married daughter, Wally! (*Calling back.*)

WALLY. (*On: calling forward.*) Well, hello, Ruth!

RUTH. (*Fading on.*) I'm only stopping by for a moment, and if you're entertaining, I won't disturb you.

WALLY. Oh, no, no; I was just going. Got to run, you know.

RUTH. I'm off to the shops to buy Len some new shirts. I hope you're not like my husband, Wally; of course, his position demands it, but I never knew a man so really fastidious.

WALLY. Well, I believe and hope the ladies like to see a man looking his best. So Hilda tells me.

RUTH. (*Interest.*) Does she? (*A curious little pause.*) You're not waiting for Hilda now? (*"of course" understood.*)

WALLY. Oh, I got her a few chocolates: wholesale.

MRS. MORGAN. Hilda said she was taking my pearls in, but that was long ago.

RUTH. Oh? The little jewellers up North Yonge?[8]

MRS. MORGAN. You know, Ruth, opposite the place where I get my flower transfers.

RUTH. (*Oddly.*) Perhaps she dropped in for a cup of coffee somewhere. (*Then with curious emphasis.*) I certainly wouldn't wait for her, if I were you, Wally.

WALLY. (*Awkwardly, as though this has been an invitation.*) Well, no, thanks very much, I'm afraid I can't. I've really got to run. Got a four o'clock appointment.

MRS. MORGAN. Let me make you another cup of tea before you go.

RUTH. Mother, it's not polite to try and detain guests against their will. Wally has lots of people to see, and he's very busy, and he has to fly.

WALLY. That's about the size of it. Uh...how if I dropped back this evening, though? (*Fading off a little.*)

MRS. MORGAN. Do that, Wally. I'll tell her, so she'll be sure to expect you.

RUTH. Have you got your hat and everything?

WALLY. (*Slightly off.*) All present and correct. Well, see you this evening, then.

SOUND: *door opens off.*

WALLY. Got to get away, or I'll never make my appointment. Four o'clock it's for.

MRS. MORGAN. (*Off.*) Goodbye, Wally. See you this evening!

SOUND: *door shuts off.*

RUTH. (*Calling.*) Has he gone?

MRS. MORGAN. (*Fading back.*) Now then, Ruth, what's the meaning of this? You practically hustled that poor man off the premises as if we didn't want to see him. Hilda's not going to thank you for this, you know.

RUTH. Mother: I've found out about Hilda.

MRS. MORGAN. (*Immediately excited.*) Sit down, Ruth, and tell me all about it.

RUTH. She's ill. There's something the matter with her.

MRS. MORGAN. I've had an uncanny feeling that something like this was going to happen. How do you know?

RUTH. Well, I saw her on the street a couple of hours ago; that's what put me on the track.

MRS. MORGAN. How?

RUTH. I know she saw me, because she looked right at me; then she dodged into the nearest store. So I knew something was happening, and I just kept quiet, and next thing, out she came, and walked off down Bloor Street.[9]

MRS. MORGAN. She said she was taking my broken necklace in.

RUTH. She did nothing of the sort. I was right behind her. Do you know where she went?

MRS. MORGAN. No, where?

RUTH. Into one of those old houses near the Medical Arts Building. I went up and looked at the brass plates, and it was full of surgeons.

MRS. MORGAN. What did she say when she came out?

RUTH. I didn't speak to her.

MRS. MORGAN. Why not? Didn't you wait?

RUTH. She ran into David Temple.

MRS. MORGAN. Oh, him! He was round *here* a week ago.

RUTH. So *that's* why she's been acting up.

MRS. MORGAN. I knew she was ill.

RUTH. Or thinks she is.

MRS. MORGAN. No, you can't tell me. I'm her mother. And I know what it is. I know as if someone had just spoken it in my ear. It's cancer.

10. The use of dogs in surgical training was introduced at Johns Hopkins University by William Halsted and Harvey Cushing in the early twentieth century (Duffy 1993, 277).

RUTH. Now, Mother, don't be silly! She probably got a sore throat or something.

MRS. MORGAN. Then why hasn't she said a word about it? I can always tell when somebody's got a growth. I should have realized long ago.

RUTH. Don't be a fool, Mother. (*Kindly, if impatiently.*)

MRS. MORGAN. (*With irritating assurance.*) Your mother's not a fool, dear. I just know. What on earth shall I do, if I lose her? (*With more feeling.*)

RUTH. Oh, come on, Mother! Hilda's as strong as a horse.

MRS. MORGAN. (*Correcting her.*) She *looks* strong, dear; but she's been delicate ever since she grew up. I don't know *what* I'll do if they have to cut her open. (*With simple hopelessness.*)

RUTH. (*Trying to pull things together.*) Mother, I only mentioned this in case you knew what was the matter. I'm sure there's nothing wrong that time won't cure.

MRS. MORGAN. (*Well away.*) She's my own daughter, Ruth; I've noticed she's not been the same these last few weeks. You can't tell *me* they aren't going to cut her open. She was foolish to go to a surgeon. They're never happy till they're cutting into you. Your poor father used to get into their labs whenever he got the chance, and it was simply terrible. Cutting up dogs[10] and all sorts of cruelty. (*Her tone is getting more and more vicious.*) I'd like to cut some of them up, and see how they'd like it.

RUTH. They have to learn somehow.

MRS. MORGAN. Cruelty is cruelty. We're told to love one another, and that doesn't mean cutting up poor dumb animals. If I ever have to be cut open, I will not have it done by a surgeon, and it worries me to think what Hilda may have to go through.

RUTH. What worries *me* is who's going to pay for it?

MRS. MORGAN. If money is truly needed in a Christian spirit, it will be provided, and that we know.

RUTH. Len and I haven't the money to spend on operations.

MRS. MORGAN. Weren't you saving for a dining room suite? I shall have to make sacrifices too.

RUTH. In any case, there's no reason why it should have to be, well, cancer. (*With a tiny hesitation on the dreadful word.*)

MRS. MORGAN. I'm never wrong about this kind of thing, Ruth. It goes in our family. I can remember knowing about it with your Aunt Nellie, and I can remember it just started as a lump, and then she was gone almost before we realized.

RUTH. But you don't have it until you're old; and Hilda's just a girl.

MRS. MORGAN. (*Rather sharply.*) Nellie was just a girl. She wasn't even fifty; she was the youngest next to me. Besides, you don't know what happened last night. My chrysanthemums burst the pot.

RUTH. It must have got cracked moving.

MRS. MORGAN. No, dear! It shattered in the middle of the night. You should have seen the mess. They outgrew the pot! I knew then it was a special warning for me!

RUTH. Such as how?

MRS. MORGAN. (*Solemn.*) It was a warning from Providence about a growth, and now it's all come true, and what on earth will become of me if Hilda dies, and ends up losing her job, I really don't know! (*Dissolving into the verge of tears.*)

RUTH. Come on, Mother, cheer up! I'm going to wait till I know what the doctor really said (*She then adds almost to herself.*) and why that Dave Temple was hanging around.

MUSIC: *low and ominous to a restaurant background.*
SOUND: *very light restaurant background.*

DAVID. So that's it, eh Hilda?

HILDA. That's it, David.

DAVID. You shouldn't have helped with your moving. Might have strained you.

HILDA. I'll be strained a lot more before we're through. This coffee's perfectly foul. See if you can find the waitress.

DAVID. I've been drinking mine.

HILDA. A woman could put up with disasters but not inconveniences.

DAVID. Is this a disaster?

HILDA. Not to me.

DAVID. Nor me. Did he say when?

HILDA. In six months. He'll be more exact later.

DAVID. Three months ago. Lake Simcoe.[11]

HILDA. (*Musing.*) I suppose. The doctor's a very nice man. Teaches himself, he says. Asked me if it gave me a pain in the eyes. I told him teaching gave me a pain in the feet and a pain in the neck. He kept calling me Mrs. Temple,[12] and both he and the nurse looked for the ring.

DAVID. You were right about getting one then. They didn't seem to realize... that...

HILDA. (*Cooly.*) That I'm not really entitled to it? Of course not, David.

DAVID. Why of course not?

HILDA. Because I *am* entitled to it. As far as I'm concerned, we've been married ten months.

DAVID. I still wish we'd made it legal. We should have done.

HILDA. Dollars and cents, David.

DAVID. Dollars and cents aren't going to count now, are they?

HILDA. No, we'll *have* to afford it now. May I have a cigarette? I feel a little shaky for some reason.

DAVID. (*Solicitous.*) Sure, honey; here you are.

HILDA. I'll be all right in a moment, I expect. Probably poisoned by the coffee.

DAVID: I think you're *glad* this has happened.

DAVID. I am glad. Because now we're going to be married; and because we're going to have a child.

HILDA. Darling! Do you want to tell your parents about the baby? Right away, I mean?

DAVID. I'd like to soon; I think they'd be very happy too. Happy as I am.

HILDA. You're happy about it?

DAVID. Very happy.

HILDA. Darling. OK, pick the time, and tell 'em; but while you're at it, tell 'em to keep it from Mother.

DAVID. Well, they're up at the cottage right now. I'll wire[13] them we're engaged, and explain when we meet.

HILDA. Don't you want to put it in a wire?

DAVID. I do not. These days telegraph companies don't send telegrams; they phone in messages, and this is no item for a rural party line.[14]

HILDA. I'll tell Mother we're engaged tonight, after supper.

DAVID. I'll call for you tonight. No need to soothe your mother now.

HILDA. I suppose. I bet Wally Turnbull called this afternoon. This is his day. I used to like him quite a lot, once; and now he's a bit of a nuisance.

DAVID. *He'll* be surprised. (*Quite pleasantly.*)

HILDA. I suppose. I think I'll go home now, David. I feel a bit upset.

DAVID. OK, let's go. I'll get a cab.

HILDA. Never mind about *that*; dollars and cents. And don't come with me. I want to save the row till after supper. You go and wire your parents; that'll give *you* something to do. And when you turn up this evening, be sure and ask mother to show you the new duplex. That may soothe her.

DAVID. Lucky you said *that*, or I'd have been off down Eglinton[15] to the old stamping ground. Fine thing when a fellow doesn't know his wife's address.

HILDA. (*Pleased at the little joke.*) Dear David. (*Then firmly.*) But I'm going to write down the address for you.

DAVID. Want some paper? Better keep me on a lead, too. Might meet a new girlfriend.

HILDA. Lend me a pencil.

DAVID. Here. You wouldn't like *that*, would you?

HILDA. (*Absent-mindedly.*) Like what?

DAVID. Me getting a new girlfriend.

HILDA. (*Going along with the gag.*) Why should I care? I'd run away with Wally Turnbull. Now here you are. This is the address: 2046 Grosvenor Street; and this is the girl's name. It's Hilda. And you remember that, Master David, or I'll have something to say to you.

DAVID. Yes, teacher. Hilda it is; and I'm very proud of her, and very happy. So let's get the glad news circulating!

*MUSIC: with a sprightly figure takes Hilda back home: and ends with a chord of
expectancy.*

MRS. MORGAN. (*Watching out of the window.*) Here she is, Ruth! She's coming
up the path. Open the door, quick!
RUTH. (*Off at the door.*) All right, Mother; I'm here!

SOUND: door opens: slightly off.

RUTH. (*Off.*) Well, *hello*, Hilda!
HILDA. (*Off.*) You gave me quite a fright. I was just going to put the key in.

SOUND: door shuts off.

RUTH. (*Fading on.*) Mother saw you coming, through the window.
HILDA. (*Fading on.*) I didn't expect to see *you* here, Ruth. Thought you spent
this time of day cooking up hot dinners for that tyrannical man of yours.
Hello, Mother. (*Casually.*)
MRS. MORGAN. (*Quite emotionally.*) Oh, Hilda, Hilda, darling!
HILDA. (*Astonished: but soothing her.*) Mother, Mother, Mother. (MRS. MORGAN
continues to cling to HILDA *and to murmur.*) What is it, dear? Ruth, what's the
matter with Mother.
MRS. MORGAN. Nothing, darling; everything's going to be all right: I *know* it is.
HILDA. (*As usual quite calm.*) What's the matter, Ruth?
RUTH. (*Rather pointedly.*) We're waiting for you to tell us.
HILDA. Waiting for *me*?
RUTH. I saw you this afternoon with Dave Temple.
HILDA. (*With blank courtesy.*) Yes?
RUTH. You'd just come out of that little surgeon's building.
MRS. MORGAN. (*Bursting out again.*) Oh, Hilda, why didn't you *tell* me! I'm
your mother; I could have comforted you; don't you realize I've been
through all this before, more than once.
HILDA. (*Slowly.*) I suppose.
RUTH. (*With gentle remonstrance.*) You should have told us you were going to
the doctor.
HILDA. I didn't want to say till afterwards.
RUTH. It might have put us in a very funny position.
MRS. MORGAN. (*Warmly.*) Sweetheart, I understand; you didn't want to worry
us. Well, you're home now, Hilda, and we must all be brave together, just
the three of us. That's the way people do nowadays. In our day, we made
a shameful secret of it; but that was wrong, oh, quite wrong. Now tell us
what the doctor said.
HILDA. He said: yes.

MRS. MORGAN. (*Suddenly becoming edgy in spite of her apparent calm.*) You see, Ruth? I had the premonition and the warning. It is cancer.

HILDA. (*Astounded.*) What on earth put *that* into your head, Mother?

MRS. MORGAN. Don't be ashamed of it, dear; it runs in the family. Several cousins had it. Aunt Nellie had it.

HILDA. (*Pulling herself together.*) Well, if that's what you were worrying about, you're wrong. It's nothing; not cancer at all. Just a—sort of stomach upset. Indigestion—overwork.

RUTH. Operation?

HILDA. No! A good rest, the doctor said, and it'll clear up eventually.

RUTH. Will it pass off naturally in due course?

HILDA. (*With an inward smile.*) Quite naturally, yes.

RUTH. Then why all the mystery? (*Flinging her arms in the air.*)

HILDA. There's no mystery.

RUTH. You didn't tell us.

HILDA. You didn't ask. I don't like a fuss.

MRS. MORGAN. (*In a loud voice.*) It's not a fuss to tell your family.

HILDA. Well, I've told you.

MRS. MORGAN. And what did he say again? (*Just too casually.*)

HILDA. I thought it was overwork, and he said yes.

MRS. MORGAN. Tell me again what he *said*, dear.

HILDA. I've told you, Mother. That's all there is to it. Got a match, Ruth?

MRS. MORGAN. On the side table, dear.

RUTH. Len and I have quit smoking. Saves a lot of money.

HILDA. I can't smoke at school; or near the school buildings.

RUTH. Ridiculous. Old-fashioned.

HILDA. The teacher must be purer than the snows of yesteryear.

MRS. MORGAN. Well, Grandpa did say: If God had meant us to smoke...

RUTH & HILDA. (*Finishing it off together.*) We'd all been born with chimneys in our heads.

HILDA. And a girl who smokes will drink...

RUTH. ...*And a girl who drinks will do anything!*

HILDA. (*With a smile.*) Wally Turnbull used to think that was true.

RUTH. (*Giggling.*) Don't be awful, Hilda! He was here this afternoon with a present for you.

HILDA. (*Positively.*) Wally's got nothing I'm interested in.

MRS. MORGAN. (*Returning to the charge in her sweetest voice.*) Hilda.

HILDA. (*Casually.*) Yes, dear?

MRS. MORGAN. Hilda, look at me.

HILDA. (*Not casually.*) Yes?

MRS. MORGAN. Hilda: is that all you have to tell your mother about this afternoon?

HILDA. (*After a pause.*) No, Mother, there *is* one thing.

MRS. MORGAN. (*Complacently.*) I knew it.

16. In other words, arrangements for the marriage were not carried out until a definite proposal was made and accepted.

HILDA. He rooked me fifteen bucks for telling me I was all right.

RUTH. Fifteen...What a waste of dough!

MRS. MORGAN. It's nothing to pay for peace of mind: if your mind is at peace.

HILDA. Why not?

MRS. MORGAN. (*With exasperating serenity.*) I don't know why not. I only know you're keeping something back.

HILDA. (*Carefully.*) I've told you what he said; that's all.

MRS. MORGAN. I haven't brought you up for twenty-five years with out knowing when there's something on your mind, and I want to know what it is. (*Hardening a little.*)

HILDA. Well, OK. There is something, yes.

MRS. MORGAN. Neither of you can ever keep anything from your mother. It only hurts me a little that you don't trust me in the first place. Out with it, dear.

HILDA. It's nothing to do with the doctor.

MRS. MORGAN. Just say what it is.

HILDA. I wanted to save it till after dinner, but you can't fool Mother. (*With a curious edge.*)

MRS. MORGAN. Say what it is.

HILDA. I'm engaged.

RUTH. Hilda!

MRS. MORGAN. (*Shocked into sincerity.*) Engaged to be *married*? Oh, my dear, Wally's a very lucky man.

HILDA. I expect he is, but I'm engaged to be married to Dave Temple.

MRS. MORGAN. (*Shocked again.*) Dave Temple! But I hardly know him.

HILDA. Why should you? You aren't marrying him.

RUTH. It's certainly sudden enough, Hilda. (*She doesn't know if she likes it or not.*)

HILDA. It may be sudden to you, but David and I have been talking it over for a long time.

MRS. MORGAN. (*Getting back on her pedestal.*) In our day the girl waited till she was asked before she did any talking over.[16]

HILDA. I waited till I was asked; otherwise he mightn't have asked me.

MRS. MORGAN. Then you've been plotting it for a long time?

HILDA. A few months.

RUTH. (*Shrewdly.*) What made you tell us now?

HILDA. We decided it was time to be getting on with it.

MRS. MORGAN. It's certainly time to talk everything over. *I* have something to say, you know.

HILDA. You didn't have anything to say when Ruth got married.

RUTH. There was still you to look after Mother. Now what happens? Len and I certainly haven't room for her.

MRS. MORGAN. Don't think of me, Ruth. Hilda doesn't. Even though she is my baby. (*On the verge of tears.*)

HILDA. I'm twenty-five.

MRS. MORGAN. Don't try and tell your own mother how old you are.

RUTH. You might have given us a chance to make arrangements.

HILDA. (*Easily.*) I'm giving you a chance. This is it.

MRS. MORGAN. I only hope *you* don't feel like this when your little girl's taken
away.

HILDA. Taken away! You see Ruth all the time.

MRS. MORGAN. Can't a mother see her daughter once in a while without
endless complaints? (*HILDA sighs.*) Or is it the funny old joke about the
mother-in-law whose daughters haven't room for her?[17]

RUTH. (*Just as sharp as her mother.*) Len and I have to keep the spare room for
his brothers.

MRS. MORGAN. (*Turning the point.*) Yes, Len thinks of his family, and Wally
thinks of his family, but I'd like to know who David and Hilda think of!

HILDA. Mostly of each other lately.

MRS. MORGAN. Selfishness never pays.

HILDA. It pays the selfish ones.

MRS. MORGAN. Oh! Ruth, did you hear that?

RUTH. What a thing to say to Mother!

HILDA. Mother's in the clear; she never has a guilty conscience.

RUTH. And I have?

HILDA. Why scratch if it isn't itching?

RUTH. Believe me, if anybody's going to have mother-in-law trouble, it's you!
If you think old Mrs. Temple is going to let her darling David fly the coop
into *your* back yard, you're crazy!

HILDA. Nag Len, Ruth; that's what he supports you for.

RUTH. Darling, I'm keeping clear of this whole mess, as of now! But how do
you think Mother and I feel when you put us in a very funny position over
this doctor, and then march in, cool as a cucumber, and tell us you're going
to marry the one and only original mother's boy.

MRS. MORGAN. And what's Wally going to say? I'm sure he's more of a man
than Dave Temple.

RUTH. What did you do to him? Twist his arm, or something? Or did you
propose to him?

HILDA. Len hung around here for long enough before you got him on the
dotted line.

MRS. MORGAN. I see we have a good deal to talk over.

HILDA. For my money, there's nothing to talk over.

MRS. MORGAN. We'll see about that, Hilda, when the time comes; tempers
have become frayed, and we'll apologize. I'm sorry for anything I've said.
Ruth?

RUTH. I'm sorry.

MRS. MORGAN. Hilda?

HILDA. I suppose.

MRS. MORGAN. And we'll talk about it again after supper.

HILDA. I shall be going out after supper.

RUTH. With David?

MRS. MORGAN. Is he going to show himself here?

HILDA. He is.

MRS. MORGAN. Then perhaps he can talk it over too. I don't doubt we shall all see reason by the time we're through.

MUSIC: *picks up the threat and passes the time.*

MRS. MORGAN. She's taking a long time getting dressed.

RUTH. Give her a chance. She wants to hit the new fiancée.

MRS. MORGAN. I'll *hit* him. You wait. I'll make them see reason. Wally's coming round later. I'll talk them out of it.

RUTH. (*Now more on HILDA's side.*) You didn't talk Len and me out of it.

MRS. MORGAN. (*Bridling.*) My dear, never for one moment did I try!

RUTH. (*Off-hand.*) Didn't you?

MRS. MORGAN. I should certainly hope not. My girls have their own lives to live. I hope I realize that. It's just my duty to advise them and make them think of someone besides themselves occasionally. And though there was some understanding with Wally Turnbull, please don't think I hold anything against David *personally*, no more than I did with Len.

RUTH. David isn't in the same position Len was.

MRS. MORGAN. Be fair, dear. He's in his father's business.

RUTH. There's a difference between a sales clerk and a banker.

MRS. MORGAN. Len's hardly a banker yet, is he, dear?

RUTH. He'll be an Assistant Manager in ten or fifteen years. Already we've been to the manager's house three times for bridge;[18] so all his work *is* getting him somewhere.

MRS. MORGAN. It's up to you, of course, if you have to make your way by gambling.

RUTH. We play for fun.

MRS. MORGAN. Your father and I could never see the fun in playing cards; but things change, and people feel they must change too.

RUTH. Well, Len doesn't smoke, and he doesn't drink, and...

MRS. MORGAN. Ruth, our mother always told us: a gambler's worse than a drunkard. A drunkard can do no more than make a beast of himself, but a gambler can lose everything for you, and never let on till the men come to take it away. And Mother certainly knew what she was talking about.

RUTH. You never told me grandpa was bad about money.

MRS. MORGAN. (*Piously.*) Whatever he was, dear, Mother made him repent before we grew up; and forgive and forget is the only Christian thing.

RUTH. (*Agitated.*) You might have told me this before. It might affect Len.

MRS. MORGAN. Len? How?

19. A guarantee of faithful conduct when dealing with financial matters. In this case, the insurance company would pay the bank a sum if Len was to misbehave in some way. Consequently, the insurance company would have to have confidence that Len would not engage in any financial crimes.

20. A recording device that originally used wax cylinders, but by the time of this play had switched to recording on Lexan (a type of plastic) by cutting grooves in the same manner as a phonograph.

RUTH. Everything must be *right* in a bank, especially family background. The temptation is enormous and the salaries are rather moderate, so they have to be sure of perfect honesty, or else the insurance companies won't put up a bond.[19]

MRS. MORGAN. (*Going pink.*) I'm sorry if I said anything wrong.

RUTH. You should have told me sooner or not at all.

MRS. MORGAN. Then simply forget I said it.

RUTH. (*Scrupulously.*) But you *have* said it. If I had to swear on the Bible, did I know any bad blood in the family? I'd have to tell them, yes.

HILDA. (*Coming on.*) I've been pinning up that slip, and I don't think it shows now.

MRS. MORGAN. (*Glad to change the subject.*) Turn round, Hilda. No, that's fine.

HILDA. Stocking seams straight?

RUTH. (*Sourly.*) Oh, straight enough.

HILDA. (*Pausing.*) What's the matter now?

RUTH. Nothing *you* need to worry about. Mother's just let out that grandpa was a gambler.

MRS. MORGAN. We have no right to judge others. Forgive us our trespasses.

RUTH. I'm not thinking of myself; it's Len. (*And it really is, too.*)

HILDA. Poor grandpa's wild oats aren't going to tickle Len at this late date.

RUTH. (*Stubbornly.*) What's bred in the bone comes out in the flesh.

MRS. MORGAN. If we're talking about breeding, you're descended from your grandmother as well, and she was a lovely person almost till the day she died.

HILDA. Even if she wasn't, we have our own lives to live.

RUTH. Len's different.

HILDA. How so?

RUTH. You don't know what a strain it is; we have to think of his position at the bank every minute. Everything we say or do is taken note of, day or night.

HILDA. Dictaphone[20] in the mattress?

RUTH. You're the coarse side of the family, Hilda. You're certainly grandpa's child.

HILDA. What's the matter? Broken your funny bone?

RUTH. (*Honestly upset.*) There's nothing funny about the way we worry and scrape; and you'll know that when you're living off David.

MRS. MORGAN. If it's my fault, I'll give back every cent you've given me. I only took it because I thought you wanted to help.

RUTH. We do, but when Hilda goes, we can't do any more, and David'll have to take over his share. (*This is her real worry.*)

HILDA. (*Sympathetically.*) If that's all that's worrying you, dear, cheer up and settle down. Of course David'll take over his share.

RUTH. (*Suspicious yet hopeful.*) How do you know? Are you sure?

HILDA. We've talked it over lots of times.

MRS. MORGAN. (*Regally.*) Not that I mind my private and personal affairs
    being discussed and debated with perfect strangers, but I do think, Hilda,
    you might tell me.
HILDA. I am telling you, dear.
MRS. MORGAN. Every so often I meet Mrs. Temple in the street; and how was
    I to know they knew all our private and personal arrangements?
HILDA. There's nothing to be ashamed of. I never care who knows the truth.
MRS. MORGAN. I know you haven't any secrets from anybody, Hilda, but
    when you're as old as I am, and living off your daughters' charity…
RUTH. Charity! Oh, Mother!
MRS. MORGAN. It makes me go hot all over when I think how I'm going to
    face that boy when he comes in the door; and you should have thought of it
    before you blurted out our business to him, Hilda.

SOUND: *doorbell rings off.*

RUTH. You sit down. I'll let him in.
HILDA. Do I look all right?
RUTH. (*Fading off.*) You look fine, darling.
HILDA. I hope so. Do I look all right, Mother?
MRS. MORGAN. You look as well as you ever do in blue, dear, even if you are a
    little tired. Sit still quietly and wait for him.

MUSIC: *a tense figure: down to Wally's background.*

WALLY. But it wasn't him. It was just little me. I was a bit surprised, because
    they put me in the front room where nobody was sitting, as if I was
    company, and after a while, and a bit of whispering here and there, Hilda
    came in—in full war paint! She was always a stunner when she had her
    glasses off, and she had lots of the old twinkle-twinkle that night. I felt
    pretty flattered that she'd got all the rigging on for yours truly, for to tell
    the truth, I had noticed we weren't as pally as we used to be, if you get the
    point. Even so, I did notice she didn't quite seem to have her eye on the
    scoreboard.

MUSIC: *out with WALLY.*

HILDA. Hello, Wally. This is a surprise seeing you.
WALLY. Oh, I can tell better than that! (*With great coyness.*) Don't tell *me* you
    weren't expecting somebody!
HILDA. (*Rather ill at ease.*) Well, yes, Wally, I was expecting somebody. You see…
WALLY. I just brought in a little package for the duchess of Grosvenor Street,
    eh? Look as if you'd stepped straight out of the silver screen.
HILDA. Do you really like it, Wally?

WALLY. (*Smiling happily.*) I like the packaging, and I like the product. I like the nice blue dress: I like what it hides, and I like what it shows.

HILDA. (*Smiling.*) Wally. And how nice of you to bring me something.

WALLY. (*Hopefully.*) No real need to open it right away.

HILDA. (*Missing the point: brightly.*) All right, I'll put it over here.

WALLY. (*Disappointed.*) It's just something a fellow in the line was able to get me specially. You can't get those sort in the regular way, you know. It's a special sort of chocolates.

HILDA. Oh; how nice of you, Wally; but I'm afraid it'll spoil my figure.

WALLY. (*Expansively.*) No, no, no: there can't be too much of you to please me. I think it's *wonderful* you're putting on weight.

HILDA. (*Alert at once.*) Oh. Is it...very noticeable?

WALLY. (*Noticing her tension.*) No offence intended. I just think the smile looks brighter when the cheeks are plumper.

HILDA. (*Relaxing.*) Oh yes, I have put a little weight on my face.

WALLY. And it makes perfection even more dandy. You know, when I see you with your hair that way, like the monkey says, where have you been all my life?

HILDA. It's sweet of you, Wally, to think of all these nice things, because, frankly, this is a special occasion for me.

WALLY. And the same goes for me, doubled in spades.[21]

HILDA. You see, I'm so fond of you Wally, I wanted you to be the first to know. I'm going to be married.

WALLY. (*After a pause.*) You're going to be married?

HILDA. Dave Temple asked me this afternoon, and I said yes, and he's coming round this evening to see Mother. He should be here any minute.

WALLY. (*After a pause.*) Dave's fond of blue, is he?

HILDA. So he says.

WALLY. (*After another pause: getting up.*) Well OK, then. Does he like hard centres?

HILDA. Well, I certainly do.

WALLY. Then, I guessed wrong again. The candy's all soft centres, I'm afraid. Don't bother opening it right now, though. There's a couple of fellows I've got to see, and I only had time to drop in for a moment. And congratulations, Hilda—no, I'm a liar—that's wrong. Congratulations for the Mister: *best wishes* for the Mrs. Best wishes, Hildy.

HILDA. Thank you.

WALLY. I'll save the congratulations till the family comes along; never do to let you have 'em now, would it? But for what they're worth you got my best wishes such as they are; and if there's ever anything you need, this makes no difference to me, you know. Just give me a ring, and I'll be right on over.

HILDA. I'll remember that, Wally.

SOUND: *doorbell off.*

WALLY. Here's the lucky guy now. I'll slip out the back way. (*He adds wistfully.*) Might make him jealous.

HILDA. (*Too heartily.*) Of course not! (*Wally sadly murmurs: no.*) I'm not going to give up *all* my boy-friends just because I'm marrying one of them.

SOUND: *door opens off.*

MRS. MORGAN. (*Off.*) Oh! Good evening.

POLICE. (*Off.*) Good evening, madam.

HILDA. (*On.*) *That's* not him.

POLICE. We're from the City Police. This 2046 Grosvenor?

MRS. MORGAN. (*Off.*) Yes. 2046 Grosvenor is certainly the address.

HILDA. Where'd you park your car?

WALLY. (*On.*) Caught a cab.

MRS. MORGAN. (*Off.*) We have nothing to do with the police; unless you're selling tickets?[22]

POLICE. (*Off.*) No, madam; we want to know if there's anybody here by the name of Hilda.

WALLY. (*On.*) They want you.

MRS. MORGAN. I'm sure Hilda hasn't done anything I wouldn't do. I'm her mother, so you can take my word for it. You see, she's a schoolteacher, and she lives right here with me.

HILDA. I'll go and see. (*Raising her voice.*) All right, Mother, I'll talk to him! Just a moment! (*Fading off.*)

SOUND: *brisk footsteps fading off then on.*

HILDA. (*On.*) My name is Hilda Morgan, officer. Can I help you?

POLICE. (*On.*) Do you happen to know a man, aged twenty-five to thirty; height five foot ten; weight a hundred and forty-five; brown hair; blue eyes; complexion fair, clear shaven, small scar on right wrist.

HILDA. (*Rather loudly.*) It isn't David...!

POLICE. (*Inquiringly.*) David?

HILDA. (*Controlled again.*) David Temple.

POLICE. Do you know him well?

MRS. MORGAN. (*On.*) Hardly at all.

HILDA. We're going to be married.

RUTH. (*Off.*) What's the matter?

HILDA. (*On.*) What's happened?

POLICE. Perhaps I'd better come inside a moment.

MRS. MORGAN. (*A gasp.*) Oh dear!

WALLY. (*Fading on.*) Anything I can do?

POLICE. The fact of the matter is, you see, there's been a traffic accident. (*With a definite fall to the voice.*)

HILDA. (*After a moment's pause.*) He's dead.

POLICE. Well…yes, miss, I'm afraid he is. We went to his home address but the people are away, and we like to get identification and there was your name on a piece of paper in his pocket…

MRS. MORGAN. (*Ever curious.*) What was that doing there?

RUTH. (*Quickly and quietly.*) Never *mind*, Mother!

HILDA. (*Firmly.*) Please tell me what to do.

POLICE. We wondered if you'd have any objection to giving us an identification.

MRS. MORGAN. My daughter doesn't have to do anything!

HILDA. You mean go and look at him?

WALLY. Does she *have* to do it?

POLICE. Certainly not, but you see…

HILDA. I don't mind looking at him…

WALLY. He may be all mashed…uh, you know…(*He tries to catch himself.*)

HILDA. (*Emphasis.*) I don't mind looking at him. I shan't be seeing him again.

WALLY. OK, then, let me go with you!

MRS. MORGAN. Oh, Wally, I wish you would!

HILDA. (*Cutting them off.*) I shall go alone, please.

POLICE. We can wait outside while you get ready.

HILDA. I'm quite ready. My coat's right here. I was expecting to go out in a few minutes anyway. Goodbye, Mother. Bye, Ruth; Wally.

MRS. MORGAN. Oh, Hilda, isn't there anything we can do?

HILDA. (*Flatly.*) Well, is there? Goodbye.

MUSIC: *firm and melancholy: under Wally as background with a vaguely ecclesiastical*[23] *flavour.*

WALLY. (*Very earnestly.*) We all have to go some day, of course, but even when it's the other fellow's turn to meet the grim reaper, it makes you think. After all, you can't take it with you, and it sure lets you know that poker games and the Casino's all right for a while, but a man's got to build up something solid by clean living and square dealing, and going to church regular Christmas and Easter, and of course for weddings and funerals. (*The sermon over he takes up his last idea in easier vein.*) I was at David's funeral myself; slipped in the back quietly. Hilda was there, naturally. Didn't wear black; didn't cry; didn't even speak to David's mom and dad much, except on the way out I saw her talking to Mrs. Temple, while the organist was finishing things off. Most people thought the girlfriend and the mother were exchanging condolences: but, how does it go? Most people are wrong, and as it turned out, they certainly were this time:

MUSIC: *during the last few lines of Wally's speech has gradually cross faded to very distant church organ playing "Abide with Me."*

MRS. TEMPLE. Please forgive me, Hilda, for taking you aside like this.

HILDA. Quite all right, Mrs. Temple.

MRS. TEMPLE. (*Who throughout, has a kind of feeble persistence that is quite irresistible.*) All during the ceremony, I thought I simply *must* speak to you, Hilda, no matter what you say.

HILDA. Please, Mrs. Temple, anything at all.

MRS. TEMPLE. You see, you have your mother and sister to comfort you. Father and I have nobody.

HILDA. You have each other. (*With a slight emphasis on the "you."*)

MRS. TEMPLE. We have each other for memories: but no hopes, Hilda.

HILDA. (*Slowly.*) No hopes, no.

MRS. TEMPLE. No hopes at all: he was everything, you know, for us.

HILDA. I know he was.

MRS. TEMPLE. Now he's gone and there's nothing left. It's as if he'd never lived.

HILDA. (*With great sincerity.*) Oh, Mrs. Temple, please, no it *isn't*.

MRS. TEMPLE. It is for Father and me; all we can do is wait our turn.

HILDA. (*Nervous.*) I'm sorry…we're both upset. I don't know what to say to you.

MRS. TEMPLE. Father doesn't know I'm speaking to you, you understand. (*This point seems very important to her.*) Look, he's over there, talking to the minister. Father knows nothing about it. But he was so glad when we heard that you two were engaged, and I was so glad too, though I had quite a good cry over it. Do you know, I didn't cry at all when I found out he was dead?

MUSIC: *the organ has stopped by now*

HILDA. Neither did I.

MRS. TEMPLE. (*Dreamily.*) Though I used to cry a lot as a girl, when I wasn't allowed to go to all the dances I thought I should…(*Suddenly.*) Well, I'm going to say it, Hilda, and you can think what you like of me. We haven't any other hope. Were you and David secretly married?

HILDA. (*Long pause.*) He told you in the telegram we were engaged. That's all.

MRS. TEMPLE. I had hopes (Father doesn't know) there might be a child.

HILDA. A child?

MRS. TEMPLE. Even if he were dead, he might have had a child. (*A query seems to run through many of these remarks.*) Then you see…I think he was fond of children. But of course you weren't married.

HILDA. No, we weren't.

MRS. TEMPLE. (*Nodding.*) No. David saw you the day he was killed?

HILDA. Yes: we saw each other in the afternoon.

MRS. TEMPLE. And then you decided to get married?

HILDA. (*Gently rejecting the implied inference.*) We'd decided *before*.

MRS. TEMPLE. But you decided to *tell* us then?

HILDA. Yes, we thought we'd tell you.

24. This could refer to the
Ladies' Auxiliary of the
Royal Canadian Legion. The
Ladies' Auxiliary is a separate
but related organization
that pursues philanthropic
ventures and offers support to
Legion activities.

MRS. TEMPLE. Why?

HILDA. We just thought you should know.

MRS. TEMPLE. (*Going straight on as if she hadn't changed the subject.*) Your sister tells me you went to see the doctor.

HILDA. (*Edgy.*) I'd been having a lot of indigestion.

MRS. TEMPLE. You went to see the doctor the same afternoon?

HILDA. Yes, I did.

MRS. TEMPLE. (*Gently bringing her argument to its climax.*) And did you send the telegram to say you were engaged before you saw the doctor—or *after?* (*There is a long pause and when the conversation resumes it seems as if they have made an unspoken understanding.*)

HILDA. I don't remember—just now.

MRS. TEMPLE. I believe it's rather important.

HILDA. If you really believe so…

MRS. TEMPLE. Indeed I do.

HILDA. Then I'll think it over very carefully; and let you know at once, if I should happen to remember.

MRS. TEMPLE. I do so hope you will.

HILDA. (*With absolute assurance and gentleness.*) You can trust me. I will.

MRS. TEMPLE. (*Breaking the mood and returning to her feather-brained repetitiousness.*) But then of course, you have your mother and sister to comfort you. Father and I have nobody.

MUSIC: *a sad feeble phrase ends the scene: background under* WALLY.

WALLY. I saw them finish their talk, but I didn't offer to see Hilda home. Bad taste: fellow shouldn't look as if he's gloating. Felt pretty low myself, so I took in a movie instead. Hamlet. When a fellow's up against it, there's nothing like the classics to make you feel things aren't all that bad, and better cheer up if I was to do Hilda any good. So thought I'd drop around in the evening. But by the time, I showed up, the shooting was almost over. I gather the fun had started with Ruth.

MUSIC: *out with* WALLY.

HILDA. (*Rather tense and on her nerves during this scene in spite of her usual air of assurance and strength.*) Hello, Ruth. Mother in?

RUTH. Ladies' Auxiliary.[24] Were you at the ceremony?

HILDA. Yes, I was at the funeral.

RUTH. Nice ceremony?

HILDA. Oh, as nice as you'd expect when they're burying the man you're engaged to. (*Then seeing* RUTH *meant well.*) But it was a lovely funeral, really; lots of flowers—music.

RUTH. That's consolation in a way, really.

HILDA. I suppose.

RUTH. You sit down and rest; I'll get you a cup of coffee.

HILDA. No thanks. (*Out it comes.*) Ruth, I guess I might as well start with you.

RUTH. (*No more than mild interest.*) Oh?

HILDA. I'm going to have a baby.

RUTH. (*After a pause.*) Oh! You fool! Are you sure?

HILDA. Doctor says so.

RUTH. I always was suspicious about that doctor business. Were you married to David?

HILDA. No. Not legally.

RUTH. Couldn't you *think*? Couldn't you remember Len's in a bank? The least breath of scandal...Well, we'll have to do something, that's certain, and argue about it afterwards. Got any ideas?

HILDA. I want to get leave of absence from the school—telling them why. Have the baby; hire a nurse for it; and go back to work.

RUTH. You can't support Mother as well.

HILDA. She'll have to go to work too.

RUTH. Perhaps *we* shan't have to chip in either. It's an ill wind. Did he know?

HILDA. Yes. He was very pleased.

RUTH. Well, we've got to think of the living. This'll finish Mother off.

HILDA. I doubt it.

RUTH. (*Conceding the point.*) Well. Probably Len's career will be finished on the spot.

HILDA. David's was.

RUTH. (*Missing the point.*) Well, of course. He was *killed*, wasn't he? Well, I'm not going to preach at you. We've got to help you for our own sake as much as yours.

HILDA. If you don't want to, you don't have to.

RUTH. I know I don't *have* to, but I'm going to all the same. (*Then softer.*) Oh, Hilda, honey, why did it have to be *you*? How much money have you got?

HILDA. About three hundred dollars.

RUTH. It's not enough. Well, we haven't much, but we've some.

HILDA. It's very kind of you, Ruth...

RUTH. Forget it. Lucky I've been a miser. We were going to get a new dining suite...Well, who the hell cares? If I hurry I can get to the bank before three o'clock. You wait here. Mother should be back any minute. Don't say a word to her till I get back!

MUSIC: *excited: ending with a suggestion of* MRS. MORGAN.

SOUND: *the door shutting off.*

HILDA. (*Raising her voice.*) That you, Ruth?

MRS. MORGAN. (*Off: fading on.*) No, it's me. So you're home, are you, Hilda?

HILDA. Yes. The funeral was over later than I thought, and I spoke to David's mother afterwards…

MRS. MORGAN. Well, I don't think you should have gone.

HILDA. Oh?

MRS. MORGAN. I don't like to intrude on people's grief.

HILDA. (*Almost with a secret smile.*) I don't think it was an intrusion. I don't think Ruth does, either.

MRS. MORGAN. You weren't married to the lad; you weren't even engaged.

HILDA. Oh, yes, we were.

MRS. MORGAN. Nothing was announced. Nothing was discussed with the parents. So there's no reason to assume things had gone very far.

HILDA. Isn't there? I'm going to have a baby.

MRS. MORGAN. (*After a scandalized pause.*) A baby!

HILDA. When I went to the doctor on Saturday, he said David and I were going to have a baby.

MRS. MORGAN. I had a premonition you and David had gone and got married regardless.

HILDA. We were not married.

MRS. MORGAN. Not married!

HILDA. Not legally.

MRS. MORGAN. (*Ashamed whisper.*) I can't believe this, Hilda. If somebody'd said you'd do a thing like this to me, I'd never have believed it. I don't know what to say. Ruth won't know what to say.

HILDA. (*Full of her secret confidence.*) I think she will.

MRS. MORGAN. (*Flatly.*) You've broken your mother's heart.

HILDA. Yours isn't the only broken heart, Mother. I don't make much fuss as a rule, but this is it. I need your help.

MRS. MORGAN. I've worked and slaved over you girls, and then for you to do a thing like this to me!

HILDA. I'm not as sure about things as you are.

MRS. MORGAN. It's not me that's sure. *Providence* has spoken, Hilda, and that we know.

HILDA. (*Hardening.*) What do you mean?

MRS. MORGAN. The wages of sin is death.

HILDA. Are you trying to tell me David was killed as a punishment for sin?

MRS. MORGAN. Don't try and blame it on *him*!

HILDA. (*Scornfully.*) I wouldn't dream of it! We were both responsible.

MRS. MORGAN. I'm well aware of *that*, thank you; why couldn't you wait till you were married?

HILDA. We were in love.

MRS. MORGAN. Your father and I didn't call that *love*. That's not the word *I'd* use.

HILDA. It's the right word.

MRS. MORGAN. Why didn't you get married?

HILDA. We couldn't. We wanted to be able to support you as well.

MRS. MORGAN. (*Flying up in a convulsion of irony.*) So that's it! *I'm* to take the blame, am I? Poor little innocent thing, didn't know what she was doing; it was all her mother's fault.

HILDA. Perhaps it was your fault.

MRS. MORGAN. (*Striking home.*) Because my children didn't bring me up properly? That's the modern idea, and it's certainly ruined you. And if it's any consolation to you, you can't come crawling to your family. I wash my hands of the whole thing.

HILDA. You aren't all my family.

MRS. MORGAN. (*Not really listening.*) You've had a good Christian home, my girl, and I'm through if this is what you make of a good Christian upbringing.

HILDA. Perhaps *you* should have had it instead of me.

MRS. MORGAN. What do you mean?

HILDA. If this is a good Christian home you're running, how about some good Christian forgiveness?

MRS. MORGAN. I can't forgive people who sin deliberately. (*Then with real emotion.*) Don't you know you've told me the most dreadful thing a mother can hear? I'd rather I'd heard you were dead.

HILDA. (*Responding to the honest note.*) I'm afraid I'm still alive, Mother; and I do need your help badly.

MRS. MORGAN. (*Recovering from her momentary weakness.*) Punishment before forgiveness. You've sinned and you must suffer for it.

HILDA. I loved him, and he's dead, and I'm going to have his baby, and we aren't married. Don't you think I'm suffering enough?

MRS. MORGAN. (*Relenting.*) I'm sure you must deserve it.

HILDA. Is that all? Am I to expect no help from you at all? (*She is incredulous.*) Very well then.

MRS. MORGAN. Come back, Hilda. I know my duty, if you don't know yours.

HILDA. (*Coldly.*) What is your duty?

MRS. MORGAN. It's my duty to smuggle you away somewhere to have your baby, and find a place to put it so that you can go back to work again. And I'll do it; but if you think I shall forgive you dragging me through this, then you're very much mistaken. Is that clear?

HILDA. If that's your damned dirty duty, I don't want it. I want your love, if you've got any. I want somebody to say they understand and they're sorry for me, and they love me.

MRS. MORGAN. Do what you like and then say you're sorry!

HILDA. I don't say I'm sorry, because I'm not sorry to have David's baby!

SOUND: *door opens off.*

MRS. MORGAN. This may be *your* idea of something to be proud of, but it isn't mine, and it isn't Ruth's!

RUTH. (*Off.*) Mother!

HILDA. Ruth knows me better than to try and put me off with talk about duty.

MRS. MORGAN. (*Raising her voice even more.*) Never mind about that! You're going to find out before you're very much older...

RUTH. (*Fading on: cutting her off.*) Mother, don't shout so! They can hear you in the street!

MRS. MORGAN. They'll all know soon enough. Tell her what you've done, Hilda, if you aren't ashamed, though why should you be ashamed to tell it when you weren't ashamed to do it?

HILDA. (*Triumphantly.*) I *have* told her, Mother, and do you know what she's done? She's gone to the bank to get some money to help me.

RUTH. And I don't know what Len'll say.

MRS. MORGAN. (*Rather taken back.*) She's doing no more than I am. I shall do my duty too.

HILDA. Ruth isn't doing her duty. She isn't doing the wisest thing, or the most moral thing, or the most dutiful thing. She's doing the *kindest* thing; she's helping me because she loves me.

RUTH. Somebody has to do something, and Hilda's had bad luck ever since she grew up, eh kid?

MRS. MORGAN. I don't see what this has to do with luck.

HILDA. Don't you?

RUTH. Well, it has.

MRS. MORGAN. You needn't look at me like that, you girls. I know there's sin in this world, and not all of it found out in *this* life.

RUTH. (*Indignantly.*) And there's human nature too, Mother.

MRS. MORGAN. That's no reason to encourage wickedness. We aren't put into this world to glorify human nature. It's a vale of tears for the sinner, and we do wrong to make it anything else.

HILDA. No need to defend yourself, Mother.

RUTH. *You* haven't anything to be ashamed of.

HILDA. And neither have I.

RUTH. Well, whatever you did, I'm sure there were reasons. Now about the money.

MRS. MORGAN. (*Going down fighting.*) I hope you're not going to squander Len's money on *her*.

RUTH. It's my money as much as his. He earned it, and I saved it; and I don't call this squandering. How much did you say you had?

HILDA. About three hundred.

RUTH. All right. Now I got out another three.

MRS. MORGAN. That was for your dining suite.

RUTH. It isn't now. That'll give you six hundred dollars.

MRS. MORGAN. (*With a nasty smile.*[25]) The price of sin is very high today.

26. A specifically Canadian term
referring to a room in a hotel
or tavern where beer is served.

27. A common adjective in the
1940s, suggesting an older
woman with an angry,
unpleasant demeanour.

RUTH. (*Angry.*) Very high, Mother, yes.

MRS. MORGAN. (*Sternly.*) Well, it's even higher than you think.

RUTH. Moralize later, Mother. For the moment, we have to be sensible, haven't we, Hilda?

MRS. MORGAN. You be sensible about wickedness, if you can. This is no time for being sensible, as you call it.

RUTH. Look at it this way, Mother. If it gets out about Hilda's baby, she's through at the school. Marg Patterson was fired because she went to beer parlours.[26]

MRS. MORGAN. They know that one thing leads to another.

RUTH. (*Ignoring this.*) Second, if it gets out about Hilda's baby, your name will be mud. You know how the old harridans'll[27] take *this* juicy item.

MRS. MORGAN. Why should the sins of the children be visited on the fathers?

RUTH. I don't know why, but they will be. And thirdly, if it gets out about Hilda's baby, Len's career at the bank will be through: we'll wait for a million years and not get anywhere.

MRS. MORGAN. (*Reluctantly.*) So?

RUTH. So it mustn't get out about Hilda's baby. It's as easy as that. And the only way to be sure is if she doesn't have it.

HILDA. I don't understand.

RUTH. I'm just explaining why you need so much money. You see, she isn't going to go through with it, Mother.

MRS. MORGAN. I won't hear of it, Ruth! It's murder.

RUTH. It's no more murder than, well, than anything else.

HILDA. Some people think so.

RUTH. Some people can afford to think so.

HILDA. (*Positively.*) No use, Ruth. It won't do.

RUTH. Why not? Nobody else knows.

HILDA. Not yet.

RUTH. I'll look after you, and you'll have a hundred over for expenses. It costs five hundred dollars.

HILDA. How do *you* know?

RUTH. From Norah Campbell.

MRS. MORGAN. That Campbell girl! I knew...

RUTH. Her sister had it done.

HILDA. Is *that* what killed her?

RUTH. Well, there is a risk. You can't call a doctor afterwards, because he has to report it. But you'll be all right. Mother and I'll be backing you up.

HILDA. (*Beginning to strike harder.*) Is *this* your idea of backing me up? Was this your only idea of sympathy? Taking David's child from him?

RUTH. Don't let's get sentimental. We've got to be practical in this world.

HILDA. Now I *am* ashamed. Horrible! (*With a shudder of disgust.*)

RUTH. It's not only for you; it's for Mother and Len and me as well.

HILDA. (*Scornfully.*) Daren't you say it's for David too?

RUTH. Well, it certainly is for David. (*Eloquently.*) Would *he* want you to disgrace your family? Would he want you to suffer miseries knowing there's no one else you can turn to?

HILDA. Don't be too sure.

RUTH. Don't you be too sure! No one else would give you their savings for a thing like this!

HILDA. Probably not. (*With inward revulsion.*)

RUTH. Then be sensible while you can. Now here's the money. I got it in twenties...

MRS. MORGAN. (*Suddenly.*) Put it away! Don't let *me* see it! I don't want to know anything about it! I'm going straight to my room and lock the door! Do whatever you decide, the pair of you, and God forgive you, but don't tell me about it!

HILDA. No need for you to leave, Mother. I'm the one that's out of place here. I'm getting out right now. I may be back. If I'm not don't be surprised.

RUTH. But Hilda, *please*...

HILDA. (*In disgust.*) Don't try to follow me, Ruth, or I'll knock you down. (*Pause.*) Goodbye, you two.

SOUND: *door shuts.*

MRS. MORGAN. Ruth, she's going to do something dreadful. You've gone too far.

RUTH. She's just being stubborn.

MRS. MORGAN. If she walks out on us, there's nowhere for her to go. I can feel she's going to do something dreadful. (*Rising intensity.*) We've lost her, Ruth, we've lost her!

RUTH. Don't be silly, Mother; she's tougher than you are.

MRS. MORGAN. I don't know what you mean.

RUTH. You're the one that's gone too far; you and your moralizing!

MRS. MORGAN. We're told we must speak out, and I've done it!

RUTH. Well, I'm going after her.

MRS. MORGAN. Do you think you should?

RUTH. What else should I do?

MRS. MORGAN. She's made up her mind; do you think it's right to stop her?

RUTH. I don't think you care what happens to her.

MRS. MORGAN. Well, if she's taken, we must bow our heads to Providence, and remember it's all for the best. I told her I'd rather I'd been told she was dead than...(*She is faltering.*)

RUTH. (*Horrified.*) Mother!

MRS. MORGAN. (*Breaking down.*) I don't know, I don't know! I'll think of something! Go and find her, and bring her back, and I'll think of something. But I can feel it's too late; I've an awful feeling we've lost her!

MUSIC: turbulent and gloomy: time passes: change to a mood of waiting.
SOUND: a little clock chimes three quarters: a pause: then the door opens and shuts off.

MRS. MORGAN. (*Calling.*) Hello, Ruth, I'm in here. (*No answer.*) I'm in here, Ruth. (*Still no answer.*) Ruth!

SOUND: footsteps have been approaching and stop.

HILDA. (*Quite near and immediately fading right on.*) Why are you sitting in the dark, Mother?

MRS. MORGAN. (*In tears.*) Oh, Hilda, Hilda, darling, it's you! I was afraid we'd lost you!

HILDA. (*Who seems to have some kind of secret triumph.*) Were you, Mother?

MRS. MORGAN. I had a feeling you were going to do something irrevocable.

HILDA. Everything is irrevocable.

MRS. MORGAN. If you'd done something terrible, people would have blamed us.

HILDA. It depends what you call terrible.

MRS. MORGAN. Oh, you're young; you're not afraid of death. Wait till you're my age; then you'll wish you'd lived a better life.

HILDA. Do you wish you'd lived a better life? (*Searchingly.*)

MRS. MORGAN. You won't shrug off dying when you're as old as me.

HILDA. Did you think I had some idea of killing myself? As though I were ashamed of David's baby? If I were going to kill myself (which I'm not) I'd wait. My life is David's life for the next six months.

MRS. MORGAN. Hilda, I've been thinking what to do. I feel responsible, in a way. I can't forgive myself. (*This is a painful confession.*)

HILDA. That's because you can't forgive me.

MRS. MORGAN. You talk as if *I* were in the wrong. If you were in the right, you wouldn't need forgiving.

HILDA. Now you're near it, Mother. Only the guilty need forgiving; and it's only the guilty you can't forgive. (*Fading off slightly.*)

MRS. MORGAN. Come back, Hilda! Where are you going?

HILDA. To pack. I'm leaving.

MRS. MORGAN. To disgrace us all.

HILDA. Do you want me to take Ruth's advice and die discretely in a back bedroom?

MRS. MORGAN. Very few die.

HILDA. You're forgetting something. This child is *wanted*.

MRS. MORGAN. Then take my advice.

HILDA. (*A pause: slightly surprised.*) What is it?

MRS. MORGAN. Even if you go away and have it, you'll ruin us when you come back with it.

HILDA. So I must have it adopted?

MRS. MORGAN. I know you won't do *that*.

HILDA. Then what must I do?

MRS. MORGAN. You must bring back a husband too.

HILDA. My husband has just been killed.

MRS. MORGAN. Wally Turnbull likes you. He's a bit wild, but what man isn't? You could make him settle down.

HILDA. (*With fatal mildness.*) If David and I had been legally married, would you have dared throw me at somebody else before I'd been a widow a week?

MRS. MORGAN. (*Making her point.*) But you *weren't* married.

HILDA. (*As if seeing that this made all the difference.*) Ah! Of course not.

MRS. MORGAN. All I want is for you to be happy and do the right thing.

HILDA. Very well, Mother; tell me what the right thing is.

MRS. MORGAN. We're all sinners, and that we know; but there is such a thing as repenting.

HILDA. By marrying Wally Turnbull?

MRS. MORGAN. (*Artfully.*) No. You're wrong there. That's what you thought; but you were wrong. *Not* by marrying him at all; unless you want to.

HILDA. Go on.

MRS. MORGAN. All I'm asking is that you don't let yourself be worried by out-worn conventions.

HILDA. (*Almost speechless.*) Oh?

MRS. MORGAN. In other words, dear; *if*…I say only, *if*…you found you were beginning to like him as much as he likes you; or even half as much. Or less.

HILDA. A quarter as much?

MRS. MORGAN. Even a little bit, then all I ask is that you remember two things. David is dead now. And your sister and I…and yourself…are all alive. Well, you know the world's ways Hilda. If Wally and you *happened* to become interested in each other; well, there'd be short memories after the baby was born.

HILDA. Thank you, Mother. You make everything very clear. You've been doing some hard thinking since I went out.

MRS. MORGAN. I hope you've done the same.

HILDA. Oh, indeed, I have.

MRS. MORGAN. My father would have turned any of us out of doors lock stock and barrel.[28]

HILDA. I'm sure he would.

SOUND: *the doorbell off.*

MRS. MORGAN. Pretend we're not in; I'll peep through the curtain and see… who (*Really astonished.*) Hilda! It's Wally!

HILDA. (*Hard.*) Wally! Did you invite him?

MRS. MORGAN. How could I have done? I didn't know you were coming back. You might have been floating in the lake for all I knew. That's why Ruth's out looking for you.

HILDA. You gave me a good start first.

SOUND: *doorbell again.*

MRS. MORGAN. Providence has given you one terrible lesson, Hilda. This is another. I hope you can take it. You open the door, and talk to him. I'll keep out of the way. (*As an afterthought.*) I worried about you, Hilda; while you were out. I thought we'd lost you, and…oh, well, please hurry up and let him in! (*She sounds quite excited.*)

MUSIC: *echoes the excitement: excited background for* WALLY.

WALLY. When I finally called round, I had to ring a couple of times. After a while, the door opened and there was Hilda. She looked a bit pale, but there was a funny gleam in her eye. She said her mother was lying down. I was pleased I'd decided to drop round, because she seemed quite glad to see me!

MUSIC: *background out with* WALLY.

HILDA. (*Rather excited: in reality she is seething with rage and indignation at her mother and delighted at the prospect of getting out permanently.*) I'm glad you called, Wally. I'm going away soon, and Mother thought I should see you, before I went.

WALLY. I don't want to bother you, Hildy. Just wanted to say, I'll always be waiting. I know how you're feeling. Must be an awful disappointment for you.

HILDA. Even disappointments can sometimes be lightened a little.

WALLY. Sure, you weren't actually married to him, were you?

HILDA. Even so, I have certain compensations. Wally: do you understand that David and I were in love with each other?

WALLY. (*Amused at this self-evident remark.*) Well, of course! You were going to marry him.

HILDA. And do you understand it'll be a very long time before I can fall in love with anybody else.

WALLY. Sure, I understand all that; it'll take months to get over it.

HILDA. Even so, would you marry me in a week or two from now. If I asked you.

WALLY. (*Simply.*) Yes, I would, Hilda. I'm no angel; never have been. Played around a bit in my time, but if we got married, that'd be out. It'd just be you as far as I'm concerned; and I'd marry you like a shot; supposing you wanted it.

29. Starting in Canada in 1949, you invested a dollar, then recruited two more investors (who each invested a dollar), and they each recruited two investors and so on. If all went well, after twelve days you would receive $2,048. The schemes were illegal (Beatty 1949).

30. Giacomo Casanova was an eighteenth-century Italian famous for his affairs with women. His name is used to signify someone with an active love life.

31. A woman who engaged in sexual activities out of wedlock. The poet Robert Browning wrote poem titled "A Light Woman" that speaks of her "nine and ninety other spoils" to which she was trying to add the friend of the poet to her long list of conquests.

HILDA. Mother wants it.

WALLY. (*Warmly.*) She's the right sort; lovely person, your mother. I really admire her. Always right in there with the good word.

HILDA. There's just one thing. I gather you've had something to do with other women.

WALLY. Honest to God, Hildy, that's right out, from now on. The past is the past; the future's what counts.

HILDA. I'm glad to hear you say that. Because there's something Mother doesn't expect me to tell you. I'm going to have a baby.

WALLY. (*After an immense pause: with forced casualness.*) Oh?

HILDA. I thought that'd change your mind. Thanks very much, Wally, anyhow.

WALLY. (*Moistening his lips.*) Wait a minute, wait a minute; take it easy. Whose is it? David's?

HILDA. Yes.

WALLY. That's why you got engaged, eh?

HILDA. He wanted to marry me for a long time. I wouldn't let him. (*With a little laugh.*) I thought I had a duty to Mother.

WALLY. It's a shock, Hildy; no use kidding. I...I don't know what to say. I didn't really think you were the kind of girl who'd...

HILDA. Play with fire? Or get burnt? Which?

WALLY. (*Thinking.*) If we got married now, the baby'd be early, but that'll happen. If we watched the arithmetic every time the wedding bells rang, there'd be a lot of surprises. It shouldn't happen, but it seems to. Lots of couples cheat a little on the deadline, so I guess we might get away with it. (*Announcing his decision.*) I'm willing, Hildy, if you are.

HILDA. Are you willing because you think I was doing right, or just because it happens all the time?

WALLY. (*Reasonably.*) Same thing. If everybody does it, sooner or later it's all right. Look at the pyramid clubs.[29] You know, Dave Temple was pretty much my colouring. We could get away with it. It'd be a lot better than adopting a kid.

HILDA. Thank you, Wally, it's very kind of you. (*A refusal.*)

WALLY. *I'm* willing.

HILDA. Because your friends'd just think you'd been cheating a little on the deadline; might make you a bit of a Casanova?[30] (*Smiling.*)

WALLY. (*Pleased.*) Oh, I wouldn't say that.

HILDA. (*With the same light smile somehow hardening.*) Just as it makes me a bit of a light woman;[31] or would if we weren't married. (*The qualification is a little overdone perhaps.*)

WALLY. Well, a girl isn't like men, you know.

HILDA. (*The light smile suddenly vanishing.*) No, the girl's the one that's caught with the evidence. But every time a man wants to be a Casanova, a girl has to help him do it, and take all the blame into the bargain. Well, if she takes the blame, she's going to take the credit.

WALLY. (*Out of his depth.*) I don't understand.

HILDA. David wanted a child. I shall give him one. Would you marry me a year from now, after I'd had the baby; after everyone knew that I'd had David's child? (*A long pause: no reply.*) I'm not ashamed of it, but I should be if I pretended it was yours.

WALLY. But what are people going to say? You can't just think of yourself, Hilda.

HILDA. (*Honestly.*) I must, Wally; and I must think of David. Everybody else thinks of duty and morality and neighbours, until the human beings are covered up with noble abstractions. And when the human beings are covered up, people can be as cruel and thoughtless as they like without hurting their consciences. Well, I can't help them; I can't play fair. I can only think of the people: David, and Mrs. Temple, and me, and the baby. Judge not that ye be not judged. If they want to judge me, I shall judge them, and be jury and executioner into the bargain. (*She is beginning to blaze.*)

WALLY. What do you mean?

HILDA. When I go away, Mother's going to be ripped apart by the neighbours; and serve her right. If she thought more of me, she might think less of them.

WALLY. Well, no one could accuse you of being soft, Hilda.

HILDA. Only a man ever thinks a woman's soft. Don't be misled, Wally. Women are as hard as rocks; that's why they find it so difficult to live together. We're only the weaker sex when it comes to weight-lifting; and even then, you mightn't like to wring out half-a-dozen blankets.

WALLY. But what are you going to do? You got to have somewhere to go.

HILDA. When I found my family didn't support me, I went to see Mrs. Temple. I've just got back. I told her everything, and I shall live with them until it's all over. Then we shall see.

WALLY. You told Mrs. *Temple*? That frail old lady?

HILDA. She's no more frail than I am; she knows what she has to do.

WALLY. She doesn't have any prejudice?

HILDA. All she had was a son. Being hard is our virtue as well as our vice. Goodbye, Wally.

MUSIC: a short figure: scarcely more than a take: down to background.[32]

WALLY. Maybe she was joking, only girls don't have a sense of humour. And if it was a joke it was a practical one. Maybe I should have taken her up. 'Course I'm married now to a real sweet little girl, and what she doesn't know won't hurt her, I mean about the others. Like I say, there's the ones to settle down with, and the ones to settle up with. But you never know which is which till it's too late. If then.

MUSIC: finale.

ANNOUNCER. Stage 49, Item 34…"Hilda Morgan," a new play by Lister
Sinclair…was produced and directed by Andrew Allan, with a musical
score composed and conducted by Lucio Agostini. Ruth Springford starred
as Hilda Morgan; Jane Mallet as her Mother, Pat Arthurs as Hilda's sister,
Ruth; Budd Knapp as Wally Turnbull; Grace Webster as Mrs. Temple; John
Drainie as David Temple; and Donald Davis as the Policeman. Sound by
David Tasker. Technical operations by Bruce Armstrong.

25 : Christmas Mummering Plays in Newfoundland (1949)

The Nineteenth Century and Forward

DENYSE LYNDE

JUST IN TIME FOR CHRISTMAS IN 1983, the folk duo Simani from Fortune Bay, Newfoundland, released the hugely popular "The Mummer's Song." Based on traditional tunes, this song tells the story of the house visit of a group of twenty or more mummers. The household tries to sort out the identities of the mummers and all are offered home brew and dance. "The Mummer's Song" was an important marker of the revival of the traditions of mummering and mummers' plays in the province that had been going on for several decades (Tye 2008).

The tradition of mummers came to Newfoundland and Labrador with the early explorers and settlers. The first of these was Sir Humphrey Gilbert. In 1583 he set sail with five ships and took with him "Morris dancers, hobby horses and May-like conceits" (Story [1969] 1990, 167). The combination of these elements became the basis of many mummering performances. Mummering really took root, however, when many Newfoundland communities were established in the nineteenth century. Records of mummering begin to appear in 1839 and into the 1840s. In 1842, for instance, Sir Richard Bonnycastle, a military officer and commanding engineer in Newfoundland, describes the Christmas festivities in St. John's, which he called "a sort of saturnalia amongst the lower classes" (Jarvis 2014, 2). Referencing mummering activities, he describes the importance of costume and mask.

Practiced in Philadelphia as well as elsewhere in the United States and parts of Ireland, mummering as it has developed in Newfoundland and Labrador has taken many forms. As "The Mummer's Song" indicates, mummering is a Christmas-time tradition that often involves costumed groups of people who visit neighbours. The term "mummering" is also used to describe the holiday of Twelfth Night, parades, and the performance of scripted mummer plays. There are, in other words, many different kinds of mummers and mummering traditions. This chapter explores some of the most popular and lasting forms of mummering.

The informal house visit is central to mummering in Newfoundland. During the Twelve Days of Christmas, visitors disguised themselves, organized themselves into groups, and visited neighbours. These groups moved from house to house. At each door, one visitor knocked and asked, "Any Mummers

FIGURE 25.1: *Winterton Jannies, ca. 1950.*
Courtesy of the Wooden Boat Museum of Newfoundland and Labrador.

'lowed in?" and if welcomed in, they all came in. The host's job was to penetrate the disguise and, if successful, the guests unmasked and enjoyed the offered food and drink. However, disguises were elaborate.[1] Mummers wore elaborate masks or covered their faces with burnt cork. Some used veils made of lace or muslin or cotton. They altered shapes of their heads using paper bags or cardboard boxes or pillowcases. They would even alter their voices. Mummers paid great attention to their costumes, or what they called their "rigout" or "janny up" or "mummer up" (Jarvis 2014, 4). The range of costumes was broad.

FIGURE 25.2: *Winterton Jannies, ca. 1950.*

Courtesy of the Wooden Boat Museum of Newfoundland and Labrador.

Some mummers wore old-fashioned clothes of relatives—"grandfather clothes"—they found stored in the attics of family homes. Some wore clothes inside out. Others used capes and dressing gowns to hide the shapes of their bodies. Men often wore women's clothes, again to heighten the disguise. The possibilities were endless.

Because there was often a lot of drinking, these visits could be quite exuberant, and indeed heavy drinking could—and sometimes did—lead to fighting. In fact, in 1860, a man was murdered during mummering festivities (Halpert [1969] 1990, 51). At the time, an effort was made by the Newfoundland Legislature to stop this tradition. Local civic and church leaders also tried to dissuade the population from participating in mummering, but the tradition continued on. Violence began to be associated with some informal house visiting, primarily in rural districts, and some evidence indicates it might have related to personal disputes and/or religious conflicts. By 1861 the violence became more widespread, which led to the government passing an act that

FIGURE 25.3: Christmas in the Olden Days *by J.W. Hayward, 1913.*

Source: 49/71, MG 334, P.K. Devine fonds, The Rooms Provincial Archives, Newfoundland and Labrador.

required individuals to receive a licence: "any Person who shall be found…
without a written License from a Magistrate, dressed as a Mummer, masked
or otherwise, shall be deemed guilty of Public Nuisance" (Fraser 2009, 75–76).
Despite this legislative effort, mummer-related disturbances continued. In
1862 an outright ban was issued, but it was mostly ignored. The love of the
Christmas tradition of the informal house visiting in costume continued.

Other mummering traditions involved the use of a hobby horse, as seen in
Figure 25.3. The hobby horse was part of the holiday season house-visiting
tradition. Judge Prowse noted in 1895 that each company of mummers "had
one or more hobby horses with gaping jaws to snap at people" (Jarvis 2014,
118). These hobby horses were operated by two or sometimes as many as six
men to form the body. Their purpose was to frighten whomever they
encountered.

Yet another tradition associated with mummering and the Twelve Days of
Christmas was singing and dancing, accompanied by the use of an "ugly stick"—
a percussion instrument made out of recycled material. Often constructed out
of a sturdy pole affixed to a heavy boot at the base, the ugly stick was covered
with bottle caps, tin cans, small bells, and other noisemakers. To "play" this

unusual instrument, the boot was thumped on the ground, causing all the noisemakers to rattle and "sing."

Another mummer performance tradition that sharply contrasted both the mummers who disguised themselves and mummers who constructed and operated frightening hobby horses was called "Hunting the Wren." This type of mummering always took place on December 26, St. Stephen's Day. Boys and girls would go from door to door with a stick, which had an image of a bird attached to it. Once the home's occupant had opened the door, these young mummers would recite a verse. At each door they would be given something to eat, or a drink of juice, or a few coins. The children usually wanted the coins, which they often then donated to the local parish.

Another important part of the mummers' tradition is the outdoor movement of mummers known as parades. According to Herbert Halpert, the anthropologist and folklorist who founded the Memorial University of Newfoundland Folklore and Language Archive, "Historically the parade and/or pageant is one of the oldest documented forms of mumming" ([1969] 1990, 48). These parades could become rowdy and even dangerous as sometimes mummers disguised as fools threatened or even struck bystanders with whips.

Finally, scripted plays were another part of the mummering tradition. Early European settlers to Newfoundland brought the tradition with them as early as the sixteenth century. Mummers' plays were hero-combat narratives in which a protagonist fights a villain. In these plays, a doctor character usually appeared to revive the fallen hero.

The structure of these hero-combat mummers' plays is clear. In reduced form, it can be divided into four parts: (1) the Presenter, (2) the Combat, (3) the Cure, and (4) the Collection (Halpert [1969] 1990, 57). In the first section, a mummer demands the room to perform a play. This person might then introduce a character who, in turn, introduces the next character, and so on. Or the first performer might introduce all the other characters. This scene is followed by the combat between the hero and the villain, which is usually very broad and physical and intended to be a lot of fun for the audience. The characters call a doctor who comes to "cure" the wounded or the dead, and the traditional ending features the company joining together in song.

"Soldiers Acting at Christmas," the first example published here, is from the memory of a resident in the 1950s who believed it reflected the plays he saw fifty years earlier. The play begins with the introduction of Father Christmas, who in turn introduces King George, whose might and authority is endorsed by the King of Egypt and a Valiant Soldier. When the Turkish Knight appears, George challenges him and a battle ensues. Of course, the Knight is struck down and the Doctor must be summoned to revive him. Duly revived, the company closes the play with a song.

The second mummers' play, which also features King George, reflects another resident's memory. It follows the general plot structure, but the central battle is extended with a George-and-the-Turk battle followed by a Turk-and-Soldier battle, again closing with a company song. The British influence is clear in both examples, as the audience is encouraged to cheer for King George and, of course, boo the evil Turkish knight.

Like the "Mummer's Song" by Simani, the resurgence of mummering in Newfoundland was also seen in theatre, first with Chris Brookes and the Mummers Troupe in 1972, which performed a version of a mummers' play. A mummers' parade was held in St. John's 2009; this event initiated a yearly parade tradition, which quickly grew. The town of Clarenville began to hold its own parade in 2013. In 2011 the provincial government honoured mummers as a "Distinctive Cultural Tradition or Practice" (Jarvis 2014, 178). Mummers and mummering are once again alive and well in Newfoundland and Labrador.

Bibliography and Further Reading

Fraser, Joy. 2009. "Mummers on Trial." *Shima: The International Journal of Research into Island Cultures* 3 (2): 70–88.

Halpert, Herbert. (1969) 1990. "A Typology of Mumming." In *Christmas Mumming in Newfoundland: Essays in Anthropology, Folklore, and History*, edited by Herbert Halpert and George M. Story, 34–61. Toronto: Published for Memorial University of Newfoundland by University of Toronto Press.

Jarvis, Dale. 2014. *Any Mummers 'Lowed In? Christmas Mummering Traditions in Newfoundland and Labrador.* St. John's, NL: Flanker Press.

Story, George M. (1969) 1990. "Mummers in Newfoundland History: A Survey of the Printed Record." In *Christmas Mumming in Newfoundland: Essays in Anthropology, Folklore, and History*, edited by Herbert Halpert and George M. Story, 165–85. Toronto: Published for Memorial University of Newfoundland by University of Toronto Press.

Tye, Diane. 2008. "At Home and Away: Newfoundland Mummers and the Transformation of Difference." *Material Culture Review / Revue de la culture matérielle* 68 (June). https://journals.lib.unb.ca/index/php/MCR/article/view/18133.

Oldtime "Mumming" Christmas Plays in Newfoundland[1]

1. Transcribed from *The Newfoundlander*, December 1949, 16–17. Many thanks to Kennedy Longaphie, student research assistant at Mount Allison University, for this transcription.

2. J.J. Peckford remembers a mummers' play introduced by an English schoolteacher Justinian M. Dowell that was performed in the early twentieth century, years ago when he was child. Mr. Moss likewise remembers the mummers' play from his childhood.

We are proud to present to readers an historic document relating to old-time Christmas folklore in Newfoundland. We are indeed grateful to Mr. J.J. Peckford, Gander Bay, and Mr. Barney Moss, Salvage, [Bonavista Bay],[2] for their interest in preserving the words and thereby giving this paper an opportunity to publish this relic of the past.

What follows is a "mumming" or mummers' play which used to be staged in many towns and villages in Newfoundland at Christmas. The play was originally brought to Newfoundland, says Mr. Moss, by early settlers from England and performed each Christmas up to about 50 years ago. Whether it is still performed in any places in Newfoundland is not known, but perhaps some readers can give further information.

Two versions of the play are presented here. The first is from the memory of Mr. Peckford, who says that it was performed at Change Islands, Fogo District, when he was a boy of 10 or 12, about 50 years ago. Mr. Peckford never saw the words in print, but he believes his version from memory is pretty near the mark.

"It was," continues Mr. Peckford, "introduced to our young people by an English schoolmaster, Mr. Justinia Dowell by name. "The soldiers, as we called them"—actors in the play—"would start St. Stephen's Day and visit all the houses in the town and would keep it up for several days. They would have quite a jolly time, and they looked very smart in their trimmed pants, white shirts and high hat with ribbons and tassels (they were dressed to kill!). They also carried swords made from birchwood, and made property, too." Mr. Peckford's version of the old mummers' play follows:

Soldiers Acting at Christmas

ROOMER (INTRODUCTION OFFICER). Room, room, gallant room, room
    required here tonight
For some of my bold champions are coming forth to fight;
Old act, new act, acts you never saw before,
For I am the very champion that brings old Father Christmas to your door.
And if you don't believe these words I say, step in Father Christmas and
    boldly declare the way.
FATHER CHRISTMAS. Here comes I old Father Christmas, welcome or
    welcome not,
I hope old Father Christmas will never be forgot;
Here comes I old Johnny Jack, my wife and family on my back,
My wife so big and my children so small.

Takes more than a crumb of bread to feed them all,
And if you don't believe these words I say, step in King George and boldly
declare thy way.

KING GEORGE. Here comes I, King George, from old England I did spring,
Some of my victorious works I am going to bring;
I fought the fiery dragon, I brought him to the slaughter,
And by those very means I'll win fair Zebra, King of Egypt's daughter.
And if you don't believe these words I say, step in King of Egypt and boldly
declare the way.

KING OF EGYPT. Here comes I, the King of Egypt, in uniform do appear;
King George, King George, thy comrade is here;
He is a man of courage bold, I am his armour-bearer
To cut down his enemies if they are any of them here.
And if you don't believe these words I say, step in Valiant Soldier and boldly
declare thy way.

VALIANT SOLDIER. Here comes I, the Valiant Soldier, Slasher is my name,
Sword and pistol by my side, I hope to end the game,
One of my brothers I saw wounded, the other I saw slain.
And by those very means I'll fight King George all on the plain. (*Takes a step.*)

Next scene

KING GEORGE. Whist, whist, bold man, what thou art telling
Apple dumplings thou are selling.
Stand where thou are and call in Brother Turk to act thy part.

VALIANT SOLDIER. Turk, Turk, come with speed, help in my time of need,
Thy time of need I do implore, I was never in such need before.

TURKISH KNIGHT. Here comes I, the Turkish Knight, come from the Turkish
land to fight;
I'll fight King George with courage bold, if his blood is hot I'll make it cold.

KING GEORGE. (*Again.*) Who art thou that speaks so bold?

TURKISH KNIGHT. Haul out thy purse and pay for satisfaction I will have
before I go away.

KING GEORGE. No satisfaction thou shan't get, while I have strength to stand,
For I don't care for no Turk stands on this English land.

They cross swords and both say.

You and I the battle try, if you conquer I will die.

TURKISH KNIGHT. I am cut down but not quite dead,
It is only the pain lies in my head,
If I once on my two legs stood,
I'd fight King George to my knees in blood.

KING GEORGE. On the ground thou dost lie, and the truth I'll tell to thee,
That if thou dost but rise again thy butcher I will be.
TURKISH KNIGHT. Come, Valiant Soldier, be quick and smart,
And with my sword I will pierce King George's heart.

Turkish Knight on his feet again, and continues.

I do not care for thee, King George, although thou art a champion bold,
I never saw that Englishman yet could make my blood run cold.
KING GEORGE. You Turkish dog, King George is here, happy for another hour
to come,
I'll cut thee and I'll hew thee, I am bound to let thee know,
I am bold King George from England before I let thee go.

The two together with crossed swords.

You and I the battle try, if you conquer I will die. (*King George falls to the
floor.*)
TURKISH KNIGHT. Now the battle I have won, thank God I am free,
And if that man do rise again his butcher will I be.
KING GEORGE. (*King George rises from the floor and strikes the Turk.*)
I suppose you thought that I was dead, but yet alive remain,
And go and tell the doctor the Turkishman is slain.
FATHER CHRISTMAS AND THE DOCTOR. Doctor, doctor, come with speed,
Help me in my time of need,
My time of need I do implore,
I was never in such need before.

Father Christmas then tries to revive the Turk himself, but with no success, He says.

Is there a doctor to be found
Can heal my son of his deadly wound?
DOCTOR. Yes, there is a doctor to be found
Can heal thy son of his deadly wound.
FATHER CHRISTMAS.
What is thy fee?
DOCTOR. Fifty guineas is my fee, but if the money is paid down,
I will do it for ten pond [*sic*].
FATHER CHRISTMAS. What can you cure?
DOCTOR. I can cure the hits, fits, palsy and the gout,
If there is any evil spirit in this man I can sure drive it out.
FATHER CHRISTMAS. What kind of medicine have you got?

DOCTOR. I have a little bit of hare's grease and mare's grease,
  The wig of a weasel and the wool of a frog,
  And twenty-four ounces of September fog.
FATHER CHRISTMAS. Where do you rub all this stuff?
DOCTOR. I rub a little to his temple, and a little to the crack-bone of his heart,
  Arise, arise, hold champion, and boldly act thy part;
  Arise, arise, my lofty man, I long to see you stand,
  Open your eyes and look about, I will take you by the hand.

The man comes to his feet.

PICKEDY WICK.[3] Here comes I, Pickedy Wick, put my hand in my pocket and
    pay what I thinks fit;
  Ladies and gentlemen, sit down to their ease,
  Put their hands in their pockets and pay what they please,
  And if you don't believe those words I say, step in Beelzebub and boldly
    clear thy way.
BEELZEBUB.[4] Here comes I Beelzebub, under my arm I carries my club;
  In my hand I keeps my pan, I thinks myself a jolly fine man.
  Money I wants, money I crave, and money I'll have to carry me to my grave.
  And if you don't believe those words I say, step in bold Hercules and boldly
    clear thy way.
BOLD HERCULES. Here comes I, bold Hercules, I boldly stem the weather,
  I took the rainbow from the skies and spliced both ends together,
  And if you don't believe those words I say, step in Jack Tar and boldly clear
    thy way.
JACK TAR.[5] Here comes I, Jack Tar, just returned from sea, sir,
  With the shiners on my breast, and what do you think of me, sir?
  I am a brisk young sailor and always on the sea,
  And now I am home, my heroes, I am full of life and glee;
  The battle will soon be over and now we will sing one song,
  And we will cheer our hardy comrades as we gladly march along.

*All the company then form into a ring, with Father Christmas in the centre, and they
sing the following ditty.*

  The pig and the bug and the bumble-bee,
  There is one more river to cross;
  The pig and the bug and the bumble-bee,
  There is one more river to cross.

  One more river and that's the river of Jordan,
  One more river, there is one more river to cross.

6. Transcribed from *The Newfoundlander*, January 1950, pp. 14–15.

7. "belly"; it is not found in the Newfoundland dictionary but is used regularly in the verse about Dame Dorothy and its variant.

Mr. Peckford gives a description of the uniforms worn by the "mumming" actors: Blue pants with red ship on the side seams, white shirt and a belt, with stars on their breast. Hats with stars on them and coloured tassels. However, Father Christmas was dressed in Father Christmas style, the doctor in professional attire, and Jack Tar in a navy suit.

Note: Space does not permit us to give Mr. Moss's version this month so it will appear in next issue.

***

Nfld's Oldtime Mummers Play[6]

Last month this paper carried the version of the old-time mummers play which used to be staged in many Newfoundland places up to about 50 years ago, and which was recorded from the memory of Mr. J.J. Peckford of Gander Bay. This month we publish below the version of Mr. Barnabas Moss of Salvage, B[onivista] B[ay]. "The Newfoundlander" is most grateful to both gentlemen for being given the opportunity of preserving this invaluable relic of old Newfoundland folk-lore. Mr. Moss says; "This is an account of the mumming play that was used on Christmas times in the early days by the first settlers in Newfoundland. They used to start out St. Stephen's Day and visit from house to house. They would keep it up for 12 days, everyone clad in war equipment that was required to do battle in those days. It's a great play, well worth resurrecting for the benefit of future generations. I have seen the old fellows at Christmas time acting it, all dressed in uniform. There's no play today can come up to the old-fashioned mumming play, because at Christmas times everyone is into it." (Note: in all cases Mr. Moss spells Christmas in the old form of "X Mass.")

BEELZEBUB. Here comes I, Beelzebub, and on my shoulder carries my club,
   And in my hand a threepenny pan; ain't I a smart jolly old man.
   If you don't believe what I do say, step in Father Christmas and clear the
      way.
   FATHER CHRISTMAS. Here comes I, old Father Christmas, all in my merry
      bloom,
   Come, gentlemen and ladies, come, give me little room;
   Room, room, brave gallant, room; give me room to rhyme
   And I will give you some revels to pass away old Christmas time.
   Old activity, new activity, the like was never seen,
   I pray you now Dim Dorthy step in.
DIM DORTHY. Here comes I, Dim Dorthy, with a fair face and a flat
      commarity,[7]

Although my commarity is but small, I'm the biggest bully of them all.

If you don't believe what I do say, step in Sir Guy and clear the way.

SIR GUY. Here comes I, Sir Guy, a man of mighty strength,

Who slew down Duncow,[8] eighty feet in length;

Is there anyone here holds King George a spleen,[9]

I'm resolved to conquer, it's for King George I'll die.

If you don't believe what I do say, step in King George and clear the way.

KING GEORGE. Here comes I, King George, a man of courage bold,

And with my glittering sword I won ten crowns of gold,

I fought the fiery dragon till I brought him to great slaughter,

And by those bloody means I won the Queen of Egypt's daughter.

Close in a closet I was kept, then upon a table rack,

And after that upon a rock of stone,

'Twas there I sat and made my grievous moan.

Then the Turkish Knight put his foot on land to fight;

To fight I would even, if I was slain, till every drop of blood would quiver in
his veins.

If you don't believe what I do say, step in, Valiant Soldier, and clear thy way.

VALIANT SOLDIER. Here comes I, the Valiant Soldier bold, Slasher is my
name,

Sword and buckle by my side in hopes to win the game;

My head is made of iron, my ribs are made of steel,

I means to fight the Turkish Knight and slay him in the field.

KING GEORGE. Hark, I hear a footstep.

VALIANT SOLDIER. That may be the Grand Turk.

KING GEORGE. If that be the Grand Turk, let him appear.

Grand Turk Enters

[GRAND TURK.] Here comes I, the Grand Turk, out of prison for to fight,

To fight King George, that man by name, if I had him what dreadful work I
make;

I would cut him and slay him as small as dust,

And send his body to the devil for a Christmas pie crust.

KING GEORGE. Stop! Stop! Don't speak so hot,

There's a man in this room thou knowest not,

I'll cut thee and slay thee and when that is done,

I will fight the bravest champion that's under the sun.

GRAND TURK. Why, King George, did I ever do you any harm?

KING GEORGE. Yes! therefore you deserve to be stabbed.

GRAND TURK. Stab for stab, I will punch you to the ground,

Where I mean to lay your body down.

10. "devil"

11. "Called ice, some tice, some old for lice" is a version of the mock Latin used by the Doctor characters.

12. An instrument of torture.

The battle is set in array between King George and the Grand Turk. King George slays the Grand Turk, his body lying dead on the ground. King George, sorry for his brother champion, calls for a doctor.

[KING GEORGE.] Doctor, doctor, come with speed,
    And help me in my time of need;
    The time of need I never saw before
    Till I saw my brother champion lying dead upon the floor.
    Is there a doctor here to be found!
DOCTOR. Yes, there's a doctor here at hand
    Who can cure your brother champion
    Of his deadly wound and make him stand.
KING GEORGE. What can you cure, noble doctor?
DOCTOR. I can cure all things: Itch, stitch, the pox, the palsy and the gout,
    And if the divil[10] is in him I can root him out.
KING GEORGE. How far have you travelled, noble sir?
DOCTOR. I've travelled from England through France and Spain,
    And always back to old England again.
    I have a little bottle in the waist band of my breeches pocket
    Called ice, some tice;[11] some gold for lice; some, the wig of a weasel;
    The wool of a frog and eighteen inches last September's fog.
    Hold it over a slow turf-fire in a wooden saucepan,
    Mixed with a hen's tooth and a cat's feather;
    Three drops to his temple and one to his heart,
    Rise up, brother, and play your part.

The dead Turk is brought to life by the doctor's medicine. The Grand Turk cries out.

[GRAND TURK.] Terrible! Terrible! The like was never seen,
    A man knocked out of seven senses into a hundred and nineteen;
    Not be bucks nor it by bears, one of the divil's whirligigs[12] blowed me up in
      the air.
    If you don't believe what I do say, step in Turkish Knight and clear the way.
TURKISH KNIGHT. Here comes I, the Turkish Knight,
    All from the Turkish land to fight;
    To fight King George or the Valiant Soldier bold, Slasher is his name;
    Show me the man before me will stand,
    I'll cut him down with my courageous hand.
VALIANT SOLDIER. I'm the man before you will stand
    And that you soon shall know,
    And if you do your worst or best
    I'll give you blow for blow.
TURKISH KNIGHT. I don't mind your words as figs.
    Neither your blows or bumps,

If you cut me off my legs,
I'll fight you on my stumps.

The battle is on between the Turkish Knight and the Valiant Soldier. The Turk, wounded, falls to the ground.

VALIANT SOLDIER. O, see, O, see, what I have done,
I have cut him down like the fallen sun;
Ten thousand more such men I'll fight,
For to maintain King George's rights.
TURKISH KNIGHT. O stop, O stop your hand, there's one thing more I crave,
If you spare me my sweet life I'll be your English slave.
VALIANT SOLDIER. Arise, arise, you Turkish dog, and to your country make
your way,
And tell unto your Turkish fleet what a champion old England bears today,
Step in Oliver Cromwell[13] and clear the way.
OLIVER CROMWELL. Here comes I, Oliver Cromwell, as you may suppose,
I conquered many nations with my copper nose;
I made the French to tremble, the Spanish to shake,
I fought the jolly Dutchmen until I made their hearts ache.
If you don't believe what I do say, step in the captain of the play.

The Captain and His Wife Appear

[THE CAPTAIN.] Here comes I, the captain of the play,
And to my men I lead the way,
As I stood on the pewter[14] rock of fame.
And on the champion bear the blame.
I'm not like some of those Turkish dogs
That go out after night and disturb the people and make a noise,
Step in the wren and clear the way.
THE WREN. The wren, the wren, the king of all birds,
St. Stephen's Day I was caught in the firs;
Although I am little my honor is great,
Rise up, Skipper, and give us a treat;
If you got no rum give us some cake.
If you fills the plate of the small,
It will not agree with those boys atall,
But if you fills it of the best,
We hope in Heaven your soul will rest.

Song follows, sung by the crowd.
Ye midwives and widows come now pay attention
To those few lines I'm now going to mention,

Of a maid in distraction who is now going to wander,
She relied upon George for the loss of her lover.
(*Chorus, after each verse.*)
Broken-hearted I'll wander,
For the loss of my lover,
My bonnie light-horseman
Was slain in the war.

Three years and six months since I left England's shore,
My bonnie light-horseman will I ever see more.
She mounted on horseback, so gallant and brave,
Amongst the whole regiment respected he was.

If I had the wings of an eagle as swift as the dove I would fly
I would cross the salt sea where my true love do lie,
And with my fond lips I would bear on his grave,
And kiss his pale cheeks so colder than clay.

END OF THE PLAY

A Dialogue on the State of the Theatre in Canada (1951)

Debating a National Theatre

JAMES HOFFMAN

IN THE LATE 1940S, Robertson Davies was asked to write a submission on theatre for a royal commission that was newly formed to assess the condition of culture in Canada. This invitation gave him the formidable task of creating not only a map of the current state of theatre, but also a blueprint for its future. That he chose to write in the creative and colourful manner of "A Dialogue on the State of the Theatre in Canada" is instructive. It reveals as much about the late 1940s in Canada as it does about Davies's own background in British theatre. To write this particular work, to bring to light his claims—and his hesitations—he peopled his dramatic dialogue with two convivial characters, Lovewit and Trueman, old friends who banter in the clubby, comfy atmosphere of Lovewit's study while preparing their/Davies's presentation to the upcoming commission.

The royal commission was formed in the post-war period of bourgeoning cultural nationalism in Canada—a time when numerous voices and organizations from previous decades reappeared, advocating for a stronger, federally supported Canadian identity, particularly in cultural matters.[1] There was concern for the precarious state of Canadian institutions. The nascent Canadian Broadcasting Corporation and the National Film Board were unsteady, as were the National Gallery, the National Museum, the Public Archives, and the universities: all lacked adequate funding and supportive federal cultural policy. Embarrassingly, major support for Canadian arts, culture, and education had been provided largely from American sources such as the Rockefeller Foundation and the Carnegie Corporation.[2] In response, the federal government decided that "it is in the national interest to give encouragement to institutions which express national feeling, promote common understanding and add to the variety and richness of Canadian life" (citing Privy Council minutes, Canada 1951a, xi).[3] In the January 1949 speech from the throne, the federal government announced the appointment of a royal commission to study the country's cultural institutions; its chair would be Vincent Massey, a man of impressive political and cultural credentials.[4] Initially faced with political reluctance and a skeptical public, the ponderously named Royal Commission on National Development in the Arts, Letters and Sciences, commonly referred to as the "Massey Commission" after its chair, commenced its work in August

1. For a comprehensive listing of activities, see Tippett 1990, especially Chapter 6.

2. By 1950 the Carnegie Corporation had donated over $7 million and the Rockefeller Foundation over $11 million in support of Canadian education, cultural, and arts institutions. For a detailed listing of grants, see Canada 1951a, Appendix V.

3. It was truly a major shift: after attending primarily to its physical and economic resources for so long, it was now time for Canada to link a nation and its culture, to address what the *Report* called "the national tradition of the future" (Canada 1951a, 4). It wouldn't be easy: the commissioners had the formidable task of selling what seemed to some as merely foisting elite culture onto the masses, a task they were careful to refute, promoting instead "a widening opportunity for the Canadian public to enjoy works of genuine merit in all fields" (Canada 1951a, 5), from mass media (radio, television, newspapers) to "high-ranking" culture (literature, music, theatre).

4. Among other appointments, Massey had been Canadian High Commissioner in London (1935–1946) and was soon to be Governor General of Canada (1952–1959). Certainly, cultural nationalism had been a concern for Vincent Massey:

FIGURE 26.1: *Robertson Davies, 1954. Source: 3744002, Walter Curtin fonds, Library and Archives Canada. © Library and Archives Canada. Reproduced with permission.*

in his book *On Being Canadian* (1948), he struggled to locate the Canadian "individuality" (30) as it differs from British or American identities. One area of focus in creating cultural unity was the arts. In his book he states that artists and writers are "interpreters of Canada...our painters have served as 'shock troops'" (34), and that Canadian writers are now showing a "new confidence in their country" (37). As for the fate of dramatic art, the future "lies largely, however, in the amateur movement" (40), worrying that it, like all arts and letters of the day in Canada, are "hemorrhaging" across the border: "we have imported our poetry and exported our poets" (42). In 1949 he had a towering occasion to do something about it.

5. One exception: with the rise of radio broadcasting in the 1920s, the federal government appointed Sir John Aird in

1949. Massey and four other commissioners crossed the country seeking a vital stocktaking of a wide range of cultural institutions in order to record and strategize "human assets...spiritual resources" (Canada 1951a, 4). The commission held hundreds of public meetings in sixteen cities in all ten provinces, received well over a thousand briefs and presentations, and attended numerous arts and cultural exhibitions and performances. Its central mandate was twofold: to conduct a "general survey of the arts, letters, and sciences in Canada" in order to make recommendations regarding national cultural institutions (Canada 1951a, 3).

Numerous individuals and groups made presentations to the commission, including many from the theatre, which, like other performing arts in Canada, had long existed without federal government attention or assistance.[5] The major theatre contribution was from Robertson Davies who, by the late 1940s, was a respected Canadian playwright, as well as a reputable newspaper editor and critic, with five one-act plays to his name, most of which had been staged by amateur and summer stock theatre companies. All were published in a single volume, *Eros at Breakfast and Other Plays* (1949), with an introduction by the noted British director Tyrone Guthrie, who called Davies "one of the pioneers of the still imaginary Canadian Theatre" (x).

1928 to chair a commission "to examine into the broadcasting situation in the Dominion of Canada and make recommendations...as to the future administration, management, control and financing thereof" (Gray 1985, 27).

6. These early plays, including *The King Who Could Not Dream* (1944), *Benoni* (1945), and *King Phoenix* (1947), "are in the nature of myth or fairy-tale" (Stone-Blackburn 1989, 130); as such, they appeared out of touch with the British "public which is a good deal more serious than any the twentieth century has hitherto known" (Sutherland 1951, 234).

7. While St. Laurent finally authorized the Massey Commission, he "was initially not predisposed to provide aid to the arts, and particularly he did not want his government to be perceived as 'subsidizing ballet dancers'" (Lindgren 2013, 181).

8. Founded by actor and teacher Konstantin Stanislavski and playwright and director Vladimir Nemirovich-Danchenko in 1898, the Moscow Art Theatre soon became noted for realistic staging, especially of the plays of Anton Chekhov. A leading venue for the promotion of Irish literary luminaries such as W.B. Yeats, Lady Gregory, Sean O'Casey, and John Synge, the Abbey Theatre of Dublin, also known as the National Theatre of Ireland, staged its first plays in 1904.

Indeed, in these early short plays, as with his first full-length play, *Fortune, My Foe* (1949), and certainly in his "Dialogue," Davies repeatedly explored the predicament of the struggling artist in a Canada he depicted as a place of cultural aridity: not a surprising perspective given his background. Born in Canada, he had studied in England at Oxford University, taking a degree in literature. He then acted at London's Old Vic Theatre under Guthrie. Returning to Canada in 1940, he first wrote plays designed for the London stage (though none succeeded there),[6] and then began a series of works about the difficulty of instituting culture in Canada—certainly a major theme in his "Dialogue."

Titled "A Dialogue on the State of the Theatre in Canada," Davies's study takes its characters and format from a British source: *Historia Histrionica: An Historical Account of the English Stage*, a "pamphlet" written in 1699 by James Wright, a lawyer with a passion for theatre. Wright's protagonists, Lovewit and Trueman, are on a mission, not unlike that of Davies's characters. They discuss, as the title page states, "The ancient Use, Improvement, and Perfection, of Dramatick Representations, in this Nation. In a Dialogue, of Plays and Players" [sic]. The two men engage in animated conversation about the origins of English theatre (mostly via medieval pageant plays) and the strength of contemporary actors and playwrights (most inferior to those of old). They also debate Jeremy Collier's controversial anti-theatre pamphlet, *A Short View of the Immorality and Profaneness of the English Stage* (1698), which characterized English Restoration theatre as corrupt.

Fun and celebratory, Davies's Lovewit and Trueman are acquaintances who seem to be created to appeal to people in a post-war Canada wary of government support for the arts, including federal politicians such as Prime Minister Louis St. Laurent.[7] Lovewit, an actor, "an Old Vic man," and Trueman, a Canadian playwright, are clearly composites of Davies and his own working theatrical background in British and Canadian theatre, so their opinions and vacillations, as much as their flashes of wit and emotion, are ostensibly influenced by Davies's personal experience in British theatre. The witty dialogue of these two characters, admitted activists and provocateurs, colourfully articulates the powerful but clearly hegemonic currents of theatre in mid-century Canada when British models of theatre were dominant. Davies thus asserts his central theme: that of lamenting the lack of a substantive local theatre in Canada while positing the need for a theatre based on national European models.

Davies's "Dialogue" appraises the present conditions of theatre and sets his discussion within a Canada waiting for the Holy Grail of a "National Theatre"—one worthy of representing nationhood like the Moscow Art Theatre in Russia or the Abbey Theatre in Ireland.[8] Davies's accomplishment in this piece is his buoyant anticipation of such a theatre, which he predicts will be celebrated as one of "the proudest possessions of the state" (Davies 1951, 392). He sees this as no easy task as it will take time to learn this theatre's needs, as well as those of the Canadian people, since Canadians have trouble recognizing "first-rate" theatre with so little opportunity to see it performed, except occasionally by

9. Formal viceregal patronage of amateur theatre began in 1907 when Governor General Grey founded the Earl Grey Musical and Dramatic Competitions, which folded when he retired in 1911. The DDF was the inspiration of another governor general, Lord Bessborough, a patron of the theatre, assisted by Vincent Massey. Except for the war years, the festival flourished as Canada's de facto national theatre until, with the establishment of professional theatre in the 1960s, it floundered and eventually folded in 1978. Davies offered considerable support for the DDF, both as governor from 1948 to 1958 and as a member of the executive committee in the early 1950s. He regularly adjudicated, spoke on panels, and conducted workshops at the festival.

10. Samuel Marchbanks is a fictional creation, which Davies used frequently to comment on cultural matters, often humorously, in his newspaper, *The Peterborough Examiner*. Davies is also excerpted, from his play *Fortune, My Foe*, in Charles F. Comfort's study of painting, "The Interpretation of a Canadian Spirit in Painting" (Canada 1951b, 412–13), in which Nicholas, an intellectual and writer, addresses the dilemma of remaining in a Canada so dominated by American culture: "But for some of us there is no choice; let Canada do what she will with us, we must stay."

foreign touring companies. Davies imagines such a theatre arising from a strong, popular theatre company—one that is led by "a first-rate artistic director," performing the great classic and modern plays. In this view, Davies was in close sympathy with Massey's notion of Canada's "national immaturity" and the consequent need for "'universal' models (especially Shakespeare)" that would enable Canadians to eventually "speak Shakespeare with a Canadian accent" (Filewod 2002, 42).

A lengthy discourse on Canadian theatre follows. Trueman looks forward to an emerging local drama, although one somewhat limited by aspects of Canada's dull national character, "her integrity, her good sense" (Davies 1951, 389–90). He sees Canada's Dominion Drama Festival (DDF)[9] as a useful model: operating under centralized decree, it fulfilled the national need to both reconcile and unify regional differences in its widely held festivals and adherence to hierarchical theatre practices, even while the country is "indifferent to it" (Davies 1951, 376): a theme that resonates strongly in the *Massey Report*.

Indeed, a considerable number of ideas expressed in Davies's "Dialogue" appear in the *Report*, notably ones that outline the paucity of theatre endeavour. Davies is directly quoted twice in the *Report* and referenced as "a well-known Canadian writer and actor" (Canada 1951a, 199). The *Report*'s theatre section opens with a three-paragraph quotation "from the correspondence of Samuel Marchbanks,"[10] Davies's fictional alter ego, who dispenses advice to a potential Canadian playwright named Fishhorn: "Now what is the Canadian playhouse? Nine times out of ten Fishhorn, it is a school hall, smelling of chalk and kids, and decorated in the Early Concrete style...Write your plays, then, for such a stage" (Canada 1951a, 192). Massey and the other members of the commission similarly note in the *Report* how "the professional theatre is moribund in Canada, and amateur companies are grievously handicapped, through lack of suitable or of any playhouses" (193). Both the "Dialogue" and the *Report* note that while iconic classical theatre—such as shown in the plays of ancient Athens or Elizabethan London—represent a glorious summit of national culture, such a theatre is rarely seen in Canada.

The *Report* also paraphrases Davies's strictures against the dangers of establishing a national theatre too much under, and therefore severely limited by, any kind of government control; the government should work merely to ease the financial burden of players travelling across the country and to remove provincial amusement taxes. Finally, at the end of Section Eighteen in the *Report*, there is an outline of how to achieve a national theatre, which is taken word-for-word from the "Dialogue": "if we can develop even one company, acting in a tent or in school halls, which can move Canadians to tears and laughter with the great plays of the past, and with great plays of the present (including perhaps a few of their own), we have the heart of a National theatre" (Canada 1951a, 199).

Thus, having established the "noble ideal" (Davies 1951, 392) of a national theatre, the two cheery comrades exit "arm in arm" to toast a presumably

11. Surprisingly, Davies disparages Canadian radio drama, which was then in its golden age.

bright and breezy future. Davies, however, remains caught between anticipating an authentic Canadian drama[11] while adhering exclusively to Eurocentric models—models that would marginalize the theatrical performances of people from Indigenous or non-Anglo origins. Thus, Davies engages in a spirited but essentially neocolonizing venture as an agent of cultural imposition in a country seen as devoid of culture. In so doing, he promotes an imagined national theatre that he believes should be created by federal cultural policy—an intervention he sees as both enabling and threatening. In these ways, "A Dialogue on the State of the Theatre in Canada" reflects Davies's theatrical aspirations as well as his conflicted cultural inheritance.

Bibliography and Further Reading

Benson, Eugene, and L.W. Conolly, eds. 1989. *The Oxford Companion to Canadian Theatre*. Toronto: Oxford University Press.

Campbell, Roy. 1930. *Adamastor, Poems*. London: Faber & Faber.

Canada. 1951a. *Report, Royal Commission on National Development in the Arts, Letters and Sciences 1949–1951*. Ottawa: Edmond Cloutier.

———. 1951b. *Royal Commission Studies: A Selection of Essays Prepared for the Royal Commission on National Development in the Arts, Letters and Sciences*. Ottawa: Edmond Cloutier.

Davies, Robertson. 1949. *Eros at Breakfast and Other Plays*. With an introduction by Tyrone Guthrie. Toronto: Clark, Irwin and Company.

———. 1951. "A Dialogue on the State of Theatre in Canada." In *Royal Commission Studies: A Selection of Essays Prepared for the Royal Commission on National Development in the Arts, Letters and Sciences*, 369–92. Ottawa: Edmond Cloutier. Reprinted in *Canadian Theatre Review*, no. 5 (Winter 1975): 16–36.

———. 1979. *The Enthusiasms of Robertson Davies*. Edited by Judith Skelton Grant. Toronto: McClelland & Stewart.

———. 1981. *The Well-Tempered Critic: One Man's View of Theatre and Letters in Canada*. Edited by Judith Skelton Grant. Toronto: McClelland & Stewart.

———. 1997. *Happy Alchemy: Writings on the Theatre and Other Lively Arts*. Edited by Jennifer Surridge and Brenda Davies. Toronto: McClelland & Stewart.

Filewod, Alan. 2002. *Performing Canada: The Nation Enacted in the Imagined Theatre*. Kamloops, BC: University College of the Cariboo.

———. 2011. *Committing Theatre, Theatre Radicalism and Political Intervention in Canada*. Toronto: Between the Lines.

———. 2015. "A Dialogue on University Theatre in the Age of the Program Prioritization Process." *Canadian Theatre Review*, no. 161, 76–79.

Fink, Howard. 1989. "Radio Drama in English." In *The Oxford Companion to Canadian Theatre*, edited by Eugene Benson and L.W. Conolly, 452–56. Toronto: Oxford University Press.

Grant, Judith Skelton. 1994. *Robertson Davies: Man of Myth*. Toronto: Penguin.

Gray, Jack. 1985. "The Performing Arts and Government Policy." In *Contemporary Canadian Theatre: New World Visions*, edited by Anton Wagner, 24–33. Toronto: Simon & Pierre.

Hartnoll, Phyllis, ed. 1951. *The Oxford Companion to the Theatre*. London: Oxford University Press.

Lee, Betty. 1973. *Love and Whisky: The Story of the Dominion Drama Festival*. Toronto: McClelland & Stewart.

Lindgren, Allana. 2013. "The National Ballet of Canada's Normative Bodies: Legitimizing and Popularizing Dance in Canada during the 1950s." In *Contesting Bodies and Nation in Canadian History*, edited by Patrizia Gentile and Jane Nicholas, 180–202. Toronto: University of Toronto Press.

Litt, Paul. 1992. *The Muses, the Masses, and the Massey Commission*. Toronto: University of Toronto Press.

Massey, Vincent. 1948. *On Being Canadian*. Toronto: J.M. Dent.

Nathan, George Jean. 1942. *The Entertainment of a Nation: or, Three Sheets to the Wind*. New York: Knopf.

Ross, Val. 2008. *Robertson Davies: A Portrait in Mosaic*. Toronto: McClelland & Stewart.

Saddlemyer, Ann. 1981. "A Conversation with Robertson Davies." *Canadian Drama* 7 (2): 110–16.

Shea, Albert, ed. 1952. *Culture in Canada: A Study of the Findings of the Royal Commission on National Development in the Arts, Letters and Sciences (1949–1951)*. Toronto: Core.

Stone-Blackburn, Susan. 1989. "Davies, Robertson." In *The Oxford Companion to Canadian Theatre*, edited by Eugene Benson and L.W. Conolly, 129–32. Toronto: Oxford University Press.

Sutherland, J.R. 1951. "England." In *The Oxford Companion to the Theatre*, edited by Phyllis Hartnoll, 222–34. London: Oxford University Press.

Tippett, Maria. 1990. *Making Culture: English-Canadian Institutions and the Arts before the Massey Commission*. Toronto: University of Toronto Press.

Wright, James. 1699. *Historia Histrionica: An Historical Account of the English Stage*. London: G. Croom.

A Dialogue on the State of the Theatre in Canada

ROBERTSON DAVIES

1. In an article, Davies talks about how the dialogue form "was immensely popular in the rural day and Sunday schools I attended" and of his participation in "innumerable dialogues" (1979, 269). He used the form a number of times in his writing: see "Chat with a Great Reader" (Grant 1994, 231-34) and "Basic Optimism" (Grant 1994, 281-83). See also the "Introduction to *Fortune, My Foe* and *Eros at Breakfast*," where he writes that the school dialogue "was a play suitable for children, always profoundly instructive, crammed with Message" (Davies 1997, 154). For a recent use of this form, see Filewod 2015.

2. A Victorian poet, cultural critic, and contemporary of Tennyson and Browning who somewhat darkly depicts the decline of religious belief, notably in his lyric poem "Dover Beach."

3. It seems that Davies had originally written a "businesslike" memorandum, but when he showed a draft to his wife, Brenda, her response was, "I thought it was a bit dull and would be much more lively as dialogue" (Ross 2008, 144). Biographer Judith Skelton Grant reports, "he revised it completely in the light of a long discussion with Michel Saint-Denis, co-director of the drama school at the Old Vic and adjudicator of [the 1950] DDF finals" (Grant 1994, 317).

Note: I have revived the characters of Lovewit and Trueman who, in a pamphlet on the condition of the English theatre in 1699, have already shown themselves admirable assistants in this sort of work. R.D.[1]

Lovewit is seated in his study. To him, Trueman in haste.

TRUEMAN. Good morning, Lovewit; I am lucky to find you at home. You have heard the news?

LOVEWIT. That we two are to prepare a memorandum on the state of the theatre in Canada for the Royal Commission? It came to me by the morning post. What a chance to speak our minds!

TRUEMAN. My dear fellow, you must contain yourself. A memorandum to a body of such solemnity and dignity will be no place for your jokes and your flights of exaggeration.

LOVEWIT. What, honest Trueman? Do you suggest that His Majesty's Commissioners are so far outside the bounds of common humanity that they cannot relish a joke now and then?

TRUEMAN. I did not say so. But I have seen some of the petitions and memoranda which have been presented to them already, and they are, as the schoolboy said of the works of Matthew Arnold,[2] "no place to go for a laugh." Indeed, I wonder if we can come up to the standard of sobriety which they have set.

LOVEWIT. Why, my dear fellow, it will be the easiest thing in the world. We will put down what we want to say in some form congenial to ourselves—as it may be, a dialogue[3]—and when it is done we will send it to a bureaucrat or a public relations counsel to be translated into the proper style, for this language of official documents is not one which any artist can master.

TRUEMAN. No literary artist would dare to touch it, for fear some of it would stick, like pitch, and ruin him. We must have plenty of tabulation of points, labelled (a), (b), and (c). And we must make a pretty show of numbers, and even Roman numerals—But no; numerals look unbusinesslike, and our age wants its artists to be as businesslike as possible.

LOVEWIT. And rightly so. But to be businesslike, and to make a parade of the apparatus of business are different things. We will be businesslike, and the press agent shall make the parade.

TRUEMAN. I know a needy, pragmatical fellow who, for a trifle of money, will supply us with a rare show of statistics to prove anything we choose to say, and these shall provide us with appendices to drag at the tail of our memorandum, and give it weight.

LOVEWIT. And I know an astrologer who has foresworn the casting of horoscopes and now gives all his time to making pie-charts for business houses.

TRUEMAN. Oh rare! The press agent, the pedant, and the astrologer shall give our memorandum the modish air of a modern state paper. But if it is to have any sense in it, Lovewit, we must provide it.

LOVEWIT. You are right. And to talk sense about the theatre demands a high degree of self control, for it is the Temple of the Passions, and too often its devotees allow the passions to escape from the temple and invade their conversation.

TRUEMAN. Let us resolve, here and now, to be as sensible as we can in what we say about the Canadian theatre.

LOVEWIT. To avoid special pleading—

TRUEMAN. Ay, and to avoid also that pitfall of those who talk of the theatre—I mean what George Jean Nathan[4] so aptly calls "ersatz profundity."

LOVEWIT. Agreed! And yet never to forget that the theatre is an art, or a compost of many arts, and that it must be treated at all times with love. For he who makes the theatre his harlot, or his little-regarded companion of the evening, or his schoolmistress, will never know her or enjoy her fairest favours. They know her best who love and serve her best.

TRUEMAN. I suppose, for a beginning, we must answer those who question whether the theatre exists at all in Canada, in any form which deserves careful consideration. Yet it seems to me that it exists here, as it does everywhere in the world, in those centres of population which are big enough to support it. For whatever the enthusiasts may say, not everyone wants the theatre, and of those who want it, not all want it on the same level.

LOVEWIT. True, for the moving-pictures supply the wants of thousands of people who would seek their entertainment in the theatre if no movies existed. But the theatre they would demand, and get, would be the theatre of windy melodrama and domestic comedy. In some countries the theatre can, and does, compete with the movies in providing this sort of fare, but it cannot be said to do so in Canada. The failure of many a Canadian travelling company, jaunting from town to town by car, and putting on its show with borrowed furniture, under the auspices of some local service club, is due to this alone: it is doing badly what the movies do much better. And when Canadian actors who have engaged in such pursuits say that Canadians are indifferent to the theatre, they delude themselves. The fact is that Canadians are indifferent to bad theatre.

TRUEMAN. I am glad to hear you say so. For it appears to me that Canadians are as responsive to first-rate work as any other people. A Canadian audience may sometimes be naive; it may be a little behind the times when confronted with the latest confection from New York or London. Sometimes we are a little provincial. But we are by no means stupid.

5. At the Old Vic Theatre Company in London from 1938 to 1940, under director Tyrone Guthrie, Davies acted in minor roles, dramaturged productions, and taught in the drama school.

6. Author, actor, director and producer, best known for his series of revue sketches, the Fridolinades, in which he played the immensely popular character, Fridolin, a streetwise teenager, as well as his plays *Tit-Coq, Bousille et les justes*, and *Hier, les enfants dansaient*. He is a major figure in the founding of Canadian theatre, especially in his native Quebec. Davies here is likely referring to *Tit-Coq*, which opened in Montreal in 1948 to a momentous reception: a two-year run, publication of the text in French, then English soon afterwards, followed by a national tour.

7. Founded in 1937 by a Roman Catholic priest, Fr. Emile Legault, to foster spiritually uplifting fare by Christian playwrights, the Compagnons de St-Laurent became professional in 1948, but despite their ambitious plans, insufficient audiences, uneven programming, and the lack of government subsidy forced the company to disband in 1952.

8. It is interesting that Davies does not acknowledge the work of the New Play Society, Toronto's first post-war professional theatre, which, since 1946, had been staging plays from the international canon as well as Canadian plays by Lister Sinclair, Morley Callaghan, and John Coulter.

9. In his plays, Anton Chekhov depicts well-formed, poignant characterizations of the shifting, troubled middle-class society in early twentieth-century Russia, while Norwegian Henrik Ibsen deeply contests the structures and values of the Victorian social order.

LOVEWIT. I agree. And I may tell you, Trueman, that I have myself been an actor in London,[5] and I have known London audiences to be naive, old-fashioned and provincial when confronted with something they did not understand. And need we suppose that a New York audience is any different? Their treatment of some fine plays certainly does not suggest it. I am with you: Canadians are as quick as anyone to recognize and applaud what is first-rate. Their reception of fine foreign artists has shown it.

TRUEMAN. It must be said, however, that they have not yet put the stamp of unmistakeable approval upon any theatre artist of their own who has not first gained some recognition abroad.

LOVEWIT. There are two answers to that. Perhaps they have not yet found an artist of the theatre so plainly of the first rank that they choose to acclaim him. And also it is almost out of the question at present for a Canadian theatre artist to be seen in all parts of the country and thus to gain national acceptance. Monsieur Gratien Gélinas[6] hopes to try the experiment soon. If he succeeds as well in English as he has done in French, he will be the man.

TRUEMAN. True: but it is not our task to prophesy. The artists of Les Compagnons de St-Laurent[7] are also working on a very high level, but while they act in French their fame will be confined to Quebec and to that very small part of the English population which knows French well enough to follow a play with pleasure—a proportion, I may say, which is even smaller than it professes itself to be. But in the English-speaking theatre who have we?

LOVEWIT. There is no one.[8] And it is impossible to say how much the fame of Fridolin and Les Compagnons owes to the fact that their audience is a compact one compared with the audience which English-speaking actors face. No one doubts their ability, but it must be allowed that they are fortunate in not having to establish their celebrity in all ten provinces.

TRUEMAN. We are agreed, then, that Canadians who care for the theatre at all are warmly responsive to first-rate theatre. And let us be generous in our definition of first-rate theatre: a classic thoroughly understood and finely presented, a display of virtuoso acting in a play of modest merit, a fine piece of ensemble work in a play of Tchekov or Ibsen,[9] a farce played with skill and gusto—any of these may, in its degree, provide that special pleasure, that sense of exhilaration and fulfillment which first-rate theatre can give. For make no mistake, friend Lovewit, the theatre is a vigorous, living, and in a certain sense, a coarse art; it is vulgar in the true sense of the word. I am always suspicious of theatre-lovers who insist that they can only endure the finest plays performed to perfection. There are many kinds of excellence in the theatre, but all are recognizable by the completeness of the special effect which they produce upon the audience, and by the unmistakeable deep satisfaction which they give.

LOVEWIT. Do you think that this completeness of effect is often achieved in the theatre in Canada?

10. Written by playwright William
Congreve and first staged
in 1695 during the British
Restoration period, the play is
a lively comedy of manners,
with besieged lovers, lost
inheritances, and deceits to
gain parental approbation,
all in genial fun and with an
agreeable finale.

11. *She Stoops to Conquer* was
written by Oliver Goldsmith
and premiered at London's
Covent Garden Theatre in 1773;
The Rivals and *The School for
Scandal* were both authored by
Richard Brinsley Sheridan: the
first opening at Covent Garden
in 1775, the second at Drury
Lane Theatre in 1777.

12. An energetic, declamatory
British actor who founded the
Allan Wilkie Shakespearean
Company (1920) and toured
widely in the UK, Australia,
New Zealand, India, the United
States, and Canada.

TRUEMAN. Sometimes, certainly, in the performances of the professional companies which visit our big cities.

LOVEWIT. Ah, but they come to us from England or from the United States; we cannot count them.

TRUEMAN. No, but we must not overlook them, for they provide examples for our native actors, and in the theatre, as in all arts, example is of the utmost value to those who would reach a high level of achievement themselves. The pity is that they come so seldom, and visit so few of our cities; for this reason we lack the constant inspiration of theatrical work on the highest level. It is an economic problem, of course. When the Old Vic visits New York it cannot come to Canada without losing money. When Gielgud brings us *Love for Love*[10] he does so at a money sacrifice, and the unfamiliarity of the play keeps people out of the theatre.

LOVEWIT. There you touch upon a point which we must not neglect. We have said that there is an audience in Canada for any sort of first-rate theatre. But there is one class of theatrical work which must be excepted, and that is the performance of unfamiliar classics. You spoke of *Love for Love*; our Canadian education is so poor in quality that virtually no Canadian who is not a university graduate in English has ever heard of its author, much less felt any anxiety to see his works on the stage. There are great realms of drama closed to us for this reason alone. In England, and to a very much lesser degree in the United States, it is possible to see plays performed which are out of the common run. But we Canadians are an illiterate people in this respect, and we fear the unknown as only the ignorant and the intellectually lazy can fear it. This is a matter, my dear Trueman, in which our country desperately needs reform.

TRUEMAN. You will start no quarrel with me on that score, and I am as good a Canadian as yourself. I think it may fairly be said that except for two or three comedies of Shakespeare, *She Stoops to Conquer* and Sheridan's *Rivals* and *School for Scandal*,[11] and two or three Ibsen bogies, a classic is rarely performed in the English-speaking theatre in this country.

LOVEWIT. An Australian told me recently that before he was eighteen he had seen twenty plays of Shakespeare performed, more or less ably, by the company which Alan [sic] Wilkie[12] maintained in that country. This experience has enriched his life in a fashion inexplicable to most of our countrymen. Have you ever asked a group of Canadian schoolteachers, professionally engaged in teaching Shakespeare, how many Shakespearean plays they have seen on the stage?

TRUEMAN. I confess that I have shrunk from such depressing investigation.

LOVEWIT. Their answers would sadden your heart and chill your blood, I promise you. What can they know about Shakespearean drama if they have never experienced it in its proper form? Who attempts to explain the works of Beethoven if he has never heard an orchestra play them?

13. A term acknowledging a continuity of lineage and belief, as
in the Christian Church, where
the succession of bishops is
believed to derive from the
original twelve apostles.

14. A highly regarded London
actor in the plays of Shaw
and Shakespeare who would
have met Davies at the Old Vic
before leaving for America
in 1939, where he appeared
on Broadway as Montague in
Romeo and Juliet with Laurence
Olivier and Vivien Leigh. May
Whitty, his wife, had a long
and successful career as a stage
and film actress in the UK and
the US.

15. A superior actor-manager
who presided over the London
stage during the final decades
of the nineteenth century. A
finely detailed and thoughtful
leading actor of many great
roles, he was also a gifted
manager, notably of the
Lyceum Theatre. In 1895 he
received the first knighthood
ever bestowed on an actor.

16. An accomplished and much-
admired London actor
who was especially noted
for working continuously
for forty years at the
Haymarket Theatre under
the management of Ben
Webster. Davies, in calling
him "Evergreen Howe," is
appreciating the actor's
enduring reputation.

17. A celebrated English actor,
best known for playing tragic,
emotionally charged roles in a
somewhat eccentric manner,
who also suffered from
controversial exploits both on
the stage and in his personal
life.

TRUEMAN. You need not confine your pity to schoolteachers alone. I think
it very likely that a majority of Canadians of good education—as education goes here—and good financial estate, have never seen a Shakespearean
play performed.

LOVEWIT. As far as the classics of the theatre are concerned, we are a nation
of ignoramuses, and the oft-advanced excuse that because we do not know
what we are missing we are none the worse for it, seems to me to be a
disgraceful evasion.

TRUEMAN. That brings us back to what I said a short time ago: I think that one
reason why we slight the classics is that we lack the example and the tradition which is wanted by those who tackle them.

LOVEWIT. Tradition! You have hit it!

TRUEMAN. Do not mistake me. A weight of tradition may be as great a handicap as none at all.

LOVEWIT. But a genuine, living tradition is constantly renewing itself, and
the theatre, perhaps more than the other arts, relies upon a living tradition. The theatre has its relics and its apostolic succession,[13] you know, and
among actors reverence for the great ones of the theatre's past is a living
and potent force.

TRUEMAN. Your phrase "apostolic succession" catches my fancy. Will you not
clarify what you mean?

LOVEWIT. With pleasure, if you will allow me a personal reminiscence. When
I was a young and unimportant actor at the Old Vic I had several conversations with Ben Webster,[14] who was himself of a great theatrical family; he
told me how, when he and May Whitty, his wife, were touring on this continent on the fifth of Sir Henry Irving's[15] visits, they helped to cheer the last
hours of an old member of the company, Henry Howe,[16] who died when
they were in Cincinnati; "Evergreen" Howe was born in 1812 of a Quaker
family, and when he wanted to go on the stage he asked advice of Edmund
Kean.[17] Webster told me of Kean's surprise; "Why, cocky, you're a Quaker!"
When Howe said that none the less he wished to act, Kean thrust his face
into the boy's and rasped, "Well, cully, can you starve?"…I tell you this story
because, as I sat in awed admiration at the feet of Ben Webster, a man with
roots deep in the theatre's past, I seemed, through his kindly acceptance of
me, to reach back into the past, through Evergreen Howe, to Kean himself.
That is tradition, Trueman. I do not pretend that it made me a better actor,
but it gave me a sense of the wonder and nearness of the great past which
made it impossible for me ever to give the theatre less than my best, whatever that best might be. And that is the thing which our Canadian actors
cannot get, although I know how powerfully many of them desire it. They
want the living tradition, and as yet there is no one to give it to them.

TRUEMAN. Acting, as a profession, is still in its infancy in Canada. We might
hope for the establishment of a native tradition if there were not strong
forces working against it. But to earn a sufficient income as an actor in

18. Despite Davies's disparagement of radio acting, some feel that Canada in fact had its first national theatre in the decades from the 1930s to the 1960s, during the country's golden age of radio, when important dramatists such as Merrill Denison, Elsie Park Gowan, Gwen Pharis Ringwood, and George Ryga were performed, often by notable actors like Frances Hyland, Douglas Rain, Lorne Greene, William Shatner, and Christopher Plummer, all of whom acted major roles in the early years of the Stratford Festival, founded in 1953 (see Fink 1989). Indeed, some of Davies's earliest dramas were written for the radio: in 1944 he wrote four short scripts publicizing the work of the Victorian Order of Nurses, then six Victory Loan playlets, all "light-hearted…but the levity missed its mark" for war weary audiences (Grant 1994, 289); none are extant.

Canada is possible only to a score or so of people. The remainder must work as radio actors in order to live.

LOVEWIT. And in saying that you explain many of their deficiencies. Radio acting[18] makes no demands upon the body; an actor whose body is untrained will never make his mark upon the stage except in a limited range of roles for which he is perfectly suited. He will be lucky if he rises above mediocrity even in those. Acting in the classics, or in a modern play which is not realistic in manner, is impossible for him, for he does not know his business.

TRUEMAN. I suspect that you do not consider radio acting as real acting.

LOVEWIT. Radio, unaided by the stage, has not produced a single actor of the first rank. The microphone imposes too many limitations. Emotions must be expressed in such a manner as to agree with the machine, for the machine is the final arbiter. The speech of even the best radio actors is unsuitable for the stage, without radical change. And what passes for sincerity in radio has nothing to do with the larger sincerity which is demanded of an actor who must fill a theatre with sound. Yet this is the work by which most of our actors have to live.

TRUEMAN. Do you consider that in general it makes bad actors of them?

LOVEWIT. Not of the wise ones. The encouraging fact is that many of these young men and women take great pains to learn to act well on the stage. They train their bodies and their voices. And when they have the chance they act in a way which gladdens the heart.

TRUEMAN. Do you refer to their performances in the summer theatres?

LOVEWIT. Yes, and anywhere that they have a chance to work under conditions which are in any way conducive to real artistic effort. I have seen them in classical plays, in commercial plays and in musical comedies and revues. They are not numerous, but there are enough of them to give us a theatre if they could live by it.

TRUEMAN. Ah, but as soon as they had reached a certain level of excellence they would get offers from the States and we would lose them.

LOVEWIT. We would lose a few of them. But there are others—some of them among the best—who would stay here. For patriotism in the arts is no less common than it is in other spheres. If they had a chance at a respectable livelihood and an honourable way of life, they would stay, and they could give us a truly fine theatre.

TRUEMAN. While such people exist it cannot be said that we are without the means to create a theatre. But so far we have said nothing of the theatre which exists widely everywhere in Canada, and flourishes triumphantly in some parts of it.

LOVEWIT. Our amateur theatre? Yes; if it flourished on such a scale, proportionately, in the U.S.A., news of the prodigy would have been spread to the uttermost ends of the earth. For where else in the world will you find a

19. Founded in 1934 by the merger
of four local drama clubs, the
London Little Theatre enjoyed
both amateur and professional
success, mounting ambitious
winter seasons of six
amateur productions led by
professional directors and
mounting Equity stock shows
in the summer. Purchasing
the Grand Theatre in 1945,
they became one of the
first amateur companies to
run an ongoing, legitimate
theatre. In 1971 the company
transitioned from amateur to
fully professional as the Grand
Theatre Company.

national amateur theatre movement comparable with our Dominion Drama Festival?

TRUEMAN. It is one of Canada's cultural glories, but Canada characteristically does not know it. The Dominion Government is indifferent to it, and hundreds of thousands of citizens either know nothing of it, or are profoundly misinformed about it. It receives no penny from the public purse. And yet it engages the attention of much of the ablest artistic talent of the country, and it provides, in its final yearly festival, a week of drama which has won the sincere admiration of extremely able professional men of the theatre, who are brought here to judge it. I cannot think of any other country in the world where a comparable effort would be so persistently snubbed by the Government. Even on the lowest level, its publicity value to the country is enormous. The libel that Canada hates the arts is more strongly supported by the resolute official slighting of the Dominion Drama Festival than in any other single matter.

LOVEWIT. Do not grow too heated, my dear fellow. It may be a blessing in disguise. The artist who is slighted by his Government is at least not under his Government's thumb. But more of this later. The curious fact, in my estimation, is that in Canada the amateurs are so much better off than the professionals.

TRUEMAN. It is a fact that some of the large amateur societies own fine theatres and have a good deal of money to spend on presenting their public performances. Such a group as the Little Theatre of London, Ontario,[19] which owns a handsome, full-sized theatre, supports a studio for experimental work, gives assistance to promising young people, and employs several persons to attend to its business all the year round, is a brilliant exception. The average amateur theatre group works in a hired hall, pays its way from year to year, and in the course of time acquires a wardrobe and some scenery. If, at the end of a season, it has paid its bills and still has enough in hand to finance some of the preparatory work for the season to come it has done well. And in addition to these groups of average success, there are struggling groups which often cannot make ends meet.

LOVEWIT. Lack of merit?

TRUEMAN. Very often, but in some cases it is because they present unpopular plays which they think should be seen. In large cities there are also groups of poor people who, as they act for poor audiences, never have quite enough money. But a few of them do work of artistic value, for all that.

LOVEWIT. When you speak of "artistic value" in an amateur performance do you mean the same thing as when you use that phrase of a professional performance?

TRUEMAN. Such a phrase cannot have a constant value, like a bar of gold of a fixed weight. But you are right to take me up in that way. When speaking of the amateur theatre one must beware of sophisticating one's standards.

20. Davies's plays, *Fortune, My Foe* and *At My Heart's Core*, while enjoying some early successes, also led to growing frustration as Davies encountered certain amateur groups carelessly altering and cutting his playscripts (notably *Fortune*) and generally disparaging his dramatic oeuvre. Meanwhile, a European response to his work informed him, "You must realize that no one, but no one, has any interest in Canada" (see Grant 1994, 318–19).

LOVEWIT. You agree with me, then, that the amateur theatre must be judged by the same standards as the professional?

TRUEMAN. I agree that the best amateur work must be judged by the same standards as the best professional work, for it has earned that compliment. When judging the work of amateurs who plainly are not the best one must use one's common sense, and some measure of charity. Do not forget, Lovewit, that I am a Canadian playwright, and I have seen my plays acted by professionals, good amateurs and bad amateurs; if I had judged them all by the same standard I should not be here to collaborate with you now upon this memorandum, for I should have slain the bad amateurs and chopped them into messes before the astonished eyes of their friends and relatives. When one has said that they, too, are God's creatures one has said absolutely all that can be said in their defence.

LOVEWIT. You speak as if there were no bad professionals.

TRUEMAN. A bad professional will bedaub your play with his own egotistical nonsense, but he will leave something of its original substance. But your bad amateur will ravish it and dance upon its corpse without any comprehension that he is doing it a disservice. But let us talk no more of bad amateurs. My gorge rises.[20]

LOVEWIT. Speak then of the good amateurs. Do you think that they ever surpass the professionals?

TRUEMAN. I will not say that they cannot do so: I say only that I have never personally seen them do so. I have seen here in Canada some fine, sensitive work by amateur actors, but it has always seemed to be lacking in the qualities which fine professional work possesses. The tragic purgation by pity and terror; the comic glory of laughter; these have never been present in their full and unmistakeable power.

LOVEWIT. Are you not a little unreasonable? These amateurs must earn their bread by other work; how can they have the same energy to give to acting that professionals have, who do nothing else?

TRUEMAN. You do not deceive me, Lovewit; you are joking. Of course what you say is half the explanation. But the real fact is that the amateurs lack the imaginative power which the professionals bring to their work. I have seen very capable amateurs; they have some technique of body and voice, and they have a certain amount of flair. But they have not the copious imaginative power which in the gifted professional actor illuminates everything he does and, in his great moments, raises acting from a craft to an art.

LOVEWIT. Yet there is truth in what I said. The actor does no work during the day, and why? Is it because he is idle? No: it is because a creative or interpretative artist needs long periods of leisure in which to prepare for the work which he is going to do. Foolish people envy him this leisure. They think how lucky he is to be paid for three hours' work a day. Yet if he is to work at the necessary pitch of intensity during those three hours, he needs the whole day free to prepare for it. It is in this respect that the amateur is

21. Certainly one of the most celebrated English actors of stage
and film of the mid-twentieth
century, Laurence Olivier was
also an important director and
actor-manager, for all of which
he was knighted in 1947.

22. Writing in *Maclean's* magazine
upon Olivier's death in 1989,
Davies elaborated on the
actor's "robust" style: "Of
the three [greatest actors of
the English-speaking stage]
Olivier must be accounted the
greatest because his range
was the greatest…as the
part [Othello] demanded the
flamboyance, the athleticism,
and the delight in heaven-
storming passion that were his
strengths" (Davies 1997, 74).

23. From *Adamastor*, poems
by South African poet Roy
Campbell, published by Faber
& Faber, 1930, 104.

at a permanent disadvantage. However seriously he may take his acting, he cannot give all of what is best in him to it. And thus he remains an amateur. Yet for all this it must be said that the best Canadian amateurs are very good indeed.

TRUEMAN. So good that if there were a professional theatre here in which an honourable livelihood could be made, many of them would be in it, and might achieve heights of which they have not dreamed.

LOVEWIT. Do you think so? I too have seen a good deal of amateur work here, and the point which has depressed me about it is its old-fashioned quality.

TRUEMAN. You mean that it lingers still in the realistic, understated mode which was popular in the 1920's? That is true.

LOVEWIT. The best actors of today have adopted a more robust style, and have left understatement to the movies, the radio and the amateurs. How thrilling the robust style can be, even in a movie, has been amply illustrated by Sir Lawrence Olivier[21] in *Henry V* and *Hamlet*. But amateurs are desperately afraid of what they call "ham." Now if they only knew it, "ham" is one thing they can never be, for "ham" is robust acting from which intelligence has been removed. If they are never robust, how can they be hams, stifle their intelligence as they may?[22]

TRUEMAN. Very often our amateurs remind me of Roy Campbell's comment on some South African novelists:

You praise the firm restraint with which they write—
I'm with you there, of course:
They use the snaffle and the curb all right,
But where's the bloody horse?[23]

They make a fetish of restraint when what they need is to cut loose.

LOVEWIT. Aha, but there you touch on what I believe to be a vital point. One can only cut loose in an act of artistic creation if one is in it up to the neck. The amateur theatre, at its best, still continues to have strong social implications. Qualities which have little to do with good acting—fairness to others, team-play, and the like—are given an exaggerated value there. For social reasons the good actor must not soar too far beyond the level of the mediocre actor. And although we must respect the ideas which lie behind such behaviour, they have nothing to do with great art.

TRUEMAN. Precisely so, for art is undemocratic and unsocial in much of its working. Nothing so cruelly and irrevocably separates man from man as the existence of unmistakeable artistic talent in one and the lack of it in another. And no one is more ruthless in his subjection of others to his needs than the great artist who is engaged in an act of creation. In the amateur theatre these facts must be kept in restraint as much as possible or the amateur theatre would cease to exist. But in the professional theatre they are the ordinary facts of existence; every professional accepts them,

24. A group of amateur actors, playwrights, and artists from Greenwich Village, New York City, who began to stage plays at the Wharf Theatre in Provincetown, Massachusetts, during the summer of 1915. Focused on giving American playwrights a chance to experiment in a supportive collective beyond the pressure of the commercial theatre or the injunctions of professional critics, the group mounted productions of worthy new playwrights such as Susan Glaspell and Eugene O'Neill. In 1918 the company continued their work at the Provincetown Playhouse in Greenwich Village. The Theatre Guild also had its origins in the Village as the Washington Square Players and similarly endured as a venue for the production of non-commercial American and foreign plays.

and they do not, in themselves, cause any friction. Though actors are, in the main, unusually genial and charitable toward one another in their private relationships, they recognize when they are at work that the superior and the inferior artist do not stand upon an equal footing. The amateur theatre is too close to private life for that.

LOVEWIT. It is really very simple. It is the economic factor which puts everything in perspective. The professional has his value and all his colleagues know it. The amateur has no unmistakeable means of determining his artistic worth.

TRUEMAN. Yet if we say these things in our memorandum will not the Commissioners think that actors are mercenary dogs who judge a man only by the fee he commands?

LOVEWIT. We may trust them to understand the matter in the way we mean it. After all, it is true in every kind of professional work that the big rewards—be they money, or honour, or public acclaim—go usually to the man whose talents give him the best claim to them.

TRUEMAN. There is always one way in which the first-rate amateur can rid himself of his disabilities.

LOVEWIT. You mean that he can become a professional?

TRUEMAN. Yes, and it may be said that the amateur who does so is in little danger of falling prey to that cynicism about his work which wrecks the careers of many professionals who have gone on the stage at the earliest opportunity. Two theatres which have exercised an incalculable influence on modern drama began as amateur theatres: I mean the Moscow Art Theatre, and the Abbey Theatre of Dublin. They were born of a great love of the theatre; when the time came to break with the disadvantages of amateurism they faced that risk bravely. But during their years of professional greatness they never lost the fresh approach and the devotion of the good amateur. And it may be said that the Theatre Guild of New York had its beginning in the amateur Provincetown Players.[24] Our Dominion Drama Festival proves to us every year that there is the raw material of a professional theatre in Canada which might rise to very great heights.

LOVEWIT. Well, let us suppose that such a devoted group of amateurs as began the Moscow Art Theatre were to try its luck in Canada; could it exist in one of our big cities?

TRUEMAN. It might, if it had adequate financial backing. Don't forget that Constantin Stanislavsky was a man of wealth. In my opinion, it would take three years for such a group to reach a point where it could pay its own way. Most of the theatrical ventures which I have had a chance to watch in Canada have died from a combination of two diseases: they were not good enough, and they were not wisely financed. The two diseases are interlocking, for lack of money leads to bad work, and bad work keeps money out of the theatre.

25. "One of the outstanding
women of the English theatre,"
according to the *Oxford
Companion to the Theatre* (1951,
63). Musically trained, Baylis
cherished opera, as well as
drama and ballet, but it was as
a producer and enthusiast that
she made her mark, notably
managing the Old Vic Theatre
where, beginning in 1914, all
of Shakespeare's plays were
presented under her watch.

26. Davies is likely referring to the
popular community concerts
that flourished in Canada in
the 1940s and 1950s. Begun in
1922 by American musician
Ward French and others in
the so-called "Organized
Audience Movement," the
strategy was to bring the
best performers—often from
New York—to medium-sized
and smaller towns by having
local volunteers organize
membership campaigns so
that presold subscriptions
would reduce financial
risk and provide personnel
support and a performance
venue. At one of these, Davies
experienced a youthful "great
revelation" after watching a
condensed version of Verdi's
opera *Rigoletto* (Davies 1979,
226).

LOVEWIT. Just a moment; I am an Old Vic man, as you know. Lilian Baylis[25] was never discouraged by lack of money.

TRUEMAN. Lilian Baylis was a financial genius; she also owned a theatre and thus had one large tangible asset; and she worked in a country and a city where the theatre counts its lovers in millions. The Canadian companies of which I speak are in a different position. If I were forming a Canadian theatre company the second man I would engage would be the best business manager I could find. And I would not seek to establish a company in one place; I would travel.

LOVEWIT. But have you not heard the moans of those who have travelled already? Where is there for them to play? In school auditoriums, which have no space for scenery, no adequate lighting, and stages which might better be described as niches in the wall. There are also town halls, skating rinks and armouries. Theatres are few, and many of them are barn-like edifices, impossible to fill and as uncomfortable, in their way, as the school auditoriums.

TRUEMAN. But if the theatre in Canada is to wait upon the establishment of well-found playhouses in every small city and large town it will wait until the crack of Doom. For—get this through your head, Master Lovewit—the theatre is not first a thing of bricks and mortar, but of players and playwrights, and if first things are to come first the inconveniences of the existing halls must be met and overcome.

LOVEWIT. Pray do not hector me, my dear friend, for I present difficulties only to draw you out.

TRUEMAN. Your pardon, honest Lovewit. But when I hear it suggested that a play cannot be done well without a perfect theatre—meaning some version of the peep-show theatre of the past two hundred years—I cannot contain my choler.

LOVEWIT. Arena staging might be tried. Fine things have been done in that manner.

TRUEMAN. Yes, and there is our old friend the fit-up—the portable stage equipment. And the depressingly educational appearance of school auditoriums could be relieved by an imaginative portable false proscenium. For a great step is taken toward stage illusion by any means which conceals from the audience that it is in the assembly hall of the Podunk Collegiate and Vocational School, where it has succumbed to boredom so often in the past.

LOVEWIT. I really do not see why a well-equipped and artistically respectable company should not travel in a circuit, as the players did in eighteenth-century England. Indeed, when one considers the success of Community Concerts in Canada,[26] one wonders if circuits might not be financed on a similar subscription plan. They would have to take in many small places, to cut the cost of travel but that would be desirable.

TRUEMAN. An advantage of such a plan would be that, as with Community Concerts, the audience and the money would be assured, and the company

27. An Irish Nationalist poet and dramatist who, along with Lady Gregory, Maud Gonne, and others, beginning in the last decade of the nineteenth century, was a key visionary and founder of the Irish Dramatic Movement that promoted the depiction of early Irish heroic legend and Celtic culture, as well as the lives of peasants and common people.

28. Vincent Massey was an amateur actor and patron of the theatre—notably as founder of Hart House Theatre in Toronto, editor of two volumes of *Canadian Plays from Hart House Theatre*, lifelong chairman of the DDF, and supporter of the Stratford Festival.

would be able to judge its expenses with its eye trained upon its income. So long as it kept the confidence of its audience, it would have little to fear.

LOVEWIT. And it would keep the confidence of its audience so long as it could provide first-rate theatrical entertainment.

TRUEMAN. That is the nub of the whole matter, for as we cannot repeat too often, more theatrical ventures are killed by their own lack of merit in a year than are killed by the neglect or malignity of the public in ten. I said that the second man I would hire, if I were charged with the task of establishing such a venture, would be a first-rate business man. The first man, and the keystone of my arch, would be a first-rate artistic director.

LOVEWIT. You would be hard set to find him.

TRUEMAN. Men of capacity are hard to find in all walks of life. He would have to be a man of fine taste, yet with a keen sense of what his audiences could be persuaded to like. He would have to keep not only his actors, but his directors, designers and technical people up to the mark. He would have to listen at all times to his business manager, and he would have to possess a good knowledge of business himself. He would have to provide, like Stanislavsky or Lilian Baylis, inspiration, instruction, succour, rebuke and a focus of faith for all who worked with him, and he would have to provide the public with a figurehead whom they could trust and admire.

LOVEWIT. You ask for a paragon.

TRUEMAN. No; merely for a man big enough for a big job. Such people are not common, nor are they cast in one mould. Can you think of three people more apparently different than Stanislavsky, W.B. Yeats[27] and Lilian Baylis? And our leader here, whoever he may be, will be like all of them, and yet not like any of them.

LOVEWIT. Come, Trueman, we agreed to stick to common sense. You are talking as though our Canadian theatre would be the work of some single remarkable figure.

TRUEMAN. Perhaps I am wrong, but I do not think so. Such a leader would collect about him the admirable single talents which exist in our country now, but which have no focus. If I write a play, to whom can I turn for an opinion which will content me? And you, Lovewit, who direct and act with a certain taste and discretion—is there anyone for whom you are ready to give your utmost, and whose banner you would follow through good times and bad? Canada has plenty of theatrical talent which is very nearly first-rate, and which would be so if it could find a catalyst—a messiah—call him what you will.

LOVEWIT. If we send a memorandum to the Commissioners saying that we want a messiah they may take us for madmen—

TRUEMAN. I doubt that. The Chairman of the Commission[28] is a notable patron of the drama, and the other Commissioners, being persons of cultivation and noble spirit, must love it too. Let us say that we need a messiah by all means, and I am sure that they would unite in the Song of Simeon if he were to appear.

LOVEWIT. Trueman, restrain your Celtic emotion! Any suggestion that the Commissioners are ready to sing a *Nunc Dimittis*[29] will undo us utterly! To imply that Commission is ready to depart, even in peace, is inexcusable impertinence! What they want from us, I venture to say, is concrete suggestion. What, in short, can the Government of Canada do about the theatre in Canada?

TRUEMAN. It could do several things. It could give reputable travelling companies, composed of Canadians, a special favourable rate on the Canadian National Railways, by making some suitable arrangement with the railway authorities. The haulage of a company and a quantity of scenery is a formidable consideration for any theatrical venture.

LOVEWIT. That would be a practical benefit certainly.

TRUEMAN. And it might induce provincial governments, at a dominion-provincial conference, to relieve reputable Canadian companies of the burdensome amusements tax which the provinces now levy.

LOVEWIT. True, for it seems unjust that the native theatre should be expected to tack onto every ticket of admission an extra charge which is not used for the furtherance of the theatre or any of the arts. If there is a case for such an impost upon any form of entertainment—which I am disposed to doubt, for it is discriminatory, and I shrewdly suspect that it has its root in a puritanical dislike of merrymaking in general—there is surely none upon the Canadian theatre, which deserves well of its country and its country's governors.

TRUEMAN. Well, there we have two benefits which might be conferred.

LOVEWIT. Both, it may be said, are negative: they let the theatre companies off certain expenses. They do not plainly give them anything.

TRUEMAN. And that, in my opinion, is as it should be. For you may as well know, Lovewit, that I oppose giving artists money from the public purse except under the most unusual circumstances: lessen their burdens, but give them no cash.

LOVEWIT. For the reason, I suppose, that I spoke of earlier: the artist who gets nothing from his Government is not under his Government's thumb.

TRUEMAN. Precisely. If the theatre is to have a patron today it must be the Government, for the Government now takes the means of patronage from private persons. But Government patronage, unless it is of the negative, unobtrusive sort which I have mentioned, or unless it operates under special safeguards, can become severely repressive in its influence. Let us suppose that some governmental scheme for a National Theatre were set at work in this country within the next five years: at every election economies are promised and the National Theatre would come under fire. That would beget a spirit of nervous tension and servility among the artists and

30. Certainly, there was concern as left-wing theatre groups threatened the complacency of the country's somewhat gentrified Dominion Drama Festival, as Toby Gordon Ryan reports on the "hostility" that socially progressive member groups like Theatre of Action encountered at the DDF: "We were made to feel that we were intruders" (Filewod 2011, 160).

31. A poet of ancient Greece and often regarded as a founder of drama, Thespis is reputed to be the first to employ an actor along with the chorus in his plays. His "car" refers to travelling with his performers in a cart.

administrators of the National Theatre which would make first-rate work impossible.

LOVEWIT. Alas, yes! And can you not imagine some Member of Parliament complaining bitterly in the Commons every time the National Theatre performed a play about people whose morals were not identical with those of his constituents? Or if he saw an actor from the National Theatre whose dress displeased him, or who wore his hair at a length deemed unbecoming in a servant of the state?[30]

TRUEMAN. Our elected representatives are already heavily burdened with public business: let us not lay upon them the responsibility of overseeing a theatre, as well.

LOVEWIT. There may come a day when a Canadian theatrical company has unmistakeably earned the right to be called a National Theatre. By that time it will have its traditions, its method of work, its individual style, and its faithful and appreciative public. If the nation chooses to offer support to it, it can accept upon honourable terms, and insist that it be allowed to know its own business better than the noble tribunes of the people. For although I am a democrat, Trueman, I do not believe that people who know nothing about the arts should be allowed to make life miserable for those who do.

TRUEMAN. Because I am a democrat, I thoroughly agree with you. And I agree, too, that a National Theatre cannot be brought into being simply by the expenditure of public money. It must grow. Set up a National Theatre, and remove it from money anxieties by a state grant, and in ten years it will have become a pension scheme for the artistically worn out, the incompetent, and the faddists.

LOVEWIT. Either that, or a new playground for the professional do-gooders. Never forget those well-meaning enemies of art. They are the people who will not allow the theatre to be its own justification. The theatre is educational and recreative. But it is not so primarily. It is first of all an art, and it is as a form of art that it stands or falls. Let people get their hands on it who regard it as means of spreading some sort of education dear to themselves, or who think that it is a social medicine, and you will kill it as dead as a doornail. But let the theatre develop freely and gloriously as an art, let it present classics and good modern plays, let it ravish the souls of its audiences with tragedy and comedy and melodrama, and it will educate and recreate them more truly and lastingly than the zealots think possible. The car of Thespis[31] must not be turned into a travelling canteen, dispensing thin gruel to the intellectually under-privileged.

TRUEMAN. Yes, if the theatre in Canada is to develop into anything of worth it cannot afford short-cuts. It must take the long way, in order that it may have time to learn not only its own business, but the special tastes and needs of our people. It is superficially attractive to think of a National Theatre created by Government fiat, but I fear the consequences. In our country officialism is splendidly developed; the art of the theatre, though

32. Arabic "*jinn*," commonly
anglicized as "genie."

33. Davies would be crucially
instrumental in the origin of
the Stratford Festival a few
years later: it was he and Dora
Mavor Moore who suggested
that Tom Patterson contact
Tyrone Guthrie to become the
all-important founding artistic
director, and of course for the
first few years the festival took
place in a large tent.

promising, is no match for it. Officialism and public interference might well prove too overpowering, and the result would be a National Theatre continually engaged in a losing fight with essentially inartistic influences.

LOVEWIT. By the bye, my dear friend, we must be careful of our use of that word "artistic" in our memorandum. Through no fault of its own it has acquired overtones of preciousness.

TRUEMAN. Yes, we must make it clear that we employ the word "artist" in its true sense of "maker." The artist is he who creates. And he must be as little as possible hampered by people whose work is not to create but to complicate, obfuscate, worry and destroy.

LOVEWIT. We are agreed then, that the Canadian theatre should thoroughly learn its job before there is any talk of a National Theatre? Even though its way may be hard?

TRUEMAN. Most certainly. Nor must we forget that to many people the words National Theatre mean a building, probably in Ottawa. Now unless such a building is a centre from which travelling companies go on tours through the length and breadth of Canada, it is a foolish extravagance. A theatre is not a thing of bricks and mortar. If a djinn[32] from the Arabian Nights were to whisk the Shakespeare Memorial Theatre from Stratford and set it down in Ottawa, with all its equipment, we would still be without a National Theatre. But if we can develop even one company, acting in a tent or in school halls, which can move Canadians to tears and laughter with the great plays of the past, and with great plays of the present (including perhaps a few of their own), we have the heart of a National Theatre.[33]

LOVEWIT. The emergence of such a company would be an interesting phenomenon; I have sometimes wondered if criticism would have any considerable part in shaping and polishing it.

TRUEMAN. Informed criticism could do much, but informed criticism is an uncommon thing in the periodicals of our country. If a critic is to be of any use to an artist, he must understand and love the art he criticises, and be must be deeply versed in its literature and its tradition, as well. He must know at least as much about the art as one of its practitioners. The hack critic, the mere reviewer, the reporter given leave to editorialize, is of no positive value and can be a real danger if he is himself a malignant or frustrated man.

LOVEWIT. Our attitude toward criticism is too deeply affected, I fear, by that of the U.S.A. There a critic is too often employed merely to give his opinion on a matter which he has not studied deeply, because he is a wit or can pass for a wit. This style of criticism is dangerous at its best, and when imitated by men of meagre gifts it is execrable.

TRUEMAN. A fine critic is himself something of an artist, and he may, in some cases, encourage an art or even bring forth new developments in it. One of the principal tasks of every good critic of the theatre is to memorialize great performances and events in its history; part of his genius is to know when these events occur, for they are not always obvious. But it is to be feared that most critics serve the theatre as a flea serves a dog—as an irritating parasite which may at times bring the dog into derision.

LOVEWIT. Do you speak as a playwright whose work has, at times, been scorned?

TRUEMAN. It may be that I do, but that does little to lessen the truth of what I have said. To have one's work condemned is unpleasant but not insupportable; to have one's work condemned irresponsibly is gall and wormwood. I think that the newspapers and periodicals have a duty in this matter which many of them neglect. But a growing theatre will make them repair their neglect.

LOVEWIT. I suppose the case of the Canadian playwright must be considered in any complete view of the Canadian theatre. I am told that a great many people in Canada write plays, and yet comparatively few Canadian plays are shown upon the stage. Are the majority so bad?

TRUEMAN. Because I am a Canadian playwright myself I must be careful how I answer you. Only a few of these manuscripts have come my way, and the thing which astonished me about them was not that many were bad, but that several were near to being very good. People whose judgement I trust, who have acted as judges in playwriting competitions, have said the same thing to me often, and they have better cause to know the facts than I. But in order to write a play one must be not only a person with some degree of literary skill, but a theatre craftsman as well. One must know not only how people talk, but how to make them talk in such a way as to complete a piece of action in two and a half hours without too much padding, or too much jumping about in the plot. One must consider the actors, and give them opportunities to show their own special skill as distinguished from your own. One must know how to build up a speech to a climax, and then how to get down from the climax without tumbling. One must not introduce characters who do not help to carry forward the story, for actors cost money and must not be wasted. And above all, one must beware of the wrong kind of subtlety, for the delicate shades which give distinction to a novel have no place in a play: the subtlety of the playwright lies in quite another direction—not less than the novelist's, but different.

LOVEWIT. Aha, you touch upon something which I have often thought, and you must forgive me if I interrupt. It has occurred to me many times that the radio has a weakening effect upon many admirable Canadian writers who occasionally write plays. Radio drama being—let us not mince words—an enfeebled echo of the real thing, encourages the sort of subtlety of which you speak. When a speech can be whispered into a microphone with such immediacy of effect that the listener may almost fancy himself sitting in the larynx, if not in the heart, of the speaker, the writer is tempted to try effects which are quite lost when transferred to the stage. But because unthinking people admire what they regard as subtlety, and condemn breadth of effect, these ineffective devices are attempted again and again.

TRUEMAN. It is this very thing which makes it so hard to put a good stage piece on the radio. A broad effect in radio is merely confusing. Alas for those who beat the drum on behalf of radio drama, the mind's eye is imperfectly hitched to the mind's ear. Hence the Procrustean "adaptation" which is necessary to crush a play into an hour's length, and make it endurable to one sense alone.

LOVEWIT. Not all Canadian playwrights, of course, suffer from the baneful influence of radio writing, but some of the most potentially brilliant of them do so.

TRUEMAN. You interrupted me in my discourse upon the things which a playwright must know. He must be able to tell a story, with a certain richness of embellishment which it is the fashion of the day to mistake for thought, entirely in dialogue and action, usually without shifting his scene from a single place. He must—

LOVEWIT. My dear fellow, please do not tell me any more of the things that he must be able to do. We do not propose, after all, to write a treatise on the playwright's craft.

TRUEMAN. Very well, let us say merely that it is a craft and that it must be learned. The best way to learn it is to write a play and see it through rehearsals and in performance. But as it costs quite a lot of money to give a play a production even in the amateur theatre, this cannot happen very often. The next best way is to see a lot of plays, and to learn from them. That can only be done where a theatre exists. I am quite sure that a robust Canadian theatre would bring forth a large body of Canadian plays, some of them good enough for export.

LOVEWIT. Hm. Do you think that people abroad would be interested in Canadian plays?

TRUEMAN. Lovewit, you disgust me! Is not the theatre of the civilized world interested in plays by and about Russians, Norwegians, Frenchmen, Swedes, Hungarians, Italians, Belgians and even? God bless us!—Irishmen and Scotchmen? Are Canadians so cut off from the charity of God and the indulgence of mankind that they alone are of no interest to their fellow-beings? Take my word for it, if the plays are good enough, the world will like them.

LOVEWIT. Hm. I am reminded of the story of a gifted young woman who asked a celebrated orchestral conductor if her sex would prevent her from getting a place in a first-rate orchestra. No, said he; you will manage it if you are able to play twice as well as any of the men. Canadian plays will have to be very good indeed to break through the prejudice which exists against them, on the ground of their origin.

TRUEMAN. I will confess to you that the agent who hawks my plays in England keeps mum about the fact that I am a Canadian. He says that it

34. By 1950, in "A Letter from Canada" published in the *New York Times Book Review* (March 19), Davies stated "Canadian drama is at its sunrise," citing the recent work of John Coulter in *Riel* (see Davies 1981, 176–78).

would work against him. Nobody thinks that there is anything odd about an Englishman or an American writing a play, but apparently it is still considered unpropitious for a play to come from Canada. Still, I think that the prejudice will be overcome and that we shall see Canadian plays performed abroad—when we have the playwrights capable of bringing that about.

LOVEWIT. It seems to me unlikely that we shall have plays which will command the attention of the outside world until we have a national drama which has roused and stirred us on our own soil.

TRUEMAN. Agreed. Nevertheless, I like to look forward to that day, whenever it may be. For I like to think that Canada will have a proud place among the nations, and I fear that her integrity, her good sense, her honest dealing and her indisputable political genius will not suffice to gain it for her. Think: do you know of any nation that the world has considered truly great which has not had one or many manifestations of great art? Canada will not become great by a continued display of her virtues for virtues are—let us face it—dull. It must have art if it is to be great, and it has more real vitality, in my opinion, in the art of the theatre than in any other save music. And I think its theatre is potentially just as good as its music and perhaps better.[34]

LOVEWIT. I agree, but art cannot be compelled. It will not flourish here simply because we wish it.

TRUEMAN. But we can remove some of the hindrances which lie in the way. I agree with you that the offer of prizes for plays, and establishment of scholarships for talented writers and actors is not the Government's responsibility, but the Government might change its ideas about taxation as it affects writers; if royalties were treated as capital gains, which they are, rather than as profits, which they are not, it would help the writer to improve his position when he has a stroke of good fortune. A writer, surely, deserves well of the state? He exploits nothing but his own talent; he does not impoverish the land; whatever he creates he creates out of nothing which anybody else wants. And yet his creations give pleasure, and in special cases they may reflect honour upon his native land. I do not suppose that the Ministers of Finance and National Revenue are conscious of the existence of authors in any real sense. Yet to the author who, after years of work, a stroke of good fortune brings a considerable sum of money, it sometimes appears that these gentlemen are simply waiting to swoop upon him and despoil him. Canadian authors who are worth their salt do not want subsidies and handouts, but they would like a chance to build up a sufficient estate to permit them to live by writing alone, and to take the time necessary to do their best work.

LOVEWIT. Very well; let us turn from the authors to the actors. Should promising artists of the theatre be given state scholarships in order to study abroad?

35. The *Massey Report*, however,
recommended that "it would
be advisable and necessary to
make provision in Canada for
the more advanced training
of young artists," such as
a "school of the National
Theatre" (Canada 1951a, 198).
The National Theatre School of
Canada opened in Montreal in
1960.

36. A director of the Old Vic
Theatre Centre (which some
saw as a potential British
National Theatre), and highly
influential in founding and
operating theatre studios
in London that combined
training and practice. On adju-
dication visits to Canada,
he advocated the forma-
tion of such a school and was
consulted in its establishment
in 1960.

37. Sometimes regarded as
France's national theatre,
the Comédie-Français was
instituted in 1680, regulated by
royal command, and through
its long and sometimes
tumultuous history, retained
a sense of the old theatrical
tradition of functioning as a
·co-operative company wherein
actors admitted to its ranks
hold full or partial shares and
the longest serving actor heads
the company.

TRUEMAN. I would rather make it possible for them to study at home. The establishment, now, of a National Theatre would be a great mistake; we do not know enough to ensure the success of such an undertaking.[35] But the time is ripe for the establishment of a Theatre Centre, where all the arts of the theatre could be studied and practised under expert supervision, and where our excellent amateurs could find the polishing they need to make them good professionals, as well as the inspiration to carry them beyond their present limited artistic vision. Government assistance in establishing such a centre would be public money well spent.

LOVEWIT. A centre? A school, you mean?

TRUEMAN. No, a practical theatre studio, not a drama school. I would strongly recommend a centre based upon the Old Vic Theatre Centre in London; Sweden has copied it, and we could find no better model. Furthermore, I have the assurance of its director, Monsieur Michel Saint-Denis,[36] that he is willing and indeed eager to help in the establishment of such a centre here. What better model than the Old Vic centre? What better advisor than the director of that centre and one of the ablest men of the theatre in the world today? If anything is to be done, Saint-Denis is your man; and it isn't every day that people of his quality offer to help a struggling art in a new country.

LOVEWIT. How is such a theatre centre financed?

TRUEMAN. By fees from each student, and by a government grant which, in the case of the Old Vic Centre, is £5,000 a year. Call it $25,000 a year for Canada, and a trifle for what it would do.

LOVEWIT. And who would head such a centre?

TRUEMAN. It would have to be a man with some experience of such a place, and I am sure that Monsieur Saint-Denis would help us to find him.

LOVEWIT. And he would be our messiah?

TRUEMAN. Perhaps: or our John the Baptist. Or even a thoroughly competent minor prophet would be a blessing. And when such a centre, and its students, were sufficiently strong we might think about a National Theatre. If the Government wants to help us, let them help us in this way: let them make it possible for us to learn. But as you see I am mistrustful of any sort of direct state patronage of the arts when the artists are not in a strong enough position to make conditions.

LOVEWIT. France, to name only one country, has had national patronage of the theatre for nearly three centuries.

TRUEMAN. Which means that such patronage began in an age when it was in effect personal patronage by persons deeply concerned about the theatre. Our modern bureaucracies are not rich in such enlightened patrons, and our succeeding ministries are almost antiseptically free from them. The Comédie-Française[37] was a product of the spirit of its time, and it had its roots in a strong popular theatre. When we have a strong popular theatre here, it will be time for us to think about a national theatre. We live in an

age of ever-increasing socialism, as you know, and it is good socialist practice to take over a going concern.

LOVEWIT. You are not to be shaken, then, in your belief that Canada does not
need a National Theatre?

TRUEMAN. Have I been talking all this while in vain? Of course I believe
that Canada needs a National Theatre! But I want Canada to have a strong
National Theatre, directed by competent artists of the theatre, and so highly
esteemed by our country and by the civilized world that it can, literally,
run its own show and be under no obligation to cringe whenever a contu-
melious parliamentarian knits his brows! I want Canada to have a National
Theatre which will be in competition with other Canadian theatres of the
first rank. I want Canada to have a National Theatre which is one of the
proudest possessions of the state, and not a drag upon the public purse! For
the theatre is one of the arts which can maintain high standards and still
pay its way; it is a truly popular art, and the people will support it when it
is unmistakeably of the first quality. I want a National Theatre in Canada
as soon as we have developed a fine native theatre which has learned to
support itself by its own efforts, asking from the Government a very little
money and a few favours as assurances of goodwill. I want, in short, a
National Theatre with its roots in the country, nourished by experience,
craftsmanship, and a noble ideal of what a theatre should be!

LOVEWIT. Honest Trueman! Give me thy hand! I have but dissembled my
agreement in order to provoke this splendid rage in thee! Pardon this tear!
'Tis but an ebullition of joy!

TRUEMAN. Enough for one morning. Come, let us to the cocktail lounge
where we may drain a bumper to the future!

Exeunt arm in arm.

27 : Tyrone Guthrie and the Festival Stage (1953)

Configuring Canada's Relationship with Shakespeare

LIZA GIFFEN

1. Not all assessments of Guthrie and his directorial approach have been articulated with unequivocal enthusiasm. Some scholars have alleged that there was an implicit imperialism underpinning Guthrie's attitude to theatre in Canada. Similarly, many of the same writers have also argued that the thrust stage at the Stratford Festival has artistic limitations and is ideologically problematic. For critiques of Guthrie and the Festival stage, see, for example, Cohen 1955, [1959] 1996, [1968] 1996; Knowles 1988, 1994, 1995, 1996; Salter 1996; Groome 2002; and Shaughnessy 2002. For more recent considerations of these issues, see Falocco 2009, 2010; and Barker and Cornford 2018.

2. The documents included in this chapter are drawn from the Stratford Festival Archives, which has a virtually complete prompt book section as well as form plans and drawings of the theatre and stage (Prompt Book Collection, Plan Collection, and Photographic Collection). The main images included here are from the original 1953 *Richard III* prompt book and are supplemented by drawings created for the publicity department for the purposes of fundraising for the festival's permanent Festival Theatre in 1956–57.

IN 1952 THE CITY OF STRATFORD, Ontario, was in a post–Second World War economic slump. Its main industries—locomotive-engine and furniture building—were suffering from the downturn, and it was looking for a way out of this situation. In January of that year, Tom Patterson, a young journalist, addressed the city council with the idea of creating a "Shakespearean Festival" in Stratford. He asked for one hundred dollars to go to New York and speak to Sir Laurence Olivier. The city agreed, even though they thought he was "either drunk or crazy" (Patterson and Gould 1987, 41). With a few alterations to the plan (Olivier was not available), Patterson eventually got in touch with Dora Mavor Moore, who, via Canadian playwright John Coulter, got in touch with the man she considered "the greatest Shakespearean director in the world": Tyrone Guthrie.[1]

Guthrie was a seasoned professional director at the time of Patterson's approach. Guthrie's previous work ranged from his beginning efforts at the Oxford Playhouse in England, experience at the BBC, directing opportunities with the Scottish National Players, producing for the CNR radio in Montreal, and assignments directing opera in New York and plays at London's Old Vic Theatre. It was, all in all, a range of experiences and experiments that had prepared Guthrie for his search for a new form of theatrical staging—a search that would lead to the new and unique Stratford Festival stage, which opened in 1953 with a production of *Richard III*, starring Alec Guinness in the title role (Figure 27.1).[2]

Prior to working at Stratford, Guthrie had previous experiences with temporary "thrust stages." At least one of these thrust stages was discovered partly by accident when a rain-disrupted *al fresco* performance of *Hamlet* at Elsinore in 1937 led to an impromptu restaging. As Guthrie explained to the press at the time, "[The audience] sat, densely packed, round three sides of a small clear space on the ballroom floor, on which most of the action passed, with the steps and little stage for occasional scenes. The effect aimed at was… the audience in the most informal and the closest possible contact with the actors" (1937, 248).

This experience inspired the fundamental principle of Guthrie's future thinking about staging: "intimacy between the actors and the players is the

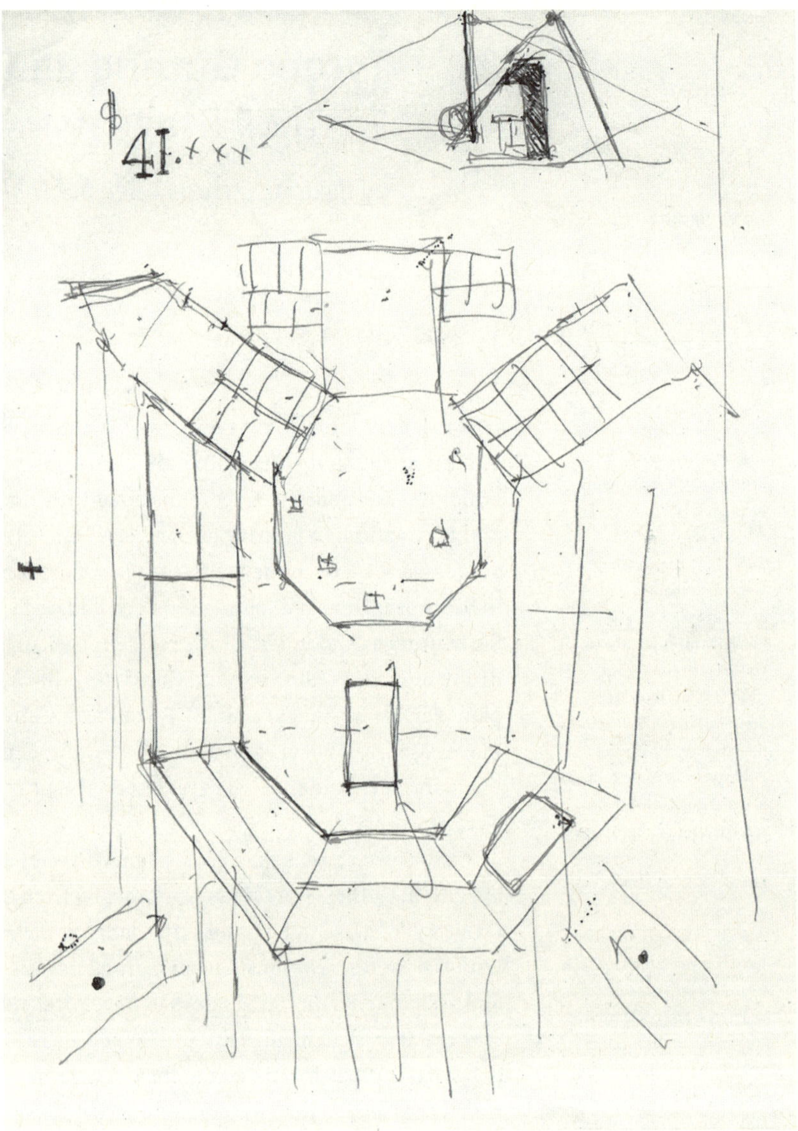

FIGURE 27.1: *Sketch of proposed festival stage from a letter to Tanya Moiseiwitsch, 1952.*
© Stratford Festival. Image courtesy of the Stratford Festival Archive.

first essential" (Guthrie 1937, 249). This nascent thrust stage concept was then elaborated ten years later in his production of *The Thrie Estaitis* in the Church of Scotland's General Assembly Hall during the 1948 Edinburgh Festival. Guthrie described the staging: "The Moderator's chair and the table before it, in the center of the hall, were enclosed under a platform attainable from each of three sides by steps. Behind and above on the fourth side, a gallery was attained by two flights of stairs. The space under the gallery could be closed or exposed at will by drawing curtains" (Guthrie 1959, 309).

In the early twentieth century, proscenium arch stages, which placed distance between audience and players, were the dominant configuration encountered in performance. Guthrie's Edinburgh Festival experience taught him that

> *one of the most pleasing effects of the performance was the physical relation of the audience to the stage. The audience did not look at the actors against a background of pictorial and illusory scenery. Seated around three sides of the stage, they focused on the actors in the brightly lit acting area, but the background was of the dimly lit rows of people similarly focused on the actors. All the time, but unemphatically and by inference, each member of the audience was being ceaselessly reminded that he was not lost in an illusion, was not at the court of King Humanitie in sixteenth century Scotland, but was in fact a member of a large audience, taking part, "assisting," as the French very properly express it, in a performance, a participation in a ritual.*
> (Guthrie 1959, 331)

The change in the relationship between the actors and the audience would be key to the creation of the design of the Festival stage at Stratford by Guthrie and his key partner, the designer Tanya Moiseiwitsch, with whom he had worked since 1945.

Moiseiwitsch was born in London and, after art studies, apprenticed as a scene painter with the Old Vic Theatre, moving to the Abbey Theatre, Dublin, in 1935, where she transformed its design aesthetic from an emphasis on realism to abstraction. In 1939 she returned to England, partly at the Old Vic under Guthrie. At Stratford-upon-Avon in the late 1940s, the Scots-Irish director and the Anglo-Russian designer developed a style of rich costuming on relatively empty stages that allowed for expressive movement and speed when changing scenes. The communion-like effect of actor-audience interaction was widely praised. "Shakespearean plays gain enormously in impact by relating actors to audience as nearly as possible...[Equally significantly] the actors were so near their audience that they could speak really low and still be heard; so near their audience that small shades of expression, subtle effects, could make their point. An audience large enough to make adequate productions pay their way can only be as near as this to the actors if the amphitheater plan be adopted" (Guthrie 1954, 147).

The first tent seating plan for the Festival stage in 1953 (Figure 27.2) and the blueprint of the Festival stage (Figure 27.3) show just how close the audience members were to the actors on stage; the whole design of the auditorium, and later the entire building that was constructed around it in 1957 (Figure 27.4), was conceived as a "machine" created to make this intimate relationship function.

This transformation of theatre space profoundly changed acting styles: creating a new and unique language of performance, combining classical

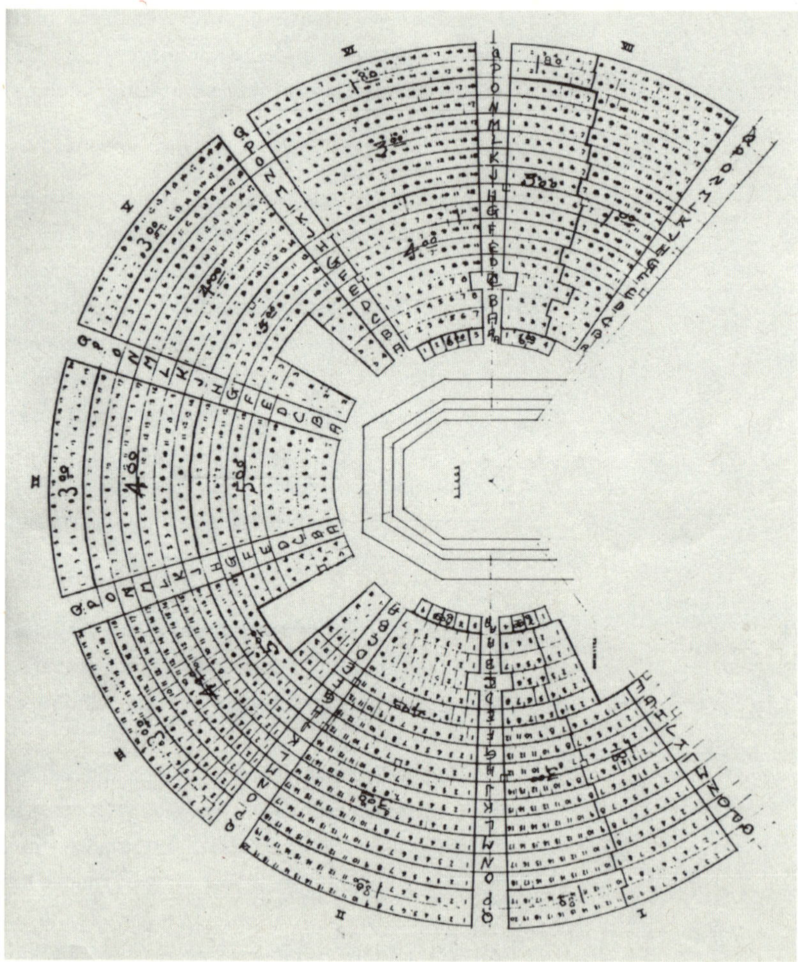

FIGURE 27.2: *Tent seating plan, 1953.* © *Stratford Festival. Image courtesy of the Stratford Festival Archive.*

techniques (such as vocal projection and controlled bodily movement) with greater naturalism in onstage speech, and defining subsequent Stratford performances. From the first, contemporary reviews noted the revolutionary connection between actor and audience that was immediately created in the first performance of *Richard III* as Guinness surveyed the auditorium, one leg dangling over the balcony, directly addressing the audience while stabbing the ledge with a dagger. A lone actor on a bare stage, speaking softly, held an audience of 2,200. The intimacy also allowed Guinness to tease out the comic elements in the role while evading caricature.

Figures 27.5 and 27.6 clearly show other elements of the new configuration, such as the introduction of voms or vomitoria (actors' entrances onto the stage running under the audience) from the front area of the auditorium and exits at the back and sides of the stage; these created fluid, fast patterns of movement based on diagonals as actors entered, crossed, and exited from multiple

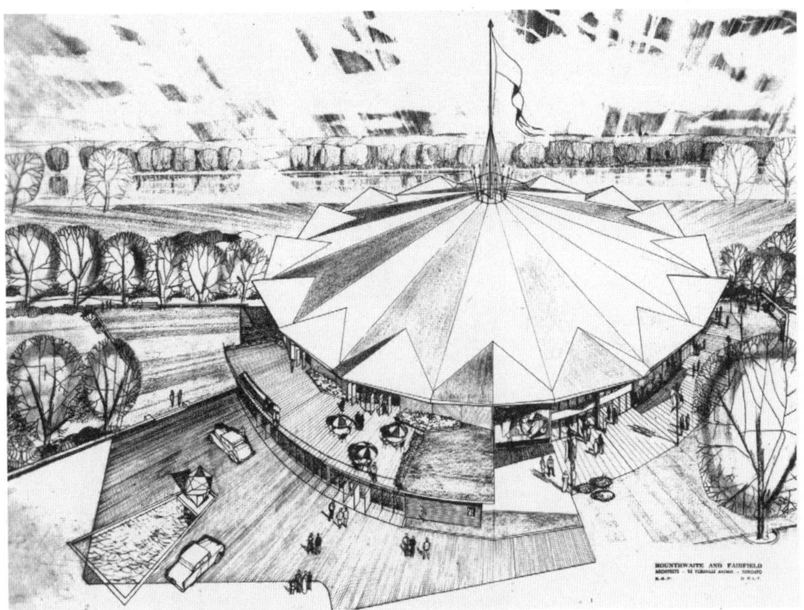

FIGURE 27.3: *Plan for theatre.*

© *Rounthwaite and Fairfield Architects. Image courtesy of the Stratford Festival Archives.*

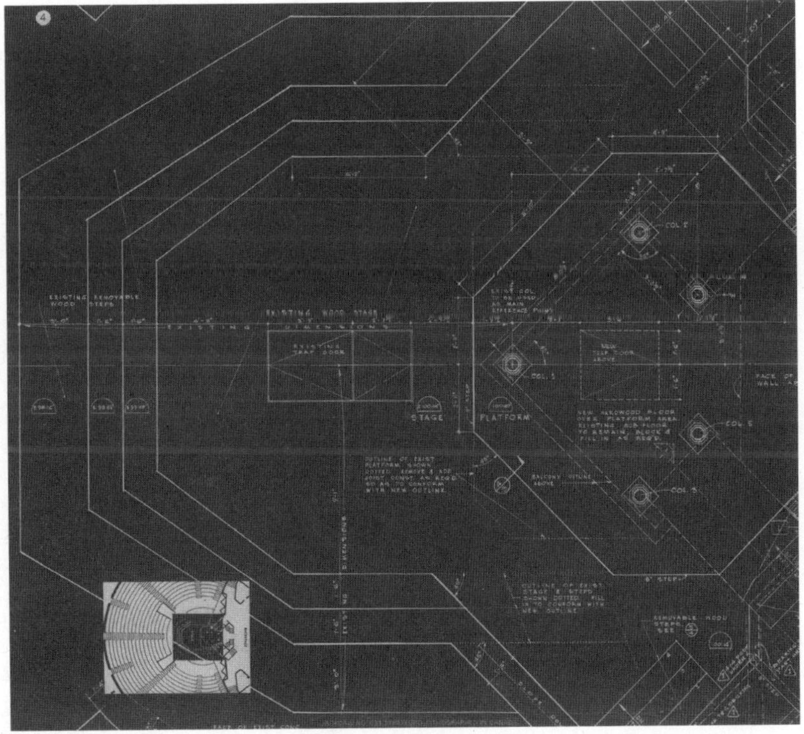

FIGURE 27.4: *Blueprint of Festival Theatre stage.*

Stage © Stratford Festival. Blueprint created by Robert Fairfield. Image courtesy of the Stratford Festival Archives.

FIGURE 27.5: *Festival stage, 1953.*

Photograph by Peter Smith & Company. Image courtesy of the Stratford Festival Archives.

FIGURE 27.6: *Tent interior, 1954.*

Photograph by Peter Smith & Company. Image courtesy of the Stratford Festival Archives.

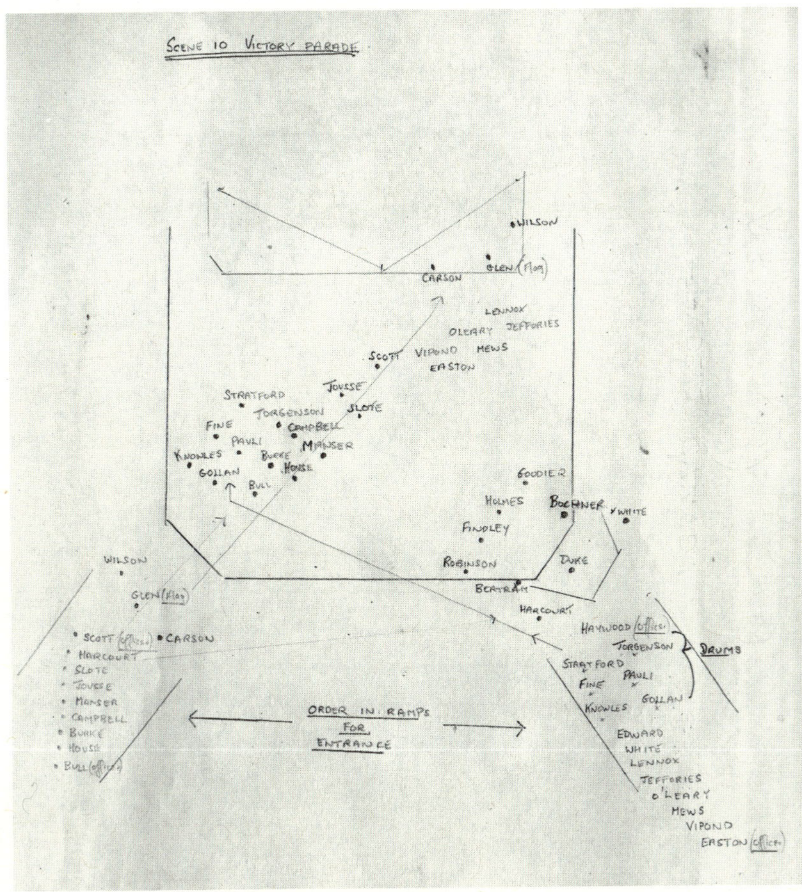

FIGURE 27.7: *Prompt script, Act III, scene 5*, All's Well That Ends Well, 1953.

© *Guthrie Estate. Images courtesy of the Stratford Festival Archives.*

directions, as can be seen from the prompt books for *All's Well That Ends Well* (Figures 27.7 and 27.8) as well as *Richard III* (Figure 27.9 and 27.10).

These prompt books look very different from later ones, with their text descriptions rather than visual expressions: these were part of a developing language of stage management at a time when lighting and sound were relatively uncomplicated. They clearly show, though, that far greater flexibility in movement and grouping was possible on this stage than on a proscenium one. That is, actors could be placed in front of each other in a more human relationship because of the multiple viewpoints afforded by the stage. At the same time, circular movement was encouraged by the configuration: then as now, actors moved around the basically bare stage, turning to change the angles at which they appeared to different sections of the audience (Figure 27.7 and 27.8). These basic patterns of movement encouraged ritual—often in the forms of processions across the full stage—as well as opening up the possibility of expressive tableaux, which could also stand as an image of wider groups,

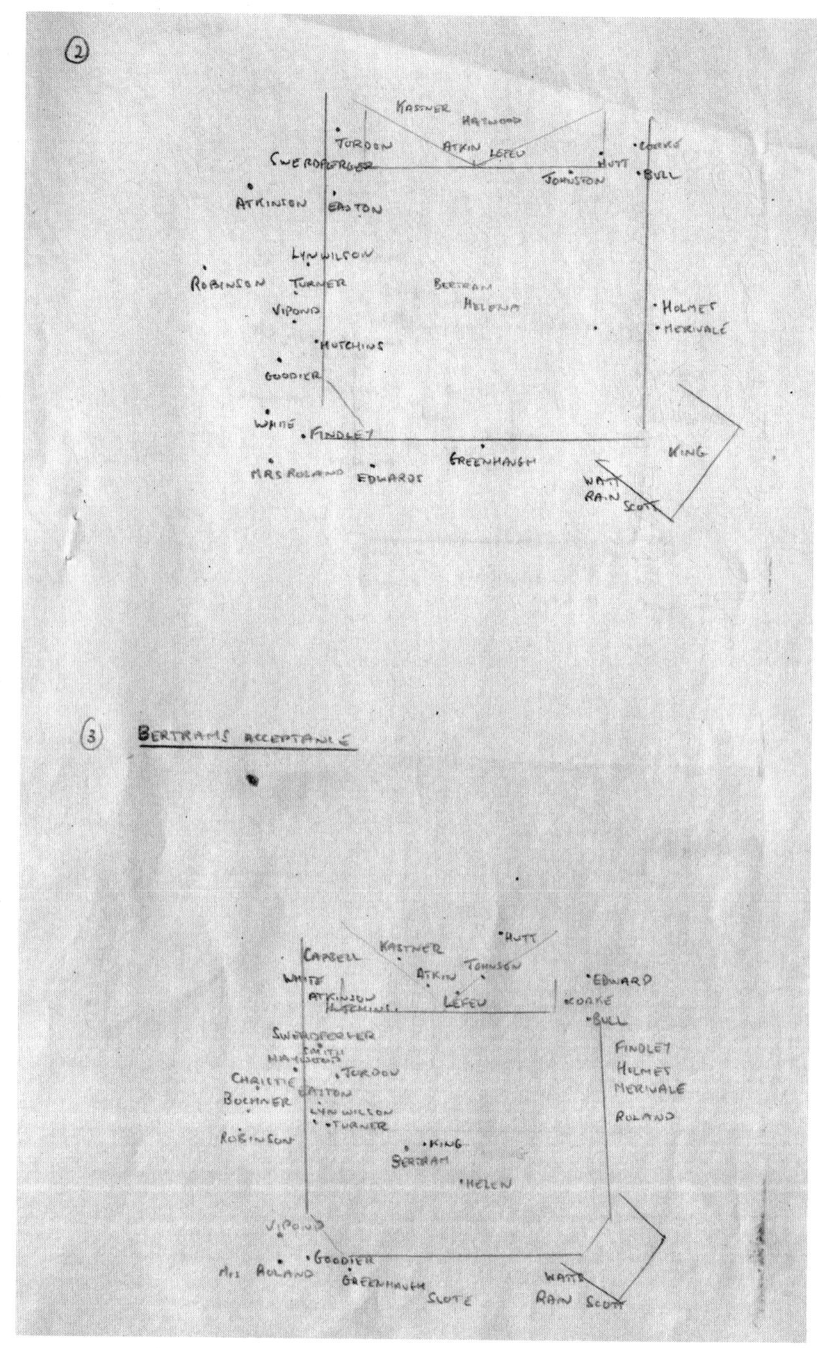

FIGURE 27.8: *Prompt script, Act II, scene 3, All's Well That Ends Well, 1953.*

© Guthrie Estate. Images courtesy of the Stratford Festival Archives.

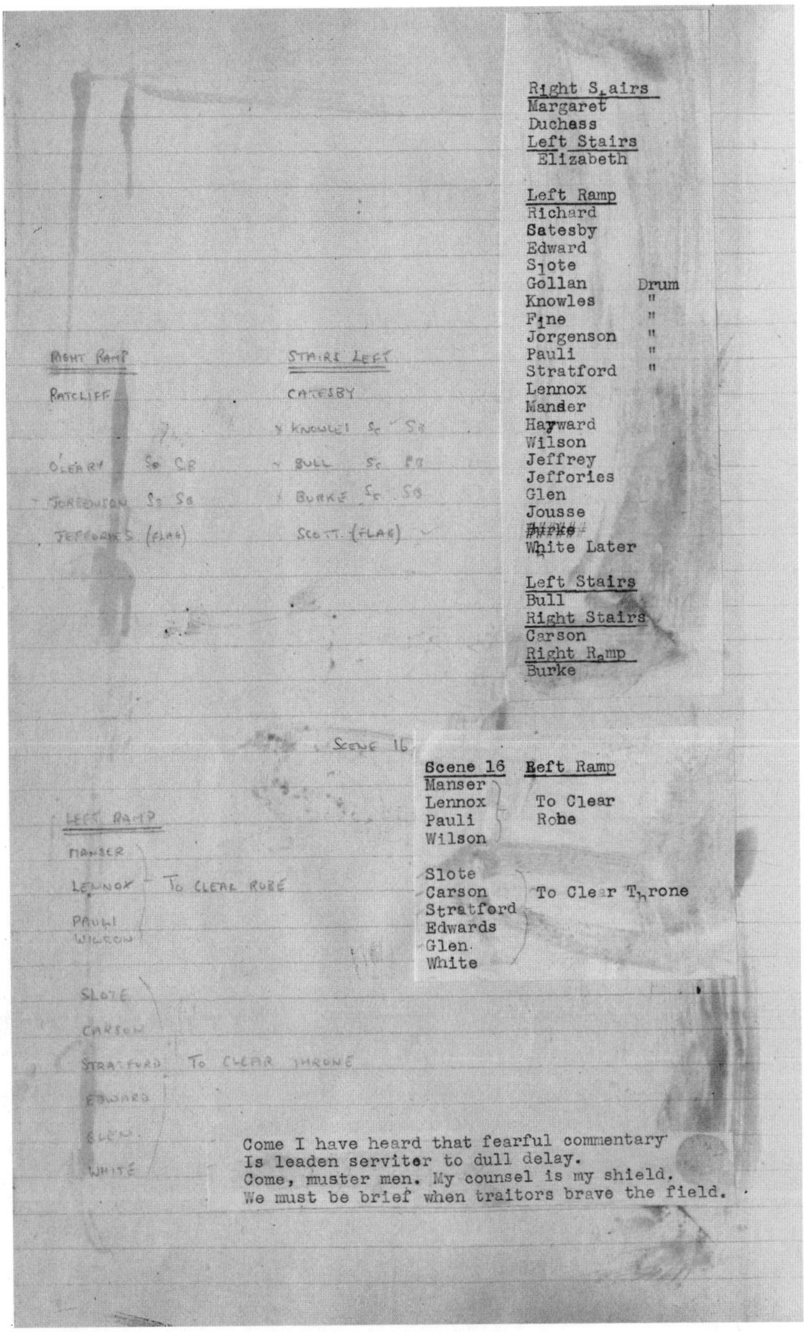

Right Stairs
Margaret
Duchess
Left Stairs
Elizabeth

Left Ramp
Richard
Satesby
Edward
Slote
Gollan Drum
Knowles "
Fine "
Jorgenson "
Pauli "
Stratford "
Lennox
Mander
Hayward
Wilson
Jeffrey
Jeffories
Glen
Jousse
Burke
White Later

Left Stairs
Bull
Right Stairs
Carson
Right Ramp
Burke

RIGHT RAMP
RATCLIFF
O'LEARY
JORGENSON
JEFFORIES (FLAG)

STAIRS LEFT
CATESBY
KNOWLES
BULL
BURKE
SCOTT (FLAG)

SCENE 16

Scene 16 Left Ramp
Manser
Lennox
Pauli
Wilson
To Clear Robe

Slote
Carson
Stratford
Edwards
Glen
White
To Clear Throne

LEFT RAMP
MANSER
LENNOX
PAULI
WILSON
TO CLEAR ROBE

SLOTE
CARSON
STRATFORD
EDWARD
GLEN
WHITE
TO CLEAR THRONE

Come I have heard that fearful commentary
Is leaden servitor to dull delay.
Come, muster men. My counsel is my shield.
We must be brief when traitors brave the field.

FIGURE 27.9: *Prompt script, Act IV, scene 3,* Richard III, *1953.*

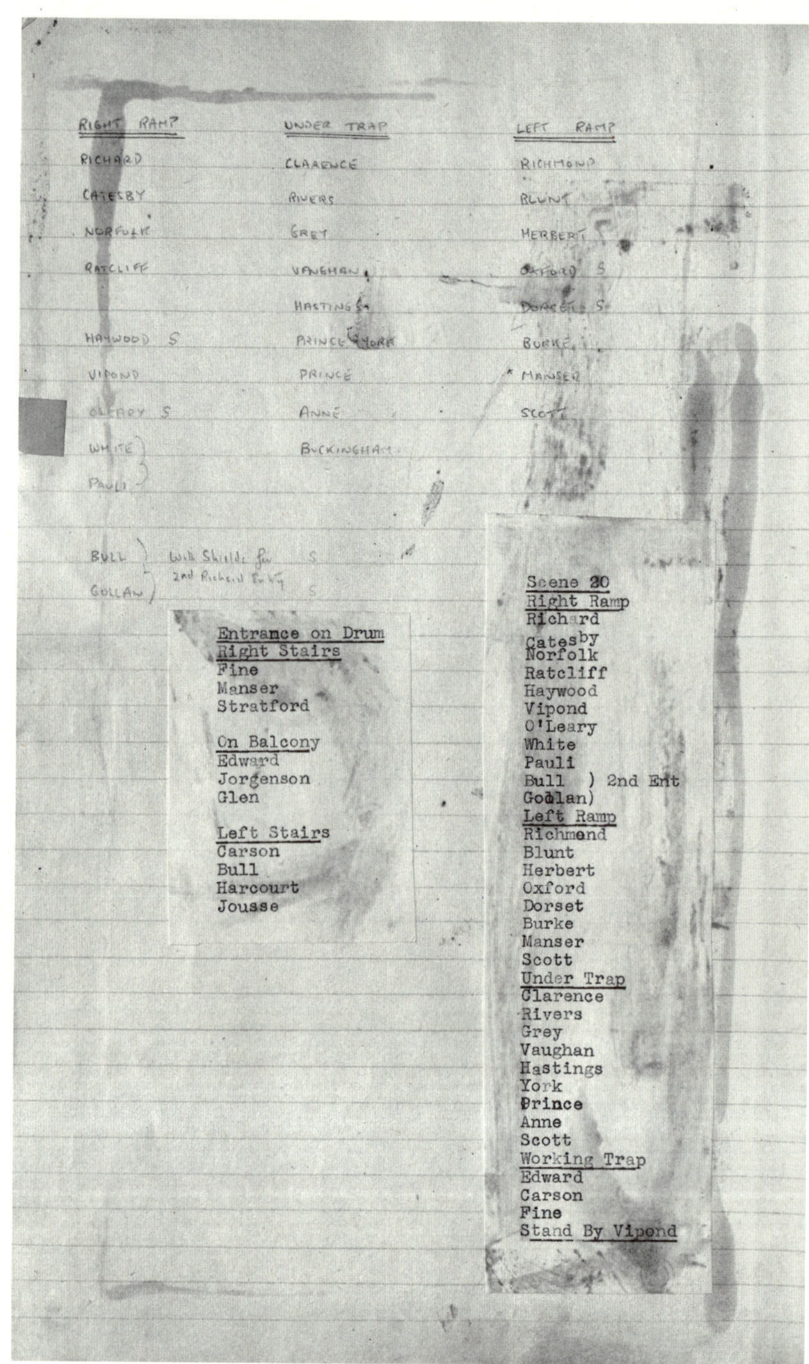

FIGURE 27.10: *Prompt script, Act V, scene 2, Richard III, 1953.*

© *Guthrie Estate. Images courtesy of the Stratford Festival Archives.*

which can be seen, in particular, in the London Street scene and Richard's coronation (Figure 27.9 and 27.10).

The latter became a meaningful ceremony as Stratford choirboys carried crucifixes through the audience and down the aisles to the steps of the main platform without layers of naturalistic scenery as Richard, dressed in a huge crimson cloak heightened by appearing against bare boards, ascended the altar at the side of the stage.

Over the years, the 1953 stage would undergo various changes and adjustments. Other theatres would use the Festival stage as a key influence when building new stages. These ranged from the large Guthrie Theatre in Minneapolis, US (1963), and the Olivier stage at the National Theatre, UK (1976).

Modestly, Guthrie had written at the end of the Stratford Festival's first season, "I do not think that we have found the complete solution. I think the principle is right and that details of what we have done will be refined and improved on, that we were practicing something which all the practitioners felt had to be done. We just happened to be fortunate and a little persistent in getting the opportunity" (quoted in Kitchin 1960, 198). Despite the awe—and the antagonism—the Festival stage sometimes evokes, it is at heart, an ongoing experiment.

Bibliography and Further Reading

Barker, Roberta, and Tom Cornford. 2018. "Tyrone Guthrie." In *The Great European Stage Directors*, vol. 3, edited by Jonathan Pitches, 115–62. London: Bloomsbury.

Cohen, Nathan. 1955. Tyrone Guthrie: A Minority Report." *Queen's Quarterly* 62 (January): 423–26.

———. [1959] 1996. "Theatre Today: English Canada." In *Canadian Theatre History: Selected Readings*, edited by Don Rubin, 223–31. Toronto: Playwrights Canada Press.

———. [1968] 1996. "Stratford after Fifteen Years." In *Canadian Theatre History: Selected Readings*, edited by Don Rubin, 252–69. Toronto: Playwrights Canada Press.

Falocco, Joe. 2009. "Conflicting Ideological Interpretations of the Founding of the Stratford Festival." *Journal of American Drama and Theatre* 21 (1) (Winter): 5–20.

———. 2010. *Reimagining Shakespeare's Playhouse: Early Modern Staging Conventions in the Twentieth Century*. Martlesham, Suffolk: Boydell & Brewer.

Groome, Margaret. 2002. "Stratford and the Aspirations for a Canadian National Theatre." In *Shakespeare in Canada: A World Elsewhere?*, edited by Diana Brydon and Irena R. Makary, 108–36. Toronto: University of Toronto Press.

Guthrie, Tyrone. 1937. "Hamlet at Elsinore." *London Mercury* 213 (July): 246–49.

———. 1954. "A Long View of the Stratford Festival." In *Twice Have the Trumpets Sounded*, Tyrone Guthrie, Robertson Davies, and Grant Macdonald, 143–93. Toronto: Clarke Irwin.

———. 1959. *A Life in the Theatre*. New York: McGraw-Hill.

Kitchin, Laurence. 1960. *Mid-century Drama*. London: Faber & Faber.

Knowles, Richard Paul. 1988. "The Legacy of the Festival Stage." *Canadian Theatre Review*, no. 54, 39–45.

———. 1994. "Shakespeare, 1993 and the Discourses of the Stratford Festival, Ontario." *Shakespeare Quarterly* 45 (2): 211–25.

———. 1995. "From Nationalist to Multinational: The Stratford Festival, Free Trade, and the Discourses of Intercultural Tourism." *Theatre Journal* 47 (1): 19–41.

———. 1996. "Shakespeare, Voice, and Ideology: Interrogating the Natural Voice." In *Shakespeare, Theory, and Performance*, edited by James C. Bulman, 95–115. London: Routledge.

Patterson, Tom, and Allan Gould. 1987. *First Stage: The Making of the Stratford Festival.* Toronto: McClelland & Stewart.

Salter, Denis. 1996. "Acting Shakespeare in Postcolonial Space." In *Shakespeare, Theory, and Performance*, edited by James C. Bulman, 117–35. London: Routledge.

Shaughnessy, Robert. 2002. *The Shakespeare Effect: A History of Twentieth-Century Performance.* New York: Palgrave Macmillan.

28 : *Zone* (1953)

Youth and Rebellion in Quebec Repertoire

SYLVAIN LAVOIE

1. Regarding his first play, Dubé was adamant in an interview, "No, forget *Le bal triste!* It was only a pretext, a sketch that required the two actors to improvise. It was purely amateur and for a single performance, which was a total failure by the way. It was not serious, or rather, it was serious in the sense that we wanted to do theatre" (Brault 2003, 66, translation mine). All translations of quotations in this introduction are mine.

BORN IN MONTREAL during the Great Depression, Marcel Dubé was barely twenty when he and a few friends established La Jeune Scène, a theatre company that staged his second play, *De l'autre côté du mur* (1952).[1] This well-received one-act drama served as the first draft of *Zone*, which begins with "the game" of a few youngsters who sneak cigarettes over the United States border; when the members of the gang are caught in their smuggling den, however, their innocence goes up in smoke with "the trial" leading to the condemnation, then "the death" of their chief.

Zone was created at the beginning of 1953 and went on to receive honours at the Festival dramatique de l'Ouest du Québec; a few months later it was performed in Victoria, as part of the Dominion Drama Festival, where it was declared the best production of the year. This positive response prompted Dubé to devote his life to writing. As he stated in 1960, "An author's first play is like his creation of the world. It already contains the essential elements of a personal dramaturgy: colours, language, characters. The five teenagers of *Zone* one day found and realized themselves through me. They were the best I could give at that stage of my life. Today they remain pivotal characters, the primary images of a world that I continue to explore" (Dubé 2013, 153).

Close to the realism and the psychological analysis that characterize typical novels of the same period, his repertoire includes *Un simple soldat* (1957), *Florence* (1957), *Le temps des lilas* (1958), *Bilan* (1960), *Les beaux dimanches* (1965), *Au retour des oies blanches* (1966), and *Un matin comme les autres* (1968). Even though these works were not necessarily written for the stage at first, they have all—except the latest—been presented in the theatre and in at least one other format (television, cinema, and/or radio); productions in more than one medium were frequent at that time. He kept writing after 1968, but none of his later plays have found a place in the history of theatre, nor are they being staged anymore.

The dates of these plays place Dubé in the chronology of Quebec theatre between Gratien Gélinas and Michel Tremblay, who, respectively, hold the titles of "Father of the French-Canadian drama" (Gélinas's *Tit-Coq* was created in 1948) and the "Father of Québécois drama" (emblematized by Tremblay's *Les belles-sœurs* in 1968). But Dubé's works should also be considered a founding moment of this national dramaturgy inasmuch as they embody a passage between two cultural states perfectly represented by *Zone*, which resonates

FIGURE 28.1: *Set of the 1953 production of* Zone.

socially and "seems revealing of the French-Canadian milieu" as a realistic yet tragic depiction "of a group of individuals living only by and for the group, under the authority of an almost sacred chief" (Godin 1988, 134).

Indeed, in 1953 the province of Quebec was under the yoke of Maurice Duplessis, whose government worked hand in hand with the Catholic Church to perpetuate conservative values against a modernizing world. This period, known as the Grande Noirceur,[2] dissipated with the sudden passing of *"le cheuf"* (mispronounced "chef" in French) in September 1959, and the subsequent election of Liberal Premier Jean Lesage a few months later. One must note, though, that the Révolution tranquille[3] that ensued also drew partial inspiration from Duplessis's attitude to maintain Quebec's autonomy from the rest of Canada.

The nationalism of the *belle province* would develop from traditional and defensive to new and modern (Vaillancourt 2012), with 1960 as its pivotal year; it soon became a movement for emancipation, as evidenced in the mottos *C'est le temps que ça change!* and *Maîtres chez nous!* chanted by Lesage's team. The Révolution tranquille was economic, social, and cultural, with protection and preservation of the French language as a strong, ongoing preoccupation—if not obsession—for Quebec. Avoiding assimilation was—and still is—a concern, but creators also struggled to free themselves from France as a literary point of reference. This is how Michel Tremblay became almost instantly the "Father of Québécois drama": a handful of (male) critics saw in his fifteen women a metaphor of the (oppressed) nation; with *Les belles-sœurs*, the real world was finally speaking,[4] and the long-muted language of Montreal streets, the so-called *joual*, could now be heard.[5]

By the mid-1960s, many leftist protest movements were reshaping the province, and until the end of the 1970s, theatre was an active vehicle for affirmation, privileging the *here* and the *now* associated with cultural and political

starting to find its place in the modernizing world.

4. For a brilliant analysis of this problematic narrative, see Hurley 2011.

5. Tit-Coq spoke a rather normative French. Twenty years later, Tremblay's characters caused a certain scandal not so much because of their somehow vulgar language, but rather because it was used against classical codes and institutions, so "the sublime was made comical, the forbidden was made accessible, and vice versa" (Robert 1998, 45).

autonomy. Collective creation—a democratic way of doing theatre—was one of the main approaches to (re)claim ownership of artistic practices. Similarly, the Parti Québécois victory in 1976 under René Lévesque would mark another step in the ascent of the separatist movement, leading to a first referendum for Quebec independence in 1980.

The English version of *Zone* in this sourcebook is Aviva Ravel's adaptation, which opened at the Saidye Bronfman Centre in April 1977; her interpretation took place in an environment that had experienced major transformations since the play premiered in 1953. For this reason, one critic wrote, "There is obviously some irony in the fact that one of Marcel Dubé's first important works is taken up for the first time since 1960 by an English-language theatre and an adaptation in English. Irony because *Zone* has marked the history of Quebec theatre of the last thirty years; irony also because we must wait until the next season for a French-language Québécois troupe to reprogram it; irony also because the Théâtre du Nouveau Monde has just created a new work [*Le réformiste*] from Marcel Dubé and it was very badly received by critics and the public" (Dassylva 1977).

It is important to note that Ravel changed certain aspects of *Zone*. First, her translation smoothed out the linguistic anomalies that many had deplored, for

6. Even though they are nick-
names that teenagers gave to
themselves—thus a certain
deal of ridiculousness—they
are significant. Tarzan was
at one point considered an
American hero, but he also
bears a great deal of racist and
sexist imagery that cinema has
certainly emphasized. Also,
the name "Tit-Noir" might
resonate in racial terms for
some readers, but when the
character explains his sobri-
quet to the Chief of Police
during the interrogation
scene, he states that the name
comes merely from the colour
of his hair; for a long time in
Quebec, many men were called
Ti-Blanc, Ti-Brun, or Ti-Noir
for this trivial reason.

7. Godin suggested that "*Zone*
is the poetic drama of dream
and love," and considered
Ciboulette to be the "axial
character" as she is "more
vividly sketched than Tarzan,
more necessary than he is
to the dramatic unity of this
play, she has the hardness and
obstinacy, the indefectible
fidelity which make the great
heroines" (1988, 141). For
playwright Sarah Berthiaume,
however, the only female
character of the play is "devoid
of any power of action," given
that her "main characteristic
is to be in love with her leader"
(Berthiaume and Lepage 2017,
51).

the youngsters spoke in a language register that was not convincingly representative of their background. Yet the fact that the characters' names were
kept in French may be understood as a way to distance them from an anglo-
phone audience.[6] Furthermore, the adaptation explicitly sets the story "in the
working-class district of Montreal's east end" where the "shaky post behind
the fence" stopped looking like the initial "poor cross, all lean, without a thief
or Christ on it" (Dubé 2013, 15). Along the same lines, Dubé originally had
Tarzan die in Ciboulette's arms, evoking the imagery of Jesus being lamented
by Mary's chaste love.[7] With these changes, Ravel erased some of the less
subtle references in an already deeply religiously inspired play. Other revisions were also made to the original plot.

It should be said of the *dramatis personæ* that two seemingly superfluous
minor characters were eliminated by Ravel: Johnny, a member of the gang
who barely appeared in the first act; and more significantly, Roger, the Chief of
Police's assistant who played an active role in the interrogation. The deletion
of Roger results in the Chief having no one to share his thoughts with at the
very end of the second act, since Ledoux leaves the commissariat with Tarzan
after the latter admits his crime. The original version would read as follows:

CHIEF. *I was hoping it wasn't him.*
ROGER. *Why, Chief?*
CHIEF. *I don't know. I was thinking about my son: he's the same age and finds
that life is easy...It feels strange to me.*
ROGER. *Tarzan is a murderer, Chief!*
CHIEF. *Only so much, only so much, Roger. He's mostly a poor creature whom
one has wanted to stifle one day, and he has revolted...He wanted to leave a
certain zone of the society where human happiness is almost impossible.*
ROGER. *I don't quite understand, Chief.*
CHIEF. *It's not important, Roger. We don't have to understand tonight, we
don't have to ask questions anymore. The job is done. Good evening Roger.*
(Dubé 2013, 116–17)

Cutting these lines gives the Chief a more rigid posture that does not reflect
his personal sympathies based on his own experiences; for the spectators, it
means that a less uncompromising point of view, coming from the authority,
isn't exposed anymore.

Every translation has gains and losses; in a way, translation is a
transaction. And this is what *Zone* is about: the difficult processes involved
in change, the arduous passage from one world to another, with adolescence
acting as a metaphor, a liminal space from which the characters are propelled
into adulthood and its accountability. Every transition, indeed, comes at a
cost, and this is how works get transformed, especially in our multicultural
context; here, the "line separating the two countries" can also be imagined
to stand between Canada's nations, as a conflict from within. Before dying,

Tarzan proclaims, "there's only one Ciboulette, but she's in two places at the same time." By looking at a play that trespasses, through its translation, the threshold of this sourcebook, we are constantly reminded of the limits of our definitions—and interpretations.

Bibliography and Further Reading

Bélanger, Julie, and Paul Poirier. 2007. "L'apparition de la locution 'Révolution tranquille'. 1ère partie." *Bulletin, Bibliothèque de l'Assemblée nationale* 36, nos. 1–2 (May): 18–19.

Berthiaume, Sarah, and Étienne Lepage. 2017. "*Zone*: Monomanie et monolithe." Issue "Répertoire québécois?" *Jeu*, no. 162, 51–53.

Biron, Michel, François Dumont, and Élisabeth Nardout-Lafarge. 2007. *Histoire de la littérature québécoise*. Montréal: Boréal.

Brault, Marie-Andrée. 2003. "Bilan: Entretien avec Marcel Dubé." Issue "Marcel Dubé: 50 ans après *Zone*." *Jeu*, no. 106, 66–73.

Dassylva, Martial. 1977. "Un simple Dubé." *La Presse*, April 18, 1977, A10.

Dubé, Marcel. 2013. *Zone*. Montréal: Leméac. First published by Éditions de la Cascade, 1955.

Godin, Jean-Cléo. 1988. "Le monde de Marcel Dubé: Mourir sa vie, vivre sa mort." In *Théâtre québécois I: Introduction à dix dramaturges contemporains*, by Jean-Cléo Godin and Laurent Mailhot, 123–69. Montréal: Hurtubise HMH.

Hurley, Erin. 2011. "Nation Reflection: Michel Tremblay's *Les belles-sœurs* and *le nouveau théâtre québécois*." In *National Performance: Representing Quebec from Expo 67 to Céline Dion*, 60–88. Toronto: University of Toronto Press.

Laroche, Maximilien. 1970. *Marcel Dubé*. Montréal: Fides.

Lavoie, Pierre. 1982. "Zone." In *Dictionnaire des œuvres littéraires du Québec*, vol. 3, edited by Maurice Lemire, 1092–95. Montréal: Fides.

Livernois, Jonathan. 2018. *La révolution dans l'ordre: Une histoire du duplessisme*. Montréal: Boréal.

Robert, Lucie. 1998. "La langue est la métaphore de l'histoire: Dire, au théâtre." *Les Cahiers d'histoire du Québec au XXe siècle* 9 (Spring): 42–48.

Vaillancourt, Yves. 2012. "The Quebec Model of Social Policy, Past and Present." In *Canadian Social Policy: Issues and Perspectives*, 5th ed., edited by Anne Westhues and Brian Wharf, 115–44. Waterloo, ON: Wilfrid Laurier University Press.

Wyczynski, Paul, ed. 1976. *Le théâtre canadien-français: Évolution, témoignages, bibliographie*. Vol. 5 of *Archives des lettres canadiennes*. Montréal: Fides.

Zone

MARCEL DUBÉ

English Adaptation by AVIVA RAVEL (1977)

CHARACTERS
   CIBOULETTE, *"Chives"*
   TARZAN
   PASSE-PARTOUT, *"Master key"*
   MOINEAU, *"Sparrow"*
   TIT-NOIR, *"Blackie"*
   LEDOUX, *detective*
   CHIEF OF POLICE

ACT I
The Game

It is autumn. The curtain rises on a set representing a backyard in the working-class district of Montreal's east end.

To the left is a rather narrow exit between two walls of deserted houses; at the back, a fence faces the city, perhaps of chicken-wire so the characters will be seen as they enter. To the right is an old dilapidated shed with a workable door that opens and closes easily. The roof of the shed, in the foreground, is superimposed over another roof, lower and further back, which is used for TARZAN's entrances in the first and third acts. A battered upholstered chair, someone's cast-off furniture, stands on an inverted wooden box, and serves as TARZAN's "throne." It leans against the fence.

The set is basically white: the colour scheme ranges from pure white to various shades of grey, then to almost total black. A gaunt and dead tree casts its shadow on the wall of the house, left, while old clotheslines cross the stage on high and are fastened to a shaky post behind the fence.

The lives of the characters as they evolve in this sad and realistic landscape will be delineated through movement, speech and an unobtrusive poetry which is both intense and melancholy.

It is not quite twilight, but we sense that the sun has bade its farewell to the city.

MOINEAU is alone on stage. He sits on a garbage can and plays a harmonica, or rather he is trying to play, since all his blowing and puffing produce neither theme

*nor melody, but a series of plaintive notes. From time to time he shakes out the
instrument on his knee. Then he resumes his playing.*

*In the background the voice of a rag pedlar is heard, a moan retreating into the
distance that mingles with the sound of his rumbling wagon. It is the well-known
chant:*

*Guenilles à vendre, guenilles à vendre
Des bouteilles, des guenilles à vendre?
[Rags, bones, bottles, Rags for sale…]*

This soon fades, but the frail sound of MOINEAU's *harmonica persists.*

Suddenly the shed door opens and TIT-NOIR *appears carrying a garbage can. He
bends over, deposits the can beside the door and straightens up.*

TIT-NOIR. Hey! Moineau! (MOINEAU *doesn't seem to hear.* TIT-NOIR *raises his
    voice.*) Moineau! Are you deaf or something?

MOINEAU *hears him. Abruptly, he comes out of his dream and stops playing.*

MOINEAU. Eh?…No, I'm not deaf. What d'you want, Tit-Noir?
TIT-NOIR. I want you to help me clean up, I've got to put the boards back now.
MOINEAU. I'm coming Tit-Noir. I'm coming. (*He slowly puts the harmonica
    away in his jacket pocket and moves quietly towards the shed.*)
TIT-NOIR. Make it snappy, the Chief should be back soon.

TIT-NOIR *disappears inside the shed while* MOINEAU, *at the threshold, confirms*
TIT-NOIR's *remark.*

MOINEAU. That's right. The sun is setting, he should've crossed over by now.

MOINEAU *enters the shed. For several moments, while the stage is empty, sounds of
the city are heard in the distance. The lights dim slightly.* PASSE-PARTOUT *enters
from the left and moves about cautiously without making a sound. He halts centre
stage and draws out of his jacket pocket several loud and colourful neckties which he
has just stolen. He looks them over with satisfaction and restores them to his pocket.
Then he moves to the shed door. He puts his eye to the keyhole to spy on* TIT-NOIR
and MOINEAU. CIBOULETTE *appears at the fence. He is caught in this position by
surprise. She halts, throws* PASSE-PARTOUT *a scornful look, then assumes an ironic
tone.*

CIBOULETTE. Hi, Passe-Partout!

PASSE-PARTOUT starts. He turns about slowly towards CIBOULETTE, feigning indifference at having been caught by surprise.

PASSE-PARTOUT. Hi Ciboulette! How are you?
CIBOULETTE. Okay. And you?
PASSE-PARTOUT. Not bad.
CIBOULETTE. Is the Chief back?
PASSE-PARTOUT. (*With a touch of malice.*) No.
CIBOULETTE. You're sure?
PASSE-PARTOUT. Yeah.
CIBOULETTE. How do you know?
PASSE-PARTOUT. (*He points to keyhole.*) 'Cause I just checked.
CIBOULETTE. Then he should be at Johnny's.
PASSE-PARTOUT. No. I rang his bell, he's not there either.
CIBOULETTE. How's that? It's late; he's usually...
PASSE-PARTOUT. Maybe they stopped off on the way.
CIBOULETTE. You think so?
PASSE-PARTOUT. There're a couple of nice restaurants on the way. And pretty girls in those nice restaurants.
CIBOULETTE. It's not like him to waste his time on things like that.
PASSE-PARTOUT. All depends. Those things are very tempting sometimes.

He draws a tie out of his pocket and looks it over with much satisfaction.
CIBOULETTE watches him.

CIBOULETTE. Passe-Partout!

PASSE-PARTOUT pretends he hasn't heard. With one sweep of the hand, he pulls off the tie he's wearing and shoves it into his pocket.

CIBOULETTE. Passe-Partout. You're stealing ties again!

PASSE-PARTOUT slips the new tie around his neck and knots it expertly; his face beams with pleasure.

PASSE-PARTOUT. How d'you like this one?...Wait till I'm through, you'll see... Now look...I've got good taste, eh? (*He flaunts himself and struts before her.*)
CIBOULETTE. You should find yourself a job instead of wasting your time stealing.
PASSE-PARTOUT. I'm in no hurry.
CIBOULETTE. You always have to be the exception.
PASSE-PARTOUT. It's none of your business. Meanwhile, *I'm* the champ. I landed more customers than the rest of you, and that's the main thing.

CIBOULETTE. I don't know about that. Today I beat you. I've got a list of ten
new ones to show the Chief.

PASSE-PARTOUT. A good thing you told me. Tomorrow I'll make sure to beat
you.

CIBOULETTE. I don't care. That's not important. What's important is to follow
orders, and you don't.

PASSE-PARTOUT. I do more.

CIBOULETTE. Maybe. But because of you we're liable to get a visit from the
police.

PASSE-PARTOUT. Don't worry about that, they don't call me Passe-Partout for
nothing...You like working in the shirt factory, Ciboulette?

CIBOULETTE. Of course not.

PASSE-PARTOUT. So why *do* you?

CIBOULETTE. Orders are orders. We've got to show that we live ordinary lives.

PASSE-PARTOUT. You shouldn't do what you don't want to.

CIBOULETTE. You don't talk like that in front of him, do you?

PASSE-PARTOUT. I don't have to. The Chief's got no false ideas about me. He
knows me.

CIBOULETTE. You think you scare him?

PASSE-PARTOUT. Only girls and cowards follow orders blindly. I'm a man.

CIBOULETTE. Tit-Noir is just as much of a man as you are, and he's not afraid
to follow orders. Every day he works at the shoe factory, from six in the
morning to three in the afternoon...No, Tit-Noir doesn't like it much, but he
knows it's necessary and safer that way.

While she speaks, PASSE-PARTOUT *casually draws out a wristwatch from his
pocket. He toys with it, weighs it in his hand. The watch gleams.*

PASSE-PARTOUT. Keep talking, you make me laugh.

CIBOULETTE. It's not funny...(*Suddenly she notices the watch.*) Passe-Partout!
What's that?

PASSE-PARTOUT. Can't you see? It's a watch.

CIBOULETTE. Where did you get it?

PASSE-PARTOUT. I bought it, Ciboulette.

CIBOULETTE. Go on. You stole it.

PASSE-PARTOUT. It's a good make. And it works real good.

CIBOULETTE. You're a crook.

PASSE-PARTOUT. I'm almost sure it's pure gold.

CIBOULETTE. You're not allowed to steal.

PASSE-PARTOUT. Now you're really making me laugh.

CIBOULETTE. The Chief has forbidden it. Those are the rules of the gang.

PASSE-PARTOUT. You know why you make me laugh? Because you talk as if
you weren't a crook yourself.

CIBOULETTE. I'm not a crook. Selling cigarettes on the black market isn't stealing.

PASSE-PARTOUT. It's stealing from the government, it's stealing from society.

CIBOULETTE. We're cheating them. We're not stealing. It's not the same.

PASSE-PARTOUT. You sure learned your lesson real good.

CIBOULETTE. I'm only telling you what I think. And if you want my advice, don't let the Chief see you with that.

PASSE-PARTOUT. He'd shut up right away if I offered it to him. He'd be real happy to wear it. He'd be proud as a rooster...Anyhow, he's not the one I wanna give it to. (*Pause.*) Aren't you interested in knowing who I'd give it to?

CIBOULETTE. To me?

PASSE-PARTOUT. Could be.

CIBOULETTE. You can keep it. I don't want it. I don't like jewellery.

PASSE-PARTOUT. It's real gold, it's beautiful, see how it shines...You'd look pretty wearing it...I could give you money, too.

CIBOULETTE. Money?

PASSE-PARTOUT. I borrowed a couple of wallets this afternoon.

CIBOULETTE. I don't need anything. I don't want to touch anything you put your dirty hands on.

PASSE-PARTOUT. My hands aren't dirty. These are the hands of a real thief. And a thief's hands are clever, they caress real good. They know all the right places.

CIBOULETTE. Leave me alone, I don't want you to touch me.

PASSE-PARTOUT. If it were him, you wouldn't say that, would you?

CIBOULETTE. There's nothing between us.

PASSE-PARTOUT. It's not because you don't want him. It's because he's too dumb to realize that you love him. Let me kiss you, and I'll give you everything. I'll steal pearls, bracelets, necklaces for you.

CIBOULETTE. No, Passe-Partout, leave me alone!

PASSE-PARTOUT. Just once, Ciboulette, only once.

PASSE-PARTOUT is interrupted by TIT-NOIR, who at this moment comes out of the shed. TIT-NOIR smiles. He is doubly pleased: he surprised PASSE-PARTOUT and he witnessed CIBOULETTE resisting him.

TIT-NOIR. Hi, Passe-Partout!

PASSE-PARTOUT. (*Assumes a flippant manner.*) Hi, there, Tit-Noir!

TIT-NOIR. That girl knows how to take care of herself, eh? She's a hard nut to crack.

PASSE-PARTOUT. Not so. "Chives" is a soft vegetable, and although it tastes a little bitter, like an onion, I'll gobble her up someday yet.

CIBOULETTE. Someday, sure. When the moon turns green.

TIT-NOIR. Listen, Passe-Partout, I'm sick and tired of breaking my back in
    that hole; three hours of washing the floor and hiding away the merchan-
    dise is enough. Stop fooling around and take over for a while. Moineau's in
    there, he'll help you.
PASSE-PARTOUT. (*In the stance of the Chief.*) What's left to do?
TIT-NOIR. Set up the two panels at the back.
PASSE-PARTOUT. The others are nailed in?
TIT-NOIR. Yeah, and make yours good and solid.
PASSE-PARTOUT. Okay. I'll go check.

PASSE-PARTOUT throws CIBOULETTE a malicious look and enters the shed.
TIT-NOIR is tired, and he sits down on TARZAN's throne. He takes a small notebook,
and a pencil stub out of his pocket and starts calculating. CIBOULETTE approaches
him slowly. Sounds of the city are heard in the distance. She leans against the wall of
the shed. She is somewhat uneasy. TIT-NOIR looks at her affectionately.

TIT-NOIR. Does he do that often?
CIBOULETTE. No, it's only the second time.
TIT-NOIR. Maybe you should tell the Chief.
CIBOULETTE. We're not kids any more.
TIT-NOIR. Yeah, you're right. (*TIT-NOIR pursues his calculations. CIBOULETTE*
    stares into space. A dog barks. TIT-NOIR again breaks the silence.) Business is
    good. I sold thirty-two hundred cigarettes in three days.
CIBOULETTE. That's a lot!
TIT-NOIR. I think I'll have a good week.
CIBOULETTE. Me too.
TIT-NOIR. You sold a lot?
CIBOULETTE. Yeah.
TIT-NOIR. How many?
CIBOULETTE. I don't know. A lot. I'll bring you the money tomorrow and you
    can put it in the cash box.
TIT-NOIR. There's no rush. I know you won't steal it. I'd better finish my book-
    keeping now. The Chief is sure to want a report on how much we took in
    last week.

He resumes his bookkeeping. As he writes he moistens the point of his pencil so his
numbers will be clear and legible. CIBOULETTE interrupts him.

CIBOULETTE. Tit-Noir!
TIT-NOIR. Yeah?
CIBOULETTE. I'm scared.
TIT-NOIR. Just relax, Ciboulette.
CIBOULETTE. I usually can, but this time I'm scared. You?

TIT-NOIR. If he's not back in ten minutes it means something's gone wrong.
    We'll have to clear out.
CIBOULETTE. He takes a chance crossing the border like that, eh?
TIT-NOIR. I never did it, but I think it's a helluva big risk.
CIBOULETTE. He had to cross over three times today.
TIT-NOIR. The border guards are getting edgy. It's a bad time to get the stuff
    across.
CIBOULETTE. You think they'd shoot at him?
TIT-NOIR. Yeah.
CIBOULETTE. Can't we do anything?
TIT-NOIR. No, we just have to wait. I've a feeling they won't be long now...
    Maybe he had trouble with the truck. It's an old one and Johnny doesn't
    take care of it much.
CIBOULETTE. Can we trust Johnny?
TIT-NOIR. Yeah. He's got nothing to worry about. He just waits at a spot at the
    side of the road about a mile from the customs. No one sees him.
CIBOULETTE. That's true.

A pause. TIT-NOIR *replaces his notebook and pencil in his pocket. Then he stands up
and moves slightly away from* CIBOULETTE, *partially turning his back on her.*

TIT-NOIR. You like him a lot, eh?
CIBOULETTE. Yes, like all of you, Tit-Noir.
TIT-NOIR. Like all of us and then some. I think you love him.
CIBOULETTE. Tit-Noir, I forbid you to...
TIT-NOIR. You got nothing to be ashamed of, Ciboulette...Everyone's got the
    right to love...Did you tell him?
CIBOULETTE. No. He mustn't know. Ever.
TIT-NOIR. Why not?
CIBOULETTE. Because.
TIT-NOIR. He loves you too, you know.
CIBOULETTE. That's not true, you shouldn't say that.
TIT-NOIR. When you keep your eyes open, you notice lots of things.
CIBOULETTE. Yeah, and you can make mistakes, too.
TIT-NOIR. Not this time. I had a good look at him and I'm sure. He pretends to
    talk tough to you like to the rest of us, but deep down inside there's love. It's
    just that he holds back.
CIBOULETTE. Why does he do that?
TIT-NOIR. He has his pride, just like you...You should talk to him.
CIBOULETTE. Never, Tit-Noir, you hear? Never. I'll never tell him.
TIT-NOIR. You're making a mistake. One day, you'll want to, but it'll be too
    late. If I loved you, I'd let you know right away.
CIBOULETTE. Then you'd make me suffer.
TIT-NOIR. How's that?

CIBOULETTE. Because you're my friend. And it would make me feel bad to
have to tell you that I like you only as a friend. I'd hate you.
TIT-NOIR. I don't get it.
CIBOULETTE. You'd turn my thoughts from him. I'd hate you for that.
TIT-NOIR. "Turn your thoughts"—that's too complicated for me, Ciboulette,
you talk like you were in a convent.
CIBOULETTE. (*Moves slowly downstage.*) No Tit-Noir, I don't go to any
convent...My name is Ciboulette and I'm only a poor street girl, that's all
I am. My parents are poor, they don't love me very much, but it doesn't
matter. I'm not waiting for them to support me. I'm sixteen, I work in a
factory and it doesn't bother me, because I'm also a smuggler. I'm part of a
gang and I have a Chief, a Chief who's stronger than anyone, a Chief who's
afraid of nothing. Together, we're planning to live happy and freer lives.
The rest doesn't matter.
TIT-NOIR. He came to our street and told us to join him. We'd never seen him
before, but he looked so sure of himself, so sincere, that we went along. He
told us we'd be somebody one day if we listened to him. We listened and
now we're making some money. We're getting stronger.
CIBOULETTE. That's why I've no right to talk to him about love, I'd mix him
up and he wouldn't be able to look at me the way he does now. To him, we're
all partners in one adventure, members of the same team.

The shed door opens and PASSE-PARTOUT *comes out. He rubs the dirt off his hands.*
MOINEAU *enters with him, an anxious expression on his face.*

PASSE-PARTOUT. We put the shed in order. Any news?
TIT-NOIR. No.
PASSE-PARTOUT. Looks bad.
MOINEAU. Maybe he was stopped at the border?...Tit-Noir?
TIT-NOIR. What?
MOINEAU. Is it true that there's a white line separating the two countries?
TIT-NOIR. No. Who told you that story?
MOINEAU. No one. I thought it up all by myself. A white line makes a clear
separation.
PASSE-PARTOUT. Yeah, but it's just as hard to steal across without a line. You
sure are pale, Ciboulette!
CIBOULETTE. I'm not paler than anyone else. I'm worried, that's all.
PASSE-PARTOUT. He should've let me try my way this time. It's a lot less
complicated. You go across with the truck, you say you've got a load of pota-
toes, they look inside, they see the sacks are the right colour, they believe
you and let you pass. He should've let me try. I offered yesterday.
TIT-NOIR. You offered because you knew he wouldn't let you.
PASSE-PARTOUT. No, I wanted him to say yes.

TIT-NOIR. You knew he'd say no. He explained right at the beginning. The American won't see anyone but him.

PASSE-PARTOUT. I'd forgotten that.

TIT-NOIR. That's easy enough to say.

PASSE-PARTOUT. Yeah, it's easy to say and what's more, it's none of your business. Let me give you a piece of advice, Tit-Noir. Keep your nose out of other people's business.

TIT-NOIR. And I want to give you the same advice, Passe-Partout. From now on, keep your hands to yourself. Leave Ciboulette alone. She's not your property, okay?

PASSE-PARTOUT. I'll do what I feel like.

TIT-NOIR. The Chief doesn't like it.

PASSE-PARTOUT. The Chief, the Chief. I bet he gets a real laugh, the way you follow him like a bunch of sheep.

CIBOULETTE. Be quiet, Passe-Partout.

TIT-NOIR. Every time he opens his mouth, he…

CIBOULETTE. You too, Tit-Noir. Shut up. You're arguing for nothing. Words won't change anything. What counts in the end is what's inside your heart.

MOINEAU. You're right, Ciboulette, words don't mean nothing. You can never tell what people are really thinking inside. You can't tell about no one. Music doesn't tell lies, music always tells the truth, not words…

As if MOINEAU wants to prove what he has just said, he brings his harmonica to his lips and begins to play. The others listen, but PASSE PARTOUT is not impressed. On the contrary, he finds it ridiculous.

PASSE-PARTOUT. You can never tell what he's playing.

CIBOULETTE. It doesn't matter, it's beautiful.

MOINEAU's feelings are hurt. He stops playing and moves towards the shed.

TIT-NOIR. Where're you going, Moineau?

MOINEAU halts at TIT-NOIR's question. He looks at them, but does not reply. He opens the door and shuts himself up in the shed. We hear him play until he comes out.

CIBOULETTE. Poor Moineau.

There is a moment of silence in which a slight feeling of anxiety permeates the air. City noises from the distance. PASSE-PARTOUT cannot bear the uneasy atmosphere. He breaks the silence.

PASSE-PARTOUT. Thirty thousand cigarettes, that's a helluva lot of money!

CIBOULETTE. He won't have to go back for two weeks.

TIT-NOIR. At the rate we're selling, I think he'll have to go next week.

Another silence. It is barely disturbed by the vague and distant sounds of the evening. This time TIT-NOIR *loses patience. He stiffens.*

TIT-NOIR. I can't stand it. I can't wait no more. It's driving me crazy.
CIBOULETTE. Go over to Johnny's, Tit-Noir. Maybe he's there.
TIT-NOIR. Maybe. You're right. Wait here. I'll go see.
CIBOULETTE. If he's not there, we'll clear out when you get back, okay?
TIT-NOIR. Okay.

TIT-NOIR *leaves by the fence and with a hurried and determined step exits right.* PASSE-PARTOUT *smiles. He takes a cigarette and slips it in the corner of his mouth.*

PASSE-PARTOUT. (*Before lighting up.*) You're getting all worked up for nothing. It doesn't pay to get so excited over someone who wouldn't do the same for us.

As he lights his cigarette, CIBOULETTE*'s attention is drawn to him. She springs at* PASSE-PARTOUT.

CIBOULETTE. Passe-Partout! You're not allowed to smoke American cigarettes! (*She pulls the cigarette out of his mouth, throws it to the ground and crushes it with her foot.*) You know damn well it could give us away.

PASSE-PARTOUT *is furious. His pride is hurt.*

PASSE-PARTOUT. We sell them, so why shouldn't we smoke them?
CIBOULETTE. Because it's not safe.
PASSE-PARTOUT. I don't give a damn.
CIBOULETTE. What if you're seen taking an American cigarette out of your pocket?
PASSE-PARTOUT. As if I'm not smart enough to look out for myself.
CIBOULETTE. You just did it in front of me, you could do it in front of a detective and get caught.
PASSE-PARTOUT. *Sure,* you see detectives all over the place. You know what, you're slowly going crazy. Now leave me alone. I don't like to be spied on and I don't like to be interfered with either, see? It's the last time I'm telling you, leave me alone.
CIBOULETTE. Act like everyone else and we'll leave you alone. Do what the Chief says.
PASSE-PARTOUT. I'll act the way I want. The Chief's not going to stop me.
CIBOULETTE. You've got no heart, Passe-Partout, he's risking his life at this very moment.

PASSE-PARTOUT. That's the role he picked for himself, and he'll play it to the
end. If he'd chosen me, I'd have played it just as good.

CIBOULETTE. You couldn't, because you don't respect the rules. You're
sneaky. To do great things you've got to have discipline. You haven't got any.
But since you swore to obey the rules, you've got no right to break them.

PASSE-PARTOUT. You're just a poor little girl, Ciboulette, and that's what
you'll be all your life if you go on like this. You keep your principles to yourself, I'll do what suits me and I'll thank you not to mix in.

CIBOULETTE. Then you can't be part of the gang.

PASSE-PARTOUT. You need me too much to let me go.

CIBOULETTE. If you want to stay, you've got to listen when we tell you you're
out of line. We obey the rules and we want them respected.

PASSE-PARTOUT. You'll always be one of the punks, one of the ordinary
soldiers that gets pushed around by the officers. You'll never know what it's
like to be independent, to get something out of it for yourself. You'll always
waste your time thinking of others.

CIBOULETTE. Go on Passe-Partout, go on! You remind me more and more of a
spider.

PASSE-PARTOUT. Watch it, Ciboulette.

CIBOULETTE. You make me sick, and I'm not afraid to shout it out loud. You
make me sick!

PASSE-PARTOUT. Shut-up, I tell you!

CIBOULETTE. He'll crush you, you'll see, like you crush a spider, to stop it
from crawling around.

PASSE-PARTOUT. Ciboulette! (*He raises an arm to her.*)

CIBOULETTE. You want to hit me? Go ahead, hit me, but you won't stop me
from telling you the truth to your face.

PASSE-PARTOUT. The truth! Is that so! *I'm* the only truth around here, the
only genuine thief. The rest of you are just playing games, if you wanna
know, you dream of being real thieves, but you're way out of it.

CIBOULETTE. Passe-Partout. You're rotten to the core.

PASSE-PARTOUT. I am what I am and I don't plan to change.

CIBOULETTE. I pity you.

PASSE-PARTOUT. Don't say that, Ciboulette!

CIBOULETTE. I pity you.

PASSE-PARTOUT. You're going too far, I'm warning you. If you say that again
I'm gonna hurt you.

CIBOULETTE. I more than pity you. Now go on, hurt me. It won't stop me from
thinking that soon enough you'll be shivering in your pants in front of him,
you'll crawl like a worm. Now go ahead, hurt me.

PASSE-PARTOUT. Soon enough! Maybe he won't be here soon. Maybe he'll
never be here again. Did you ever think he might get shot? Did you ever
think he might die? If he were dead, you'd have pitied me for nothing, you
wouldn't get to see me shaking...And what if I was to become the strongest

one around here? Stronger than anyone? And what if I was Chief right now?

CIBOULETTE. (*Cries out.*) Stop it!

PASSE-PARTOUT. (*He laughs.*) Now it's my turn to pity you. Now *you're* the one that's shaking.

CIBOULETTE. You'll pay for this, Passe-Partout. I don't care if you hurt me, but you'll pay for what you said behind his back.

PASSE-PARTOUT. We'll see about that.

TIT-NOIR enters. He is distressed. He moves towards CIBOULETTE.

TIT-NOIR. He's not there.

CIBOULETTE. You're sure?

TIT-NOIR. Yeah. Johnny's mother is worried, too.

CIBOULETTE. What did the Chief tell us to do if he wasn't back on time, Tit-Noir?

TIT-NOIR. We take off, in case the police stopped them and forced them to talk. We've gotta make ourselves scarce so they won't get us, too.

CIBOULETTE. Then that's what we'll do right now.

TIT-NOIR. Where's Moineau?

PASSE-PARTOUT. Can't you hear him?

TIT-NOIR opens the shed door.

TIT-NOIR. Moineau! Come quick. We gotta scram.

PASSE-PARTOUT. Where'll we go?

TIT-NOIR. Doesn't matter. The main thing is we don't stay here together.

MOINEAU, who has stopped playing, comes slowly out of the shed.

MOINEAU. I'm staying. I'm the guard.

TIT-NOIR. Never mind that. You can't stick around here now. It's not safe.

CIBOULETTE. The cops could be here any minute.

MOINEAU. I'll tell the police there's no one here and the shed is empty.

TIT-NOIR. You can't stay, Moineau. They'll arrest you just the same and take you to the station. They'll force you to talk. Come on.

CIBOULETTE. It's probably a false alarm, but we can't take a chance.

MOINEAU. Okay, you're right. I'll go with you.

They move towards the fence exit. TARZAN appears on the roof of the shed. He carries a sack on his back.

TARZAN. Stay where you are! I'm back.

Dumbfounded, the others turn around, their voices subdued with surprise and admiration.

ALL. Tarzan!

TARZAN. I got through...Moineau! Catch. (*TARZAN throws him the sack. MOINEAU catches it awkwardly and almost falls over in the process. The others laugh.*) Okay, cut it out. (*TARZAN springs and jumps down—to MOINEAU.*) Hide that in the shed. And be quick about it.

MOINEAU obeys promptly.

TARZAN. You, Tit-Noir, run over to Johnny's and bring the rest.

TIT-NOIR. Yes, Tarzan.

TARZAN. (*To PASSE-PARTOUT.*) Are the orders ready for tomorrow?

PASSE-PARTOUT. No, Tarzan. We were waiting 'til you got back.

TARZAN. Okay. Start wrapping them up. When Tit-Noir gets back he'll help you.

PASSE-PARTOUT. Okay, Tarzan, right away.

PASSE-PARTOUT enters the shed. TARZAN is alone with CIBOULETTE. He steals a glance at her, then suddenly aware of his fatigue, sits down on his throne. CIBOULETTE watches him out of the corner of her eye.

TARZAN. (*Under his breath.*) They didn't get me...I got through...They'll never get me.

CIBOULETTE. You ran a long way? You're tired? (*She approaches him slowly.*)

TARZAN. I ran a long way. Does it show?

CIBOULETTE. Yeah. Your eyes are...different.

TARZAN. It doesn't mean a thing.

CIBOULETTE. It means that you're tired, that's all.

TARZAN. It means I got the job done and that I'm tired. That's all it means.

CIBOULETTE. Of course, that's all it means. Your tiredness always shows in your eyes. (*An uneasy silence ensues. CIBOULETTE looks at TARZAN anxiously.*) They gave you a hard time?

TARZAN. No more than usual.

CIBOULETTE. You don't usually come back so late.

TARZAN. Mind your own business.

CIBOULETTE. I just mentioned it. That's all.

TARZAN. Don't worry about me. I'll always come back

CIBOULETTE. I wasn't worried. I was just curious.

TARZAN. So what are those frowns doing on your forehead?

CIBOULETTE. We waited a long time, we were afraid.

TARZAN. The others don't show their feelings, try to be like them. Besides, you
    don't have to be afraid. Nothing'll happen to you. I always fix it so you won't
    be in danger.

CIBOULETTE. I know that, Tarzan.

TARZAN. You're too young to have your face all messed up from frowning. (*He
    rises and moves slightly towards centre stage.*) Wait, Ciboulette, you'll have lots
    of time for that.

CIBOULETTE. You mean I'll be unhappy one day?

TARZAN. I mean that one day you'll be in love—and it's the same thing.

CIBOULETTE. I don't think so. When I'm in love, I won't have any more trou-
    bles.

TARZAN. That's what people think, but it's a lie.

CIBOULETTE. Who told you? Have you ever been in love?

TARZAN. No...I've seen others.

CIBOULETTE. Won't you ever love anyone, Tarzan?

TARZAN. (*Looking at her.*) Maybe...someday.

CIBOULETTE. When?

TARZAN. When I can, when I find a sensible girl.

CIBOULETTE. Am I sensible, Tarzan?

TARZAN. You make me nervous with all your questions. Leave me alone. I've
    got important business to attend to.

CIBOULETTE. I'm sorry, I didn't mean to make you mad.

TARZAN. It's not your fault. Listen, Ciboulette, I just want one thing from you.
    Stay as you are. I let you into our gang because you're strong and brave. I
    don't want you to turn sentimental on me all of a sudden. You understand?

CIBOULETTE. Yes, Tarzan.

TARZAN. Good. We won't talk about it any more. Now I have to take care of
    Passe-Partout. (*He sits on his throne, and calls out.*) Passe-Partout!

PASSE-PARTOUT emerges from the shed almost immediately.

TARZAN. Passe-Partout, I wanna talk to you.

PASSE-PARTOUT. What d'you wanna know, Tarzan?

TARZAN. First of all, I wanna know if you found a job.

PASSE-PARTOUT. Not yet. I've been to lots of places, they never need me.

TARZAN. That's no excuse. If you haven't found a job by tomorrow, don't come
    back here again.

PASSE-PARTOUT. But...

TARZAN. Now shut up! I don't wanna hear nothing more. The others don't
    make excuses, they do what they're supposed to. When I asked you to join
    the gang, I told you the rules and you agreed to follow them. Right.

PASSE-PARTOUT. That's right, Tarzan.

TARZAN. I warned you, I told you that sometimes it would be hard for you
    to obey orders, but it was absolutely necessary. I invented a system that

doesn't put you in any danger, I take all the risks...all the risks...you understand, Passe-Partout?

PASSE-PARTOUT. Yes, Tarzan.

TARZAN. And in a couple of years from now, we'll have money and we'll live like human beings. No one'll be able to force us to work like dirty slaves in their factories, no one'll push us around. We won't throw away our lives like the poor devils who let themselves be exploited by everybody.

PASSE-PARTOUT. Yes, Tarzan.

TARZAN. In the meantime, to keep the police off our backs, we've got to make out that we're living ordinary lives, just like everyone else. We've got to work so no one'll suspect what we're doing. That way, people won't think we're bums, and they won't blame us for all sorts of crimes.

PASSE-PARTOUT. Yes, Tarzan.

TARZAN. We're not murderers...we're not criminals...we never killed nobody.

PASSE-PARTOUT. We never killed nobody, Tarzan, we're not murderers.

TARZAN. If we do kill one day, it's because we had to. Because we had no choice.

PASSE-PARTOUT. Yes, Tarzan, yes.

TARZAN. This is the last time I'm going to talk to you about this, Passe-Partout...and you, Ciboulette, anything to report?

CIBOULETTE. There is something about...

TIT-NOIR enters the yard carrying two sackfuls of cigarettes. TARZAN's attention is drawn to him.

TARZAN. Hide 'em away quick and don't leave a single trace. Tit-Noir!

TIT-NOIR. Yeah?

TARZAN. Tell Moineau I wanna talk to him.

TIT-NOIR. Right now?

TARZAN. Yeah, right now. You'll finish wrapping the orders by yourself.

TIT-NOIR. Sure.

TIT-NOIR goes into the shed. TARZAN turns to CIBOULETTE.

TARZAN. Go on, Ciboulette.

CIBOULETTE. All the girls at work smoke. I've got ten new customers.

TARZAN. Okay. But be careful. Watch out for your boss.

CIBOULETTE. There's nothing to be afraid of. He'll never notice.

MOINEAU. (*Appears at the shed door.*) You wanna talk to me, Chief?

TARZAN. Yeah, come here. Did you guard the place good today?

MOINEAU. Yes, Chief.

TARZAN. Don't call me "Chief," call me Tarzan.

MOINEAU. Yes, Chief.

TARZAN. You understand what I just said?

MOINEAU. Yeah, yeah...excuse me, Chief...I mean Tarzan.

TARZAN. Anything happen today?

MOINEAU. A man came by.

TARZAN. What?

MOINEAU. A man came by.

TARZAN. What man?

MOINEAU. I don't know. I never saw him before. All I can say is that he was a real gentleman with a raincoat and a hat. Yeah, that's it, a grey hat.

TARZAN. And the raincoat?

MOINEAU. Dark blue, I think.

TARZAN. That doesn't tell me a thing...You were alone?

MOINEAU. Passe-Partout was in the shed, getting cigarettes for a customer.

PASSE-PARTOUT. Why didn't you tell me when I came out, Moineau?

MOINEAU. I only report to the Chief.

TARZAN. Don't you know it's forbidden to take cigarettes out during the day?

PASSE-PARTOUT. It was for a good customer...

TARZAN. That's no reason...What time was it, Moineau?

MOINEAU. About two.

TARZAN. Was Passe-Partout in the shed for a long time?

MOINEAU. About five minutes I think.

TARZAN. Did you talk to the guy?

MOINEAU. I asked him what he was looking for.

TARZAN. And what did he say?

MOINEAU. He said he wasn't looking for anything special, he was just passing by. I told him he had no business here, that this was my yard and I wanted to be alone. So he smiled and left.

TARZAN. Passe-Partout!

PASSE-PARTOUT. Yeah.

TARZAN. Did anyone follow you here?

PASSE-PARTOUT. No.

TARZAN. You didn't see anyone when you left the yard?

PASSE-PARTOUT. No one.

TARZAN. You're sure?

PASSE-PARTOUT. Yeah, I'm sure...there was no one, I swear.

TARZAN. I don't like this story too much. It gives me the creeps. (*To* MOINEAU.) When you saw him, did you think he was looking for something?

MOINEAU. I don't know but his eyes went all over.

TARZAN. It sounds fishy. (*On edge.*) And I don't like it. I don't like it. Tit-Noir! (*TIT-NOIR comes out of shed. TARZAN moves towards him.*) Tit-Noir, Moineau saw a man hanging around here this afternoon...

TIT-NOIR. Uh? Here?

TARZAN. Yeah. He was wearing a grey hat and a dark blue raincoat. Does that mean anything to you?

TIT-NOIR. No, it doesn't mean a thing.

TARZAN. Okay, we'll get out of circulation for a couple of days. Are the orders ready?

TIT-NOIR. Yes.

TARZAN. Anything lying around that shouldn't be?

TIT-NOIR. Everything's hidden. You can't even notice the panels…It looks like an empty shed.

TARZAN. Perfect. Now has everybody got that straight? Don't come back here till you hear from me.

PASSE-PARTOUT. What about our customers?

TARZAN. You'll fill the most urgent orders tomorrow; the rest'll have to wait. Tell 'em that new stock'll be coming in soon, but you don't know when. We can't take any chances. If we're really in danger, and that guy is a cop, he'll be back to have another look, so we've got to make him think he's on the wrong track. You understand?

ALL. Sure, I got it…

TARZAN. Oh, I forgot! There's good news. Next month we'll be selling in bulk. We'll still have our regular customers but we'll also have a dozen new ones who'll buy in quantity.

PASSE-PARTOUT. And you'll smuggle it all in by yourself?

TARZAN. Yes. The American said we'd talk about a new arrangement next time.

PASSE-PARTOUT. Then we'll be making twice as much money, eh?

TARZAN. Yes. And that's why we have to be twice as careful. We don't wanna get caught just when things are going good. Okay, now get your parcels in the shed and get moving.

TARZAN has not completed his sentence when we see a man at the fence. He is dressed precisely as MOINEAU has described.

LEDOUX. Good evening!

The others stiffen and retreat slowly.

MOINEAU. It's him, Tarzan.

LEDOUX. You seem to be busy. Sorry to disturb you.

He moves in and looks around. TARZAN puts himself in his way.

TARZAN. What can we do for you?

LEDOUX. Nothing much. I just have a few words to say to one of you here.

TARZAN. No one knows you around here.

LEDOUX. I'm not so sure about that. (*He pushes* TARZAN *aside brusquely, and moves towards* PASSE-PARTOUT *who recoils.* LEDOUX *grabs him by the collar.*) You, you know me, don't you?

PASSE-PARTOUT. No. I don't know you and I got nothing to say to you.

LEDOUX. Then you must've lost your memory. Let me help you find it again, uh?

While he speaks, LEDOUX *grabs* PASSE-PARTOUT *by the arm so he is unable to move. With his free hand, he searches for a wallet in* PASSE-PARTOUT*'s inner jacket pocket.*

LEDOUX. You remember this, don't you?...You're not very professional, my boy, your hand shook and you touched me three times. Afterwards, I followed you for twenty minutes and you didn't even notice.

LEDOUX *pushes* PASSE-PARTOUT *off roughly and turns towards the exit. Once again* TARZAN *gets in his way.*

TARZAN. Check if anything's missing.

LEDOUX. (*He checks.*) No, nothing's missing. Besides, I'm certain he didn't have time to open it, or he'd have found a little card that would've given him a big surprise.

LEDOUX *takes several dollars out of the wallet and offers the money to* TARZAN.

LEDOUX. Is this where they sell American cigarettes?

TARZAN *dives his hand into his jacket pocket.* LEDOUX *observes this gesture and concludes that* TARZAN *is armed. He looks* TARZAN *in the eye and slips the money back in his wallet.*

TARZAN. We don't sell cigarettes. Not American or Canadian. This isn't a restaurant.

LEDOUX. Sorry, I must've been misinformed. (*He makes a move to leave, then halts. He surveys them.*) You know what happens when you play with fire.

LEDOUX *exits. For a moment the characters remain frozen in their places. Then they turn slowly to* PASSE-PARTOUT, *who is overcome by fear.* TARZAN *walks slowly towards him.*

PASSE-PARTOUT. Don't hit me, Tarzan, don't hit me. I'll never do it again, I swear!

TARZAN. (*Very calmly.*) I warned you, Passe-Partout. How many times've I
warned you, Passe-Partout? And you don't wanna listen, you really don't
wanna listen. This time, I've had enough!

PASSE-PARTOUT retreats.

TARZAN. You wanna be a wise guy, eh? You wanna be an exception, eh? All
right then, go back to your dump and don't ever come back here again!
PASSE-PARTOUT. No, Tarzan, no!
CIBOULETTE. Don't, Tarzan, let him go.
TARZAN. Quiet, Ciboulette! We'll show him who's boss around here, we'll
prove that we're not just fooling around. Rats like him don't deserve no
sympathy, no pity.

*PASSE-PARTOUT tries to escape by the rear exit, but TARZAN trips him and he
stumbles.*

TIT-NOIR. Tarzan, let him go!
TARZAN. Shut up! I'm the Chief, I'm in charge here.

He grabs PASSE-PARTOUT roughly and raises him to eye level.

TARZAN. I didn't force nobody to be with us. You hear, Passe-Partout? And
I didn't force you. Now, I don't ever wanna see your ugly puss around here
again.

TARZAN hits him in the face. PASSE-PARTOUT collapses. TARZAN pulls him up.

TARZAN. All you had to do was behave like the others. But no, you had to have
your own way, your own filthy way…I want you to scram and forget all
about us. If you ever betray us, I'll give you something to remember, you
hear? We can get along without you. Now scram!

*TARZAN shoves him violently through the opening in the fence. At precisely this
moment we hear a police whistle in the distance. PASSE-PARTOUT returns immediately. He is frightened. TARZAN pays no attention to him, but turns to the others.*

TARZAN. (*Cries out.*) It's the cops! (*Pointing to the opening in the fence he says to
CIBOULETTE and TIT-NOIR.*) You two, out that way.

*They exit quickly. We hear the whistles again. TARZAN points to the left and
addresses MOINEAU and PASSE-PARTOUT.*

TARZAN. Moineau, you go that way. I'll catch up with you.

Whistle blasts. TARZAN *remains alone, centre stage. He draws a gun out of his jacket pocket and hides it under his throne. Then he moves to left exit. But* MOINEAU *and* PASSE-PARTOUT *have been driven back into the yard, and* TARZAN *can't escape. Repeated whistles.*

PASSE-PARTOUT. They're coming through the lane!
TARZAN. This way!

He directs them to the opening in the fence. Again they are driven back by TIT-NOIR *and* CIBOULETTE, *who are retreating into the yard. The whistle blasts are heard at closer intervals. Searchlights roam the walls.*

TIT-NOIR. We can't, they're coming in between the shacks.
TARZAN. We're surrounded!
TIT-NOIR. What'll we do?
TARZAN. We'll try anyway. Each man for himself!

They try to escape. Sirens and whistle blasts ring out in the night; the whole area is illuminated by searchlights.

ACT II
The Trial

At the Police Station. The room is gloomy and bare. The CHIEF *is seated at his desk. In front of the desk, a stool on which the accused will sit in turn when they are interrogated. At the back, a coat rack and chair. There are waiting rooms on either side of the office. The young people wait on the bench to the left before they are called in. After the interrogation, they exit to the right. An exit at the rear leads to the infirmary.*

LEDOUX *enters. We immediately recognize him as the man in the blue raincoat and grey hat.*

LEDOUX. Good evening, Chief. (*He removes his coat and hangs it on the rack.*)
CHIEF. Good evening, Ledoux.
LEDOUX. They're in there, Chief. I think we got them all. We seized some sixty thousand cigarettes in their shed. (*He prepares coffee for himself and the* CHIEF.)
CHIEF. Congratulations, Ledoux.
LEDOUX. You want to question them right away?
CHIEF. Yes, but first I want to know how you got onto them.
LEDOUX. Well, Chief, it was a real stroke of luck. As you know, I've been in charge of investigating District 7 for the past few weeks. Reports show that the smuggling in of American cigarettes has reached alarming proportions.

But until today, I hadn't found anything. I was even getting a bit discouraged. I was walking along Sherbrooke, not thinking of anything, minding my own business, when suddenly I was jostled by this kid at an intersection. I felt a hand sliding into my pocket. I pretended I hadn't noticed he borrowed my wallet, and I followed him. He led me into a lane. I hid there while he disappeared into a yard. Until that moment I didn't think I'd find anything special. So a few minutes later I just wandered into the yard after him. I found a tall skinny kid in there, not too smart either, who seemed upset to see me. I put on an innocent expression and went back to hide in the lane. A few minutes later, I see my thief leaving with a package under his arm. So I follow him. He leads me around for fifteen minutes and then he stops in front of one of those rich houses in the neighbourhood. He rings the bell and goes in. I wait at the street corner. When he comes out, the package is gone. I let him get away and I went over to the house.

CHIEF. That's where you discovered he had just sold two thousand cigarettes and you phoned me.

LEDOUX. Exactly. Afterwards I put in a request for a police squad. I posted them in the lanes so the yard was completely surrounded. I went in first and discovered there were five of them including, by the way, one young girl. I got my wallet back, returned to my men, and gave the signal. We moved in on them, they tried to get away, but no one escaped.

CHIEF. Good. Did you find any guns on them?

LEDOUX. No. We searched, but we didn't come up with anything. At first, I thought the kid, who seems to be their leader, had a gun. I frisked him but he was clean.

CHIEF. All right then, let's start right now. Save the toughest ones 'til last.

LEDOUX. It'll be easy to get those kids to talk.

CHIEF. Don't count on any confessions, Ledoux. You still get these stubborn kids who dream of being heroes.

LEDOUX. I tell you they'll talk, Chief. (*At exit.*) You come in first. (*To CHIEF.*) The first kid doesn't seem to be all there, so don't be surprised…(*MOINEAU enters.*) In there, and sit down.

MOINEAU goes to the stool but remains standing.

CHIEF. Sit down.

MOINEAU does not move. LEDOUX sits him down roughly.

LEDOUX. You're deaf?

MOINEAU. No, I'm taking my time.

CHIEF. Your name?

MOINEAU. Moineau.

CHIEF. Your real name.

MOINEAU. Moineau. I don't have no other.

LEDOUX. I warned you, Chief. He's not all there.

MOINEAU. Why did you say that?

LEDOUX. You don't look very smart.

MOINEAU. Before you talk, you should have a good look at yourself in the mirror.

LEDOUX. (*Grabs him by the collar.*) Listen, my boy!...

CHIEF. Okay, Ledoux, let him go (*To* MOINEAU.) Your age?

MOINEAU. Twenty, more or less.

CHIEF. What do you do for a living?

MOINEAU. All sorts of things. One day I do one thing, the next day I do something else. That way I never get bored.

LEDOUX. The Chief asked you a straight question, give him a straight answer.

MOINEAU. I answered as best I could. How do you expect me to say I do one particular thing if I'm always doing different things?

LEDOUX. Why were you loafing this afternoon?

MOINEAU. I wasn't loafing, I was playing my harmonica.

LEDOUX. And what do you do in the evenings?

MOINEAU. I talk to my friends.

CHIEF. And how do you spend your time when you're not playing your harmonica, and you're not talking to your friends?

MOINEAU. All depends. Sometimes I read a bit.

LEDOUX. What do you read?

MOINEAU. Comic books.

LEDOUX. Some reading!

MOINEAU. That's right, I like Superman best.

CHIEF. And when you're not reading?

MOINEAU. I work.

CHIEF. Where?

MOINEAU. Here and there.

CHIEF. (*Harder.*) Where?

MOINEAU. Sometimes for the neighbours.

CHIEF. What do you do for the neighbours?

MOINEAU. Whatever they ask me to. I don't choose my jobs.

CHIEF. Along with all these little jobs, you don't also smuggle cigarettes, by any chance?

MOINEAU does not reply.

LEDOUX. You were asked a question, my boy.

MOINEAU. I don't know what you mean.

CHIEF. You never delivered American cigarettes anywhere?

MOINEAU. Never. People sometimes ask me to deliver parcels, but I never look to see what's inside.

LEDOUX. Acting innocent, eh?

CHIEF. That's right, Moineau, you're acting innocent. But that kind of act doesn't carry much weight here. What if I told you that we have proof, that we've followed you many times, that we can even tell you the days, the hours and the addresses, that we caught you red-handed and you never even knew it.

MOINEAU. So why ask me if you already know everything?

CHIEF. Because we want to know more. We're missing one little detail, but it's the most important one...

LEDOUX. See, it's like this: if you give us the information, you'd be doing us a favour. And when you do someone a favour, you get a reward.

CHIEF. In other words, we'd like to know the name of your supplier, and where he operates.

LEDOUX. You see, we're not asking much.

CHIEF. Practically nothing.

MOINEAU. I never smuggled nothing, I don't know what you're talking about.

LEDOUX. You're lying. We found sixty thousand cigarettes in your shed.

CHIEF. What were you planning to do with those cigarettes?

LEDOUX. You wanted to smoke them all, I suppose?

CHIEF. Come on, tell us the name of your supplier.

MOINEAU is silent.

LEDOUX. Answer. Answer or you'll go straight to prison.

MOINEAU remains silent.

CHIEF. You don't want to say anything, eh?

MOINEAU. No, I'm no traitor.

CHIEF. Sure, Moineau. You're too honest for that...But if you say you're no traitor, that means there's something to betray. You *are* a traitor, Moineau, like all the others who'll come in after you. They'll all wind up talking. The best thing you can do for yourself now, is to tell us everything you know, so you won't make your case worse than it is.

LEDOUX. Go on, tell us what it is you don't want to betray. No sense wasting our time. We'll find out everything in the end anyhow.

MOINEAU. You're wrong. You won't find out nothing from me...maybe I don't look very smart, but I can be stubborn.

CHIEF. And you won't let anything out, eh?

MOINEAU. No.

CHIEF. Why not?

MOINEAU. Because I don't know nothing. 'Cause you ask too many questions, 'cause I'm tired and I feel like playing some music. Why don't you leave me alone? I never did nothing to you.

CHIEF. Of course you didn't do anything to us, but you've gone against the law, and *we* represent the law, my boy. If you don't want trouble with the police you must respect the laws, you hear? Why did you become a smuggler, Moineau? To get rich?

MOINEAU. No.

CHIEF. Why then?

MOINEAU. To earn some money.

CHIEF. So you *do* smuggle!

MOINEAU. You just told me you knew.

CHIEF. That was a little trick to make you talk. You see, we always find out what we want to know…You say you smuggle to earn money, which brings us right back to what I said before: you want to get rich.

MOINEAU. No. I want to earn some money to study music…to buy myself a new harmonica (*He shows his own harmonica.*), a real one with lots of keys and notes.

LEDOUX. I warned you, Chief, he's not all there…

CHIEF. On the contrary, Ledoux, I find him very intelligent.

MOINEAU. If you're saying that to get me to talk, you're barking up the wrong tree.

CHIEF. If I promised you a new harmonica, like the one you want, would I still be barking up the wrong tree?

MOINEAU. Yes. Because I know that with Tarzan, I'll have one some day.

CHIEF. Who is Tarzan?

MOINEAU. Our Chief. *He* won't talk, you'll see.

CHIEF. And if we put you all into prison, your Tarzan will really be able to help you, won't he?

MOINEAU. Doesn't matter. We'll get out one day, and we'll be somebody, just like he promised.

CHIEF. You really like your Chief, don't you?

MOINEAU. Yes.

CHIEF. Why?

MOINEAU. Because he's going to save us. With him I'll have everything I ever wanted. I'll be a musician.

CHIEF. Good. I've heard enough out of him. Take him out and bring in the next one.

LEDOUX. Okay, Chief.

CHIEF. But keep him on hand, we may use him later on.

LEDOUX. (*To MOINEAU.*) Come on, let's go. (*MOINEAU is about to exit at the left, but LEDOUX pushes him towards the right.*) No, this way.

CHIEF. That's a good beginning. It'll all become clear soon, very clear.

LEDOUX. Yeah, but you're not pushing them hard enough, Chief, you're too soft.

CHIEF. It's not necessary, Ledoux. When we start questioning them over and over again, they're bound to contradict themselves. Besides, I figure that one told me a great deal, when he talked about his Chief. Patience, Ledoux, you'll see soon enough.

LEDOUX calls in TIT-NOIR. He enters smiling and very much at ease. He is followed by LEDOUX.

TIT-NOIR. (*To the CHIEF.*) Good evening, sir.
LEDOUX. Sit down.
TIT-NOIR. (*Sits.*) Thank you, sir, you're very kind.
CHIEF. Your name?
TIT-NOIR. Tit-Noir.
LEDOUX. That's a nickname.
TIT-NOIR. I know, but it's not my fault...When I was young, I had black hair so my father called me...
LEDOUX. All right, all right...
TIT-NOIR. As you like, but you're missing out on a damn good story.
LEDOUX. What's your real name?
TIT-NOIR. I don't like it much, it's dumb.
LEDOUX. This is no time for kidding around.
TIT-NOIR. All right, sir. You asked for it, it's Arsène.
LEDOUX. Arsène what?
TIT-NOIR. Arsène Larue.
CHIEF. What does your father do?
TIT-NOIR. He's dead, sir. One night he got plastered...
CHIEF. And you?
TIT-NOIR. Me? I'm not dead, sir.
CHIEF. What do *you* do?
TIT-NOIR. I support my mother.
CHIEF. Do you work?
TIT-NOIR. Yeah, in a ladies' shoe factory, sir.
CHIEF. The name of the company?
TIT-NOIR. Rubber and Shoe Leather Limited, sir.
CHIEF. What exactly is your job?
TIT-NOIR. I make the little heels, that's what the women wear out most...
CHIEF. What are your hours?
TIT-NOIR. From six in the morning to three in the afternoon.
CHIEF. And afterwards?
TIT-NOIR. Afterwards?
CHIEF. Yes, afterwards.
TIT-NOIR. After what, sir?
CHIEF. What do you do when you finish work?
TIT-NOIR. I go home. My old lady always needs me.
LEDOUX. Except for this evening?
TIT-NOIR. Except this evening, sir.

CHIEF. Listen, kid, we don't have time to fool around; we know you're
involved in smuggling American cigarettes, we have...

TIT-NOIR. You must've been misinformed, sir.

CHIEF. No, we have positive proof.

TIT-NOIR. Show me.

LEDOUX. Mind your manners, kid. You don't talk like that to the Chief.

TIT-NOIR. How are you supposed to talk?

LEDOUX. *First* you listen, *then* you answer.

TIT-NOIR. But when he lies, I have to interrupt.

LEDOUX. No, first you'll listen to what he has to say. Then you answer like
you're supposed to.

TIT-NOIR. (*To the* CHIEF.) Go ahead, I'm listening.

CHIEF. Well, we're convinced that you've been smuggling. Your friend just
told us.

TIT-NOIR. Poor Moineau, you must've tortured him.

CHIEF. Not at all. We were simply gentle, just like we'll be with you, if you
co-operate.

TIT-NOIR. I don't believe you. You must've hurt him. Otherwise he
wouldn't've talked.

LEDOUX. You're wrong, it's exactly like the Chief says, everything went
quietly. In the strictest confidence.

CHIEF. We would've liked to know more, but after he said that the five of you
were smuggling to make a little money, we figured he had told us enough.

LEDOUX. So we very gently conducted him to the waiting room next door.

TIT-NOIR. He shouldn't've talked, he should've kept quiet.

CHIEF. Like you would've done in his place.

TIT-NOIR. Right, I wouldn't have talked.

CHIEF. So if I understand clearly, you also confess.

TIT-NOIR. What??

CHIEF. That the five of you are involved in smuggling.

TIT-NOIR. No, I admit nothing.

CHIEF. But yes, you do. You said that Moineau should've kept quiet. Therefore,
you admit that you have something to hide.

LEDOUX. And in *this* instance, the little something...is smuggling.

CHIEF. There you are!

TIT-NOIR. You bastards!

CHIEF. We're doing our job, my boy...Now let's go on to something else. Where
do you get your stock? Who is your supplier?

TIT-NOIR. (*Pauses, looks at the two men.*) Questions like that have to go unan-
swered.

CHIEF. You'd better be serious, my boy.

TIT-NOIR. But I can't answer, sir.

LEDOUX. Why not?

TIT-NOIR. Because I don't know nothing and I don't understand what you're talking about. It sounds Greek to me.

CHIEF. So now it's your turn to be tricky, eh?

TIT-NOIR. No, sir. I'm simply trying to make you see that you won't trap me no more.

LEDOUX. You don't know what you're losing by taking that attitude, my boy. People who confess are rewarded.

TIT-NOIR. For ten thousand bucks I'll admit to anything you want, sir.

LEDOUX. (*Bullying him.*) Cut the dumb jokes, this is no time to kid around.

CHIEF. Can you tell us what got you started in this sort of business?

TIT-NOIR. No.

CHIEF. You're making a mistake. I'm ready to take everything into consideration.

TIT-NOIR. To make me sing louder.

CHIEF. Not at all. If you have good reasons, there's a chance that we'll be able to lighten your sentence, and you'll be free in no time.

TIT-NOIR. Gimme whatever sentence you like, I don't care.

LEDOUX. You're wrong to take that attitude. Very wrong.

CHIEF. You're not betraying anyone or confessing if you tell us why you're involved in smuggling.

TIT-NOIR. (*He looks at them.*) There's only one reason, sir.

CHIEF. Tell me, I'm listening.

TIT-NOIR. Later on, when I get married, I want my children to live good, my wife too. Because one day I'll get married, sir. That may surprise you, but I'll do it, you know!

CHIEF. It doesn't surprise me at all. Go on.

TIT-NOIR. I couldn't ever do what I wanted with my life 'cause my parents were poor.

CHIEF. What did you want to do?

TIT-NOIR. I wanted to study and become a...a priest.

CHIEF. I see.

TIT-NOIR. When I was twelve, I dreamed about it, but now I know that...

The telephone rings and cuts TIT-NOIR *off in mid-sentence. The* CHIEF *lifts the receiver and motions to* TIT-NOIR *to remain where he is.*

CHIEF. Hello!...Yes yes, it's me...What?...When?...Yeah...What was that?...No clue, no trace?...Do you suspect anyone?...All right...I'm busy now with something else...Yes, yes, pursue it at your end...keep me posted...Bye.

The CHIEF *hangs up and ponders for a moment. Then he turns to* LEDOUX.

CHIEF. Take him out.

LEDOUX. Yes, Chief. (*To* TIT-NOIR.) Come on, let's go.

TIT-NOIR. (*He protests and is dragged out.*) But I haven't finished my story! You're not very polite!

LEDOUX. If you're so anxious to talk, we'll call you in later. In the meantime, keep your little friend company. (*They exit.* LEDOUX *returns immediately.*) What happened, Chief?

CHIEF. An American border guard was killed by a bullet from a .38 revolver about six o'clock this afternoon while making his rounds in the woods. They didn't find his body until nine this evening. I'll be conducting the investigation here; Spencer has already begun on the other side.

LEDOUX. Shall we stop the interrogation, then?

CHIEF. No, no. My investigation begins right here.

LEDOUX. Any ideas, Chief? I don't think these kids are capable of...

CHIEF. They can help. Someone's been selling them cigarettes and someone's been smuggling them in. We've got to get to the bottom of this. Bring in the girl, Ledoux, and let's go carefully.

LEDOUX. Right away, Chief. Do we push harder?

CHIEF. Harder, but not too hard, you understand?

LEDOUX exits. CIBOULETTE *enters with* LEDOUX. *She moves to the stool, sits without looking at anyone.*

CHIEF. Your name?

CIBOULETTE. It won't mean anything to you.

CHIEF. We need the information for our files.

LEDOUX. Give us your name.

CIBOULETTE. Ciboulette.

LEDOUX. So now we're dealing in vegetables!

CHIEF. What are your first and last names?

CIBOULETTE. My name is Ciboulette.

CHIEF. Are you afraid we'll inform your parents?

CIBOULETTE. Do what you like. They couldn't care less.

CHIEF. Okay. We'll take care of that later. Do you know why you're here?

CIBOULETTE. I think so.

CHIEF. Do you admit you've been smuggling?

CIBOULETTE. I admit nothing. I only know that you arrested me.

CHIEF. We have proof.

CIBOULETTE. So what more do you want?

CHIEF. We'd like to know where you get your cigarettes.

LEDOUX. Who sells them to you?

CIBOULETTE. You're wasting your time, I won't talk.

CHIEF. Naturally.

LEDOUX. That's what the others said. However, since you've been brought in, the situation got worse and we've decided to use force to make you talk.

CIBOULETTE. You've no right.

LEDOUX. An American border guard was killed this afternoon while making his rounds in the woods.

CIBOULETTE is gripped with fear which she is unable to hide. She recollects the strange look on TARZAN's face when he returned from his last trip.

CHIEF. And more often than not, border guards are killed by smugglers.

CIBOULETTE. (*Repeating TARZAN's words.*) "We're not murderers...we're not criminals...we never killed no one."

LEDOUX. You'll have to prove it.

CHIEF. A border guard is an officer of the law. It's a serious crime to kill a border guard.

CIBOULETTE. You're making up lies to make me talk. But you won't succeed, you won't succeed.

LEDOUX. Take it easy and answer our questions.

CIBOULETTE. No.

LEDOUX. You'll do what we tell you.

CIBOULETTE. I can't, I don't know anything.

CHIEF. Did you receive any cigarettes today?

CIBOULETTE. No.

CHIEF. Were you expecting any?

CIBOULETTE. No.

LEDOUX. Don't try to get out of it: you'll tell us what you know.

CIBOULETTE. I've got nothing to tell.

CHIEF. Your expression changed when we told you about the border guard.

CIBOULETTE. That's not so.

CHIEF. Oh yes, it *is*.

LEDOUX. We both saw it.

CHIEF. Listen, my child, I'm ready to help you. I've even considered letting you go. There's only one condition: you must answer all our questions. What were you doing when you were arrested? Were you waiting for someone?

CIBOULETTE. No.

CHIEF. What were you doing?

CIBOULETTE. Nothing. We were talking.

CHIEF. What were you saying?

CIBOULETTE. Words, just words.

LEDOUX. What time were you expecting them?

CIBOULETTE. What?

LEDOUX. The cigarettes.

CIBOULETTE. We weren't waiting for cigarettes.

LEDOUX. All right then, when was the last time you received a shipment.

CIBOULETTE. I don't remember, I wasn't there.

LEDOUX. So you *did* receive them, right?

CIBOULETTE. Yes, we "received" them.

CHIEF. Who brought them?

CIBOULETTE. I don't know. A man.

CHIEF. His name?

CIBOULETTE. No one ever told me.

LEDOUX. You never heard his name mentioned by any of the others?

CIBOULETTE. No. And I never saw him.

CHIEF. You're lying.

LEDOUX. You're lying, and you'll go straight to prison and life in prison isn't very funny.

CIBOULETTE. Put me in prison, see if I care.

LEDOUX. You're saying that because you don't know what prison is.

CIBOULETTE. I'm saying that because it's what I think.

CHIEF. Who brings the cigarettes?

LEDOUX. Tell us.

CIBOULETTE. You won't get anything from me, I won't talk.

CHIEF. Then you *do* know *something*.

LEDOUX. You know the murderer.

CHIEF. What's his name?

LEDOUX. His name.

CHIEF. His name.

CIBOULETTE. Stop it, you're driving me crazy!

CHIEF. Talk and we'll let you go.

LEDOUX. We won't question you any more.

CHIEF. You'll be free.

LEDOUX. We only want a name.

CHIEF. Just a name and you'll free the others.

LEDOUX. It's not much to ask.

CHIEF. It's hardly anything.

CIBOULETTE. I don't know, I don't know anything!

LEDOUX. Yes you *do*. You think we're stupid?

CHIEF. We're sure you know, it's written all over your face.

CIBOULETTE. (*Covers her face with her hands.*) There's nothing written on my face.

CHIEF. Yes, there is.

CIBOULETTE. No.

LEDOUX. Even if you cover it, we can still see right through your hands. Come on, tell us.

CHIEF. Let yourself go. Tell us, you'll see how easy it is.

LEDOUX. And then you'll be free.

CHIEF. Try. Just open your mouth and it's all over.

LEDOUX. What are a couple of words?

CIBOULETTE. Leave me alone, leave me alone I tell you!

CHIEF. We'll leave you alone afterwards.

LEDOUX. After the confession, we swear. (*He touches her shoulder.*)

CIBOULETTE. Don't touch me, you've no right to touch me.

CHIEF. So talk. That's all you have to do.

LEDOUX. If you want to get out.

CHIEF. Talk.

LEDOUX. Talk.

CHIEF. Otherwise we won't leave you alone...

LEDOUX. We'll drive you to the very end...

CHIEF. Until you tell us what you know...

LEDOUX. Until you confess...

CHIEF. Until you shout it out loud...

CIBOULETTE. (*She rises, a helpless expression on her face, and cries out.*) No!...I won't talk!...I won't talk! (*She feels faint.*) Tarzan! Tarzan! Help me!

She sways. LEDOUX *catches her in time. Her head falls back and her body goes limp.*

CHIEF. Take her to the infirmary, Ledoux, and tell them she broke down.

LEDOUX. Okay, Chief.

CHIEF. And come back at once!

LEDOUX *leaves with* CIBOULETTE *in his arms.*

CHIEF. They know something about this murder, I feel it. When we mentioned the border guard, the girl was very frightened. In the state she's in, we obviously can't question her again tonight. But we've got to make the others talk.

LEDOUX *returns.*

CHIEF. (*To* LEDOUX.) This Tarzan they all talk about, seems to command a lot of respect.

LEDOUX. He's the eldest of the five. I'm keeping him for last. I think he's going to be very hard to handle.

CHIEF. What sort of kid *is* he?

LEDOUX. Proud, self-confident, an arrogant look in his eyes. I think he's their leader.

CHIEF. I see. We'll take care of him right away. Bring him in, Ledoux.

LEDOUX. Yes, Chief.

LEDOUX *exits.*

LEDOUX. (*Off.*) Okay, you, "Tarzan," move.

LEDOUX *pushes* TARZAN *into the office.* TARZAN *is on edge. He sees that* CIBOULETTE *is no longer there. He loses control and charges at the* CHIEF.

TARZAN. What have you done to Ciboulette? You're just a bunch of cowards,
    that's what you are, a bunch of yellow cowards!
LEDOUX. (*Grabs him and forces him to sit.*) Sit down and shut up. It'll be
    healthier for you.
TARZAN. I know Ciboulette, I'm sure she didn't talk. I'm...
CHIEF. Silence! Your name?
TARZAN. They call me Tarzan.
CHIEF. Okay, we've heard that joke before.
TARZAN. What joke?
CHIEF. Your real name. Tell us.
TARZAN. If I feel like it.
LEDOUX. That's not how you answer questions around here. (*Hits TARZAN on
    the back of the head.*)
TARZAN. My name is François Boudreau.
CHIEF. Age?
TARZAN. Twenty-one.
CHIEF. You're an adult. You're responsible for your actions. What's your occu-
    pation?
TARZAN. I'm an orphan.
CHIEF. Your occupation.
TARZAN. Nothing.
CHIEF. Where do you live?
TARZAN. At my uncle's, when I feel like it.
CHIEF. Why only when you feel like it?
TARZAN. Because me and my uncle don't get along too good. When I can,
    I sleep somewhere else.
CHIEF. Are you the leader of the group?
TARZAN. I am.
CHIEF. Why do you smuggle?
TARZAN. To earn a living.
CHIEF. Can't you earn an honest living?
TARZAN. Honest work doesn't mean a thing. I want to live better than those
    poor fools in the slums.
CHIEF. I see. You know that smuggling is against the law, don't you?
TARZAN. I don't give a damn about the law.
CHIEF. Laws are made for everybody, my boy.
TARZAN. Not for me.
CHIEF. Especially for you.
TARZAN. No, sir.
CHIEF. And why not for you?
TARZAN. I have my reasons.
CHIEF. You want to tell me?
TARZAN. It wouldn't interest you.
CHIEF. As you like, but I'm ready to listen.

TARZAN. You wouldn't understand. You're not here for that, you're here to make me talk. And when you've learned all you want to know you'll be very pleased with yourself, you'll sit back in your chair and boss everybody around…you couldn't understand.

CHIEF. Okay. I tried to help you out, you could have defended yourself, but…

TARZAN. I didn't come here to defend myself and I don't intend to.

CHIEF. Okay. Later you may regret that attitude…Now, let's go over everything. You're the fourth to come in here. The other three talked. Thanks to them we're not too badly informed. We know that the five of you smuggle and you do it to improve your standard of living. The girl told us that cigarettes are delivered to your shed (*TARZAN smiles.*), there you fill your orders and deliver them to your customers. You probably run the whole business…All that is clear enough. We're missing only one small detail. The others couldn't help us, because they didn't know, but you can since you're the leader.

TARZAN. Don't kid yourself, you'll never make me talk.

CHIEF. They all say that. But you'll weaken in the end. We have very good methods for loosening tongues, you know. And we can use them on you.

TARZAN. It's the same thing in detective films, they always start by scaring the guy, but if he's strong, and not a kid, he keeps quiet until the very end, and it's the police who come up against a brick wall.

CHIEF. That's true. But you're not in the movies here—and you don't stand a chance.

TARZAN. I'm not counting on chances, I'm counting on myself.

CHIEF. (*Hard.*) That's enough. You brought the others into this business, eh?

TARZAN. I didn't force anyone. We talked it over before, and we knew what we were doing.

CHIEF. Are you sorry you were caught?

TARZAN. No. When you're a real man, you don't regret what you've done even if you fail.

CHIEF. Even if you corrupted a sixteen-year-old girl?

TARZAN. I didn't corrupt her. Ciboulette is worth all of us, she's the strongest, the most sincere. She's worth more than you, many times over.

LEDOUX. (*Hits him again.*) I told you to watch it…

CHIEF. Let him go, Ledoux. (*To TARZAN.*) You're right. Ciboulette is a strong and sincere young girl, but she was very frightened. If she hadn't fainted, she probably would've told us everything we want to know.

TARZAN. That's not so!

LEDOUX. Oh, yes it is.

CHIEF. Where were you this afternoon?

TARZAN. I dunno…somewhere in town.

CHIEF. Can you be more precise?

LEDOUX. You weren't down at the border by any chance, were you?

TARZAN. (*Startled.*) Doing what?

LEDOUX. Taking in a bit of fresh air, maybe.

CHIEF. Did anyone see you in town this afternoon?

TARZAN. Yeah, lots of people.

LEDOUX. Who, for instance?

TARZAN. Everyone I met on the street.

CHIEF. That's no alibi.

LEDOUX. Can you name anyone?

TARZAN. You think I made a list?

LEDOUX. Where did you hide your gun?

TARZAN. I never had a gun.

LEDOUX. I don't believe you. You had one when I first visited you today.

TARZAN. I didn't. I made a move to scare him, and he believed it.

CHIEF. A border guard was killed this afternoon while making his rounds in the woods.

TARZAN *is slightly startled.*

LEDOUX. Does that mean anything to you?

TARZAN. No.

LEDOUX. A man, who was doing his job, was killed.

CHIEF. Now, in our opinion, there's an obvious connection between this crime and the smuggling that's going on in the province. Since you're the chief of a smuggling ring, you can probably help us find the guilty party.

LEDOUX. Those who help the police get rewarded.

CHIEF. It can even free those who don't deserve it.

TARZAN. What d'you want from me?

CHIEF. One piece of information. Who supplies you with cigarettes. (TARZAN *is silent.*) I suppose they fall into your lap straight from heaven.

TARZAN. We had them for sale, for us that was the main thing.

LEDOUX. Someone delivered them to you?

TARZAN. (*Offers this information eagerly.*) Someone delivered them, like Ciboulette said.

CHIEF. Who was it?

TARZAN. I never saw his face. He wore a mask.

CHIEF. This guy's having a good time, he's enjoying himself.

LEDOUX. (*Approaching* TARZAN.) We'll see if we can't change his tune.

CHIEF. (*To* TARZAN.) Listen, my boy, we don't have time to waste.

TARZAN. You're waiting for me to give you all the details. You *are* wasting your time. I'm the accused, I'm not on your side, I won't help you.

LEDOUX. We'll soon see about that. (*He seizes him by the collar and raises his fist to him.*)

TARZAN. You can hit me all you like, it won't help. I took plenty of beatings in my life: at school, at my uncle's, in the street. I took them and I hit back. I've been hardened enough and I can take more. It won't make me talk.

LEDOUX. See what I told you, Chief, a real tough customer—hard as a rock.

CHIEF. We'll see—even the hardest rocks crack. (*He approaches* TARZAN.) Listen, in the infirmary, a young girl is frightened because we asked her a couple of questions too many. All we've got to do is bring her back here and we'll know a lot more. Surely you don't want us to do that?...Answer me, is that what you want?

TARZAN. No.

CHIEF. All right, you'll have to answer our questions yourself.

TARZAN. I told you everything. I don't know nothing more.

LEDOUX. We're not stupid.

TARZAN. I won't talk.

CHIEF. Then the girl will.

TARZAN. You've no right.

CHIEF. You're afraid, eh?

TARZAN. I'm not afraid. Ciboulette won't talk, I know that. But I don't want you to hurt her.

CHIEF. It's up to you.

LEDOUX. Your choice.

TARZAN. I won't say nothing. Ciboulette won't talk either.

CHIEF. Even if we force her to?

TARZAN. She won't talk.

CHIEF. We'll see. Take him away, Ledoux, and bring back the girl.

TARZAN. No! You've no right, you've no right. That's filthy, that's a dirty trick! (LEDOUX *grabs hold of him and forces him out.*) Ciboulette, Ciboulette! Don't talk...Don't be scared...they've no right...Ciboulette! (*The rest of his words are lost.*)

CHIEF. Stay here, Ledoux. It didn't work.

LEDOUX. But it was a good manoeuvre, Chief. We could make that girl talk.

CHIEF. No, there must be another way. Bring the last one in, Ledoux.

LEDOUX returns.

LEDOUX. What about the girl?

CHIEF. Later, maybe as a last resort.

LEDOUX. Okay, Chief. (*Exits.*)

CHIEF. There must be one rotten apple in the bunch.

LEDOUX. (*Pushes* PASSE-PARTOUT *into the office.*) Okay, you, inside! Walk!

PASSE-PARTOUT. Don't push, don't push, I didn't do nothing. (*He rushes towards the* CHIEF.) I didn't do nothing, sir. I didn't know, it's not my fault.

CHIEF. We'll soon see. Sit down.

PASSE-PARTOUT. Okay, sir. (*He sits on the stool.*)

CHIEF. Well, you seem to be in a receptive frame of mind. What's your name?

PASSE-PARTOUT. Passe-Partout.

LEDOUX. So now it's keyholes! Why the hell can't you have names like normal
    people?

PASSE-PARTOUT. I'm sorry, it's a habit. My name's René Langlois.

CHIEF. Your age?

PASSE-PARTOUT. Twenty.

CHIEF. You have parents?

PASSE-PARTOUT. Yes.

CHIEF. Do you work?

PASSE-PARTOUT. No. I sell cigarettes to earn a living and bring some money
    into the house.

CHIEF. And your father?

PASSE-PARTOUT. He drinks away his pay. *I* support my mother.

LEDOUX. You also steal wallets on the side? Right?...This is the thief I was
    telling you about, Chief.

CHIEF. Why don't you work like everyone else?

PASSE-PARTOUT. I tried, lots of times, but it never works out. I'm always fired
    after a couple of days.

LEDOUX. Is it because they think you're not trustworthy?

PASSE-PARTOUT. No. They say I don't do the job good enough. (*Pause.*) I swear
    I'm telling the truth, sir.

CHIEF. Okay. You're accused of smuggling and pickpocketing. You don't deny
    it?

PASSE-PARTOUT. I did it for my mother.

CHIEF. You don't deny it, then?

PASSE-PARTOUT. Oh, no.

CHIEF. Good. So far, so good. Now all we need is a little more information. We
    know about your delivery system. All that's clear. Now tell us about your
    supplies.

PASSE-PARTOUT. You mean how we store the supplies?

LEDOUX. We know that. At the moment, your shed is empty. What we're
    really interested in, is how the cigarettes are brought across the border.

PASSE-PARTOUT. (*Cautiously.*) Is this information very important to you?

LEDOUX. Of the utmost importance.

PASSE-PARTOUT. I'm sorry I can't talk. I can't betray my friends.

LEDOUX. Are you sure you can't?

PASSE-PARTOUT. Practically...Unless...

CHIEF. Unless what?

PASSE-PARTOUT. Unless the help I give you is taken into consideration.

CHIEF. Occasionally such services *are* taken into consideration.

PASSE-PARTOUT. How, for instance?

CHIEF. We might, for instance, release the suspect on bail until the trial, or
    soften the evidence brought in against him.

PASSE-PARTOUT. That's very interesting.

CHIEF. Isn't it?

PASSE-PARTOUT. You mean if I give you the information, you'll let me and
the others go?

CHIEF. In view of the extreme importance of this service, yes.

PASSE-PARTOUT. I understand, I'm not squealing on anyone, I'm only serving
the law.

LEDOUX. You're just serving the law like an honest citizen, that's all.

CHIEF. Come on, talk, we're listening.

PASSE-PARTOUT. You have to question *me*.

CHIEF. Who supplies you with cigarettes?

PASSE-PARTOUT. An American, from the States.

CHIEF. His name?

PASSE-PARTOUT. I don't know. He gives 'em to us cheap and we sell them at a
profit.

CHIEF. Does he deliver them in person?

PASSE-PARTOUT. No way. We had to go and get them.

CHIEF. From the States?

PASSE-PARTOUT. Of course. We took care of it ourselves. We snuck across by
the woods.

LEDOUX. Have you ever done it?

PASSE-PARTOUT. No. Tarzan's always the one. We wanted to take his place
sometimes but...

*The two policemen freeze. They realize that they are close to their goal. They become
very interested, serious, but remain discreet.*

CHIEF. Good. When was the last time he made the trip?

PASSE-PARTOUT. He went across today.

CHIEF. This afternoon?

PASSE-PARTOUT. Yes.

LEDOUX. What time did he get back?

PASSE-PARTOUT. About seven-thirty. Yeah, that's it, he was late.

CHIEF. Usually he's not back so late?

PASSE-PARTOUT. No. Today we even thought he got picked up.

CHIEF. Good. That's all we wanted to know. Anything else to add?

PASSE-PARTOUT. No...(*He starts to rise.*)

LEDOUX. Just a minute. When he crosses the border, is he armed?

PASSE-PARTOUT. I don't think so.

CHIEF. Sit back down there. Ledoux, bring Tarzan in right away. Now we lean
on him.

LEDOUX. Yes, Chief.

LEDOUX exits. PASSE-PARTOUT rises.

PASSE-PARTOUT. What about me?

CHIEF. You sit there quietly and say nothing.

PASSE-PARTOUT. You're not going to question him in front of me, are you?

CHIEF. Yes. To make sure you're telling the truth.

PASSE-PARTOUT. I only told the truth.

CHIEF. That's what we mean to find out. And when you're not being questioned, keep quiet. Remember our little understanding, eh?

TARZAN and LEDOUX enter. TARZAN halts. He is taken aback for a moment when he sees PASSE-PARTOUT, then throws him a hard look.

CHIEF. Give him a seat.

LEDOUX brings the chair from the back of the room.

LEDOUX. (*To TARZAN.*) Sit down.

LEDOUX and the CHIEF look at him but remain silent.

TARZAN. What more do you want? I told you all I have to say.

CHIEF. You're gonna have to say it again.

TARZAN. (*He is silent. He looks at PASSE-PARTOUT.*) Why are you questioning me in front of Passe-Partout?

CHIEF. We have our reasons. You see, we changed our minds before and decided to question Passe-Partout instead of the girl.

LEDOUX. You see, we're human. (*A pause. LEDOUX approaches him.*) You don't think we're human?

TARZAN. Is that all you've got to ask?

CHIEF. Ah! No. We've got lots more. But now, we're in no hurry.

A pause. TARZAN looks at PASSE-PARTOUT, who lowers his eyes.

LEDOUX. Do you still claim that the cigarettes are delivered to you?

TARZAN. Yes.

LEDOUX. He still says so, Chief.

CHIEF. Ask him if the man wears a mask like in the movies?

TARZAN does not reply.

LEDOUX. (*Casually.*) Where were you this afternoon?

TARZAN. You already asked me that.

LEDOUX. I'm asking you again.

TARZAN. I was in town.

LEDOUX. Exactly where in town?

TARZAN. Here and there.

CHIEF. Anyone see you?

TARZAN. Lots of people.

LEDOUX. Who, for instance?

TARZAN. Everyone I met on the street.

LEDOUX. You're consistent enough, but it's no alibi.

CHIEF. Give us an alibi.

LEDOUX. You still haven't given us an alibi.

TARZAN. I don't need one.

CHIEF. A contrary testimony informs us that you stole across the border this afternoon and that you yourself smuggled in the cigarettes.

TARZAN. (*He turns abruptly towards* PASSE-PARTOUT, *looks at him furiously.*) That's not true. (*Then he bursts out laughing.*) Boy, that's a good one! That's what Passe-Partout told you, eh? And you fell right in.

CHIEF. This is no time to laugh, explain yourself.

TARZAN. I beat up Passe-Partout this evening because he disobeyed me. I humiliated him in front of the others. So, when you told him about the murdered border guard, he made up this crazy story to revenge himself, that's all.

CHIEF. Could be, if we weren't so certain it's not a crazy story.

LEDOUX. Because we didn't tell him about the murder. We set a trap and he fell right in.

CHIEF. We told him that the others had confessed and if he also co-operated, his sentence wouldn't be too tough.

PASSE-PARTOUT. You see, Tarzan, it's like they said, it's not my fault, they trapped me...

TARZAN. (*Jumps at* PASSE-PARTOUT.) You filthy sonuvabitch, Passe-Partout, you'll pay for this.

He is about to hit PASSE-PARTOUT, *but* LEDOUX *seizes him, leads him back to his chair and forces him to sit.*

LEDOUX. Easy does it, my friend. You're not laughing now, are you?

CHIEF. Admit it, you crossed the border this afternoon.

TARZAN. (*Firmly.*) No.

CHIEF. Take that one out, Ledoux. We don't need him any more.

LEDOUX. Yes, Chief. (*To* PASSE-PARTOUT.) You come here.

LEDOUX *and* PASSE-PARTOUT *exit right.*

CHIEF. What time did you cross the border?

TARZAN. I didn't cross.

CHIEF. What time was it?

TARZAN. I didn't cross.

CHIEF. Listen, kid! The way you acted in front of Passe-Partout is proof enough that you lied. Now we're certain you crossed the border today.

TARZAN. If you're certain why...

CHIEF. Quiet! *I'm* doing the talking. Here *you're* not the Chief, my boy. Moreover, you've never *been* a chief. You put yourself outside the law and you dragged the others along with you. You'll pay for what you did yourself, and for the others too. Listen carefully. When you leave here we'll know everything we want to know. I advise you, then, to answer our questions properly; otherwise, we'll take extreme measures. We've got the right, you know, because you're of age, and there's a link between this case and a serious crime. A man was killed. I've no right to accuse you, but I do have the right to suspect you, and I've also the right to get the information as soon as possible. You'll have to prove that you didn't kill this man. You understand?

TARZAN. I don't have to prove anything...

CHIEF. Don't think you can get away with it because you're the leader of a gang and you got a bunch of kids to obey you. As I just told you, you've never been a *real* leader. A real leader is obeyed wholeheartedly, because his men love him, *you* they obey out of self-interest. They would've deserted you one day.

TARZAN. That's not true, my men love me.

CHIEF. You're living under an illusion. One after the other they've come before me; one after the other, they talked. They didn't say much, that's true, but enough to make me understand that they're only following you for their own personal gain.

TARZAN. Prove it.

CHIEF. The first one smuggles to buy a new harmonica, to become a musician; the second, to safeguard the future of his unborn children; the third is living in a melodrama—he steals to support his mother because his father is a drunkard.

TARZAN. You're forgetting Ciboulette.

CHIEF. Yes. But you'll admit you've got very little to be proud of there. She broke down and when she leaves here, she'll have a police record. Are you proud of *that*?...Answer me...She's marked for life, you, *too, and* the others. Are you proud of that? Be honest.

TARZAN. No.

CHIEF. Ciboulette was frightened for herself, that's why she fainted. True, she didn't say much, she even put us on the wrong track saying that the cigarettes were delivered to your shed, but if the interrogation had gone on, she'd have revealed her selfish motives, just like the others.

TARZAN. Not Ciboulette.

CHIEF. She, too. Except maybe she's not interested in getting rich, maybe it's *you* she's interested in. In the long run, she may not give a damn about smuggling; other things are going on inside her little head. But you understand nothing, and it's *your* fault that she's marked for life.

TARZAN. It's not true. You've no right to say that.

CHIEF. Moreover, you were betrayed…you better understand *that* right now. You're alone. You can't run away from your conditions like heroes in the movies. Your head is full of illusions and dreams. Now your dreams are dead, Tarzan. You're alone; like all of us are alone in life, my boy. Even at the very moment when we believe that friends are behind us, we're alone like stones.

TARZAN. It's true that suddenly I do feel alone, they seem so far away. I see their faces but I can hardly recognize them.

LEDOUX. You see, keeping silent is just not worth it.

CHIEF. Definitely not worth it.

LEDOUX. Admit you stole across the border this afternoon.

TARZAN. Yes, I crossed the border this afternoon. But I didn't kill the border guard!

CHIEF. No one says you did, not at all.

TARZAN. Now leave me alone. I told you all you wanted to know.

CHIEF. We still have one or two more questions.

LEDOUX. The American who sells you cigarettes—what's his name?

TARZAN. Stone. Mr. Stone.

LEDOUX. His address?

TARZAN. He never gave it to me. We met at a certain spot and he sold me the cigarettes. I never knew his first name, either.

CHIEF. We believe you.

LEDOUX. You seem to be telling the truth.

TARZAN. Let me go now, I told you everything. I'll give you the details tomorrow. I'm too tired now. (*He rises.*)

LEDOUX. You should sit when you're tired, sit down.

TARZAN. (*Uneasy.*) What more do you want?

LEDOUX. Nothing much, don't get excited.

CHIEF. What time did you cross the border today?

TARZAN. I don't know. I crossed three times.

CHIEF. The *first* time, about what time was that?

TARZAN. It was very hot, close to noon I'd say.

LEDOUX. The second time?

TARZAN. Three o'clock, maybe.

CHIEF. And the last?

TARZAN. I don't remember.

CHIEF. You must remember. What time was it?

TARZAN. Probably about six. (*He rises.*)

LEDOUX. Not so fast, sit down. Relax. (*Sits him down.*)

CHIEF. Did you meet anyone in the woods?

TARZAN. No.

LEDOUX. That's strange. Since the war, the border hasn't been watched as carefully as it is now.

CHIEF. If you'd met a border guard what would you have done?

TARZAN. I don't know. I would've hidden.

CHIEF. Have you ever hidden from a border guard before?

TARZAN. Often.

LEDOUX. Are you armed when you cross the border?

TARZAN. No.

CHIEF. How many cigarettes did you bring across today?

TARZAN. A lot.

CHIEF. How many?

TARZAN. Thirty thousand.

CHIEF. Without a gun?

TARZAN. Without a gun.

CHIEF. You take risks.

TARZAN. That's my choice.

CHIEF. You risk your life too, you know.

TARZAN. It's my life.

CHIEF. Very noble, but your cause is rotten.

TARZAN. Fighting for your life is not a rotten cause!

LEDOUX. And since you enjoy taking risks, you steal across unarmed?

TARZAN. Yes.

CHIEF. We believe you. That's just about all we wanted to know. (*Pretends that his dossier is complete.*) So, when you saw the border guard, you hid, eh?

TARZAN. Yes.

CHIEF. Oh no, you just said you didn't see him.

LEDOUX. (*Sits him down roughly.*) You mustn't start lying to us again, my boy. Too bad. Things were going so well. Now we've got to start all over again.

CHIEF. Did he see you?

TARZAN. Who?

LEDOUX. The border guard.

TARZAN. No.

CHIEF. What time was it?

TARZAN. During the second trip, about three.

CHIEF. If he'd seen you, would you have fired at him?

TARZAN. No, I wasn't armed!

LEDOUX. What *would* you have done?

TARZAN. I don't know. I'd have let him approach.

LEDOUX. And you'd have tried to disarm him?

TARZAN. Maybe.

CHIEF. But he didn't see you?

TARZAN. No.

LEDOUX. He was a Canadian, right?

TARZAN. No, American.

LEDOUX. That's what I meant.

CHIEF. That's right, an American was killed...Was he a big man?

TARZAN. Medium.

CHIEF. Fat?

TARZAN. Thin.

LEDOUX. Was he old?

TARZAN. About thirty, maybe.

CHIEF. Then you had a good look at him, right?

TARZAN. He walked close by me.

CHIEF. The colour of his eyes?

TARZAN. Black.

CHIEF. Well! You say he didn't see you, yet you saw the colour of his eyes!

TARZAN. I saw his eyes: two big black eyes.

CHIEF. He must've been pretty absent-minded not to have seen you.

LEDOUX. He was probably singing a little tune to pass the time of day.

CHIEF. That's it, eh?

TARZAN. I don't know.

CHIEF. What time was it?

TARZAN. Three o'clock.

CHIEF. And the first trip?

TARZAN. At noon.

CHIEF. And the last?

TARZAN. At six.

CHIEF. *Where* were you coming from?

TARZAN. From Landmark Road two miles from the American border.

CHIEF. Where were you going to?

TARZAN. A truck waits for me at the side of the road about a mile from the
Canadian side.

CHIEF. The truck driver's name?

TARZAN. (*He hesitates.*) It's...I'm the driver. I rent the truck.

CHIEF. So you walk three miles?

TARZAN. Yes.

LEDOUX. Three miles there, three miles back, you walked six miles.

TARZAN. Yes.

LEDOUX. And eighteen, in all, to make three trips.

TARZAN. Yes.

LEDOUX. Pretty fast considering you have to go through the woods.

CHIEF. You certainly weren't taking many precautions.

TARZAN. I'm used to it. I know my way.

CHIEF. Maybe you don't actually cover three miles each time?

TARZAN. Maybe not.

LEDOUX. And all you saw was a border guard.

TARZAN. Yes.

LEDOUX. Are you sure he didn't see you?

TARZAN. Yes.

CHIEF. Why?

TARZAN. I don't know. I don't know any more...you're asking too many questions.

LEDOUX. How come he didn't see you?

CHIEF. I suppose he was too far away.

TARZAN. That's right, he was too far away.

LEDOUX. No, just a minute ago, you said you saw him from up close. You even knew the colour of his eyes.

CHIEF. Was he near you, or was he far away?

TARZAN. He was...neither near...or far.

LEDOUX. Then he wasn't anywhere! Come on, answer! Did he walk by, or didn't he?

TARZAN. He walked by right in front of me. I was hiding, that's all.

LEDOUX. Was he big?

TARZAN. Yes.

LEDOUX. You just said he was medium.

CHIEF. Why did you say he was medium? I suppose from far he looked big, and from near, he looked medium. Distance changes your perspective. But he can't be near and far at the same time, so he can't be big *and* medium.

LEDOUX. It doesn't make sense. It's one or the other.

CHIEF. Was he fat?

TARZAN. Thin.

CHIEF. What time was it?

TARZAN. Three o'clock.

LEDOUX. He saw you and you fired at him.

TARZAN. No, I wasn't armed.

CHIEF. Why did you say you carried a .38?

TARZAN. I didn't say that.

LEDOUX. Yes you did.

CHIEF. At the beginning of your testimony you said: "I always carry a .38 when I cross the border."

LEDOUX. You don't remember?

TARZAN. I said that I risk it and cross without a gun.

CHIEF. You have a bad memory.

LEDOUX. You're confused, my boy.

CHIEF. Soon we won't know what you said and what you didn't say.

LEDOUX. And neither will you.

CHIEF. Come on, refresh your memory—you always need to do that.

LEDOUX. Here, let me help you out...When did you cross the first time?

TARZAN. At noon.

CHIEF. And the second?

TARZAN. Three o'clock.

LEDOUX. And the last?

TARZAN. Six!

CHIEF. That's right. Interesting how the number six keeps turning up. Six miles there and back, six hours for three trips, and the last trip was also at six.

LEDOUX. And the border guard was six feet tall.

CHIEF. That's true, he was six feet tall.

LEDOUX. And you said he was thin, eh?

TARZAN. No.

CHIEF. Yes, that's what you said: thin, with black eyes.

TARZAN. Yes, his eyes were black, I saw them, I told you. I remember that.

CHIEF. Then he wasn't too far when he went by?

LEDOUX. Maybe he was even close?

CHIEF. Very close?

TARZAN. Yes.

CHIEF. And the sun was shining?

LEDOUX. Pretty afternoon sunshine?

TARZAN. Yes...the sun was shining...or rather it wasn't it was close to evening.

CHIEF. Then it wasn't three o'clock?

LEDOUX. You just said you saw him during the second trip.

CHIEF. But if it wasn't evening, then it must've been during the last trip at six then.

TARZAN. No.

CHIEF. So when was it?

TARZAN. I don't know, I don't know.

LEDOUX. Admit it, you fired at him. Everything was in your favour.

TARZAN. No.

CHIEF. Yes.

LEDOUX. With a .38.

TARZAN. No! No! No!

CHIEF. With a .38 at point-blank. He died immediately.

TARZAN. That's not true.

LEDOUX. What? That he didn't die immediately?

TARZAN. That I fired at him. That's not true.

CHIEF. Afterwards, you saw that his eyes were black.

TARZAN. No.

LEDOUX. Yes. He bled a lot. You were afraid, it was your first crime.

TARZAN. No.

CHIEF. Where did you put your gun?

TARZAN. I didn't have a gun.

CHIEF. We must have the murder weapon.

TARZAN. You won't have it.

CHIEF. Then you confess.

TARZAN. No. You're forcing me to talk and I'm saying things that aren't true.
LEDOUX. The truth's coming out now.
CHIEF. We must ask a lot of questions to get at the truth!
LEDOUX. We must question you to the bitter end. We must break down all of
    your resistance!
CHIEF. Confess!
LEDOUX. Confess!
CHIEF. Confess, Tarzan!

The CHIEF *moves towards the back wall. He presses a button. A very strong reflector
on the ceiling is lit and beamed on* TARZAN*'s head.*

TARZAN. I didn't do it!

LEDOUX *seizes* TARZAN *by the hair and shoulders. He holds his face in the beams.*

TARZAN. Not the light...not the light...I'm not a murderer!
CHIEF. Look straight into the light, it tells the truth.
TARZAN. Turn it off, turn it off!
LEDOUX. Some criminals can't stand the light...
CHIEF. Because they're afraid.
TARZAN. Turn it off, turn it off!
CHIEF. Confess!
TARZAN. You're driving me crazy, turn off the lights!
LEDOUX. Confess!
CHIEF. Tell us you killed him!
TARZAN. (*In one loud scream.*) Yes, I did it!...turn it off...I did it, I did it!...

The CHIEF *turns off the light.* LEDOUX *releases* TARZAN, *who slumps down in
the chair, covers his face with his hands, and sobs. We hear fragments of* TARZAN*'s
speech.*

TARZAN. He walked by...he looked into my eyes...he opened his mouth to
    speak...I fired!...he fell...he fell like a tree...he couldn't cry out...he couldn't
    speak, his words were caught in his throat...

He sobs. A long silence. The tension is broken.

CHIEF. (*Softly.*) Take him away.

TARZAN *rises automatically.*

CHIEF. Do you have anything else to add?
TARZAN. No...that's all...Ciboulette...release her...let her go...

CHIEF. The others will be released tomorrow. After your trial, they won't feel
    like starting over again.
TARZAN. Ciboulette…Tell her…tell her that I…no, don't tell her nothing.
CHIEF. Take him outside. (LEDOUX *leads him out.*)

LEDOUX exits. The CHIEF *shows visible signs of fatigue. He sits at his desk and files
away his papers. Then, after several moments he lifts the receiver and dials.*

CHIEF. Hello! Get me Inspector Spencer, in Plattsburg, please…

*As the scene ends, the harmonica plays its melancholy music. The music fades into
the stillness of the night.*

ACT III
The Death

*The scene is the same as Act I. It is a dull autumn evening. From the distance is heard
the sorrowful and plaintive music of the harmonica. The music seems to arise out of
the depths of human suffering.* MOINEAU *is alone on stage. He sits on* TARZAN'*s
throne and reads a comic book. Apparently, he is very much intrigued by what he is
reading, for he bites his fingernails.* PASSE-PARTOUT *is inside the shed. He nails
boards, comes out, fixes the exterior wall, then exits quietly.*

*The characters are dressed more warmly than they were in the previous acts and
should appear to be somewhat cold. After a while,* CIBOULETTE *enters. Her pace is
slow and her face no longer glows with the fervour we had witnessed in the first act.
It is as though she is living in a bad dream, and her face is as sad as that of an abandoned child. She leans against the fence.*

CIBOULETTE. Hi, Moineau.
MOINEAU. (*Greets her.*) Hi, Ciboulette! (*Continues reading.*)

Silence.

CIBOULETTE. You're reading?
MOINEAU. Yeah.

Silence.

CIBOULETTE. What're you reading?
MOINEAU. An adventure story. I'm almost finished.
CIBOULETTE. Does it have a happy ending?
MOINEAU. No. They spoiled it. Those they call the "bad guys," are punished by
    the "good guys."

Pause.

CIBOULETTE. You think he'll be convicted, Moineau? (*Silence.*) Moineau! I'm
    talking to you!
MOINEAU. Wait a minute…I got two more pictures.

*He finishes reading, closes his comic book carefully, folds it and slides it into his
pocket.*

MOINEAU. Something you want to know?
CIBOULETTE. I want to know if you think they'll convict him.
MOINEAU. I'm afraid so. Usually, when you kill someone, they hang you.
CIBOULETTE. With a rope?
MOINEAU. Yeah.
CIBOULETTE. Around the neck?
MOINEAU. Yeah.
CIBOULETTE. Is hanging an ugly way to die?
MOINEAU. It's not pretty. Sometimes they show you in the comics. Their necks
    are all stretched and their tongues hang out.
CIBOULETTE. We'll defend him at the trial, Moineau. We'll save him. Tarzan
    was never ugly, he mustn't be hanged. Besides, he won't let them, he'll
    escape.
MOINEAU. You think so?
CIBOULETTE. Yes.
MOINEAU. It's hard. In prison they guard you real good.
CIBOULETTE. Then he'll die?
MOINEAU. Maybe.
CIBOULETTE. What do you think, does he have a chance?
MOINEAU. Not much. Because if they don't hang him, they'll throw him in
    prison for life.
CIBOULETTE. For his whole life?…But that can't be. Moineau!…Remember
    one evening in July, when he came back from a trip, he was all sweaty, and
    his shirt was wide open and you could see his bare chest. He sat with us on
    Tit-Noir's stairs, he looked at us one after the other with his eyes so full of
    life, and he told us his adventures until late into the night. You remember,
    Moineau? Remember how happy he was to be alive, and more than that, to
    be free?
MOINEAU. Yes, Ciboulette.
CIBOULETTE. But now, it's all over. No more adventures, no more freedom.
MOINEAU. No more nothing.

Silence.

CIBOULETTE. We had a beautiful Chief, eh Moineau?

MOINEAU. Yeah, a *real* one.

PASSE-PARTOUT enters carrying boards. He sees MOINEAU and CIBOULETTE, and halts. He has lost none of his former arrogance and deceptive masculinity. Moreover, his appearance suggests that he has done something dishonest.

PASSE-PARTOUT. Well! We have a visitor...Hi, Ciboulette.
CIBOULETTE. Hi, Passe-Partout. So you're here.
PASSE-PARTOUT. Does it bother you?
CIBOULETTE. No. I was just wondering what's so interesting around here?
PASSE-PARTOUT. You never *know* what you can find in a deserted old shed.
CIBOULETTE. They took everything.
PASSE-PARTOUT. Of course, what did you expect? They came in, and ten minutes later, the place was cleaned out...Even though our *Chief* assured us there was no danger, that it was all very well organized...We had a good Chief, but I think he was too much of a dreamer.
CIBOULETTE. Passe-Partout!
PASSE-PARTOUT. It's true, Ciboulette.
CIBOULETTE. Passe-Partout, he's going to die.
PASSE-PARTOUT. Sure, what do you expect? At least if he hadn't fired! But no, he had to take himself serious, act the hero to the very end.
CIBOULETTE. He defended himself, that's all.
PASSE-PARTOUT. As if there was no other way to save your skin.
CIBOULETTE. There was no other way, that's why he did it.
PASSE-PARTOUT. Why not admit he goofed, eh?
MOINEAU. I keep wondering who betrayed him. Because he was betrayed, eh?
PASSE-PARTOUT. Who can tell? We'll probably never know.
CIBOULETTE. But we might suspect someone, anyway.
PASSE-PARTOUT. Why're you looking at *me*, Ciboulette? Are you referring to me?
CIBOULETTE. I didn't say that.
PASSE-PARTOUT. That's just as well, because if you were...
CIBOULETTE. I didn't say that, but when I look you straight in the eye, you turn your head away, and there's a strange look on your face.
PASSE-PARTOUT. No girl's eyes are gonna scare *me*. I can look anybody in the eye. You're seeing the old Passe-Partout, not the new one. The new Passe-Partout is not scared.
CIBOULETTE. You're not scared but you can't look at people. You're not scared but maybe you're ashamed.
PASSE-PARTOUT. I've never been ashamed, you hear?! Not in front of anyone.
CIBOULETTE. Not even in front of us when Tarzan beat you up?
PASSE-PARTOUT. I wasn't ashamed. You were four against one. If it was just him and me, I would've beat him easy.

CIBOULETTE. You hear that, Moineau? *He* would've beaten him, he's scared of his own shadow. Look out, Passe-Partout!

PASSE-PARTOUT turns around quickly. He realizes he was ridiculed. He is livid with rage.

CIBOULETTE. (*Laughs.*) You see?

PASSE-PARTOUT. Never mind, you won't laugh at me for long! Ever since we were released, you watch me, you spy on me. You're jealous because I'm alive, because *I'm* not accused of murder and Tarzan is, because I'm free! But from now on, things are gonna be different around here.

MOINEAU. You don't know what you're talking about.

PASSE-PARTOUT. As for *you*, mind your own business. I'm the new Chief, you understand? (*He sits on* TARZAN*'s throne.*) The throne is vacant and I'm taking it…And you're gonna listen to me.

CIBOULETTE. Listen to you? Have you taken a good look at yourself lately?

MOINEAU. There's no new Chief. After Tarzan's trial, we'll all go home and we won't ever come back here again.

PASSE-PARTOUT. That's what *you* think, but I've found a way to keep us together.

CIBOULETTE. You think we'll obey just anyone?

PASSE-PARTOUT. I found a way to force you.

MOINEAU. You're going about it the wrong way.

CIBOULETTE. Don't make us laugh…It's all over without Tarzan.

PASSE-PARTOUT. Get that out of your heads.

CIBOULETTE. We'll leave you all alone, Passe-Partout.

PASSE-PARTOUT. Even if I tell you I just found the cash box and I've got all the money right here inside my pocket.

MOINEAU. Even so. Only part of that money belongs to you. You'll put the rest back.

CIBOULETTE. Don't pay attention to him, Moineau. He's lying. The police took the money when they took the cigarettes.

PASSE-PARTOUT. You're wrong. Tit-Noir hid it real good, they never touched it.

CIBOULETTE. And you think you can buy us with our own money?

PASSE-PARTOUT. Why are you against me? Tarzan is a murderer, and you respect *him*.

MOINEAU. Tarzan is a man and you're a rat; it's not the same, Passe-Partout.

PASSE-PARTOUT. (*Furious; advances towards* MOINEAU.) Say that again and we'll see who's a…

MOINEAU. You're a rat, Passe-Partout, that's what you are.

PASSE-PARTOUT. (*Slaps* MOINEAU.) Say it again.

MOINEAU. Rat.

PASSE-PARTOUT. (*Slaps him once more.*) Had enough?

CIBOULETTE. (*Coming between them.*) That's enough. You hit him 'cause you
know he won't fight back. But if Moineau wanted to, he could break every
bone in your body.

PASSE-PARTOUT. Easier said than done. I'm stronger than anyone. And I hit
when I want and *who* I want, and I say *yes* or *no* when *I* feel like it…Now
we'll get back to work right away, and forget the dumb things Tarzan made
us do. I've got everything organized, the plans are all worked out in my
head. So what if American cigarettes cost twenty cents less than Canadian,
you'll never get rich on that. From now on we'll smuggle in bigger things,
we'll get serious, we'll…

MOINEAU. You're talking into thin air, Passe-Partout.

PASSE-PARTOUT. I know that talking to *you* is like talking into thin air. But
I'll see to it that you stay in line.

MOINEAU. No.

PASSE-PARTOUT. You never answered Tarzan back, you called him big Chief,
and snapped to attention, and all the time you were shivering in your
pants, and you'll do the same for me.

MOINEAU. No.

PASSE-PARTOUT. You wanna play my little game again?

He makes for MOINEAU *but* CIBOULETTE *stands in his way.*

CIBOULETTE. Let's see you try.

PASSE-PARTOUT. *You* won't stop me. I'll make you crawl too, I'll make you
shiver. Get out of my way.

CIBOULETTE. No.

PASSE-PARTOUT. Get out of my way, or else I'll testify against Tarzan at the
trial.

CIBOULETTE. It doesn't matter, *three* of us will testify for him. Give back the
money. We need it for a lawyer.

PASSE-PARTOUT. They'll find him guilty anyhow. Get out of my way.

CIBOULETTE. You won't touch Moineau again.

PASSE-PARTOUT. You wanna get hit instead?

CIBOULETTE. You're afraid to hit me, you can't.

PASSE-PARTOUT. I'm not afraid.

CIBOULETTE. So look me straight in the eye.

PASSE-PARTOUT. I'm looking you straight in the eye.

CIBOULETTE. If you've never seen hate before, that's what you see right now.

PASSE-PARTOUT. Right now I see that you'll love me, that you'll kiss me too
one day.

CIBOULETTE. That's because you don't see good. If you looked good, you'd see
a snake wrapped around you, ready to strangle you.

PASSE-PARTOUT. You make me laugh.

CIBOULETTE. So laugh. (*She spits in his face.*)

PASSE-PARTOUT. (*Gripped with rage.*) Ciboulette! You don't spit in your leader's face!
MOINEAU. Leave her alone, Passe-Partout!

PASSE-PARTOUT grabs her by the neck.

PASSE-PARTOUT. You'll be punished. Now *I'll* do the strangling.
MOINEAU. (*Looks on helplessly, at a loss for what to do.*) You asked for it.

*MOINEAU throws himself on PASSE-PARTOUT. Armed with sudden strength,
MOINEAU clutches him in both arms, then gives him one violent shove. PASSE-
PARTOUT is thrown five or six feet and practically loses his balance. He cries out in
rage and frustration.*

PASSE-PARTOUT. I'm the Chief!...I give the orders and you'll obey me, you
hear?!...I'm your Chief, I'm your...

*But they have stopped listening to him. Instead, they are alerted to TIT-NOIR who
races towards them, running and speaking all at once.*

TIT-NOIR. Tarzan's escaped. Tarzan's escaped...Tarzan got away! Listen, guys,
Tarzan has escaped. He's escaped!

*TIT-NOIR appears at the fence, noble and courageous like a messenger out of a
Greek tragedy.*

MOINEAU. For real?

*This is bad news for PASSE-PARTOUT. He recovers, then quietly sneaks away left,
and disappears.*

TIT-NOIR. I was at home listening to the radio, they stopped the program to
make the announcement.
CIBOULETTE. (*In awe.*) They stopped the program?
TIT-NOIR. Yes. They said, "A young criminal has escaped from the prison
where he has been detained pending his forthcoming trial." Then they gave
his name and description and said the police are going after him.
MOINEAU. Are you sure they meant *him*?
TIT-NOIR. Yes, Moineau.
CIBOULETTE. You think he'll come here?
TIT-NOIR. Could be. He'll need money to leave the country.
MOINEAU. (*Becomes aware of PASSE-PARTOUT's disappearance.*) Tit-Noir!
Passe-Partout is gone. He's got our money.
TIT-NOIR. What do you mean? The cash box was there yesterday.

CIBOULETTE. Passe-Partout was just here. He ran away when he heard the
news.

TIT-NOIR enters the shed.

TIT-NOIR. (*Returns.*) You're right. He stole it all.
MOINEAU. We've got to find him.
TIT-NOIR. Yes. Stay here, Ciboulette, wait for Tarzan. If he gets here before
us, tell him we'll soon be back.
CIBOULETTE. Yes, but hurry, we don't have time to lose.
TIT-NOIR. We won't be long.

*They leave. CIBOULETTE moves slowly, dreamily, downstage. There is music in
the background. Then the music is quickly drowned out by the roar of police sirens.
CIBOULETTE halts. She listens as the sound draws closer. She moves rapidly
towards the back and sees a police car approach. The car stops nearby. A door slams
shut. Then CIBOULETTE moves to TARZAN's throne and sits with both hands on her
knees. She does not stir. LEDOUX enters carrying a flashlight and revolver. He halts
in his footsteps and looks at CIBOULETTE. He makes a bee-line for the shed and
enters. CIBOULETTE rises and moves quickly to the fence. She leans against it close
to the opening. She looks into the distance, surveys the surrounding area, watching
out for Tarzan. The door of the shed opens and LEDOUX comes out. CIBOULETTE
flattens herself against the fence and feigns innocence. She gazes towards the
far right.*

LEDOUX. You shouldn't be here. You hear me? You should be at home.
CIBOULETTE. There's nothing to do at home. I'd rather be here.

LEDOUX moves to exit then turns about.

LEDOUX. We'll catch him you know and if he resists, we'll shoot him down like
a dog.
CIBOULETTE. Who're you talking about?
LEDOUX. You know damn well who I'm talking about.

*He exits running. We hear the car door shut. The automobile starts up and drives
away accompanied by the roar of the siren. Music fades in. CIBOULETTE moves
downstage once more. She suddenly hears her name. The music comes to a halt.*

TARZAN. (*Off.*) Ciboulette!
CIBOULETTE. Tarzan! Where are you?
TARZAN. (*Off.*) Here, on the other side of the shed. Are they all gone?
CIBOULETTE. Yes. You can come out now.

TARZAN appears on the roof where he first appeared in Act I.

TARZAN. I was hiding. I heard what he said.

CIBOULETTE. Did you recognize him?

TARZAN. Yeah. (*He drops down into the yard.*) I didn't see his face but I recognized his voice.

CIBOULETTE. You've run a long way. You're tired?

TARZAN. Yeah, Ciboulette.

CIBOULETTE. Your throne is still there, you can sit down.

TARZAN. Yeah, I'll sit, Ciboulette.

CIBOULETTE. Tit-Noir and Moineau are chasing Passe-Partout. He ran away with our money.

TARZAN. They'll be back soon?

CIBOULETTE. As soon as they catch him. They know you escaped and you need money to get away.

TARZAN. They don't have to go to all that trouble.

CIBOULETTE. Of course they do. If you can get across the border, you'll have to eat, take a train, stay at a hotel.

TARZAN. I told you it's not necessary.

CIBOULETTE. I don't understand.

TARZAN. I'll explain later. We have other things to talk about now.

The sound of sirens is heard.

CIBOULETTE. Sirens...they're going away...they're far away now.

TARZAN. They'll search somewhere else in the meantime, then they'll be back, you'll see.

The sound of the sirens fades out.

CIBOULETTE. I knew you'd escape.

TARZAN. They got me with all their talk and their questions, but I fixed them.

CIBOULETTE. How did you do it?

TARZAN. I'd been planning it for three days. I thought about it all the time. And tonight I tried my luck, took a chance, and I made it. It happened like in a movie. When the guard came to bring me supper, I pretended I was asleep and just as he was about to leave, I jumped him like a tiger, and knocked him out. The rest was luck and nerve...Now I'm here, Ciboulette.

CIBOULETTE. Yes, Tarzan.

Pause.

TARZAN. Ciboulette. You know what the police told me?

CIBOULETTE. No.

TARZAN. That you would have betrayed me if they'd kept you any longer. Is
     that true?
CIBOULETTE. You believed them?
TARZAN. No, but I asked myself a lot of questions in prison.
CIBOULETTE. If I had betrayed you, I would've died.
TARZAN. Did they hurt you?
CIBOULETTE. It's over…I don't want to talk about it.

Silence.

TARZAN. Ciboulette! I want to ask you something…You're not ashamed of me?
CIBOULETTE. Why should I be?
TARZAN. Because I killed a man.
CIBOULETTE. If you hadn't killed him, wouldn't he have killed you?
TARZAN. I don't know any more…I thought about you a lot in prison.
CIBOULETTE. Yes?
TARZAN. I thought about escaping, and you. I knew that Passe-Partout
     betrayed me, but I didn't think about that. I said to myself: Ciboulette is
     all alone now. I thought: Tit-Noir and Moineau can't help her and Passe-
     Partout will try to hurt her…I thought: maybe she's unhappy and it's my
     fault. They're all unhappy and I did it to them. They have a bad name now;
     their lives are no longer the same. And I said to myself: I'd like to get out
     and see Ciboulette, take her hand and go to the movies to see a jungle film,
     or a film about love…I want her to be happy, I want to be happy too, like
     everybody else walking on the street on Saturday night…And I said it over
     and over again and I couldn't stop thinking of you.
CIBOULETTE. I've been thinking about you for a long time, Tarzan. From the
     very first day, I've held you in my heart.
TARZAN. And you never told me?
CIBOULETTE. I tried, but I couldn't.
TARZAN. Why not?
CIBOULETTE. It was too hard. I was afraid of the words.
TARZAN. And now that I'm condemned to die, and the police are looking for
     me, can you say them now?
CIBOULETTE. Yes. Because you began first. Because I feel so calm tonight. I'm
     calm because you're with me, because you said you were thinking of me.
TARZAN. I'm calm too, because we're all alone for the first time. For the first
     time in my life I'm going to tell a girl that I love her.
CIBOULETTE. Tarzan! Look at me first, look at me good. I'm ugly, my hair is
     straight like strings, and my teeth are crooked. Look at me!
TARZAN. I *am* looking at you, Ciboulette, and I see you as I've always seen you.
     True, you're not beautiful like the women in the movies, but your name is
     Ciboulette and your eyes are full of light.
CIBOULETTE. Hold me, Tarzan.

TARZAN. Let me look at you first. I want to have your image firm in my mind
    before I touch you. I close my eyes, I look inside my head to make sure that
    all the colours are there, that your features are engraved like on a sculp-
    ture, that nothing's missing. It's all there now, Ciboulette. I open my eyes
    and the picture hasn't changed; there's only one Ciboulette, but she's in two
    places at the same time: here in front of me and inside my head. In front of
    me for just one minute but inside me forever. (*He goes towards her and takes
    her head in his hands.*)
CIBOULETTE. Kiss me softly. (*He kisses her lips gently.*) Now kiss me hard like
    a real lover. (*He kisses her. Then she pulls away.*) Am I doing it right? Do I look
    like a real lover?
TARZAN. Yes, Ciboulette.
CIBOULETTE. Am I sensible, too?
TARZAN. More than any other girl.
CIBOULETTE. What does sensible mean?
TARZAN. It means "someone who understands."
CIBOULETTE. Kiss me again, Tarzan.

They embrace. Then they hear voices and they separate.

TIT-NOIR. We got him, we got him, Tarzan.

MOINEAU and TIT-NOIR enter holding PASSE-PARTOUT between them.

MOINEAU. He was hiding in Johnny's yard.
PASSE-PARTOUT. Let me go, you're hurting me, let me go!
MOINEAU. Yeah, sure we'll let you go. Hold on.

*MOINEAU throws TIT-NOIR a look. TIT-NOIR understands the signal. Together
they give him one hard shove and PASSE-PARTOUT falls flat on his face at
TARZAN's feet.*

MOINEAU. Here he is, Chief.
TIT-NOIR. Special delivery.

*A long pause. TARZAN thinks things over and says nothing. PASSE-PARTOUT does
not dare get up.*

MOINEAU. What'll we do with him, Chief?
TARZAN. (*In a voice unlike his own.*) Don't call me Chief, call me Tarzan.
TIT-NOIR. You want us to beat the hell out of him, Tarzan?
TARZAN. No. There's no time for that, we'd only dirty our hands. (*To PASSE-
    PARTOUT.*) Get up, Passe-Partout. (*PASSE-PARTOUT rises slowly, very much
    afraid.*) Hand over the money.

PASSE-PARTOUT. What money, Tarzan? I've got no money.

TARZAN. You know what I mean. Hand it over. Fast. We're in a hurry! All of it! (*PASSE-PARTOUT slowly draws the money out of his pocket and hands it to TARZAN.*) Now you can go, Passe-Partout.

MOINEAU and TIT-NOIR express surprise.

TIT-NOIR. What!

TARZAN. Go, right now, Passe-Partout, because if you're not gone in ten seconds, I'll beat the hell out of you.

PASSE-PARTOUT looks at the others and backs out. TIT-NOIR kicks him in the shins and trips him.

PASSE-PARTOUT. No, don't hit me! Don't hit me!

TARZAN. Tit-Noir! Let him go...*I give the orders around here.*

PASSE-PARTOUT. (*Climbing to his feet.*) Thank you, Tarzan, thank you, I didn't betray you, I didn't betray you...it wasn't me...I didn't squeal...

TARZAN. (*Cries loudly.*) Get out!

PASSE-PARTOUT runs off.

CIBOULETTE. Now, you must go too. You're in danger if you stay here any longer.

TARZAN. Not yet. I'll divide the money up first.

TIT-NOIR. You're crazy!

MOINEAU. We don't want it. You need it, not us.

TARZAN. You need it as much as me, and who gave you permission to answer back?...Here, Tit-Noir, take this. (*He offers him a wad of bills.*)

TIT-NOIR. No, Tarzan, I won't take it.

TARZAN. This is the last time I'll be asking you to obey me, Tit-Noir. The last time...Take it: you'll need it if you want to get married some day. (*He puts the money inside TIT-NOIR's pocket.*) Now for your share, Moineau. With this, you'll study music, and become a good musician and no one'll ever tell you you don't know how to play.

MOINEAU. When you're gone, I won't care about music.

TARZAN. By tomorrow you'll forget what you just said. Take your money, you earned it. (*TARZAN forces the money into MOINEAU's hand, then turns his back on them and moves a bit upstage.*) There's one last thing you can do for me...I want you to leave me alone with Ciboulette. Go, don't say a word, it's the only favour I'm asking you.

TIT-NOIR. Tarzan, I...

TARZAN. Do what I ask, Tit-Noir.

MOINEAU. (*To TIT-NOIR.*) Come...Goodbye, Chief...Good luck, Tarzan. (*He puts the harmonica to his lips, begins to play, and leaves slowly.*)
TIT-NOIR. Goodbye, Tarzan...Be careful...

They exit. The music fades. CIBOULETTE turns to TARZAN.

CIBOULETTE. Why did you do that?
TARZAN. The rest is for you...I never gave you anything...It'll be my first gift. Buy yourself anything you want...Don't give any of it to your parents...Buy a dress, a necklace, a bracelet...buy yourself new shoes and a little hat for Sundays.

TARZAN puts the money into her hand and closes her fingers over it.

CIBOULETTE. You've changed so much in just one minute.
TARZAN. I didn't come here to take the money, I came to kiss you and tell you I love you.
CIBOULETTE. Then you must go and if you really love me, you'll take me with you. The money'll be for both of us.
TARZAN. I can't do that, Ciboulette.
CIBOULETTE. Why not?
TARZAN. Because I'm done for. You don't think I can get away, do you?
CIBOULETTE. *You* can do anything you want to.
TARZAN. Wake up, Ciboulette, that's all over now. My name is François Boudreau, I killed a man, I escaped from prison and I'm sure they'll shoot me.
CIBOULETTE. No, to me, you're still Tarzan.
TARZAN. No. I'm not Tarzan. Can't you see I've become a coward?
CIBOULETTE. No, you're not a coward. You're afraid, that's all. I was afraid too when they questioned me. I was so afraid to betray you that my blood ran cold.
TARZAN. I promised you a good life, and I couldn't give it to you. I failed, it's all my fault.
CIBOULETTE. Passe-Partout betrayed you, it's *his* fault.
TARZAN. If he hadn't betrayed me, they'd have gotten me some other way. That's why I didn't punish him and that's why I don't want your money. I wouldn't touch money that doesn't mean anything to me, because it's all over now. I killed a man! Had I loved you, I wouldn't have killed. I realized that in prison. But it's too late.
CIBOULETTE. You mean we could've been married and had children?
TARZAN. Maybe.
CIBOULETTE. And now we can't?
TARZAN. No. Never.

CIBOULETTE. Tarzan! Let's get married, right now. Come to our castle, we
still have a few moments to live our love. Come.
TARZAN. You'd be twice as unhappy afterwards.
CIBOULETTE. I don't care. I'm only a young girl, I'm not sensible or beautiful,
but I can give you my life.
TARZAN. No, *you* must live. Your eyes are full of life. You must be as strong as
you always were, even if I must leave you forever.
CIBOULETTE. When a boy and girl really love each other, they must live *and*
die together; otherwise it's not true love.

The sound of sirens is heard.

TARZAN. What I once told you is true, anyone in love with me is bound to be
unhappy.
CIBOULETTE. No. This is a bad dream, we must wake up before it's too late.
TARZAN. It *is* too late, Ciboulette. Listen, you can hear the sirens. Moineau,
Tit-Noir, Passe-Partout are gone, I'll never see them again. We're now lost
and alone in the very yard where we dreamed of being happy one day.
You're here in my arms, shivering from the cold like a little bird. My eyes
are wide open, I can see the houses, the darkness, and you. I know that I'm
going to die, but my only wish is that you stay in my arms.
CIBOULETTE. Kiss me...one last time...so I won't hear the voices of death. (*He
kisses her, in an act of hopeless love.*) Now, you'll go, Tarzan. You'll overcome
your fears. You won't think about me any more. You're clever enough to
escape.

The sirens draw closer.

TARZAN. So you'll have believed in me 'til the very end. I shouldn't've come
back, Ciboulette; it would've been less painful for you.
CIBOULETTE. No, Tarzan, you did the right thing. What's important now is
that you leave.
TARZAN. You're right, Ciboulette.

TARZAN *releases her and moves towards the fence. He looks out for a moment, then
returns.*

TARZAN. It won't be long now. In five minutes this place will be swarming
with cops. I can feel them coming now.
CIBOULETTE. You must hurry.
TARZAN. Yes, Ciboulette.

He draws away from her and moves to the left. He looks into the lane then returns.

TARZAN. They'll spot me there right away.

CIBOULETTE. On the roof, the way you came.

TARZAN. Yes, there's no other way.

He edges towards the roof, looks about, then approaches his throne, lifts the box, takes his revolver and returns to CIBOULETTE.

TARZAN. Listen. I know they'll get me 'round some corner or other...If I *could* escape, I would, but it's impossible.

CIBOULETTE. You have one chance in a hundred and you've got to take it.

TARZAN. No. It's too late. I'd rather die here, than on the street.

He checks the revolver and puts it in his pocket.

TARZAN. I'll wait for them. When they get here, shut yourself up in the shed so you won't get hurt. If they fire at me, I'll defend myself to the very end; if they don't, I'll surrender and they'll take me away.

The sound of the sirens fades out.

CIBOULETTE. You're a coward, Tarzan.

TARZAN. Ciboulette!

CIBOULETTE. You don't want to take a chance any more, you don't want to fight, you've become weak. That's why you gave me the money. Take back your money and save yourself!

TARZAN. It won't do me any good.

CIBOULETTE. If you're still a man, do as I say. It'll help you live in another place, it'll help you stay alive.

TARZAN. It's no use trying to live when you know you've killed somebody.

CIBOULETTE. You're looking for a way out to justify your cowardice. Take your money and try to get away.

TARZAN. No.

CIBOULETTE. Yes. (*She throws the money at him.*) It's yours, not mine. I didn't work for money, I worked for *you*. I worked for a Chief. You're not a Chief any more.

TARZAN. We only had one minute left, and you destroyed it.

CIBOULETTE. Like you'll destroy my whole life, if you choose to surrender.

TARZAN. You're *also* betraying me, Ciboulette. You're all the same; you, Passe-Partout, everyone. I'm all alone like I was at the police station. Let them come now, let them take me away! (*He walks about the stage.*) What are you waiting for?! Why don't you shoot? I know you're there, I know you're all over the place. Go ahead and shoot...

CIBOULETTE. (*Throws herself at him.*) Tarzan, it's not true what I just said. Please go, you have a chance, take it, if you love me...I love you with all my

heart...and that's why I want you to go; maybe somewhere there's a place
where you can live. I would die right now, if I knew, just for one moment,
that you would live.

TARZAN looks at her for a moment, takes her head in his hands and kisses her gently.

TARZAN. Bonsoir, Ciboulette.
CIBOULETTE. Bonsoir, François...

*TARZAN climbs up to the roof, and disappears. A smile lights up CIBOULETTE's
face.*

CIBOULETTE. He'll get through, he's bound to get through...Tarzan is a man.
Nothing can stop him. Tarzan is the strongest of them all. He'll never die.
(*Three gun shots ring out.*) Tarzan! Tarzan, come back! (*Pause.*) Tarzan!
Answer me!...It's not my fault...it's because I believed in you so much.
He can't hear me...Death has taken him away, death has stolen his heart.
Sleep...and I shall keep watch over you...I don't know how to love you like
a real lover, I know I'm not sensible, I'm not even pretty. I can't do anything
right. I wanted to save you, but I lost you instead. Part of me has died with
you. Sleep and let my image remain with you forever.

Breaking Constraints of Race and Theatrical Form
at the Black Theatre Workshop

CLARENCE S. BAYNE

1. One production influenced by these three productions was *Seashango*, written in the early 1960s by Errol Sitahal, and directed by Sitahal on December 8, 1974, at Revue Theatre. The script was based on African beliefs and West African religious tradition. Another early production was *The Black Experience*, which I wrote and directed, and in 1975 also premiered at Revue Theatre. *The Black Experience* was based on African American and Caribbean rhythms as well as the dramatic tension between Christian religious beliefs and traditional African belief system.

THE BLACK THEATRE WORKSHOP (Le Theatre BTW Inc.) evolved out of the experiments of the Black Workshops of the Drama Committee of the Trinidad and Tobago (T-and-T) Association, Montreal (October 1965–1985). It is the oldest surviving professional English-speaking Black theatre company in Canada (Bayne 2001). The year 2018 marked the fiftieth anniversary of its existence as the Black Theatre Workshop and its forty-eighth professional season. The association was created to meet the needs of Trinidadian students, scholars, and cultural leaders seeking to honour and remain connected to their Caribbean culture in Montreal. This desire to connect with Caribbean culture is evident in the T-and-T Association's production of Johnny Cayonne's two "calypsoperas": *Calypso in the Flesh* (at the Revue Theatre, Montreal, September 1, 2, and 9, 1966), and *Fact and Fancy* (at Westmount High School, Montreal, June 26–29, 1968). *How Now Black Man* by Lorris Elliott was conceived, written, and workshopped between 1967 and 1969. An important contribution to this creative moment, *How Now Black Man*, along with Cayonne's "calypsoperas," established the artistic style of the emerging Black Theatre Workshop—an artistic style that lasted well into the next decade.[1]

It took several years to develop *How Now Black Man*, which began as an ambitious and innovative concept originally shaped in a basement apartment in the McGill University student ghetto in 1964 and was chosen to be the first production presented by the Black Workshop of the T-and-T Association (thus the name Black Theatre Workshop, or BTW). The script was completed in 1969 and offered to the CBC, but it was rejected as not suitable for TV. That same year, the Drama Committee of the T-and-T Association called a meeting to announce the departure of Cayonne for Toronto and to discuss plans for a permanent Black Workshop, which would be administered by the Drama Committee, and would be dedicated to creating Black Canadian performing arts and literature. The plan was approved, establishing the framework for the workshopping of *How Now Black Man*.

By mid-1969, three professional artists from Trinidad and Tobago, who were working and living in Montreal, were recruited to help stage *How Now Black Man*: Herbert Webb, teacher of drama and English, Vanier College; Errol Sitahal, actor and drama teacher, Vanier College; and Cynthia Allen, actress, director, and film scriptwriter, in Communications Arts, Loyola Campus. Later,

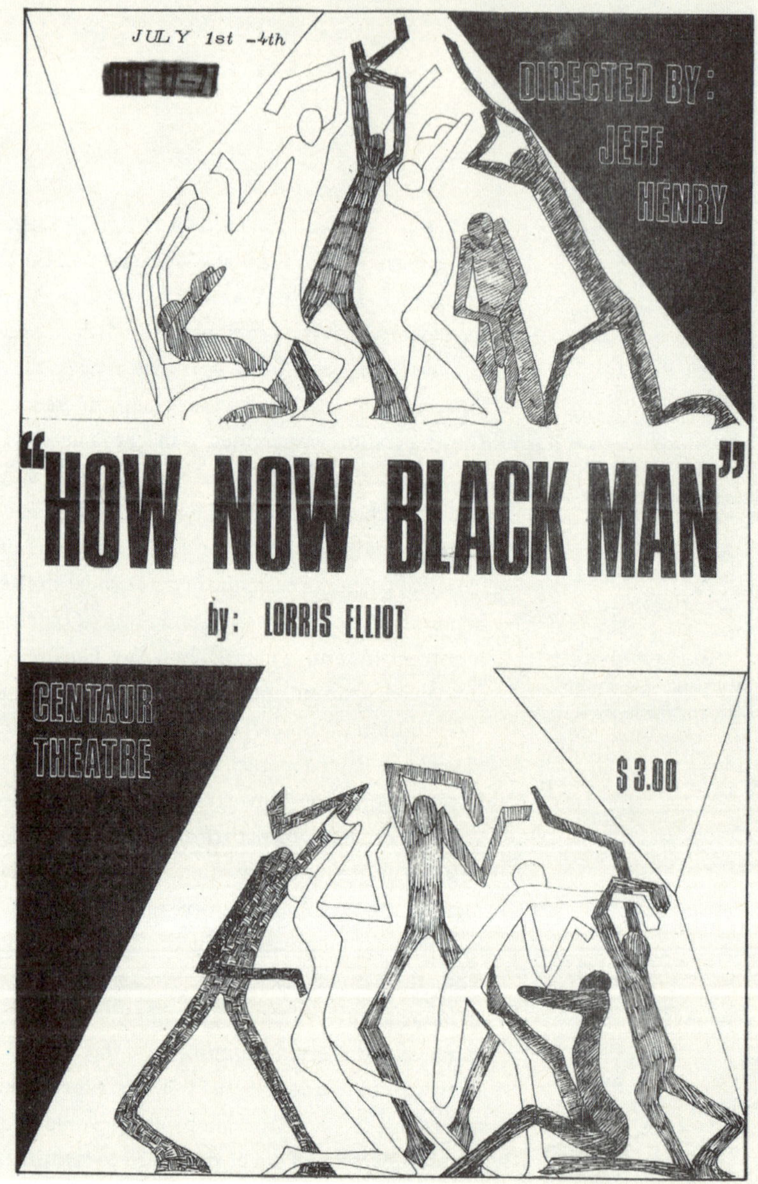

FIGURE 29.1: *Original poster for* How Now Black Man *at the Black Theatre Workshop, Montreal, 1970. Graphic Design by Robert Ruckus.* Courtesy of the Black Theatre Workshop.

2. Literary critics have stated that although reading Harris's work is challenging, it is rewarding in many ways. Harris has been admired for his exploration of the themes of conquest and colonization as well as the struggles of colonized peoples. See Harris 1985.

3. Prior to the T-and-T Drama Committee Black Workshops (1968), there were Black minstrel shows in Montreal and Quebec performed by Black American minstrels. Most importantly—and more respectfully—the Negro Theatre Guild/Negro Theatre Club emerged in Little Burgundy's Black neighbourhoods out of the local Blacks' (racialized as coloured and negro) interest in theatre for teaching Black pride, as well as for cultural expression, enlightenment, and social development.

4. In the winter of 1969, over two hundred students occupied the ninth floor of the Henry F. Hall Building on the campus of Sir George Williams University (now part of Concordia University) in Montreal. The students were protesting racial discrimination at the university after six students had lodged a complaint of racism against a biology professor. The university reviewed and ultimately rejected the complaint. The sit-in was the students' response. The police eventually intervened and a violent clash ensued. This incident is generally viewed as a pivotal moment in the history of Black activism in Canada.

Jeff Henry, choreographer and dance master at the National Theatre School, joined the workshops on my invitation and became the director of Lorris Elliott's play.

Elliott was born on December 30, 1931, in Scarborough, in the Republic of Trinidad and Tobago. By fourteen, he had completed high school. He came to Canada in the late 1950s, enrolled at the University of British Columbia in Vancouver, and was awarded a BA (with honours) in English in 1962. He then moved to Montreal in 1964 as a lecturer at McDonald College, McGill University. He submitted a thesis on James Baldwin to UBC for his MA in English in 1965. He later enrolled in the University of Montreal where he received his PHD in 1974, specializing in twentieth-century literature. His thesis, "Time, Self, and Narrative: A Study of Wilson Harris's 'Guiana Quartet,'" is a study of the renowned Guyanese poet and novelist.[2] Harris's epic style greatly influenced the style used in *How Now Black Man* and Elliott's other work (Metzger, n.d.).

How Now Black Man is of critical importance because in the context of Black Canadian literature it is a deliberate break with classical British style and form in playwrighting. Moreover, it was written by a West Indian immigrant teaching English literature at McGill University, and was produced, directed, and performed mostly by Blacks from the African diaspora. It reinforced and extended the search that I conducted with Arthur Goddard, Johnny Cayonne, and Leon St. Martin for a uniquely Afro-Caribbean theatre rooted in Trinidad traditions of social rebellion and criticism (Liverpool 1990) that combined fact and fantasy (Rohlehr 1990). After a year of creating the management structure of the Black Workshop, and six months of training in diction, singing, movement, dance, acting, and drumming, the artists involved opened *How Now Black Man* at the Centaur Theatre in June 1970. Inspired by the success of the production, and acting on behalf of the expanded Black Workshop membership, I convinced the T-and-T Association to accept a proposal for the Black Workshop to become an independent theatre company. In 1972 the Black Theatre Workshop of Montreal was incorporated as a non-profit company and continues to operate to this day.

The Black Theatre Workshop was not the first group to present theatre by or about people of African ancestry in Montreal or Canada.[3] But in terms of its longevity, it surpasses any other known Black theatre company. Its initial style and mission were radical Black theatre. In its early years, the company's revolutionary and celebrative confidence reflected the Black power movement of the 1960s that was partly responsible for the Sir George Williams student riot of 1969.[4] The aims and artistic orientation of the Black Theatre Workshop differed significantly from the American avant-garde style of the Revue Theatre and the traditional Black American plays (e.g., *All God's Chillun Got Wings* and *The Emperor Jones*) of the Negro Theatre Club that preceded it. These two companies produced work that may be considered inspirational theatre: informing, enlightening, thought-provoking, and socially provocative. But it

5. The play *How Now Black Man*, which follows this introduction, refers to itself as a "series of things."

6. Elliott spoke with the author about *How Now Black Man* numerous times over the years since the production's premiere.

7. Elliott later acknowledged that he liked the presentational aspects of Henry's directing but felt that it tended to detract from the meaning and intent of the work (Elliott in conversation with the author).

8. In their speeches and writings, Malcolm X and Stokely Carmichael, who were prominent leaders in the civil rights movement in the United States, justified the use of violence by oppressed peoples as part of liberation from slavery and the owners of capital. Elliott's Black struggle was more transformative and all-inclusive of humanity.

was not Black radicalism or revolutionary theatre in the sense that the Black Theatre Workshop productions were.

The Black Theatre Workshop entered the Montreal arts scene in the mid-1960s at a time of questioning, a time of "the rhetoric of NO" (Fabrizio, Karkas, and Menmuir 1970) on North American campuses. The countries of the Black diaspora were experiencing a transformation from Crown colony government and colonial capitalism to various forms of social and political independence. Therefore, it is not surprising that Caribbean scholars on Montreal campuses created cultural instruments like plays, or "series of things,"[5] that for a Black theatre workshop based on Afro-Caribbean cultures would be seen as a potent tool to fight against class injustice, the so-called cultural superiority of imperial forces, colonial capitalism, and Eurocentrism.

Cayonne's *Calypso in the Flesh* and *Fact and Fancy* used African and Caribbean movement, the "*kaiso*," and Caribbean folklore to tell stories about life in the West Indies. Several years later, my play *The Black Experience* built on this style using stories from the Caribbean and Afro-American ghettos. It explored the conflict between the indolence of Colonial American Negroes and revolutionary African American Blacks (Jones 1963) using song, dance, and the spoken word rooted in the rhythmic structures of the calypso and reggae traditions. *The Black Experience* is about liberation.

How Now Black Man also addresses issues of liberation and reconciliation, but on a universal level. As Elliott explained, *How Now Black Man* is about the conflict of opposites: disharmony based on power and the use of power to assign value, meaning, and rewards that reflect preferences based on non-influencing and or perceived differences.[6] It is an epic that resembles in scope and language Milton's poetic discourses in *Paradise Lost* and *Paradise Regained*. It uses a classical style that lends itself to argument (the Voice) and, at times, uses a logic and voice that are devoid of emotion or sensitivity (the Man). This structure seems intended to symbolize the functionalism of art and life in Western and European civilizations. But Jeff Henry, the director of *How Now Black Man* and a specialist in Black and African dance forms, gave preference to dance and movement, seemingly moderating the centrality of the voice of reason. This choice became a point of conflict between the dance choreographer and the playwright, and the cancellation of the play was only narrowly avoided.[7]

To understand Elliott's views, one needs to know that he did not support actions to ascribe futility to the Black and Caribbean experience or the human experience more generally. He saw the human struggle as essential and central to human evolution: a response to challenges on the journey in the search for "paradise lost." In this way, *How Now Black Man* is about Blacks and the Black struggle, but not a promotion of the Malcolm X or Stokely Carmichael conceptualizations of Black power.[8] Elliott's central purpose, in other words, was to explore the conflict that arises between opposites: a life near to and in harmony with nature versus life evolving away from nature and

9. Wilson Harris described his writing as epic with nonlinear events/happenings and metaphor as a substantive component of his prose/dialogue. See Harris 1985; Ashcroft 1989.

out of harmony with nature. *How Now Black Man* deals with matters of life and death that apply to all humanity (Elliott 1971).

This expansive and inclusive approach is evident in the structure of *How Now Black Man*. Acts are replaced by a "series of things": happenings that allow an interpretation of life emerging out of and responding to a multiplicity of unpredictable events. It is a literary style akin to what Wilson Harris (1985) has described as "quantum writing,"[9] which allows the author great flexibility. Elliott uses a combination of directorial text and the logic of a disembodied mind (the Voice) that moves from the subconscious to conscious self to provide a ritual language. Symbolically, events happen around the construct of a pyramid of actors that symbolizes a Maslowian hierarchy of the needs of humanity, while also serving as a literary device similar to the chorus in early Greek tragedy.

Encapsulating Elliott's views, the rituals of Thing Four, the final happening in *How Now Black Man*, demonstrate how self-righteousness and refusal to respect the humanity of others eventually becomes self-destruction. The character named Figure 3 in the play encounters death and cries out for help:

> *Come spirits of the dark. Kind spirits, come; pull off the mask and let myself emerge, born into new life, strengthened and refreshed. Pull off the mask. (Pulls desperately at it.) Unmask me here and let me breathe the wholesome air again.*

As this character seeks and finds redemption, the actor falls "into the general pattern of the dance which is being performed by the others." Through reconciliation, they become one with the now fully formed "pyramid of humanity." And so Endeth the Final Thing.

Bibliography and Further Reading

Adler, Joyce Sparer. 2003. *Exploring the Palace of the Peacock: Essays on Wilson Harris.* Kingston: University of the West Indies Press.

Ashcroft, Bill, Gareth Griffiths, and Helen Tiffin. 1989. *The Empire Writes Back: Theory and Practice in Post-Colonial Literatures.* London: Routledge.

Austen, David. 2013. *Fear of a Black Nation: Race, Sex, and Security in Sixties Montreal.* Toronto: Between the Lines.

Bayne, Clarence. 1968. "The Roots of White Racism." *Expression* (Winter): 7–9. https://bscportal.files.wordpress.com/2015/08/expression-special-conference-1968-papers.pdf.

———. 2001. "Le Black Theatre Workshop de Montréal: Un nouveau bilan." *Annuaire* 29 (Printemps): 141–42.

Best, Lloyd, and Winston Franco. 1968. "Two Views of the Conference of Black Writers." *Expression* (Winter): 33–47. https://bscportal.files.wordpress.com/2015/08/expression-special-conference-1968-papers.pdf.

Black, Ayanna, ed. 1992. *Voices: Canadian Writers of African Descent.* Toronto: HarperCollins.

Elliott, Lorris. 1971. Notes about the play, Theatre program, "How Now Black Man." Centaur Theatre.

———. 1982. *Coming for to Carry, A Novel in Five Parts*. Toronto: William-Wallace.

Elliott, Lorris, ed. 1985. *Other Voices: Writings by Blacks in Canada*. Toronto: William-Wallace.

Fabrizio, Ray, Edith Karkas, and Ruth Menmuir. 1970. *The Rhetoric of NO*. New York: Holt, Rinehart and Winston.

Harris, Wilson. 1960. *Palace of the Peacock*. London: Faber & Faber.

———. 1985. *Carnival*. London: Faber & Faber.

———. 1990. *The Four Banks of the River of Space*. London: Faber & Faber.

Hebert, Paul. 2015. "A Microcosm of the General Struggle: Black Thought and Activism in Montreal, 1960–1969." PHD diss., University of Michigan.

"How Now Black Man." 1971. Theatre program, Centaur Theatre.

James, C.L.R. 1938. *Black Jacobins: Tousaint L'Ouverture and the San Domingo Revolution*. London: Secker & Warburg.

Jones, LeRoi. 1963. *Blues People: The Negro Experience in White America and the Music That Developed from It*. New York: William Morrows.

Liverpool, Hollis U.L. 1990. *Kaiso and Society*. Diego Martin, Trinidad: Juba.

Metzger, Sheri Elaine. n.d. "Elliott, Lorris 1931–1999." Contemporary Black Bibliography. Encyclopedia.com. Accessed October 25, 2021. https://www.encyclopedia.com/education/news-wires-white-papers-and-books/elliott-lorris-1931-1999.

Naipaul V.S. 1963. *The Middle Passage: The Caribbean Revisited*. London: A. Deutsch.

———. 1967. *The Mimic Men*. London: A. Deutsch.

Rohlehr, Gordon. 1990. *Calypso and Society in Pre-independence Trinidad*. Port of Spain, Trinidad: G. Rohlehr.

Williams, Eric. 1994. *Capitalism and Slavery*. Chapel Hill: University North Carolina Press.

How Now Black Man

LORRIS ELLIOTT

A PROLOGUE
To a series of "things" that happen on stage

Now that the entire audience (if any at all turns up) is seated in their respective places (or not), all the lights go out. Total silence prevails. Then, quite unexpectedly, a voice, coming from all corners of the hall, not very loud but quite distinct and without any emotional inflexions:

VOICE. Mankind, (*A pause.*) I cannot say, "welcome here now" because where we are at and when involves no here and now. In fact, though in space, we're out of space; and, though in time, we're out of time. Here, there, anywhere, nowhere, somewhere, now, then, soon, am, was and always will be—that's where we're at and when, assembled not to witness a performance or to listen to some long awaited message or to purge some basic fears or guilt but to experience entirely and collectively things happening here on stage out of life but in life—life itself in time and out of time— things which for the necessity of identity we have labelled with a question to which there is no answer given nor ever was nor ever will be; in fact, no question either; nor statement too; just another thing—just another being. (*Lights go on in the audience.*) Ladies and gentlemen, "How Now Black Man" is not a play, a piece of propaganda, musical, ballet, nor opera; it is just a thing made up of happenings involving several actors here on stage—in fact, several black actors, not to raise issues but to draw you into life and death for a brief while. (*Total darkness again; the voice continues.*) And now mankind, and now mankindand nowmankindand nowmankind and now— (*Voice fades off as if some hand has lifted the arm from off a well-worn disc.*)

The stage (representing somewhere anywhere anytime) is completely black. Drum beats, slow and heavily pulsating, are heard in the background. Gradually the blackness of the stage gives way to a dark-bluish lighting; the beat of the drums increases in tempo. Eventually, against the bluish background, the dim outline of several human forms can be seen slumped in various postures of apathy (or perhaps, resignation).

Soon the blue lighting of the stage changes to a lurid yellow which steadily increases in intensity (somewhat like the rising sun). The tempo of the drumming rises to a frenzy.

At this point, the slumped bodies betray some movement (though barely perceptible) as if some reptilian forms of life, emerging from their calcic encasements, were slowly twitching themselves to life. Moreover, faint whimperings can be heard.

Suddenly the crescendo of drumming stops. An extremely bright light at rear center stage bursts into brilliance, dazzling the audience for a while. A long piercing cry is heard (apparently coming from all angles of the stage). As the light decreases in intensity and the screaming ceases as abruptly as it had begun, the audience discerns several black bodies dressed in black tights and gazing upwards in the attitude of adoration.

Music (an ensemble of instruments and voices) is now heard; it is obviously jazz, but with sacred overtones (something like "Cristo Redentor" or the Donald Byrd album, A New Perspective). The actors, until then rigidly stationary, begin a carefully rehearsed series of rhythmic movements, yet remaining rooted to their respective spots. They are very self-confident, full of pride and dignity in their performance. Each, however, is completely self-involved, very conscious of his own physical attractiveness and completely oblivious of the others and of the audience.

On closer examination, one recognizes that these actors, though all Negroes, differ considerably in physical appearance. In fact, the various ethnic strains that have filtered into their Negro stock can be detected. Few, however, have preserved the original characteristics untainted.

As the music swings into a more relaxed tempo, they begin to hum (or to chant) obviously quite touched by the beauty of the tune. Gradually, as they begin to weave in and out among each other, they seem to become aware of each other's presence. They move upstage and downstage (without any apparent pattern) as if every action was spontaneous—dictated by the dynamics of the music.

As they meet and greet each other, it is obvious that their actions and reactions are most exaggerated: attitudes of surprise, rapture, awe, and so on can be observed. Above the music, which has now quieted down considerably, popular words of welcome are heard:

VOICES. (*At intervals.*) Say hey, man. Hi, brother. Hi, sister. What's up, baby? Cool it, baby. What ya doing, manchile? Nothing, womanchile.

Soon they all have met and greeted each other. The sounds of welcome subside. Still moving as if spontaneously, each actor seems to deliberately seek his original position. Meanwhile, they resume the former attitudes of self-concern and of oblivion. One feels that one has just witnessed a brief moment of togetherness that was sincere, profound and inevitable. One also feels, however, that this subsequent withdrawal into self is also significant and inevitable.

Without any warning, the ensemble ceases its music entirely. The actors, having returned to their original positions, freeze, gazing upwards as before. The bright light at rear center stage flashes once more, dazzling all. Piercing scream is also heard. As the light decreases in intensity, drum beats can be heard in the background. The tempo is at first quite fast; but it gradually reduces itself, at the same time becoming softer. Soon it is quite slow and heavily pulsating. Now that the light no longer dazzles, one can discern against the steadily darkening background, the human forms slumped in various postures of inertia, as if some spring of life that had been set in motion within them had now wound itself out and left them, like life-size plastic dolls, crumpled helplessly on the floor.

Within a few minutes, the stage reduces itself to darkness and the drums roll to a sudden stop. And all is silent!

HERE ENDETH THE FIRST OF THE THINGS TO HAPPEN ON STAGE

***

HERE BEGINS THE SECOND "THING"

The stage is entirely black. There is a strange silence. Soon, however, sounds like the howling of wind on a tempestuous night come out of the dark. Soon other sounds, mysterious and unidentified, are heard. In fact, one seems to detect the sound of chariot wheels, as if some ancient traveller, for a long time now lost and lonely, were fighting the elements in an effort to find home. At first, it is vague and in the distance; however, it soon gets louder as if getting closer.

Then suddenly a voice is heard. It is distinct and fairly loud; in fact, it is unique and somewhat inhumanlike, like that of a broadcaster who shouts through a microphone into an echo-chamber. Moreover, there is a note of tiredness, of mild frustration and of bewilderment in it, as if some prophet, endeavouring a long time now to sing the meaning of some phenomenon coeval with time, has finally realized his failure and now gives expression to his helplessness.

VOICE. How now, black man? (*A pause. The wind continues to howl.*)
VOICE. How now, black man? (*Sounding more earnest, more intense, the voice repeats itself. A slightly longer pause. The wind again.*)
VOICE. Black man, how now? (*The wind, for a brief moment, increases in intensity and then subsides.*)

At this point, the audience becomes aware of a presence on stage. Soon the darkness lessens, revealing in dim outline, silhouettelike, a close gathering of bodies, pyramid-like. Some are sitting at the base, some squatting at different levels, others standing right up and leaning over as if to form the apex. Then in unison, as if the pyramid spoke out of its entire body up through the apex, a sound.

PYRAMID. Yea man. Black man. Black woman too. Yea, man. That we are, man. Black manchile and black womanchile. Yea man. That's where we're at man; was always at, man and will always be, man. (*The wind rises again, sounding like a most inhuman moan. Soon it subsides. A pause.*)

VOICE. Alas, black man, so true, so very true. Indeed, I know too well! (*A pause ensues. Then a tired sigh, like the wind, is heard.*)

VOICE. But who art thou, black man? Why like the night so dark? So enigmatic, like the night, deep night, mysterious night? (*The voice seems more tired than before, more earnest—almost pleading like.*).

VOICE. Alas, alas. So full of life, black man, and yet so much like death itself, so very much like death. (*Thunder, the wind again.*) Most fascinating! So often cursed, but frequently admired. So much like night; like death itself. (*The elements again rise up and then subside.*)

VOICE. (*Heartrending in its agony.*) Alas, black man. Black man, I die. Indeed, I perish fast. Blinded by the light of my intelligence, which did never penetrate thy darkness, thy blackness so profound, I grope about, floundering desperately on and drowning in the quicksands of my intellect, finding no true escape within the whiteness of the day.

A flash of lightening lights up the stage. Thunder, the wind. The pyramid still dimly visible seems to have grown in stature.

PYRAMID. Yea man. Say hey, man. But hear them drums, man.

The audience now realizes that what was the thunder has now become the obvious beating of a drum. Moreover, the howling of the winds gives way to the pleasant but unobtrusive sound of woodwinds.

PYRAMID: But hear them drums, man. The drums they talk, man; they set the rhythm, man. The darkness comes to life; the sounds of night begin. (*The darkness of the stage decreases gradually and the pyramid becomes more obvious.*) Say man, you feel the beat, man. Night beat, earth beat—boom-boom; heart beat, life beat—boom-boom; pulse beat, soul beat—boom-boom.

The stage is quite brighter now; the individuals that make up the pyramid can be distinguished. Soon, in well-rehearsed movements, the structure comes apart. Each individual continues its routine, moving to different parts of the stage, but as part of a totality of movement.

The pyramid now no longer speaks in unison, but in separate voices. Individuals from various parts of the stage speak the following sequence while performing their routine.

PYRAMID 1. Ah! Yes man. Hear them drums, man. Earth beat, night beat, heart beat, life beat. Soul, man, soul.

PYRAMID 2. True man. Black man, black woman too. Man-chile and woman-chile. Man beat and woman beat. Life beat and heart beat, heart-to-heart beat, man.

PYRAMID 3. Come man. Come hear them drums, man. Come hear them drums beat out the rhythm, man. Life rhythm, man—boom-boom. Earth rhythm, man— boom-boom. Sex rhythm too—boom-boom. Come man, come meet the beat, man. Move man, move to the beat, man.

The actors now have begun to move in ritualistic fashion, as if they are acting out the age-old rites of fertility and of sex—contorting, moaning, sighing, as if in rapture and in pain. The tempo quickens rapidly.

PYRAMID 4. Aha man. Beat faster, man. Put life in it, man. Life out of life; man. Life into life.

PYRAMID 5. Beat man, beat. Let the tempo rise, man. Come man, come. Come to the climax fast, man.

PYRAMID 6. And blow the flute too, man. Blow out the tune, man. Sweet, blow sweet, man. Like money, man. Ah, man.

PYRAMID 7. True man, true. Blow the line through, man. Weave through the rhythm, man. And hold the beat tight, man; hold the whole thing tight.

PYRAMID 8. Up to the climax now, man. Beat faster now and harder. Right up to the climax, now. Now man, now.

PYRAMID 9. Life out of life, life into life, man. Full it up now, up to bursting point. Life out of life, man. Let it burst out now.

The drums have now reached a climax—a crescendo. The flute plays loudly, as loudly as it can. The dancers gyrate, bump and grind, as if in a frenzy. The look upon their faces is a strange blend of rapture and of pain. Above the seeming bedlam, various cries are heard:

Ah man. Sweet man. Now man. This is life, man. Good man, soul man.

And now the stage gets gradually darker. In the dimness, the individuals could be seen coming together. Finally the stage is completely black. Soon, a dazzling flash, like lightening, lights up the stage; it is suspended for a while, revealing the pyramid of human beings again, as solid, as motionless and as enigmatic as before. Then blackness fills the stage. The wind blusters again. Chariot wheels are heard. Then a long sigh—as if some weary traveller had felt some burden lifted from his aged

VOICE. A Miracle, indeed. (*Pause.*) At last, black man, and none too soon, thou
hast spoken to me. And I have heard thy voice—the voice of blackness in
entirety—black man and woman too, black night, black earth, black death,
which is the voice of life itself and of eternity.

*The wind blows more calmly now. A soft yellow light now floods the stage /like
dawn/, revealing the pyramid of bodies dismantling itself. The individuals, now
moving apart, assume an easy manner in various attitudes of friendliness. Some
recline upon the floor, others walk casually around as if in meditation. The sound of
wind again; also soft swishing sounds, like surf. And then, another long sigh of relief.*

VOICE. A miracle for sure, black man. Out of thy awesome blackness, out
of the very blackness, the pale whiteness of my reason has been intensified and made brilliant. And, moreover, the cold fires of my intellect, once
smouldering within me, now incandesce, fanned by the heat of thy passion.
Deep within me, too, where once the flame of knowledge flickered sickly
on, each minute threatening to put out itself, small embers, struck from thy
solid pyramid of darkness now flit about in lively dance, like fairy sprays.

*The yellow light gets brighter. Soft rhythmic drums can now be heard in the back-
ground. Occasionally, other sounds of tropical life can be detected. And now, a figure
gaily dressed in flowing robes moves on-stage, unnoticed by the others, and makes his
way downstage towards the audience.*

VOICE. Black man, black woman too, earth child, night child, death child,
life child. Thou art both am and was and will forever be. Like Time itself,
forever present and not to be denied; yet so often quite neglected or grudg-
ingly acknowledged. Like Time itself, most tolerant of fond pretentiousness
and vile pomposity, until such trivialities threaten to become subversive. (*A
pause. A sigh.*)

*By this time, the figure has made his way to front center, where he stands and looks
around as if in search of some distant presence.*

FIGURE. (*Totally unaware of any other people on stage and without confronting
the audience, speaking lyrically but with a heavy accent.*) I heard the sounds of
Africa, blest Africa—earth center. I see hot sweltering jungles glistening
with rain-drenched vegetation; hot blinding desert-land swirling with
the wind-blown sands; hot bristling flat-lands teeming with fleet-footed

herds of animals. (*He moves around as if in a trance, pausing occasionally as if to meditate.*)

VOICE. (*As if inspired.*) Black man and woman too, thou art no product of Immaculate Conception, nor wast thou moulded in the workshop of some blanched divinity, to wear the semblance of His pride and vanity. Oh no, thine was and is and ever will be the pristine agony of struggle slowly upwards out of the deepest regions of the womb of earth; thine the rhythmic ingress into life out from the darkest caverns of cold, uncompromising death; thine the painful issuing forth of being out of the vast frozen fields or nothingness; thine too a deliberate evolvement of entity out of the tortuous labyrinths or chaos.

The figure now suddenly stops and turns to the audience, pointing a finger in their direction.

FIGURE. Look, 'way off in the distance! Look and there you'll see tall men, proud men of giant stature, descendants of the sons of earth, the sons and daughters of an ancient royalty. See! See how beautiful they are! Black bodies glistening in the sun with freely flowing sweat. Look, man! Look and see how gracefully they move, like panthers of the night, on up the steep slopes along the beaten tracks to where Earth rears her head high up to show the frozen whiteness that struggles (O so vain!) to put out her heat. (*A pause, still trancelike.*)

During this speech the other actors, members of the pyramid, have realized his presence and drawn closer to him—yet remaining in the background—and now sit or stand or squat closely observing him.

VOICE. (*Somewhat more intense.*) Black man, thou wast not, art not, will not ever be called to the mythic fields of Paradise, there to be tempted with the promise of eternal happiness and then to yield (how else?) to the temptations of some mythic fiend disguised as a limp phallus and thence to be driven out into the world of suffering, quite fallen and disgraced! (*Panting with emotion.*) No such vain efforts to eke out eternal comfort from the throes of life; no such vain efforts to disguise pale cowardice in the ethereal splendour of mythology.

FIGURE. (*Stopping again and pointing to a different section of the audience.*) And see, see over there, where tiny springs of life, flowing out from deep within her massive mountain-bulk, trickle slowly onwards. Watch how they meet and flow together, joining their waters in a common stream. And now exulting in togetherness, they shoot off, gathering new speed each minute. Look and listen, as they hurtle onwards, splintering themselves against the jagged rockface, then reunite; now listen, as they drop sheer downwards

in death-defying plunge deep within the frothing foam-fringed pool and
disappear.

*At this point, another figure is seen standing to the right rear of stage. He is also quite
gaily dressed but in a more conventional summer attire.*

But see, see there! They reappear! And now, with no less urgency but with
much more assurance, they hurry on along the flatter land, seeking most
unrelentlessly to lose themselves deep down within the waters of the
ocean-home, thence to be born again with greater purity and to return
once more to Mother-earth. (*Moving around with a puzzled look upon his face,
all the while observed by the other individuals and by the other figure.*)
VOICE. (*Sounding like an oracle of old.*) Black man, earth man. No fall hast thou
experienced, except the falling out of life into the very blackness at the core
of life and so into new life. Time's contemporary thou art, borne high aloft
upon the flood of life, drawn under into the dark waters of death, and up
again on to the surface, as the Fates conspire.

*During this speech, the second figure has made his way through the various bodies
closer to the first one.*

FIGURE. (*Pointing again in another direction as if he has just discovered the solution to his puzzlement.*) There, on the flatlands; there, lying on the banks and
reaching far out to drink and feel the surge of life within them, or waiting
patiently to thrust the pointed end of some firm sapling deep into some
hidden prey! No idle games of hunt and kill you see there, but the grave
process of survival. (*More calmly.*) Black brothers of the taller men they are,
though as you see of much smaller size. And yet, within their tiny frames,
there throbs an even greater life-force; for these are the darlings of the
Earth, most faithful in their loyalty. Look, see how their eyes gleam sharply
out of mud-smeared faces, flashing with the knowledge of all things—
ancient knowledge out of ancient head, head of ancient man all smeared
with mud.

*Second figure has now reached center stage and stands facing the speaker who at
the completion of his speech seems to have awakened from his trance and noticed the
other.*

FIGURE 2. (*Also lyrically, but more liltingly and with a lighter accent.*) I hear you
speak and recognise your voice. (*He smiles, but the other still maintains an
unrevealing face. The others follow the happenings keenly.*)
VOICE. Black man, thou art the integer of life and not the component. Thou
art the tiger and the lamb, the Dragon and the Dragonkiller. Thou art the
shadow and the substance, the body and the soul. Thou art the ego and the

id—and super ego too. (*Now strangely serene.*) The infant Spring feels itself
come alive in thee; the aged Winter sees reflected in thy eyes the deepest
mysteries he knows. Within thee too, the youthful pulse of Summer throbs,
and Autumn more mature, conceals her cherished store.

FIGURE 2. (*During this speech,* FIGURE 2 *stands smiling in admiration, turns and
surveys the scene, contemplating the others for a while. Now he confronts the
former speaker.*) How well do I recall your voice, your ancient voice. (*As if
inspired by some pleasant recollections.*) Ah yes, that ancient voice that echoes
all the mysteries of the earth, that ancient voice that speaks the meaning of
all things for those who hear and understand such language, which is the
language of the night and of the dark earth. I hear you and I understand.
(*Smiles; so too the other actor.*)

FIGURE 2. You see, that land of yours is mine as well. Once upon a time, a
long time ago, that land gave birth to me and to my brothers and my sisters
too. But since that time, a long time now, we were quite roughly seized and
taken far away to other lands, and scattered here and there throughout
strange fields to dwell among pale ghostly forms. (*Serious now and with great
dignity.*) But our roots, reaching deep down within earth-center, remain
unbroken. And now, the land, anxious to reclaim her offsprings, cries
out, and we begin to gravitate. (*Somewhat more relaxed.*) I too have felt the
heat and seen my brothers glisten with the sweat of labour under a sun no
cooler. I too have swallowed the cool waters of the earth and snared the fish
from out the murky depths. I too have dared to snatch new life from the
cold mouth of death. Ah, yes indeed! that ancient voice that rolls so rhythmically on through life and death, I've heard and felt it strong within me.

VOICE. I too have heard thee speak, black man. I too have seen thee proud and
constant in thy destiny. I too have watched thy struggles and thy successes,
thy dying into life and living out of death. But, to be true, the full meaning
of thy words have once again eluded me. I cannot understand the logic of
thy actions, the reasons for thy confidence.

FIGURE 2. (*During the last speech, the figures, completely oblivious to the voice,
pace back and forth, absorbed in thought, with smiles upon their faces. Pausing
now.*) But I did never understand why my hot blood rose up and seemed
to want to burst the veins that held it on its course, when histories of pale
kings and emperors were whispered in my ear. (*With rising emotion.*) But
I have heard your voice. (*Calmer now.*) And I am calm. No more will I be
angry. For now, indeed, my recollections have been touched deep down,
and dark fate that cannot be denied has revealed itself. And now, I'm home
again; I'm home to stay this time.

The stage now brightens somewhat, revealing the individuals regrouping themselves.

VOICE. O woebetide! My light of knowledge that just recently did seem to
glow more brilliantly now quivers sickeningly once more; its little flame

seems helpless once again, engulfed within the dark impenetrable that enfolds thee.

A pause. Thunder and blustering wind. A flash of lightening reveals the pyramid reformed, motionless and still.

VOICE. And so, I'm still excluded from the knowledge of your lot. (*Rising in intensity.*) Since this is so, I must protect myself against thee. In order to preserve myself and to be proud of what I am, I must again endeavour to destroy thy blackness. And if I fail in this, as I have so many times before, I must deny most irrevocably the fact of thy existence.

The stage suddenly grows dark. Wintery winds bluster menacingly; thunder rolls most ominously.

VOICE: On on, there is so little time. Ah, woe is me. Why should such be my destiny?

Chariot wheels are heard fading amidst the threatening elements. Flashes of lightning light up the stage, revealing the pyramid. It does not move or speak. Total darkness descends upon the stage.

AND SO, ANOTHER "THING" HAS DONE ITSELF IN; THAT IS, IF IT EVER MANAGES TO COME TO LIFE.

***

HERE BEGINS THE THIRD "THING"

Stage entirely black. Out of the darkness, a loud rumbling, like the trembling of the earth is heard. Then a long weird-sounding cry. A sudden lighting of the front stage reveals a witch-doctor figure. He wears a mask, obviously smeared with mud. Nevertheless, he does not present the image of the traditional witch doctor. He appears to be much more dignified, more serious and involved. After a while the rumbling subsides.

WITCH DOCTOR *now performs a ritualistic dance. Jerking his head to the left, he shades his eyes with the left hand and leans forward as if scanning the far distant region in that direction. Then he draws himself up slowly. Lowering his left hand, he now holds up the other and performs the scanning action—to the right this time. Then he straightens himself up once again. Quite unexpectedly, he throws himself up into the air, his body arched and curved somewhat to the left, his hands above his head. Suddenly, he falls to the floor, kneeling upon his left knee; the right knee supports the right elbow. Slowly, his head falls forward into the palm of his right hand. Moving in a dancelike routine, he brings himself up to the squat position, both hands upon the hips, toes pointing outwards. Then jerking his head to the left then to the right, like an ancient hooded viper, he turns slowly around in a complete circle, at the same time performing several little jumps. Facing the audience once more, he freezes in the squat position, his head slightly inclined. Lifting his hands above his head, palms together but racing outwards, he raises his head up. He then speaks above the rumbling which is considerably less now. His voice is not very loud, but mysteriouslike—like a priest chanting a litany. In fact, the following scene is to be performed in the manner of some ancient religious ritual.*

WITCH DOCTOR. Oh me. Oh mine! Oh yeah, oh yeah, oh yeah! Listen and hear my brothers, my black brothers and my black sisters too. Listen to the mountain talk—tall tall big mountain that holds her head up high, her great big earth-body, like our bodies, black and firm, and glistening in the sun most beautifully. (*Pause. At this time, the blackness downstage slowly lightens, revealing the dim outline of the pyramid.*) Up high upon her head, she holds afar the whiteness icy cold that threatens—ah, but in vain—to chill her heat and freeze up the tiny streams that bring new life to us from deep within her bulk. (*He now begins to move, improvising all the while.*) Yeah, oh yeah! Earth-mother, proud mother of the night—and of that other child, so quite unlike herself. Listen to the voice, my sisters, my brothers, listen to the voice—a voice you seldom hear, because she seldom speaks. Listen to the wisdom she holds silent, womb-deep within her body. Listen to the painful truth that cannot be avoided.

Now the pyramid is quite visible; however, the stage is not brilliantly lit—it is just bright enough to permit visibility.

PYRAMID. (*Swaying as it talks in unison.*) Ayee, ayee, ayee! We listen and we hear; we hear the sound not loud but reaching gut deep to start a pain within us. We listen and we feel the life astir within us.

The WITCH DOCTOR, who for a while had remained frozen within the spotlight, now begins to improvise again. A lurid yellow light now floods the stage and the pyramid in the background begins to come apart.

WITCH DOCTOR. I feel the pain myself; But do not be afraid; hold up the head manchile. And do not cry, sweet womanchile. It is the truth, my brothers; you cannot shut it out, my sisters. (*With renewed vigour all the individuals of the pyramid now begin to improvise as well.*) Hold up the head—the head, black like Mother-earth that rises high high up. And feel the pain. And when you fall—for fall you must—to get right up again and hold the head up higher will make you strong—strong enough to hear the words more clearly and bear the pain more calmly.

PYRAMID. (*Individual voices from different parts of the stage.*) The pain. The pain gets worse. But hold the head up high. And if you fall, get up again. And hold the head up higher.

Definite efforts are now being made to follow the improvised movements of the witch-doctor. His movements become more exaggerated and more laborious—something like a dance of strength, determination and endurance.

WITCH DOCTOR. Now boom the drums, the big big drums, the big deep drums. (*The sound of drums, almost funereal.*) The big drums, the deep ones, the boom deep drums. (*The others have now fallen into the pattern of the movements.*) Feel the pain, sweet womanchile, the wombdeep pain; the gutdeep pain, manchile. But hold the heads up high. Boom the big deep drums. Feel the pain and fall, but rise again to feel the pain again. But keep them heads up high.

PYRAMID VOICES. Gut-pain. Wombdeep pain. Hold up the head. Fall down. Get up, again. Lift the head up, man. Eyes dark with pain. Black pain. Head up, up high.

WITCH DOCTOR. (*The rate of the speech becomes gradually less, so too the rate of his movements.*) Roll out the drums, roll hard, manchile; roll the big drums out. Listen to the earth, sweet womanchile. I know the pain gets worse. Listen to the earth, for you must fall. And soon, soon now.

The drums roll, growing in intensity. The rumbling of the earth rises up for a moment, but soon gives way to the drums. There is a bright flash of light. The witch-doctor, as if with a final effort, leaps high into the air and falls unto the stage. All the others follow suit. They remain still as the stage darkens. Total silence prevails. Then a pale yellow light reveals the actors struggling to their feet. They are all soon standing and, with slow difficult steps, they re-form the pyramid. The witch doctor, however, remains still on the floor. As the pyramid takes shape the light brightens for a moment then slowly the stage darkens. Blackness and total silence.

***

THE FOURTH "THING" (IF NEEDED)

Stage in total darkness. After a while, the sounds of footsteps can be heard. A spotlight, flashing upon left front stage, picks up a figure, strutting slowly but confidently across to center stage. As it nears front-center, it pauses, carefully brushes itself off in a manner of self-adoration and looks in the direction of the audience. It smiles and struts a few more paces. It is obvious that the figure is clad in a thin tightly fitting white garment which covers his entire body. Reaching center-stage, it stops and flicks an imaginary object from the sole of its foot with a cane it carries in its hand. Facing the audience, it crosses its left foot over the right and leans heavily upon the cane.

FIGURE 1. A good world, isn't it? So clean and bright and beautiful. And what a gorgeous day! No clouds at all; all shining bright and white! (*Pauses, straightens up and lifts his cane, twirling it slowly.*) Know who I am? I am the man. Indeed, I am the man, the only man, essential man, created in the image of HIM who made all things, all creatures too—all the world indeed. Oh yes! I AM the man. I AM THE MAN. (*Struts to his right, then to his left; moves backwards, then forwards, quite unhurriedly. His broad smile almost resembles a sneer.*) He, proud maker of all things, made me, like HIM, most white and wonderful, gifted with the talents to perform all things—except perhaps to make new life—and put me here upon HIS earth to be his sole executor, to oversee HIS works and keep His systems working. And as a grand reward—by no means undeserving—he has given to me sole rights to all that's good and valuable; to me alone, he has granted privileges to enjoy all comforts here; for me alone, he has provided all necessities—fish, flesh and fowl, all creatures of the land, the air and of the waters. Through me alone, he speaks and acts—through me, the darling of creation. My words, therefore, like his must be infallible; my deeds inevitable. (*Smiling, as if quite reassured that all he has said is true, he bows with a great flourish to the left, to the right and to center.*)

At this point the rest of the stage is flooded with a yellowish light that reveals the outline of the pyramid, but much smaller than in the previous scenes.

FIGURE 1. (*Looking around in a questioning manner, yet not aware of the presence of the pyramid, it now speaks in a less confident manner.*) Indeed, I am the man. But now, I cannot stay much longer. I must be off. Farewell, indeed, for I must be about my Father's business; the Lamb must be attended to and I must go.

Twirling his cane, he turns and struts, still smiling but somewhat embarrassed, across stage to the right and off. The spotlight which has been following him all the time goes out, leaving the stage in darkness. Soon other footsteps are heard, not as sturdy as before. The spotlight, like before, picks up another figure at left front stage; it is similarly dressed but looks slightly dingy. Moreover, it looks older. As it moves across the stage, not strutting but with an attempt at grandeur, it comes nearer center stage. Pausing, it lifts the cane up as if about to twirl it, but does not. Instead it contemplates the cane for a while, then turns to the rear as if listening. Soon it seems to recover its composure and, moving to center stage, begins to speak.

FIGURE 2. It is indeed a lovely day, despite the many clouds. The sun still shines, though not as radiant as before. And I am still the man! (*Looking at

himself, as if to make sure, he becomes aware of some change in his appearance.
Somewhat startled and self-conscious, he continues.) Oh no! I have not fallen.
Surely I AM the man! made by the maker of all things, in HIS image, bright
and white and wonderful. (*Pauses. Contemplates himself again.*) Indeed, I am
the man.

*Now a faint sound is heard, gradually getting louder. It is the clinking of chains being
dragged and the meaning of people at some kind of strenuous task. Although the
noises subside a little, they are heard even as the figure speaks.*

FIGURE 2. Indeed, 'tis also true. The black fiend, whom the all-powerful
creator hurled deep down into the center of the earth to suffer everlasting
pain within hot fires there, he who in vain tries to o'erthrow the Maker and
to possess his world and all therein—he, fiend that he is, reaching up from
his fiery earth-grave, tries desperately to cast a shadow on my brightness,
to make my whiteness sullied. But he is doomed to failure. The world's still
mine to profit by. (*Looking round as the noises of the chains and the moans rise
up again, he seems to gain new confidence.*) For I have made myself secure.
Indeed, so cunning that I am!

*Now the rear stage brightens just a little, revealing the pyramid to the right—still
smaller than in the other scenes. One notices that it sways as if about to fall apart.
The figure, however, continues completely unaware of this new development.*

FIGURE 2. I have reached far—far into the darkest regions of the land, where
dwell the offsprings of that most infernal one, and I have seized many, O
so many, of the black hordes that pay homage to him, and I have brought
them out into the region of the light and chained them to the earth—the
very earth, where deep beneath the blackest of them all wallows in his
fiery pools and shapes his deeds most foul. Alas, so futile are his efforts!
(*The sounds grow louder.*) I am indeed the man. (*A smile upon his face.*) Listen!
Listen as the black legions, descendants of the arch-enemy, bemoan their
lot. (*He seems to be quite proud of himself.*) Naked in the bright light of day,
they labour to make fertile and preserve that which the enemy of man
determines to destroy. A just reward, imposed by me, the Man. Next to
my whiteness, the blackness of their evil, the darkness of their ignorance,
becomes more obvious. Indeed, they are no better than the lowly beasts
that roam the fields quite unaware of everything. In fact, their lot's the
worse!

*At this point, the rear stage darkens and the pyramid disappears. However, the
moaning and groaning continues. But now a new sound can be distinguished: the
singing of the blues most soulfully. On the figure's face the attitude of pride blots itself
out, leaving in its place a painful look of puzzlement. He turns to look into the dark*

and seems to withdraw within himself. As he turns around and begins to speak, his voice sounds almost pleading-like.

FIGURE 2. What strange sounds now fill my ear? Is it from out the darkness that it comes? What could it mean that sound so soulful, so melancholy, yet so comforting? Surely, the sons and daughters of the dark could not possess a gift so rare? Oh no, it is not possible. (*Turns to look around once more, pauses, then whirls around in amazement—a look of horror upon his face.*) Do you see what I see? From out the deepest shadows where the black creatures toil, not voices only, but flashes of pure whiteness, like ivory of the purest quality! (*For a while it seams that he would swoon, but he pulls himself together, smoothens his attire, holds up his head. The smile he tries to bring about looks more like a silly grin.*) Ha! It is the fiend! 'tis he who from the darkness tries, with the blackest of his arts, to trick me and to confound my thinking. Ha, ha. Oh most foul deception! All alas, in vain. The Man still triumphs. (*At this point, the pyramid appears at left stage which has now lightened somewhat. The figure now speaks in a tone of obvious anxiety.*) But now—my time runs out and I must depart. I leave the prince of darkness and his subjects to their doom. (*He starts to make his way towards the right exit.*) Ah yes, I must now be about my father's business. The lamb must be protected or else the white fleece perishes.

Glancing fearfully to the rear, which has now gone dark, he makes a feeble attempt to twirl his cane; it falls; he retrieves it, pretending to be in the act of bowing to the audience, but he stumbles and nearly falls. His forward movement takes him right across the stage. The spotlight goes out as he makes his rather abrupt exit. Stage in darkness. Immediately the rolling of voices. They grow silent as a voice, echoing with authority sounds out.

VOICE. Hear ye, hear ye! Through the mercy of His means and by the mercy of my means, thou shalt be free. (*Cheers resound—cries of "Bravo, Ole, etc."* *The drum rolls again, then silence.*) Let the chains be severed. (*The sound of hammering against chains; the chains fall heavily to the floor. More cheering.*) 'Tis done. Let the trumpets sound, the drums roll loudly and the cymbals clash. Go proclaim the deed abroad.

Sounds drums in martial fashion is heard. From the back of the dark stage comes the murmuring of celebration; a parade seems to be moving off. However, the stage lightens gradually revealing the dim outline of people bent and suffering limping slowly across the stage. Soon all is quiet and the stage is dark again.

After a few minutes, a figure, dressed like the previous ones and carrying a similar cane, is picked up at left front stage by the spotlight. It is obviously an older person. This time it resembles a clown, wearing a mask with a fixed smile painted upon it; the

*shoes are pointed outward, extending beyond the tips of the toes. It comes capering
across the stage in a most awkward manner, but it is obviously quite proud of its
athletic prowess. Suddenly, it comes to a halt at center stage.*

FIGURE 3. And there they go in honour of the deed that I have done most
recently. Off to proclaim my greatness, the greatness of the Man—for
indeed, I am the MAN, bright and white and wonderful. (*Twirls stick in
the manner of a drum-major.*) 'Tis true, the black fiend, determined still to
o'erthrow the Maker (fond hope!) still tries to smudge the whiteness of His
favourite, the Man, and to confound the brightness of His world with his
thick darkness. But he is doomed to fail. Confined within his fiery earth-
grave, he suffers everlasting agony, and the painful frustration of perpetual
disappointment. (*Throws cane into the air and catches it.*) But I the Man,
through the mercy of my means, has seen it fitting to unchain his legions
here on earth. Because I willed it so, no fetters bind him longer to the land.
(*Bowing with a great flourish.*) And so, for this, I'm more the Man, the Man
supreme. But they, poor creatures, though no longer bound, yet still are
burdened by their horrid blackness; though free, they flounder helplessly,
according to the very nature of their lesser being. (*Shakes head as if in pity
of their lot, despite the evergrinning face he wears.*) Alas, it is inevitable; 'tis
the privilege of me alone, who am the Man, to prosper and be happy in the
glory of this world.

*At this stage, the pyramid still smaller than before can be recognized, this time at
rear center stage behind him. He seems to be about to make his exit. He speaks,
however.*

FIGURE. But I must be about my father's business and keep the white lamb
pure. I must preserve the whiteness of its fleece. (*Just at this point, the final
bars of some soulful song are heard, then shouts of approval, hand clapping
and encores. He pauses and turns slowly around, as the stage goes black and the
pyramid disappears.*) What is this sudden ecstasy? Who else besides the Man
deserves such obvious praise? (*Looks around in confusion, raises his hands
in protest. Just then sounds of a large crowd cheering enthusiastically as they
witness some thrilling sport or athletic competition.*) More sounds of praise!
And louder than before! Who dares compete with me for the glory of
success? (*Looks around again as if trying to pierce the darkness beyond the spotlight that encircles him. Turns front, obviously about to panic, despite the smiling
face.*) The little lamb must be protected; I must attend my father's business.

*Just as he is about to rush offstage, the stage lightens enough to reveal the dim
outlines of the pyramid, still small. In fact, the darkness seems to have come alive. A
bedlam of sounds arises; laughter, moaning, singing, orations, heckling, jazz, drums,
porter's cries, cheers, boos, sounds of football, baseball, boxing, etc.*

The figure who stood frozen at first, retreats to the edge of the front stage, as if about to jump into the audience. Darkness descends upon the rest of stage. With the spotlight following him, he rushes into the darkness, flaying wildly with his cane—the face still smiling. Stumbling wearily about, he falls upon knees and elbows. The sounds subside. He rises cautiously, then brandishing his cane in the direction of the darkness.

FIGURE 3. Away, away, you spirits of the dark. I will not yield to you. I feel new strength well up inside of me and I must rise or else the lamb will perish. (*Turns to face the rear of stage.*) Show! (*In a menacing attitude, his voice trembling with fear and anger, despite the grinning mask.*) Reveal yourselves! Assume some form that can be recognised, despite your horrid blackness. (*Holding the cane aloft, he peers into the dark, then turns to face the audience.*) I am the Man, who calls upon the creatures of the dark, the legions of the fiend, the arch-enemy or Him who made me Man. (*The bedlam again startles him. He regains his composure, after a while, as the bedlam subsides. As if he has gained some new insights.*) Ha! I see it now. The sharp light of my intellect has pierced the darkness round about. It is the fiend once again, who gathering all his forces, makes one final desperate attempt to crush and overthrow the rightful heir of this fair land. (*Seems to gain confidence.*) And so, the Man must be about his father's business and keep the white lamb safe. Or else, aged Chaos, blind sire of the prince of darkness, would rise again. (*Pausing, as if to ponder his next move. Then reassured.*) The Man must act immediately. It is inevitable. (*With renewed courage he turns to face the darkness, looking like Napoleon from the rear. With a loud demanding voice, yet somewhat desperate.*)

FIGURE 3. Reveal yourselves! Show, or be damned forever! (*The stage now gets brighter revealing the pyramid in center stage rear, still smaller than before.*) Behold! (*Like a judge passing a sentence of doom.*) Behold the black legions, descendants of blind Chaos, arch-enemy of Him, through the mercy or whose means I have just recently set free. (*Pyramid begins to come apart.*) See how with ingratitude they threaten to invade the whiteness of His and my domain. (*The members of the pyramid, at this time, have begun to spread out in a slowly increasing circle.*) See how they threaten to destroy the lamb of innocence! (*Pauses, trembling with fear as the outermost members have approached within the circle of the spotlight.*) It must be done. The fair world of the Omnipotent must be protected. All else must be destroyed as sacrifice, in order to preserve his glorious works untainted.

Pulling a revolver from a slit in the upper regions of his garment, which had been carefully concealed, he turns and fires repeatedly at the circle of figures. They do not fall; in fact, they move with greater dignity and firmness. The final shot seems to have set off a reverberation of noises: sounds of battle, anthem-like music, groans, triumphant cries, sounds of protest and of rioting, etc. All of which suggest the happenings of the history of mankind. As the noise becomes louder, the circle of humanity begins to close towards the center. Soon the pyramid begins to form itself. The lights begin to dim.

The figure, meanwhile recoils in astonishment. He drops his cane and begins to cough and grasp his throat as if asphyxiated by the din. He behaves in the manner of a man being strangled. In fact, he seems to be trying to prevent his left hand from strangling himself with his right hand. All the while, his clownlike smile remains fixed. The stage is now completely dark, leaving only the spotlight, within which the figure stumbles about, in apparent agony. He speaks haltingly.

FIGURE 3. Black devils! Fiends! Kill! Kill! Shoot the black hordes! Protect the lamb. (*A fit of coughing.*) I am the man—I must survive. I must prevail. All else must perish to this end. Not me! (*With obvious bravado.*) I will not let it be, black fiends. (*Now he falls, rises, falls again, then struggles to his feet once more.*) The Man must rise again. (*Much feebler now.*) The lamb must be protected. The darkness must be stifled. (*The spotlight begins to fade.*) Kill the black devils of the earth. (*Almost whimpering now.*) Not me. (*Falls.*) Not me. (*Rises halfway with great difficulty.*) I am—am—I am—the—the— (*Crumples to the floor. Slowly pulsating drums begin. The stage brightens a little, revealing the outline of the pyramid, swaying slightly. A scream pierces the air, but the drums do not cease, the actors seem quite undisturbed by it. Suddenly the figure struggles to his feet; as if possessed, he clutches desperately at the still smiling mask and at the rest of his attire, which seem to be the cause of his agony. The mask, however, remains fixed; the clothes though thin remain untorn. Still pulling at the mask.*) I am the—the—I am the—the—the— (*Clutching more desperately at the mask.*) Kill—kill—the black—fi—fi— (*He falls heavily to the floor with a most heartrending cry.*)

The stage goes black for a while, as the drums roll out more loudly. They soften again. The stage lightens a little, revealing the figure lying on the floor. Slowly he rises to kneeling position and whimperinglike.

FIGURE 3. Help me, or I perish. (*More sincerely.*) Oh please! Save me, or I fall. (*Slumping somewhat.*) Too late, too late—the lamb—its white fleece now wears—wears the tiger spots. (*A little calmer now, but not strongly.*) The world's in danger now, alas!

He falls upon his back, his hands still clutching the mask. The stage goes black and the drums roll out. Soon a bright yellow light floods the stage, revealing the pyramid as in the previous scenes. The figure, lying on the stage, begins to stir. Sobbing sounds are heard. Then a voice.

FIGURE 3. Dear spirits of the dark. Alas! Come help me save the world, this world of ours. (*Rising slowly and gathering strength.*) And help me free myself. (*Quite earnest now.*) Help me to escape this most constricting garb. (*Clutches at the mask.*) Come spirits of the dark. Kind spirits, come; pull off the mask and let myself emerge, born into new life, strengthened and refreshed. Pull off the mask. (*Pulls desperately at it.*) Unmask me here and let me breathe the wholesome air again.

With a cry of agony, he falls to the floor, totally exhausted. The tempo of the drumming quickens. The pyramid of bodies sways faster and faster, then seems to explode, sending its parts in all directions. The actors improvise, moving in a frenzy of action, as if possessed by some demonic spirit. It continues until it becomes almost unbearable. Then all collapse as the drumming comes to a sudden stop.

There is a loud clap of thunder. A flash like lightening lights up the stage. Rumblings are heard, like during an earthquake. Then silence. Suddenly, from rear center stage a solitary light, like a sun, illuminates the stage. The actors are in the same positions as when they had fallen. Eventually, however, the figure in white stirs, rubs his eyes—in fact, where the eyes are on the mask he still wears—and passes his hands over his entire body as if to confirm that he is still whole. He rises to his knees, looks around for a while, then seems to remember where he is and what the scene before him means. Now he bends forward upon his hands and knees and like a creeping infant he moves among the bodies, touching each person lightly upon the forehead, thus awakening them. Soon he has roused them all. Slowly they raise themselves upon one elbow, looking at the figure who has now made his way to the center of the group. Getting off his hands, he sits back upon his heels and lowers his head as if in supplication. He holds his hands clasped firmly against his breast. And softly.

FIGURE 3. Awake sweet manchile; sweet womanchile awake. It is the dawning of the day. (*A little louder now.*) Come, come my brothers; come my sweet sisters. Come lend a hand to one who, for a while—for much too long a while, had lost his way and stumbled blindly in the dazzling glare of life. (*Pauses, lowers head, then raises it again.*) Come lend a hand that, like the lowly serpent, I may escape this timeworn flimsiness, this fondly grinning mask, this entire masquerade, that threatens to destroy the essential being that I am. Come lend a hand that, bursting through this pale exterior, once the proud confines of myself, I may emerge most joyfully into the harmony of life and earth. (*Falls to the floor.*)

Drums, happy drums speak out. The light at rear center stage goes out. The actors can be seen in the pale yellow light that is left, moving closer to the prostrate figure. Soon it is completely encircled. Obvious movements of unveiling can be detected. It all resembles some ancient forgotten ritual. The drumming now reaches a crescendo. Then in one total movement, the actors throw up their hands and rise. Shuffling their feet, they begin to move backwards. The spotlight flashes on the figure still lying on the stage, but now clad entirely in black, his mask and shedded garment lying on the stage a little way from him. Soon he begins to move—slightly at first, then more vigorously—as if the victim of a sudden spasm. Jerking spasmodically, he rises to his feet like Ledean born emerging from its giant swan's egg. As he straightens up, the spotlight widens and merges with the other light, flooding the entire stage. Soon the jerky movements end and he begins to move more smoothly, falling into the general pattern of the dance which is being performed by the others. The drums meanwhile have softened, but they still maintain their happy rhythm. As the light darkens, the figure has completely merged with the others; in fact, he cannot be distinguished. Meanwhile voices are heard.

VOICES. Hey man. Hi, brother; hi, sister. What's up baby? Nothing, manchile. Keep the faith, baby. Cool it, womanchile. Say hey, man. Yea, man; it's the life, man.

Total darkness now falls upon the entire theatre. No sounds are heard now. Then suddenly, a crash like thunder. A bright flash lights up the stage and is suspended for a while. At center stage, there can be seen the bold outline of the pyramid of bodies, standing tall, firm, mysterious, enigmatic and silent. The light goes out, leaving the entire theatre dark for a few seconds.

HERE ENDETH THE FINAL THING
THAT IS
OF COURSE
IF WE EVER GET
THIS
FAR

30 : Theatre in the Canada Pavilion at Expo 67 (1967)

A "Meeting Place"

ERIN HURLEY

ON EVERY EVENING BUT MONDAY from May 10 to October 27, 1967, a cast of nine performed a *"revue canadienne"* to full houses in the theatre of the Canada Pavilion at the 1967 International and Universal Exhibition, more widely known as "Expo 67." A meeting of "the broad farce of the English music-hall and the acidulous comedy of the Parisian revue," this Canadian revue featured an almost-balanced cast of four francophones and five anglophones (Expo [International Exhibitions Bureau] 1967, 31); of the nine, four were women and five were men (Figure 30.1). For approximately fifty minutes each evening, the well-known performers sang and danced, performed pantomimic bits, did impressions, and acted in comic sketches that would "make pleasant, satirical, funny, emotional, and other comments on Expo and the people visiting Expo" (31). Out of this "bilingual and bicultural" combination of talents (hailing from Toronto and Montreal, and standing in for "English Canada" and "French Canada") would arise a specifically Canadian national performance—as well as an evening of laughter and mutual (mis)understanding about the common experience of visiting Expo 67.[1] This chapter aims to contextualize and introduce this popular show, whose significance lies in its harmonizing representation of Canada, its bicultural artistic team, and its popular form.

The 1967 International and Universal Exhibition was held from the spring to the fall of that year in Montreal, Canada's largest city at the time and the cultural centre of French Canada. Governed and regulated by the Paris-based Bureau international des expositions, such events have been organized regularly since the mid-nineteenth century in Europe, Asia, and the Americas as showcases for "industrial progress and national prestige" on the world stage ("About World Expos," n.d.) and as fosterers "of nationalistic sentiment among their citizens" (Rydell and Kroes 1994, 50). As Expo 67 was a "First-Category" International and Universal Exposition,[2] it was incumbent on the planners to foreground the unifying agenda and broadly humanist values of the international exhibition movement. It did so through its theme of "Terre des hommes / Man and His World" and in the organization of its grounds. For instance, the landscape design allowed no boundary markers between pavilions; signage, street furniture, and graphics were uniform across the site; and the whole was

---

1. Particularly cheeky press reports on this theatrical offering dubbed it the "bi and bi" show, in reference to the Royal Commission on Bilingualism and Biculturalism, which ran from 1963 to 1969.

2. From 1928 to 1972, world exhibitions were divided by the Bureau international des expositions into two categories, whereby Universal and International Exhibitions of the First Category are organized around a universal theme, may not exceed a duration of six months, may not repeat in the same country more than once every fifteen years, and at which each participating nation builds its own pavilion. Second-Category exhibitions are specialized, may be held more frequently in a single country, and the host country builds the pavilions (Jasmin 1997, 18–19.)

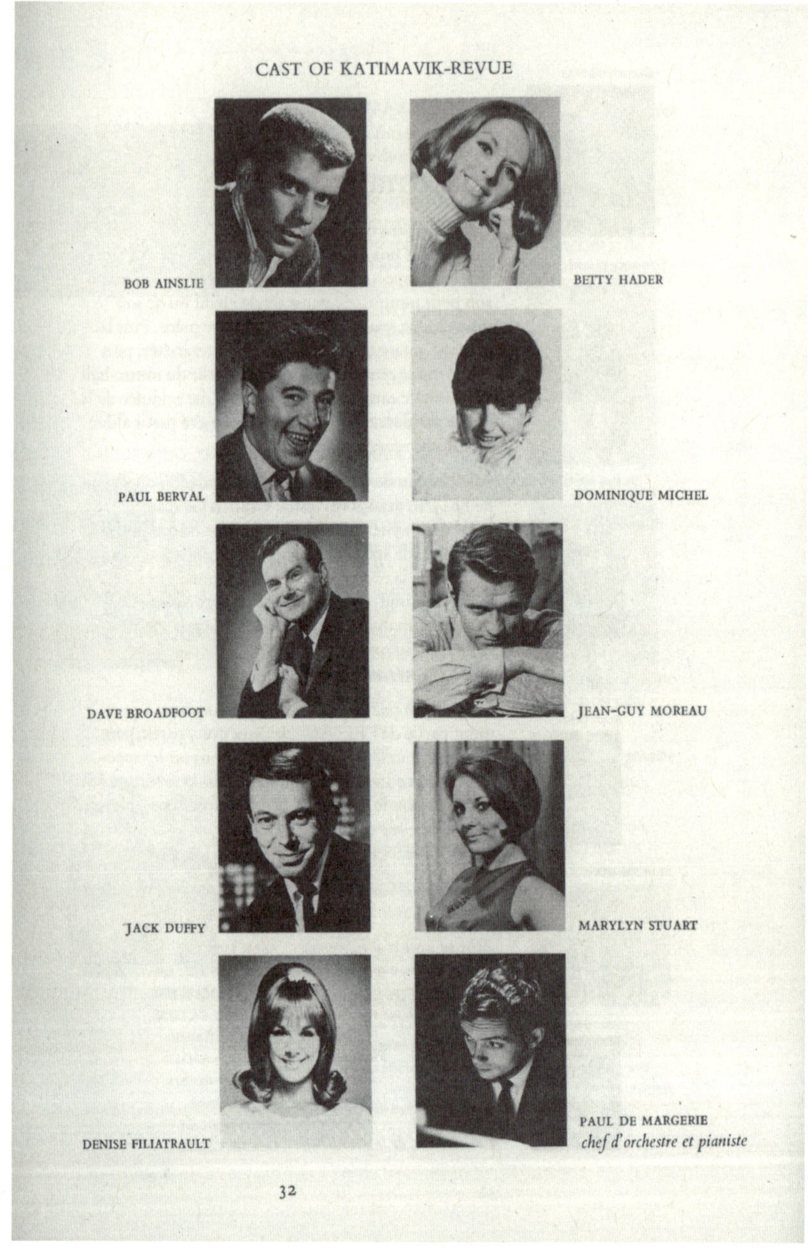

FIGURE 30.1: *Photograph page of the cast of the* Katimavik-Revue.

File 00797, Sam Gesser—Katimavik. Courtesy of the Jewish Public Library Archives, Montreal.

interconnected by transportation networks (Gold and Gold 2016, 118).
However, the built environment was still primarily organized by national
pavilions, interspersed with exhibition areas of companies (e.g., Kodak),
institutions of civil society (e.g., trade unions, faith-based organizations), and
the fair's thematic pillars (e.g., "Man the Explorer"). Here, visitors could be

3. The 400 hectares of the Expo site welcomed the pavilions of 62 nations, 3 US states, 3 Canadian regions (Ontario, the Atlantic provinces, and the Western provinces), plus the "Indians of Canada Pavilion," and 268 companies and organizations along with more than 55 million visits over the 83 days of Expo (Curien 2007, 28).

4. In their entry on Expo 67 in *Mondo Canuck*, Geoff Pevere and Greig Dymond cite the international press on this matter, including London's *Observer*, as follows: "Expo 67 isn't just a world's fair, it has glitter, sex appeal, and it's given impact and meaning to a word that has neither: Canadian" (1996, 54). Elsewhere, I maintain that much of Canada's sex appeal at Expo 67 was provided by Expo hostesses (Hurley 2011, 31–59).

5. Under their aegis, 2,008 "projects of a lasting nature" were funded to a total of $14,073,806 by the Commission in 1967 and 1968 (Davies 1999).

6. Gimby's bilingual "Ca-na-da" held the record for "the highest-selling Canadian single in history" until 1985, with over 300,000 copies purchased (Pevere and Dymond 1996, 57).

both edified and entertained in seeing "the world for a shilling," as promised by the first world's fair, London's 1851 Crystal Palace (Leapman 2001), as well as in gaining access to the full range of activities of contemporary society, including arts and culture.[3] As such, patrons could have a bratwurst in the German beer garden between taking in a fashion show of Canadian design and a tour of the International Fine Arts exhibit or a ride on the Gyrotron in the amusement park, La Ronde. Fifty-five million entrances later, Expo 67 largely fulfilled its universalist purposes, as well as its nationalist ones—it both garnered international acclaim as a meeting place of nations and made Canada "sexy."[4]

Expo 67 was also the keystone event of Canada's Centennial celebrations, meant to endorse a unified vision of the country on its one hundredth birthday since Confederation. The celebrations were overseen by the Centennial Commission, established in 1964 to "promote interest in the Centennial and to plan programs and projects related to the Centennial's historical significance" (Standing Committee on Canadian Heritage 2012, 4).[5] To stage such a harmonious and celebratory national image,

> the Centennial Commission drew up plans and sought proposals for events on the national and the community scale. They supported a number of monumental national initiatives, including the flagship Expo 67 and the National Arts Centre [in Ottawa], but also embraced smaller and more mobile events, such as the travelling Centennial Train exhibition and iconic appearances by Bobby Gimby singing his "Ca-na-da" song with choirs of children. (Filewod 2018, 48)[6]

Some argue that the Centennial celebrations, and Expo 67 in particular, papered over tensions between Canada and Quebec, where secularism, an educated francophone bourgeoisie, and a growing state bureaucracy had transformed the social, cultural, and political landscape in the years following 1960—an epoch of prosperity and social change known as the Quiet Revolution. Certainly, the fact that this International and Universal Exposition happened at all, never mind its successful burnishing of Canada's image, was taken as another proof of Quebec's increasing capabilities for self-governance (Curien 2006). For instance, social scientist Pauline Curien (2007) argues that Quebec discovered its own "genius" and powers at Expo as much as it discovered the rest of the world. By 1967 Quebec's independence movement had already produced *indépendantiste* political parties (the Parti Québécois was the result of a 1968 merger of three such groups) and the Front de libération du Québec (active from 1963 to 1972), a radical separatist group that committed terrorist acts, including bombings, against representatives of Canadian federalism and Anglo-American capitalist imperialism in their quest for sovereignty. Sovereigntist aspirations were fanned during the Expo summer by French Prime Minister Charles de Gaulle's famous "Vive le Québec libre" call from the balcony of Montreal City Hall.

From de Gaulle's *coup de théâtre* to the costuming of Expo's national pavilion hostesses in the "traditional dress" of their countries to the immersive environments of the Quebec pavilion, "theatre" was everywhere at the 1967 International and Universal Exhibition, a pervasiveness consistent with the centrality of display to world's fairs. Augmenting Expo 67's attractions was a kind of cultural Olympiad called the World Festival: a "unique programme of the performing arts, spectaculars, sports and folkloric entertainments from six continents" (*World Festival* 1967). This World Festival—organized and operated by the Theatre Division of the exposition—brought the likes of the Kabuki Theatre of Japan, the National Theatre of Great Britain, the Paris Opera Ballet, and the Cameri Theatre of Israel to the three theatres of downtown Montreal's recently constructed Place des Arts.[7] To accommodate additional companies and acts of a more popular nature, the Expo architects designed three large performance venues on the Expo site itself, including the 2,000-seat "Expo-Théâtre" and the modular 33,170-seat Autostade, which received (among other attractions) Carol Channing in *Hello, Dolly!* and the Shell Centennial [Car] Rally 4000, respectively. The third new performance venue— "entirely devoted to popular entertainment"—was the 1,500-seat "Jardin des étoiles" (Canadian Corporation 1969, 2309).

In addition to these new venues were the numerous theatre spaces built into the national, commercial, and thematic pavilions whose programming was the purview of the pavilion sponsors. Among these was the home of the "Canadian revue": a 500-seat theatre at the heart of an Arts Centre (Figure 30.2) on the 11.5-acre Canada Pavilion site, the biggest of the fair. Nestled amidst a library, a gallery, a restaurant, and a café, the Arts Centre theatre sat adjacent to the main Canada Pavilion, topped with its distinctive, climbable, nine-storey, inverted-pyramid structure dubbed the "Katimavik," or "meeting place" in Inuktitut.

But what Canadian performances would populate these purpose-built venues on the grounds of the Canada Pavilion? Such was the challenge issued to Samuel Gesser, the Montreal impresario hired as *"conseiller artistique"* of the performing arts division of the Canadian Government participation at Expo 67. A music promoter and producer who made his name in the 1950s by producing "more than 100 original records [of Canadian folk music] for [the influential U.S. folk label] Folkways," Gesser used his extensive knowledge of Canadian musicians to curate an impressive roster, evenly balanced between French-language and English-language artists, who filled sixty-five hours per week in the Arts Centre theatre and the exterior bandshell ("A Finding Aide" 2006). As the Theatre and Bandshell schedule documents (Figure 30.3) show, organists, soloists, chamber music groups, and jazz and folk musicians all made appearances, alongside Les Feux-Follets, Canada's first professional folk-dance troupe. And yet, in this abundant offer of Canadian performing arts in both official languages, there was no theatre. Gesser had expressed a concern that was not particularly uncommon among cultural elites at the time when

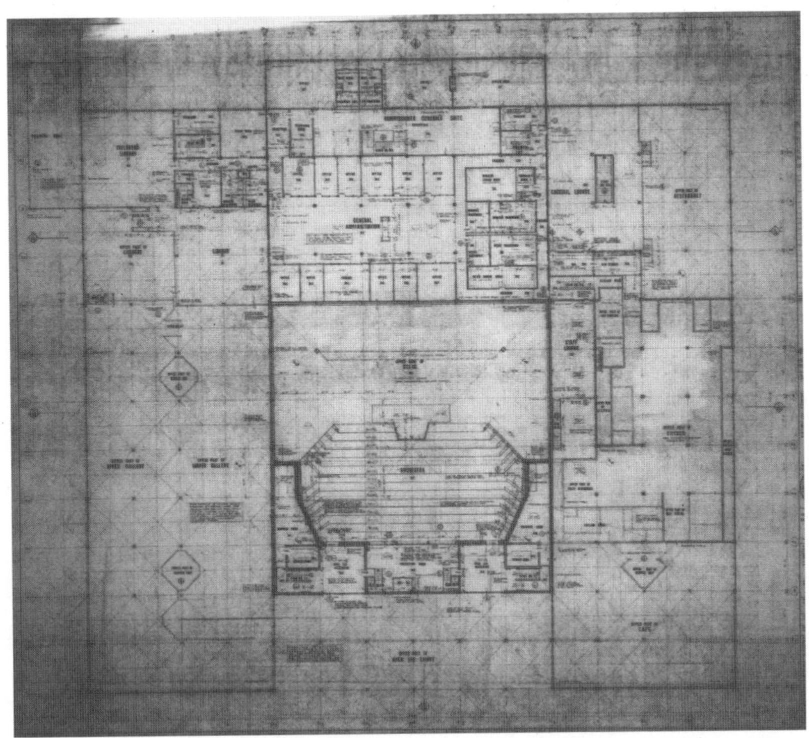

FIGURE 30.2: *Architectural plan of the theatre in the Canada Pavilion's Arts Centre, 1966–67.*

File I-131450, Department of Industry, Trade and Commerce fonds, Library and Archives Canada. © Government of Canada. Reproduced with the permission of Library and Archives Canada.

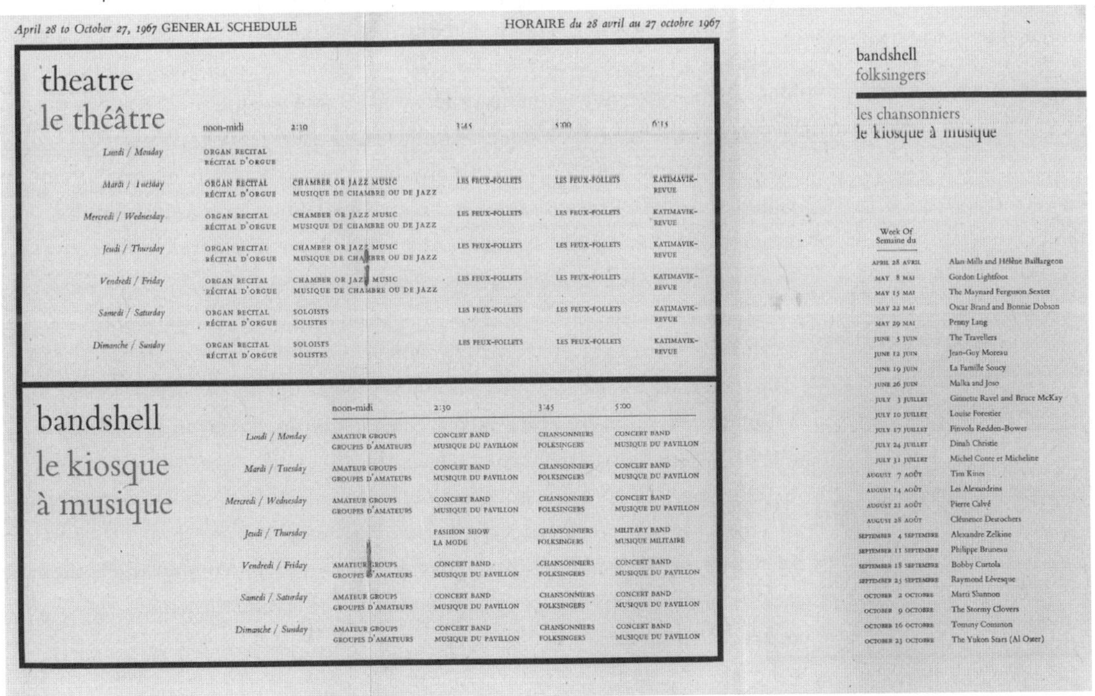

April 28 to October 27, 1967 GENERAL SCHEDULE

HORAIRE du 28 avril au 27 octobre 1967

theatre / le théâtre

	noon-midi	2:30	3:45	5:00	6:15
Lundi / Monday	ORGAN RECITAL / RÉCITAL D'ORGUE				
Mardi / Tuesday	ORGAN RECITAL / RÉCITAL D'ORGUE	CHAMBER OR JAZZ MUSIC / MUSIQUE DE CHAMBRE OU DE JAZZ	LES FEUX-FOLLETS	LES FEUX-FOLLETS	KATIMAVIK-REVUE
Mercredi / Wednesday	ORGAN RECITAL / RÉCITAL D'ORGUE	CHAMBER OR JAZZ MUSIC / MUSIQUE DE CHAMBRE OU DE JAZZ	LES FEUX-FOLLETS	LES FEUX-FOLLETS	KATIMAVIK-REVUE
Jeudi / Thursday	ORGAN RECITAL / RÉCITAL D'ORGUE	CHAMBER OR JAZZ MUSIC / MUSIQUE DE CHAMBRE OU DE JAZZ	LES FEUX-FOLLETS	LES FEUX-FOLLETS	KATIMAVIK-REVUE
Vendredi / Friday	ORGAN RECITAL / RÉCITAL D'ORGUE	CHAMBER OR JAZZ MUSIC / MUSIQUE DE CHAMBRE OU DE JAZZ	LES FEUX-FOLLETS	LES FEUX-FOLLETS	KATIMAVIK-REVUE
Samedi / Saturday	ORGAN RECITAL / RÉCITAL D'ORGUE	SOLOISTS / SOLISTES		LES FEUX-FOLLETS	KATIMAVIK-REVUE
Dimanche / Sunday	ORGAN RECITAL / RÉCITAL D'ORGUE	SOLOISTS / SOLISTES	LES FEUX-FOLLETS	LES FEUX-FOLLETS	KATIMAVIK-REVUE

bandshell / le kiosque à musique

	noon-midi	2:30	3:45	5:00
Lundi / Monday	AMATEUR GROUPS / GROUPES D'AMATEURS	CONCERT BAND / MUSIQUE DU PAVILLON	CHANSONNIERS FOLKSINGERS	CONCERT BAND / MUSIQUE DU PAVILLON
Mardi / Tuesday	AMATEUR GROUPS / GROUPES D'AMATEURS	CONCERT BAND / MUSIQUE DU PAVILLON	CHANSONNIERS FOLKSINGERS	CONCERT BAND / MUSIQUE DU PAVILLON
Mercredi / Wednesday	AMATEUR GROUPS / GROUPES D'AMATEURS	CONCERT BAND / MUSIQUE DU PAVILLON	CHANSONNIERS FOLKSINGERS	CONCERT BAND / MUSIQUE DU PAVILLON
Jeudi / Thursday		FASHION SHOW / LA MODE	CHANSONNIERS FOLKSINGERS	MILITARY BAND / MUSIQUE MILITAIRE
Vendredi / Friday	AMATEUR GROUPS / GROUPES D'AMATEURS	CONCERT BAND / MUSIQUE DU PAVILLON	CHANSONNIERS FOLKSINGERS	CONCERT BAND / MUSIQUE DU PAVILLON
Samedi / Saturday	AMATEUR GROUPS / GROUPES D'AMATEURS	CONCERT BAND / MUSIQUE DU PAVILLON	CHANSONNIERS FOLKSINGERS	CONCERT BAND / MUSIQUE DU PAVILLON
Dimanche / Sunday	AMATEUR GROUPS / GROUPES D'AMATEURS	CONCERT BAND / MUSIQUE DU PAVILLON	CHANSONNIERS FOLKSINGERS	CONCERT BAND / MUSIQUE DU PAVILLON

bandshell folksingers / les chansonniers — le kiosque à musique

Week Of / Semaine du	
APRIL 28 AVRIL	Alan Mills and Hélène Baillargeon
MAY 8 MAI	Gordon Lightfoot
MAY 15 MAI	The Maynard Ferguson Sextet
MAY 22 MAI	Oscar Brand and Bonnie Dobson
MAY 29 MAI	Penny Lang
JUNE 5 JUIN	The Travellers
JUNE 12 JUIN	Jean-Guy Moreau
JUNE 19 JUIN	La Famille Soucy
JUNE 26 JUIN	Malka and Joso
JULY 3 JUILLET	Ginnette Ravel and Bruce McKay
JULY 10 JUILLET	Louise Forestier
JULY 17 JUILLET	Finvola Redden-Bower
JULY 24 JUILLET	Dinah Christie
JULY 31 JUILLET	Michel Conte et Micheline
AUGUST 7 AOÛT	Tim Kines
AUGUST 14 AOÛT	Les Alexandrins
AUGUST 21 AOÛT	Pierre Calvé
AUGUST 28 AOÛT	Clémence Desrochers
SEPTEMBER 4 SEPTEMBRE	Alexandre Zelkine
SEPTEMBER 11 SEPTEMBRE	Philippe Bruneau
SEPTEMBER 18 SEPTEMBRE	Bobby Curtola
SEPTEMBER 25 SEPTEMBRE	Raymond Lévesque
OCTOBER 2 OCTOBRE	Marti Shannon
OCTOBER 9 OCTOBRE	The Stormy Clovers
OCTOBER 16 OCTOBRE	Tommy Common
OCTOBER 23 OCTOBRE	The Yukon Stars (Al Oster)

FIGURE 30.3: *Weekly schedule of the theatre and the bandshell of the Canada Pavilion.*

File 00797, Sam Gesser—Bandshell Schedule Expo '67. Courtesy of the Jewish Public Library Archives, Montreal.

8.	Indeed, his first play, *Tit-Coq* (1948), which starred a Fridolin-like main character played by Gélinas himself, toured the country (in English) after more than three hundred performances in its first run in French in Montreal.

a self-consciously Canadian drama and theatre was still being forged: "the theatre may be the most difficult to achieve [of the performing arts programming in the theatre and the bandshell]. Nothing or very little has been done as far as we know—and we wonder what will come of it" (Davidson 1966). To resolve this issue required a shift in practice—from curating and presenting to creating and producing.

Into this gap of programming and imagination stepped the mainstays of Canadian popular theatre of the day. Invited by the commissioner of the Canadian Government Pavilion to "produce an attraction in the two official languages" (Brown 1966), Gratien Gélinas and the comedy duo Johnny Wayne and Frank Shuster ultimately realized the vision of a Canadian national performance as reflecting an officially bilingual and bicultural country. Gélinas was a legendary monologist, vaudevillian, and playwright who is widely credited as having founded a national Quebecois theatre with his revue character, Fridolin, "initially an endearing street urchin, evolving into a good-humoured critic of social norms and individual foibles" whose monologues anchored annual variety shows between 1938 and 1946 (Doucette 2010, 229). In his long and varied career, which included founding the Comédie-Canadienne theatre in Montreal, Gélinas advocated for a French Canadian national and popular theatre, while also working regularly with his English-speaking counterparts.[8] Less bilingual than Gélinas but equally committed to home-grown entertainment, the Jewish Torontonians Johnny Wayne and Frank Shuster also made their name in variety performance as writer-performer-stagers of satirical comic sketches in the 1930s and 1940s. With their "unique brand of literate farce, a mixing of witty or high-toned satire with low comedy and slapstick" (Rutherford 1990, 210), Wayne and Shuster conquered American and Canadian airwaves; in the US, they were Ed Sullivan's most frequent guests and at home they appeared regularly on CBC radio and then television until Wayne's death in 1990. Drawing on their shared contacts and collective experience, Gélinas plus Wayne and Shuster created a one-hour, $255,950 variety entertainment called *Katimavik-Revue*: a name that both signalled its location next to the nine-storey "Katimavik" atop the Canada Pavilion and pointed to the show's purpose as another kind of "meeting place."

Billed as a satirical take on Expo 67 and its visitors, the *Katimavik-Revue* took the form of a variety entertainment—a combination of sketches, songs, dance numbers, and set-pieces. Popular entertainments historian Don B. Wilmeth notes that the revue form "was not simply a string of speciality acts but [its program] was devised especially for the production," which was held together by both a "theme or current political, social or theatrical events" and an ensemble of performers (1982, 165–66). Figure 30.4 is the "rough outline" of the revue developed largely, it seems, by Wayne and Shuster, in which one can see the kinds of numbers projected for the program and the people in charge of executing them.

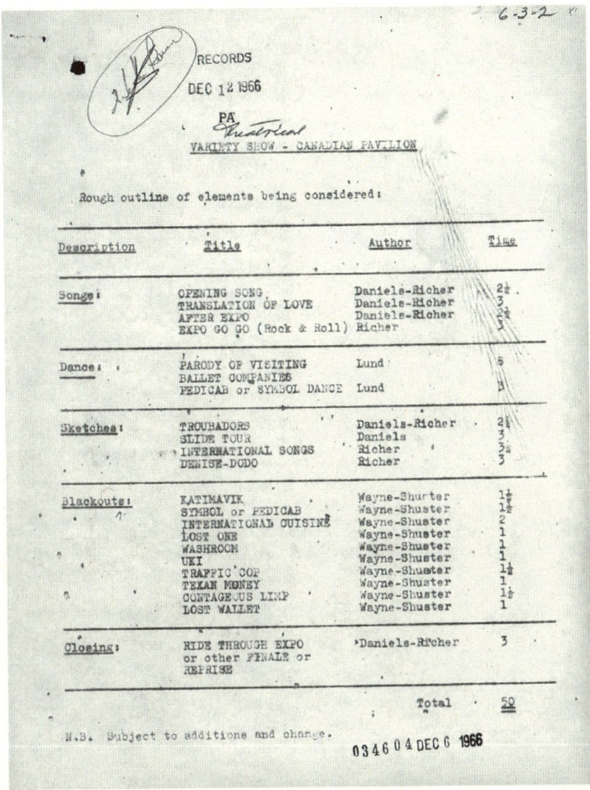

RECORDS
DEC 12 1966

PA

VARIETY SHOW - CANADIAN PAVILION

Rough outline of elements being considered:

Description	Title	Author	Time
Songs:	OPENING SONG	Daniels-Richer	2½
	TRANSLATION OF LOVE	Daniels-Richer	3
	AFTER EXPO	Daniels-Richer	2½
	EXPO GO GO (Rock & Roll)	Richer	3
Dance:	PARODY OF VISITING BALLET COMPANIES	Lund	5
	PEDICAB or SYMBOL DANCE	Lund	3
Sketches:	TROUBADORS	Daniels-Richer	2½
	SLIDE TOUR	Daniels	3
	INTERNATIONAL SONGS	Richer	3½
	DENISE-DODO	Richer	3
Blackouts:	KATIMAVIK	Wayne-Shurter	1½
	SYMBOL or PEDICAB	Wayne-Shuster	1½
	INTERNATIONAL CUISINE	Wayne-Shuster	2
	LOST ONE	Wayne-Shuster	1
	WASHROOM	Wayne-Shuster	1
	UKI	Wayne-Shuster	1
	TRAFFIC COP	Wayne-Shuster	1½
	TEXAN MONEY	Wayne-Shuster	1
	CONTAGEOUS LIMP	Wayne-Shuster	1½
	LOST WALLET	Wayne-Shuster	1
Closing:	RIDE THROUGH EXPO or other FINALE or REPRISE	Daniels-Richer	3
		Total	50

N.B. Subject to additions and change.

0346 04 DEC 6 1966

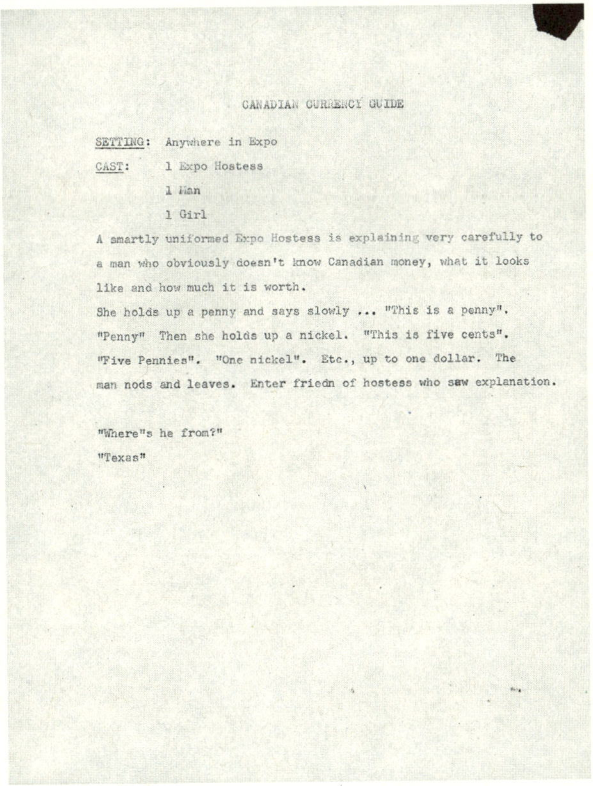

CANADIAN CURRENCY GUIDE

SETTING: Anywhere in Expo

CAST: 1 Expo Hostess

         1 Man

         1 Girl

A smartly uniformed Expo Hostess is explaining very carefully to
a man who obviously doesn't know Canadian money, what it looks
like and how much it is worth.
She holds up a penny and says slowly ... "This is a penny".
"Penny" Then she holds up a nickel. "This is five cents".
"Five Pennies". "One nickel". Etc., up to one dollar. The
man nods and leaves. Enter friedn of hostess who saw explanation.

"Where"s he from?"
"Texas"

FIGURE 30.6: *Handwritten notes.* Revues-idées–Exposition universelle, 1963, Gratien Gélinas fonds, MG30-D406, vol. 7, Library and Archives Canada. Courtesy of the Estate of Gratien Gélinas.

FIGURE 30.7: *Annotated typescript of "Preliminary Routine."* Katimavik Revue, Expo '67, Script, Frank Shuster fonds, MG31-D251, vol. 21, Library and Archives Canada. Courtesy of the Frank Shuster and Johnny Wayne Estates.

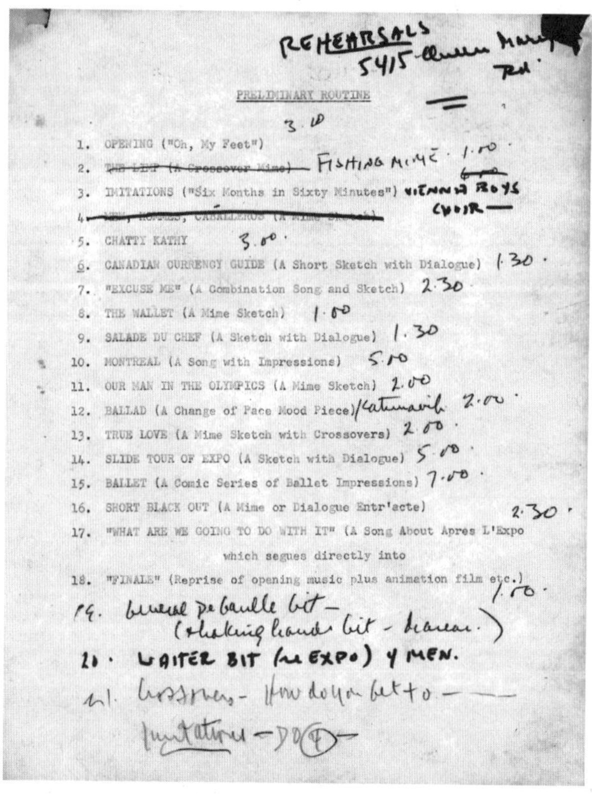

9. Daniels went on to pen many
    episodes of the *Mary Tyler
    Moore* show, among others,
    while Gilles Richer's sitcom
    television show, *Moi et l'autre*—
    in which *Katimavik-Revue*
    performers Denise Filiatrault
    and Dominique Michel
    starred—was a huge hit for
    Radio-Canada from 1966 to
    1971. In 1967 choreographer
    and director Alan Lund was
    touring *Anne of Green Gables*,
    the musical he had directed
    that would come to know a
    certain success.

10. "Go-go" was a type of popular
    dance music in Quebec in the
    1960s.

Wayne and Shuster are in charge of the "Blackouts"—short, rapid-fire gags that do not advance plot and that end abruptly in a blackout (see Figure 30.5). Two television writers, Stan Daniels and Gilles Richer, are charged with the sketches (of approximately three minutes each and thus double the length of the blackouts) and with the songs (two-and-a-half to three minutes each), while Alan Lund choreographs the two dances.[9]

The notes in Figure 30.6, in the hand of Gélinas, were scribbled down in 1963, the year after Montreal was awarded the 1967 International and Universal Exposition. As Gélinas would not be brought into the Canada Pavilion entertainment project until 1966, these notes represent an imagined contribution to an imagined revue at Expo 67. Still, one can't help but wonder if his ideas for "*Le gogo de l'expo*" were discussed with Gilles Richer, who is credited with the song "Expo Go Go (Rock & Roll)" for the revue.[10]

The undated typed listing of numbers for the *Katimavik-Revue* in Figure 30.7 is annotated by Shuster, who tracks the running times of each segment of the show. Like Gélinas, Shuster kept detailed records of his professional activities; unlike Gélinas, Shuster filed drafts of sketches from this production. His marginalia on these typewritten pages and his handwritten notes on others point to Shuster's active role in rehearsals in Montreal, which newspaper and magazine coverage indicates took place in March and April 1967. Here, we see the dynamism of the revue as numbers are cut, replaced, and added; the revue form's internal variety is also on display—a "change of pace mood piece" sits between two mime sketches and amid other "bits" including songs, dances, and impressions.

Like Expo as a whole, the *Katimavik-Revue* also had to straddle the universalist aspirations of the international exposition movement and the nationalist agendas at play in the Canada Pavilion. Expo's internationalism was specifically highlighted in two types of acts: impressions and "crossovers"—literally, performers crossing the stage via the conceit of immediately recognizable situations or relations (e.g., a bickering couple). Impressions of Expo's celebrity visitors were performed and included French, American, and Quebecois luminaries such as Maurice Chevalier and Brigitte Bardot, Ed Sullivan and Frank Sinatra, and Gilles Vigneault and Monique Leyrac. In the "Vamp with Crossovers" number in Figure 30.8, each national pavilion named (Russia, Cuba, Japan, etc.) can be reached through an ethnic joke.

In keeping with Gesser's other performing arts programming, the revue trumpeted its "Canadian-ness" in its bicultural artistic team, and in its resolute—if not thorough—bilingualism. Of the extant textual materials for the show, only the songs—"Oh My Feet / *Mes pieds*" (Figure 30.9), "*Qu'allons nous en faire* / What are we going to do with it?," and "Imitations"—show French and English intermingling to produce a common set of meanings. In the extant sketches and blackouts where the languages are mixed, the mixing is used either for linguistic puns or for clear comic effect—to make a joke at

FIGURE 30.8: *Manuscript of "Vamp with Crossovers."* Katimavik Revue, Expo '67. Script, Frank Shuster fonds, MG31-D251 vol. 21, Library and Archives Canada. Courtesy of the Frank Shuster and Johnny Wayne Estates.

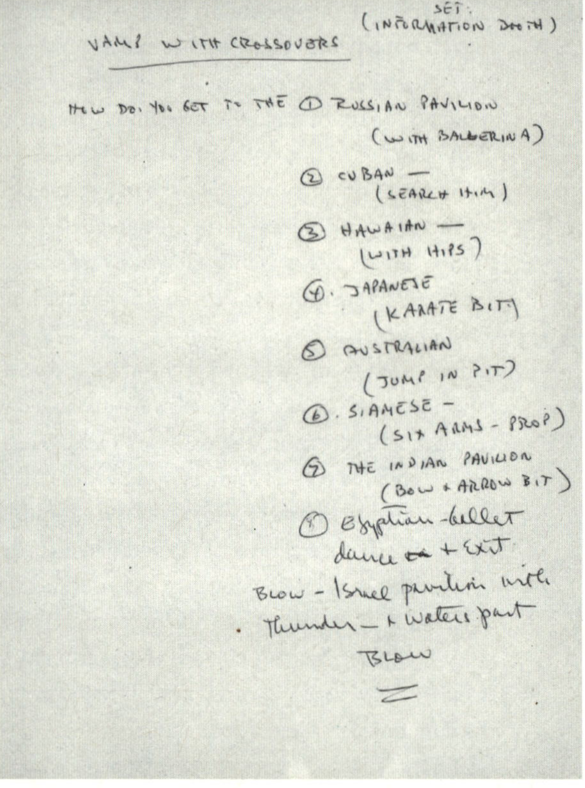

SET: (INFORMATION BOOTH)
VAMP WITH CROSSOVERS
HOW DO YOU GET TO THE ① RUSSIAN PAVILION
(WITH BALLERINA)
② CUBAN — (SEARCH HIM)
③ HAWAIAN — (WITH HIPS)
④ JAPANESE (KARATE BIT)
⑤ AUSTRALIAN (JUMP IN PIT)
⑥ SIAMESE — (SIX ARMS – PROP)
⑦ THE INDIAN PAVILION (BOW + ARROW BIT)
⑧ Egyptian ballet dance + exit
BLOW — Israel pavilion with Thunder — + waters part
BLOW

FIGURE 30.9: *Typescript of opening song "Oh My Feet / Mes pieds."* Katimavik Revue, Expo '67. Script, Frank Shuster fonds, MG31-D251 vol. 21, Library and Archives Canada. Courtesy of the Frank Shuster and Johnny Wayne Estates.

(Pre Show with Slides)
OPENING

Oh all the stunning pavillons
And oh, all the folks in their millions
And oh, my feet
Oh, les spectacles formidables
Oh, inventions incroyables
Oh,
(E) My feet
Ah, et la place des nations, magnifique !
Ah, that superb underwater display
And ah ....
Oh ....
Hou .... mes pieds !

OPENING (2)

Oh, all those rides at "La Ronde"
Oh, tous les grands de ce monde
Oh,
(F) mes pieds
Oh, the enchanting "village"
Oh, quel charmant paysage
Oh,
(E) mes pieds
Ah, all the lights and excitement and music
Ah, les structures, les formes insolites
Ah ....
Oh ....
Hou .... my feet !

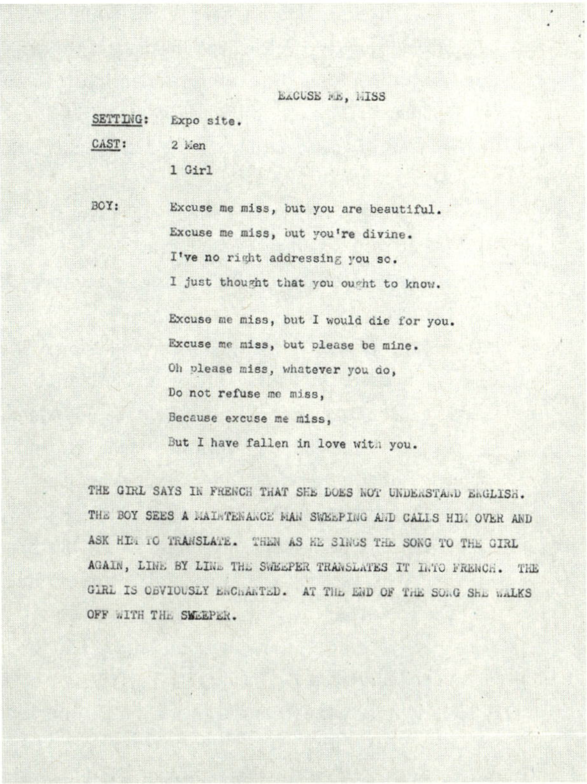

EXCUSE ME, MISS

SETTING: Expo site.

CAST: 2 Men
1 Girl

BOY: Excuse me miss, but you are beautiful.
Excuse me miss, but you're divine.
I've no right addressing you so.
I just thought that you ought to know.

Excuse me miss, but I would die for you.
Excuse me miss, but please be mine.
Oh please miss, whatever you do,
Do not refuse me miss,
Because excuse me miss,
But I have fallen in love with you.

THE GIRL SAYS IN FRENCH THAT SHE DOES NOT UNDERSTAND ENGLISH. THE BOY SEES A MAINTENANCE MAN SWEEPING AND CALLS HIM OVER AND ASK HIM TO TRANSLATE. THEN AS HE SINGS THE SONG TO THE GIRL AGAIN, LINE BY LINE THE SWEEPER TRANSLATES IT INTO FRENCH. THE GIRL IS OBVIOUSLY ENCHANTED. AT THE END OF THE SONG SHE WALKS OFF WITH THE SWEEPER.

FIGURE 30.10: *Typescript of sketch, "Excuse Me, Miss." Katimavik Revue, Expo '67. Script, Frank Shuster fonds, MG31-D251 vol. 21, Library and Archives Canada. Courtesy of the Frank Shuster and Johnny Wayne Estates.*

the expense of a character who doesn't understand one or the other language, for instance, as in "Excuse Me, Miss" (Figure 30.10).

Canada's original theatre creation for Expo 67 presented a humorous and harmonious image of the country on its one-hundredth birthday to an international audience. In bringing together the Montreal- and Toronto-based artistic teams, the *Katimavik-Revue* performed a humanist nationalism. That is, like Expo itself, the revue both pointed to national and linguistic distinctions and reconciled them in spectacle. The revue form's use of thematic unity and a common ensemble allowed the numbers' and performers' internal variety to be showcased but still contained by the overarching structure and the comic tone of the show, which reflected the tertiary position of speakers of languages other than Canada's two official tongues. The documents featured in this chapter take on special significance since, to my knowledge, there exists no publicly available recording nor photo documentation of the *Katimavik-Revue*.

Bibliography and Further Reading

"About World Expos." n.d. Bureau international des expositions. Accessed September 10, 2018. https://www.bie-paris.org/site/en/about-world-expos.

Brown, H. Leslie. 1966. Letters to Gratien Gélinas and Wayne and Shuster, March 1, 1966. RG20, vol. 1898, folder 6-3-2-1, Special Events–Performing Arts–Variety Show, Library and Archives Canada.

Canadian Corporation for the 1967 World Exhibition. 1969. *General Report on the 1967 World Exhibition*. Vol. 4, *Department of Operations*. Ottawa: Queen's Printer.

Curien, Pauline. 2006. "Une catharsis identitaire: L'avènement d'une nouvelle vision du Québec à l'Expo 67." *Anthropologie et Sociétés* 30 (2): 129–51. doi:10.7202/014117ar.

———. 2007. "Expo 67: La découverte d'un Québec éblouissante." *Cap-aux-Diamants*, no. 89, 25–28.

Davidson, Hugh. 1966. "Overall Budget for Theatre, Bandshell & Entertainment Therein." Memo from Davidson to Mr. Leslie Brown, February 24, 1966. RG20, vol. 1897, folder 6-3-1-1, Special Events–Performing Arts–Variety Show, Library and Archives Canada.

Davies, Helen. 1999. "The Politics of Participation: A Study of Canada's Centennial Celebration." PHD diss., University of Manitoba.

Doucette, Leonard E. 2010. "Gratien Gélinas." In *Oxford Companion to Theatre and Performance*, edited by Dennis Kennedy. Oxford: Oxford University Press. https://www.oxfordreference.com/view/10.1093/acref/9780199574193.001.0001/acref-9780199574193-e-1482.

Expo (International Exhibitions Bureau). 1967. "Katimavik-Revue." In *Theatre and Bandshell: Performances, Canadian Government Pavilion, Expo 67*, 31–32. Ottawa: Queen's Printer.

Filewod, Alan. 2018. "A Confederation Minstrel Show: *The Centennial Play* of 1967." *Canadian Theatre Review* 174 (Spring): 48–51.

"A Finding Aide to the Samuel Gesser Fonds." 2006. Jewish Public Library Archives, Montreal.

Gesser, Sam. 1966. Memo to Gratien Gélinas, copied to H. Leslie Brown and Gilles Richer, "Variety Show–Canadian Pavilion re: Rough outline of the elements being considered," December 6, 1966. RG20, vol. 1898, folder 6-3-2-1, Special Events–Performing Arts–Variety Show, Library and Archives Canada.

Gold, John R., and Margaret M. Gold. 2016. *Cities of Culture: Staging International Festivals and the Urban Agenda, 1851–2000*. London: Routledge.

Hurley, Erin. 2011. *National Performance: Representing Quebec from Expo 67 to Céline Dion*. Toronto: University of Toronto Press.

Jasmin, Yves. 1997. *La petite histoire d'Expo 67: L'Exposition universelle et international de Montréal comme vous ne l'avez jamais vu*. Montréal: Québec/Amérique.

Leapman, Michael. 2001. *The World for a Shilling: How the Great Exhibition of 1851 Shaped a Nation*. London: Headline.

Pevere, Geoff, and Dymond Greig. 1996. "When We Were Fab: Expo '67." In *Mondo Canuck: A Canadian Pop Culture Odyssey*, 50–57. Scarborough, ON: Prentice Hall Canada.

Riar, Inderbir Singh. 2014. "Expo 67, or the Architecture of Late Modernity." PHD diss., Columbia University.

Rutherford, Paul. 1990. *When Television Was Young: Primetime Canada, 1952–1967*. Toronto: University of Toronto Press.

Rydell, Robert, and Rob Kroes. 1994. *Buffalo Bill in Bologna: The Americanization of the World, 1869–1992*. Chicago: University of Chicago Press.

Standing Committee on Canadian Heritage. 2012. *Canada's 150th Anniversary in 2017: Report of the Standing Committee on Canadian Heritage*. September 2012. 41st Parliament, 1st Session.

Wilmeth, Don B. 1982. "The Musical Revue and Early Musical Theater." In *Variety Entertainment and Outdoor Amusements: A Reference Guide*, 165–84. Westport, CT: Greenwood Press.

The World Festival: Programme for Performing Arts and Activities, Expo 67, Montreal Canada. 2nd ed. Universal and International Exhibition of 1967, Montreal, Canada, April 28–October 27, 1967. Accessed September 29, 2021. https://www.worldsfairphotos. com/expo67/brochures/world-festival.pdf.

31 : *Lament for Confederation* (1967)

Assertions of Sovereignty

JENN COLE

1. The Idle No More movement began as a protest against Bill c-45, a bill tabled by the federal government under Stephen Harper in 2012, which threatened to claw back the rights of Indigenous people in Canada in the service of capitalist resource extraction through changes to the Indian Act, the Navigable Waters Protection Act, and the Environmental Assessment Act. Idle No More has since evolved into an international Indigenous-led movement calling "on all people to join in a peaceful revolution which honours Indigenous sovereignty and which protects the land, the water, and the sky" (Idle No More 2020). The Truth and Reconciliation Commission spent six years travelling to all parts of Canada to hear from more than six thousand Indigenous people who had been taken from their families as children, often forcibly, and placed in residential schools. The process has resulted in calls to action towards reconciliation that require the nation-state of Canada to reconsider "virtually all aspects of Canadian society" as outcroppings of genocide (Truth and Reconciliation of Canada 2015).

2. "Turtle Island" is a traditional name for the land mass that extends across the Americas based on Anishinaabe and Haudenosaunee creation stories. In certain Northwest Coast and Inuit nations,

CHIEF DAN GEORGE, born Geswanouth Slahoot in 1899, was Chief of Tsleil-Waututh First Nation in British Columbia from 1951 to 1963, a film and stage actor, a poet, and an Indigenous rights activist (McCardle 2007). His mother was Squamish and his father Tsleil-Waututh. George lived on the Burrard Band Reserve all his life, where most of the men in his community worked at a nearby lumber mill (CBC 1973). One of his most well-known poems and performances is the 1967 "Lament for Confederation." Performed for Centennial celebrations, recorded by the CBC, and widely published in the late 1960s, the poem was taken up again many times on the celebration of Canada's 150th by critics who felt the poem's powerful message had not been well heeded. In the context of the Truth and Reconciliation Commission's 94 Calls to Action and in an era marked by Idle No More, intensive land defences by Indigenous nations, and Indigenous resurgence movements, George's poem is hugely valuable for contemporary study.[1]

Chief Dan George began acting late in life. Before that, he worked as a bus driver, construction worker, longshoreman, logger, and itinerant musician. He began acting at the age of sixty as Ol' Antoine in a CBC show called *Cariboo Country*. When asked to audition for a new iteration of the role in a Hollywood film version of the show *Smith!*, George followed the advice of his wife, Amy, who told him to take the role to show other Indigenous people what they could achieve (Mortimer 1981, 25). Métis actor and champion of Indigenous performance in Canada, Marrie Mumford (2019) describes how she and Indigenous actors across Turtle Island were cheering for George, recognizing the force of his achievements in representing the talents and values of Indigenous communities and performers.[2] George changed the way that the film industry portrayed Indigenous people. He refused to play demeaning Indigenous roles and advised directors and scene partners, altering scripts when necessary, to ensure that none of the ridicule he describes in his "Lament" would continue (CBC 1973). Sometimes, George delivered his lines so powerfully that his scene partners would break character, being moved to tears (Mortimer 1981, 26). At the peak of his career, George delivered an Oscar-nominated performance of Old Lodge Skins, alongside Dustin Hoffman, in Arthur Penn's 1970 film *Little Big Man*. George also performed in *The Ecstasy of Rita Joe*, George Ryga's play about a murdered Indigenous woman, at the Vancouver Playhouse Theatre Company in 1967 and at the National Arts Centre

FIGURE 31.1: *Chief Dan George at Empire Stadium, July 1, 1967. The photograph was reprinted in the* Vancouver Sun *on July 2, 2015, with the caption, "On Canada's 100th birthday, Chief Dan George silenced a crowd of 32,000 with his 'Lament for Confederation' at Empire Stadium."* Photograph by Glenn Baglo. Material republished with the express permission of Vancouver Sun, a division of Postmedia Network Inc.

as its inaugural play in 1969. In 1971 George was made an Officer of the Order of Canada. The Chief Dan George Theatre, in the Department of Theatre at the University of Victoria, is named after him.

Chief Dan George performed "Lament for Confederation" with his children on July 1, 1967, at the Empire Stadium in Vancouver as part of Canada's centenary celebration of Confederation. The festivities at the stadium, with the exception of George's public lament, jubilantly honoured Canada's history and achievements. The day's events, offering a performative portrait of a relatively new nation, included chuck wagon races, military displays, acrobatic demonstrations, and a history pageant with nearly four thousand performers

(Dobie 1967b, 1–2). Large-scale displays of nationalism were also taking place in Montreal and Ottawa. At the same time, a train was crossing the country, its cars filled with museum displays depicting Canada since the beginning of its colonization processes—processes the exhibitions labelled "settlement" (*Confederation Train* 1967). Likewise, the event at the Empire Stadium focused on a Canadian history that, as George's "Lament" addresses, overlooked the experiences of Indigenous nations: "My nation was ignored in your history textbooks—they were little more important in the history of Canada than the buffalo that ranged the plains." Chief Dan George's performance reminded his audience what settler Canadians were so good at omitting from their histories: the vital presence of Indigenous Peoples, their sovereignty as nations, and that the country was founded on land theft and cultural genocide.

George's "Lament" was an important public critique of the founding of Canada through violent colonization, ecological destruction, and systemic racism. The criticism was so powerful that George's daughter, Amy George, was worried he would be killed for giving the speech (Kane 2017). As Leonard George, Dan George's son, expressed, "To stand up and tell the truth in such a profound way, he had no idea how the public would take to that" (Kane 2017).

"Lament for Confederation" begins, "How long have I known you, Oh Canada? A hundred years? Yes, a hundred years. And many, many *seelanum* more. And today, when you celebrate your hundred years, Oh Canada, I am sad for all the Indian people throughout the land." Already, in this opening address, George positions Canada as a new nation, meeting much, much older Coast Salish nations, whose calendar unapologetically continues to revolve around moons, not the settler calendar year. George's opening address also positions itself as a lamentation that a celebration like Confederation necessitates. While Canada was celebrating its one hundred years, there was plenty to be unhappy about if one paused to think about what that one hundred years had meant for Indigenous people. In response to the question, "Oh Canada, how can I celebrate with you?," George offers a list of the state's failings vis-à-vis Indigenous people. He describes life before colonization:

> *For I have known you when your forests were mine; when they gave me my meat and my clothing. I have known you in your streams and rivers where your fish flashed and danced in the sun, where the waters said come, come and eat of my abundance. I have known you in the freedom of the winds. And my spirit, like the winds, once roamed your good lands.*

In this passage, we witness deep spiritual and material connection to the land and a relationship of reciprocity between Indigenous people and our other relatives—tree nation, fish nation, sacred water—a relationship based upon taking care of one another. George has written elsewhere about family experiences that reflect spiritual and cultural values of Indigenous Peoples of Turtle Island:

My father loved the earth and all its creatures. The earth was his second mother. The earth and everything it contained was a gift from See-see-am… and the way to thank this great spirit was to use his gifts with respect.

I remember, as a little boy, fishing with him up Indian River and I can still see him as the sun rose above the mountain top in the early morning…I can see him standing by the water's edge with his arms raised above his head while he softly moaned…"Thank you, thank you." It left a deep impression on my young mind.

And I shall never forget his disappointment when once he caught me gaffing for fish "just for the fun of it." "My son" he said, "The Great Spirit gave you those fish to be your brothers, to feed you when you are hungry. You must respect them. You must not kill them just for the fun of it."

This then was the culture I was born into and for some years the only one I really knew or tasted. This is why I find it hard to accept many of the things I see around me. (George 2003, 35–36)

In his "Lament," George turns this image of reciprocal relationship with the land so that we see it distorted through the processes of colonialism. He says,

Oh Canada, how can I celebrate with you this centenary, this hundred years? Shall I thank you for the reserves that are left to me of my beautiful forests? For the canned fish of my rivers? For the loss of my pride and authority, even among my own people? For the lack of my will to fight back? No!

The salmon are now in tins. The autonomy to roam freely through the forests mutates to the image of reserves, which count for 0.36 per cent of the total land mass in Canada. These are not centenary conditions worth celebrating. Nor do they merit any thanks. George's "Lament" interrupts the 1967 celebration and calls for reflection by his immediate audience and by the Canadian nation-state. This performance conjures an opportunity for settler Canadians to move beyond the colonial forgetting of history books and beyond the mockeries of Indigenous people in popular entertainment. It asks them to expect to see Indigenous people in the seats of government.

The "Lament" is also a call to Indigenous uprising or rebirth. Through prayer to the Creator, George calls for a spiritual awakening of Indigenous people in the new context of this broken nation-to-nation relationship with Canada. Indigenous people will "rise up," they will "rise again," and George will

see our young braves and our chiefs sitting in the houses of law and government, ruling and being ruled by the knowledge and freedoms of our great land…So shall the next hundred years be the greatest in the proud history of our tribes and nations.

3. The CBC studio recording of
Chief Dan George's "Lament
for Confederation" is available
online, through CBC Archives:
https://www.cbc.ca/player/
play/937471043585.

George performed the poem accompanied by his children, who drummed and sang a song George had composed called "Prayer Song," which was later adopted by Coast Salish Chiefs as the Coast Salish Anthem (tsleilwautt 2015). George joined his children in song following the delivery of the text. The presence of Coast Salish song as part of a national celebration is hugely significant. On a day when Canada's forefathers were being recognized and celebrated from coast to coast, the George family publicly reclaimed and asserted their right to sing their songs in their language, practices that were banned alongside Indigenous gatherings by amendments to the Indian Act in 1884 and further suppressed by early church authorities, government policies, and residential schools. Singing in their own nation's language, the George family activated personal and political interventions into colonial history and an equally colonial present. George describes how his grandparents "were the great tribal singers and dancers of [his] tribe." But

> then the church came. And that was the beginning of the end of our way of life. The first mass celebrated on the North Shore took place right down in my grandfather's smokehouse. They told my grandmother, "You must forget your pagan ways." And from then on, she was forbidden by the church to sing or dance. From that time, no one ever heard her sing another song in public. And that was very hard for her. For it was part of her life as an Indian.
> (Mortimer 1981, 22)

The church's suppression of Indigenous song coincided with government restrictions on singing, dancing, and ceremony—policies aimed to erase the practices that grounded Indigenous people in their cultures and Indigenous identities. The presence of the Prayer Song as part of "Lament" both signalled and overturned Canada's suppression of Indigenous cultures.

According to newspapers, following George's soliloquy, the crowd of somewhere near thirty-two thousand sat for a moment in stunned silence and then burst into applause. Nevertheless, according to Dan George's son, Leonard George, some audience members threw garbage at George as they left the stadium (Kane 2017). But to look at the reception of George's performance, beyond the immediate audience response at the stadium, means to look to how the Canadian government and settler culture responded to George's call for historical reckoning in his "Lament," as well as at how Indigenous people responded to the call to rise up.

The centenary Canada Day performance was not taped, but the text appeared in newspapers in July of 1967. A few months later, the CBC created a studio recording of the "Lament" that was shown on *The 7 O'Clock Show* on November 27, 1967.[3] George also performed the poem again on CBC's *Very Interesting People*, hosted by Lorraine Thompson in 1973.

Prime Minister Lester B. Pearson was not present in Vancouver—he was in Ottawa with the Queen—but he certainly might have wanted to read George's performance text, since it was in part addressed to him. Following George's performance, Pearson's speeches to press representatives, international political figures, and graduating university classes demonstrate that the prime minister was very engaged by centenary activities. He used lessons learned in the 1967 celebrations to communicate about what it meant to be Canadian to the public. But he didn't listen to George.

In his addresses during Canada's centenary year, Prime Minister Pearson repeatedly described what centenary celebrations had taught him, but his takeaways from 1967 celebrations are steeped in colonial amnesia. Not only is George's performance not mentioned a single time in any of Pearson's addresses from July to September 1967, but Indigenous people are not mentioned a single time either. Instead, the prime minister perpetuated the concept of terra nullius, that Canada was created on "undiscovered," empty land—a concept that organizations such as the United Nations, the Supreme Court of Canada, and the Truth and Reconciliation Commission have subsequently urged the Canadian government to reject because of its illegality and violent consequences (Assembly of First Nations 2018).

According to Prime Minister Pearson, the events celebrating Confederation had helped to "restore and strengthen confidence in the country" (Prime Minister's Remarks 1967). He acknowledged that "'Centennial and Expo 67 and all that' is doing something to us" but its effects, given the stakes raised by George in his performance, are disappointingly void of attention to Indigenous Peoples:

> We are beginning to realize that Canadians can do anything that is required of them in this new century; as long as we work together in unity, as Canadians, cherishing our different cultures and traditions, and our special provincial ties and loyalties, for these things are good, provided they do not obstruct age full realization of the greater destiny of a united Canada, or hinder the building of a great nation strong at home and respected in its contribution to peace and good relations in the world. (Notes 1967)

Lodged firmly in the context of fraught English and French Canadian relations, Pearson's propagandizing the notion of "unity" implicitly refuses the presence and sovereignty of Indigenous nations while promoting a picture of co-operative founding French and British nations. Pearson validated "unity which recognizes that when Confederation was signed a hundred years ago there were two founding peoples. Or…'paternal races'" (Prime Minister's Remarks 1967). He also said,

> My belief in this country is a very simple one. I believe in a Canadian Confederation which is one sovereign state, but which is based on two languages and cultural groups who were there when the country was founded. The Fathers of Confederation understood this. (Transcript 1967)

The "Fathers of Confederation," one remembers, includes Sir John A. MacDonald, who has been hugely criticized for implementing genocidal policies that starved Indigenous people and required that Indigenous children attend residential schools. That Pearson asks for the nation to understand itself in the terms of its founding fathers' perspectives indicates that active reception of George's performance at government levels was impeded by the kind of colonial racism that embraced the Doctrine of Discovery and terra nullius. Pearson's addresses also point to how a colonial fantasy that ignored Indigenous sovereignty was necessary to uphold Confederation in a celebratory way.

What has changed? During the year of Canada's 150th birthday celebration—noted by many to be a dishonest birthdate for a nation settled on territory where hundreds of sovereign Indigenous nations have lived vibrantly for millennia—critics of Canada's celebrations reflected on Chief Dan George's "Lament" and on how far we've come since then. For instance, George's grandson, Chief Rueben George, noting the disproportionately high numbers of Indigenous children in government care, inadequate funding for housing and education, and the lack of clean water in First Nations communities, wrote, "There hasn't been much improvement in how Canada treats First Nations since George's speech" (Kane 2017). In another reflection piece, Sidd Bobb (2017), Chief Dan George's great-grandson, who owns and operates Aanmitaagzi/Big Medicine Studio on Lake Nipissing with Penny Couchie (Ojibwe/Mohawk), wrote that "much has changed and much remains the same." He writes about suicide among Indigenous youth and about rising up against feelings of shame, fear, and sadness caused by growing up in violence and alcoholism—experiences that have long links to colonialism, as George's "Lament" indicates. Bobb compares having to fish in his home territory hiding under a blanket at night to avoid criminalization to being made to lurk in the shadows as an Indigenous artist. He calls on the Canadian government to bring back the salmon to the Fraser River and to support Indigenous performance by Indigenous artists. We know George's "Lament" was significant for Indigenous people because it has been taken up again in the context of Canada's 150th birthday.

George's performance legacy continues. The current field of Indigenous performance, including dance, theatre, text-based plays, and film, is robust. Indigenous artists are representing themselves in varied and vital ways that challenge performance norms and generate specifically Indigenous artistic works. This does not mean that mainstream representation and funding of Indigenous performance is beyond critique, but it is worth noting that Indigenous performers are "rising up." Festivals like Weesageechak and Talking Stick, Indigenous performance programs at universities, the opening of the Indigenous Theatre at the National Arts Centre, the first Indigenous Fringe Festival at Nozhem First Peoples' Performance Space, the proliferation of Indigenous performance and dance companies—these are all signs that

4. Chief Dan George's grandson's performance of the "Prayer Song" from "Lament for Confederation" can be viewed online at https://www.youtube.com/watch?v=hrzveOSwHZw.

Indigenous people are disrupting the colonial story, taking storytelling into their own hands.

In George's performance of "Lament," the call to rise up like the thunderbird gains volume and momentum. According to the Squamish Lil'wat Cultural Centre website, Thunderbird is considered a grandfather figure who cares for the people. He sends gifts to the people in their time of need and can bring thunder and lightning to impose law, order, and protocol (Squamish Lil'wat 2016). George's "Lament" should not be taken as a pleading call to the Canadian government to be permitted to enter Parliament or legal systems, providing Indigenous people assimilate. It is an announcement that Indigenous people are coming, supported by their knowledges and sovereign relationships to this land, and that they will occupy sovereign spaces grounded in the power of their cultures. In George's home nation, the Tsleil-Waututh Sacred Trust continues to defend the land according to their sacred responsibility in court against government and corporate destruction of the land through pipelines (Tsleil-Waututh Nation 2018). His family and nation are both still singing the song.[4]

Bibliography and Further Reading

Assembly of First Nations. 2018. *Dismantling the Doctrine of Discovery*. http://www.afn.ca/wp-content/uploads/2018/02/18-01-22-Dismantling-the-Doctrine-of-Discovery-EN.pdf.

Bobb, Sid. 2017. "Chief Dan George's Great-Grandson Reflects." *Anishinaabek News*, May 13, 2017. http://anishinabeknews.ca/2017/05/13/chief-dan-georges-great-grandson-reflects/.

Bolten, Mike. 1967. "Chief Silences Birthday Crowd." *Vancouver Province*, July 3, 1967, 1, 7.

CBC. 1973. "Dan George." *Very Interesting People*. February 12, 1973. VHS recording. Library and Archives Canada.

———. n.d. "Lament for Confederation – Chief Dan George 1967." CBC Archives-Celebrations. Accessed October 30, 2021. https://www.cbc.ca/player/play/937471043585.

Confederation Train. 1967. "Modern Settlement." Exhibited in Coach Number 3. Contact sheet. Library and Archives Canada.

Dobie, George. 1967a. "Oh Canada – What a Birthday!" *Vancouver Province*, July 3, 1967, 1, 7.

———. 1967b. "'Twas a Happy Birthday!" *Vancouver Sun*, July 3, 1967, 1–2.

Findlay, Len. 2004. "Intent for a Nation." *English Studies in Canada* 30 (2) (June): 39–48.

George, Chief Dan. 1967. "A Lament for Confederation." *Vancouver Sun*, July 4, 1967, 6.

———. 2003. *The Best of Chief Dan George*. Surrey, BC: Hancock House.

Hopper, Tristan. 2018. "This Is What Sir John. A Macdonald Did to Indigenous People." *National Post*, August 28, 2018. https://nationalpost.com/news/canada/here-is-what-sir-john-a-macdonald-did-to-indigenous-people.

Idle No More. 2020. "About the Movement—Vision." https://idlenomore.ca/about-the-movement/.

Indigenous Corporate Training. 2017. "Reflections in 2017 on the 1967 Centennial Speech of Chief Dan George." *Indigenous Corporate Training* (blog), February 23, 2017.

https://www.ictinc.ca/blog/reflections-in-2017-on-the-1967-centennial-speech-of-chief-dan-george.

Kane, Laura. 2017. "Dan George's 'Lament for Confederation' Remembered." *Durham Region*, June 28, 2017. https://www.durhamregion.com/news-story/7396073-dan-george-s-lament-for-confederation-remembered/.

McCardle, Bennett. 2007. "Dan George." *Canadian Encyclopedia*. August 12, 2007. https://www.thecanadianencyclopedia.ca/en/article/dan-george.

Mortimer, Hilda. 1981. *You Call Me Chief: Impressions of the Life of Chief Dan George.* Toronto: Doubleday Canada.

Mumford, Marrie. 2019. Informal conversation with Jenn Cole, January 3, 2019.

National Arts Centre and Western Canada Arts Centre. 2008. *The Ecstasy of Rita Joe Study Guide.* https://nac-cna.ca/pdf/eth/0809/rita_joe_guide.pdf.

"1967 and 'Lament for a Confederation.'" 2016. *CanLit Guides*, UBC. http://canlitguides.ca/canlit- guides-editorial-team/indigenous-literary-history-1960s-1990/1967-and-lament-for-a-confederation/.

North Vancouver Museum and Archives. 2017. *The Chief Dan George Story and Coast Salish Ways: Teacher's Package.* https://monova.ca/wp-content/uploads/2014/04/CDNV_DISTRICT_HALL-3360931-v1-Chief_Dan_George_Grades_3-5_Teacher_s_Package.pdf.

Notes for the Prime Minister's Address at the Convocation of Dalhousie University, Halifax. 1967. July 14, 1967. Lester B. Pearson fonds, Speeches (N9), MG26-N9, vol. 44, Library and Archives Canada.

Prime Minister's Remarks at the Canadian Weekly Newspaper Association Banquet, Chateau Laurier. 1967. September 8, 1967. Lester B. Pearson fonds, Speeches (N9), MG26-N9, vol. 44, Library and Archives Canada.

Rogers, Janet. 2017. "Has Anything Changed?: Revisiting Chief Dan George's Iconic 'Lament for Confederation.'" *CBC Opinion*, November 27, 2017. http://www.cbc.ca/2017/has-anything-changed-revisiting-chief- dan-george-s-iconic-lament-for-confederation-1.4079657.

Squamish Lil'wat Cultural Centre. 2016. "The Thunderbird." https://shop.slcc.ca/learn/the-thunderbird/.

Transcript of the Prime Minister's Remarks at the Liberal Caucus Dinner, House of Commons, Ottawa. 1967. Sunday, September 24, 1967. Lester B. Pearson fonds, Speeches (N9), MG26-N9, vol. 44, Library and Archives Canada.

Truth and Reconciliation Commission of Canada. 2015. *Honouring the Truth, Reconciling for the Future: Summary of the Final Report of the Truth and Reconciliation Commission of Canada.* https://publications.gc.ca/collections/collection_2015/trc/IR4-7-2015-eng.pdf.

tsleilwautt. 2015. "Coast Salish Anthem—Chief Dan George Prayer Song—by Gabriel George." YouTube video, May 17, 2015. https://www.youtube.com/watch?v=hrzveOSwHZw.

Tsleil-Waututh Nation. 2018. "Statement Re Federal Government Pipeline Purchase Announcement." May 29, 2018. https://twnsacredtrust.ca/statement-regarding-federal-court-appeal-case/.

Lament for Confederation

CHIEF DAN GEORGE (GESWANOUTH)

How long have I known you, Oh Canada? A hundred years? Yes, a hundred years. And many many "seelanum" more. And today, when you celebrate your hundred years, oh Canada, I am sad for all the Indian people throughout the land.

For I have known you when your forests were mine; when they gave me my meat and my clothing. I have known you in your streams and rivers where your fish flashed and danced in the sun, where the waters said come, come and eat of my abundance. I have known you in the freedom of your winds. And my spirit, like the winds, once roamed your good lands.

But in the long hundred years since the white man came, I have seen my freedom disappear like the salmon going mysteriously out to sea. The white man's strange customs which I could not understand, pressed down upon me until I could no longer breathe.

When I fought to protect my land and my home, I was called a savage. When I neither understood nor welcomed this way of life, I was called lazy. When I tried to rule my people, I was stripped of my authority.

My nation was ignored in your history textbooks—they were little more important in the history of Canada than the buffalo that ranged the plains. I was ridiculed in your plays and motion pictures, and when I drank your firewater, I got drunk—very, very drunk. And I forgot.

Oh Canada, how can I celebrate with you this centenary, this hundred years? Shall I thank you for the reserves that are left to me of my beautiful forests? For the canned fish of my rivers? For the loss of my pride and authority, even among my own people? For the lack of my will to fight back? No! I must forget what's past and gone.

Oh, God in Heaven! Give me back the courage of the olden Chiefs. Let me wrestle with my surroundings. Let me again, as in the days of old, dominate my environment. Let me humbly accept this new culture and through it rise up and go on,

Oh God! Like the Thunderbird of old I shall rise again out of the sea; I shall grab the instruments of the white man's success—his education, his skills, and with these new tools I shall build my race into the proudest segment of your society. Before follow the great Chiefs who have gone before us, oh Canada, I shall see these things come to pass.

I shall see our young braves and our Chiefs sitting in the houses of law and government, ruling and being ruled by the knowledge and freedom of our great land. So shall we shatter the barriers of our isolation. So shall the next hundred years be the greatest in the proud history of our tribes and nations.

Previously Published Documents

"Acadius, or Love in a Calm." 1774. *The Nova Scotia Gazette*, February 1, 1774, 3.

Cockings, George. 1766. *The Conquest of Canada*. London: J. Cooke Bookseller.

Curzon, Sarah Anne. 1882. "Sweet Girl Graduate." *The Grip-Sack: A Receptacle of Light Literature, Fun and Fancy*, July 1882, 43–55.

Davies, Robertson. 1951. "The Theatre: A Dialogue on the State of the Theatre in Canada." In *Royal Commission Studies: A Selection of Essays Prepared for the Royal Commission on National Development in the Arts, Letters and Sciences*, 369–92. Ottawa: King's Printer.

Dubé, Marcel. 1982. *Zone*. Translated by Aviva Ravel. Toronto: Playwrights Canada.

Elliott, Lorris. 1985. "How Now Black Man, Part 4." In *Other Voices: Writings by Blacks in Canada*, edited by Lorris Elliott. Toronto: Williams-Wallace Publishers.

Gauvreau, Claude. 2009. "The Good Life." In *Total Refusal / Refus global: The Manifesto of the Montréal Automatists*, translated by Ray Ellenwood, 49–69. Holstein, ON: Exile Editions.

George, Chief Dan. 2004. "Lament for Confederation." In *The Best of Chief Dan George*, by Chief Dan George and Helmut Hirnschall, 12–13. Surrey, BC: Hancock House Publishers.

Johnson, E. Pauline. 1893. "A Red Girl's Reasoning." *The Dominion Illustrated Monthly*, February 1893, 19–28.

"Nfld's Oldtime Mummers Play." 1950. *The Newfoundlander*, January 1950, 14–15.

"Oldtime 'Mumming' Christmas Plays in Newfoundland." 1949. *The Newfoundlander*, December 1949, 16–17.

Pickthall, Marjorie. 1922. *The Wood Carver's Wife*. Toronto: McClelland & Stewart.

Ryan, Oscar. 1976. "Unity." In *Eight Men Speak and Other Plays from the Canadian Workers' Theatre*, edited by Richard Wright and Robin Endres, 97–106. Toronto: New Hogtown Press.

Sinclair, Lister. 1987. "Hilda Morgan." In *All the Bright Company: Radio Drama Produced by Andrew Allan*, edited by Howard Fink and John Jackson, 67–101. Kingston, ON: Quarry Press.

Tremayne, William. 1918. *The Man Who Went*. Boston: Walter H. Baker and Company.

Voaden, Herman. 1993. "Rocks." In *A Vision of Canada: Herman Voaden's Dramatic Works, 1928–45*, edited by Anton Wagner, 181–218. Toronto: Simon & Pierre.

Contributors

CLARENCE S. BAYNE, past president and founder of the Black Theatre Workshop (BTW), was born in Trinidad and Tobago, Port of Spain, West Indies, and came to Canada in 1955 to study at the University of British Columbia. He is best known for his contributions in the arts and culture and work to foster and develop a Black Canadian theatre and literature.

KYM BIRD is an Associate Professor of Drama at York University in the Department of Humanities and Director of the Graduate Program in Interdisciplinary Studies. She is a leading researcher in the field of early Canadian women's drama, about which she has written several groundbreaking articles. Her book *Redressing the Past: The Politics of Early English-Canadian Women's Drama, 1880–1920* won the Association of Canadian Theatre Research Saddlemyer book prize. Her anthology *Blowing up the Skirt of History: Recovered and Reanimated Plays by Early Canadian Women Dramatists, 1876–1920* (McGill-Queen's University Press, 2020) is the first of its kind to collect early Canadian women's plays.

JUSTIN A. BLUM is an Assistant Professor of Drama at the University of Lethbridge, where he teaches theatre history, dramaturgy, playwriting, dramatic literature and works as a dramaturg and translator. His writing has appeared in collections and journals including *Theatre Research in Canada*, *Nineteenth-Century Theatre and Film*, and *Theatre Topics*.

AMY BOWRING is the Executive and Curatorial Director at Dance Collection Danse. She has curated several live and virtual exhibitions, teaches at Ryerson University's School of Performance, and has published widely. Her book *Navigating Home: Artists of the NL Dance Project* was released in fall 2019 (Dance Collection Danse Press/Presse).

JILL CARTER is an Anishinaabe-Ashkenazi theatre worker based in Tkaronto/Gchi Kiiwenging. She also works as an Assistant Professor with the Centre for Drama, Theatre and Performance Studies; the Transitional Year Programme; and Indigenous Studies at the University of Toronto.

JENN COLE (mixed-ancestry Algonquin) is an Assistant Professor of Gender and Social Studies at Trent University, Associate Artistic Producer for Nozhem First Peoples Performance Space, and co-editor of *Gatherings*, a handmade chapbook for theatre and performance scholars to share creative work. She researches performance practices and histories that illuminate Indigenous presence, cosmologies, and stories from the Land in her home territory of the

Kiji Sibi watershed and along the Odenabe River, where she currently lives, in Michi Saagiig territory.

CYNTHIA COOPER is Head, Collections and Research, and Curator, Dress, Fashion and Textiles at Montreal's McCord Museum. She is the author of *Magnificent Entertainments: Fancy Dress Balls of Canada's Governors General, 1876–1898* (Goose Lane Editions and Canadian Museum of Civilization, 1997). She takes a particular interest in dress entangled within Canadian identity projects.

HEATHER DAVIS-FISCH is an Associate Professor in English and Theatre at the University of the Fraser Valley. She is the author of *Loss and Cultural Remains in Performance: The Ghosts of the Franklin Expedition* (Palgrave, 2012) and editor of *Canadian Performance Histories and Historiographies* and *Past Lives: Performing Canada's Histories* (both Playwrights Canada Press, 2017).

MOIRA DAY is a Professor of Drama at the University of Saskatchewan. A former co-editor of *Theatre Research in Canada / Recherches théâtrales au Canada*, she has published and lectured widely in the field of Canadian theatre, with a particular focus on women and prairie theatre prior to 1960.

RAY ELLENWOOD is Professor Emeritus at York University and author of *Egregore: A History of the Montréal Automatist Movement* (Exile Editions, 1992, French trans. Jean Antonin Billard, 2014). He has published numerous translations and articles relating to the Automatists, including their manifesto, *Refus global*, and two books of plays by Claude Gauvreau.

ALAN FILEWOD was a Professor of Theatre Studies at the University of Guelph until his retirement in 2018. His most recent books include *Reliving the Trenches: Memory Plays by Veterans of the Great* War (Wilfrid Laurier University Press, 2021) and a critical edition of the banned communist play *Eight Men Speak* (University of Ottawa Press, 2013).

HOWARD FINK was the founding Director of the Concordia Centre for Broadcasting Studies and Head of the Radio Drama Project and is Director of the Radio Drama Archives. He led the collection of the 18,000 radio-drama scripts (CNR, CRBC, and CBC). With Professor John Jackson, he prepared an up-to-date descriptive Radio Drama Bibliography and edited several collections of the best scripts, including the anthology *All the Bright Company: Radio Drama produced by Andrew Allan* (1989), which includes Lister Sinclair's *Hilda Morgan*.

LIZA GIFFEN is an archivist who has worked at The Women's Library (UK), Business Archives Council of Scotland, Leeds University, the National

Archives (UK), and the publishers DC Thomson. She is the former Director of
Archives at the Stratford Festival.

J. PAUL HALFERTY is an Assistant Professor in Drama Studies at University
College Dublin where he is also Director for the Centre of Canadian Studies.
His work has been published in *Theatre Research in Canada*, *Canadian Theatre
Review*, and in the anthology *Queer Theatre in Canada*. He also researches queer
theatre and performance in Ireland, most recently publishing "Performing
Politics: Queer Theatre in Ireland, 1968 to 2017" in the *Palgrave Handbook of
Contemporary Irish Theatre and Performance* (2018).

JAMES HOFFMAN is Professor Emeritus of Thompson Rivers University. His
research interest is the theatre history of British Columbia. Notable publications include a biography of George Ryga, plus edited collections of Ryga's
plays and novels, scholarly articles on British Columbia's first play, early
theatre schools and companies, and theatre criticism. He has donated his
British Columbia Theatre Papers to the University of Victoria Library, and his
George Ryga Papers to the University of Calgary Library.

ERIN HURLEY, former president of the Canadian Association for Theatre
Research, is a specialist in modern Quebec theatre at McGill University.
Author of *National Performance* (University of Toronto Press, 2011) and *Theatre
and Feeling* (Palgrave Macmillan, 2010), Hurley's recent scholarship appears in
Theatre Annual, *Revue d'historiographie du théâtre*, and in the edited volume
Performance Studies in Canada (eds. Levin and Schweitzer, McGill-Queen's
University Press, 2017). As part of the research group SEPT-QC, she collabo-
rated with the lead authors (David, Guay, Jacques, and Jubinville) on *Le théâtre
contemporain au Québec, 1945–2015: Essai de synthèse historique et socio-esthétique*
(Les Presses de l'Université de Montréal, 2020).

JOHN JACKSON is Professor Emeritus of Sociology at Concordia University,
Montreal, and a researcher with Concordia's Centre for Broadcasting and
Journalism Studies of which he was co-founder in 1972. He is co-author of
Mediated Society: A Critical Sociology of Media (Oxford University Press, 2011)
and author of *Community and Conflict* (Canadian Scholars Press, 1998). He has
co-edited two anthologies on radio drama.

STEPHEN JOHNSON is Professor Emeritus of Theatre and Performance
Studies at the University of Toronto. He researches performance and popular
culture, and the performance of race, in the nineteenth and twentieth centuries. He is Principal Investigator for the research project Gatherings: Archival
and Oral Histories of Canadian Performance.

SASHA KOVACS is an Assistant Professor at the University of Victoria. Her research, teaching, and creative practice focus on Canadian theatre historiography. Her work has been published in the *Canadian Theatre Review*, *Theatre Research in Canada*, and *Canadian Performance Histories and Historiographies* (Playwrights Canada Press, 2017).

SYLVAIN LAVOIE is a PHD candidate (Humanities) at Concordia University, where he has taught drama and performance. He is also a part-time professor at the University of Ottawa and at the National Theatre School. Since 2018, he has been acting as the Editorial Director of the "scène_s" collection at Les Herbes rouges publishing company.

LOUIS PATRICK LEROUX is a Professor and Associate Dean of Research in the Faculty of Arts and Science at Concordia University. He leads the Montreal Working Group on Circus Research. Recent titles include *Contemporary Circus* (with K. Lavers and J. Burtt; Routledge, 2019), *Cirque Global: Quebec's Expanding Circus Boundaries* (co-edited with with C. Batson; McGill-Queen's University Press, 2016), *Le jeu des positions: Discours du théâtre québécois* (co-edited with H. Guay; Nota Bene, 2014), and the forthcoming *Estie toastée des deux bords: Les formes populaires de l'oralité chez Victor-Lévy Beaulieu* with S. Dubois (Presses de l'Université de Montréal).

ALLANA C. LINDGREN is the Dean of the Faculty of Fine Arts at the University of Victoria. Recent co-edited publications include *The Modernist World*, *Renegade Bodies: Canadian Dance in the 1970s*, and *Moving Together: Dance and Pluralism in Canada*. She is also the Dance Editor for the *Routledge Encyclopedia of Modernism*.

DENYSE LYNDE is a Professor at Memorial University of Newfoundland and Labrador, specializing in Canadian and Newfoundland drama. She edited *The Breakwater Book of Contemporary Newfoundland Plays* (vol. 3, 2016) and contributed an article on Newfoundland's Memorial Day to *Canadian Theatre Review* (vol. 174, 2018). She is presently working on a monograph on artistic fraud.

ERIN JOELLE MCCURDY is a Toronto-based dance scholar and historian interested in intersections between dance and visual art. Her work has recently appeared in the anthology *Curating Live Arts: Critical Perspectives, Essays, and Conversations on Theory and Practice*. She has a PHD in Communication and Culture (Ryerson and York Universities).

WING CHUNG NG is a historian of modern China and the Chinese diaspora. His main publications include *The Chinese in Vancouver, 1945–1980: The Pursuit of Identity and Power* (UBC Press, 1999), and *The Rise of Cantonese Opera* (University of Illinois Press and HKU Press, 2015). Currently, he is working on a biography of Master Wong Toa (1914–2015), whose career of unrivalled longevity sheds considerable light on the trans-Pacific history of Cantonese opera.

GLEN F. NICHOLS was Director of Drama from 2010 to 2018 at Mount Allison University, where he taught drama literature and theatre. In the early 2000s he was president of the Canadian Association for Theatre Research and later editor of *Theatre Research in Canada* for six years. He has published in a number of journals.

CODY POULTON is Professor Emeritus of Japanese literature and theatre in the Department of Pacific and Asian Studies at the University of Victoria. Author of numerous books on Japanese theatre, he has also translated kabuki and contemporary Japanese drama. He is a co-editor of *The Columbia Anthology of Modern Japanese Drama* (Columbia University Press, 2014).

VK PRESTON is an Assistant Professor of History at Concordia University and principal investigator of the SSHRC-funded Insight Development project New Directions in Seventeenth-Century Performance Research: Intangible Baroques. VK's writing appears in *Theatre Journal, The Futures of Dance Studies, TDR / The Drama Review,* and elsewhere.

DANIEL J. RUPPEL is a performance researcher, translator, and theatre creator whose work carries him across languages, eras, and oceans. He completed his doctorate at Brown University, and teaches courses in aesthetics and art history at Roger Williams University in Bristol, Rhode Island. His research employs documents of "joyous and triumphant" entry ceremonies to articulate the performative construction of a French empire on both sides of the Atlantic.

JORDAN STANGER-ROSS is Professor of History at the University of Victoria and the Project Director of Landscapes of Injustice, a SSHRC Partnership Grant–funded project on the dispossession of Japanese Canadians. He has published widely in the area, including *Landscapes of Injustice: A New Perspective on the Internment and Dispossession of Japanese Canadians* (McGill-Queen's University Press, 2020).

PAUL J. STOESSER is former Technical Director (Graduate) at the University of Toronto's Centre for Drama, Theatre and Performance Studies, where, in addition to Canadian theatre history, his teaching included praxis-based scenography and production techniques. Dr. Stoesser is a past member of the Associated Designers of Canada and a charter member of the Canadian Institute for Theatre Technology. He is also the company designer and a founding member of Toronto Laboratory Theatre.

CHRISTL VERDUYN is Professor Emerita of English and Canadian Studies at Mount Allison University. Her research and teaching interests include Canadian and Québécois literature with a focus on women's writing and minority writing, and she is the author, editor, or co-editor of several books and numerous articles in these areas.

ANTHONY J. VICKERY's research focuses on the business and logistics of commercial theatre in the United States and Canada from the late nineteenth century to the present day. He currently teaches theatre history courses in the Theatre Department at the University of Victoria.

ANTON WAGNER was one of the founding executive members of the Association for Canadian Theatre History in 1976. He received PhDs in drama and theatre from the University of Toronto and from York University. His many publications include *Establishing Our Boundaries: English Canadian Theatre Criticism* (University of Toronto Press, 1999).

JERRY WASSERMAN is Professor Emeritus of English and Theatre at the University of British Columbia, a former Head of the Department of Theatre and Film, and editor of *Modern Canadian Plays*. An actor with over two hundred professional theatre, film, and TV credits, he is currently theatre critic for the *Vancouver Sun* and a member of the BC Entertainment Hall of Fame.

Index

This index covers the book's introduction, as well as the introduction to each chapter. The contents of the plays and transcripts are not indexed. Figures indicated by page numbers in italics.